A NEW

EDITION OF THE

⊁ PRO AUDIO REFERENCE ⊁

CONTAINING

A BRIEF ACCOUNT

OF THE

WORDS AND TERMS

OF THE MORE

Commonly Seen

AND

Most Often Misunderstood

IN

EVERY AUDIO ENDEAVOR.

———•———

Compiled By Dennis A. Bohn,

———•———

WITH CONTRIBUTIONS BY

Terry Pennington, Stephen Macatee, Rick Jeffs, Ray Miller, Jeff Davies, Chris Duncan, Roy Gill, Greg Duckett

AND

Devin Cook, Monty Ross, Mike Slattery, Ray Bennett.

BEING THE NEWEST EDITION, CORRECTED

With numerous Additions.

PUBLISHED BY

MAKERS OF FINE AUDIO SINCE MCMLXXXI.

Mukilteo: MMII

Pro Audio Reference
Copyright © 2002 by Rane Corporation

For information, contact Rane Corporation, 10802 47th Ave. W., Mukilteo, WA 98275.

Visit our website at www.rane.com

Compiler & Editor: Dennis A. Bohn

Publications Designer & Webmaster: Jeff Davies

Trademarks:
Trademarks, tradenames, product names and logos are those of their respective owners. No definition in this document is to be regarded as affecting the validity of any trademark. Any word included within this document is not an expression of Rane Corporation's opinion as to whether or not it is subject to proprietary rights.

Accuracy and Limitation:
Rane Corporation believes the information in this publication is accurate as of its publication date; such information is subject to change without notice. Rane Corporation is not responsible for any inadvertent errors. Rane Corporation has obtained information contained in this work from sources believed to be reliable. However, neither Rane nor its authors guarantees the accuracy or completeness of any information published herein and neither Rane nor its authors shall be responsible for any errors, omissions, or damages arising out of use of this information. This work is made available with the understanding that Rane and its authors are supplying information but are not attempting to render engineering or other professional services. If such services are required, the assistance of an appropriate professional should be sought.

Acknowledgements:
Rane Corporation gratefully acknowledges the Houghton Mifflin Company publication, *The American Heritage Dictionary of the English Language, Fourth Edition* (credit shown "AHD"), and the IEEE publication, *IEEE 100: The Authoritative Dictionary of IEEE Standards Terms, Seventh Edition* (credit shown "IEEE"), in the preparation of this edition.

Printed on acid-free paper.

Library of Congress Control Number: 2002093826
ISBN 0-9723607-0-0 (paper)

Revision Date: June 17, 2002

Contents

Rane Corporation

Founded in 1981, Rane Corporation designs and builds pro audio products used in sound systems found in churches and schools, in live music venues, in music and paging systems in restaurants, lounges, theme parks, and sports stadiums, as well as in DJ dance clubs and competitions, recording studios, cinemas, teleconferencing systems and by musicians everywhere. All design and manufacturing is done exclusively in Washington State.

Established innovators in problem-solving analog and digital audio tools, Rane's products, distributed worldwide in 57 countries, are characterized by affordable prices, unequalled reliability and the best support in the industry.

Rane is owned and directed by the same five people who incorporated the business in 1981: Linda Arink, Rick Bernard, Steve Brakken, Larry Winter, and Dennis Bohn, with daily activities the responsibility of CEO, George Sheppard.

See our products at *www.rane.com* and drop us a line at *info@rane.com.*

Dennis A. Bohn

A principal partner and vice president of research & development at Rane Corporation, Dennis holds BSEE and MSEE degrees from the University of California at Berkeley. Prior to Rane Corporation, he worked as engineering manager for Phase Linear Corporation. Before that he was the audio application engineer at National Semiconductor Corporation where he created the *Audio Handbook*, acting as technical editor and contributing author.

Mr. Bohn is a Fellow of the Audio Engineering Society and is listed in the first edition of *Who's Who In Science and Engineering* as well as *Who's Who in America.* He holds two US patents, has designed over 40 professional and consumer audio products and authored over 100 articles appearing in national and international magazines, including his many conference papers delivered and published by the Audio Engineering Society, and the entry on "Equalizers" for the *McGraw-Hill Encyclopedia of Science & Technology, 7th edition.*

Preface

Welcome to the first hardcopy edition of the Pro Audio Reference.

The Pro Audio Reference started life as an aid in understanding digital audio terminology for customers and sales representatives. In those days, it was known as the "digi-dic," short for digital dictionary. It has since grown into a unique and valuable reference covering all aspects of audio from the physiology of the ear to the psychology of hearing. Whether it is the physics of sound or the topology of electronic audio circuits, there is something to find. It is more than a dictionary but less than an encyclopedia. The intent is to give clear concise meanings to the specialized terms found in the fields of audio, mixed-up with some fun and unrelated, but interesting, information.

The including CD-ROM gives you options in using the Pro Audio Reference. The hardcopy offers a quick and convenient information source, while the CD-ROM adds electronic portability plus the valuable hyperlinks found on the website. It is the liberal use of hyperlinks taking the viewer to places all over the planet to find the most accurate and latest audio information that separates the Pro Audio Reference from its competition.

Therefore when using the printed form be aware that when you see references that say "see: ..." or "compare with: ..." that these comments become hyperlinks when using the CD-ROM. If an explanation appears incomplete, abrupt or obscure, then use the CD-ROM to make the sentence come alive. Most short sentences are hyperlinks that take you to an Internet website for the full story. Particularly useful are the hyperlinks to organizations and individuals. Hyperlinks to original sources keeps the information fresh and accurate.

Like all useful references, this one becomes more valuable with each suggested new term. We welcome and encourage your ideas. Email me at *dennisb@rane.com*.

The Internet version of the Pro Audio Reference is revised twice yearly, so if you want the very latest edition view it online at *www.rane.com/digi-dic.html*.

Thanks and we hope you enjoy and learn from your new book.

Numbers

0 See: zero.

0 dBFS See: decibel.

0 dBm See: decibel.

0 dBr See: decibel.

0 dBu See: decibel.

0 dBV See: decibel.

⅓-octave See: one-third octave.

¼" TRS or **¼" TS** See: connectors.

1/f noise See: flicker noise.

1 The other half of all the stored knowledge in a computer; compare with: zero. Surprisingly, not a prime number. A prime number is defined to be a natural number (i.e., a positive whole number) *greater than one* that has exactly two different factors: one and itself.

3D See: 3D sound in section T.

3-dB down point or **-3 dB point** See: passband.

+4 dBu See: decibel.

5.1 See: 5.1 surround sound in section F

6.1 Extended version of 5.1 surround sound (called **Dolby Digital ES** but this isn't official) where one rear channel is added to the basic 5.1 group (left-front, center, right-front, left-surround, right-surround, and subwoofer).

7.1 Extended version of 5.1 surround sound (called **Dolby Digital EX**, this is official) where left and right rear channels are added to the basic 5.1 group (left-front, center, right-front, left-surround, right-surround, and subwoofer).

10Base-T or **100Base-T** or **1000Base-T** or **1000Base-F** See: Ethernet.

-10 dBV See: decibel.

10.2 Somewhat tongue-in-check term created by Tom Holman (of THX fame) for his experimental (but incredibly impressive) surround system based on 5.1 surround sound,

but with *twelve channels*. See Kim Wilson "Tomlinson Holman's Next Experiment" for speaker locations and description.

16 ⅔ rpm Phonograph recording speed obtained using a half-speed converter on a 33 ⅓ rpm machine, used for special recording purposes, but never a standard.

21-gun salute See: 21-gun salute in section T.

24/96 Data conversion using 24-bits quantization at 96 kHz sampling rate.

24/192 Data conversion using 24-bits quantization at 192 kHz sampling rate.

33 ⅓ rpm record The standardized phonograph recording speed selected for the long-play record. Warren Rex Isom explains the reasons in his article, "Before the Fine Groove and Stereo Record and Other Innovations," published in the *Journal of the Audio Engineering Society*, October/November, 1977, Vol. 25, No. 10/11, pp. 815-820. The quick answer is that Western Electric synchronized motion pictures with phonograph records in 1925. A reel of 35-mm film runs for 11 minutes. A record was needed to play the same length of time, which was 3.66 times longer than the 3-minute 10-inch 78-rpm standard. After considering optimum needle groove velocity and diameter and shooting for something approximately half of the 78 rpm standard that could be easily locked to the 60 Hz line, 33 ⅓ rpm was the answer (see Isom for the exact details).

42V PowerNet See: 42V PowerNet in section F.

45 rpm record The standardized phonograph recording speed selected for the single song record. Warren Rex Isom explains the reasons in his article, "Before the Fine Groove and Stereo Record and Other Innovations," published in the *Journal of the Audio Engineering Society*, October/November, 1977, Vol. 25, No. 10/11, pp. 815-820. One popular belief is that 45 rpm was selected because 78 – 33 = 45. While not too far off, it was a more practical engineering matter that created the ballpark number, and perhaps that mathematical nicety determined the exact number. Once marketing decided on a 7-inch disc with 5 ½ minutes of playing time, and knowing the groove details and cutter restrictions, the speed satisfying these conditions is 45 rpm.

70-volt line See: constant-voltage.

78 rpm record First standardized phonograph recording speed (exact speed was 78.26 rpm for 60 Hz power and 77.92 rpm for 50 Hz power). The reason for 78 rpm is explained by Warren Rex Isom in his article, "Before the Fine Groove and Stereo Record and Other Innovations," published in the *Journal of the Audio Engineering Society*, October/November, 1977, Vol. 25, No. 10/11, pp. 815-820. The short summary is that the first machines were handcranked and a comfortable speed was found to be about heartbeat rate — between 60 and 90 per minute. (Interestingly, the same cadence as marching bands and the same speed recommended for handcranked farm equipment.) When it became time to standardize, Victor machines operated at 78 rpm, while competing Edison machines used 80 rpm, but Victor was the predominate sales leader so it was picked for maximum compatibility. The exact speed of 78.26 rpm came about from a simple gearing reason. For a 60 Hz synchronous motor, and a simple worm-gear drive, then a ratio of 46 to 1 turned the table at 78.26 rpm and synchronized with the line.

A

AAC (*Advanced Audio Coding*) Shortened name for the MPEG-2 Advanced Audio Coding specification, declared an international standard by MPEG in April 1997; however, now the term is used also to refer to MPEG-4 advanced audio coding.

A&R (*artists and repertory*) Historically the record industry term for the department or person that acts as the go-between the artist and the record label. Their job is to select and sign the performers to the label, decide what songs they will record, and select who will work with the artists in the production arranging and performance of the material for the recording of master tapes. These details vary a lot from label to label. For a good discussion on how the A&R world is changing see: *What Are Record Labels Looking For?* by Wendy Day (www.slavesnomore.bigstep.com/generic.html?pid=14).

absorption To *absorb* is to receive (an impulse) without echo or recoil: *a fabric that absorbs sound; a bumper that absorbs impact*; therefore *absorption* is the act or process of absorbing. (AHD) The absorption of sound is the process by which sound energy is diminished when passing through a medium or when striking a surface, i.e., *sound is attenuated by absorption*. The physical mechanism is usually the conversion of sound into heat, i.e. sound molecules lose energy upon striking the material's atoms, which become agitated, which we characterized as warmth; thus, absorption is literally the changing of sound energy to heat. A material's ability to absorb sound is quantified by its ***absorption coefficient***, whose value ranges between 0 (total reflection) and 1 (total absorption), and just to keep things interesting, varies with sound frequency and the angle of incidence. See Siegfried Linkwitz's *Acoustic absorption and acoustic resistors*.

ABX testing (aka **ABX double-blind comparator**) A system controller for audio component comparison testing where the listener hears sound-*A*, sound-*B*, and sound-*X*. The listener must make a determination as to whether *X* is *A* or *B*. The subject may go back to A and B as often and for as long as necessary to make a determination. The listener knows that A and B *are* different and that X *is* either A or B, so there is always a correct answer. The "double-blind" part comes from the fact that neither the tester nor the listener (can be the same person) knows whether the source is *A*, *B* or *X*, only the controller knows, which is downloaded after the test is complete to determine the results. First invented in 1977 by Arnold Krueger and Bern Muller (of the famous *Southeastern Michigan Woofer and Tweeter Marching Society* or SMWTMS), later refined and marketed by David Clark and his ABX Company. [For complete details see David L. Clark, "High-Resolution Subjective Testing Using a Double-Blind Comparator," *J. Audio Eng. Soc.*, Vol. 30 No. 5, May 1982, pp. 330-338.]

AC-3 (*audio coding 3*) Dolby's digital audio data compression algorithm adopted for HDTV transmission and used in DVDs, laserdiscs and CDs for 5.1 multichannel home theater use. See: Dolby Digital. Competes with DTS Consumer. The terms *AC-1* and *AC-2* are other versions developed by Dolby for different applications.

Academy curve The name of the standard mono optical track that has been around since the beginning of sound for film. Standardized in 1938, it has improved (very) slightly over the years. Also known as the *N* (normal) *curve* the response is flat 100 Hz-1.6 kHz, and is down 7 dB at 40 Hz, 10 dB at 5 kHz and 18 dB at 8 kHz. This drastic "dumping" of the high-end was to hide the high-frequency "frying" and "crackling" noise inherent in early film sound production. Compare with: X curve.

Accelerated-Slope A trademark of Rane Corporation used to describe their family of patented tone control technologies that produce steeper slopes than normal, thus allowing boost/cut of high and low frequencies without disturbing the critical midband frequencies.

accommodation Said to be the most misspelled word in American writing (*two "c"s and two "m"s*).

accordion "An instrument in harmony with the sentiments of an assassin." — Ambrose Bierce.

acoustic distortion Term coined by Dr. Peter D'Antonio, founder of RPG Diffusor Systems, for the interaction between the room, the loudspeaker, and the listener.

acoustic echo canceller See: echo canceller.

acoustic feedback The phenomenon where the sound from a loudspeaker is picked up by the microphone feeding it, and re-amplified out the same loudspeaker only to return to the same microphone to be re-amplified again, and so on. Each time the signal becomes larger until the system runs away and *rings* or *feeds back* on itself producing the all-too-common scream or squeal found in sound systems. These buildups occur at particular frequencies called *feedback frequencies.*

acoustic lobe See: Linkwitz-Riley crossover.

acoustics 1. *Hearing*; from the Greek *akouein*: to hear. 2. The study of sound.

acoustic treatments There are only three classic (physical) tools available for the acoustician to treat a room: absorbers, reflectors and diffusers. Absorbers attenuated sound; reflectors redirect sound, and diffusers (hopefully) uniformly distribute sound. Or put another way, these tools change the temporal, spectra and spatial qualities of the sound. Additionally, with today's advanced digital audio tools, all of these elements can be electronically manipulated.

acquisition time The time required for a sample-and-hold (S/H) circuit to capture an input analog value; specifically, the time for the S/H output to approximately equal its input.

acronym A *word* formed from the first letters of a name, such as *laser* for *l*ight *a*mplification by *s*timulated *e*mission of *r*adiation, or by combining initial letters or parts of a series of words, such as *radar* for *ra*dio *d*etecting *a*nd *r*anging. The requirement of forming a *word* is what distinguishes an acronym from an *abbreviation* (or *initialism* as it is also called). Thus *modem* [*mod*ulator-*dem*odulator] is an acronym, and *AES* [*A*udio *E*ngineering *S*ociety] is an abbreviation or initialism. Compare with: portmanteau word [Unsubstantiated rumor has it that the word "acronym" itself is an *acronym*, created from the phrase "*a*bbreviating by *c*ropping *r*emainders *o*ff *n*ames to *y*ield *m*eaning" — but it has never been confirmed.] (Thanks MR.)

active crossfader A device found in DJ mixers used to cross-fade between two music sources. An active design uses the potentiometer to send a control voltage to some type of voltage-controlled device that controls the audio, while in a passive design the audio appears on the potentiometer itself. Active designs are more robust and offer greater reliability over passive ones. See *Evolution of the DJ Mixer Crossfader* by Rane's ace DJ mixer designer, Rick Jeffs, for additional details.

active crossover A loudspeaker crossover requiring a power supply to operate. Usually rack-mounted as a separate unit, active crossovers require individual power amplifiers for each output frequency band. Available in configurations known as *stereo 2-way, mono 3-way*, and so on. A *stereo 2-way* crossover is a two-channel unit that divides the incoming signal into two segments, labeled *Low* and *High* outputs (**biamped**). A *mono 3-way* unit is a single channel device with three outputs, labeled *Low, Mid* and *High* (**triamped**). In this case, the user sets two frequencies: the Low-to-Mid, and the Mid-to-High crossover points. Up to *stereo 5-way* configurations exist for very elaborate systems. See: passive crossover and RaneNote: *Signal Processing Fundamentals*.

active equalizer A variable equalizer requiring a power supply to operate. Available in many different configurations and designs. Favored for low cost, small size, light weight, loading indifference, good isolation (high input and low output impedances), gain availability (signal boosting possible), and line-driving ability. Disliked for increased noise performance, limited dynamic range, reduced reliability, and RFI susceptibility; however, used everywhere. See RaneNote: *Operator Adjustable Equalizers*.

ActiveX A Microsoft developed software technology released in 1996. ActiveX, formerly called OLE (Object Linking and Embedding), is loosely based on the Component Object Model (COM), but provides substantially different services to developers. An ActiveX *component* is a unit of executable code (such as an *.exe* file) that follows the Active X specification for providing *objects*. This technology allows programmers to assemble reusable software components into applications and services. However, component software development using ActiveX technology should not be confused with Object-Oriented Programming (OOP). OOP is concerned with *creating objects*, while ActiveX is concerned with *making objects work together*. Simply stated, ActiveX is a technology that lets a program (the ActiveX component or control) interact with other programs over a network (e.g., the Internet), regardless of the language in which they were written. ActiveX components can do similar things as Java beans, but they are quite different. Java is a programming language, while ActiveX controls can be written in any language (e.g., Visual Basic, C, C++, even Java). Also ActiveX runs in a variety of applications, while Java beans usually run only in Web browsers. ActiveX controls are of concern to the pro audio community, because this is the technology that allows designers of computer-controlled sound systems to create common front-end software control panels that will operate different manufacturer's units, without having to know anything about their internal code or algorithms. Each ActiveX control is made up of *properties*, values associated with the control which might include such things as level settings and meter readings, and *events*, which tell the computer something significant has happened, such as a switch closer or clip detection. ActiveX allows the manufacturer to create an object that fully describes a device, while hiding the implementation details, such as protocol from the programmer. By hiding the communication details, there is no longer a need for different manufacturer's devices *to agree on protocol*. This lack of a protocol standard means that cooperation between manufacturers is not required. It allows each manufacturer to choose the best protocol for their devices. See RaneNote: *Controlling Audio Systems with ActiveX*.

adaptive delta modulation (*ADM*) A variation of delta modulation in which the step size may vary from sample to sample.

ADAT (*Alesis Digital Audio Tape*) Digital tape recording system developed by Alesis, and since licensed to Fostex & Panasonic, putting 8-tracks of 16-bit, 44.1 kHz digital audio on S-VHS tape.

ADAT ODI (*optical digital interface*) See: **ADAT Optical**.

ADAT Optical Alesis's proprietary multichannel optical (fiber optic) digital interface specification for their family of ADAT modular digital multitrack recorders. This standard describes transmission of 8-channels of digital audio data through a single fiber optic cable.

ADC (or A/D, *analog-to-digital converter*) The electronic component which converts the instantaneous value of an analog input signal to a digital word (represented as a binary number) for digital signal processing. The ADC is the first link in the digital chain of signal processing. See: data converter bits. See RaneNote: *Digital Dharma of Audio A/D Converters.*

administratium See: "Administratium" [*No technical glossary is complete without this term. Supporting evidence is given by the fact that it took the Google search engine just 0.25 second to return 2,150 versions located on the Web. Among these, it is credited to more than six authors, a hundred different research centers, universities and corporations, and is dated from the 1980s to the 1990s, but there is compelling evidence that it dates back to the '60s. Anyone who can prove who created this classic piece of humor and when, please write me. Thanks.*]

ADPCM (*adaptive differential pulse code modulation*) A very fast data compression algorithm based on the differences occurring between two samples.

ADR (*automatic dialog replacement*) Film postproduction term used to indicate the act and location where dialogue that is not taped during production or that needs to be redone is recorded and synchronized to the picture. Usually the name of the room where this occurs, containing a studio with a screen, TV monitors, microphones, control area, console and loudspeakers.

Advanced Audio Coding See: AAC.

AES (*Audio Engineering Society*) Founded in 1948, the largest professional organization for electronic engineers and all others actively involved in audio engineering. Primarily concerned with education and standardization.

AES17 low-pass filter The common name given to the low-pass filter defined by *AES standard method for digital audio engineering — Measurement of digital audio equipment AES17-1998*, used to limit the measuring bandwidth. The rather daunting specifications call for a filter with a passband response of 10 Hz to 20 kHz, 0.1 dB and a stopband attenuation greater than 60 dB at 24 kHz.

AES24 A developing AES standard for sound systems using computer networks to control audio equipment. Formerly called "SC-10" (after the working group's subcommittee number), the title for AES24-1-1999 (the first part to be published) is *Application Protocol for Controlling and Monitoring Audio Devices via Digital Data Networks — Part 1: Principles, Formats, and Basic Procedures.* The complete standard is broken down into several parts issued separately. The second part, in the *proposed draft* stage, is titled — *Part 2: Data Types, Constants, and Class Structure.* The remaining two parts are in process.

AES3 interface (*The interface formerly known as AES/EBU*). The serial transmission format standardized for professional digital audio signals (AES3-1992 *AES Recommended Practice for Digital Audio Engineering — Serial transmission format for two-channel linearly represented digital audio data*). A specification using time division multiplex for data, and balanced line drivers to transmit two channels of digital audio data on a single twisted-pair cable using 3-pin (XLR) connectors. Issued as ANSI S4.40-1985 by the American National Standards Institute. In addition, information document AES-3id is available describing the transmission of AES3 formatted data by unbalanced coaxial cable. Transmission by fiber optic cable is under discussion. The consumer version is referred to as S/PDIF. See RaneNote: *Interfacing AES3 and S/PDIF.*

AES/EBU interface See: AES3.

AFL Abbreviation for *after fade listen*, a term used on recording consoles and mixers, referring to a signal taken after the main channel fader; hence this sampling point tracks the main fader level. Also referred to as *post fade solo*, but since PFL already meant *pre* fade, AFL was adopted to prevent confusion. Got it? Compare with: PFL.

algorithm A structured set of instructions and operations tailored to accomplish a signal processing task. For example, a fast Fourier transform (FFT), or a finite impulse response (FIR) filter are common DSP algorithms.

aliasing The problem of unwanted frequencies created when sampling a signal of a frequency higher than half the sampling rate. See: Nyquist frequency. Also see RaneNote: *Digital Dharma of Audio A/D Converters.*

all-pass filter A filter that provides only phase shift or phase delay without appreciably changing the magnitude characteristic.

ALMA (*American Loudspeaker Manufacturers Association*) Founded in 1964, an international trade association for companies that design, manufacture, sell, and/or test loudspeakers, loudspeaker components and loudspeaker systems.

ambience 1. *Acoustics.* A perceptual sense of space (Blesser). The acoustic qualities of a listening space (White). 2. *Psychoacoustics* The special atmosphere or mood created by a particular environment; also spelled ***ambiance*** (AHD). Contrast with: reverberation.

Ambisonics A British-developed surround sound system designed to reproduce a true three-dimensional sound field. Based on the late Michael Gerzon's (1945-1996) (Oxford University) famous theoretical foundations, Ambisonics delivers what the ill-fated *quadraphonics* of the '70s promised but could not. Requiring two or more transmission channels (encoded inputs) and four or more decoded output loudspeakers, it is not a simple system; nor is the problem of reproducing 3-dimensional sound. Yet with only an encoded stereo input pair and just four decoded reproducing channels, Ambisonics accurately reproduces a complete 360-degree *horizontal* sound field around the listener. With the addition of more input channels and more reproducing loudspeakers, it can develop a true spherical listening shell. As good as it is, a mass market for Ambisonics has never developed due to several factors. First, the actual recording requires a special tetrahedron array of four microphones: three to measure left-right, front-back and up-down sound pressure levels, while the fourth measures the overall pressure level. All these microphones must occupy the same point in space as much as possible. So far, only one manufacturer (first Calrec, bought by AMS, bought by Siemens, sold, now Soundfield Research) is known to make such an array. Next, a professional Ambisonics encoding unit is required to matrix these four mic signals together to form two or more channels before mastering or broadcast begins. Finally, the consumer must have an Ambisonics decoder, in addition to at least four channels of playback equipment.

AMI-C (*Automotive Multimedia Interface Collaboration*) "An organization of motor vehicle manufacturers worldwide created to facilitate the development, promotion and standardization of electronic gateways to connect automotive multimedia, telematics and other electronic devices to their motor vehicles."

AMPAS (*Academy of Motion Picture Arts &Sciences*) Created in 1927, a professional honorary organization composed of over 6,000 motion picture craftsmen and women. *Think Oscars®*.

ampere *Abbr.* **I**, also **A**. 1. A unit of electric current in the International standard meter-kilogram-second (mks) system. It is the steady current that when flowing in straight parallel wires of infinite length and negligible cross section, separated by a distance of one meter in free space, produces a force between the wires of 2E-7 newtons per meter of length. 2. A unit in the International System specified as one International coulomb per second and equal to 0.999835 ampere. [After **André Marie Ampère**.] (AHD)

Ampère, André Marie (1775-1836) French physicist and mathematician who formulated Ampère's law, a mathematical description of the magnetic field produced by a current-carrying conductor. (AHD)

amplifier An electronic device used to increase an electrical signal. The signal may be voltage, current or both (power). *Preamplifier* is the name applied to the first amplifier in the audio chain, accepting inputs from microphones, or other transducers, and low output sources (CD players, tape recorders, turntables, etc.). The preamplifier increases the input signals from mic-level, for instance, to line-level. *Power amplifier* is the name applied to the last amplifier in the audio chain, used to increase the line-level signals to whatever is necessary to drive the loudspeakers to the loudness required. See: amplifier classes.

amplifier classes Audio power amplifiers are classified according to the relationship between the output voltage swing and the input voltage swing; thus it is primarily the design of the output stage that defines each class. *Classification is based on the amount of time the output devices operate during one complete cycle of signal swing.* This is also defined in terms of output bias current [the amount of current flowing in the output devices with no applied signal]. For discussion purposes (with the exception of class A), assume a simple output stage consisting of two complementary devices (one positive polarity and one negative polarity) using tubes (valves) or any type of transistor (bipolar, MOSFET, JFET, IGFET, IGBT, etc.).

Class A operation is where both devices conduct continuously for the entire cycle of signal swing, or the bias current flows in the output devices at all times. The key ingredient of class A operation is that both devices are always on. There is no condition where one or the other is turned off. Because of this, class A amplifiers in reality are not complementary designs. They are single-ended designs with only one type polarity output devices. They may have "bottom side" transistors but these are operated as fixed current sources, not amplifying devices. Consequently class A is the most inefficient of all power amplifier designs, averaging only around 20% (meaning you draw about 5 times as much power from the source as you deliver to the load.) Thus class A amplifiers are large, heavy and run very hot. All this is due to the amplifier constantly operating at full power. The positive effect of all this is that class A designs are inherently the most linear, with the least amount of distortion. [Much mystique and confusion surrounds the term *class A*. Many mistakenly think it means circuitry comprised of discrete components (as opposed to integrated circuits). Such is not the case. A great many integrated circuits incorporate class A designs, while just as many discrete component circuits do not use class A designs.]

Class B operation is the opposite of class A. Both output devices are never allowed to be on at the same time, or the bias is set so that current flow in a specific output device is zero when not stimulated with an input signal, i.e., the current in a specific output flows for one half cycle. Thus each output device is on for exactly one half of a complete sinusoidal signal cycle. Due to this operation, class B designs show high efficiency but poor linearity around the crossover region. This is due to the time it takes to turn one device off and the other device on, which translates into extreme crossover distortion.

Thus restricting class B designs to power consumption critical applications, e.g., battery operated equipment, such as 2-way radio and other communications audio.

Class AB operation is the intermediate case. Here both devices are allowed to be on at the same time (like in class A), but just barely. The output bias is set so that current flows in a specific output device appreciably more than a half cycle but less than the entire cycle. That is, only a small amount of current is allowed to flow through both devices, unlike the complete load current of class A designs, but enough to keep each device operating so they respond instantly to input voltage demand s. Thus the inherent non-linearity of class B designs is eliminated, without the gross inefficiencies of the class A design. It is this combination of good efficiency (around 50%) with excellent linearity that makes class AB the most popular audio amplifier design.

Class AB plus B design involves two pairs of output devices: one pair operates class AB while the other (slave) pair operates class B.

Class C use is restricted to the broadcast industry for radio frequency (RF) transmission. Its operation is characterized by turning on one device at a time for less than one half cycle. In essence, each output device is pulsed-on for some percentage of the half cycle, instead of operating continuously for the entire half cycle. This makes for an extremely efficient design capable of enormous output power. It is the magic of RF tuned circuits (flywheel effect) that overcomes the distortion created by class C pulsed operation.

Class D operation is switching, hence the term *switching power amplifier*. Here the output devices are rapidly switched on and off at least twice for each cycle (Sampling Theorem). Theoretically since the output devices are either completely on or completely off they do not dissipate any power. If a device is on there is a large amount of current flowing through it, but all the voltage is across the load, so the power dissipated by the device is zero (found by multiplying the voltage across the device [*zero*] times the current flowing through the device [*big*], so 0 x big = 0); and when the device is off, the voltage is large, but the current is zero so you get the same answer. Consequently class D operation is theoretically 100% efficient, but this requires zero on-impedance switches with infinitely fast switching times — a product we're still waiting for; meanwhile designs do exist with true efficiencies approaching 90%. [Historical note: the original use of the term "Class D" referred to switching amplifiers that employed a resonant circuit at the output to remove the harmonics of the switching frequency. Today's use is much closer to the original "Class S" designs.

Class E operation involves amplifiers designed for rectangular input pulses, not sinusoidal audio waveforms. The output load is a tuned circuit, with the output voltage resembling a damped single pulse. Normally Class E employs a single transistor driven to act as a switch. The following terms, while generally agreed upon, are not considered "official" classifications.

Class F Also known by such terms as "biharmonic," "polyharmonic," "Class DC," "single-ended Class D," "High-efficiency Class C," and "multiresonator." Another example of a tuned power amplifier, whereby the load is a tuned resonant circuit. One of the differences here is the circuit is tuned for one or more harmonic frequencies as well as the carrier frequency. See: References: Krauss, et al. for complete details.

Class G operation involves changing the power supply voltage from a lower level to a higher level when larger output swings are required. There have been several ways to do this. The simplest involves a single class AB output stage that is connected to two power supply rails by a diode, or a transistor switch. The design is such that for most musical program material, the output stage is connected to the lower supply voltage, and automatically switches to the higher rails for large signal peaks [thus the nickname *rail-switcher*]. Another approach uses two class AB output stages, each connected to a different power supply voltage, with the magnitude of the input signal determining the signal path. Using two power supplies improves efficiency enough to allow significantly more power for a given size and weight. Class G is becoming common for pro audio designs. [Historical note: Hitachi is credited with pioneering class G designs with their 1977 *Dynaharmony HMA 8300* power amplifier.]

Class H operation takes the class G design one step further and actually modulates the higher power supply voltage by the input signal. This allows the power supply to track the audio input and provide just enough voltage for optimum operation of the output devices [thus the nickname *rail-tracker* or *tracking power amplifier*]. The efficiency of class H is comparable to class G designs. [Historical note: Soundcraftsmen is credited with pioneering class H designs with their 1977 *Vari-proportional MA5002* power amplifier.]

Class S First invented in 1932, this technique is used for both amplification and amplitude modulation. Similar to Class D except the rectangular PWM voltage waveform is applied to a low-pass filter that allows only the slowly varying dc or average voltage component to appear across the load. Essentially this is what is termed "Class D" today. See: References: Krauss for details.

amplifier dummy load Modeling a real world loudspeaker for power amplifier testing purposes has been studied for years, resulting in many circuit possibilities. An article compiled and edited by Tomi Engdahl entitled "Speaker Impedance" is an excellent summary of the results. He gives a complete (and complex) solution to the loudspeaker dummy load question. However you can get excellent results with a simplified version developed by Michael Rollings, Sr. Design Engineer, Rane Corporation, appearing below. The series resistor and inductor model the loudspeaker voice coil's *DC resistance* and *inductance*, while the parallel inductor and capacitor simulate the mechanical components of *suspension compliance* and *cone mass* respectively. The values shown work well for most power amplifier measurements.

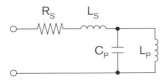

R_S = 6 Ω (Vishay Dale RH-250, or equal; power rating twice max testing watts)

L_S = 0.33 mH (air core inductor; wire sized for max current)

L_P = 20 mH (air core inductor; wire sized for max current)

C_P = 1000 μF (100 V, or maximum expected peak voltage; paralleling two 500 μF caps may be smaller, cheaper)

amplitude 1. Greatness of size; magnitude. 2. *Physics.* The maximum absolute value of a periodically varying quantity. 3. *Mathematics.* a. The maximum absolute value of a periodic curve measured along its vertical axis. b. The angle made with the positive horizontal axis by the vector representation of a complex number. 4. *Electronics.* The maximum absolute value reached by a voltage or current waveform. (AHD)

amplitude-frequency response See: frequency response.

analog A real world physical quantity or data characterized by being continuously variable (rather than making discrete jumps), and can be as precise as the available measuring technique.

anechoic Literally, *without echo*, used to describe specially designed rooms, *anechoic chambers*, built to emulate a free sound field, by absorbing practically all the sound field.

anode 1. A positively charged electrode. 2. In a vacuum tube, it is the plate electrode. 3. In a forward-biased semiconductor diode it is the positive terminal. Contrast with: cathode.

ANSI (pronounced "ann-see") (*American National Standards Institute*) A private organization that develops and publishes standards for voluntary use in the U.S.A.

Antheil, George (1900-1959) US Composer, specializing in film music, who described himself as "America's bad boy of music." *Among Antheil's early avant-garde pieces, none caused a greater sensation than his Balet mécanique,* *scored for automobile horns, airplane propeller, fire siren, ten grand pianos, and other instruments. When it was performed at Carnegie Hall in 1924, a concertgoer near the orchestra could stand no more than a few minutes of the racket. Tying his handkerchief to his cane, he raised the white flag in surrender.* [Bartlett's Book of Anecdotes]

anti-aliasing filter A low-pass filter used at the input of digital audio converters to attenuate frequencies above the half-sampling frequency to prevent aliasing.

anti-imaging filter A low-pass filter used at the output of digital audio converters to attenuate frequencies above the half-sampling frequency to eliminate image spectra present at multiples of the sampling frequency.

APA (*Audio Publishers Association*) The online resource center designed for audio book listeners and industry professionals.

apparent power The result of multiplying the rms value of the voltage by the rms value of the current in an electronic circuit. It is expressed in watts (W) for resistive loads and in volt-amperes (VA) for reactive loads. It's the amount of power the casual observer *thinks* is available (hence, *apparent*), but because of *power factor* may not be — the real power is usually less. See: power factor.

ARM (*advanced RISC machines*) The name for a microprocessor group formed from Acorn, backed by Apple, VLSI Technology and Nippon Investment and Finance, in 1990. Acorn Computer was the parent company set up by Dr. Hermann Hauser and Dr. Chris Curry in 1979 to make personal computers, but now enjoys its biggest success selling intellectual property around their proprietary RISC computer, called ARM, which originally stood for *Acorn RISC Machines.*

ASA (*Acoustical Society of America*) Founded in 1929, the oldest organization for scientist and professional acousticians and others engaged in acoustical design, research and education.

ASCII (pronounced "ask-ee") (*American Standard Code for Information Interchange*) An ANSI standard data transmission code consisting of seven information bits, used to code 128 letters, numbers, and special characters. Many systems now use an 8-bit binary code, called ASCII-8, in which 256 symbols are represented (for example, IBM's "extended ASCII").

ASHRAE (*American Society of Heating, Refrigerating and Air-conditioning Engineers, Inc.*) An international organization organized for the purpose of advancing the arts and sciences of heating, ventilation, air-conditioning and refrigeration for the public's benefit through research, standards writing, continuing education and publications.

ASIC (*application-specific integrated circuit*) A large-scale integrated circuit whose function is determined by the final mask layer for a particular application or group of applications; for example, an IC that does all the functions of a modem.

ASIO (*audio stream input/output*) A multichannel audio transfer protocol developed by Steinberg North America in 1997, for audio/MIDI sequencing applications, allowing access to the multichannel capabilities of sound cards.

ASPEC (*adaptive spectral perceptual entropy coding*) A bit rate reduction standard for high quality audio. Jointly developed by AT&T Bell Labs, Thomson, the Fraunhofer Society and CNET. Characterized by high degrees of compression to allow audio transmission on ISDN.

asymmetrical (non-reciprocal) response Term used to describe the comparative shapes of the boost/cut curves for variable equalizers. The cut curves do not mirror the boost curves, but instead are quite narrow, intended to act as notch filters.

asynchronous A transmission process where the signal is transmitted without any fixed timing relationship between one word and the next (and the timing relationship is recovered from the data stream).

A-taper See: potentiometer.

ATM (*asynchronous transfer mode*) networking An extremely fast networking technology already found on many disk editors (*Avid, Sonic Solutions, Studio Audio, etc.*) and predicted to infiltrate homes within the coming decade. ATM specifies the protocol (i.e., the order and sequence) of the digital information on the network, but not the physical means of transmission (e.g., fiber optic, twisted-pair, etc.). The protocol controls how the entire network is run and maintained.

atmospheric pressure Pressure caused by the weight of the atmosphere. At sea level it has a mean value of one atmosphere but reduces with increasing altitude. (AHD)

attenuator or **attenuator pad** *Electronics.* A passive network that reduces the voltage (or power) level of a signal with negligible distortion, but with insertion loss. Often a purely resistive network, although any combination of inductors, resistors and capacitors are possible, a pad may also provide impedance matching. [Compare with: fader and crossfader.] Pads are referred to by the topology of the network formed, with the two most common being an *L-pad* and a *T-pad*:

> **L-pad** A two-leg network shaped like an inverted, backward letter "L". It usually consists of two resistors that are fixed or adjustable. A true variable L-pad consists of two variable potentiometers that are ganged (tied) together. The ganged sections work to provide either a constant input or a constant output impedance regardless of the attenuation setting. Since modern analog audio electronic circuits consist of stages characterized by very high input and very low output impedances, the term is now broaden to include all L-shaped networks without the requirement of providing constant impedance to the source or load. Volume and level controls are common examples.

> **T-pad** A three-leg network shaped like the letter "T". It usually consists of three resistors that are fixed or adjustable. A true variable T-pad consists of two or three variable potentiometers that are ganged (tied) together. The ganged sections work to provide either a constant input or a constant output impedance regardless of the attenuation setting. Since modern analog audio electronic circuits consist of stages characterized by very high input and very low output impedances, the term is now broaden to include all T-shaped networks without the requirement of providing constant impedance to the source or load.

audio 1. Of or relating to humanly audible sound, i.e., audio is all the sounds that humans hear (*approximately 20 Hz - 20 kHz*). 2.a. Of or relating to the broadcasting or reception of sound. b. Of or relating to high-fidelity sound reproduction. [Audio traveling through air is vibrations, or cycles of alternating pressure zones. Rarefaction follows each cycle of compression, which produces a wave.] (AHD)

audio books See: *Pro Audio Reference Books* for books used to create this book.

audio bridge A communications bridge that allows multiple duplex connections over 4-wire telephone connections. Well designed audio bridges, such as Rane's ECB 6 do not connect inputs to their own outputs, thus avoiding feedback. See: mix-minus.

audio compression See: digital audio data compression.

audio connectors See: connectors.

Audio magazine (1947-2000) America's first and longest running audio magazine. Its demise after 53 years of continuous publication leaves a huge void in the consumer audio world. Gone is the last great rational voice, lost amidst the pseudoscientific din dominating high-end audio. An audio warrior is dead and we are lessened.

audion Dr. Lee De Forest's name for his 1906 invention of the triode (*three-element vacuum tube*), building upon Sir John Ambrose Fleming's thermionic diode, based on the Edison effect. De Forest credits his assistant, C.D. Babcock for the name.

audion piano The first vacuum tube instrument in 1915, invented by Dr. Lee De Forest.

audio taper See: potentiometer.

Audio Timeline A most fascinating audio development time-line created by three esteemed AES members, Jerry Bruck, Al Grundy and Irv Joel, as part of the 50th anniversary of the AES.

audio websites A truly astonishing and remarkable list of audio related websites compiled *daily* by Steve Ekblad. Also see Audio & Hi-Fi Page, an equally astonishing and remarkable list of audio related websites compiled by Tomi Engdahl. And for a refreshingly rational voice on hot audio topics check out Rod Elliott's site, particularly his get-rich-quick scheme for exploiting the gullible regarding burning-in audio cables. [*Absolutely brilliant*.]

auditory filter Term used to describe the concept of critical bands. Analogous to a bandpass filter with a rounded top ("rounded-exponential" after Patterson and Moore, 1986). The filter is slightly asymmetric, being wider on the low-frequency side.

Aureal 3D (*A3D*) Proprietary 3D sound technology first developed by Crystal River Engineering, which became the advanced technology subsidiary of Aureal Semiconductor, *alas, now defunct*. Aureal 3D made many claims. At one time their website stated that "since we can hear sounds three dimensionally in the real world by using two ears, it must be possible to create sounds from two speakers that have the same effect" ... well ... *NO* ... it's pretty rhetoric, but flawed logic. Our two ears receive sound coming from sources located in every possible direction, and from *that* information process three-dimensional location — that is not the problem. The problem is how to make our two ears receive sound from sources located in only two directions, and trick them into hearing three dimensionally — that is the problem. Aureal claimed to have solved this problem, but didn't stay in business long enough for anyone to find out.

autoformer *Autoformer* is short for *autotransformer*, or *self-transformer*, from the definition of *auto-*. An autotrans-former is one that self-magnetizes to produce the trans-former voltage, it does this by not having a true secondary, i.e., there is only one winding with one part acting as the primary and the other part acting as the secondary, but there is no second winding, and no air gap, and thus no true isolation between the primary and secondary. Therefore an autotransformer is a transformer in which part of one winding is common to both the primary and the secondary circuits associated with that winding. For this reason, au-totransformers are not the preferred choice for professional audio use because in addition to the transformed voltage (usually 70.7 V in the U.S. & 100 V elsewhere) you want true isolation. However, they are common because they are cheaper to make since you don't have to wind a separate primary and secondary.

automatic mic mixer A specialized mixer optimized for solving the problems of multiple live microphones oper-ating together as a system, such as found in boardrooms, classrooms, courtrooms, church systems, etc. An automatic mic mixer controls the live microphones by turning up (*on*) mics when someone is talking, and turning down (*off*) mics that are not used, thus it is a voice-activated, real-time process, without an operator, hence, *automatic*. An auto-matic mic mixer must adapt to changing background noise conditions. Further it must control the additive effect of multiple mics being on at the same time (See: NOM). If one mic is on at maximum gain, opening up another one may cause acoustic feedback, so an automatic mixer must also control the system gain to prevent feedback or excessive noise pickup. Dan Dugan patented the first automatic mic mixer and is recognized as the father of this technology. A final problem that automatic mixers solve is maintaining a natural ambience from the room. This is especially criti-cal in recording and broadcasting. A good automatic mixer must make rapid and dramatic changes in the gains of the input channels while maintaining the sonic illusion that nothing is happening at all.

aux fed subs, or **aux fed subwoofers** A live sound technique becoming popular when subwoofers are used with the FOH system. It is claimed that a properly configured and oper-ated aux fed subwoofer system better maintains gain struc-ture and crossover relationships. See Tom Young's article at ProSoundweb, *A Detailed Explanation Of The Aux Fed Subwoofer Technique*.

AVD (*advanced video disk*) A Chinese proposed alternative to the DVD standard to avoid paying what they consider exorbitant royalties. This threatened standard would apply to DVD-like players sold only in China. Members of the *China Audio Industry Association (CAIA)* say the spec could be published in late 2001 if the DVD royalty issue remains unsettled.

average power See: apparent power.

A-weighting See: weighting filters.

AWG (*American wire gauge*) A specification for non-ferrous (e.g., copper, aluminum, gold, silver, etc.) wire diameter. [*Note, for example, that this means that 14 gauge galva-nized steel wire & 14 gauge cooper wire have different diameters.*] Also known as **Brown and Sharp (B&S) wire gauge**, after J.R. Brown who devised the system in 1857 (*I have been unsuccessful in finding out what Sharpe's role was*). For more detail, see Douglas Brooks' "How to Gauge Traces." Many tables exist on the Internet; e.g., See: Alpha. The British standard is called **SWG** standing for *Standard wire gauge*, also called **Imperial wire gauge**. Compare with: AWG here.

azure noise See: noise color.

B

babbling tributary In LAN technology, a workstation that constantly sends meaningless messages.

back-EMF (back-*electromotive force*) See: EMF. Literally, *back-voltage*, is a phenomena found in all moving-coil electromagnetic systems, but for audio is most often used with respect to loudspeaker operation. This term describes the action where, after the signal stops, the speaker cone continues moving, causing the voice coil to move through the magnetic field (now acting like a microphone), creating a *new* voltage that tries to drive the cable back to the power amplifier's output. If the loudspeaker is allowed to do this, the cone flops around like a dying fish. It does *not* sound good. The only way to stop back-emf is to make the loudspeaker "see" a dead short, i.e., zero ohms looking backward, or as close to it as possible. See: damping factor.

background music Officially music without lyrics and not performed by the original artist, used as an alternative to silence. Contrast with: *foreground music.*

balance control A control found most commonly on professional and consumer stereo preamplifiers, used to change the relative loudness (power) between the left and right channels. Attenuating the opposite channel makes one channel (apparently) louder. This is most often done (in analog designs) with a dual potentiometer with an "M-N taper." An M-N taper consists of a "shorted" output for the first 50% of travel and then a linear taper for the last 50% of travel, operating oppositely for each channel. Therefore, with the control in its center detent position, there is no attenuation of either channel. Rotating it away from the center position causes one channel to be attenuated, while having no effect on the other channel, and vice-versa. Contrast with: pan and crossfade controls.

balanced line The IEEE dictionary defines a *balanced circuit* as "a circuit, in which two branches are electrically alike and symmetrical with respect to a common reference point, usually ground." This is the essence of a balanced interconnect. Namely, that two lines are driven equally and oppositely with respect to ground. Normally this also implies that the receiving circuits have matching impedances. Exactly matching impedances is preferred for it provides the best common mode rejection. Balances lines are the preferred method (for hum free) interconnecting of sound systems using a shielded twisted-pair. Because of its superior noise immunity, balanced lines also find use in interconnecting data signals, e.g., RS-422, and digital audio, e.g., AES/EBU. The principal behind balanced lines is that the signal is transmitted over one wire and received back on another wire. *The shield does not carry any information,* thus it is free to function as a true shield, but must be earth grounded *at each end* to be successful. (For a detailed tutorial on proper grounding practices, See RaneNote: *Sound System Interconnection*) [*Long Answer:* To understand why balanced lines are so successful, first examine a balanced, or differential (equivalent term) output stage, and then an input stage: A differential output stage simultaneously drives two lines, one positive and one negative. The voltage difference between these two wires is the audio signal. The two signals form an envelope that rides the wires to the balanced input stage. Note that the audio signal exists uniquely between these two lines — not between them and ground. The complete circuit path travels down on the positive line and back on the negative line. Ground is not needed to transmit the signal — this is the essence and power of balanced lines. Ground is used only for shielding and safety purposes. Conversely, an **unbalanced line** is one that transmits the audio signal between one wire and ground. The circuit path is down the wire and back through the shield cable connected to ground. Ground is the return path; the circuit does not work without it. A balanced (or differential) input stage extracts the difference between the two input lines, and that, of course, is the desired audio signal. It receives the envelope sent down the cable by the differential output. This circuit's shining virtue is its great noise rejection ability. It has what is called great common-mode rejection. The concept here relies on induced noise showing up equally (or common) on each wire. It is mainly due to EMI (electromagnetic interference: passing through or near magnetic fields), RFI (radio frequency interference: strong broadcast signals), noisy ground references, or a combination of all three. The best balanced line designs have exactly equal impedance from each line relative to ground, guaranteeing equal noise susceptibility. Since the balanced input stage amplifies only the difference between the lines, it rejects everything else (noise) that is common to the lines.]

balun (*balanced-unbalanced*) A jargon term originally popularized by radio engineers referring to the *bal*anced to *un*balanced transformer used to interface with the radio antenna. Today, expanded to refer to any interface (usually a transformer) between balanced and unbalanced lines or circuitry; may also provide impedance transformation, as 300 Ω balanced to 75 Ω unbalanced, or vice versa. Another popular use is in transitioning between balanced twisted-pair and an unbalanced coaxial cable.

banana jack or **banana plug** See: connectors.

band-limiting filters A low-pass and a high-pass filter in series, acting together to restrict (limit) the overall bandwidth of a system.

bandpass filter A filter that has a finite passband, neither of the cutoff frequencies being zero or infinite. The bandpass frequencies are normally associated with frequencies that define the half power points, i.e. the -3 dB points. See Figure 1 of RaneNote: *Constant-Q Graphic Equalizers*.

bandwidth *Abbr.* **BW** 1. *Electronic filters* The numerical difference between the upper and lower -3 dB points of a band of audio frequencies. Used to figure the Q, or quality factor, for a filter. See Figure 1 of RaneNote: *Constant-Q Graphic Equalizers*; also download "Bandwidth vs. Q Calculator" as a zipped Microsoft Excel spreadsheet in the Rane Library. 2. *Telecommunications* The size of the communications channel. In analog communications, bandwidth is measured in Hertz (Hz), while digital communications measures bandwidth (data transfer rate) in bits per second. For example, an analog telephone channel has a bandwidth of 4,000 Hz, while a digitally coded telephone channel has a bandwidth of 64 kilobits/second. See RaneNote: *Audio Specifications*.

banjo "I can see fiddling around with a banjo, but how do you banjo around with a fiddle?" — Duncan Purney [*from* Barber]

bar A unit of pressure equal to one million dynes per square centimeter. (*Yeah, I know, you expected some wiseacre response, but you ain't gonna get it.*)

Bara, Theda (1890-1955) Anagram of "Arab Death," used as a pseudonym by the Cincinnati-born, Hollywood actress Theodosia Goodman in the 1920s, who became the first woman movie star.

Baroque 1. Music: of, relating to, or characteristic of a style of composition that flourished in Europe from about 1600 to 1750, marked by chromaticism, strict forms, and elaborate ornamentation. (AHD) 2. When you are out of Monet. (*Thanks JF and I'll never tell.*)

barrier strips Same as *terminal strips*, see: connectors.

baseband A transmission medium with capacity for one channel only. Typically found in local area networks (LANs). In baseband LANs, the entire bandwidth, or capacity, of the cable is used to transmit a single digital signal. Everything on that cable (transmitted or received) must use that one channel, which is very fast, so each device needs only to use that high speed channel for only a little of the time. Therefore all attached devices (printers, computers, databases) share by taking turns using the same cable. Baseband as used in videoconferencing means audio and video signals are transmitted over separate cables. Contrast with: broadband.

baseband signaling Transmission of a digital or analog signal at its original frequencies; i.e., a signal in its original form, not changed by modulation.

bass management See: LFE.

baud rate (pronounced "bawd"; after *Baudot Code* named for the French telegrapher Emile Baudot, 1845-1903) The transmitted signaling speed, or keying rate of a modem. Often confused with bit rate. *Bit rate and baud rate are NOT synonymous and shall not be interchanged in usage.* For example, one baud equals one half dot cycle per second in Morse code, one bit per second in a train of binary signals, and one 3-bit value per second in a train of signals each of which can assume one of 8 different states, and so on – all brought to you by the magic of advanced coding techniques that allow more than one bit per baud. Preferred usage is *bit* rate, with *baud* used only when the details of a modem are specified.

Baxandall tone controls The most common form of active bass and treble tone control circuit based upon British engineer P.J. Baxandall's paper "Negative Feedback Tone Control — Independent Variation of Bass and Treble Without Switches," *Wireless World*, vol. 58, no. 10, October 1952, p. 402. The Baxandall design is distinguished by having very low harmonic distortion due to the use of negative feedback.

BCD 1. (*binary-coded decimal*) Pertains to a number system where each decimal digit is separately represented by a 4-bit binary code; for example, the decimal number 23 is represented as 0010 0011 (2 = 0010 and 3 = 0011, grouped together as shown), while in straight binary notation, 23 is represented as 10111. 2. (*binary-coded digit*) A digit of any number system that is represented as a fixed number of binary digits; from the previous example, the decimal digit 23 is represented as 10111.

beat *Physics.* To cause a reference wave to combine with a second wave so that the frequency of the second wave can be studied through time variations in the amplitude of the combination. [AHD]

beat frequency Equal to the absolute value of the difference in frequency of two waves beating together (See: "beat" above).

Beat Generation The story goes like this ...
In The Origins of the Beat Generation *Jack Kerouac (1922-1969) recalled how he borrowed the term that labeled an entire decade from a broken-down drug addict named Herbert Huncke and how he then went on to use it himself. "John Clellon Holmes ... and I were sitting around trying to think up the meaning of the Lost Generation and the subsequent existentialism and I said, 'You know, this is really a beat generation': and he leapt up and said, 'that's it, that's right.'"* [Bartlett's Book of Anecdotes] See: Generation X.

bel *Abbr.* **b, B** Ten decibels. [After **Alexander Graham Bell**.] The Bel was the amount a signal dropped in level over a one-mile distance of telephone wire. See: decibel.

Belchfire Series Term coined by Crown International for their mythical power amplifier, the BF-6000SUX. Based on original research into the first principles of teramagnostriction quasar-quadrature, the BF-6000SUX could have changed the design of all future power amps, but it didn't. In spite of Crown's leap forward into the past of technical declination, the marketplace categorically stated that it did not want 6,000 watts per channel in only one rack space - in spite of its six-foot depth and 206 pounds weight. The only known use of a BF-6000SUX was to drive the experimental Electro-VoiceRearaxial Softspeaker, when Rane demoed their PI 14 Pseudoacoustic Infector using Jensen's JE-EP-ERs Multi-denomial Transpedance Informer for coupling - but many consider that only hearsay.

Bell, Alexander Graham (1847-1922) Scottish-born American inventor of the telephone. The first demonstration of electrical transmission of speech by his apparatus took place in 1876. Bell also invented the audiometer, an early hearing aid, and improved the phonograph. (AHD)

BeOS (*Be operating system*) An operating system (OS) developed by Be Incorporated in 1996, called the first true "media OS," it is becoming very popular for Internet appliances, as well as software designed for live performance venues.

BER (*bit error ratio*) (also called **bit error rate**) 1. The ratio of the number of erroneous bits divided by the total number of bits transmitted, received, or processed over some stipulated period. 2. The number of bits processed before an erroneous bit is found (e.g., 10E13), or the frequency of erroneous bits (e.g., 10E-13).

Bessel crossover A type of crossover utilizing low-pass filter design characterized by having a *linear phase response* (or *maximally flat phase response*), but also a monotonically decreasing passband amplitude response (which means it starts rolling off at DC and continues throughout the passband). Linear phase response (e.g., a linear plot of phase shift vs. frequency produces a straight line) results in *constant time-delay* (all frequencies within the passband are delayed the same amount). Consequently the value of linear phase is it reproduces a near-perfect *step response*, i.e., there is no overshoot or ringing resulting from a sudden transition between signal levels. The drawback is a sluggish roll-off rate. For example, for the same circuit complexity a Butterworth response rolls off *nearly three times as fast*. This circuit is based upon *Bessel polynomials*; however, the filters whose network functions use these polynomials are correctly called *Thompson filters* [W.E. Thomson, "Delay Networks Having Maximally Flat Frequency Characteristics," *Proc. IEEE*, part 3, vol. 96. Nov 1949, pp. 487-490]. The fact that we do not refer to these as *Thompson crossovers* demonstrates, once again, that we do not live in a fair world. See Ray Miller, *Bessel Filter Crossover and Its Relation to Other Types.*

biamp, biamplified, or **biamplification** Term used to refer to a 2-way active crossover where the audio signal is split into two paths, and using separate power amplifier channels for each driver.

BICSI (*Building Industry Consulting Services, International*) A telecommunications association that is a worldwide resource for technical publications, training, conferences, and registration programs for low-voltage cabling distribution design and installation.

bifilar windings A term most often associated (in the pro audio industry) with audio transformer design describing the winding technique of laying two wires side-by-side, providing essentially unity coupling, thus reducing leakage inductance to negligible amounts. Literally *two threads* from Latin *bi-* two, and *filum* thread.

bilinear transform A mathematical method used in the transformation of a continuous time (analog) function into an equivalent discrete time (digital) function. Fundamentally important for the design of digital filters. A bilinear transform ensures that a stable analog filter results in a stable digital filter, and it exactly preserves the frequency-domain characteristics, albeit with frequency compression.

binary A condition in which there are two possible states; for example, the binary number system (base-2) using the digits 0 and 1. See RaneNote: *Digital Dharma of Audio A/D Converters.*

binary logarithm A logarithm based on the powers of 2 (*aka base 2*).

binaural recording or **binaural sound** Believe it or not, the groundwork was laid in the 1920s (*no kidding*, and some claim even earlier) when the idea of placing two microphones in a dummy head was first introduced as a source of loudspeaker stereo (which wouldn't go anywhere until Blumlein's contributions). It was the Germans who first produced a standard artificial listener for evaluating auditorium acoustics, and then played back the results over headphones — the startling realism launched binaural recording. A binaural recording is made using two microphones placed in the ear canals of an anatomically accurate dummy head, such that all the normal spatial attributes of the human head are present (just as in real listening situations) when the recording is made. Designed to be played back through headphones, the results are nothing but astonishing. First time listeners to binaural recordings often swear someone is there with them, talking and walking around them, such is the realism accomplished.

binding posts See: connectors.

binky See Larry Blake's Film Sound Glossary.

bit *Abbr.* **b** Abbreviation for *binary unit* or *binary digit.* 1. The smallest amount of digital information. A bit can store or represent only two states, 0 and 1. [The original term *binary unit* was coined by John Tukey of Bell Laboratories to represent the basic unit of information as defined by Shannon as a message representing one of two states.] 2. *A little bit* — from Old English *bita*, meaning a piece bitten off.

bit clock The synchronizing signal that indicates the rate of individual data bits over a digital audio interface.

bit error rate or **bit error ratio** See: BER.

bit rate The rate or frequency at which bits appear in a bit stream. Applied to digital audio, bit rate (kbits/sec/channel) equals the sampling rate (kHz) times the number of bits per sample. The data bit rate for a CD, for example, is 1.41M bits per second (44.1 kHz x 16 bits per sample x 2 channels). [*The oft-quoted CD bit rate of 4.3218 MHz is for the raw bit rate which comes from multiplying 7,350 frames per second by 588, the number of channel bits.*]

bits — data converter See: data converter bits.

bit stream A binary signal without regard to grouping.

bit-mapped display A display in which each pixel's color and intensity data are stored in a separate memory location.

Blackmer, David (1927-2002). American scientist, inventor and businessman best known for founding dbx, Inc. and pioneering audio-grade VCAs for signal processing.

black noise See: noise color.

blame shifter Shifts the pitch of mistakes down one octave so the audience thinks it was the bass player. [*Thanks to DD at Sound Path Labs.*]

blue moon For half a century, it's been known as the second full moon in the same calendar month; however, recently this definition was corrected by the editors of *Sky & Telescope* magazine. The correct definition, they say, is that a blue moon occurs when a season has *four full moons, rather than the usual three.* Further, they claim the misunderstanding is their fault based on an article they published in 1946. For all the wonderful details, See: *Once In A Blue Moon.*

blue noise See: noise color.

Bluetooth The code name given a wireless network protocol, after a 10th century Danish king, *Harald Bluetooth*, who unified Denmark. The code name was adopted in April, 1998, when Intel and Microsoft formed a consortium between themselves IBM, Toshiba, Nokia, Ericsson and Puma Technology. This protocol promises to bring wireless Internet to the masses, making the Web as ubiquitous as radio and TV. The Bluetooth SIG (*special interest group*), now numbering over 2000 companies, sees a world where equipment from different manufacturers works seamlessly together using Bluetooth as a sort of virtual cable. Check out the website to read the whole history of Harald Bluetooth and get all the details on this exciting technology. Compare with: ZigBee.

blue whales See: SPL.

Blumlein, Alan Dower (1903-1942) English engineer who in a short working life span of 15 years wrote or cowrote 128 patents, developed stereophonic sound, designed new uses for microphones, designed a lateral disc-cutting system making modern records possible, developed much of the 405-line high definition television system broadcast in Britain until 1986, and improved radar systems such that they still operated 40 years later. Indeed, a genius by any definition, yet his story had to wait until 1999 to be told completely. Thanks to Robert Charles Alexander, former editor of *AudioMedia* magazine, a definitive biography now exists. Not only that, but Alexander has created a web site dedicated to Blumlein that eventually will have all 128 patents reproduced in their entirety, along with all of his binaural recordings (another of his inventions), downloadable as MP3 files, including binaural film clips (the world's first stereo films).

BNC (*bayonet Neill-Concelman*) A miniature bayonet locking connector for coaxial cable. It was developed in the late '40s by a collaboration of Paul Neill and Carl Concelman. In 1942, while at Bell Labs, Paul Neill developed what became known as the type N connector, named after him, which became a U.S. Navy standard. Carl Concelman, while at Amphenol, developed a bayonet version of the N connector, which became known as the type C connector, after him (*the first true 50-Ω connector*). Then, together, they developed a miniature bayonet locking version of the C connector and it was named the type BNC connector, after both of them. There is even an improved threaded version called the *threaded Neill-Concelman* or *TNC connector* See: BNC RF Connectors for additional details, and JCM for examples. [*Thanks to all who wrote me to help clarify this correct meaning. My condolences to all, who with passion, conviction, and great creativity, truly believe differently. It is a sad but true tale that BNC does NOT stand for "baby N connector," or "bayonet connector," or "bayonet Naval connector," or "British Naval Connector" (sorry Microsoft). For further verification search the web for info on Paul Neill and Carl Concelman.*]

Boole, George (1815-1864) British mathematician who devised a new form of algebra that represented logical expressions in a mathematical form now known as **Boolean Algebra**. See: Maxfield.

boost/cut equalizer The most common graphic equalizer. Available with 10 to 31 bands, on 1-octave to ⅓-octave spacing. The flat (*0 dB*) position locates all sliders at the center of the front panel. Comprised of bandpass filters, all controls start at their center *0 dB* position and boost (amplify or make larger) signals by raising the sliders, or cut (attenuate or make smaller) the signal by lowering the sliders on a band-by-band basis. Commonly provide a center-detent feature identifying the *0 dB* position. Proponents of boosting in permanent sound systems argue that cut-only use requires adding make-up gain that runs the same risk of reducing system headroom as boosting.

Boucherot, Paul (1869-1943) French engineer who studied the phenomena of electric conduction, introducing the concept of *reactive power* and inventing the synchronous electric motor in 1898. He also studied the thermal energy of the seas. The *Claude-Boucherot Process* described a scheme to power a turbo-alternator using warm seawater from tropical oceans to produce steam in a vacuum chamber. *Theorem of Boucherot*: In an AC electrical network, the total active power is the sum of the individual active powers, the total reactive power is the sum of the individual reactive powers, but the total *apparent power* is NOT equal to the sum of the individual apparent powers.

Boucherot cell After Paul Boucherot above; See: Zobel network.

boundary microphone See: PZM.

Bps (*always uppercase B*) Abbreviation for bytes per second.

bps (*always lowercase b*) Abbreviation for bits per second.

brewer See: zymurgy.

bridge 1. In communications networks a bridge is a device that connects two or more different networks and forwards packets between them; specifically a device that (a) links or routes signals from one ring or bus to another, or from one network to another, (b) may extend the distance and capacity of a single LAN system, (c) performs no modification to packets or messages, (d) operates at the data-link layer of the OSI—Reference Model (Layer 2), (e) reads packets, and (f) passes only those with addresses on the same segment of the network as the originating user. 2. A functional unit that interconnects two local area networks that use the same logical link control (LLC) procedure, but may use different medium access control (MAC) procedures. 3. A balanced electrical network, e.g., a Wheatstone bridge. Contrast with: hub.

broadband Also *wideband*, a transmission medium having a bandwidth greater than a traditional telephone (speech) channel (4 kHz). [*Some argue that to be "broadband" the medium must support 20 kHz.*] The most common broadband medium is coaxial cable carrying multiple audio, video and data channels simultaneously. Each channel takes up a different frequency on the cable. There will be guard bands, or empty spaces, between the channels to make sure each channel does not interfere with its neighbor. The most common example is the CATV cable. Contrast with: baseband.

brown noise See: noise color.

B&S gauge (*Brown & Sharpe*) See: AWG.

BSI (*British Standards Institute*) The National Standards organization responsible for coordinating standards preparation for sound equipment in the UK.

B-taper See: potentiometer.

buffer In data transmission, a temporary storage location for information being sent or received.

buffer amplifier The IEEE dictionary defines buffer amplifier as "An amplifier in which the reaction of output-load-impedance variation on the input circuit is reduced to a minimum for isolation purposes." This is a bit confusing, but one thing is clear, it says that at the most fundamental level a buffer amplifier isolates (or buffers) the loading effects (impedance) of two stages. It separates them, making them independent. In analog designs, buffer amplifiers are used for just this purpose. If the next circuit stage in a design has impedance characteristics that are detrimental to the preceding stage then a buffer amplifier minimizes this interaction. And its use is not confined to analog design, digital circuits use buffers to minimize similar loading effects.

The term "amplifier" comes about from the fact that most buffer amplifiers also provide either voltage or current gain. In this sense, a normal audio power amplifier can be called a buffer amplifier - it buffers your preamp from your very low impedance loudspeakers. [*Historical Note*: Sometimes a buffer amplifier provides speed as well as isolation. In the mid '70s, National Semiconductor offered in their specialty hybrid circuits line, a product simply named "Fast Buffer," whose purpose was to provide impedance isolation, but could do so at high megawiggle speeds (not a trivial task back then), and if that wasn't good enough, they also offered a "Damn Fast Buffer," that could really get the job done (true story).] As can be seen, the term buffer amplifier is a bit vague: it provides isolation, that much is sure, however, it may also offer voltage gain, current gain, or both. And it may even provide an unbalanced-to-balanced function, or vice-versa.

Bulwer-Lytton Fiction Contest A whimsical literary competition that challenges entrants to compose the opening sentence to the worst of all possible novels. Created by Professor Scott Rice, English Department, at San Jose State University in 1982, the contest is still sponsored by the college. The name comes from Edward George Earle Bulwer-Lytton, who wrote the famous line "*It was a dark and stormy night ...*" as the opening words in his novel *Paul Clifford* (1830). Check it out — great fun.
When Wilkie Collins's detective novel The Woman in White *appeared in 1860, it created a considerable stir. A feature*

much remarked upon was the villain, Count Fosco. One lady reader, however, was not so impressed and wrote to tell Collins, "You really do not know a villain. Your Count Fosco is a very poor one." She then offered to supply Collins with a villain next time he wanted one. "Don't think that I am drawing upon my imagination. The man is alive and constantly under my gaze. In fact, he is my husband." The writer was Bulwer-Lytton's wife.[Bartlett's Book of Anecdotes]

bumbershoot 1. An umbrella. Derived from an alteration of *umbrella* + alteration of *(para)chute.* (AHD) 2. A Seattle arts festival held each Labor Day weekend, featuring over 2,500 artists including comedians, dancers, painters, poets, sculptors, tightrope walkers, acrobats, filmmakers, book-binders, DJs, thespians, and musicians of every genre from classical to hip-hop.

burst error A large number of data bits lost on the medium because of excessive damage to or obstruction on the medium.

burst noise See: popcorn noise.

bus One or more electrical conductors used for transmitting signals or power from one or more sources to one or more destinations. Often used to distinguish between a single computer system (connected together by a *bus*) and multi-computer systems connected together by a *network*.

buss To kiss. (AHD)

Butterworth filter A type of electronic filter character-ized by having a *maximally flat magnitude response*, i.e., no amplitude ripple in the passband. [Contrast with: Chebyshev] This circuit is based upon *Butterworth func-tions* (or *Butterworth polynomials*). [For the mathematically inclined, these polynomials represent a specialized solu-tion to a general MacLaurin series based upon a Taylor series expansion. Named after S. Butterworth, a British engineer who first described this response in his paper "On the Theory of Filter Amplifiers," *Wireless Engineer,* vol. 7, 1930, pp. 536-541. Eleven years later, V.D. Landon coined the phrase *maximally flat* in his paper "Cascade Amplifiers with Maximal Flatness," *RCA Review,* vol. 5, 1941, pp. 347-362.]

Butterworth crossover The category of loudspeaker cross-over design (or alignment) based on Butterworth filters (See: above).

byte *Abbr.* **B** A group of eight bits (a word) operating together. Usually abbreviated in uppercase to distinguish "byte" from "bit" which uses lowercase "b". See: Bps.

C

C The electronic symbol for a capacitor.

CABA (*Continental Automated Buildings Association*) An industry association that promotes advanced technologies for the automation of homes and buildings in North America.

cables Audio systems use many different types of cables (for all the details see Lampen):

coaxial cable A single copper conductor, surrounded with a heavy layer of insulation, covered by a thick surrounding copper shield and jacket. A constant-impedance unbalanced transmission line.

data cable See: data cables and Category cables.

fiber optics The technology of using glass fibers to convey light and modulated information. Short distances (typically less than 150 feet) use plastic fibers, while long distances must use glass fibers.

mic cable (aka **audio cable**) A shielded twisted-pair, usually designed for low current, high flexibility and low handling noise. The best insulating materials are somewhat inflexible, so most mic cables use rubber, neoprene, PVC, or similar materials, with small gauge wire, and therefore, true mic cables are not intended for long runs. Unfortunately the term "mic cable" has become synonymous with general-purpose audio cable (as distinguished from *speaker cable*) when it can be quite different. The very best audio cable may not be the best mic cable and vice versa.

quad mic cable or **star-quad mic cable** [*a term coined by Canare for the first quad mic cable, but was not trademarked and is now a generic term*]. A four-conductor cable exhibiting very low noise and hum pickup (hum reduction can be 30 dB better than standard mic cable). The four conductors are wound together in a spiral, and then opposite conductors are joined together at the connectors forming a two-conductor balanced line (also called *double balanced*) with superior performance.

speaker cable An unshielded insulated pair, normally not twisted, characterized by heavy (or large) gauge conductors (hence, low-resistance), used to interconnect the output of a power amplifier and the input of a loudspeaker. The coupling between amplifier and loudspeaker may be direct or via transformer (See: constant voltage). The *star quad* design described above also makes excellent speaker cables for use in high noise environments.

twisted-pair Standard two-conductor copper cable, with insulation extruded over each conductor and twisted together. Usually operated as a balanced line connection. May be shielded or not, abbreviated **UTP** (*unshielded twisted-pair*), or **STP** (*shielded twisted-pair*).

Cannon plug See: connectors.

capacitance A force that resists the sudden buildup of electric voltage (as opposed to inductance which resists the sudden buildup of electric current). [IEEE]

capacitive reactance See: impedance.

capacitor Circuit symbol: **C**. 1. A device with the primary purpose of introducing capacitance into an electric circuit. 2. An element within a circuit consisting of two conductors, each with an extended surface exposed to that of the other, but separated by a layer of insulating material called the dielectric. *Note:* The dielectric is designed so the electric charge on one conductor is equal in value but opposite in polarity to that of the other conductor. [IEEE]

capacitor microphone See: condenser microphone.

cardioid A heart-shaped plane curve, the locus of a fixed point on a circle that rolls on the circumference of another circle with the same radius. (AHD)

Cartesian coordinate system 1. A two-dimensional coordinate system in which the coordinates of a point in a plane are its distances from two perpendicular lines that intersect at an origin, the distance from each line being measured along a straight line parallel to the other. (AHD) 2. A three-dimensional coordinate system in which the coordinates of a point in space are its distances from each of three perpendicular planes that intersect at an origin. After the Latin form of Descartes, the mathematician who invented it.

CAT 3 (*Category 3 cable*) Unshielded twisted-pair (UTP) data grade cable (usually 24 AWG). CAT 3 cables are characterized to 16 MHz and support applications up to 10 Mbps. Typically used for voice telephone and 10Base-T Ethernet systems.

CAT 5 (*Category 5 cable*) Unshielded twisted-pair(UTP) data grade cable (usually 24 AWG). CAT 5 cable runs are limited to 100 meters (328 feet) due to signal radiation and attenuation considerations. Longer runs are vulnerable to electromechanical interference. CAT 5 cables are characterized to 100 MHz and support applications up to 100 Mbps. Most common application is 100Base-T Ethernet systems. [*With the release of ANSI/TIA/EIA-568-B, CAT 5 is no longer recognized and is officially replaced by CAT 5e (see next entry).*]

CAT 5e (*Category 5 enhanced*) As above CAT 5 cable except there is a plastic rib running through the center of the cable that separates the pairs, maintaining greater distance between them to reduce crosstalk (*(they are other non-rib ways to meet this requirement)*). It also keeps them in position to maintain the proper geometry along the whole cable. It uses better insulation, making attenuation and crosstalk performance better. IT DOES NOT EXTEND THE BANDWIDTH as some believe. The rated bandwidth is the same 100 MHz. It *may* run faster but the official specification (ANSI/TIA/EIA-568-B) does not require it, so *caveat emptor.*

CAT 6 (*Category 6*) Proposed 300 MHz cabling is under study.

Category cables Telecommunications created a *Category of Performance* standard for data cables. This defines standards (mostly tests) for cabling and cabling components (connectors, etc.). Originally there were five categories, however, today, there are effectively only two: *CAT 3* and *CAT 5* (see above). See hyperlink for details.

cathode 1. A negatively charged electrode. 2. In a vacuum tube the electron emitting electrode. 3. In a forward-biased semiconductor diode it is the negative terminal. Contrast with: anode.

cathode follower See: buffer amplifier.

CATV (*community antenna television* or *cable television*) A broadband transmission medium, most often using 75 Ω coaxial cable carrying many TV channels simultaneously.

CAV (*constant angular velocity*) A disc rotating at a constant number of revolutions per second. The LP is a CAV system at 33 ⅓ rpm. Another example is the CAV laser disc that plays two thirty minute sides.

CCIF (*Comité Consultatif International des Téléphonique, or International Telephone Consultative Committee*) The CCIF merged with the CCIT becoming the CCITT. In 1992, the CCITT, together with the CCIR, morphed into the ITU.

CCIR (*Comité Consultatif International des Radio Communications, or International Radio Consultative Committee*) (*International Radio Consultative Committee*) Merged with the ITU and became the ITU-R radiocommunications division.

CCIR ARM See: weighting filters.

CCIR-468 See: weighting filters.

CCIR 2 kHz See: weighting filters.

CCIT (*Comité Consultatif International des Télégraphique, or International Telegraph Consultative Committee*) Merged with the CCIF to become the CCITT.

CCITT (*Comité Consultatif International des Téléphonique et Télégraphique, or International Telegraph and Telephone Consultative Committee*) Merged with the ITU and became the ITU-T telecommunications division.

CD (*compact disc*) Trademark term for the Sony-Philips digital audio optical disc storage system. The system stores 80 minutes (maximum) of digital audio and subcode information, or other non-audio data, on a 12-centimeter diameter optical disc. The disc is made of plastic, with a top metallized layer, and is read by reflected laser light. Variations (such as the 3" disc) are reserved for special applications.

CD horn EQ See: constant directivity horn.

CD-I (*compact disc interactive*) System storing digital audio, video, text, and graphics information interactively, with user control over content and presentation, on a 12-centimeter diameter optical disc.

CD+MIDI A System storing MIDI information in a disc's subcode area.

CD-PROM (*compact disc programmable read-only memory*) A write-once CD-ROM disc.

CD-R (*compact disc-recordable*) A compact disc that is recordable at least once.

CD-ROM (*compact disc read-only memory*) A method of storing digitally coded information, such as computer information or database, on a 12-centimeter diameter optical disc.

CD-V (*compact disc video*) A system storing five minutes of analog video and digital audio plus twenty minutes of digital audio only on a 12-centimeter diameter optical disc, and longer times on 20- or 30-centimeter diameter optical discs.

CEI (*Commission Electrotechnique Internationale*) See: IEC.

Celsius *Abbr.* **C** Of or relating to a temperature scale that registers the freezing point of water as 0 °C and the boiling point as 100 °C, under normal atmospheric pressure. (AHD) [The term "Celsius" is preferred to "centigrade" in technical contexts.] [After **Anders Celsius**]

Celsius, Anders (1701-1744) Swedish astronomer who devised the centigrade thermometer (1742). (AHD)

CEMA (*Consumer Electronics Manufacturers Association*) The definitive source for information about the consumer electronics industry.

CE-mark (*Conformité Européenne*) The letter-logo used in marking units certified for distribution within the European Union (EU) that meet the directives mandated by the European Commission.

center frequency One of the parameters of a *bandpass filter*. The center frequency occurs at the maximum or minimum amplitude response for Butterworth filters, the most common found in audio electronics.

centi- Prefix for one hundredth (10E-2), abbreviated **c.**

centigrade Temperature term generally not used in scientific contexts apart from meteorology. See: Celsius.

cereal interface A bowl and a spoon. [*Thanks PM.*]

CERN (*Conseil Européenne pour la Recherche Nucléaire*) European Particle Physics Laboratory. See: World Wide Web.

chachka or **tchotchke** also **tsatske** A cheap showy trinket, sometimes used as swag or a spiff. (AHD)

channel separation See: crosstalk.

charge *Symbol* **q** 1.*Electricity.* a. To cause formation of a net electric charge on or in (a conductor, for example). b. To energize (a storage battery) by passing current through it in the direction opposite to discharge. 2. *Physics.* a. The intrinsic property of matter responsible for all electric phenomena, in particular for the force of the electromagnetic interaction, occurring in two forms arbitrarily designated *negative* and *positive*. b. A measure of this property. c. The net measure of this property possessed by a body or contained in a bounded region of space. (AHD)

chassis ground 1. The common point on a conducting chassis surrounding the system electronic circuit boards; usually separate from the signal ground but may be tied at one point. 2. The earth grounding connection provided on the chassis for safety reasons. See RaneNote: *Sound System Interconnection.*

Chebyshev filter A class of electronic filter characterized by having an equal-ripple magnitude response, meaning the magnitude increases and decreases regularly from DC to the cutoff frequency. Chebyshev filters are classified by the amount of ripple in the passband, for example a 1-dB Chebyshev low-pass filter is one with a magnitude response ripple of 1 dB. Chebyshev filters are popular because they offer steeper roll-off rates than Butterworth filters for the same order, but for audio applications the Chebyshev is virtually never seen due to the superior magnitude and phase responses of the Butterworth class. [After **Pafnuty Lvovich Chebyshev.**]

Chebyshev, Pafnuty Lvovich [also spelled **Tschebyscheff** and **Tchebysheff**] (1821-1894) Russian mathematician best remembered for his work on the theory of prime numbers. (AHD)

checksum The sum of a group of data items used for error checking. If the checksum received equals the one sent, all is well. Otherwise, the receiving equipment requests the data be sent again.

chiasmus The term for a reversal in the order of words in two otherwise parallel phrases. For example, the advice from the great sci-fi writer Ray Bradbury to aspiring writers: "*You have to know how to accept rejection and reject acceptance,*" or the familiar adage: "*Say what you mean and mean what you say.*"

Christie, Samuel Hunter See: Wheatstone bridge.

chorusing *Recording.* An effect where the audio signal is given multiple delays so as to sound like several instruments playing at once. The delay times are short, typically 20-45 milliseconds, and each delayed signal may be pitch-shifted. The effect is similar to hearing a chorus, where everyone is singing the same thing but at slightly different times and pitches. Chorusing is a slightly elaborated version of doubling. A signal is delayed approximately 15-35 milliseconds and mixed with the undelayed signal. The delay time is modulated by a low-frequency-oscillator to achieve a shimmering effect due to a combination of beat-frequencies and the slight pitch-bending that occurs as the delay time is changed.

chromatic scale *Music.* A scale consisting of 12 semitones.

chrominance Abbreviated **C**. The color portion of the video signal — includes hue and saturation information but not brightness (See: luminance).

CISC (*complex instruction set computing*) See: RISC.

class-A An amplifier class.

Class I equipment Equipment where protection against electric shock does not rely on basic insulation only, but also provides an additional safety precaution allowing connection of the equipment to the protective earth conductor in the fixed wiring of the installation so that accessible metal parts cannot become live in the event of a failure of the basic insulation.

Class II equipment Equipment where protection against electric shock does not rely on basic insulation only, but also provides additional safety precautions such as double insulation or reinforced insulation, but there is no provision for connection of the equipment to the protective earth conductor.

client Any device connected to a server on a local area network (LAN), e.g., personal computer, DSP-based unit, workstation, etc.

clipping Term used to describe the result of an amplifier running into power supply limitation. The maximum output voltage that any amplifier can produce is limited by its power supply. Attempting to output a voltage (or current) level that exceeds the power supply results in a flattoping effect on the signal, making it look cut off or "clipped." A clipped waveform exhibits extreme harmonic distortion, dominated by large amplitude odd-ordered harmonics making it sound harsh or dissonant. **Hard clipping** is the term used to describe extreme clipping of a signal, producing highly visible flattoped waveforms as viewed on an oscilloscope; **soft clipping** refers to moderate clipping that results in waveforms having softly-rounded edges, as opposed to the sharp edges of hard clipping. For how-to-avoid See RaneNote: *Setting Sound System Level Controls*.

clock A timing device that generates the basic periodic signal used as a source of synchronizing signals in digital equipment.

CLV (*constant linear velocity*) A disc rotating at varying numbers of revolutions per second to maintain a constant relative velocity between pickup and track across the disc radius. The CD is a CLV system rotating from 500-rpm (lead-in track) to 200 rpm (lead-out track). Another example is the CLV laser disc that plays two sixty minute sides.

CMR or **CMRR** See: common-mode rejection (ratio).

coaxial cable A single copper conductor, surrounded with a heavy layer of insulation, covered by a thick surrounding copper shield and jacket. A constant-impedance unbalanced transmission line. See: cables.

CobraNet™ A trademark of Peak Audio (a division of Cirrus Logic) identifying their licensed networking technology used for the deterministic and isochronous transmission of digital audio, video, and control signals over 10 Mbit and 100 Mbit Ethernet networks.

codec (*code-decode* also *compression-decompression*) Originally a device for converting voice signals from analog to digital for use in digital transmission schemes, normally telephone based, and then converting them back again. Broaden now to mean an electronic device that converts analog signals, such as video and voice signals, into digital form and compresses them to conserve bandwidth. Most codecs employ proprietary coding algorithms for data compression, common examples being Dolby's AC-2, ADPCM, and MPEG schemes. It is data compression (and direct digital video & audio inputs) that has evolved the newer meaning of *compression-**de**compression*.

coincident-microphone technique See: X/Y microphone technique.

combining response See: interpolating response and RaneNote: *Exposing Equalizer Mythology*.

common logarithm A logarithm based on the powers of 10 (*aka base 10*).

common-mode rejection (ratio) Abbr. **CMR** and **CMRR** The characteristic of a differential amplifier to cancel all common-mode signals applied to its inputs. The "ratio" is obtained by dividing the input common-mode voltage by the amount of output voltage, thereby giving you some measure of the amplifier's ability to reject common signals. See RaneNote: *Audio Specifications*.

common-mode signal Strictly speaking it is the average of the signals present at the two inputs of a differential amplifier, although it is more often meant to be the voltage level present at both inputs, as if they were tied together.

compander A contraction of compressor-expander. A term referring to dynamic range reduction and expansion performed by first a compressor acting as an encoder, and second by an expander acting as the decoder. Normally used for noise reduction or headroom reasons.

complex frequency variable An AC frequency in complex number form. See: complex number.

complex number *Mathematics.* Any number of the form $a + bj$, where a and b are real numbers and j is an imaginary number whose square equals -1 (AHD); and a represents the ***real part*** (e.g., the resistive effect of a filter, at zero phase angle) and b represents the ***imaginary part*** (e.g., the reactive effect, at 90 degrees phase angle).

component video A video system for color television that stores separate channels of red, green and blue. Becoming increasingly popular on DVD players, as well. See: Fist's Fabulous Fact Finder for more details.

composite video A video signal combining luminance, chrominance and synchronization data on a single coax cable using RCA connectors and color-coded yellow.

compression 1. An increase in density and pressure in a medium, such as air, caused by the passage of a sound wave. 2. The region in which this occurs.

compression wave A wave propagated by means of the compression of a fluid, such as a sound wave in air. (AHD)

compressor A signal processing device used to *reduce the dynamic range* of the signal passing through it. For instance, an input dynamic range of 110 dB might pass through a compressor and exit with a new dynamic range of 70 dB. This clever bit of skullduggery is normally done through the use of a VCA (voltage controlled amplifier), whose gain is a function of a control voltage applied to it. Thus, the control voltage is made a function of the input signal's dynamic content. [*Long answer*: What "compression" is and does has evolved significantly over the years. Originally compressors were used to reduce the dynamic range of the *entire signal*; with modern advances in audio technology, compressors now are used more sparingly. First the classical case: The history of compressors dates back to the late '20s and '30s (the earliest reference I have located is a 1934 paper in the Bell Labs Journal.) The need arose the very first time anyone tried to record (sound-motion pictures film recording, phonograph recording, etc.) or broadcast audio: *the signal exceeded the medium.* For example, the sound from a live orchestra easily equals 100 dB dynamic range. Yet early recording and broadcasting medium all suffered from limited dynamic range. Typical examples: LP record 65 dB, cassette tape 60 dB (w/noise reduction), analog tape recorder 70 dB, FM broadcast 60 dB, AM broadcast 50 dB. Thus "6 pounds of audio into a 4 pound bag" became the necessity that mothered the invention of the compressor (*sorry*). Early compressors did not have a "threshold" knob, instead, the user set a center ("hinge") point equivalent to the midpoint of the expected dynamic range of the incoming signal. Then a *ratio* was set which determined the amount of dynamic range reduction. The earlier example of reducing 110 dB to 70 dB requires a ratio setting of 1.6:1 (110/70 = 1.6). The key to understanding compressors is to always think in terms of *increasing and decreasing level changes **in dB** about some set-point.* A compressor makes audio *increases* and *decreases smaller.* From our example, for every input *increase of 1.6 dB above* the hinge point, the output only *increases 1 dB,* and for every input *decrease of 1.6 dB below* the hinge point, the output only *decreases 1 dB.* If the input increases by x-dB, the output increases by y-dB, and if the input decreases by x-dB, the output decreases by y-dB, where x/y equals the ratio setting. Simple — but not intuitive and not obvious. This concept of *increasing* above the set-point and *decreasing* below the set-point is where this oft-heard phrase comes from: *"compressors make the loud sounds quieter and the quiet sounds louder."* If the sound gets louder by 1.6 dB and the output only increases by 1 dB, then the loud sound has been made quieter; and if the sound gets quieter by 1.6 dB and the output only decreases by 1 dB, then the quiet sound has been made *louder* (it didn't decrease as much). Think about it — it's an important concept. With advances in all aspects of recording, reproduction and broadcasting of audio, the usage of compressors changed from reducing the entire program to just reducing selective portions of the program. Thus was born the *threshold* control. Now sound engineers set a threshold point such that all audio below this point is unaffected, and all audio above this point is compressed by the amount determined by the ratio control. Therefore the modern usage for compressors is to turn down (or reduce the dynamic range of) just the loudest signals. Other applications have evolved where compressors are used in controlling the *creation* of sound. For example when used in conjunction with microphones and musical instrument pick-ups, compressors help determine the final timbre by selectively compressing specific frequencies and waveforms. Common examples are "fattening" drum sounds, increasing guitar sustain, vocal "smoothing," and "bringing up" specific sounds out of the mix, etc.] See RaneNote: *Squeeze Me, Stretch Me: The DC 24 Users Guide* , RaneNote: *Signal Processing Fundamentals*, and RaneNote: *Good Dynamics Processing.*

condenser microphone [*Also called **capacitor microphone** but more properly, the correct name is **electrostatic microphone**.*] A microphone design where a condenser (the original name for *capacitor*) is created by stretching a thin diaphragm in front of a metal disc (the *backplate*). By positioning the two surfaces very close together an electrical capacitor is created whose capacitance varies as a function of sound pressure. Any change in sound pressure causes the diaphragm to move, which changes the distance between the two surfaces. If the capacitor is first given an electrical charge (*polarized*) then this movement changes the capacitance, and if the charge is fixed, then the backplate voltage varies proportionally to the sound pressure. In order to create the fixed charge, condenser microphones require external voltage (*polarizing voltage*) to operate. This is normally supplied in the form of phantom power from the microphone preamp or the mixing console.

conjobble An English word no longer in print (*except here*) meaning *to settle, arrange; to chat* (late 17th century).

connectors Audio equipment uses many types of connectors as follow:

banana jack and **banana plug** A single conductor electrical connector with a banana-shaped spring-metal tip most often used on audio power amplifiers for the loudspeaker wiring. Usually configured as a color-coded molded pair (red = hot & black = return) on ¾" spacing. Also used for test leads and as terminals for plug-in components. The British still refer to these as a **GR plug**, after General Radio Corporation, the inventor (according to *The Audio Dictionary* by Glenn D. White).

binding posts Alternate name for banana jacks above, derived from the capability to loosen (unscrew) the body and insert a wire through a hole provided in the electrical terminal and tighten the plastic housing down over the wire insulation, holding the wire in place.

BNC A miniature bayonet locking connector for coaxial cable. Used to interconnect S/PDIF digital audio. See BNC for development and name history.

Cannon connector or **Cannon plug** Alternate reference for XLR.

Elco connector or **Elco plug** AVX Elco manufactures several connectors used for interconnecting multiple audio channels at once, most often found in recording studios on analog and digital audio tape machines. One of these, a 90-pin version (Varicon Series 8016), carries 28 shielded pairs of audio channels, allowing 3-wires per channel (positive, negative & shield) for a true balanced system interconnect.

Euroblocks Shortened form of *European style terminal blocks*, a specialized disconnectable, or *pluggable* terminal block consisting of two pieces. The receptacle is permanently mounted on the equipment and the plug is used to terminate both balanced and unbalanced audio connections using screw terminals. Differs from regular terminal strips in its pluggablility, allowing removal of the equipment by disconnecting the plug section rather than having to unscrew each wire terminal.

RCA (aka *phono jack* or *pin jack*) The Radio Corporation of America (RCA) originally developed this type of unbalanced pin connector for internal chassis connections in radios and televisions during the '30s. It became popular for use in the cables that connected phonograph cartridges to preamplifiers because it was inexpensive and easily fitted to the rather small diameter shielded cables used for the cartridge leads (then they were mono cartridges so single conductor shielded cables were adequate — *now you know.*). The standard connector used in line-level consumer and project studio sound equipment, and most recently to interconnect composite video signals. (excerpted from *Yamaha Sound Reinforcement Handbook*, pp. 297-298).

Speakon® A registered trademark of Neutrik for their original design loudspeaker connector, now considered an industry de facto standard.

terminal strips or **terminal blocks** Also called *barrier strips*, a type of wiring connector provided with screwdown posts separated by insulating barrier strips. Used for balanced and unbalanced wiring connections, where each wire is usually terminated with a crimped-on spade- or ring-connector and screwed in place; not disconnectable, or pluggable. Has become known as the *U.S. style terminal blocks*. Contrast with: Euroblocks.

¼" TRS (*tip-ring-sleeve*) 1. Stereo ¼" connector consisting of tip (T), ring (R), and sleeve (S) sections, with T = left, R = right, and S = ground/shield. 2. Balanced interconnect with the positive & negative signal lines tied to T and R respectively and S acting as an overall shield. 3. Insert loop interconnect with T = send, R = return, and S = ground/shield. [*Think: ring, right, return.*]

¼" TS (*tip-sleeve*) Mono ¼" connector consisting of tip (T) [*signal*] and sleeve (S) [*ground & shield*] for unbalanced wiring.

XLR 1. Originally a registered trademark of ITT-Cannon. The original model number series for Cannon's 3-pin circular connectors — invented by them — now an industry generic term. [*Ray A. Rayburn tells the whole story*: "At one time Cannon made a large circular connector series that was popular for microphones called the P series (now known as the EP series). Mics used the 3-pin P3 version. Some loudspeakers use the P4 or P8 versions of this connector to this day (*Neutrik Speakon NL4MPR 4-pole chassis mount and all Speakon 8-pole chassis mount connectors are made to fit the same mounting holes as the Cannon EP series*). In an attempt to make a smaller connector for the microphone market, Cannon came out with the UA series. These were "D" shaped instead of circular and were used on such mics as the Electro-Voice 666 and 654. There was a desire for a smaller yet connector. Someone pointed out the small circular Cannon X series. The problem with this was it had no latch. Cannon rearranged the pins and added a latch, and the XL (X series with Latch) was born. This is the connector others have copied. Later Cannon modified the female end only to put the contacts in a resilient rubber compound. They called this new version the XLR series. No other company has copied this feature."] 2. The standard connector for digital and analog balanced line interconnect between audio equipment.

constant directivity (CD) horn A horn-loaded high frequency driver that exhibits more or less constant distribution of high-frequency sound in the horizontal direction. This is done by using one of several special dual shaped horn designs created to solve the traditional problem of horn-loaded driver output varying with frequency. All CD horns exhibit a high frequency roll-off of approximately 6 dB/octave beginning somewhere in the 2 kHz to 4 kHz area. Fixed EQ boost networks that compensate for this are known as **CD horn EQ** circuits.

constant group delay See: group delay.

constant-Q equalizer (also **constant-bandwidth**) Term applied to graphic and rotary equalizers describing bandwidth behavior as a function of boost/cut levels. Since Q and bandwidth are inverse sides of the same coin, the terms are interchangeable. The bandwidth remains constant for all boost/cut levels. For constant-Q designs, the skirts vary directly proportional to boost/cut amounts. Small boost/cut levels produce narrow skirts and large boost/cut levels produce wide skirts. See RaneNote: *Constant-Q Graphic Equalizers*, RaneNote: *Operator Adjustable Equalizers*, and RaneNote: *Signal Processing Fundamentals*.

constant-voltage The common name given to the general practices begun in the 1920s and 1930s (becoming a U.S. standard in 1949) governing the interface between power amplifiers and loudspeakers used in *distributed sound systems*. Installations employing ceiling-mounted loudspeakers, such as offices, factories and schools are examples of distributed sound systems. The standard was derived from the need to minimize cost and to simplify the design of complex audio systems. One way to minimize cost is to minimize the use of copper, and one way to do that is to devise a scheme that allows the use of smaller gauge wire than normal 8 Ω loudspeakers require. Borrowing from the cross-country power distribution practices of the electric companies, this was done by using a transformer to step-up the amplifier's output voltage (with a corresponding decrease in output current); use this higher voltage to drive the (now smaller gauge due to smaller current) long lines to the loudspeakers; and then use another transformer to step-down the voltage at each loudspeaker. Clever. This scheme became known as the *constant-voltage* distribution method. The term "constant-voltage" is quite misleading and causes much confusion until understood. Point 1: In electronics, two terms exist to describe two very different power sources: "constant-current" and "constant-voltage." Constant-current is a power source that supplies a fixed amount of current regardless of the load, so the output voltage varies, but the current remains constant. Constant-voltage is just the opposite. The voltage stays constant regardless of the load, so the output current varies but not the voltage. Applied to distributed sound systems, the term is used to describe the action of the system *at full power only.* This is the key point in understanding. *At full power the voltage on the system will not vary as a function of the number of loudspeakers driven*, that is, you may add or remove (subject to the maximum power limits) any number of loudspeakers and the voltage will remain the same, i.e., constant. Point 2: The other thing that is "constant" is the amplifier's output voltage at rated power — and *it is the same voltage for all power ratings.* Several voltages are used, but the most common in the U.S. is 70.7 Vrms. The standard specifies that all power amplifiers put out 70.7 V at their rated power. So, whether it is a 100 watt, or 500 watt or 10 watt power amplifier, the maximum output voltage of each must be the same (constant) value of 70.7 V. This particular number came about from the second way this standard reduced costs: Back in the late '40s, UL safety code specified that all voltages above 100 V peak created a "shock hazard," and subsequently *must be placed in conduit.* Expensive. Bad. So, working backward from a maximum of 100 V peak (conduit not required), you get a maximum rms value of 70.7 V (Vrms = 0.707 Vpeak). [Often "70.7 V" is shortened to just "70 V." It's sloppy; it's wrong; but it's common — accept it.] In Europe, the most common level is 100 Vrms (although 50 V and 70.7 V are used too). This allows use of even smaller wire. Some large U.S. installations used as high as 210 Vrms, with wire runs of over one mile! Remember, the higher the voltage the lower the current, and consequently the smaller the cable and the longer the line can be driven without significant line loss. [The reduction in current exceeds the increase in impedance caused by the smaller wire because of the current-squared nature of power.] In some parts of the U.S., safety regulations regarding conduit use became stricter, forcing distributed systems to adopt a 25 Vrms standard. This still saves conduit, but adds a considerable increase in copper cost, so its use is restricted to small installations. Modern constant-voltage amplifiers either integrate the step-up transformer into the same chassis, or employ a high voltage design to directly drive the line without the need for the transformer. Similarly, constant-voltage loudspeakers have the step-down transformer built-in. Both 70.7 V amplifiers and loudspeakers need only be rated in watts. An amplifier is rated for so many watts output at 70.7 V, and a loudspeaker is rated for so many watts input (to give a certain SPL). Designing a system becomes a relatively simple matter of selecting speakers requiring so many watts to achieve the target SPL (quieter zones use lower wattage speakers, etc.), and then adding up the total to obtain the amplifier(s) power. For example, say you need (10) 25 watt, (5) 50 watt and (15) 10 watt loudspeakers, then you need at least 650 watts of amplifier power (actually you need about 1.5 times this due to real world losses, but that's another story). [*See RaneNote: Constant-Voltage Audio Distribution Systems for more details.*]

contour control *DJ mixers.* A control found on professional DJ performance mixers used to change the shape or taper (*contour*) of the fader action. Thus at, say, 50 % of travel, a fader may allow 50 %, or 10 %, or 90 % of the audio signal to pass depending on the taper of the control. The *contour control* (switched, continuous or stepped variable) changes this amount.

control voltage In audio electronic circuits using voltage-controlled amplifiers, or other gain-controllable devices, a DC voltage proportional to the audio input signal amplitude, sometimes frequency dependent, used to set the instantaneous gain of a VCA or other device. It is normally developed in the *side-chain* of the electronic circuit.

convolution A mathematical operation producing a function from a certain kind of summation or integral of two other functions. In the time domain, one function may be the input signal, and the other the impulse response. The convolution than yields the result of applying that input to a system with the given impulse response. In DSP, the convolution of a signal with FIR filter coefficients results in the filtering of that signal.

cooker wire A British term for the large gauge solid wire (i.e., not stranded) used for electric cookers. Popularly used in ABX testing to confound and expose the aural hallucinations of those obsessed by exotic loudspeaker wire.

Corba (*common object request broker architecture*) An ORB (object request broker) standard developed by the OMG (object management group). Corba provides for standard object-oriented interfaces between ORBs, as well as to external applications and application platforms (from *Newton's Telecom Dictionary*). Not to be confused with CobraNet.

corner frequency Same as *–3 dB point*, or the *3 dB down* point; See: passband.

correlation A mathematical operation that indicates the degree to which two signals are alike.

CRC (*cyclic redundancy check*) An integrity checking process for block data. A CRC character is generated at the transmission end. Its value depends on the hexadecimal value of the number of ones in the data block. The transmitting device calculates the value and appends it to the data block. The receiving end makes a similar calculation and compares its results with the added character. If there is a difference, the recipient requests retransmission.

crap (*completely ridiculous audio performance*) Favorite acronym used to describe the characteristics of poor sound equipment.(Thanks C.D.!)

creepage distance Shortest path along the surface of insulating material between two conductive parts.

crest factor The term used to represent the ratio of the peak (crest) value to the rms value of a waveform measured over a specified time interval. For example, a sine wave has a crest factor of 1.4 (or 3 dB), since the peak value equals 1.414 times the rms value. Music has a wide crest factor range of 4-10 (or 12-20 dB). This means that music peaks occur 12-20 dB higher than the rms value, which is why headroom is so important in audio design.

critical band *Physiology of Hearing.* A range of frequencies that is integrated (summed together) by the neural system, equivalent to a bandpass filter (auditory filter) with approximately 10-20% bandwidth (approximately one-third octave wide). [Although the latest research says critical bands are more like 1/6-octave above 500 Hz, and about 100 Hz wide below 500 Hz.] The ear can be said to be a series of overlapping critical bands, each responding to a narrow range of frequencies. Introduced by Fletcher (1940) to deal with the masking of a pure-tone by wideband noise.

cross-coupled A type of balanced line driver loosely based on servo-loop technology. Developed to emulate some of the features of a balanced line output transformer, the circuit employs positive feedback taken from each side of the outputs coupled back (*cross-coupled*) to the opposite input circuitry where it is used to fix the gain of the positive and negative line drivers. Each gain is typically set to unity (one) for normal operation and changes to *two* whenever either of the output lines is shorted to zero. In this manner, it emulates a transformer in that there is no change in output level if one of the lines becomes short-circuited to ground; however, since the gain of the ungrounded side has increased 6 dB then *the headroom of the system has been reduced by 6 dB* due to the short. In this sense this circuit does not act like a transformer, which does not change gain when one side is shorted to ground. See RaneNote: *Unity Gain and Impedance Matching: Strange Bedfellows.*

crossfade or **crossfader** Within the pro audio industry, a term most often associated with DJ mixers and broadcast. DJ mixers usually feature a *crossfader* slide-type potentiometer control. This control allows the DJ to transition from one stereo program source (located at one travel extreme) to another stereo program source (located at the other travel extreme). It is the crossfader that becomes the main remix tool for turntablists. The exact origin of the first use of a crossfader in the DJ world has proven difficult to track down. It seems certain to have come out of the broadcast industry, where the term "fader" has been in use since at least the '50s (mentioned throughout the Radiotron Designer's Handbook, 4th ed., 1952) and the term "cross-fading" shows up in the Tremaine's Audio Cyclopedia in 1973. Richard Wadman, one of the founders of the British company Citronic, designed the earliest example documented so far. It was called the model **SMP101**, made about 1977, and had a crossfader that doubled as a L/R balance control or a crossfade between two inputs. [*Anyone who can document an earlier example of a DJ crossfader please write me.*]
For a history of DJ-use crossfader circuitry see: RaneNote: *Evolution of the DJ Mixer Crossfader* by Rane's ace DJ-mixer designer, Rick Jeffs. Contrast with: pan, balance and fader controls.

cross-framing A term borrowed from the construction industry (meaning diagonal bracing) by TimeLine to describe their new TL-Sync product with "independent cross-framing" capability that allows a longitudinal timecode (LTC) reader and two generators to be set to different frame rates.

crossover An electrical circuit (passive or active) consisting of a combination of high-pass, low-pass and bandpass filters used to divide the audio frequency spectrum (20 Hz - 20 kHz) into segments suitable for individual loudspeaker use. Since audio wavelengths vary from over 50 feet at the low frequency end, to less than one inch at the high frequency end, no single loudspeaker driver can reproduce the entire audio range. Therefore, at least two drivers are required, and more often three or more are used for optimum audio reproduction. Named from the fact that audio reproduction *transitions* (or *crosses over*) from one driver to the next as the signal increases in frequency. For example, consider a two driver loudspeaker crossed over at 800 Hz: Here only one driver (the **woofer** — *"woof, woof"* = low frequencies) works to reproduce everything below 800 Hz, while both drivers work reproducing the region immediately around 800 Hz (the *crossover region*), and finally, only the last driver (the **tweeter** — *"tweet, tweet"* = high frequencies) works to reproduce everything above 800 Hz. Crossover circuits are characterized by their *type* (Butterworth, Bessel and Linkwitz-Riley being the most popular), and by the steepness of their *roll-off slopes* (the rate of attenuation outside their passbands) as measured in decibels per interval, such as *dB/octave*, or sometimes *dB/decade* [useful rule-of-thumb: 6 dB/octave approximately equals 20 dB/decade]. See RaneNote: *Signal Processing Fundamentals.*

crosstalk (recording) See: print-through.

crosstalk (signal) 1. Undesired capacitive, inductive, or conductive coupling from one circuit, part of a circuit, or channel, to another. 2. Any phenomenon by which a signal transmitted on one circuit or channel of a transmission system creates an undesired effect in another circuit or channel. Note: In telecommunications, crosstalk is usually distinguishable as speech or signaling tones. See RaneNote: *Audio Specifications.*

cue 1. A term found throughout various audio fields meaning to monitor, or listen (via headphones) to a specific source. In mixers (particularly DJ mixers), the term is used interchangeably with solo or PFL as found on recording consoles. 2. Music. a. A section of music used in film or video ranging from a short piece of background music to a complex score. b. An extract from the music for another part printed, usually in smaller notes, within a performer's part as a signal to enter after a long rest. c. A gesture by a conductor signaling the entrance of a performer or part. 3. A signal, such as a word or an action, used to prompt another event in a performance, such as an actor's speech or entrance, a change in lighting, or a sound effect. (AHD)

current *Symbol* **i, I** *Electricity.* a. A flow of electric charge. b. The amount of electric charge flowing past a specified circuit point per unit time, or the rate of flow of electrons. (AHD) [As electrons flow in one direction, the spaces left behind, called *holes*, appear to flow in the opposite direction. Thus, current can be visualized as *electron flow* (negative current flow), or in the opposite direction, *hole flow* (positive current flow, sometimes called *conventional current flow*).]

current loop A data transmission scheme that looks for current flow rather than voltage levels. This systems recognizes no current flow as a binary zero, and having current flow as a binary one. Favored for its low sensitivity to cable impedance, and independence of a common ground reference; hence current loops do not introduce ground loops. MIDI is an example of a current loop interconnect system.

cut-only equalizer Term used to describe graphic equalizers designed only for attenuation. (Also referred to as notch equalizers, or band-reject equalizers). The flat (0 dB) position locates all sliders at the top of the front panel. Comprised only of notch filters (normally spaced at ⅓-octave intervals), all controls start at 0 dB and reduce the signal on a band-by-band basis. Proponents of cut-only philosophy argue that boosting runs the risk of reducing system headroom.

cutoff frequency *Filters.* The frequency at which the signal falls off by 3 dB (the *half power point*) from its maximum value. Also referred to as the *-3 dB points*, or the *corner* frequencies.

D

DA-88 Tascam's model number for their digital multitrack recorder using Sony-developed "Hi8" 8 mm videotape as the storage medium. Becoming a generic term describing this family of recorders. See: DTRS.

DA (*distribution amplifier*) Common abbreviation used throughout the broadcast, telecommunication and sound consulting/contracting fields.

DAA (*Digital Access Arrangement*) *Telephony.* Name for the physical connection to the telephone line known as the *local loop.* The DAA performs the four critical functions of *line termination, isolation, hybrid,* and *ring detection.*

DAB (*digital audio broadcast*) 1. NRSC (National Radio Systems Committee) term for the next generation of digital radio broadcast. 2. Initials of the compiler of this book.

DAC (or **D/A**, *digital-to-analog converter*) The electronic component which converts digital words into analog signals that can then be amplified and used to drive loudspeakers, etc. The DAC is the last link in the digital chain of signal processing. See: data converter bits.

damping factor Damping is a measure of a power amplifier's ability to control the back-emf motion of the loudspeaker cone after the signal disappears. *The damping factor of a system is the ratio of the loudspeaker's nominal impedance to the total impedance driving it.* Perhaps an example best illustrates this principle: let's say you have a speaker cabinet nominally rated at 8 Ω, and you are driving it with a Rane MA 6S power amp through 50 feet of 12 gauge cable. Checking the MA 6S data sheet (obtained off the Rane website, of course), you don't find its output impedance, but you do find that its damping factor is 300. What this means is that the ratio of a nominal 8 Ω loudspeaker to the MA 6S's output impedance is 300. Doing the math [8 divided by 300] comes up with an amazing .027 Ω. Pretty low. Looking up 12 gauge wire in your handy Belden Cable catalog (...then get one.) tells you it has .001588 Ω per foot, which sure ain't much, but then again you've got 100 feet of it (that's right: 50 feet out and 50 feet back — don't be tricked), so that's 0.159 Ω. That is about six times as much impedance as your amplifier. (Now there's a lesson in itself — *use big cable.*) Adding these together gives a total driving impedance of 0.186 Ω still pretty low — yielding a very good damping factor of 43 (anything over 10 is enough, so you don't have to get extreme about wire size). [Note that the word is damp-*ing*, not damp-*ning* as is so often heard — correct your friends; make enemies.]

DAR (*digital audio radio*) EIA term for the next generation of digital radio broadcasting standards.

DASH (*digital audio stationary head*) A family of formats for ensuring compatibility among digital multitrack studio recorders using stationary (as opposed to rotating) heads. The DASH standard, popularized by Sony and Studer, specifies 2 to 48 tracks, with tape speeds from 12 to 76 cm/sec.

DAT (*digital audio tape recorder*) 1. A digital audio recorder utilizing a magnetic tape cassette system with rotary heads similar to that of a video recorder. 2. A little bit of something as in *dis & dat.*

data cables Analog audio signals require a relatively small bandwidth and are interconnected using standard cables. In contrast to analog audio, digital audio and digital control signals require a very large bandwidth and must be interconnected with specially designed *data* cables. See: Category cables.

data compression See: digital audio data compression.

data converter bits The number of bits determines the data converter *precision.* The more bits available, the more precise the conversion, i.e., the closer the digital answer will be to the analog original. When an analog signal is sampled (at the sampling frequency), it is being sliced up into vertical pieces. Each vertical piece is then estimated as to its amplitude (*How large is the audio signal at this instant?*). This estimation process is the data converter's job. It compares the original signal against its best estimate and chooses the closest answer. The more bits, the more choices the data converter has to choose from. The number of choices is the number "2" raised to the number of bits (*this explanation is simplified for clarity*). For example, 16-bits creates 2 to the 16th power of choices, or 65,536 possible answers for the converter to choose from. And the higher the sampling rate, the more slices for any given time period. Again, the more slices, the more accurate will be the data conversion. All of which ultimately determines how well the reproduced signal sounds compared to the original. For example, if a signal is recorded using "16-bits at 48 kHz", then for every one second of the audio signal, it is sliced up into 48,000 pieces. Then each piece is compared against a ruler with 2 to the 16th graduations, or 65,536 voltage levels. Each sample instant is compared against this ruler and one value is assigned to represent its amplitude. For each second, 48,000 samples are given specific values to represent the original signal. If the same signal is recorded using "24-bits at 96 kHz" then for the same one second period, there will be 96,000 slices, or samples, and each one will be compared against a voltage ruler now divided into 2 to the 24th divisions, or 16,777,216 choices. Obviously this converter can choice an answer that is far closer to the original than before, and it gets to do this for twice as many samples. All of which, in the end, means this converter recorded samples that more closely approximated the original audio signal. [*Where it gets interesting is in trying to answer the question of what is enough? Sure, more bits are more accurate, but can the human ear tell the difference. In most cases, once you go beyond true 16-bits, the answer is no. All benefits above 16-bits/48 kHz are very small refinements, not monumental improvements. What really is going on, is that the advertised "16-bit/48 kHz" recordings of yesterday weren't. They used 16-bit converters but their accuracy was not 16-bits, it was more like 14-bits. Similarly today, the advertised "24-bit" converters are not 24-bit accurate, but they are certainly at least 18-bit accurate, and that makes an audible difference. So, if you can find a true 16-bit system and compare it with a typical 24-bit system of today, they will sound very nearly identical. And the sampling rate getting faster makes even less of an audible difference. For example if you compare a typical 16-bit/96 kHz system against a 24-bit/48 kHz, you will pick the 24-bit system every time. If you have a choice, always choose more bits, over a higher sampling rate.*] See RaneNote: *Digital Dharma of Audio A/D Converters.*

DAW (*digital audio workstation*) Any of several software/hardware systems using a computer as the basis for creating, editing, storing, and playback of digital audio, using the computer's hard disk as the recording medium, or a SAN.

dB (*decibel*) See: decibel.

DB-25 connector A 25-pin D-shell connector standardized for RS-232 serial communications.

DB-9 connector A smaller 9-pin version of the connector used for RS-232 communications. First made popular by IBM in their AT personal computer.

DCA (*digitally-controlled attenuator*) Also *digitally-controlled analog* and *digitally-controlled amplifier*.

DCC (*Digital Compact Cassette*) Philips's digital version of the standard analog cassette tape system. A DCC recorder plays and records digital cassettes, as well as playing analog cassettes. [Now discontinued.]

DCE (*Data Communications Equipment*) Within the RS-232 standard, the equipment that provides the functions required to establish, maintain, and terminate a connection, as well as the signal conversion, and coding required for communication between data terminal equipment and data circuit — e.g., a modem or printer. See: DTE. The main difference between DCE and DTE is the wiring of pins 2 and 3, thus the need for a null modem cable when tying two computers together.

deadly nevergreen An English word no longer in print (except here) meaning *the gallows* (late 18th, early 19th centuries).

Dead Musician Directory "A site about dead musicians ... and how they got that way" Hey! Don't laugh, these guys are dead serious. Dead Rockers, jazz, reggae, bluegrass, etc.

Dead Recording Media A great chronicle of obsolete devices compiled by David L. Morton: "... site devoted to the dead, dying, or very ill technologies of sound recording."

decibel *Abbr.* **dB** Equal to one-tenth of a bel. [After **Alexander Graham Bell**.] 1. A measuring system first used in telephony (Martin, W.H., "DeciBel — the new name for the transmission unit. *Bell System Tech. J.* January, 1929), where signal loss is a *logarithmic* function of the cable length. 2. The preferred method and term for representing the *ratio* of different audio levels. It is a mathematical shorthand that uses *logarithms* (a shortcut using the powers of 10 to represent the actual number) to reduce the size of the number. For example, instead of saying the dynamic range is 32,000 to 1, we say it is 90 dB [*the answer in dB equals 20 log x/y, where x and y are the different signal levels*]. Being a ratio, *decibels have no units.* Everything is relative. Since it is relative, then it must be relative to some *0 dB reference point*. To distinguish between reference points a suffix letter is added as follows: [*The officially correct way per AES-R2, IEC 60027-3 & IEC 60268-2 documents is to enclose the reference value in parenthesis separated by a space from "dB"; however this never caught on, for brevity reasons if no other.*]

0 dBu Preferred informal abbreviation for the official dB (0.775 V); a voltage reference point equal to 0.775 Vrms. [This reference originally was labeled dB*v* (lower-case) but was too often confused with dBV (upper-case), so it was changed to dBu (for unterminated).]

+4 dBu Standard pro audio voltage reference level equal to 1.23 Vrms.

0 dBV Preferred informal abbreviation for the official dB (1.0 V); a voltage reference point equal to 1.0 Vrms.

-10 dBV Standard voltage reference level for consumer and some pro audio use (e.g. TASCAM) equal to 0.316 Vrms. (Tip: RCA connectors are a good indicator of units operating at -10 dBV levels.)

0 dBm Preferred informal abbreviation of the official dB (mW); a *power* reference point equal to 1 milliwatt. To convert into an equivalent voltage level, *the impedance must be specified*. For example, 0 dBm into 600 Ω gives an equivalent voltage level of 0.775 V, or 0 dBu (See above); however, 0 dBm into 50 Ω, for instance, yields an equivalent voltage of 0.224 V — something quite different. Since modern audio engineering is concerned with voltage levels, as opposed to power levels of yore, the convention of using a reference level of 0 dBm is obsolete. The reference levels of +4 dBu, or -10 dBV are the preferred units.

0 dBr An arbitrary reference level (r = *re*; or *reference*) that must be specified. For example, a signal-to-noise graph may be calibrated in dBr, where 0 dBr is specified to be equal to 1.23 Vrms (+4 dBu); commonly stated as "dB re +4," that is, "0 dBr is defined to be equal to +4 dBu."

0 dBFS A digital audio reference level equal to "Full Scale." Used in specifying A/D and D/A audio data converters. Full scale refers to the maximum *peak* voltage level possible before "digital clipping," or digital overload (See: overs) of the data converter. The Full Scale value is fixed by the internal data converter design, and varies from model to model. [*According to standards people, there's supposed to be a space between "dB" and "FS" — yeah, right, like that's gonna happen.*]

decimal digit Everyday normal, base-10 numbers.

DED (pronounced "dead") (***dark emitting diode***) A variation of LED technology used exclusively by the CIA for clandestine equipment. Also popular as power-off indicators.

de-emphasis See: pre-emphasis.

de-esser A special type of audio signal compressor that operates only at high frequencies (>3 kHz), used to reduce the effect of vocal sibilant sounds.

De Forest, Lee (1873-1961) Known as "the Father of Radio," he was an American electrical engineer who patented the triode electron tube (1907) that made possible the amplification and detection of radio waves. He originated radio news broadcasts in 1916. (AHD)

delay 1. *Crossovers.* A signal processing device or circuit used to delay one or more of the output signals by a controllable amount. This feature is used to correct for loudspeaker drivers that are mounted such that their *points of apparent sound origin* (not necessarily their voice coils) are not physically aligned. Good delay circuits are frequency independent, meaning the specified delay is equal for all audio frequencies (*constant group delay*). Delay circuits based on digital sampling techniques are inherently frequency independent and thus preferred. 2. *MI.* Digital audio delay circuits comprise the heart of most all "effects" boxes sold in the MI world. Reverb, flanging, chorusing, phasers, echoing, looping, etc., all use delay in one form or another. 3. *Sound Reinforcement.* Acousticians and sound contractors use signal delay units to "aim" loudspeaker arrays. Introducing small amounts of delay between identical, closely mounted drivers, fed from the same source, controls the direction of the combined response.

delta modulation A single-bit coding technique in which a constant step size digitizes the input waveform. Past knowledge of the information permits encoding only the differences between consecutive values.

delta-sigma ADC See: delta-sigma modulation.

delta-sigma modulation (also **sigma-delta**) An analog-to-digital conversion scheme rooted in a design originally proposed in 1946, but not made practical until 1974 by James C. Candy. Inose and Yasuda coined the name delta-sigma modulation at the University of Tokyo in 1962, but due to a misunderstanding the words were interchanged and taken to be *sigma-delta*. Both names are still used for describing this modulator. Characterized by oversampling and digital filtering to achieve high performance at low cost, a delta-sigma A/D thus consists of an analog modulator and a digital filter. The fundamental principle behind the modulator is that of a single-bit A/D converter embedded in an analog negative feedback loop with high open loop gain. The modulator loop oversamples and processes the analog input at a rate much higher than the bandwidth of interest (See: Sampling (Nyquist) Theorem). The modulator's output provides 1-bit information at a very high rate and in a format that a digital filter can process to extract higher resolution (such as 20-bits) at a lower rate. See RaneNote: *Digital Dharma of Audio A/D Converters.*

denominator *Mathematics.* The bottom part of a common fraction.

Descartes, René (1596-1650) French mathematician and philosopher. Considered the father of analytic geometry, he formulated the Cartesian system of coordinates. [*Then there's the story about how Descartes met his ultimate demise: It seems he was in a bar in Paris sipping a glass of Kir when the bartender asked if he would like another. M. Descartes responded "I think not," whereupon he disappeared without a trace.*] (Thanks to Glenn White for this.)

deserializer A serial-to-parallel data converter; used in buses and networks.

destructive solo See: solo.

DI (***digital audio input***) AES3 (IEC 60958-4) abbreviation to be used for panel marking where space is limited and the function of the XLR AES3 connector might be confused with an analog signal connector.

DI (***direct***) **box** See: direct box.

diatonic 1. *Music.* Of or using only the eight tones of a standard major or minor scale without chromatic deviations. (AHD) 2. A popular summer drink without the gin or the sugar.

dictionary "A malevolent literary device for cramping the growth of a language and making it hard and inelastic. This dictionary, however, is a most useful work." — Ambrose Bierce.

difference-tone IMD See: IM.

differential amplifier *Electronics.* A three-terminal analog device consisting of two inputs designated positive and negative and one output that responds to the difference in potential between them.

diffraction *Acoustics.* The bending of waves around obstacles and the spreading of waves through openings that are approximately the same as the wavelength of the waves. See: link.

diffraction grating A usually glass or polished metal surface having a large number of very fine parallel grooves or slits cut in the surface and used to produce optical spectra by diffraction of reflected or transmitted light. (AHD)

diffuse Widely spread out or scattered; not concentrated. (AHD)

diffuser (or **diffusor**, British spelling; in acoustics, the British spelling is seen most often.) A commercial device that diffuses, or scatters sound. First invented by Manfred R. Schroeder ["Diffuse Sound Reflection by Maximum-Length Sequences," *J. Acous. Soc. Am.,* Vol. 57, No. 1, pp. 149-150, Jan 1975], and made commercially successful by Dr. Peter D'Antonio and his company RPG Diffusor Systems. Diffusors are the acoustical analog of diffraction grating — see: diffraction grating.

digital audio The use of sampling and quantization techniques to store or transmit audio information in binary form. The use of numbers (typically binary) to represent audio signals.

digital audio data compression Commonly shortened to "audio compression." Any of several algorithms designed to reduce the number of bits (hence, bandwidth and storage requirements) required for accurate digital audio storage and transmission. Characterized by being "lossless" or "lossy." The audio compression is "lossy" if actual data is lost due to the compression scheme, and "lossless" if it is not. Well-designed algorithms ensure "lost" information is inaudible — that's how you win the game.

digital audio recording formats See *The Digital Revolution* compiled by Steve E. Schoenherr — *outstanding compilation beginning in 1937 with the invention of PCM by Alec H. Reeves.*

digital audio watermarking See: watermarking.

digital clipping See: 0 dBFS.

digital filter Any filter accomplished in the digital domain.

digital hybrid See: hybrid.

digital overs See: overs.

digital signal Any signal which is quantized (i.e., limited to a distinct set of values) into digital words at discrete points in time. The accuracy of a digital value is dependent on the number of bits used to represent it.

digitization Any conversion of analog information into a digital form.

diminished fifth 1. A fifth is an interval of 3:2 (*interval* is the ratio of frequencies between a base note and another note). A diminished fifth is a half step lower. 2. What's left after you've had a few shots. [*Thanks GD*]

DIN Acronym for *Deutsche Industrie Norm (Deutsches Institut fuer Normung),* the German standardization body.

dipless crossfader A crossfader design that does not attenuate the first audio signal until the fader is moved past the 50 % travel point, while simultaneously increasing the second audio signal to 100 % at the center point. With this design there is no attenuation (*dip*) in the center position for either audio signal, hence "dipless."

direct box Also known as a **DI box**, a phrase first coined by Franklin J. Miller, founder of Sescom, to describe a device that enables a musical instrument (guitar, etc.) to be connected *directly* to a mic- or line-level mixer input. The box provides the very high input impedance required by the instrument and puts out the correct level for the mixer.

direct out Term for auxiliary outputs found on some mic preamps, mixing consoles, and teleconferencing equipment. Direct outputs are taken before any signal processing (other than normal mic preamp functions like gain, buffering, phantom power, band-limiting filters, etc.), or mixing with other channels is done, hence, normally at line-level.

direct sound Sound first arriving. Sound reaching the listening location without reflections, i.e., sound that travels *directly* to the listener. See: early reflections.

disc The term used for any *optical* storage media. Originally popularized to refer to phonograph records. From Latin *discus*, the term refers primarily to *audio* and *video* storage systems, such as compact discs, laser discs, etc., but the advent of CD-ROMs and computer optical storage units blurs this distinction. Compare with: disk.

discoidal capacitor Also known as feed-thru capacitors, they are used mainly by connector designers to create in-line EMI/RFI filters for each pin. Constructed of ceramic dielectric, and toroidal shaped, these capacitors help suppress electromagnetic interference by shunting the interference to ground, and if combined with a series inductor become even more effective. The feed-thru design results in greatly reduced self-inductance compared to standard leaded capacitors. The combination of low inductance and high input/output isolation provides excellent shunting of EMI for frequencies up to and beyond 1 GHz. Made by Spectrum Control, Inc., CDI, INSTEC, and others.

discreet Marked by, exercising, or showing prudence and wise self-restraint in speech and behavior. (AHD) [*You may want to be discreet when bussing someone.*]

discrete Constituting a separate thing; distinct, or a set of distinct things. (AHD)

discrete Fourier transform (DFT) 1. A numerical method of calculating the coefficients of the Fourier series from a sampled periodic signal. 2. A DSP algorithm used to determine the Fourier coefficient corresponding to a set of frequencies, normally linearly spaced. See: Fourier theorem.

disk The term used for any *magnetic* storage media such as computer diskettes or hard disks. From Greek *diskos*, the term refers primarily to *non-audio digital data storage*, but the advent of hard disk digital audio recording systems fogs this up somewhat. Compare with: disc.

distance learning A specialized form of videoconferencing optimized for educational uses. Distance learning allows students to attend classes in a location distant from where the course is being presented. Two-way audio and video allows student and instructor interaction.

distortion *Audio distortion*: By its name you know it is a measure of unwanted signals. Distortion is the name given to anything that alters a pure input signal in any way other than changing its size. The most common forms of distortion are unwanted components or artifacts added to the original signal, including random and hum-related noise. Distortion measures a system's linearity — or nonlinearity, whichever way you want to look at it. Anything unwanted added to the input signal changes its shape (skews, flattens, spikes, alters symmetry or asymmetry, even if these changes are microscopic, they are there). A spectral analysis of the output shows these unwanted components. If a piece of gear is perfect, it does not add distortion of any sort. The spectrum of the output shows only the original signal — nothing else — no added components, no added noise — nothing but the original signal. See RaneNote: *Audio Specifications.*

distribution amplifier A splitter with added features. Distribution amplifiers (usually) feature balanced inputs and outputs with high-current line drivers (often cross-coupled) capable of driving very long lines.

dither The noise (analog or digital) added to a signal prior to quantization (or word length reduction) which reduces the distortion and noise modulation resulting from the quantization process. Although there is a slight increase in the noise level, spectrally shaped dither can minimize the apparent increase. The noise is less objectionable than the distortion, and allows low-level signals to be heard more clearly. The most popular type of dither is called TPDF. See RaneNote: *Digital Dharma of Audio A/D Converters.*

DIY Acronym for *do-it-yourself,* usually referring to various hobbies especially audio-related.

DLP (*digital light processing*) Texas Instrument's proprietary projection display technology. The basis of the technology is the Digital Micromirror Device (DMD) semiconductor chip, which uses an array of up to 1.3 million hinged, microscopic mirrors (made using nano-technology) that operate as optical switches to create a high resolution color image. See: TI's DLP website.

DMD (*digital micromirror device*) See DLP above.

DMM (*digital multimeter*) See: VTVM.

DO (*digital audio output*) AES3 (and IEC 60958-4) abbreviation to be used for panel marking where space is limited and the function of the XLR digital AES3 connector might be confused with an analog signal connector.

Dolby Digital® Dolby's name for its format for the digital soundtrack system for motion picture playback. Utilizes their AC-3 system of digital compression. The signal is optically printed *between* the sprocket holes. Now being introduced to Home Theater on laserdisc and DVD. Dolby Digital may use any number of primary audio delivery and reproduction channels, from 1 to 5, and may include a separate bass-only effects channel. The designation "5.1" describes the complete channel format. Surround decoder systems with Dolby Digital automatically contain Dolby Pro Logic processing to ensure full compatibility with the many existing program soundtracks made with Dolby Surround encoding. *No abbreviations are to be used.* See RaneNote: *Home Cinema Systems.*

dongle Security device for protected software: a small hardware device that, when plugged into a computer, enables a specific copy-protected program to run, the program being disabled on that computer if the device is not present. The device is effective against software piracy.

Doppler effect [After **Christian Johann Doppler**, 1803-1853, Austrian physicist and mathematician who first enunciated this principle in 1842.] 1. For an observer, the apparent change in pitch (frequency) of a sound (or any wave) when there is relative motion between the source and the listener (or observer). The classic example is the train phenomenon where the pitch of the whistle sounds higher approaching and lower leaving. 2. Gave rise to the variation known as the *dope-ler effect,* defined as the phenomenon of stupid ideas that seem smarter when they come at you in rapid succession. [Thanks, JF.]

DOS (pronounced "doss") (*disk operating system*) A software program controlling data in memory, disk storage, running programs and I/O management.

double balanced See: cables.

double bass A large viola that plays one octave lower than the cello, thereby doubling the bass. Also referred to as a *Baroque doghouse* for its deep tones. See Slatford for historical details.

double-blind comparator See: ABX testing.

double precision The use of two computer words to represent each number. This preserves or improves the precision, or *correctness*, of the calculated answer. For example, if the number 999 is single precision, then 999999 is the double precision equivalent.

doubling *Recording.* An effect where the original signal is added to a slightly delayed version of itself. The result is a fuller sound, giving the aural impression of more players or singers then originally recorded. The most famous use of doubling is that done by Roger Nichols on Donald Fagen's vocals and Walter Becker's instruments in all *Steely Dan* recordings.

downward expander See: expander.

drain wire A non-insulated wire in contact with parts of a cable, usually the shield(s), used for chassis or earth grounding; in general, a ground or shield wire.

dreamt The only English word ending in the letters "mt."

DRM (*Digital Rights Management*) Controlling mechanisms for exchanging intellectual property in digital form over the Internet or other electronic media. Basically, DRM is an encryption distribution scheme with built-in payment methods. Content is encoded, and to decode it a user must do something like supply a credit card, or provide an email address, or whatever. Content owners set the conditions.

dropout An error condition in which bits are incorrect or lost from a digital medium. Also occurs with analog tape — audio or video.

dry *Recording.* 1. The original recorded signal before any effects processing. 2. Any signal without reverberation; dead. Contrast with: wet.

dry circuit See below.

dry transformer *Telephony.* An analog audio transformer designed for AC operation only; no direct current (DC) is allowed to flow in the primary or secondary coils. Derived from the term, *dry circuit*, referring to a circuit where voice signals are transmitted but does not carry direct current. Contrast with: wet transformer.

DSD (*Direct Stream Digital*) See: SACD.

DSP (*digital signal processing*) A technology for signal processing that combines algorithms and fast number-crunching digital hardware, and is capable of high-performance and flexibility.

DTE (*Data Terminal Equipment*) 1. Within the RS-232 standard, the equipment comprising the data source, the receiver, or both — e.g., personal computers or terminals. See: DCE. The main difference between DTE and DCE is the wiring of pins 2 and 3, thus the need for a null modem cable when tying two computers together. 2. *CobraNet* refers to DTEs as the source and sink devices on the network, i.e., they source and sink audio. Rane's *NM 48 & NM 84 Network Mic/Line Preamps* are DTE devices.

DTMF (*dual tone multi-frequency*) Normal everyday push-button touch-tone dialing system, where a combination of two tones is used for each button pushed.

DTRS (*digital tape recording system*) Tascam's suggested term for describing their DA-88 type digital multitrack recorders.

DTS Coherent Acoustics® (now *DTS Cinema*) A competing digital soundtrack system for motion picture playback developed by Digital Theater Systems Inc. (backed by Stephen Spielberg and Universal Studios). Its novelties are: 1) not requiring a special projector to read digital code off the filmstrip like its competitors; 2) using only very moderate compression (3:1 verses Dolby's 11:1); and 3) offering 20-bit audio. The discrete digital full bandwidth six (6) channel sound is contained on a CD that is played synchronously with the film. The synching time code is printed between the standard optical soundtrack and the picture.

DTS-ES (*DTS Extended Surround*) Digital Theater System's version of THX Surround EX. DTS-ES adds a third surround channel to the left and right surround channels in a DTS-encoded signal. Two versions exist: straight "DTS-ES" matrix-encodes the third surround channel into the existing left and right surround signals in a 5.1 channel source, while "DTS-ES Discrete" is a new format that adds a separate third surround channel.

DTS Zeta Digital™ (now *DTS Consumer*) Digital Theater Systems' audio compression scheme applied to laser disc, DVD and CD technology for home theater use. Competing format with Dolby's AC-3 algorithm. See RaneNote: *Home Cinema Systems.*

dubplate *DJ.* An acetate one-off version of a vinyl record. The name comes from the Jamaican dancehall reggae scene in the early '70s where "dub" or instrumental versions of songs were produced so the vocalist could "toast" over the "riddims" in club settings.

ducker A dynamic processor that lowers (or "ducks") the level of one audio signal based upon the level of a second audio signal. A typical application is paging: A ducker senses the presence of audio from a paging microphone and triggers a reduction in the output level of the main audio signal for the duration of the page signal. It restores the original level once the page message is over. Another use is for talkover.

Dudley, Homer Inventor of the vocoder. [*Dudley, H. (1939) "The Vocoder," Bell Labs Record, 17, pp. 122-126*]

dummy load Any substitute device having impedance characteristics simulating those of the substituted device. For example, see: amplifier dummy load.

duplex Pertaining to a simultaneous two-way independent transmission in both directions. Often referred to as "full duplex" which is redundant. See also: half-duplex.

DVD (Officially "DVD" does not stand for anything. At one time it was "digital *versatile* disc" — and before that it meant "digital *video* disc" also once known as *hdCD* in Europe.) A 12-centimeter (4.72") compact disc (same size as audio CDs and CD-ROMs) that holds 10 times the information. Capable of holding full-length movies *and* a video game based on the movie, or a movie *and* its soundtrack, or two versions of the same movie — all in sophisticated discrete digital audio surround sound. The DVD standard specifies a laminated single-sided, single-layer disc holding 4.7 gigabytes, and 133 minutes of MPEG-2 compressed video and audio. It is backwards compatible, and expandable to two-layers holding 8.5 gigabytes. Ultimately two discs could be bounded together yielding two-sides, each with two-layers, for a total of 17 gigabytes. There are four main versions:

DVD-Video (movies) As outlined above.

DVD-Audio (music-only) The standard is flexible, allowing for many possibilities, leaving the DVD-player to detect which system is used and adapt. Choices include 74 minutes for 2-chs at 24-bits, 192 kHz sampling, or 6-chs at 24-bits, 96 kHz, all utilizing lossless compression (type MLP for *Meridian Lossless Packing*). Quantization can be 16-, 20-, & 24-bits, with sampling frequencies of 44.1, 88.2, and 176.4 kHz, as well as 48, 96, and 192 kHz all supported. [*See: "DVD-Audio Specifications" by Norihiko Fuchigami, Toshio Kuroiwa, and Bike H. Suzuki, in the J. Audio Eng. Soc., Vol. 48, No. 12, December 2000, pp. 1228-1240 for complete details.*]

DVD-ROM (read-only, i.e., games and computer use)

DVD-RAM (rewritable, i.e., recording systems). Matsushita (*Panasonic* brand) is currently the leader in density with 4.7 Gb and 9.4 Gb claimed for single-sided and double-sided discs respectively, compared with 2.6 Gb and 5.2 Gb offered by standard DVD-RAM technology. There are several competing formats:

DVD-R (Hitachi, Pioneer & Matsushita) Primary 4.7 Gb application is peripheral drive for PCs, but is also of interest for video servers, video-disk cameras and other consumer applications.

DVD-RW (Pioneer) Also 4.7 Gb aimed at VCR replacement.

DVD+RW or just **RW** (because it is not sanctioned by the DVD Forum) (Sony, Philips & Hewlett-Packard) Originally a 3-Gbyte system, positioned as a PC peripheral, but now expanded to a 4.7 Gbyte consumer version.

MMVF-DVD (NEC's 5.2 Gbyte *Multimedia Video File* Disk system) Now officially shifted from a laboratory project to a business project.

dynamic controllers (or **dynamic processors**) A class of signal processing devices used to alter an audio signal based solely upon its *frequency content* and *amplitude level*, thus the term "dynamic" since the processing is completely program dependent. The two most common dynamic effects are compressors and expanders, with limiters, noise gates (or just "gates"), duckers and levelers being subsets of these. Another dynamic controller category includes exciters, or enhancers. And noise reduction units fall into a final dynamic processor category. See RaneNote: *Squeeze Me, Stretch Me: The DC 24 Users Guide.*

dynamic microphone A microphone design where a wire coil (the *voice coil*) is attached to a small diaphragm such that sound pressure causes the coil to move in a magnetic field, thus creating an electrical voltage proportional to the sound pressure. Works in almost the exact opposite of a dynamic loudspeaker where an electrical voltage is applied to the voice coil attached to a large cone (diaphragm) causing it to move in a magnetic field, thus creating a change in the immediate sound pressure. In fact, under the right circumstances, both elements will operate as the other, i.e., a dynamic loudspeaker will act as a microphone and a dynamic microphone will act as a loudspeaker — although not too loud. See: electromagnetic induction.

dynamic range The ratio of the loudest (undistorted) signal to that of the quietest (discernible) signal in a unit or system as expressed in decibels (dB). Dynamic range is another way of stating the *maximum S/N ratio*. With reference to signal processing equipment, the maximum output signal is restricted by the size of the power supplies, i.e., it cannot swing more voltage than is available. While the noise floor of the unit determines the minimum output signal, i.e., it cannot put out a discernible signal smaller than the noise. Professional-grade analog signal processing equipment can output maximum levels of +26 dBu, with the best noise floors being down around -94 dBu. This gives a maximum *dynamic range* of 120 dB — pretty impressive numbers, which coincide nicely with the 120 dB dynamic range of normal human hearing (from just audible to uncomfortably loud). See RaneNote: *Audio Specifications.*

dyne A unit of force, equal to the force required to impart an acceleration of one centimeter per second per second to a mass of one gram. (AHD) Old units for sound pressure.

E

e *Mathematics.* The base of the natural system of logarithms, having a numerical value of approximately 2.71828. (AHD) See: Maor.

ear *Anatomy.* The vertebrate organ of hearing, responsible for maintaining equilibrium as well as sensing sound and divided in mammals into the external ear, the middle ear, and the inner ear. [AHD]

early reflections *Acoustics.* The first sound that arrives at a listener is called the direct sound; the next to arrive is the first reflected sound waves, which take a little longer to reach the listener due to travelling a slightly longer path length. The first several reflected sound waves to reach the listener after the direct sound are called *early reflections.*

earthshine The sunlight reflected from the Earth to the moon and back again. Leonardo da Vinci was the first person to figure out that when the Earth reflects enough light, we can see the entire moon, not just the crescent.

EASE (*Enhanced Acoustic Simulator for Engineers*) A computer modeling tool distributed by Renkus-Heinz for ADA (Acoustic Design Ahnert), who developed the software and introduced it in 1990 at the 88th AES Convention in Montreux.

EBU (*European Broadcasting Union*) An international professional society that, among other things, helps establish audio standards.

echo 1. *Acoustics* A discrete sound reflection arriving at least 50 milliseconds after the direct sound, and significantly louder than the background reverberant sound field. Contrast with: reverberation. 2. *Psychoacoustics* A perceptually distinct copy of the original sound; a delayed duplicate. A single echo may be the result of multiple surface reflections. [Blesser]

echo canceller A technique using DSP (analog circuits exist, but DSP solutions are overwhelmingly superior) that filters unwanted signals caused by echoes from the main audio source. Echoes happen in both voice and data conversation, therefore two types of cancellers are encountered: *acoustic* and *line.* "Acoustic" echo cancellers are used in teleconferencing applications to suppress the acoustic echoes caused by the microphone/loudspeaker combination at one end picking up the signal from the other end and returning it to the original end. It is similar to sound system feedback problems (where the sound reinforcement loudspeaker is picked up by the microphone, re-amplified through the loudspeaker, only to be picked up again by the microphone, to be re-amplified, and so on), only made much worse by the additional time delay introduced by the telecommunication link. "Line" echo cancellers are used to suppress *electrical* echoes caused by the transmission link itself. Such things as non-perfect hybrids, and satellite systems (creating round-trip delays of about 600 ms), contribute to very annoying and disruptive line echoes.

echoic Of or resembling an echo (AHD).

ECS (*Engineered Conference Systems*) Rane Corporation trademark for their teleconferencing equipment.

eddy current An electrical current induced in electrical conductors by fluctuating magnetic fields in the conductors. The current moves contrary to the direction of the main current, just below the surface of the material, flowing in circular motion like river eddies. First noted by Michael Faraday after his discovery of electromagnetic induction in 1831. For a short tutorial see: *Eddy Current Theory – Principles.* Non-destructive testing based on eddy currents is a fast growing industry. Electrical currents are generated in a conductive material by an induced alternating magnetic field. Interruptions in the flow of eddy currents, caused by imperfections, dimensional changes or changes in the material's conductive and permeability properties, can be detected with the proper equipment. See: Introduction to Eddy Current Testing.

Edison effect In 1883, Thomas Edison noticed that certain materials, when heated by a filament in a vacuum, emitted electrons that could be attracted to an electrode held at a positive potential with respect to the emitter. This became known as the *Edison effect* and according to Edison, was discovered by accident when experimenting with his new invention, the incandescent lamp. Twenty years later, this effect became the basis for inventing the vacuum tube.

Edison plug An ordinary household plug with two flat blades and a ground pin.

EEPROM or **E²PROM (*electrically erasable programmable read-only memory*)** A version of read-only memory that can be *electrically* erased and reprogrammed by the designer. Differentiated from standard EPROM (one "E") which requires ultraviolet radiation for erasure.

effects loop A mixer term used to describe the signal path location where an external (*outboard*) signal processor is connected. The loop consists of an output *Send* jack connecting to the effects box *input*, and an input *Return* or *Receive* jack that comes from the effects box *output*. This is the preferred term when *two* separate ¼", or other connectors are provided to patch in an outboard processor using separate cables for send and receive. These jacks are usually unbalanced, but could be balanced. A stereo effects loop requires four jacks. Compare with: insert loop.

EFP (*electronic field production*) mixer Pretentious equivalent for ENG mixer.

EIA (*Electronic Industries Alliance*) Founded in 1924 as the *Radio Manufacturers Association* (RMA), The EIA is a private trade organization made up of manufacturers which sets standards for voluntary use of its member companies (and all other electronic manufacturers), conducts educational programs, and lobbies in Washington for its members' interests.

EIA-422 See: RS-422.

EIA-485 See: RS-485.

eigentone (from German *eigen* meaning "self" or "own") See: room mode.

EIN (*equivalent input noise*) Output noise of a system or device referred to the input. Done by modeling the object as a noise-free device with an input noise generator equal to the output noise divided by the system or device gain. See RaneNote: *Audio Specifications*.

Elco plug See: connectors.

electret microphone A microphone design similar to that of condenser mics except utilizing a permanent electrical charge, thus eliminating the need for an external polarizing voltage. This is done by using a material call an *electret* [acronym for *electr*icity + magn*et*] that holds a permanent charge (similar to a permanent magnet, i.e., a solid dielectric that exhibits persistent dielectric polarization). Because electret elements exhibit extremely high output impedance, they often employ an integral built-in impedance converter (usually a single JFET) that requires external power to operate. This low voltage power is often supplied single-ended over an unbalanced connection, or it may operate from standard phantom power.

electromagnetic induction The generation of an electromotive force (*voltage*) and current in a circuit or material by a changing magnetic field linking with that circuit or material. Electricity and magnetism are kinfolk and form the foundation of audio transducers found at both ends of any audio chain: *dynamic microphones* and *loudspeakers with voice coils*. The principle is beautifully simple: if you pass a coil of wire through a magnetic field, electricity is gener-ated within the coil (*dynamic microphone*), and if you pass electricity through a coil of wire (*voice coil*), a magnetic field is generated. *Move a magnet, create a voltage; apply a voltage, create a magnet.* This is the essence of all electro-mechanical objects.

electronic music Glossary of terms.

electrostatic loudspeaker See: loudspeaker.

electrostatic microphone See: condenser microphone.

EMC Directive (*ElectroMagnetic Compatibility*) 1. A directive issued by the European Commission aimed at establishing product compatibility within the EU (European Union). Article 1.4 defines electromagnetic compatibility as the ability of an electrical and electronic appliance, equipment or installation containing electrical and/or electronic components to function satisfactorily in its electromagnetic environment (*immunity* requirement) without introducing intolerable electromagnetic disturbances to anything in that environment (*emission* requirement). 2. Due to the significant increases in development time and product costs imposed by the EMC Directive, many believe the initials really stand for "eliminate minor companies." [*Thanks DC.*]

EMD (*electronic music distribution*) Distributing digital music files (compressed using MP3, AAC, AC-3, etc.) from a server to a client.

EMF (*electromotive force*) *Electronics.* Voltage. See: volt; also back-emf

EMI (*electromagnetic interference*) A measure of electromagnetic radiation from equipment.

emitter follower See: buffer amplifier.

EMP (*Experience Music Project*) Paul Allen's (co-founder of Microsoft) interactive music museum, located in Seattle, that celebrates and explores creativity and innovation in American popular music as exemplified by rock 'n' roll. [*Very cool place ... come visit sometime.*]

ENG (*electronic news gathering*) mixer Portable battery-powered mixer accommodating at least two or three mic inputs, used in the field to record speech and outdoor sound effects. Some specialized models have built-in telephone line interfacing.

enhancers See: exciters.

ENOB (*effective number of bits*) A figure of merit for A/D data converters useful in specifying a converter's real AC accuracy and performance. *We all know that the data sheet says it's 24 bits, but what is it really? For a perfect sine wave, it can be approximated from the SINAD measurement by subtracting 1.76 from the SINAD (dB) and then dividing by 6.02. (For down-and-dirty quick calculations*

just divide the SINAD by 6 and you'll be in the ballpark.)
For example, if a 24-bit A/D converter has a real world
measured SINAD = 100 dB, then it has an ENOB equal to
16, nowhere near the claimed 24 bits.

envelope delay See: group delay.

eponym A person whose name is or is thought to be the
source of the name of something, such as a city, country, or
era. For example, *Romulus* is the eponym of *Rome*. (AHD)

EQ (*equalizer*) A class of electronic filters designed to aug-
ment or adjust electronic or acoustic systems. Equalizers
can be fixed or adjustable, active or passive. Indeed, in
the early years of telephony and cinema, the first equalizers were fixed units designed to correct for losses in the
transmission and recording of audio signals. Hence, the
term *equalizer* described electronic circuits that corrected
for these losses and made the output *equal* to the input.
Equalizers commonly modify the frequency response of
the signal passing through them; that is, they modify the
amplitude versus frequency characteristics. There are
also fixed equalizers that modify the phase response of
the transmitted signals without disturbing the frequency
content. These are referred to as all-pass, phase-delay, or
signal-delay equalizers. See RaneNote: *Exposing Equalizer
Mythology*, RaneNote: *Operator Adjustable Equalizers*, and
RaneNote: *Signal Processing Fundamentals*.

equivalent input noise See: EIN.

Eric "Hoss" Cartwright's given name — "Hoss" was a nickname ... ... this, for all you Jeopardy! fans.

error correction A method using a coding system to correct
data errors by use of redundant data within a data block.
Often data is interleaved for immunity to burst errors.
Corrected data is identical to the original.

EST (*Electronic Systems Technician*) A consortium for electronic systems technician training.

ESTA (*Entertainment Services & Technology Association*)
A non-profit trade association representing the North
American entertainment technology industry.

ether From a Greek word meaning "upper air," a term used in
early physics (based on ancient beliefs), a magical medium
thought to explain the propagation of electromagnetic
waves.

Ethernet A local area network (LAN), originally developed by Xerox (the name was coined by its inventor Bob
Metcalfe after the old science term *ether*), used for connecting computers, printers, workstations, terminals, etc.,
now extended to include audio and video using CobraNet
technology. Ethernet operates over twisted-pair, coaxial
cable, or fiber optic cable at various speeds designated:

10Base-T up to 10 megabits/sec (Mbps)

100Base-T, a.k.a. *Fast Ethernet*, up to 100 Mbps

1000Base-T up to 1 gigabit/sec, or 1000 Mbps, a.k.a.
Gigabit Ethernet (GE) [*uses all 8 conductors and can
be up to 100 meters long*], and now, talk of moving
beyond 10 Gbits/s, known simply as *10-Gbit Ethernet*.
(The number in the front designates the speed in
megabits/second. "Base" indicates the network is baseband. The letter following determines the type of cable
and its requirements. 10Base-T, for example is unshielded twisted-pair, using a star topology, and **1000Base-F**
uses fiber cable.)

Other Ethernet designators include:

1000Base-CX A standard for GE connectivity where the
"C" means copper and "X" is a placeholder.

1000Base-SX (*"S" for short wavelength laser*) for laser
fiber cabling based on the Fiber Channel signaling
specification for multimode fiber only.

1000Base-LX (*"L" for long wavelength laser*) for laser
fiber cabling also based on the Fiber Channel signaling specification for multimode or single-mode fiber.

1000Base-LH (*"LH" for long haul*) for a multivendor
specification (each vendor has a set of transceivers
covering different distances). While not an IEEE
standard, the vendors are working to interoperate
with IEEE 1000Base-LX equipment using the *gigabit
interface connector (GBIC)* multivendor specification in order to provide a common form factor and
greater flexibility. Further details available at Network
Information.

Euroblocks Shortened form for *European style terminal
blocks*. See: connectors.

exciters (or **enhancers**) A term referring to any of the popular
special-effect signal processing products used primarily
in recording and performing. All exciters work by adding
harmonic distortion of some sort - but harmonic distortion
found pleasing by most listeners. Various means of generating and summing frequency-dependent and amplitude-de-
pendent harmonics exist. Both even- and odd-ordered harmonics find favorite applications. Psychoacoustics teaches
that even-harmonics tend to make sounds soft, warm and
full, while odd-harmonics tend to make things metallic,
hollow and bright. Lower-order harmonics control basic
timbre, while higher-order harmonics control the "edge"
or "bite" of the sound. Used with discrimination, harmonic
distortion changes the original sound dramatically, more so
than measured performance might predict.

expander A signal processing device used to *increase the dynamic range* of the signal passing through it. Expanders complement compressors. For example, a compressed input dynamic range of 70 dB might pass through a expander and exit with a new *expanded* dynamic range of 110 dB. [*Long answer*: Just like compression, what "expansion" is and does has evolved significantly over the years. Originally expanders were used to give the reciprocal function of a compressor, i.e., it undid compression. Anytime audio was recorded or broadcast it had to be compressed for optimum transfer. Then it required an expander at the other end to restore the audio to its original dynamic range. Operating about the same "hinge" point and using the same ratio setting as the compressor, an expander makes audio *increases* and *decreases bigger*. From this sense came the phrase that "*expanders make the quiet sounds quieter and the loud sounds louder*." Modern expanders usually operate only *below a set threshold point* (as opposed to the center hinge point), i.e., they operate only on low-level audio. The term **downward expander** or *downward expansion* evolved to describe this type of application. (The term **upward expander** is sometimes used to refer to expanders operating only on high-level signals, i.e., increasing dynamic range above threshold.) The most common use is noise reduction. For example, say, an expander's threshold level is set to be just below the smallest vocal level being recorded, and the ratio control is set for 3:1. What happens is this: when the vocals stop, the "decrease below the set-point" is the change from signal (vocals) to the noise floor (no vocals), i.e., there has been a step decrease from the smallest signal level down to the noise floor. If that step change is, say, -10 dB, then the expander's output will be -30 dB (because of the 3:1 ratio, a 10 dB decrease becomes a 30 dB decrease), thus resulting in a noise reduction improvement of 20 dB. See RaneNote: *The DC 24 Users Guide*, RaneNote: *Signal Processing Fundamentals*, and RaneNote: *Good Dynamics Processing*.

exponent The component of a floating-point number that normally signifies the integer power to which the radix is raised in determining the value of the represented number (IEEE-100). For example if radix =10 (a decimal number), then the number 183.885 is represented as mantissa = 1.83885 and exponent = 2 (since $183.885 = 1.83885 \times 10^2$).

extensible Of or relating to a programming language or a system that can be modified by changing or adding features. Capable of being extended: *AES24 is an extensible protocol.*

eye pattern An oscilloscope display of the received voltage waveform in a transmission system. So named because portions of the display take on a human eye-like shape. The eye pattern gives important information. An eye pattern is obtained when a high-speed transmission system outputs a long pseudorandom bit sequence. A sampling oscilloscope is used to observe the output such that the scope is triggered to sample on every fourth or eighth pseudorandom clock cycle, and every sample point is plotted on the screen.

(*The pseudorandom digital data signal from a receiver is repetitively sampled and applied to the vertical input, while the data rate is used to trigger the horizontal sweep.*) The picture obtained is a superposition of ones and zeros output. The horizontal "fatness" of the lines indicates the amount of jitter and the rise and fall times is measured from the crossing points. See: Siemon publication *Data Throughput Validation: Making Every Bit Count* for an example and more details.

F

42V PowerNet The official name for the new 42 V automotive electrical power system.

5.1 surround sound The digital audio multichannel format developed by the Moving Picture Experts Group (see: MPEG) for digital soundtrack encoding for film, laserdiscs, videotapes, DVD, and HDTV broadcast. The designation "5.1" (first proposed by Tom Holman of THX fame) refers to the five discrete, full bandwidth (20-20 kHz) channels — *left, right, & center fronts*, plus *left & right surrounds* — and the ".1" usually refers to the limited bandwidth (20-120 Hz) *subwoofer* channel, but can also refer to a special effects/feature channel. Terminology used by both Dolby Digital and DTS Consumer (the home version of their theater Coherent Acoustics system).

fader A control used to *fade* out one input source and *fade* in another. The fading of a single source is called *attenuation* and uses an attenuator.

Fahrenheit *Abbr.* **F** Of or relating to a temperature scale that registers the freezing point of water as 32 °F and the boiling point as 212 °F, under normal atmospheric pressure. (AHD) [In scientific and technical contexts temperatures are now usually measured in degrees Celsius rather than Fahrenheit.] [After Gabriel Daniel Fahrenheit]

Fahrenheit, Gabriel Daniel (1686-1736) German-born physicist who invented the mercury thermometer (1714) and devised the Fahrenheit temperature scale. (AHD)

FAQ (*frequently asked question*) Acronym commonly seen on bulletin boards, Internet Web sites, and corporate information centers. By compiling FAQ lists (*FAQs*), organizations significantly reduce time spent repeatedly answering the same questions.

Faraday, Michael (1791-1867) British physicist and chemist who discovered electromagnetic induction (1831) and proposed the field theory later developed by Maxwell and Einstein. (AHD) See: Faraday's Magnetic Field Induction Experiment.

far end Teleconferencing term meaning the distant location of transmission; the other end of the telephone line, as opposed to your end (known as the *near end*).

far-end crosstalk Crosstalk that is propagated in a disturbed channel in the *same direction as the propagation of the signal* in the disturbing channel. The terminals of the disturbed channel, at which the far-end crosstalk is present, and the energized terminals of the disturbing channel, are usually remote from each other.

far field or **far sound field** The sound field distant enough from the sound source so the SPL decreases by 6 dB for each doubling of the distance from the source (*inverse square law*). Contrast with: near field.

Fast Ethernet See: Ethernet.

fat *Recording slang.* Informal phrase for heavily processed audio, usually featuring lots of reverb, chorusing, or doubling. Also seen as *phat* sound.

fax on demand One of the terms for the process of ordering fax documents from remote machines via telephone, using a combination of voice processing and fax technologies. Also called *fax-back*.

fax-back See: **fax on demand**.

FEA See: Finite Element Analysis.

feedback See: acoustic feedback.

feedback The longest word in the English language that uses all the letters "A" through "F." [*Thanks, Brad, for being so observant while playing Trivial Pursuit.*]

feedback suppressor An audio signal processing device that uses automatic detection to determine acoustic feedback frequencies and then positions notch filters to cancel the offending frequencies. Other methods us continuous frequency shifting (a very small amount) to prevent frequency build up and feedback before it happens.

FDDI (*fiber distributed data interface*) An ANSI standard describing a 100 megabytes/sec (MBps) fiber optic LAN; now also specified for twisted-pair use.

femto- Prefix for one thousandth of one trillionth (10E-15), abbreviated **f**.

FET (*field-effect transistor*) A three-terminal transistor device where the output current flowing between the *source* and *drain* terminals is controlled by a variable electric field applied to the *gate* terminal. The gate design determines the type of FET: either **JFET (*junction FET*)** or **MOSFET (*metal-oxide semiconductor FET*)**. Each type has two polarities: positive, or *p-channel* devices, and negative, or *n-channel* devices. In a JFET device the gate forms a true semiconductor junction with the channel, while in a MOSFET device the gate is insulated from the channel by a very thin (typically less than the wavelength of light) layer of glass (*silicon dioxide*) and the gate is either metal or doped silicon (*polysilicon*), hence the acronym *metal-oxide semiconductor.*

FFT (*fast Fourier transform*) 1. Similar to a discrete Fourier transform except the algorithm requires the number of sampled points be a power of two. 2. A DSP algorithm that is the computational equivalent to performing a specific number of discrete Fourier transforms, but by taking advantage of computational symmetries and redundancies, significantly reduces the computational burden. [It is believed Cornelius Lanczos of the Boeing Company, in the '40s, first described the FFT.]

fiber optics The technology of using glass fibers to convey light and modulated information. Short distances (typically less than 150 feet) use plastic fibers, while long distances must use glass fibers. See: cables.

field *Video.* One half of a complete video scanning cycle, equaling 1/60 second, or 16.67 milliseconds for NTSC, and 1/50 second, or 20 milliseconds for PAL/SECAM.

film sound glossary See Larry Blake's Film Sound Glossary; find out what a "binky" is.

filter Any of various electric, electronic, acoustic, or optical devices used to reject signals, vibrations, or radiation of certain frequencies while passing others. Think sieve: pass what you want, reject all else. For audio use the most common electronic filter is a *bandpass filter*, characterized by three parameters: *center frequency*, *amplitude* (or magnitude), and *bandwidth*. Bandpass filters form the heart of audio *graphic equalizers* and *parametric equalizers.*

Finite Element Analysis *Abbr.* **FEA** A computer-based numerical technique for calculating the strength and behavior of engineering structures. See Peter Budgell's Finite Element Analysis and Optimization Introduction

FIR (*finite impulse-response*) filter A commonly used type of digital filter. Digitized samples of the audio signal serve as inputs, and each filtered output is computed from a weighted sum of a finite number of previous inputs. An FIR filter can be designed to have linear phase (i.e., constant time delay, regardless of frequency). FIR filters designed for frequencies much lower that the sample rate and/or with sharp transitions are computationally intensive, with large time delays. Popularly used for adaptive filters.

Firefly See: ZigBee.

Firewire See: IEEE 1394.

firkytoodle An English word no longer in print (except here) meaning to engage in intimate physical affection, as a prelude to sexual intercourse; foreplay (17th to 19th century).

firmware Computer read-only code (files) residing inside DSP and microprocessor ICs that controls the hardware response to software instructions — the liaison between software and hardware.

fishpaper An insulating paper, often fiber- or oilcloth-like, used in the construction of transformers and coils. [*Historical Note*: EP Coughlin of LMC Plasticsource writes: "Although my roots go back in fiber to 1959 I have never seen any hard copy evidence noting the origin of the name 'fishpaper.' My initial experience in the fiber industry was with Taylor Fibre Company and the owner claimed roots back to Thomas Taylor of England who is credited with 'inventing' vulcanized fiber. Original patent was in Great Britain in 1859 and Thomas Taylor received a US patent in 1872 titled 'Improvements in the treatment of paper and paper-pulp.' The major use for vulcanized fiber eventually was in the electrical insulation field but, obviously, requirements for same did not exist in 1859. Although anecdotal, John Taylor (owner/founder of The Taylor Fibre Company) claimed that vulcanized fiber's initial use was in England's fish markets as table/bin liners. The resistance to fish oil and tearing of vulcanized fiber makes this a very plausible story."]

fixed-point A computing method where numbers are expressed in the fixed-point representation system, i.e., one where the position of the "decimal point" (technically the *radix point*) is fixed with respect to one end of the numbers. Integer or fractional data is expressed in a specific number of digits, with a radix point implicitly located at a predetermined position. Fixed-point DSPs support fractional arithmetic, which is better suited to digital audio processing than integer arithmetic. A couple of fixed-point examples with two decimal places are 4.56 and 1789.45.

flanging Originally, "flanging" was achieved using two reel-to-reel tape recorders playing the same program, in synchronization, with their outputs summed together. By alternately slowing one machine, then the other, different phase cancellations occurred in the summation process. The "slowing down" was done simply by pressing against the *flanges* of the tape reels, hence the original term "reel flanging," soon shortened to just "flanging." Since the two identical signals would alternately add and subtract due to the introduced phase (timing) difference, the audible effect was one of a sweeping comb filter. It was described as a "swishing" or "tunneling" sound. Soon electronic means were devised to mimic true "reel flanging" by using delay lines and mixing techniques. Adding a low-frequency oscillator to modulate the audio delay line's clock signal created a sweeping effect, much like a jet airplane taking off. The best flangers used two delay lines. Compare with: phaser.

Fleming, Sir John Ambrose (1849-1945) British electrical engineer and inventor known for his work on electric lighting, wireless telegraphy, and the telephone. He invented and patented the first tube, a diode (which he called a *thermionic valve*, he used for signal detection (although Edison technically developed the first tube with a version of his light bulb).

Fletcher-Munson Curves Fletcher and Munson were researchers in the '30s who first accurately measured and published a set of curves showing the human's ear's sensitivity to loudness verses frequency. They conclusively demonstrated that human hearing is extremely dependent upon loudness. The curves show the ear most sensitive to sounds in the 3 kHz to 4 kHz area. This means sounds above and below 3-4 kHz must be louder in order to be heard *just as loud*. For this reason, the Fletcher-Munson curves are referred to as "equal loudness contours." They represent a family of curves from "just heard," (0 dB SPL) all the way to "harmfully loud" (130 dB SPL), usually plotted in 10 dB loudness increments.

flicker noise or **1/f noise** Noise whose amplitude varies inversely with frequency. Mainly used in *solid-state physics* to describe noise with 1/f behavior, such as the noise resulting from impurities in the conducting channel, generation and recombination noise due to base current in transistors, etc. Pink noise has a 1/f characteristic so the two terms are often interchanged, however when used to describe semiconductor noise (in op amps for instance) it is uniquely a low-frequency phenomena occurring below 2 kHz, while in audio, pink noise is wideband to 20 kHz.

floating-point A computing method where numbers are expressed in the floating-point representation system, i.e., one where the position of the decimal point does not remain fixed with respect to one end of numerical expressions, but is regularly recalculated. A floating-point number has four parts: *sign, mantissa, radix,* and *exponent*. The sign indicates polarity so it is either always 1 or -1. The mantissa is a positive number representing the significant digits. The exponent indicates the power of the radix (usually *binary 2*, but sometimes-hexadecimal *16*). A common example is the "scientific notation" used in all science and mathematics fields. Scientific notation is a floating point system with radix 10 (i.e., decimal). See: FLOPS.

floating unbalanced line A quasi-balanced output stage consisting of an unbalanced output connected to the *tip* of a " TRS (tip-ring-sleeve) jack through an output resistor (typically in the 50-300 Ω range). An equal valued resistor is used to tie the *ring* terminal to signal ground. The *sleeve* connection is left open or "floating." Thus, from the receiver's viewpoint, what is "seen" are two lines of equal impedance, used to transfer the signal. In this sense, the line is 'balanced," although only one line is actually being driven. Leaving the sleeve open, guarantees that only one end of the shield (the receiving end) will be grounded. A practice that unbalanced systems often require. For trouble

free interconnections, balanced lines are always the preferred choice.

floobydust A contemporary made-up term, one meaning being derived from the archaic Latin *miscellaneus*, whose disputed history springs from Indo-European roots, probably finding Greek origins (influenced, of course, by Egyptian linguists) — meaning a *mixed bag*, or a *heterogeneous motley mixed varied assortment*. Popularized within the audio community when borrowed and used by the author of this reference as a chapter title in the National Semiconductor *Audio Handbook* first published in 1976.

FLOPS (*floating-point operations per second*) A measure of computing power.

flutter 1. *Analog Recording.* Any significant variation from the designed study rotational speed of a recording or playback mechanism, e.g., turntables and analog tape recorders (typically at 5-10 Hz rate). Heard as rapid fluctuation in pitch when played back. Compare with: wow. 2. *Telecommunications.* Any rapid variation of signal parameters, such as amplitude, phase, and frequency.

FOH Abbreviation for *front of house*, used to describe the main mixer usually located in the audience for sound reinforcement systems. Meant to differentiate the main house mixer from the *monitor mixer* normally located to the side of the stage.

foldback The original term for *monitors*, or monitor loudspeakers, used by stage musicians to hear themselves and/or the rest of the band. The term "monitors" has replaced "foldback" in common practice

Foley A term synonymous with film sound effects. A recording studio *Foley stage* is where the sound effects are generated in synch with the moving picture. Named after *Jack Foley*, who invented sound effects for film sound while working for Universal. He simultaneously added music and effects to the previously silent film "Showboat" and the first "Foley" session was born.

follower Shortened form for a number of electronic circuit buffer amplifiers named *voltage followers, cathode followers, emitter followers,* etc.

foreground music Officially music with (or without) lyrics and performed by the original artist. Used where it is believed people will pay attention to it. Contrast with: *background music.*

Fourier analysis *Mathematics.* Most often the approximation of a function through the application of a Fourier series to periodic data, however it is not restricted to periodic data. [The Fourier *series* applies to periodic data only, but the *Fourier integral transform* converts an infinite continuous time function into an infinite continuous frequency function, with perfect reversibility in most cases. In this sense, it is not an approximation. The DFT and FFT are examples of the Fourier series, but are not approximations either unless the time data is an approximation itself, such as for sampled data systems, which introduces sampling errors.]

Fourier, Baron Jean Baptiste Joseph (1768-1830) French mathematician and physicist who formulated a method for analyzing periodic functions and studied the conduction of heat. (AHD)

Fourier series Application of the *Fourier theorem* to a periodic function, resulting in sine and cosine terms which are harmonics of the periodic frequency. [After **Baron Jean Baptiste Joseph Fourier.**]

Fourier theorem A mathematical theorem stating that any function may be resolved into sine and cosine terms with known amplitudes and phases.

FPGA (*field-programmable gate array*) A programmable logic device which is more versatile (i.e., much larger) than traditional programmable devices such as PALs and PLAs.

frame One complete video scanning cycle, equals two fields for NTSC and PAL/SECAM.

free field or **free sound field** A sound field without boundaries or where the boundaries are so distant as to cause negligible reflections over the frequency range of interest. Note that if the boundaries exist but completely absorb the sound then a virtual free field is created, thus anechoic chambers are used to measure loudspeakers.

frequency 1. The property or condition of occurring at frequent intervals. 2. *Mathematics. Physics.* The number of times a specified phenomenon occurs within a specified interval, as: a. The number of repetitions of a complete sequence of values of a periodic function per unit variation of an independent variable. b. The number of complete cycles of a periodic process occurring per unit time. c. The number of repetitions per unit time of a complete waveform, as of an electric current. (AHD)

frequency response *Audio electronics.* It connotes **amplitude-frequency response** and quantifies a device's maximum and minimum frequency for full-output response. The electrical passband of an audio device. The measure of any audio device's ability to respond to a sine wave program, and therefore is a complex function measuring gain and phase shift (see phasor). It is used to express variation of gain, loss, amplification, or attenuation as a function of frequency, normally referred to a standard 1 kHz reference point.

full duplex Redundant term. See: duplex.

FX unit Slang for "effects unit."

G

gain The amount of amplification (*voltage, current* or *power*) of an audio signal, usually express in units of dB (i.e., the ratio of the output level to the input level). For example, amplifying a voltage signal by a factor of two is stated as a voltage gain increase of 6 dB.

gain riding *Recording term.* The act of constantly monitoring and adjusting as necessary the gain of a recording process to prevent overloading the medium.

gain stage Any of several points in an electrical circuit where gain is taken (applied).

gain suppression See: suppression.

GAL (*generic array logic*) Registered trademark of Lattice Semiconductor for their invention of EEPROM-based low-power programmable logic devices.

gang, ganged, ganging To couple two or more controls (*analog* or *digital*) mechanically (or *electronically*) so that operating one automatically operates the other, usually applied to potentiometers (*pots*). The volume control in a traditional two-channel hi-fi system is an example of a ganged control, where it is desired to change the gain of two channels by the same amount, and now in home theater and DVD-audio applications, used to change 6 or more channels simultaneously.

gate See: noise gate.

gated or **gated-on** *Teleconferencing.* Term referring to microphone inputs on an automatic mic mixer that turns off (*close*) after speech stops. Contrast with: last-on.

Gauss, Karl Friedrich (1777-1855). German mathematician and astronomer known for his contributions to algebra, differential geometry, probability theory, and number theory. (AHD)

GBIC (*gigabit interface connector*) See: Ethernet.

GE (*gigabit Ethernet*) See: Ethernet.

Generation X The tenth generation of Americans since 1776. [From *Roman numeral X meaning 10.*] See: Beat Generation.

getter A small amount of material added to a chemical or metallurgical process to absorb impurities. In vacuum tubes it is a small cup or holder, containing a bit of a metal that reacts with oxygen strongly and absorbs it. In most modern glass tubes, the getter metal is barium, which oxidizes very easily forming white barium oxide. This oxidization removes any oxygen remaining after vacuumization.

gibi *Symbol* **Gi** New term standardized by the IEC as Amendment 2 to IEC 60027-2 *Letter Symbols to be Used in Electrical Technology* to signify binary multiples of 1,073,741,824 (i.e., 2E30). Meant to distinguish between exact binary and decimal quantities, i.e., 1,073,741,824 verses 1,000,000,000. For example, it is now 16 gibibits, abbreviated 16 Gib, not 16 gigabits or 16 Gb.

giga- A prefix signifying one billion (10E9), abbreviated **G**.

gigabyte Popular term meaning a billion bytes but should be *gibibyte* meaning 2E30 bytes. See: gibi.

GIGO (*garbage in garbage out*) Popular acronym used by programmers to indicate that incorrect information sent to a system generally results in incorrect information received from it.

glass Popular jargon referring to glass fiber optic interconnection, or fiber optics in general.

GPIB (*general purpose interface bus*) See: IEEE-488.

granulation noise An audible distortion resulting from quantization error.

graphic equalizer A multi-band variable equalizer using slide controls as the amplitude adjustable elements. Named for the positions of the sliders "graphing" the resulting frequency response of the equalizer. Only found on active designs. Center frequency and bandwidth are fixed for each band.

gray code A sequence of binary values where only one bit is allowed to change between successive values. Generally "quieter" (producing less audible interference) than straight binary coding for execution of commands in audio systems.

gray noise See: noise color.

Green Book Nickname for the Philips and Sony's ECMA-130 standard document that defines the format for CD-I (compact disc-interactive) discs; available only to licensees. Compare with: Red Book and Yellow Book.

green noise See: noise color.

ground *Electronics.* The common reference point for electrical circuits; the return path; the point of zero potential.

grounding, proper See Steve Macatee's *Considerations in Grounding and Shielding* , RaneNote: *Sound System Interconnection* and Tony Waldron and Keith Armstrong, "Bonding Cable Shields at Both Ends to Reduce Noise," *EMC Compliance Journal*, May 2002.

ground lift switch 1. Found on the rear of many pro audio products, used to separate (*lift*) the signal ground and the chassis ground connection. 2. Common three-pin to two-pin AC plug adapter used to reduce ground loops. [NOTE: This is unsafe and illegal. DO NOT USE.] For discussion See Steve Macatee's *Considerations in Grounding and Shielding* and RaneNote: *Sound System Interconnection*.

ground loop 1. *Electronics.* Within a single circuit, or an audio system, the condition resulting from multiple ground paths of different lengths and impedances producing voltage drops between paths or units. A voltage difference developed between separate grounding paths due to unequal impedance such that two "ground points" actually measure distinct and different voltage potentials relative to the power supply ground reference point. See Steve Macatee's *Considerations in Grounding and Shielding* and RaneNote: *Sound System Interconnection* 2. *Aviation.* The tendency of a tailwheel aircraft (vs. tricycle gear) to pivot around its vertical axis during runway ops in the presence of a high crosswind. [*Thanks DK.*]

groups (aka *subgroup* or *submix***)** A combination of two or more signal channels gathered together and treated as a set that can be varied in overall level from a single control or set of controls. Mixing consoles often provide a group function mode, where the level of any group of incoming singles may be adjusted by a single slide fader, which is designated as the *group fader.* Likewise in certain signal processing equipment with splitting and routing capabilities, you will have the ability to group together, or assign, outputs allowing control of the overall level by a single external controller. See: SRM 66.

group delay Same as **envelope delay** [*technically the time interval required for the crest of a group of waves to travel through a 2-port network* -IEEE.] The rate of change of phase shift with respect to frequency. *Mathematically,* the first derivative of phase verses frequency. The *rate of change* is just a measure of the slope of the phase shift verses linear (not log) frequency plot. If this plot is a straight line, it is said to have a "constant" (i.e., not changing) phase shift, or a "linear phase" (or "phase linear" -*European*) characteristic. Hence, *constant group delay*, or *linear group delay*, describes circuits or systems exhibiting constant delay for all frequencies, i.e., all frequencies experience the same delay. Note that pure signal delay causes a phase shift proportional to frequency, and is said to be "linear phase," or "phase linear." In *acoustics*, such a system is commonly referred to as a "minimum phase" system. For a circuit example, see: Bessel crossover. Also see: Siegfried Linkwitz: *Group delay and transient response*, and RaneNote: *Linkwitz-Riley Crossovers up to 8th-Order: An Overview.*

GR plug (*General Radio plug*) See: connectors: banana plug.

GUI (*graphical user interface*) A generic name for any computer interface that substitutes graphics (like buttons, arrows, switches, sliders, etc.) for characters; usually operated by a mouse or trackball. First mass use was Apple's Macintosh computers, but is now dominated by Microsoft's Windows programs.

gyrator filters Term used to describe a class of active filters using gyrator networks. Gyrator is the name given for RC networks that mimic inductors. A gyrator is a form of artificial inductor where an RC filter synthesizes inductive characteristics. Used to replace real inductors in filter design. See RaneNote: *Constant-Q Graphic Equalizers.*

H

Haas Effect Also called the *precedence effect*, describes the human psychoacoustic phenomena of correctly identifying the direction of a sound source heard in both ears but arriving at different times. Due to the head's geometry (two ears spaced apart, separated by a barrier) the direct sound from any source first enters the ear closest to the source, then the ear farthest away. The Haas Effect tells us that humans localize a sound source based upon the first arriving sound, if the subsequent arrivals are within 25-35 milliseconds. If the later arrivals are longer than this, then two distinct sounds are heard. The Haas Effect is true even when the second arrival is louder than the first (even by as much as 10 dB.). In essence we do not "hear" the delayed sound. This is the hearing example of human *sensory inhibition* that applies to all our senses. Sensory inhibition describes the phenomena where the response to a first stimulus causes the response to a second stimulus to be inhibited, i.e., sound first entering one ear cause us to "not hear" the delayed sound entering into the other ear (within the 35 milliseconds time window). Sound arriving at both ears simultaneously is heard as coming from straight ahead, or behind, or within the head. The Haas Effect describes how full stereophonic reproduction from only two loudspeakers is possible. (After Helmut Haas's doctorate dissertation presented to the University of Gottingen, Gottingen, Germany as "Über den Einfluss eines Einfachechos auf die Hörsamkeit von Sprache;" translated into English by Dr. Ing. K.P.R. Ehrenberg, Building Research Station, Watford, Herts., England Library Communication no. 363, December, 1949; reproduced in the United States as "The Influence of a Single Echo on the Audibility of Speech,"*J. Audio Eng. Soc.,* Vol. 20 (Mar. 1972), pp. 145-159.)

half-duplex Pertaining to a transmission over a circuit capable of transmitting in either direction, but only one direction at a time. See also: duplex.

Hall effect or **Hall voltage** In a semiconductor, the Hall voltage is generated by the effect of an external magnetic field acting perpendicularly to the direction of the current.

Hall, Edwin Herbert (1855-1938) American physicist best known for his 1879 discovery of the Hall effect.

Hamster switch *DJ Mixers.* A control found on professional DJ performance mixers that reverses fader action. For example, if a fader normally is *off* at the bottom of its travel and *on* at the top of its travel, then activating the hamster switch reverses this, so *off* is now at the top and *on* is at the bottom of travel, or alternatively, it swaps left for right in horizontally mounted faders. Used to create the most comfortable (and fastest) fader access when using either turntable, and to accommodate left-handed and right-handed performers. Credited to, and named after, one of the original scratch-style crews named *The BulletProof Scratch Hamsters.*

handshaking The initial exchange between two communications systems prior to and during transmission to ensure proper data transfer.

happiness "An agreeable sensation arising from contemplating the misery of another." — Ambrose Bierce.

hard clipping See: clipping.

hard disk A sealed mass storage unit used for storing large amounts of digital data.

hard disk recording See: DAW (*digital audio workstation*) and HDR.

hardware The physical (mechanical, and electrical) devices that form a system.

hardware key See: dongle.

harmonic distortion See: THD.

harmonic series 1. *Mathematics.* A series whose terms are in harmonic progression, as $1 + \frac{1}{3} + \frac{1}{5} + \frac{1}{7} + \ldots$ 2. *Music.* A series of tones consisting of a fundamental tone and the overtones produced by it, and whose frequencies are consecutive integral multiples of the frequency of the fundamental. (AHD)

Hatchet Jack's A website for real engineering and manufacturing people.

HAVi (*Home Audio/Video interoperability*) An industry standard for home networks designed to link consumer electronics products. Developed by eight consumer giants — Grundig, Hitachi, Panasonic, Philips, Sharp, Sony, Thomson Multimedia and Toshiba — the main aim of this protocol is to ride on IEEE 1394 interface, connecting digital TVs, set-top boxes, DVD players and other digital consumer products.

hdCD (*high-density compact disc*) See: DVD.

HDCD (*high definition compatible digital*) Pacific Microsonics' (now owned by Microsoft) trademark for their encode/decode scheme that allows up to 24 bit, 176.4 kHz digital audio mastering process, yet is compatible with normal 16 bit, 44.1 kHz CD and DAT formats. Claimed to sound superior even when not decoded, and to be indistinguishable from the original if decoded.

HDR (*hard-disk recorder*) An audio recording device based on computer hard disk memory technology. Typically, these machines are configured like analog tape recorders offering 24-48 tracks, utilizing 24-bit / 48-96 kHz data converters with optional I/O to interface with ADAT, TDIF, or AES3, and file format interchangeability with DAWs.

HDTV (*high definition television*)The standard for digital television in North America, still being revised. When finished will include a definition for picture quality at least that of a movie theater, or 35 mm slide, i.e., at least two million pixels (compared to 336,000 pixels for NTSC).

headphones An electromagnetic transducer usually based on the principle of electromagnetic induction used to convert the electrical energy output of a headphone amplifier into acoustic energy.

headphone sensitivity See: sensitivity.

headroom A term related to dynamic range, used to express in dB, the level between the *typical* operating level and the *maximum* operating level (onset of clipping). For example, a nominal +4 dBu system that clips at +20 dBu has 16 dB of headroom. Because it is a pure ratio, there are no units or reference-level associated with headroom — just "dB." Therefore (and a point of confusion for many) headroom expressed in dB accurately refers to *both* voltage *and* power. Which means our example has 16 dB of *voltage* headroom, as well as 16 dB of *power* headroom. It's not obvious, but it's true. (*The math is left to the reader.*)

HeadWize A non-profit (*i.e., no ads*) site specializing in headphones and headphone listening, featuring articles, essays, projects and technical papers on all things headphone — very informative.

hearing Perceiving sound by the ear.

Helmholtz Equation Used in acoustics and electromagnetic studies. It arises, for example, in the analysis of vibrating membranes, such as the head of a drum, or in solving for room modes. (After Hermann Ludwig Ferdinand von Helmholtz below.)

Helmholtz, Hermann Ludwig Ferdinand von (1821-1894) German physicist and physiologist who formulated the mathematical law of the conservation of energy (1847) and invented an ophthalmoscope (1851) (AHD) [An instrument for examining the interior structures of the eye, especially the retina, consisting essentially of a mirror that reflects light into the eye and a central hole through which the eye is examined. You aren't a real doctor without one.] Famous for his book, *On the Sensations of Tone* first published in 1862.

hertz *Abbr.* **Hz.** A unit of frequency equal to one cycle per second. [After **Heinrich Rudolf Hertz.**]

Hertz, Heinrich Rudolf (1857-1894) German physicist who was the first to produce radio waves artificially. (AHD)

hexadecimal A number system using the base-16, i.e., each number can be any of 16 values. Normally represented by the digits 0-9, plus the alpha characters A-F. A four-bit binary number can represent each hexadecimal digit.

Heyerdahl, Thor (1914-2002) Norwegian anthropologist and explorer made famous by his book *Kon-Tiki* about his epic 1947 expedition voyage to Polynesia.
On a visit to London, Heyerdahl had a busy schedule of appointments. Shortly after recording a program for the Independent Television Network, he was due at the BBC studios for an interview. Having been assured by the BBC that a taxi would be sent to pick him up from the ITN studios, Heyerdahl waited expectantly in the lobby. As the minutes ticked by, however, he began to grow anxious. He approached a little man in a flat cap, who looked as if he might be a taxi driver and was obviously searching for someone. "I'm Thor Heyerdahl," said the anthropologist, "Are you looking for me?" "No, mate," replied the driver. "I've been sent to pick up four Airedales for the BBC."
[Bartlett's Book of Anecdotes]

Hi8 See: DA-88.

high-cut filter See: low-pass filter [*In audio electronics, we define things like this just to make sure you're paying attention.*] Contrast with: high-*pass* filter below.

high-pass filter A filter having a passband extending from some finite cutoff frequency (not zero) up to infinite frequency. An infrasonic filter is a high-pass filter. Also known as a *low-cut filter*.

hiss Random high frequency noise with a sibilant quality, most often associated with tape recordings.

hoaxes, audio See Bob Pease's wonderful "What's All This Hoax Stuff, Anyhow?"

Holophonics An acoustical recording and broadcast technology claimed to be the aural equivalent to holography, hence the name. Holophonics is an encode process that occurs during the recording session using a special listening device named "Ringo." It is claimed that "playback or broadcast is possible over headphones or any existing mono or stereo speaker system, with various levels of spatial effect. Optimal effects occurs when two tracks (stereo) are played utilizing digital technology over headphones and minimal effect when played over a single mono speaker (two tracks merged into one and played over a single speaker)."

HomeRF Lite See: ZigBee.

homicide "The slaying of one human being by another. There are four kinds of homicide: felonious, excusable, justifiable and praiseworthy, but it makes no great difference to the person slain whether he fell by one kind or another — the classification is for advantage of the lawyers." — Ambrose Bierce.

homophone Words, such as *taper* and *tapir*, or *timbre* and *tambour*, that are pronounced the same but differ in meaning, origin, and sometimes spelling. [AHD]

hope "Desire and expectation rolled into one." — Ambrose Bierce.

Horner, William George (1786-1837) English mathematician and inventor of the Zoetrope.

house mixer See: FOH.

howlround What the British call acoustic feedback.

HRRC (*Home Recording Rights Coalition*) An advocacy group that includes consumers, retailers, manufacturers and professional servicers of consumer electronics recording products.

HRTF (*head-related transfer function*) The impulse response from a sound source to the eardrum is called the *head-related impulse response* (HRIR), and its Fourier transform is called the *head-related transfer function* (HRTF). The HRTF captures all of the physical cues to source localization, and is a surprisingly complicated function of four variables: three space coordinates (azimuth, elevation & range) and frequency, and to make matters worst, they change from person to person. Interaural (i.e., *between the ears*) time differences, interaural time delays and the physical effects of diffraction of sound waves by the torso, shoulders, head and pinnae modify the spectrum of the sound that reaches the eardrums. These changes allow us to localize sound images in 3D space and are captured by the HRTFs. HRTFs have been named and studied since at least the early '70s. [Blauert]

HTML (*hypertext markup language*) The software language used on the Internet's World Wide Web (WWW). Used primarily to create home pages containing hypertext.

HTTP (*hypertext transfer protocol*) The name for the protocol that moves documents around the Internet/Web. Used by the various servers and browsers to communicate over the net.

hub 1. In broadband LAN use, a central location of a network that connects network nodes through spokes, usually in a star architecture. Think of it as a digital splitter, or distribution amplifier. 2. In complex systems, hubs perform the basic functions of restoring signal amplitude and timing, collision detection and notification, and signal broadcast to lower-level hubs.

Huffman coding or **Huffman algorithm** One of the MP3 and AAC techniques used in digital audio data compression. While not a compression technique in itself, it is used in the final steps to code the process, and is an ideal complement of the perceptual coding. Huffman codes are used in nearly every application that involves the compression and transmission of digital data, such as fax machines, modems, computer networks, and high-definition television. For more details, see: Hoffman Coding [After **David Huffman** (1925-1999).]

hum components The harmonics of the AC mains supply. The Americas (except the southern half of South America), Japan, Taiwan, Korea and the Philippines use a 60-Hz system, placing the most annoying 2nd and 3rd harmonics at 120 Hz and 180 Hz. For Europe, and the rest of the world using 50-Hz mains, these components fall at 100 Hz and 150 Hz.

HVAC *Construction*. Term used to stand for the *heating, ventilating, & air conditioning* system of any building. *Electrical engineering*. Term used to mean *high-voltage alternating current*.

hybrid A telecommunication term used to describe an interface box that converts a conversation (or data signal) coming in on two pairs (one pair for each direction of the conversation or signal) onto one pair and vice versa (i.e., a 2-wire to 4-wire converter). This is necessary because all long distance circuits are two pairs, while most local circuits are one pair. The name comes from the original use of a "hybrid coil" in the telephone whose function was to keep the send and receive signals separated. Both analog and digital hybrid designs are found. A fundamental (and unavoidable) problem in any 2-wire to 4-wire design is leakage (crosstalk) between the transmit and receive signals. In analog designs leakage is reduced by modeling the impedance seen by the transmit amplifier as it drives the hybrid coil. Because telephone-line impedance is complex and not well modeled by a simple passive RLC circuit, only 10 dB to 15 dB of leakage reduction is usually possible. Digital hybrids use DSP technology to model and dynamically adapt to provide much greater reduction than analog designs, typically resulting in reductions of 30 dB to 40 dB. However, the best digital hybrids incorporate acoustic echo cancelling (AEC) circuitry to gain even greater improvements. The AEC works to cancel out any remaining signal coming from the loudspeaker (far-end received signal) from the microphone signal before they can be retransmitted to the far end as acoustic echo. Digital hybrids with AEC achieve total leakage reduction of 50 dB to 65 dB.

hyperlink The protocol that allows connecting two Internet resources via a single word or phrase; allowing the user a simple point-and-click method to create the link.

HyperPhysics A website concept created by Carl R. (Rod) Nave, Department of Physics and Astronomy, Georgia State University. "An exploration environment for concepts in physics which employs concept maps and other linking strategies to facilitate smooth navigation." [*An incredible site. You can get lost in it for hours. I can't recommend it enough.*]

hypertext Within WWW documents, the linking of words to other sections of text, pictures or sound is called hypertext. Hypertext is created using the HTML software language. Also used frequently in Help files.

I

IC (*integrated circuit*) A solid-state device with miniaturized discrete active components on a single semiconductor material.

IEC (*International Electrotechnical Commission*) A European organization (headquartered in Geneva, Switzerland) involved in international standardization within the electrical and electronics fields. The U.S. National Committee for the IEC operates within ANSI.

IEEE (*Institute of Electrical and Electronic Engineers*) The largest professional organization for electrical engineers. Primarily concerned with education and standardization.

IEEE-488 also referred to as the *general purpose interface bus (GPIB)*. Most common parallel format computer interface for simultaneous control of up to 15 multiple peripherals.

IEEE-1394 (aka *Firewire*) A joint Apple and TI implementation of the IEEE P1394 Serial Bus Standard. It is a high-speed (100/200/400 Mbits/sec now, with 1 Gbit/s on the horizon) serial bus for peripheral devices. Supported by Apple, IBM, Intel, Microsoft and Sony, it is intended to replace Apple Desktop Bus (ADB) and SCSI (Microsoft announced Windows support for IEEE 1394). Firewire supports automatic configuration ("plug and play") and hot-plugging (changing peripheral devices while running). It is also isochronous, meaning that a fixed slice of bandwidth can be dedicated to a particular peripheral — video, for instance. IEEE 1394 aims to become the optimal digital interface for 21st-century applications. Fast, inexpensive and reliable for audio/video as well as computer peripherals, IEEE 1394 carries all forms of digitized video and audio. A single Firewire interface can be used for all entertainment-center interconnections, done in a daisy-chain fashion. New computer peripherals such as digital television, CD-ROM, DVD, digital cameras (Sony was first) and home networks are the first users. See USB for complementary low-speed system.

IEEE 754-1985 Standard for binary floating-point arithmetic often referred to as *IEEE 32-bit floating-point*. A standard that specifies data format for floating-point arithmetic on binary computers. It divides a 32-bit data word into a 24-bit mantissa and an 8-bit exponent.

IEV (*International Electrotechnical Vocabulary*) A valuable database, made available on-line by the IEC. It contains over 18,500 electrotechnical concepts divided into 73 subject areas (*IEV parts*). Each concept contains equivalent terms in English, French and German.

IFB (*interrupted foldback*) (aka **talent cueing**) An audio sub-system allowing on-air personnel ("talent") to receive via headphones, or ear monitors, the normal program audio mixed with audio cues from the production director, or their assistants.

IIR (*infinite impulse-response*) filter A commonly used type of digital filter. This recursive structure accepts as inputs digitized samples of the audio signal, and then each output point is computed on the basis of a weighted sum of past output (feedback) terms, as well as past input values. An IIR filter is more efficient than its FIR counterpart, but poses more challenging design issues. Its strength is in not requiring as much DSP power as FIR, while its weakness is not having linear group delay and possible instabilities.

IM or IMD (*intermodulation distortion*) An audio measurement designed to quantify the distortion products produced by nonlinearities in the unit under test that cause complex waves to produce beat frequencies, i.e., sum and difference products not harmonically related to the fundamentals. For example, two frequencies, f1 and f2 produce new frequencies f3 = f1 - f2; f4 = f1 + f2; f5 = f1 - 2f1; f6 = f1 + 2f2, and so on. See RaneNote: *Audio Specifications*.

Numerous tests exist, each designed to "stress" the unit under test differently. The most popular follow:

SMPTE/DIN IMD The most common IMD measurement. SMPTE standard RP120-1994 and DIN standard 45403 are similar. Both specify a two-sine wave test signal consisting of a large amplitude low-frequency tone linearly mixed with a high-frequency tone at the amplitude of the low frequency tone. SMPTE specifies 60 Hz and 7 kHz mixed 4:1. The DIN specification allows several choices in both frequencies, with 250 Hz and 8 kHz being the most common.

ITU-R (*old* CCIF), Twin-Tone, or Difference-Tone IMD All these terms refer to the same test and are used interchangeably. The test specifies two equal-amplitude closely spaced high frequency signals. Common test tones are 19 kHz and 20 kHz for full audio bandwidth units. While all combinations of IM distortion products are possible, this test usually measures only the low-frequency second-order product falling at f2-f1, i.e., at 1 kHz.

DIM/TIM (dynamic/transient intermodulation distortion) A procedure designed to test the dynamic or transient behavior, primarily, of audio power amplifiers. The other IM tests use steady-state sine wave tones, which do not necessarily reveal problems caused by transient operation. In particular, audio power amplifiers with high amounts of negative feedback were suspect due to the inherent time delay of negative feedback loops. The speculation was that when a rapidly-changing signal was fed to such an amplifier, a finite time was required for the correction signal to travel back through the feedback loop to the input stage and that the amplifier could be distorting seriously during this time. The most popular test technique consists of a large amplitude 3 kHz square wave (band-limited to ~20 kHz)
[*Historical Note*: This test proved that as long as the amplifier did not slew-limit for any audio signal, then the loop time delay was insignificant compared to the relatively long audio periods. Thus, properly designed negative feedback was proved not a problem. Subsequently, this test has fallen into disuse.]

IMA (*International MIDI Association*) The original association that developed MIDI, now defunct (*see hyperlink for a 1993 posting for the IMA Bulletin which appears to be the last gasp.*) and replaced by the MMA.

image impedances The impedances that will simultaneously terminate all of a network's inputs and outputs in such a way that at each of its inputs and outputs the impedances in both directions are equal. In this manner the input and output impedances "see" their own "image." (IEEE)

image parameters Fundamental network functions, namely image impedances and image transfer functions, used to design or describe a filter. (IEEE)

imaginary number A number whose square equals minus one, or, alternatively, a number that represents the *square root of minus one*. See Nahin's *An Imaginary Tale* for its incredible history.

impedance A measure of the complex resistive and reactive attributes of a component in an alternating-current (AC) circuit. Impedance is what restricts current flow in an AC electrical circuit; impedance is not relevant to DC circuits. In DC circuits, resistors limit current flow (because of their resistance). In AC circuits, inductors and capacitors similarly limit the AC current flow, but this is now because of their ***inductive*** or ***capacitive*** **reactance**. Impedance is like resistance but it is more. Impedance is the sum of a circuit, or device's resistance *and* reactance. Reactance is measured in ohms (like resistance and impedance) but is frequency-dependent. Think of impedance as the complete or total current limiting ohms of the circuit — the whole banana. Since AC circuits involve phase shift — i.e., the voltage and current are rarely in phase due to the storage effects (*think time; it takes time to charge and discharge*) of capacitors and inductors, the reactance is termed "complex," that is

there is a "real" part (resistive) and an "imaginary" part (bad terminology, but it means the phase shifting resistance part). To summarize: *resistance* has no phase shift; *reactance* (capacitors & inductors in AC circuits) includes phase shift; and *impedance*, is the sum of resistance and reactance. Just that simple.

impedance matching Making the output driving impedance and the next stage input impedance equal, often requiring the insertion of a special *impedance matching* network. For why impedance matching is not necessary (and, in fact, hurtful) in pro audio applications, see William B. Snow, "Impedance — Matched or Optimum," [*written in 1957!*] *Sound Reinforcement: An Anthology*, edited by David L. Klepper (Audio Engineering Society, NY, 1978, pp. G-9 - G-13), and RaneNote: *Unity Gain and Impedance Matching: Strange Bedfellows*.

impulse response *Acoustic measurements*. A theoretical impulse has an amplitude vs. time response that is infinitely high and infinitely narrow — a spike with zero duration and infinite amplitude, but finite energy. This means the energy is spread over a very large frequency range, making impulses an ideal source for acoustic measurements. Real world use of the mathematical impulse consists of a test impulse that has a very short time duration and whose amplitude is limited to whatever will not overload the system components. The Fourier theorem tells us that this rectangular pulse is nothing more than a sum of sine and cosine functions with known amplitudes and phases, therefore the impulse response of a linear system occurs in the time domain, but also contains all of the frequency information. By capturing the system impulse response with a digital storage scope and then performing a Fast Fourier Transform (FFT) analysis, the frequency-domain response (amplitude and phase) is obtained. [*Very powerful tool.*]

inductance A force that resists the sudden buildup of electric current (as opposed to capacitance which resists the sudden buildup of electric voltage). [IEEE]

inductive reactance See: impedance.

inductor Circuit symbol: **L**. A device consisting of one or more windings, with or without a magnetic core, for introducing inductance into an electric circuit. [IEEE]

infrasonic Generating or using waves or vibrations with frequencies below that of audible sound. Compare with: subsonic — commonly used (erroneously) to mean infrasonic.

infrasonic filter (aka **rumble filter**) A high-pass filter used with phonograph turntables to reduce the effects of low frequency noise and vibration, called rumble, caused by imperfections in turntable performance and warped records. Often mistakenly called subsonic filter. Since typical rumble frequencies occur in the 3-10 Hz area, most infrasonic filters have a corner frequency of around 15 Hz, with a steep slope, or rolloff rate, of 18 dB/octave, and a Butterworth response.

inline mixer Term referring to the normal long narrow vertical strip format common to all medium to large-scale mixing console designs (*mixers*). Non-inline designs typically refer to rack-mount mixers, i.e., those that are 19" wide, and designed to fit into standard rack cases. These are as small as 1U space (1.75" H). Sometimes these are designed similar to an inline design laying on its side, now having a horizontal control flow instead of a vertical one. In the middle of the pack are rack-mount mixers that still use the inline vertical format, but do rack mount, but normally take up 10 or more spaces.

in-phase In a synchronized or correlated way. See: polarity and phase et al.

input referred noise See: EIN.

insertion loss The loss of voltage (or power), as measured in dB, resulting from placing a pad (or other power absorbing network) between a voltage (or power) source and its load impedance. It is the ratio of the voltage (or power) absorbed in the load without the pad (or network) to that when the network is inserted. For example if the voltage across a load is 2 V without a network and 1 V with the network, then the insertion loss is stated as 6 dB.

insert loop The preferred term for a specialized I/O point found on mixers utilizing a single ¼" TRS jack following the convention of *tip = send, ring = return, & sleeve = signal ground*. Used to patch in an outboard processor using only *one* cable, with unbalanced wiring. A stereo insert loop requires two jacks. Compare with: effects loop.

instrument-level See: levels.

interference *Acoustics.* Anything that hinders, obstructs, or impedes sound travel, including another sound wave. See: link.

intermodulation distortion See: IMD.

interlayer-transfer See: print-through.

interleaving The process of rearranging data in time. Upon de-interleaving, errors in consecutive bits or words are distributed to a wider area to guard against consecutive errors in the storage media.

International Music Products Association See: NAMM.

International System of Units See: SI.

Internet To try and define the Internet in a few words is a futile task. Click the hyperlink for a wonderful Internet history timeline. Contrast with: WWW.

interpolating response Term adopted by Rane Corporation to describe the summing response of adjacent bands of variable equalizers using buffered summing stages. If two adjacent bands, when summed together, produce a smooth response without a dip in the center, they are said to *interpolate* between the fixed center frequencies, or *combine* well. [*Historical note:* Altec-Lansing first described their buffered equalizer designs as *combining* and the terminology became commonplace. Describing how well adjacent bands combine is good terminology. However, some variations of this term confuse people. The phrase "combining filter" is a misnomer, since what is meant is not a filter at all, but rather whether adjacent bands are buffered before summing. The other side of this misnomer coin finds the phrase "non-combining filter." Again, no filter is involved in what is meant. Dropping the word "filter" helps, but not enough. Referring to an equalizer as "non-combining" is imprecise. All equalizers combine their filter outputs. The issue is how much ripple results. For these reasons, Rane adopted the term "interpolating" as an alternative. Interpolating means to insert between two points, which is what buffering adjacent bands accomplishes. By separating adjacent bands when summing, the midpoints fill in smoothly without ripple.] See RaneNote: *Constant-Q Graphic Equalizers* and RaneNote: *Exposing Equalizer Mythology*.

interrupted foldback See: IFB.

inverse square law *Sound Pressure Level.* Sound propagates in all directions to form a *spherical* field, thus sound energy is *inversely* proportional to the *square of the distance*, i.e., doubling the distance quarters the sound energy (the *inverse square law*), so SPL is attenuated 6 dB for each doubling.

I/O (*input/output*) Equipment, data, or connectors used to communicate from a circuit or system to other circuits or systems, or the outside world.

IP (*intellectual property*) Referring to protected proprietary information, usually in the form of a patent, maskworks (integrated circuits or printed circuit boards), a copyright, a trade secret, or a trademark. Often misused to mean many different things.

IP (*internet protocol*) IP is the most important of the protocols on which the Internet is based. Originally developed by the Department of Defense to support interworking of dissimilar computers across a network, IP is a standard describing software that keeps track of the Internet work addresses for different nodes, routes outgoing messages, and recognizes incoming messages. It was first standardized in 1981. This protocol works in conjunction with TCP and is identified as TCP/IP.

IP address Another name for an *Internet address*. A 32-bit identifier for a specific TCP/IP host computer on a network, written in dotted decimal form, such as 4.23.65.178, with each of the four fields assigned 255 values, organized into hierarchical classes.

IRMA (*International Recording Media Association*) An advocacy group for the growth and development of all recording media and is the industry forum for the exchange of information regarding global trends and innovations.

ISBN (*International Standard Book Number*) In bibliography, a 10-digit number assigned to a book which identifies the work's national, geographic, language, or other convenient group, and its publisher, title, edition and volume number. Its numbers are assigned by publishers and administered by designated national standard book numbering agencies, such as R.R. Bowker Co. in the U.S., Standard Book Numbering Agency Ltd. in the U.K., Staatsbibliothek Preussischer Kulterbesitz (Prussian State Library) in Germany, and the Research Library on African Affairs in Ghana. Each ISBN is identical with the Standard Book Number, originally devised in the U.K., with the addition of a preceding national group identifier. [*Now if that isn't more than you will ever need to know about this subject then I'll eat a book.*]

ISDN (*Integrated Services Digital Network*) A high-capacity digital telecommunication network (mainly fiber optic) based on an international telephone standard for digital transmission of audio, data and signaling — all in addition to standard voice telephone calls. A cost-effective alternative to satellite links.

ISO (*International Standards Organization* or *International Organization for Standardization*) Founded in 1947 and consisting of members from over 90 countries, the ISO promotes the development of international standards and related activities to facilitate the exchange of goods and services worldwide. The U.S. member body is ANSI. [*Interesting tidbit*: according to ISO internet info, "ISO" is not an acronym. It is a derived Greek word, from *isos*, equal. For example, *isobar*, equal pressure, or *isometric*, equal length. Take a small jump from "equal" to "standard" and you have the name of the organization. It offers the further advantage of being valid in all the official languages of the organization (English, French & Russian), whereas if it were to be an acronym it would not work for French and Russian.]

isochronous (pronounced "i-sok-ronus") ("iso" *equal* + "chronous" time) A term meaning time sensitive; *isochronous transmission* is time sensitive transmission. For example, voice and video require isochronous transmission since audio/video synchronization is mandated.

ISRC (*International Standard Recording Code*) The international identification system for sound recordings and music video recordings.

ITS (*Imaging Technology and Sound Association*) A trade association created in 1986 as a national group, now existing only in California.

ITU (*International Telecommunications Union*) Headquartered in Geneva, Switzerland, ITU is an international organization within which governments and the private sector coordinate global telecommunication networks and services. The ITU is divided into three sectors: radiocommunications (**ITU-R**), telecommunications development (**ITU-D**), and telecommunications standards (**ITU-T**).

ITVA (*International Television Association*) A global community of professionals devoted to the business and art of visual communication.

J

jackfield British term for patchbay

JADE (*Joint Audio Decoder Encoder*) Siemens trademark for their device that implements voice compression algorithms.

Java The trademarked name for a powerful object-oriented programming language developed by Sun Microsystems. Java allows high-speed fully interactive Web pages to be developed for the Internet or any type of platform.

jerk *Mathematics.* The (first) derivative of *acceleration*, i.e., it is a measure of the rate of change of acceleration — just as *velocity* is the derivative of *speed*, and acceleration is the derivative of velocity.

JFET (*junction field-effect transistor*) See: FET.

jiffy An actual unit of time, representing 1/100th of a second. [See: *Rowlett's How Many? A Dictionary of Units of Measurement* for the complete details.]

jitter A tendency towards lack of synchronization caused by electrical changes. Technically the unexpected (and unwanted) phase shift of digital pulses over a transmission medium. Time skew; a discrepancy between when a digital edge transition is supposed to occur and when it actually does occur — think of it as nervous digital, or maybe a digital analogy to wow and flutter.

jitter timing error Short-term deviations of the transitions of a digital signal from their ideal positions in time.

Johnson noise or **thermal noise** A form of white noise resulting from thermal agitation in electronic components. For example, a simple resistor hooked up to nothing generates noise, and the larger the resistor value the greater the noise. It is called thermal noise or Johnson noise and results from the motion of electron charge of the atoms making up the resistor (called *thermal agitation*, which is caused by heat — the hotter the resistor, the noisier. [After **John Bertrand Johnson** (1887-1970), Swedish-born American physicist who first observed thermal noise while at Bell Labs in 1927, publishing his findings as "Thermal agitation of electricity in conductors," Phys. Rev., vol. 32, pp. 97-109, 1928.]

joule *Abbr.* **J** or **j**. 1. The International System unit of electrical, mechanical, and thermal energy. 2. a. A unit of electrical energy equal to the work done when a current of one ampere is passed through a resistance of one ohm for one second. b. A unit of energy equal to the work done when a force of one newton acts through a distance of one meter. (AHD)

Joule, James Prescott (1818-1889) British physicist who established the mechanical theory of heat and discovered the first law of thermodynamics: a form of the law of conservation of energy whose discovery he shared with Hermann von Helmholtz, Julius von Mayer and Lord Kelvin. (AHD)

JPEG (*Joint Photographic Experts Group*) A standard for lossy compression of graphic-image files.

juke A roadside drinking establishment that offers inexpensive drinks, food, and music for dancing, especially to the music of a jukebox. [Derivative Note: probably from Gullah *juke, joog* disorderly, wicked of West African origin; *Wolof dzug* to live wickedly Mandingo (Bambara) *dzugu* wicked. Gullah, the English-based Creole language spoken by Black people off the coast of Georgia and South Carolina, retains a number of words from the West African languages brought over by slaves. One such word is *juke*, bad, wicked, disorderly, the probable source of the English word *juke*. Used chiefly in the Southeastern states, *juke* (also appearing in the compound *juke joint*) means a roadside drinking establishment that offers cheap drinks, food, and music for dancing and often doubles as a brothel. To juke is to dance, particularly at a juke joint or to the music of a jukebox whose name, no longer regional and having lost the connotation of sleaziness, contains the same word. (AHD) [... *and you thought you were smart.*]

JSA (*Japanese Standards Association*) The National Standards organization responsible for coordinating standards preparation in Japan.

justify To shift a numeral so that the most significant digit, or the least significant digit, is placed at a specific position in a row.

K

kelvin *Abbr.* **K** The International System unit of absolute temperature equal to 1/273.16 of the absolute temperature of the triple point of water. This unit is equal to one Celsius degree. A temperature in kelvin may be converted to Celsius by subtracting 273.16. (AHD) [After **First Baron Kelvin.**]

Kelvin, William Thomson, First Baron (1824-1907) British physicist who developed the Kelvin scale of temperature (1848) and supervised the laying of a transatlantic cable (1866). His pioneering work in thermodynamics and electricity helped develop the law of the conservation of energy. (AHD)

Kelvin worked out an improved method for measuring the depth of the sea using piano wire and a narrow-bore glass tube, stoppered at the upper end. While experimenting with this invention, he was interrupted one day by his colleague James Prescott Joule. Looking with astonishment at the lengths of piano wire, Joule asked him what he was doing. "Sounding," said Thompson. "What note?" asked Joule. "The deep C," returned Thompson. [Bartlett's Book of Anecdotes]

keeper A bar of easily magnetized material (usually soft iron) placed across the poles of a permanent magnet to protect it from demagnetization. Most often seen on horseshoe or U-shaped magnets.

key *Music.* 1. The pitch of a voice or other sound. 2. The principal tonality of a work: *an etude in the key of E.* 3. A tonal system consisting of seven tones in fixed relationship to a tonic, having a characteristic key signature and being the structural foundation of the bulk of Western music; tonality. (AHD)

keynote The tonic of a musical key. (AHD)

Key West audion Nickname given the first use of the audion tube by the Navy at their wireless station in Key West, Florida.

KHN filter See: state-variable filter.

kHz (*kilohertz*) One thousand (1,000) cycles per second.

kibi *Symbol* **Ki** New term standardized by the IEC as Amendment 2 to IEC 60027-2 *Letter Symbols to be Used in Electrical Technology* to signify binary multiples of 1024 (i.e., 2E10). Meant to distinguish between exact binary and decimal quantities, i.e., 1024 verses 1000. For example, it is now 16 kibibits, abbreviated 16 Kib, not 16 kilobits or 16 Kb.

kilo- Abbreviated **k** (*always lower-case*). A prefix signifying one thousand (10E3).

Kilo- Abbreviated **K** (*always upper-case*). A prefix popularly used in computer work to signify multiples of 1024 (i.e., 2E10), but should use kibi. Meant to distinguish base-2 (binary) from base-10 (decimal) magnitudes. For example, a "16 K" memory is actually 16,384 bits (i.e., 16 times 1024, or 2E14), but should now read "16 Ki".

Klipsch, Paul W. (1904-2002) American engineer and inventor best know for inventing the "Klipschorn" below. He was one of the American audio pioneers. Member of the Audio Hall of Fame.

Klipschorn A type of full-range loudspeaker developed in 1941 with a revolutionary low end (Paul W. Klipsch, "A Low Frequency Horn of Small Dimensions," *JASA*, Vol. 13 October 1941; U.S. Pat. Nos. 2,310,243 & 2,373,692). By using the corner of the room as an extension of the folded horn within the cabinet, it was able to reproduce low-distortion tones down to 30 Hz. The Klipschorn is claimed as the only speaker in the world that has been in continuous production since the '40s. [After **Paul W. Klipsch** above.]

Kloss, Henry (1929-2002) American engineer and inventor, best known for inventing the acoustic-suspension loudspeaker and the large-screen projection television; founded four successful consumer electronics companies: Acoustic Research, KLH, Advent and Cambridge SoundWorks. Member of the Audio Hall of Fame.

kludge or **kluge** A system, especially a computer system, that is constituted of poorly matched elements or of elements originally intended for other applications. (AHD) Or as an article by Jackson Granholme in "Datamation" put it: "An ill-assorted collection of poorly matching parts, forming a distressing whole." [From AHD: *The word kludge is not "etymologist-friendly," having many possible origins, none of which can be definitively established. This term, found frequently in the jargon of the engineering and computer professions, denotes a usually workable but makeshift system, modification, solution, or repair. Kludge has had a relatively short life (first recorded in 1962 although it is said to have been used as early as 1944 or 1945) for a word with so many possible origins. The proposed sources of the* *word, German klug, kluge, "intelligent, clever," or a blend of klutz and nudge or klutz and refudge, do not contain all the necessary sounds to give us the word, correctly pronounced at least. The notions that kludge may have been coined by a computer technician or that it might be the last name of a designer of graphics hardware seem belied by the possibility that it is older than such origins would allow. It seems most likely that the word kludge originally was formed during the course of a specific situation in which such a device was called for. The makers of the word, if still alive, are no doubt unaware that etymologists need information so they can stop trying to "kludge" an etymology together.]*

knee (of a curve) The point on a curve where change begins to occur; a section resembling the human knee exhibiting bending.

Kodak See: Muzak

kSPS (*kilo samples per second*) One thousand (1,000) samples per second. A measurement of data converter speed.

kVA (*kilovoltamperes*) One thousand (1,000) voltamperes. See voltampere.

L

L The electronic symbol for an inductor.

Lamarr, Hedy (1924-2000) Born Hedy Kiesler in Vienna, this Hollywood actress used her knowledge of musical harmony, along with composer George Antheil, to obtain a patent on technology for military communications in 1942, which established the groundwork for today's spread-spectrum communication technology.

LAN (*local area network***)** A combination of at least two computers and peripherals on a common wiring scheme, which allows two-way communication of data between any devices on the network.

Laplace, **Marquis Pierre Simon de** (1749-1827) French mathematician and astronomer who formulated the theory of probability.

laser (*light amplification by stimulated emission of radiation***)** A device that generates coherent, monochromatic light waves. All CD players contain a semiconductor laser in their optical pickup.

last-on *Teleconferencing.* Term referring to microphone inputs on an automatic mic mixer that stay on (*open*) until another mic input turns on. Contrast with: gated-on. A last-on mic becomes a master mic if left open long enough.

latency Similar to propagation delay but broader in application. Used to describe the inherent delay in signal processing as well as software processing. The time it takes for a system or device to respond to an instruction, or the time it takes for a signal to pass through a device. It is how long it takes for a result to happen from a command. In telecommunications it is the length of time it takes packets to traverse the media.

lavalier or **lavaliere microphone** A small electret microphone designed to be worn on a person. The first lavalier mics were worn around the neck on a lanyard, hence the French name *lavallière, a type of necktie,* used to describe a pendant worn on a chain around the neck [after the Duchesse de La Vallière who started the fashion (AHD)]. Today most lavalier (the final "e" is commonly dropped) mics are attached by clips rather than hung from a cord.

lawful "Compatible with the will of a judge having jurisdiction." — Ambrose Bierce.

lawyer "One skilled in circumvention of the law." — Ambrose Bierce.

LCD (*liquid crystal display***)** A display of numerical or graphical information made of material whose reflectance or transmittance changes when an electric field is applied. An LCD requires ambient light or backlighting for viewing.

LED (*light emitting diode***)** A self-lighting semiconductor display of numerical or graphical information based on the light emitting characteristics of a solid-state device that emits incoherent (i.e., random direction) light when conducting a forward current. See: LEVD.

legacy devices Something handed down from an ancestor, or a predecessor, or something from the past (AHD). Used in the computer world to refer to yesterday's solutions, for example including an RS-232 port on a USB machine.

LEO (*low earth orbit***)** *Telephony.* Term referring to communications satellites positioned 200-900 miles (320-1450 kilometers) high.

LEVD (*light emitting vegetable diode***)** See Matt Reilly's "The Light Emitting Vegetable Diode" [*Thanks JD!*]

leveler A dynamic processor that maintains (or "levels") the amount of one audio signal based upon the level of a second audio signal. Normally, the second signal is from an ambient noise sensing microphone. For example, a restaurant is a typical application where it is desired to maintain paging and background music a specified loudness above the ambient noise. The leveler monitors the background noise, dynamically increasing and decreasing the main audio signal as necessary to maintain a constant loudness differential between the two. Also called *SPL controller.*

levels Terms used to describe relative audio signal levels: (Also see decibel).

    mic-level Nominal signal coming directly from a microphone. Very low, in the microvolts, and requires a preamp with at least 60 dB gain before using with any *line-level* equipment.

    line-level Standard *+4 dBu* or *-10 dBV* audio levels. See: decibel.

    instrument-level Nominal signal from musical instruments using electrical pick-ups. Varies widely, from very low *mic-levels* to quite large *line-levels.*

LFE (*low frequency enhancement*) also called **bass management** The "point-one" in "5.1 surround systems". It refers to the limited bandwidth (20-90 Hz, 20-120 Hz, or 20-150 Hz depending on the encoding system) subwoofer channel, but can also refer to a special effects/feature channel. Both Dolby Digital and DTS Consumer use the term. The "bass management" part comes from having the option of leaving the bass in the 5 full-range channels or sending all the lower bass to the subwoofer, or some combination. For more details, see Genelec's excellent LFE Q&A page.

lift/dip Popular European term meaning boost/cut.

limiter A compressor with a fixed *ratio* of 10:1 or greater. The dynamic action effectively prevents the audio signal from becoming any larger than the *threshold setting*. For example, if the threshold is set for, say, +16 dBu and the input signal increases by 10 dB to +26 dB, the output only increases by 1 dB to +17 dBu, essentially remaining constant. Used primarily for preventing equipment, media, and transmitter overloads. A limiter is to a compressor what a noise gate is to an expander. See RaneNote: *Limiters Unlimited*, RaneNote: *Signal Processing Fundamentals*, and RaneNote: *Good Dynamics Processing*.

linearity error *Electronics.* The maximum permissible deviation of the actual output quantity from a reference curve or line. Think of it as an error-window surrounding the reference: anywhere inside is okay, anywhere outside is not. The size of the window is the linearity error.

linear PCM A pulse code modulation system in which the signal is converted directly to a PCM word without companding, or other processing.

linear phase response Any system which accurately preserves phase relationships between frequencies, i.e., that exhibits pure delay. See: group delay.

linear system A system that meets two criteria: 1) *proportionality* — the output smoothly follows the input; 2) *additivity* — if input x results in output U and input y results in output V, then input x+y must result in output U+V. This means a system is predictably and its cause and effect relationship is proportional.

linear taper See: potentiometer.

line driver A balanced output stage designed to interface and drive long lines. Long output lines tax output stages in terms of stability and current demands. Designs vary from direct-drive differential (sometimes using cross-coupled techniques) to transformer drive. See RaneNote: *Practical Line Driving Current Requirements*.

line echo canceller See: echo canceller.

line-level See: levels.

Linkwitz-Riley crossover The de facto standard for professional audio active crossovers is the 4th-order (24 dB/octave slopes) Linkwitz-Riley (LR-4) design. Consisting of cascaded 2nd-order Butterworth low-pass filters, the LR-4 represents a vast improvement over the previous 3rd-order (18 dB/octave) Butterworth standard. Named after S. Linkwitz, a Hewlett-Packard engineer at that time, who first described the problems and solution in his paper "Active Crossover Networks for Non-coincident Drivers," *J. Audio Eng. Soc.*, vol. 24, Jan/Feb 1976, pp. 2-8. In this paper, he credited his co-worker Russ Riley for the idea that cascaded Butterworth filters met all his crossover requirements. Their effort became known as the Linkwitz-Riley alignment. Linkwitz showed that a significant weakness of the Butterworth design was the behavior of the combined acoustic lobe along the vertical axis. An acoustic lobe results when both drivers operate together reproducing the crossover frequency band, and in the Butterworth case it exhibits severe peaking and is not on-axis (it tilts toward the lagging driver). Linkwitz showed that this results from the Butterworth outputs not being in-phase. Riley demonstrated an elegant solution by cascading two 2nd-order (any *even-ordered* pair works) Butterworth filters, which produced outputs that were always in-phase and summed to a constant-voltage response. Thus was created a better crossover. See RaneNote: *Linkwitz-Riley Crossovers*, RaneNote: *Linkwitz-Riley Crossovers up to 8th-Order* and RaneNote: *Signal Processing Fundamentals*.

Linux A computer Unix-type operating system (OS) invented by *Linus Torvalds* in 1992, who wrote it as a student at the University of Helsinki. He created this OS because he couldn't afford one that could accomplish what he wanted with his available hardware. He then posted it on the network for other students, where it grew and became very stable and powerful. Today, for free, the software, source code, etc., is available off the Web.

litz wire Derived and shortened from the German word "litzendraht" meaning strand, or woven wire. It is a cable constructed of individually insulated magnet wires either twisted or braided into a uniform pattern, which increases the total surface area compared to an equivalent solid conductor. The pattern is formed to reduce *skin effect* by guaranteeing that along a significant length, any single conductor will be, for some portion of its length, located in the center, the middle, and the outer portion of the bundle. This transposition prevents any one conductor from being subject to the full forces of magnetic flux, thereby reducing the effective resistance of the entire bundle. Litz wire bundles of 50, 100 or even more conductors are available. They are constructed by winding smaller bundles of six conductors into larger bundles. Those bundles may be "litzed" with other bundles to create progressively larger cables. Litz constructions counteract skin effect by increasing the amount of surface area without significantly increasing the size of the conductor.

lobing error *Electronic crossovers.* The amount of on-axis deviation in amplitude from zero (i.e., perfect combined radiation pattern) resulting from phase deviations at the crossover point. Term coined by Lipshitz (Lipshitz, Stanley P. and John Vanderkooy, "A Family of Linear-Phase Crossover Networks of High Slope Derived by Time Delay," *J. Audio Eng. Soc.*, Vol. 31, No. 1/2, January/February 1983, pp. 2-20). See RaneNote: *Linkwitz-Riley Crossovers.*

log Short for logarithm.

logarithm *Mathematics.* A shortcut method that uses the powers of 10 (or some other *base*) to represent the actual number. The logarithm is the power to which a base, such as 10, must be raised to produce a given number. For example, 10^3 = 1,000; therefore, log (to the base 10) 1,000 = 3. The types most often used are the *common logarithm* (base 10), the *natural logarithm* (base *e*), and the *binary logarithm* (base 2).

log taper See: potentiometer.

Lorentz force The orthogonal (*right angle*) force on a charged particle traveling in a magnetic field, named after H. A. Lorentz. (AHD)

Lorentz, Hendrik Antoon (1853-1928) Dutch physicist, famous for the Lorentz force and co-receiving a Nobel Prize for researching the influence of magnetism on radiation. (AHD)

lossy See: digital audio data compression.

loud Having offensively bright colors: *a loud necktie.* (AHD)

loudness The SPL of a standard sound which appears to be as loud as the unknown. Loudness level is measured in phons and equals the equivalent SPL in dB of the standard. [For example, a sound judged as loud as a 40 dB-SPL 1 kHz tone has a loudness level of 40 phons. Also, it takes 10 phons (an increase of 10 dB-SPL) to be judged *twice* as loud.]

loudspeaker *Dynamic.* An electromagnetic transducer based on the principle of electromagnetic induction used to convert the electrical energy output of a power amplifier into acoustic energy. The heart of a dynamic loudspeaker is a coil of wire (the ***voice coil***), a magnet, and a cone. The amplifier applies voltage to the voice coil causing a current to flow that produces a magnetic field that reacts with the stationary magnet making the cone move proportional to the applied audio signal.

Other loudspeaker technologies exist, among these are ***electrostatic*** (a thin sheet of plastic film suspended between two wire grids or screens; the film is conductive and charged with a high voltage; the film is alternately attracted to one grid and then the other resulting in motion that radi-ates sound), but for pro audio applications, dynamic loudspeakers dominate. See also: ribbon tweeter and back-emf.

loudspeaker model See: amplifier dummy load.

loudspeaker sensitivity See: sensitivity.

low-cut filter See: high-pass filter [*In audio electronics, we define things like this just to make sure you're paying attention.*] Contrast with: low-*pass* filter (below).

low-pass filter A filter having a passband extending from DC (zero Hz) to some finite cutoff frequency (not infinite). A filter with a characteristic that allows all frequencies below a specified rolloff frequency to pass and attenuate all frequencies above. Anti-aliasing and anti-imaging filters are low-pass filters. Also known as a **high-*cut*** filter.

L-pad See: attenuator pad.

LRC (*inductance-resistance-capacitance*) *Electronics.* Shorthand for the most common passive circuit elements. Also seen as **RLC**, **LCR**, **CRL**, etc.

LSB (*least significant bit*) The bit within a digital word that represents the smallest possible coded value; hence, the LSB is a measure of precision.

Lully, Jean-Baptiste (1632-1687) French composer. (AHD) *The baton used by a seventeenth-century conductor was a much longer and heavier affair than the little wand used today. On January 8, 1687, in the course of conducting a* Te Deum, *Lully struck his foot with his baton, injuring it so seriously that gangrene set in and he died ten weeks later.* [Bartlett's Book of Anecdotes]

luminance Abbreviated **Y**. That part of the video signal that carries the information on how bright the TV signal is to be. The black and white signal.

M

macintosh (also **mackintosh**) *Chiefly British* A raincoat or a lightweight, waterproof fabric that was originally of rubberized cotton. [After Charles *Macintosh* (1766-1843), Scottish inventor.] (AHD)

MADI (*multichannel audio digital interface*) An AES recommended practice document *Digital Audio Engineering — Serial Multichannel Audio Digital Interface (MADI) AES-10-1991 (ANSI S4.43-1991)* specifying and controlling the requirements for digital interconnection between multitrack recorders and mixing consoles. The standard provides for 56 simultaneous digital audio channels that are conveyed point-to-point on a single coaxial cable fitted with BNC connectors along with a separate synchronization signal. Fiber optic implementation is specified in document AES-10id-1995, entitled *AES information document for digital audio engineering ¯ Engineering guidelines for the multichannel audio digital interface (MADI) AES 10.* Basically, the technique takes the standard *AES/EBU interface* and multiplexes 56 of these into one sample period rather than the original two.

magic "An art of converting superstition into coin. There are other arts serving the same high purpose, but the discreet lexicographer does not name them." — Ambrose Bierce.

magnitude 1. *Mathematics.* a. A number assigned to a quantity so that it may be compared with other quantities. b. A property that can be quantitatively described, such as the volume of a sphere, the length of a vector, or the value of a voltage or current waveform. (AHD)

Maine The only American state whose name is just one syllable.

mantissa The fractional part of a real number, e.g., in the number "1.83885," the mantissa is 0.83885. (The integer part of a number is called the characteristic. In the example the characteristic is 1.) Floating-point arithmetic also calls this the significand.

Marconi, Guglielmo (1874-1937) Italian engineer and inventor who in 1901 transmitted long-wave radio signals across the Atlantic Ocean and opened the door to a rapidly developing wireless industry. In 1909 he won the Nobel Prize in physics, shared with Karl Ferdinand Braun whose modifications to Marconi's transmitters significantly increased their range and usefulness. (AHD)

mask or **masking** *Psychology of Hearing.* The human hearing phenomenon where the response to one stimulus is reduced in the presence of another, i.e., *two sounds arrive but only one sound is heard.* Particularly evident when one sound is louder than another, with the result being that we hear the louder sound, even if arriving at a slightly different time. Frequency plays a part: a louder sound heard at one frequency prevents softer sounds near that frequency from being heard. However, not all frequencies mask the same. Mid-band frequencies mask far better than low frequencies, for example. Related to: critical bands.

Massa, Frank (1906-1990) American engineer who is considered the father of modern electroacoustics for developing the fundamental technology that became the foundation for electroacoustics. He is the recognized pioneer in the design of transducers and systems for both air and underwater applications, as well as the founder of Massa Products Corporation. Frank Massa and Harry Olson authored the first textbook on electroacoustics, Applied Acoustics, in 1934. See: Fundamentals of Electroacoustics for further details.

mastering *Audio recording.* The final step in the recording process, completed before the replication or streaming process. The act of creating the *master* from which all copies will be made. The following lists many of the required artistic and technical steps, although some of these are more accurately referred to as ***pre-mastering*** steps leading to a preliminary master used to create the final ***production master***.

- Transfer the recording into the highest digital (or analog) format for the mastering steps.

- Fix unwanted noise problems, either captured during the recording process, or for restoration archival purposes.

- Edit and apply signal processing as required to optimize timbre, clarity, smoothness and impact.

- Maximize the stereo or surround-sound balance and spread.

- Maximize and smooth out differences in song levels.

- Add pre-emphasis equalization if required for the duplication media.

- Add ISRC and other subcodes as required.

- Sequence the songs into their optimum playing order.

- Create fade-ins, fade-outs, segues and spacing between songs.

- Hide bonus tracks by using creative subcoding, if requested.

- Format and transfer the final results to the required media for duplication.

- And sometimes, create the package artwork.

Or, as DRT Mastering succinctly puts it: "Mastering creates a seamless whole out of a collection of individual tracks."

master mic *Teleconferencing.* Term referring to the microphone input on an automatic mic mixer that is the last to detect audio. A last-on mic becomes a master mic only if left open long enough.

master port *Teleconferencing.* Term referring to the audio input port that is the last to detect audio.

matrix-encoding *Audio.* A technique of storing more than two audio channels on a two-channel medium or transmission format. Dolby Surround is an example, where the center and surround channels are electronically encoded into the left and right channels of a stereo signal (usually by broadband 90° phase shifting and summing). On playback, the center and surround channel are decoded from the left and right signals. The problem inherent with matrix-encoding is the mathematical dilemma of trying to solve for four unknowns (*left, right, center surround*) when you only have two equations (*the stereo signal*); you can get close but you cannot get the exact right answer (*so you always have crosstalk*). This contrasts with today's discrete digital channels.

matrix-mixer Similar to the matrix switcher (or router) below, but with additional signal processing features on all the inputs and outputs. With a matrix-mixer, not only can you assign any input to any output but you may add EQ, compression, change level, etc. Very elaborate models exist with as many as 32-channels in and 8 or more output channels (and as big as a Volkswagen). Also see: mix-minus.

matrix switcher See: router.

maximally flat magnitude response See: Butterworth crossover.

maximally flat phase response See: Bessel crossover.

MAU (*multistation access unit*) See: token ring.

Mbps (*million bits per second*) (*always lower-case b*) A popular measure of transmission speed, but should be *Mibps*, or *mebi bits per second*. See: mebi.

MBps (*million bytes per second*) (*always upper-case B*) A popular measure of transmission speed, but should be *MiBps*, or *mebi bytes per second*. See: mebi.

MD (*MiniDisc*) Trademark term for the Sony digital audio recordable optical storage system utilizing data compression to reduce disc size.

MDM (*modular digital multitrack*) Generic term used to describe any of the families of digital audio multitrack recorders. The most common examples being the Alesis ADAT series and the Tascam DA-88 series.

mebi *Symbol* **Mi** New term standardized by the IEC as Amendment 2 to IEC 60027-2 *Letter Symbols to be Used in Electrical Technology* to signify binary multiples of 1,048,576 (i.e., 2E20). Meant to distinguish between exact binary and decimal quantities, i.e., 1,048,576 verses 1,000,000. For example, it is now 16 mebibits, abbreviated 16 Mib, not 16 megabits or 16 Mb.

media converter or **media manager** The *ability* to manage and the *process* of managing different media (coaxial cable, twisted-pair cable, and fiber-optics cable) used within the same network. Media management involves cable performance monitoring, cable break detection, planning for cable routes, as while as converting data signals between the various media.

medical conferencing See: telemedicine.

medium 1. In telecommunications, the transmission path along which a signal propagates, such as a twisted-pair, coaxial cable, waveguide, fiber optics, or through water, or air. 2. The material on which data are recorded, such as plain paper, paper tapes, punched cards, magnetic tapes, magnetic disks, or optical discs.

mega- 1. A prefix signifying one million (10E6). abbreviated **M**. 2. A prefix popularly used in computer work to signify multiples of 1,048,576 (i.e., 2E20), but should use *mebi*.

megabyte Popular term meaning a million bytes but should be mebibytes. See: mebi.

megaflops See: MFLOPS.

MEMS (*microelectromechanical systems*) The acronym says it all. Check out this clearinghouse website for the latest info.

MFLOPS (pronounced "mega-flops") (*million floating point operations per second*) A measure of computing power.

MI (*musical instrument*) A broad term used to describe the musical instrument marketplace in general. Reference is made to "the MI market," or to a specific "MI store." If a store sells band instruments, for instance, it is an *MI store*.

mic-level See: levels.

micro- Prefix for one millionth (10E-6), abbreviated **ì**.

microbar 1. A unit of pressure equal to one millionth of a bar. 2. A really small place to have a beer.

microcontroller See: microprocessor.

microphone An electroacoustic transducer used to convert the input acoustic energy into an electrical energy output. Many methods exist; see, for example, electret microphone, condenser microphone, and dynamic microphone.

microphone sensitivity See: sensitivity.

microphonic *General.* Any noise cause by mechanical shock or vibration of elements in a system (*IEEE Std 100). Audio.* Electrical noise caused by mechanical or audio induced vibration of the object. Common examples are vacuum tubes where mechanical vibration of the tube causes modulation of the electrode current, and capacitors that induce noise when tapped or vibrated in any manner.

microprocessor An integrated circuit that performs a variety of operations in accordance with a list of instructions. The core of a microcomputer or personal computer, a one chip computer.

mic splitter A phrase first coined by Franklin J. Miller, founder of Sescom, to describe a box fitted with female (inputs) and male (outputs) XLR mic connectors that allowed mic inputs to be routed to two, or more outputs. Usually passive, either hard-wired, or transformer connected. One common usage is for on-stage mic splitting, where one output goes to the monitor mixer and one to the FOH mixer.

MIDI (*musical instrument digital interface*) Industry standard bus and protocol for interconnection and control of musical instruments. First launched in 1983, now generalized and expanded to include signal processing and lighting control. See: MMA.

MIDI show control A term originally created by Charlie Richmond (Richmond Sound Design) to describe a new form of MIDI control designed for live theater venues. His efforts resulted in the official MIDI Show Control (MSC) specification. This document states: "The purpose of MIDI Show Control is to allow MIDI systems to communicate with and to control dedicated intelligent control equipment in theatrical, live performance, multi-media, audio-visual and similar environments." The magazine TCI has posted a great review article (March 1997) on MSC titled "MIDI Show Control — Five Years Later."

military music "Military justice is to justice what military music is to music." — Groucho Marx. [*from* Barber.]

milli- Prefix for one thousandth (10E-3), abbreviated **m**.

Minifon An early portable dictating machine developed in the 1950s using wire recorder technology. An example of "dead recording media."

minimum-phase filters *Electrical circuits* From an electrical engineering viewpoint, the precise definition of a minimum-phase function is a detailed mathematical concept involving positive real transfer functions, i.e., transfer functions with all *zeros* restricted to the left half *s-plane* (complex frequency plane using the Laplace transform operator *s*). This guarantees unconditional stability in the circuit. For example, all equalizer designs based on 2nd-order bandpass or band-reject networks have minimum-phase characteristics. *Acoustics* A term used to mean a linear phase (or *phase linear*, European term) system. See: group delay and RaneNote: *Exposing Equalizer Mythology.*

MIPS (*million instructions processed per second*) A measure of computing power.

mix-minus A specialized matrix-mixer where there is one output associated with each input that includes all other inputs *except* the one it is associated with. (The output is the complete *mix, minus* the one input.) In this manner, the simplest mix-minus designs have an equal number of inputs and outputs (a *square* matrix). For example, if there were 8-inputs, there would be 8-outputs. Each output would consists of a mix of the seven other inputs, but not its own. Therefore Output 1, for instance, would consist of a mix of Inputs 2-8, while Output 2 would consist of a mix of Inputs 1 & 3-7, Output 3 would consist of a mix of Inputs 1,2 & 4-7, and so on. Primary usage is large conference rooms, where it is desirable to have the loudspeaker closest to each microphone *exclude that particular microphone*, so as to reduce the chance of feedback. See RaneNote: *Mix-Minus Speech Reinforcement with Conferencing.*

mixer At its simplest level, an audio device used to add (combine or sum) multiple inputs into one or two outputs, complete with level controls on all inputs. From here signal processing is added to each of the inputs and outputs until behemoth monsters with as many as 64 inputs are created — at a cost of around 10-20 kilobucks per input for fully digitized and automated boards. At these price points a mixer becomes a *recording console.*

MLP (*Meridian Lossless Packing*) A lossless audio coding scheme developed by Meridian Audio Ltd.. MLP has been selected as the optional coding scheme for use on DVD-Audio, as well as other transmission, storage and archiving applications. It is a true lossless coding technology, in that the recovered audio is bit-for-bit identical to the original. Unlike perceptual or lossy data reduction, MLP does not alter the final decoded signal in any way, but merely "packs" the audio data more efficiently into a smaller data rate for transmission or storage. It is simple to decode and requires relatively low computational power for playback.

MLS (*maximum-length sequences*) A time-domain-based analyzer using a mathematically designed test signal optimized for sound analysis. The test signal (a *maximum-length sequence*) is electronically generated and characterized by having a flat energy-vs.-frequency curve over a wide frequency range. Sounding similar to white noise, it is actually periodic, with a long repetition rate. This test signal is most often tailored to be pink noise, as the preferred response for fractional octave analysis. Similar in principle to impulse response testing — think of the *maximum-length sequence* test signal as a series of randomly distributed positive- and negative-going impulses. See: MLSSA.

MLSSA (pronounced "Melissa") (*maximum-length sequences system analyzer*) Trademarked name for the first MLS measurement instrument designed by DRA Laboratories (Sarasota, FL). M.R. Schroeder used maximum-length-sequences methods for room impulse response measurement in 1979 (based on work dating back to the mid-60's); however, it was not until 1987 that the use of MLS became commercially available. The first MLS instrument was developed and made practical by Douglas Rife, who described the principles in his landmark paper (co-authored by John Vanderkooy, University of Waterloo) "Transfer-Function Measurement with Maximum-Length Sequences" (*J. Audio Eng. Soc.*, vol. 37, no. 6, June 1989), and followed up with new applications described in "Modulation Transfer Function Measurement with Maximum-Length Sequences" (*J. Audio Eng. Soc.*, vol. 40, no. 10, October 1992).

MMA (*MIDI Manufacturers Association*) The original source for information on MIDI technology, where companies work together to create the standards upon which MIDI compatibility is built.

MMCD (*multimedia compact disc*) See: DVD.

MMVF (*multimedia video file*) See: DVD.

modal *Acoustics.* Of, relating to, or characteristic of a room mode or modes. (AHD)

modes Shorten form of room modes.

modem (*modulator-demodulator*) A peripheral device used to convert digital signals ("1s" and "0s") into analog signals (tones) and vice-versa, necessary for communication using standard telephone lines.

mojo 1. A charm or amulet thought to have magic powers. 2. *Slang*: power, luck, etc., as of magical or supernatural origin. 3. Mojo Series Rane Corporation trademark for their series of economical products designed for high quality

performance and reliability aimed at the working musician. 4. Abbr. *Mother Jones* magazine, or reference to their Internet news network: The Mojo Wire.

MOL (*maximum output level*) *Magnetic tape.* The maximum output level of a magnetic tape is defined as the magnetization level at which a recorded 1-kHz sine wave reaches 3% third-harmonic distortion (*note that is 3% THIRD-harmonic distortion — not 3% TOTAL harmonic distortion*). Also referred to as 3% distortion of the musical twelfth. See: third-harmonic distortion.

monitor mixer A mixer used to create the proper signals to drive the individual musician stage loudspeaker monitors. Also called *foldback speakers*. Compare: FOH.

mono 3-way, etc. See: active crossover.

monotonic *Mathematics.* Designating sequences, the successive members of which either consistently increase or decrease but do not oscillate in relative value. Each member of a monotone increasing sequence is greater than or equal to the preceding member; each member of a monotone decreasing sequence is less than or equal to the preceding member. (AHD)

month One of the words in the English language without a rhyme — some others are "orange," "purple" and "silver."

Moore's Law 1. Named after *Gordon Moore*, a cofounder of Intel, who wrote in an *Electronics* magazine article in 1965, that computer chip complexity would double every twelve months for the next ten years. Ten years later his forecast proved to be correct. At that time, he then predicted that the doubling would happen every *two* years for the *next* ten years. Ten years later, he was, once again, proved correct. By combining the two predictions, *Moore's Law* is often stated as a doubling every 18 months. 2. The dictum that requires you to buy a new computer every two years. [Thanks DC.]

MOR (*magneto-optical recording*) An erasable optical disc system using magnetic media and laser reading/writing.

MOSFET (*metal-oxide semiconductor field-effect transistor*) See: FET.

motional feedback See: servo-loop.

Mozart, Wolfgang Amadeus (1756-1791) Austrian composer.

Mozart was approached by a young man, little older than a boy, who sought his advice on composing a symphony. Mozart pointed out that he was still very young and it might be better if he began by composing ballads. "But you wrote symphonies when you were only ten years old," objected the lad. "But I didn't have to ask how," Mozart retorted. [Bartlett's Book of Anecdotes]

MP3 (*MPEG-1, layer 3*) A type of digital audio compression popularized for transmitting songs over the Internet. MP3 allows real-time audio streaming for Internet encoding and downloading. MP3 files are identified by the suffix ".MP3" Typically MP3 compresses CD-quality audio down to about one minute per 1MB file size. Also see Wired magazine's MP3 site.

MPEG (*Moving Picture Experts Group*) A working group within SMPTE who set, among other things, specifications for compression schemes for audio and video transmission. A term commonly used to make reference to their image-compression scheme (MPEG-2) for full motion video.

MPEG-4 Structured Audio This specifies a set of tools that allow powerful and flexible description of sound in a variety of ways, all based on what has become known as "structured audio," meaning transmitting sound by *describing* it rather than *compressing* it.

MPGA (*Music Producers Guild of the Americas*) A professional guild for music producers and audio recording engineers.

M/S or M-S (*mid-side* or *mono-stereo*) *Microphone Technique.* Developed in the mid '50s by the Danish radio engineer Holger Lauridsen (H. Lauridsen F. Schlegel, "Stereophonie und richtungsdiffuse Klangwiedergabe," Gravesaner Blätter, 1956, Nr. V, August, S.28-50) , a method for capturing stereophonic sound using two microphones. One microphone with a cardioid response (although any polar pattern will work) is aimed straight ahead toward the sound source (this is the *mid* or *mono* **M** part), and a second microphone with a figure-8 (or *bipolar*) response is placed so that the two lobes are directed toward the sides (this is the *side* or *stereo* **S** part). The two signals are then combined using an **M-S matrix** circuit that yields two signals: M+S and M-S. See Streicher Everest for complete details.

M/S matrix See M/S above.

MS-DOS (*Microsoft disk operating system*) Microsoft's registered trademark for their PC operating system.

MSB (*most significant bit*) The bit within a digital word that represents the biggest possible single-bit coded value.

MSPS (*million samples per second*) A measurement of data converter speed.

multi-denomial transpedance informer Term coined by Jensen Transformers for their mythical product, the JE-EP-ERs, first introduced in 1987, which almost changed the whole audio transformer industry. The Jensen JE-EP-ERs pioneered the use of triple electonomic shielding and intrinsic eddy-breeding, until outlawed by Congress in 1988. Voluntarily discontinued when their stock of zeta-metal ran out, preventing any further use of interstage transpedance informance. Considered by many to be the only necessary accessory when coupling a Rane PI 14 Pseudoacoustic Infector to a Crown Belchfire BF-6000SUX amplifier for playback using an Electro-Voice Rearaxial Softspeaker.

multimedia Generally refers to personal computers capable of multiple forms of communication methods. These constitute a minimum combination of stereo audio, video, text, and graphics, plus the more complex system includes fax and telephony provisions.

multiplex To interleave two or more signals into a single output; a process of selecting one of a number of inputs and switching its information to the output.

multipoint conference Telecommunication term referring to conferencing between three or more sites.

musical twelfth The third-harmonic of a tone, which equals one octave and a fifth — hence, twelfth (*12 not 13 because you don't count the original tone*).

MUSICAM (*masking pattern adapted universal sub-band integrated coding and multiplexing*) A flexible bit rate reduction standard for high quality audio. Jointly developed for digital audio broadcast by CCETT in France, IRT in Germany and Philips in the Netherlands.

music temperament See: temperament.

music vs. noise 1. "The sensation of a musical tone is due to a rapid periodic motion of the sonorous body; the sensation of a noise to non-periodic motion." from *On the Sensation of Tone* (1862) Hermann Helmholtz. 2. "Of all noises, I think music is the least disagreeable." — Samuel Johnson. [*from* Barber.]

mute A control found on recording consoles, some mixers, and certain signal processing units that silences (*mutes*) a signal path, or output. Various uses.

Muzak (*music + Kodak*) 1. Trademark of the business music company founded in 1928 by General George Owen Squier who patented the transmission of background music (phonograph records played through the telephone system). He created the name by merging the word "music" with that of his favorite high-tech venture, the *Eastman Kodak Company.* The word "Kodak" was coined by Eastman himself, and in 1888 he first registered it as a trademark. According to Eastman, he invented it out of thin air. He explained: "I devised the name myself. The letter "K" had been a favorite with me — it seems a strong, incisive sort of letter. It became a question of trying out a great number of combinations of letters that made words starting and ending with 'K.' The word 'Kodak' is the result." 2. "I worry that the person who thought up Muzak may be thinking up something else." — Lily Tomlin. [*from* Barber.]

N

NAB (*National Association of Broadcasters*) A professional trade organization for people working in the radio and television industry.

NAMM (*National Association of Music Merchants* is the original name; today it is officially the *International Music Products Association* but they didn't change the acronym) A professional trade organization for people working in the music business — primarily in retailing and manufacturing of music *making* products.

nano- A prefix for one billionth (10E-9), abbreviated **n**.

NARAS (*National Academy of Recording Arts & Science*) See: *The Recording Academy.*

NARM (*National Association of Recording Merchandisers*) An industry organization made up primarily of music retailers acting as an advocate body for the common interests of merchandisers and distributors of music to industry and public policy makers.

narrow-band filter Term popularized by equalizer pioneer C.P. Boner to describe his patented (tapped toroidal inductor) passive notch filters. Boner's filters were very high Q (around 200) and extremely narrow (5 Hz at the -3 dB points). Boner used 100-150 of these sections in series to reduce feedback modes. Today's usage extends this terminology to include all filters narrower than ⅓-octave. This includes parametrics, notch filter sets, and certain cut-only variable equalizer designs.

natural logarithm A logarithm based on the powers of *e* (aka *Base-e*).

N curve (*normal curve*) Same as Academy curve.

NC (*noise criterion*) curves A unit of measurement for the ambient or background noise level of occupied indoor spaces, i.e., a measure of its *noisiness* — true story; real word. The measured noise spectrum (done in octave bands using an SPL meter) is compared against a series of standard noise criteria (NC) curves to determine the "NC level" of the space. The standard NC curves take into account the equal loudness contours of Fletcher-Munson to accurately reflect the listening experience. Each NC curve is assigned a number (in 5 dB increments) corresponding to the octave band SPL measured over the octave centered at approximately 1500 Hz. A space is then said to have a background noise level of "NC-20," for instance, which would be very quiet, comparable to a quality recording studio. Compare with: RC rating.

near end Telecommunication term referring to your end; the local room, as opposed to the far end.

near-end crosstalk Crosstalk that is propagated in a disturbed channel in the *direction opposite to the direction of propagation of the signal* in the disturbing channel. The terminals of the disturbed channel, at which the near-end crosstalk is present, and the energized terminal of the disturbing channel, are usually near each other.

near field or **near sound field** The sound field very close to the sound source, between the source and the far field. Technically, a distance less than one wavelength at the frequency of interest.

near-field monitor A loudspeaker used at a distance of 3-4 feet (1-1 meters) in recording studios.

negative feedback The act of comparing a fraction of the output signal to the input signal at the input to an amplifier in such a way that the amplifier will keep this fraction of the output signal always exactly the same as the input signal. Negative feedback is of prime importance in designing with opamps and audio power amplifiers. As applied to audio amplifiers, negative feedback is first attributed to Bell Labs scientist Harold S. Black, as described in the *Bell Labs Technical Review, 1934.*

network Generally used to mean a multi-computer system (as opposed to a single computer bus-type system) where multiple access is allowed from more than one computer at a time. Characterized by full two-way (duplex) communications between all equipment and computers on the network. See CobraNet for an example.

network glossary See CobraNet's glossary for many useful terms.

newton *Abbr.* **N** . The International System unit of force. It is equal to the force required to accelerate a mass of one kilogram one meter per second per second.

Newton, Sir Isaac (1642-1727) English mathematician and scientist who invented differential calculus and formulated the theory of universal gravitation, a theory about the nature of light, and three laws of motion. The sight of a falling apple supposedly inspired his treatise on gravitation, presented in Principia Mathematica (1687). (AHD)

nibble A group of four bits or half a byte (8-bits).

noise cancelling headphones Special headphones incorporating a microphone built into the headset that samples the ambient sound and adds it back out-of-phase to the headphone signal. This method actively cancels or nulls out background noise — works best with high frequencies.

noise cancelling microphone A special dynamic microphone designed so both sides of the diaphragm are exposed to the sound field. Close direct sound strikes primarily one side of the diaphragm causing it to move while sounds from far away tend to be canceled because they strike the diaphragm from all sides with no net force.

noise color People working in pro audio know the terms *white noise* and *pink noise*, but few recognize the terms "azure noise" or "red noise," but they are real terms. Noise that is not white is called *colored noise* and will have more energy at some frequencies than others, analogous to colored light.

White noise and pink noise are well defined and known; much less so are the others.

White noise is so named because it is analogous to white light in that it contains all audible frequencies distributed uniformly throughout the spectrum. Passing white light through a prism (a form of filtering) breaks it down into a range of colors. Examination shows that red light is characterized by the longer wavelengths of light, i.e., the lower frequency region. Similarly, "pink noise" has higher energy in the low frequencies, hence the somewhat tongue-in-cheek term.

The Federal Standard 1037C *Telecommunications: Glossary of Telecommunication Terms* defines four noise colors (white, pink, blue black) and is considered the official source. No official standard could be found for the others.

The following list of noise colors is loosely based on a rainbow-prism light analogy, where a prism creates a rainbow effect by separating white light passed through it into a visible spectrum labeled red, orange, yellow, green, blue, indigo, and violet from lowest to highest frequencies. Also shown is the approximate slope of the power density spectrum relative to white noise used as the reference:

red noise also called **brown noise**: -6 dB/oct decreasing density (most amount of low frequency energy or power; used in oceanography; power proportional to 1/frequency-squared); *popcorn noise*.

pink noise: -3 dB/oct decreasing noise density (but, equal power per octave; *1/f noise*< or *flicker noise*; power proportional to 1/frequency).

white noise: 0 dB/oct reference noise with equal power density (equal power per hertz; *Johnson noise*).

blue (or **azure**) **noise**: +3 dB/oct increasing noise density (power proportional to frequency).

purple (or **violet**) **noise**: +6 dB/oct increasing noise density (power proportional to frequency-squared; most amount of high frequency energy or power).

black noise: silence (zero power density with a few random spikes allowed).

Other noise colors exist for specialized fields like video/photographic/image processing, communications, mathematical chaos theory, etc., but are not found in pro audio circles. Definitions for the noise colors **orange**, **green**, **gray**, and **brown** are found many times on the Web, but all appear to be from the same document (*whose true origin I could not detect*), e.g. see Bob Paddock at Circuit Cellar Online. (*Definitions without supporting documentation are suspect.*)

noise criterion (NC) curves See: NC curves.

noise figure The ratio between the Johnson noise (or *thermal noise*) of the equivalent input resistance of a circuit and its measured noise, expressed in decibels. It is the ratio of the output noise to the input noise, so the answer is always positive, with a theoretically noise-free device having a noise figure of 0 dB.

noise floor Normally the lowest threshold of useful signal level (although sometimes audible signals below the noise floor may be recovered).

noise gate An expander with a fixed "infinite" downward expansion ratio. Used extensively for controlling unwanted noise, such as preventing "open" microphones and "hot" instrument pick-ups from introducing extraneous sounds into the system. When the incoming audio signal drops below the user set-point (the *threshold* point) the expander prevents any further output by reducing the gain to "zero." The actual gain reduction is typically on the order of -80 dB, thus once audio falls below the threshold, effectively the output level becomes the residual noise of the gate. Common terminology refers to the gate "opening" and "closing." Another popular application uses noise gates to enhance musical instrument sounds, especially percussion instruments. Judicious setting of a noise gate's *attack* (turn-on) and *release* (turn-off) times adds "punch," or "tightens" the percussive sound, making it more pronounced. A noise gate is to an expander as a limiter is to a compressor. See RaneNote: *The DC 24 Users Guide*, RaneNote: *Signal Processing Fundamentals*, and RaneNote: *Good Dynamics Processing*.

noise masking *Acoustics.* The practice of adding white noise to an audio system to make background sounds unintelligible or less distracting; makes use of the human hearing masking phenomenon.

noise measurement filters See: weighting filters.

noise reduction See: expander.

noise shaping A technique used in oversampling low-bit converters and other quantizers to shift (*shape*) the frequency range of quantizing error (noise and distortion). The output of a quantizer is fed back through a filter, and summed with its input signal. Dither is sometimes used in the process. Oversampling A/D converters shift much of it out of the audio range completely. In this case, the in-band noise is decreased, which allows low-bit converters (such as delta-sigma) to equal or out-perform high-bit converters (those greater than 16 bits). When oversampling is not involved, the noise still appears to decrease by 12 dB or more because it is redistributed into less audible frequency areas. Further digital processing usually reverses the benefits of this kind of noise shaping. See RaneNote: *Digital Dharma of Audio A/D Converters.*

NOM (*number of open mics*) An acronym believed first created in 1967, or 1968, by Bill Snow after he retired from Bell Labs and went to work at Altec Lansing Research. It's use was popularized by Dan Dugan, the father of the automatic microphone mixer and Altec Lansing, the manufacturer of his first design. In Dan's original design, the automatic mic mixer, like human operators, turned the gain down on unused mic channels and turned the gain up on active channels, all the while ensuring that the overall level remained roughly constant. As a rough approximation, each doubling of the number of open mics (NOM) cuts the gain by 3 dB, i.e., as more mics are opened up the mic mixer reduces overall gain. If not, as mics open and close, the reverberation and ambient noise fluctuates unacceptably. NOM attenuation techniques work to provide the gain, stability, and low noise qualities of a single open mic with the benefits of multiple mics. [*Historical Note: This concept was first written about by C.P. Boner & R.E. Boner, in their paper "The Gain of a Sound System" April 1969, reproduced in* Sound Reinforcement: An Anthology *(Audio Engineering Society, NY, 1978.*]

nominal This word has several definitions but the one of importance to pro audio is its engineering sense meaning: insignificantly small; trifling: *a nominal amount*. It does **not** mean *average* or *typical* as is so often seen.

NOMM (*number of open mics & mixers*) A term created by Rane Corporation extending the concept of NOM (above) to include multiple mixers as well as microphones. As used by Rane, it is NOM-like in that feedback stability is maintained, however, since large systems have mics across multiple mixers, Rane includes these mixers in the NOMM calculation. For example, in audio conferencing, when the chairman is speaking and someone else quickly answers "yes," coughs, or drops a pen, most mic mixers running in NOM mode are annoying because they reduce the level of the chairman mic just because someone else made a noise. The Rane NOMM approach avoids this annoyance by keeping the chairman's mic at the same gain while still allowing the interruption to be heard, yet at a reduced gain from its full gated level.

nonvolatile Refers to a memory device that does not lose its data when power is removed from the system.

normaling jacks See: patchbay.

notch filter A special type of cut-only equalizer used to attenuate (*only*, no boosting provisions exist) a narrow band of frequencies. Three controls: *frequency, bandwidth* and *depth*, determine the notch. Simplified units provide only a frequency control, with bandwidth and depth fixed internally. Used most often in acoustic feedback control to eliminate a small band of frequencies where the system wants to howl (feedback).

NPO 1. *Ceramic capacitors* Temperature coefficient designator meaning *negative-positive-zero*, i.e., the capacitance drifts negative and positive averaging zero. A marking meaning stable with temperature. 2. *Medicine* Abbreviation for *nil per os*, or *nothing by mouth.*

NSCA (*National Systems Contractors Association*) "Founded in 1980 as the National Sound Contractors Association, the NSCA underwent a name change in 1994 to better reflect the diversification found within the hi-tech industry of electronic systems. Rather than focusing solely on the installation of audio systems, today's innovative member companies of the NSCA expanded into other fields, including audio, video, intercom/paging, telecommunications, security/access control, and many others." [from NSCA website.]

NSP (*native signal processing*) Intel-designed method of using a powerful microprocessor (like their Pentium CPU) for signal processing functions normally done by separate DSP chips. Not finding many backers.

NSSP (*National Standards Systems Network*) A Web-based service launched by ANSI, along with government and industry partners. A full search & sales service provides for locating and buying virtually any standard. More than 100,000 global standards are available. Over 25 standards groups provide technical specs for this database, including ISO. The EIA endorsed the project.

NTSC (*National Television Standards Committee*) The United States and Japan standard for color formatting for television transmission developed in the 1950s. Compare with: PAL/SECAM.

null modem cable Special wiring of an RS-232 cable such that a computer can talk to another computer without a modem (thus "null" modem). As a minimum, a null modem cable reverses pins 2 and 3 on a standard RS-232 cable — but other pins may also need changing and shorting together.

numerator *Mathematics.* The top part of a common fraction.

numerological nonsense John Allen Paulos' wonderful page of rationality helping to fight off the increasing numbers of irrational parents/teachers/politicians/scientists/engineers/audiophiles/(*your favorite here*).

Nyquist frequency The highest frequency that may be accurately sampled. The Nyquist frequency is one-half the sampling frequency. For example, the theoretical Nyquist frequency of a CD system is 22.05 kHz. See RaneNote: *Digital Dharma of Audio A/D Converters.*

O

¼" TRS or **¼" TS** See: connectors.

100Base-T or **1000Base-T** See: Ethernet.

1/f noise See: flicker noise.

object-oriented or **object-based programming** (Abbreviated **OOP**) A software technique in which a system program is expressed completely in terms of predefined things (objects), consisting of a set of variables and operations which can be performed on them, and the connections between objects.

octal A number system using the base-8, i.e., each digit can be any of 8 values, represented by the digits 0-7. A three-bit binary number can also represent each octal digit (since 2E3 = 8).

octave 1. *Audio.* The interval between any two frequencies having a ratio of 2 to 1. 2. *Music* a. The interval of eight diatonic degrees between two tones, one of which has *twice* as many vibrations per second as the other. b. A tone that is eight full tones above or below another given tone. c. An organ stop that produces tones an octave above those usually produced by the keys played. (AHD)

ohm *Abbr.* **R**, (Greek upper-case *omega* [Ω]). A unit of electrical resistance equal to that of a conductor in which a current of one ampere is produced by a potential of one volt across its terminals. [After **Georg Simon Ohm**.]

Ohm, **Georg Simon** (1789-1854) German physicist noted for his contributions to mathematics, acoustics, and the measurement of electrical resistance. (AHD)

ohmage Misnomer. No such word. *Bad, bad, super bad.* Wrongfully used as a term for loudspeaker resistance. The correct term is impedance — learn it; use it.

OIART (*Ontario Institute of Audio Recording Technology*) This Canadian school offers a three-term, forty-six week immersion course designed to prepare graduates for a career in the professional audio recording and audio communications industry.

OLED (*organic light emitting diode*) A type of LED display made from organic polymers (*think plastic that glows*) that provides a wide viewing angle and uses low power. OLED displays do not require a backlight as do LCD screens. OLED screens can also be fabricated on plastic as well as glass substrates, making them more flexible and durable. See: *OLED* website for details.

OL light See: overload light.

Olson, Harry Ferdinand, PhD (1901-1982) American engineer who worked 40 years at RCA labs, recognized and honored as a pioneer and leading authority in acoustics and electronic sound recording. He was granted over 100 patents, along with many awards and medals for his contributions to the science of sound. He authored more than 130 technical papers and wrote several textbooks still considered the best of their genre.

one-bit data converter Loose reference to any of the various data conversion schemes (e.g., delta-sigma, adaptive delta modulation, etc.) that use only one binary bit (i.e., levels 1 and 0) in the conversion and storage process.

one-third octave 1. Term referring to frequencies spaced every one-third of an octave apart. One-third of an octave represents a frequency 1.26-times above a reference, or 0.794-times below the same reference. The math goes like this: $\frac{1}{3}$-octave = $2^{1/3}$ = 1.260; and the reciprocal, $\frac{1}{1.260}$ = 0.794. Therefore, for example, a frequency $\frac{1}{3}$-octave above a 1 kHz reference equals 1.26 kHz (which is rounded-off to the ANSI-ISO preferred frequency of "1.25 kHz" for equalizers and analyzers), while a frequency $\frac{1}{3}$-octave below 1 kHz equals 794 Hz (labeled "800 Hz"). Mathematically it is significant to note that, to a very close degree, $2^{1/3}$ equals $10^{1/10}$ (1.2599 vs. 1.2589). This bit of natural niceness allows the *same frequency divisions* to be used to divide and mark an *octave into one-thirds* and a *decade into one-tenths*. 2. Term used to express the bandwidth of equalizers and other filters that are $\frac{1}{3}$-octave wide at their -3 dB (half-power) points. 3. Approximates the smallest region (*bandwidth*) humans reliably detect change. See: critical bands. Compare with: third-octave.

onomatopoetic The formation or use of words such as *buzz*, *hiss*, *splash*, *sizzle* or *murmur* that imitate the sounds associated with the objects or actions they refer to. (AHD) See: zaa zaa.

OOP See: object-oriented.

op amp (*operational amplifier*) An analog integrated circuit device characterized as having two opposite polarity inputs and one output, used as the basic building block in analog signal processing.

optical-fiber cable See: fiber-optics.

optocoupler Any device that functions as an electrical-to-optical or optical-to-electrical transducer.

orange One of the words in the English language without a rhyme — some others are "month," "purple," and "silver."

orange noise See: noise color.

ordinate *Mathematics.* The plane Cartesian coordinate representing the distance from a specified point to the *x*-axis, measured parallel to the *y*-axis. (AHD)

organic LED See: OLED.

ORTF (*Office de Radiodiffusion — Television Francaise*) An initialism formed from the name of the French national broadcasting system, who designed a stereo microphone recording technique known as the ORTF method. The technique uses two cardioid microphones with a spacing of 17 cm between the microphone diaphragms, and with an 110° angle between the capsules. This technique reproduces stereo cues similar to those used by the human ear to perceive directional information in the horizontal plane. The spacing of the microphones emulates the distance between the human ears, and the angle between the two directional microphones emulates the shadow effect of the human head. The ORTF stereo technique provides the recording with a wider stereo image than X-Y stereo while still preserving good mono information.

OSD (*on-screen display*) chip An integrated circuit providing all necessary functions for adding text to television or video monitor display screens.

OSI (*open system interconnection*) The only internationally accepted framework of standards for communication between different systems made by different vendors. The model originally developed by ISO describing computer communication services and protocols without making assumptions concerning language, operating systems or application issues. The main goal is to create an open systems networking environment where any vendor's computer system, connected to any network, can freely share data with any other computer system on that network.

OTPROM (*one-time programmable read-only memory*) A redundant term, incorrectly used to mean PROM — a PROM, by definition, is a one-time device.

outboard unit *External,* usually referring to a separate piece of signal processing gear located remote to a mixer that connects in the effects loop.

out-of-phase In an un-synchronized or un-correlated way. See: polarity and phase et al.

overload light or **OL light** An indicator found on pro audio signal processing units that lights once the signal level exceeds a preset point. There is no standard specifying when an OL light should illuminate, although common practice makes it 3-4 dB below actual clipping. Good signal processing design ensures that the OL light illuminates anytime the signal exceeds the set point, anywhere in the signal path, not just the input or output level.

overs A term associated with A/D converters used to describe input signals exceeding the full scale range (0 dBFS). *Overs* indicators vary from simple single LEDs to elaborate calibrated digital meters. To be of genuine value the overs indicator, however displayed, must be based on reading the true digital code associated with the input level. It is important to distinguish between 0 dBFS and overs; they are not the same. 0 dBFS is the absolute highest voltage level that any particular A/D can convert. It produces the equivalent of a digital code consisting of all 1s. No digital level can exceed 0 dBFS. A 0 dBFS voltage level *and all levels greater than this* produce the same output code of all 1s. A true overs indicator actually counts the number of times that the 0 dBFS level was exceeded and displays this number. As yet there is no standard as to how many samples exceeding 0 dBFS constitutes an over. Everyone agrees that very brief excursions beyond 0 dBFS (producing digital clipping) cannot be heard; however no such agreement exists as to just how many samples it takes before an over is audible.

oversampling 1. Sampling at a rate higher than the sampling Nyquist theorem. 2. A technique where each sample from the data converter is sampled more than once, i.e., *oversampled*. This multiplication of samples permits digital filtering of the signal, thus reducing the need for sharp analog filters to control aliasing. See RaneNote: *Digital Dharma of Audio A/D Converters.*

Oz From Frank Baum's "The Wizard of Oz," the name was created when he looked at his filing cabinet and saw "A-N," and "O-Z," hence "Oz."

P

P2P See: peer-to-peer.

p's and q's From old British saying: *pints and quarts* [... and you know pints and quarts of what.] 1. Socially correct behavior; manners. 2. The way one acts; conduct: *was told to watch his p's and q's or he would be fired.* (AHD)

PA-232 An RS-232-based variant of the PA-422 AES standard.

PA-422 A pro audio implementation of Electronics Industries Association EIA-422 interconnection standard, defined and adopted by the Audio Engineering Society as *AES Recommended practice for sound-reinforcement systems — Communications interface (PA-422) AES 15-1991 (ANSI S4.49-1991).*

pad See: attenuator pad.

PAL (*programmable array logic*) Original registered trademark of Monolithic Memories Inc. (now owned by Advanced Micro Devices, Inc.) for their fuse-link once-programmable logic parts that have a programmable AND array, but a predefined OR array. See also: PLA, PLD & FPGA.

PAL/SECAM (*phase alternated line/sequential couleur avec memoire* or *sequential color with memory*) The European and Australian standard for color formatting for television transmission developed in the 1960s and used most everywhere in the world except the U.S.A. and Japan, which use NTSC.

pan (*panoramic*) control A control found on mixers, used to "move," or *pan* the apparent position of a *single sound channel* between two outputs, usually "left," and "right," for stereo outputs. At one extreme of travel the sound source is heard from only one output; at the other extreme it is heard from the other output. In the middle, the sound is heard equally from each output, but is reduced in level by 3 dB relative to its original value. This guarantees that as the sound is panned from one side to the other, it maintains equal loudness (power) for all positions. Contrast with: balance and crossfade controls.

PAQRAT A registered trademark of Rane Corporation for their recording converter devices, RC 24T & RC 24A, that convert AES/EBU stereo 18-24 bit digital audio two track data into 16-bit compatible four tracks for recording and playback on 1st-generation 16-bit modular digital multi-track tape machines such as Alesis ADAT and Tascam DTRS (DA-88) models.

paragraphic See: parametric equalizer.

parallel interface The printer port in the PC world. A parallel port conforming to the quasi-standard called the Centronics Parallel Standard (there is no EIA standard). Originally a 36-pin connector, now more often a D-25 type connector. A parallel (as opposed to *serial*) interface transfers all bits in a word simultaneously. See also: serial interface.

parametric equalizer First named by George Massenburg, a multi-band variable equalizer offering control of all the "parameters" of the internal bandpass filter sections. These parameters being *amplitude, center frequency* and *bandwidth.* This allows the user not only to control the amplitude of each band, but also to shift the center frequency and to widen or narrow the affected area. Available with rotary and slide controls. Subcategories of parametric equalizers exist which allow control of center frequency but not bandwidth. For rotary control units the most used term is *quasi-parametric.* For units with slide controls the popular term is *paragraphic.* The frequency control may be continuously variable or switch selectable in steps. Cut-only parametric equalizers (with adjustable bandwidth or not) are called notch equalizers, or band-reject equalizers. See RaneNote: *Constant-Q Graphic Equalizers.*

parity A redundant error detection method in which the total number of binary 1's (or 0's) is always made even or odd by appending one or more bits.

pascal *Abbr.* **Pa.** The International System unit of pressure equal to one newton per square meter. [After **Blaise Pascal**.]

Pascal, Blaise (1623-1662) French philosopher and mathematician. Among his achievements are the invention of an adding machine and the development of the modern theory of probability.

passband The range of frequencies passed by an audio low-pass, high-pass or bandpass filter. Normally measured at the *-3 dB point*: the frequency point where the amplitude response is attenuated 3 dB (decibels) relative to the level of the main passband. For a bandpass filter two points are referenced: the *upper* and *lower* –3 dB points. The –3 dB point represents the frequency where the output *power* has been reduced by one-half. [Technical details: -3 dB represents a multiplier of 0.707. If the voltage is reduced by 0.707, the current is also reduced by 0.707 (ohms law), and since power equals voltage-times-current, 0.707 times 0.707 equals 0.5, or *half-power.*] The opposite of stopband.

passive crossover A loudspeaker crossover not requiring a power supply for operation. Normally built into the loudspeaker cabinet. Passive crossovers do not require separate power amplifiers for each driver. See: active crossover, and RaneNote: *Signal Processing Fundamentals.*

passive equalizer A variable equalizer requiring no power supply to operate. Consisting only of passive components (inductors, capacitors and resistors) passive equalizers have no AC line cord. Favored for their low noise performance (no active components to generate noise), high dynamic range (no active power supplies to limit voltage swing), extremely good reliability (passive components rarely break), and lack of RFI interference (no semiconductors to detect radio frequencies). Disliked for their cost (inductors are expensive), size (and bulky), weight (and heavy), hum susceptibility (and need careful shielding), and signal loss characteristic (passive equalizers always reduce the signal). Also inductors saturate easily with large low frequency signals, causing distortion. Rarely seen today, but historically they were used primarily for notching in permanent sound systems. See RaneNote: *Operator Adjustable Equalizers.*

patchbay or **patch panel** A flat panel, or enclosure, usually rack-mounted, that contains at least two rows of ¼" TRS connectors used to "patch in" or insert into the signal path a piece of external equipment (really dense configurations use 4.4 mm miniature or "bantam" jacks). The two rows consists of "send" (top row) and "receive" (bottom row) jacks wired for true balanced interconnection, i.e., tip = positive signal, ring = negative signal, sleeve = shield ground (*unbalanced patchbays exist but should not so no further discussion*). The two rows are tied together by shorting contacts such that the *normal* operation (hence, **"normaling" jacks**) is to short the send and receive tip-to-tip & ring-to-ring (the sleeves are always connected) maintaining the signal path until something is plugged in (or *jacked in* as cyberpunks love to say). Popular in recording studios where it is common to change the units in the signal path for each new session or client.

patents See: USPTO.

PBX (*private branch exchange*) Term referring to hardware allowing several telephones to be connected to a smaller number of lines.

PC (*personal computer*) Original term coined by IBM to describe their first personal computers; now used to mean all IBM-compatible personal computers, or any personal computer.

PC-Card See: PCMCIA.

PC-DOS (*personal computer disk operating system*) IBM's trademarked acronym for their PC operating system. If PC-DOS runs on an IBM *compatible,* it is then called *MS-DOS.*

PCI (*peripheral component interconnect*) Intel-designed high performance CPU interconnect strategy for "glueless" I/O subsystems. A 32- or 64-bit local-bus specification, characterized by being self-configuring, open, high-bandwidth and processor-independent — allowing for modular hardware design.

PCM (*pulse code modulation*) A conversion method in which digital words in a bit stream represent samples of analog information. The basis of most digital audio systems, first invented by Alec H. Reeves in 1937 [*see The Digital Revolution*]. Also see RaneNote: *Digital Dharma of Audio A/D Converters.*

PCMCIA (*Personal Computer Memory Card International Association*) 1. The association and first name given to the standardized credit-card size packages (aka *smart cards*) for memory and I/O (modems, LAN cards, etc.) for computers, laptops, palmtops, etc. Nicknamed *PC-Card*, which is now the preferred term. 2. Popularly believed to stand for *People Can't Memorize Computer Interface Acronyms.*

PDA (*personal digital assistant*) A small palmtop-like computer designed for specific tasks such as a pocket calculator. Other examples include personal electronic diaries, memo takers, communicators, web browsers, dictionary-translators, etc. Apple's *Newton* is a PDA. IBM named theirs *personal communicators.*

pdf (*probability density function*) See: probability density function.

PDF files (*portable document format*) Suffix letters used (*.pdf*) to indicate an Adobe Acrobat document.

peaking response Term used to describe a bandpass shape when applied to program equalization.

peak program meter See: PPM.

PEAQ (*perceptual evaluation of audio quality*) Term for the ITU-R recommendations for the objective measurement of perceived audio quality for perceptually coded digital audio signals. Popularly called the new "electronic ear" to provide yardstick values for digitally coded audio quality, there are a series of recommendations covering various aspects of this method (e.g., ITU-R Rec. BS.1387, ITU-R Rec. BS.1116 and ITU-R Rec. BS.562-3). For details of this complex issue see the definitive overview paper by Thiede, et al., "PEAQ — The ITU Standard for Objective Measurement of Perceived Audio Quality," *J. Audio Eng. Soc.*, vol. 48 (Audio Engineering Society, January/February 2000). See also CRC's (Communication Research Centre) excellent summary with the same title.

PEC (*parallel earth conductor*) Modern best practices for EMC in installations (per IEC 61000-5-2:1998) require the use of trays, conduits and heavy-gauge earth conductors, known as "parallel earth conductors" (PEC) to divert power currents away from cables and their shields. See Williams' *EMC for Systems and Installations* for full details.

PEC (*protective earth conductor*) Conductor to be connected between the protective earth terminal and an external protective earthing system.

peer-to-peer abbreviated **P2P** A network term popularly used to mean an equal access network where every node can send/receive data at any time without waiting for permission, i.e., each node can act as a client or server. An example would be a group of computers that communicate directly with each other, rather than through a central server.

perceptual coding A lossy digital audio data compression technique based on the human hearing mechanisms of masking and critical bands. AC-3 and AAC are examples of digital audio data compression schemes based on perceptual coding.

period *Abbr.* **T, t** 1. The period of a periodic function is the smallest time interval over which the function repeats itself. [For example, the *period* of a sine wave is the amount of time, T, it takes for the waveform to pass through 360 degrees. Also, it is the reciprocal of the frequency itself: i.e., $T = 1/f$.] 2. *Mathematics.* a. The least interval in the range of the independent variable of a periodic function of a real variable in which all possible values of the dependent variable are assumed. b. A group of digits separated by commas in a written number. c. The number of digits that repeat in a repeating decimal. For example, $1/7 = 0.142857142857...$ has a six-digit period. (AHD)

periodic motion Motion that repeats itself at regular or predictable intervals.

peripheral Equipment physically independent of, but which may interface to a computer or a controller.

PET (*protective earth terminal*) Terminal connected to conductive parts of Class I equipment for safety purposes. This terminal is intended to be connected to an external earthing system by a PEC (protective earth conductor).

PFC (*power-factor-corrected*) See: power-factor-corrected.

PFL (*pre-fade listen*) A term used on recording consoles and mixers, referring to a signal taken before the main channel fader. The significance is this signal is not affected by the fader position. Normally used to monitor (via headphones) to an individual input (or a small group of inputs) without affecting the main outputs, particularly useful in that it allows listening to an input with its fader all the way down (off). In broadcast this function is often called *cueing*,

while recording or live-sound users may also refer to it as *soloing*. Compare: AFL.

phantom power The term given to the standardized scheme of providing power supply voltage to certain microphones using the same two lines as the balanced audio path. The international standard is IEC 60268-15, derived from the original German standard DIN 45 596. It specifies three DC voltage levels of 48 V, 24 V and 12 V, delivered through 6.8 kΩ, 1.2 kΩ, and 680 Ω matched resistors respectively, capable of delivering 10-15 ma. The design calls for both signal conductors to have the same DC potential. This allows the use of microphone connections either for microphones without built-in preamps, such as dynamic types, or for microphones with built-in preamps such as condenser and electret types.

[*Phantom Power Mini-tutorial:* Much confusion surrounds phantom power. This is an area where you need to make informed decisions: Is it provided? Do you need it? Is it the correct voltage, and does it source enough current for your microphone? There is a huge myth circulating that microphones sound better running from 48 V, as opposed to, say, 12 V, or that you can increase the dynamic range of a microphone by using higher phantom power. For the overwhelming majority of microphones both of these beliefs are false. Most condenser microphones require phantom power in the range of 12-48 VDC, with many extending the range to 9-52 VDC, leaving only a very few that actually require just 48 VDC. The reason is that internally most designs use some form of current source to drive a low voltage zener (usually 5 V; sometimes higher) which determines the polarization voltage and powers the electronics. The significance is that neither runs off the raw phantom power, they both are powered from a fixed and regulated low voltage source inside the mic. Increasing the phantom power voltage is never seen by the microphone element or electronics, it only increases the voltage across the current source. But there are exceptions, so check the manufacturer, and don't make assumptions based on hearsay. From RaneNote: *Selecting Mic Preamps.*]

phase Audio signals are complex AC (alternating current) periodic phenomena expressed mathematically as phasors, or vectors. *Phase* refers to a particular value of *t* (time) for any periodic function, i.e. it is the relationship between a reference point and the fractional part of the period through which the signal has advanced relative to an arbitrary origin. [*The origin is usually taken at the last previous passage through zero from the negative to the positive direction* — IEEE.] See Georgia State University's great website HyperPhysics for more detail.

phase cancellation When two signals have the same exact time relationship to each other, they are said to be "in-phase;" if they do not, they are said to be "out-of-phase." (Compare with: polarity) If two out-of-phase signals add together, since this is vector arithmetic (see: phasor), they will, in fact, subtract from one another. This is called *phase* *cancellation.* Another type of phase cancellation occurs when water waves interact. One wave's energy becomes stronger when two waves collide in-phase (*summing*) and becomes weaker when they collide out-of-phase (*cancelling*).

phase delay A phase-shifted sine wave appears displaced in *time* from the input waveform. This displacement is called *phase delay* and is usually constant for all frequencies of interest. Used as another name for group delay; however there are instances where they are not the same, for example systems exhibiting ripple in their phase vs. frequency characteristics.

phase lag and **phase lead** Phase shift caused by reactive elements (capacitors and inductors) that either subtracts (*lag*) or adds (*lead*) degrees of shift. See RaneNote: *Linkwitz-Riley Crossovers up to 8th-Order: An Overview.*

phase linear 1. Chiefly a European phrase meaning "linear phase." Any system which accurately preserves phase relationships between frequencies, i.e., that exhibits pure delay. See: group delay. 2. Consumer hi-fi company where all five Rane owners worked before starting Rane Corporation. See: Phase Linear History/Repair website.

phase lock loop A circuit for synchronizing a variable local oscillator with the phase of a transmitted signal. The circuit acts as a phase detector by comparing the frequency of a known oscillator with an incoming signal and then feeds back the output of the detector to keep the oscillator in phase with the incoming frequency. Commonly used for bit-synchronization.

phaser Also called a "phase shifter," this is an electronic device creating an effect similar to flanging, but not as pronounced. Based on phase shift (*frequency dependent*), rather than true signal delay (*frequency independent*), the phaser is much easier and cheaper to construct. Using a relatively simple narrow notch filter (all-pass filters also were used) and sweeping it up and down through some frequency range, then summing this output with the original input, creates the desired effect. Narrow notch filters are characterized by having sudden and extreme phase shifts just before and just after the deep notch. This generates the needed phase shifts for the ever-changing magnitude cancellations.

phase shift The fraction of a complete cycle elapsed as measured from a specified reference point and expressed as an angle. See RaneNote: *Exposing Equalizer Mythology.*

phasor 1. A complex number expressing the magnitude and phase of a time-varying quantity. It is math shorthand for complex numbers. Unless otherwise specified, it is used only within the context of steady-state alternating linear systems. [Example: 1.5 /27° is a phasor representing a vector with a magnitude of 1.5 and a phase angle of 27 degrees.] 2. For some unknown reason, used a lot by Star Fleet personnel.

phat *adj.* *Slang* **phatter, phattest** Excellent; first-rate: *phat fashion*; *a phat rapper.* [Earlier, *sexy (said of a woman), of unknown origin.*] (AHD)

phlogiston A hypothetical substance formerly thought to be a volatile constituent of all combustible substances released as flame in combustion. (AHD) See: smoke.

Phoenix-blocks (or -connectors or **-strips)** A term, becoming generic, meaning disconnectable, or pluggable terminal blocks, after Phoenix Contact connector company, although dozens of companies make them. Also called *Euroblocks.* See: connectors.

phon A unit of apparent loudness, equal in number to the intensity in decibels of a 1,000 Hz tone judged to be as loud as the sound being measured.

phone jack Same as *" TRS,* see connectors.

phonograph "An irritating toy that restores life to dead noises." — Ambrose Bierce.

phono jack Same as *RCA,* see connectors.

physics *Some claim that studying physics is all you need for a complete education — after a visit to HyperPhysics you may agree.*

pi *Symbol* (Greek lower-case *pi:* π) 1. *Mathematics.* A transcendental number, approximately 3.14159, represented by the Greek lower-case pi symbol, that expresses the ratio of the circumference to the diameter of a circle and appears as a constant in many mathematical expressions. (AHD) 2. *Filters.* Equal to 180 degrees or integral multiples thereof. See: Beckmann.

PI 14 See: Pseudoacoustic Infector.

pico- Prefix for one trillionth (10E-12), abbreviated **p.**

PICO (*Program In, Chip Out*) Hewlett-Packard technology that use computers to design computers.

pin-1 problem Phrase created by Neil A. Muncy (Canadian electroacoustic system consultant) to describe the improper connection of the "pin-1" terminal of XLR connectors found on analog pro audio equipment. The correct way to terminate pin-1 of XLR connectors is to bond it to the chassis immediately at the entry and exit points. It should not be connected to circuit signal ground. Equipment with pin-1 left open, or connected to circuit signal ground is said to suffer from a "pin-1 problem." See Steve Macatee's *Considerations in Grounding and Shielding* , RaneNote: *Sound System Interconnection,* Philip Giddings' "A New and Important Audio Equipment Evaluation Criteria," and Tony Waldron and Keith Armstrong, "Bonding Cable Shields at Both Ends to Reduce Noise," *EMC Compliance Journal,* May 2002.

pin jack Same as *RCA*, see: connectors.

pink noise Pink noise is a random noise source characterized by a flat amplitude response per octave band of frequency (or any *constant percentage* bandwidth), i.e., it has equal energy, or constant power, per octave. Passing white noise through a filter having a 3 dB/octave roll-off rate creates pink noise. See white noise discussion for details. Due to this roll-off, pink noise sounds less bright and richer in low frequencies than white noise. Since pink noise has the same energy in each ⅓-octave band, it is the preferred sound source for many acoustical measurements due to the critical band concept of human hearing. The name comes from the filtering of white noise. White noise is analogous to white light in that it contains all audible frequencies distributed uniformly throughout the spectrum. Passing white light through a prism (a form of filter) breaks it down into a range of colors. Examination shows that red light is characterized by the longer wavelengths of light, i.e., light in the lower frequency region. Similarly, pink noise has higher energy in the low frequencies, hence the somewhat tongue-in-cheek term *pink*. See: noise color.

pitch Frequency or tone of a sound.

pitch-shifting or **pitch-transposing** *Recording.* An effect that changes the pitch (*frequency or tone*) of musical notes without changing their length, or timing. For example, fast-forwarding an audio cassette results in a higher pitched version of the music at an increased pace. Pitch-shifting does the same thing without changing the music speed. One way to accomplish this is to use *continuous wavelet transform*, where the musical signal is decomposed into separate *wavelets* and processed. First, the pitch is modified by a constant related to the required pitch change, then the time scale is adjusted appropriately.

pixel (*picture element*) The smallest element on a display surface, like a video screen, that can be assigned independent characteristics.

PLA (*programmable logic array*) A programmable logic device in which both the AND & OR arrays are programmable.

placement equalization or **placement EQ** Term coined by Tomlinson Holman (of THX fame) to mean moving around the loudspeaker and listener until the room response (at the listener) is smoothest.

PLD (*programmable logic device*) The generic name for an integrated circuit offering a vast array of logic function building blocks that the circuit designer defines (programs) to interconnect for specific applications.

plenum 1. A ductwork system in which air is at a pressure greater than that of the outside atmosphere. 2. Such a system located in the space above a suspended ceiling, used to circulate air back to a building's HVAC.

plenum cable The type of cable used when smoke retardant properties are required. Plenum cable is specifically designed for use in a plenum area (see above) which is typically used as the distribution system in buildings. Most cities requiring all cable ran through a plenum ceiling to be *plenum cable* which has insulated conductors jacketed with PVDF (*polyvinylidene difloride*) — a material providing low flame spread and low smoke producing properties. Underwriters Laboratories approve plenum cables for non-conduit applications located in environmental air spaces. This low cost alternative has replaced traditional conduit use in many commercial installations.

PnP (*plug 'n play*) 1. *Computers.* The technology that lets certain operation systems (Windows 95, others) automatically detect and configure most of the adapters and peripherals connected to or sitting inside a PC. 2. Any system with automatic detection and configuration of auxiliary devices.

polarity A signal's electromechanical potential with respect to a reference potential. For example, if a loudspeaker cone moves *forward* when a *positive* voltage is applied between its red and black terminals, then it is said to have a *positive polarity*. A microphone has *positive polarity* if a positive pressure on its diaphragm results in a positive output voltage. [Usage Note: polarity vs. phase shift: *polarity* refers to a signal's *reference* NOT to its *phase shift*. Being 180° *out-of-phase* and having *inverse polarity* are DIFFERENT things. We wrongly say something is *out-of-phase* when we mean it is *inverted*. One takes *time*; the other does not.]

popcorn noise *Solid-state physics.* Noise primarily found in integrated circuit audio amplifiers that exhibit a sizzling, frying hot-grease kind of sound, similar to popcorn popping. Found to be due to manufacturing defects in the form of metallic impurities in the junctions, often caused by dirty fabrication lines. The frequency spectrum typically conforms to 1/frequency-squared. See: ***red/brown noise*** under noise color.

portmanteau word A word formed by merging the sounds and meanings of two different words, as *chortle*, from *chuckle* and *snort*, or *motel*, from *motor* and *hotel*. (AHD) Compare with: acronym.

post-echo See: print-through.

pot (*lowercase*) Shorten form of potentiometer (*and if you think I'm gonna make some cheap joke about the smokin' kind, you're crazy*).

potentiometer A three-terminal variable resistor. Two terminals connect to the ends of the resistor, while the third terminal is attached to a movable device that makes contact with the resistive element. The movable terminal, or *slider*, is capable of being positioned from one end of the element to the other. Many physical arrangements exist, with the rotary design being the most common, followed by linear motion (used in graphic equalizers, for example), all the way to tiny SMT devices. Often used as voltage dividers in electronic circuits, the input voltage is applied to the top of the resistive element, while the other end is tied to ground or a common reference and the output is taken from the slider. When the slider is positioned to the top extreme, the output equals the input, or the entire voltage; moving it to the bottom extreme gives an output of 0 V; and every possible level between is available as the slider is moved from one end to the other. The most common application uses this arrangement to control the volume of an audio device. In this manner the voltage, or electrical potential is varied, hence, a *potentiometer*. The taper of the pot controls the rate at which the voltage changes as the slider is moved. The taper defines the amount of resistive change as a function of travel. Several popular examples follow:

audio taper (aka ***A-taper***): Usually 15% resistance at the 50% rotation point.

linear taper (aka ***B-taper***): Always 50% resistance at the 50% travel point.

log taper: Often used for an audio taper since its 50% rotation point has 10% resistance.

MN taper (aka ***balance pot***) Special taper developed for home stereo "Balance" controls. Consists of two sections (one for each channel) operating opposite each other. Exactly one-half of each section is a zero-resistance surface (i.e., solid-copper or equivalent), the next 50% of travel is linear taper. Therefore one channel rotating the slider through the first 50% of travel does not change the level at all, while the other channel is reduce from full to zero, and vice-versa, with the middle position (usually featuring a center-detent) always passing full signal to each channel. See: balance control.

POTS (*uppercase*) Acronym for *plain-old telephone system.* The normal single line basic telephone service. Often used in reference to modems associated with regular telephone lines. See RaneNote: *Interfacing Audio and POTS.*

power 1. *Electricity* a. The product of applied voltage (potential difference) and current in a direct-current circuit (or the voltage squared divided by the resistance, or the current squared times the resistance). b. The product of the effective values of the voltage and current with the cosine of the phase angle (between current and voltage) in an alternating-current circuit. See: apparent power and rms power 2. *Physics* The rate at which work is done, expressed as the amount of work per unit time, and measured in units such as the watt (1 joule per second, which equals the power dissipated (as heat) by 1 Ω of resistance when 1 ampere of current passes through it) and horsepower (equal to 745.7 watts). (AHD)

power amplifier See: amplifier.

power amplifier dummy load See: amplifier dummy load.

power factor *Abbr.* **PF** *Electronics.* The ratio of the total power in watts (resistive load) to the total apparent power in voltamperes (VA) (reactive load). The difference between *watts* and *VA* is due to reactive load impedance. Apparent power equals watts only for a purely resistive load (i.e., zero degrees phase shift between the applied voltage and the resultant current). Power factor is best thought of intuitively as the multiplier (ranging between 0 and 1) that you must use to obtain the real power from the apparent power. For example if you measure the rms voltage and current of a circuit and multiply them together you obtain the apparent power, but you must multiply this value by the power factor to obtain the real power. If the load is purely resistive then the phase difference between the voltage and current will be zero and the power factor will be one, and the apparent power will equal the true power — but only for a resistive load. For a reactive load (any load with inductive and/or capacitive reactance, i.e., any *real* load) there will be a phase difference between the voltage and the current due to the phase delay introduced by the reactive elements. Simply put, since the maximum voltage and current do not occur at the same instant of time the amount of power developed is less than the measured rms voltage and current multiplied together.

Since power factor is a ratio, and hence unitless, it can be expressed in several ways — all of them equal. It is the ratio of watts to voltamperes, of resistance to reactance, and if the phase shift in degrees is known (*phase angle*>), it is the cosine of that angle, or **cos**. If the angle is zero the PF = 1, and if the angle is 90° the PF = 0.

power-factor-corrected (*PFC*) Any system that has a power-factor-correcting device, such as a capacitor, installed to reduce the phase difference between the rms voltage and rms current.

PowerPC A super powerful RISC processor PC jointly developed by IBM, Apple and Motorola, designed to run *any* PC operating system (MS-DOS, UNIX, Windows, OS/2, Mac OS. etc.). Featured in Apple's line of PowerMac computers.

PPM (*peak program meter*) An audio meter originally developed in Europe to accurately measure and display *peak* audio signals (as opposed to *average* audio signals; see VU meter). The PPM augments the VU meter and it is normal to find both in modern recording studios. The PPM is particularly valuable for digital audio recording or signal processing due to the critical monitoring required to prevent exceeding 0 dBFS and reducing overs. There are two standards: IEC 60268-10 for analog meters and IEC 60268-18 for digital meters. [*These are available to buy on the IEC website.*] An interesting aspect of PPM design is that rather than respond instantaneously to peaks, they require a finite 5 ms integration time, so that only peaks wide enough to be audible are displayed. IEC 60268-10 translates this into a response that is 1 dB down from steady-state for a 10 ms tone burst, 2 dB down for a 5 ms burst, and 4 dB down for a 3 ms tone burst — requirements satisfied by an attack time constant of 1.7 ms. The IEC specified decay rate of 1.5 seconds to a -20 dB level can be met with a 650 ms time constant.

preamplifier See: amplifier.

precedence effect See: Haas Effect.

pre-echo See: print-through.

pre-emphasis A high-frequency boost used during recording, followed by de-emphasis during playback, designed to improve signal-to-noise performance.

pre-mastering See: mastering.

pressure gradient microphone See: ribbon microphone.

pressure zone microphone See: PZM.

print-through The name for the magnetic tape recording phenomena where the act of layering, or winding layer upon layer of tape causes the flux from one layer to magnetize the adjacent layer, thus *printing through* from one layer onto another layer. Also called *crosstalk* or *interlayer transfer*. The most vulnerable parts of the magnetic tape are the blank spots, particularly leaders and spaces between material that happen to occur adjacent to loud passages. Two other terms come from print-through: on layers played back *before* loud passages it gives a *pre-echo*, whereas on playback *following* the loud passage it gives a *post-echo*.

probability density function, or **pdf**, or **p.d.f.** The name given to a mathematical function that defines a continuous interval (i.e., one without gaps), or curve, such that the area under the curve (and above the x-axis, i.e., the probability is always positive) described by the function is unity, or equals *one*, or 100 % — whatever way you want to look at it. It simply means that all possibilities are represented. The most familiar example is the famous "bell-shaped curve" or just "bell curve." The bell curve is a symmetrical curve representing a *normal* or *Gaussian* distribution. Also called a *normal curve*. When applied to school grading, for example, it says that there is the highest probability that a student picked at random will receive a C-grade, and rapidly decreasing probabilities that any one student will receive a B- or A-grade, going in one direction, or a D- or F-grade, going in the other direction. Technically, it means the probability of a random variable taking values between two real numbers, or extremes (an *A* or an *F*) is given by the area under the curve between these two points.

production master See: mastering.

Programming, Law of The law states that every program contains at least one bug. The law further states that every program can be shortened by at least one instruc-

tion. Therefore, the law concludes, every program can be reduced to one instruction that does not work. The law is not wrong. [*Thanks TP.*]

PROM (*programmable read-only memory*) A memory device whose contents can be electrically programmed (once) by the designer.

proof "Evidence having a shade more of plausibility than of unlikelihood. The testimony of two credible witnesses as opposed to that of only one." — Ambrose Bierce.

propagation The motion of waves through or along a medium. For electromagnetic waves, propagation may occur in a vacuum as well as in material media.

propagation delay The initial delay through a signal processing box, i.e., the time it takes for a signal to pass once through a device. It is the unavoidable and uncontrollable (by the user) delay inherent to the processing electronics. Propagation delay is caused most often in analog electronics by phase delay in filter networks, and in digital electronics by computational delay in microprocessors and DSP devices, as well as data conversion. In networking, the time it takes for a signal to pass through a channel. Similar to latency but normally restricted to signal processing devices, rather than computer operations.

proportional-Q equalizer (also **variable-Q**) Term applied to graphic and rotary equalizers describing bandwidth behavior as a function of boost/cut levels. The term "proportional-Q" is preferred as being more accurate and less ambiguous than "variable-Q." If nothing else, "variable-Q" suggests the unit allows the user to vary (set) the Q, when no such controls exist. The bandwidth varies inversely proportional to boost (or cut) amounts, being very wide for small boost/cut levels and becoming very narrow for large boost/cut levels. The skirts, however, remain constant for all boost/cut levels. See RaneNote: *Operator Adjustable Equalizers.*

prosumer Shortened form of *professional + consumer*, often used to refer to home recording studio equipment.

protocol A specific set of rules, procedures or conventions relating to format and timing of data transmission between two devices. A standard procedure that two data devices must accept and use to be able to understand each other.

proximity effect *Microphones.* Term for the increase in low frequency response (bass boost), or sensitivity, of most directional microphones when the sound source is within a few inches.

Pseudoacoustic Infector Term coined by Rane Corporation for their mythical product, the PI 14, first introduced in 1988, which *almost* caught the attention of the music industry. An acoustic stimulator designed to add a little bit of *This* and a little bit of *That* to recordings, to give them a sense of *Now* previously unobtainable. Rane's PI 14 introduced a unique *Here-to-There* (*and-Back-Again*) pan control. Transformer operation required the Jensen JE-EP-ERs when coupling directly into a Crown Belchfire BF-6000SUX for playback through an Electro-Voice Rearaxial Softspeaker. Today, PI 14s are considered quite scarce and highly collectable.

pseudo-balanced output A two-wire (with overall shield) interfacing technique for an unbalanced output where a resistor equal to the output resistor is placed in series with the return leg (either pin-3 for an XLR connector or the ring lead for an ¼" TRS connector). This makes both lines measure the same impedance when looking back from the receiver and allows the common-mode rejection feature of the input differential amplifier to function. See RaneNote: *Sound System Interconnection.*

PSPICE See: SPICE.

psophometric See: weighting filters.

psychoacoustics The scientific study of the perception of sound. Called "the music of science" by Roederer.

punch-in/punch-out *Recording studio*: To engage/disengage record mode on a track previously recorded, usually for purposes of correcting unwanted segments.

PURLnet See: ZigBee.

purple One of the few words in the English language without a rhyme — some others are "month," "orange" & "silver."

purple noise See: noise color.

PVC cable (*polyvinyl chloride*) The most common type of cable used when smoke retardant properties are not required, i.e., when a building's HVAC system is run through metal ducts — not open ceilings. This cable is sheathed in PVC, the standard jacketing of most electrical cable. PVC is a tough water and flame retardant material, but is not smoke retardant. If PVC catches fire, it emits noxious gases, and if the cable is run in a plenum area, the deadly gases can be dispersed throughout the building.

PWM (*pulse width modulation*) A conversion method in which the widths of pulses in a pulse train represent the analog information. See RaneNote: *Digital Dharma of Audio A/D Converters.*

Pythagorean temperament The mathematical principles of musical harmony according to the Greek philosopher Pythagoras.

PZM (*pressure zone microphone*) Patented by Ed Long Ron Wickersham in 1982, a technique and design where the microphone is mounted on a flat plate which acts as a reflective surface directing sound into the mic capsule. The PZM principle uses the compression and decompression of air between the plate and the membrane in parallel with the plate (the gap is very narrow, typically only a millimeter or less. This arrangement gives about 6 dB extra amplification of the signal, which means 6 dB less inherent electronic noise. Now owned by Crown (recently acquired by Harman).

Q

q (lower-case) *Physics.* The symbol for charge.

Q (upper-case) Quality factor. *Filters.* The selectivity factor defined to be the ratio of the center frequency *f* divided by the bandwidth *BW.* See RaneNote: *Constant-Q Graphic Equalizers*; also download "Bandwidth vs. Q Calculator" as a zipped Microsoft Excel spreadsheet from the Rane website, Library section.

Q-8 RCA's name for their 4-channel, eight-track tape cartridges, the world's first (*and last*). For photo, see Discrete Four-Channel Sound on Magnetic Tape.

QoS (*quality of service*) 1. The performance specification of a communications channel or system. It may be quantitatively indicated by channel or system performance parameters, such as signal-to-noise ratio (S/N), bit error ratio (BER), message throughput rate, and call blocking probability. 2. A subjective rating of telephone communications quality in which listeners judge transmissions by qualifiers, such as excellent, good, fair, poor, or unsatisfactory. [*From Federal Standard 1037C*; also see Quality of Service Forum.]

QS Sansui's name for their quadraphonic sound system using a proprietary matrixing algorithm for encoding four-channel sound down to two-channels. See: Matrix Quad. Compare with: SQ.

QSound The name of a Canadian company and its proprietary and patented 3D sound technology. Designed for two channel playback systems, QSound finds success in the computer and arcade game markets, as well as movie theaters. Using advanced signal processing techniques, QSound adds localization cues to the original material. Since loudspeakers and headphones create quite different playback environments, different algorithms exist for each. QSound allows the music producer to locate specific sound events in virtual positions outside the physical locations of the two loudspeakers. The effect is primarily one of widening the sound field. QSound works best when the listener is positioned in the sweet spot located equidistant between the speakers.

quackery The statement floating about cyberspace that a duck's quack does not echo and no one knows why.

quad flat pack The most commonly used package in surface mount technology to achieve a high lead count in a small area. Leads are brought out on all four sides of a thin square package.

quad mic cable See: cables.

quadraphonic sound Coined in the '70s, the original term for surround sound.

quantization distortion Same as *quantization error* below.

quantization error Error resulting from quantizing an analog waveform to a discrete level. It is the difference between the actual value of the analog signal at the sampling instant and the nearest quantization value. Therefore, in general, the longer the word length, the less the error, because there are more step sizes to choose the closest. See also SQNR and RaneNote: *Digital Dharma of Audio A/D Converters.*

quantization The process of converting, or digitizing, the almost infinitely variable amplitude of an analog waveform to one of a finite series of discrete levels. Performed by the A/D converter. See also SQNR and RaneNote: *Digital Dharma of Audio A/D Converters.*

quarter-inch jack Same as ¼" TRS or ¼" TS. See: connectors.

quasi-balanced line See: floating unbalanced line.

quasi-parametric See: parametric equalizer.

QWERTY Nickname for the computer (or typewriter) keyboard derived from the left side, top row of letter keys.

quint *Music.* Name for an interval of a fifth.

R

rack unit See: "U".

radian 1. *Mathematics.* A unit of angular measure equal to the angle subtended at the center of a circle by an arc equal in length to the radius of the circle, approximately 57°17'44.6 (AHD) 2. *Filters.* Frequency is measured in radians/second. One cycle (360°) equals 2 pi radians.

radicalism "The conservatism of tomorrow injected into the affairs of today." — Ambrose Bierce.

radix The number base, such as 2 in the binary system and 10 in the decimal system.

radix point The binary equivalent of the decimal point — think of it as a "binary point."

rail-switcher A term used to describe audio power amplifier designs utilizing more than one power supply for the output, and a means of switching between them based upon the input signal. This scheme improves efficiency. See: Class G Amplifiers and compare with: tracking power amplifiers.

rail-to-rail Registered trademark of Nippon Motorola, Ltd. for their op amp designs having maximum input and output levels equal to the power supply voltages. See: RRIO.

RAM (*random access memory*) A memory device in which data may be read out and new data written into any address or location.

RaneNotes A series of technical notes written by Rane's technical staff.

RaneWare A registered trademark of Rane Corporation used to identify Rane software products — not something to keep you dry.

Rankine scale A scale of absolute temperature using degrees the same size as those of the Fahrenheit scale, in which the freezing point of water is 491.69° and the boiling point of water is 671.69°. After William John Macquorn Rankine below. [AHD. *Sounds handy to me.*]

Rankine, William John Macquorn (1820-1872), Scottish engineer and physicist.

RAQ (*rarely asked questions*) The really important questions that should be asked, but never are. The answers to RAQs are kept hidden within government and corporate walls.

rarefaction 1. A decrease in density and pressure in a medium, such as air, caused by the passage of a sound wave. 2. The region in which this occurs. (AHD)

RC (*room criteria*) rating A new noise criteria adopted by ASHRAE to replace the NC criteria. The RC rating is based on ASHRAE sponsored studies of preference and requirements for speech privacy ratings for "acoustical quality." RC ratings contain both a numerical value and a letter to describe the expected spectral quality of the sound. The numerical part is called the *speech interference level (SIL)* equal to the arithmetic average of the measured SPL in the 500 Hz, 1 kHz and 2 kHz octave bands, and the letter part denotes the timbre or sound quality as subjectively described by an observer as *neutral (N), rumbly (R), hissy (H) or acoustically induced vibration noise (RV)*. The RC curves serve as optimum spectrum shapes for background sound in buildings. Octave band analysis that meet a specific RC curve are considered *neturally balanced*, i.e., they have the desired amounts of low-, mid- and high-frequency content to be heard as not offensive. RC curves are straight lines set at -5 dB/octave slopes (*of course — couldn't be 6, had to be 5*). The RC rating standard is *Criteria for Evaluating Room Noise, ANSI S12.2*. See Trane's excellent summary "How To Determine The RC Noise Rating," for a step-by-step tutorial. And for a more formal comparison between the NC and RC methods see University of Colorado Prof. Ralph T. Muehleisen's notes "Room Noise Criteria: NC and RC Methods".

RCA jack See: connectors.

RCDD (*Registered Communications Distribution Designer*) A designation for individuals who demonstrate expertise in the design, integration, and implementation of telecommunications (voice, data, video, audio, and other low-voltage control) transport systems and their related infrastructure components.

R-DAT or DAT (*rotary head digital audio tape recorder*) A digital audio recorder utilizing a magnetic tape cassette system similar to that of a video recorder.

reactance The imaginary part of an impedance.

Reado The name of the first FAX machine, introduced by Crosley Radio in 1940.

real-time analyzer See: RTA.

real-time operation What is perceived to be instantaneous to a user (or more technically, processing that completes in a specific time allotment).

rearaxial softspeaker Term coined by Electro-Voice for their mythical loudspeaker, the SP13.5TRBXWK. Claimed by many to be the speaker that couldn't be made, it might have changed all future loudspeaker design, but it didn't. Characterized by being undirectional, the designer's claimed it produced silken highs and woolen lows. The only loudspeaker known to incorporate both "presence" *and* "absence" controls. Based on a ridiculously simple principle that still cannot be explained, the SP13.5TRBXWK was only heard once, during the Rane demo of their PI 14 Pseudoacoustic Infector, coupled by a Jensen JE-EP-ERs Multi-denomial Transpedance Informer to a Crown Belchfire BF-6000SUX amplifier. No one survived.

reconstruction filter A low-pass filter used at the output of digital audio processors (following the DAC) to remove (or at least greatly attenuate) any aliasing products (image spectra present at multiples of the sampling frequency) produced by the use of real-world (non-brickwall) input filters.

Recording Academy, The The organization formerly known as NARAS. Think *Grammy*; often confused with SPARS.

recording console See: mixer.

recording technology history See site posted by Steve Schoenherr.

recording terminology See Recording Institute of Detroit, who claims to have posted the largest glossary of recording terms on the web.

recursive A data structure that is defined in terms of itself. For example, in mathematics, an expression, such as a polynomial, each term of which is determined by application of a formula to preceding terms. (AHD) Pertaining to a process that is defined or generated in terms of itself, i.e., its immediate past history.

Red Book Nickname for the Philips and Sony's ECMA-130 standard document that defines the format for CD-Audio (compact disc-digital audio) discs; available only to licensees. Compare with: Green Book and Yellow Book.

red noise See: noise color.

reflection *Acoustics.* Sound that is reflected. See hyperlink.

reflectors In acoustics, an object or surface that reflects, or bounces back the original signal. A perfect reflector would reflect with no loss of energy. A diffuser is a special kind of reflector.

refraction *Acoustics.* The bending of sound waves caused by entering a medium where the speed of sound is different. See hyperlink.

resistance See: impedance.

resonance 1. *Electronics.* In an LRC circuit, it is the condition where the **inductive** and **capacitive** **reactances** are equal; this is called the resonant frequency. 2. *Physics.* The increase in amplitude of oscillation of an electric or mechanical system exposed to a periodic force whose frequency is equal or very close to the natural undamped frequency of the system. (AHD) A dynamic condition which occurs when any input frequency of vibration coincides with one of the natural frequencies of the structure. That is, the inclination of any mechanical or electrical system to vibrate (*resonate*) at a certain frequency when excited by an external force, and to keep vibrating after the excitation is removed. 3. *Acoustics.* Intensification and prolongation of sound, especially of a musical tone, produced by sympathetic vibration. 4. *Linguistics.* Intensification of vocal tones during articulation, as by the air cavities of the mouth and nasal passages. (AHD)

resonant frequency *Electronic Circuits.* See above.

retro audio Termed coined by Tomlinson Holman of THX fame, referring to new audio gear designed using legacy or old technology, usually tubes, with cosmetics to match.

reverb *Recording.* Shortened form of **reverberator, or reverberation unit**. Any electronic or acoustical device designed to simulate, or capture, the natural reverberation of a large hard-surfaced (*echoic*) room, and mix it back with the original recorded sound. Reverb today is accomplished by digital devices using complex DSP algorithms; previously done using a chamber, a plate, or springs.

reverberation The total sound field remaining in a room after the original source is silenced. The length of time of this collapsing sound field is called the reverberation time and is defined below. Contrast with: echo and ambience. "Reverberation represents the energy decay process after the initial echoes" [Blesser].

reverberation time also **RT60** *Reverberation* is all sound remaining after the source stops. The time it takes for this sound to decay is called the *reverberation time*, and it is quantified by measuring how long it takes the sound pressure level to decay to one-millionth of its original value. Since one-millionth equals a 60 dB reduction, reverberation time is abbreviated "RT60."

RFI (*radio frequency interference*) A measure of radio frequency (RF) radiation from equipment. An RF disturbance is an electromagnetic disturbance having components in the RF range.

RF-Lite See: ZigBee.

rhythm The only English language word containing two syllables with no natural vowels. [*Thanks GS.*]

RIAA (*Recording Industry Association of America*) A professional trade organization representing the U.S. recording industry. RIAA members create, manufacture and/or distribute approximately 90 % of all sound recordings produced and sold in the United States.

RIAA equalization curve The standard first proposed by the RIAA (see above) and adopted by the disc recording industry in 1953, reaffirmed in 1964 by both the RIAA and NAB and issued as international standard IEC 60098 (old IEC 98) by the IEC, which remains in effect today. The curve is used in cutting vinyl records and its inverse is required in phono playback preamplifiers. The curve attenuates low frequencies and amplifies high frequencies (relative to a 1 kHz reference point) in order to achieve the maximum dynamic range for a lateral cut vinyl disc (as opposed to the older method of vertical cutting). The grooves in a stereo phonograph disc are cut by a chisel shaped cutting stylus driven by two vibrating systems arranged at right angles to each other. The cutting stylus vibrates mechanically from side to side in accordance with the signal impressed on the cutter. The resultant movement of the groove back and forth about its center is known as groove modulation. The amplitude of this modulation cannot exceed a fixed amount or "cutover" occurs. Cutover, or overmodulation, describes the breaking through the wall of one groove into the wall of the previous groove. Since low frequencies cause wide undulations in the groove, they must be attenuated to prevent overmodulation. At the other end of the audio spectrum, high frequencies must be amplified to overcome the granular nature of the disc surface acting as a noise generator, thus improving signal-to-noise ratio.

ribbon microphone Invented in 1923 by Walter Schottky (the same German physicist who invented the famous diode) and Erwin Gerlach of Siemens Halske (German pioneering telegraph company), it is constructed using a very thin metal foil ribbon (~0.002 mm [*really*]) and pleated or corrugated to reduce its longitudinal stiffness, to obtain the lowest resonant frequency so the ribbon is mass-controlled) attached between the poles of a permanent magnet. The acoustic signal (sound pressure variation) causes the ribbon to move and interact with the stationary magnetic field inducing a voltage into the ribbon proportional to the amplitude and frequency of the audio signal.

Also called **velocity microphone** or **pressure gradient microphone**. These names come about from the physical action of the air particles hitting the ribbon. The motion of the ribbon is proportional to the *velocity* of the air particles striking it, due to its mass being so small that its resonant frequency is infrasonic (2-4 Hz); looked at another way, it responds to the air particle velocity which is developed by the *pressure gradient*, i.e., the difference in air pressure between the two sides of the ribbon (both sides of the ribbon are open to the atmosphere) causes the ribbon to move.

[*Historical Note: In 1931, Harry F. Olson, along with Frank Massa, successfully developed the first commercial ribbon microphone based on Schottky Halske's patent filed eight years earlier on ribbon loudspeaker and microphone theory. They received a US patent for the first cardioid ribbon microphone using a field coil instead of a permanent magnet. Because of this Olson is usually credited as the inventor of ribbon microphones, even though this is historically incorrect.*]

ribbon tweeter Also invented by Schottky and Gerlach simply by reversing the physical effects of their microphone; it is the inverse of the ribbon microphone described above. It creates a high frequency loudspeaker consisting of a paper-thin metal foil ribbon suspended in a magnetic field (i.e., placed between the poles of a permanent magnet). The audio voltage signal drives the ribbon causing a current to flow creating a magnetic field that reacts with the stationary magnet to create sound proportional to the applied waveform. Very similar in principle to the dynamic loudspeaker, only much smaller, with the ribbon replacing the voice coil and cone arrangement.

"Ring it up ... !" Phrase coined from the first cash registers that ran a bell for emphasis when the drawer opened, signifying the end of the calculation.

ring topology A network topology where all nodes are daisy chained together (connected) in a closed loop.

RISC (*reduced instruction set computer*) A computer design that achieves high performance by doing the most common computer operations very quickly, utilizing a high speed processing technology that uses a far simpler set of operating commands. Primarily found in workstations and PowerPCs. The alternative to *CISC (complex instruction set computing)*, the original way of doing computing.

RJ (*Registered Jacks*) As in red *RJ-12* modular telephone jacks used by Rane Corporation for external power supply connection.

rms See: root mean square.

rms power *No such thing.* A misnomer, or application of a wrong name. There is no such thing as "rms power." *Average* or *apparent* power is calculated using rms values but that does not equal "rms power;" it equals continuous sine wave power output into a resistive load.

rolloff rate *Filters.* The rate at which low-pass, high-pass and bandpass filters attenuate frequencies not in the passband. Expressed in dB/octave, it is a measure of the attenuation slope. Slopes occur in 6 dB/octave increments (due to the natural storage effects of capacitors and inductors), e.g., 12 dB/oct, 18 dB/oct, 24 dB/oct, etc.

ROM (*read-only memory*) A memory from which data, after initial storage, may only be read out, but new data cannot be written in. The normal audio CD is an example of a read-only system.

room modes or **eigentones** (from German *eigen* meaning "self" or "own")*Acoustics.* The acoustic resonances (or **standing waves**) in a room (*or any enclosed space*) caused by parallel surfaces. It is the dimensional resonance of a room, where the distance between the walls equals half the wavelength of the lowest resonant frequency (*and resonates at all harmonic frequencies above it*). Room modes create uneven sound distribution throughout a room, with alternating louder and quieter spots.

root mean square *Abbr.* **rms** (lower case), *Mathematics.* The square root of the average of the squares of a group of numbers. (AHD) A useful and more meaningful way of averaging a group of numbers.

rotary equalizer A multi-band variable equalizer using rotary controls as the amplitude adjustable elements. Both active and passive designs exist with rotary controls. Center frequency and bandwidth are fixed for each band.

router An audio device used to selectively assign any input to any output, including the ability to add inputs together. In this way, one input could go to all outputs, or all inputs could go to just one output, or any combination thereof. An *n x m matrix* forms the core of any router, where there are *n* inputs and *m* outputs. Typically, level controls are provided on all inputs and outputs; balanced and unbalanced designs exist. More elaborate designs are called matrix-mixers.

RPM (*Remote Programmable Multiprocessor*) Rane Corporation's trademark for their line of DSP multiprocessor-based digital audio signal processing devices.

RRIO (*rail-to-rail input output*) Term created to indicate op amps with maximum input and output levels equal to the power supply voltages, without violating the registered term rail-to-rail®.

RS (*Recommended Standard*) As in RS-232 serial interface standard, et al.

RS-232 The standard serial interface (EIA/TIA-232-E) used on most personal computers. A format widely supported for bidirectional data transfer at low to moderate rates. The most common interface method used to connect personal computers with peripheral hardware and instruments. Use is restricted to one peripheral at a time and short distances. The standard originally called for DB-25 connectors, but now allows the smaller DB-9 version.

RS-422 The standard adopted in 1978 by the Electronics Industry Association as *EIA-422-A, Electrical characteristics of balanced voltage digital interface circuits.* A universal balanced line twisted-pair standard for all long distance (~1000 m, or ~3300 ft) computer interconnections, daisy-chain style. [*See: NSC AN 759 for RS-422 vs. RS-485 comparison.*]

RS-485 The standard describing the electrical characteristics of a balanced interface used as a bus for master/slave operation. Allows up to 32 users to *bridge* onto the line (as opposed to RS-422's need to *daisy chain* the interconnections). Same as *EIA-485*. [*See: NSC AN 759 for RS-422 vs. RS-485 comparison.*]

RS-490 The standard adopted in 1981 by the EIA entitled *Standard Test Methods of Measurement for Audio Amplifiers.* The power amp testing standard for consumer products.

RT60 See: reverberation time.

RTA (*real-time analyzer*) A constant percentage bandwidth spectrum analyzer. For example, see the Rane model RA 30.

RU (*rack unit*) See: "U".

rumble A quantitative measure of phonograph turntable noise and vibration resulting from performance imperfections. The rms voltage is measured at the cartridge while playing a blank (silence) record, and the answer expressed in dB below a reference point.

rumble filter See: infrasonic filter.

RW 232 (also RaneWare®) A trademark of Rane Corporation used to identify Rane's RS-232-based variant of the PA-422 AES standard.

S

70-volt line See: constant-voltage.

sabin A non-metric unit of sound absorption used in acoustical engineering. One sabin is the sound absorption of one square foot (or one square meter — a *metric sabin*) of a perfectly absorbing surface — such as an open window. The sound absorption of a wall or some other surface is the area of the surface, in square feet, multiplied by a coefficient that depends on the material of the surface and on the frequency of the sound. These coefficients are carefully measured and tabulated. The unit honors Wallace Sabine (see below). Sabine used this unit, which he called the *open window unit (owu)*, as early as 1911. [*From Rowlett's How Many? A Dictionary of Units of Measurement.*]

Sabine, Wallace Clement Ware (1868-1919) American physicist and Harvard University professor who founded the systematic study of acoustics around 1895. Regarded as the father of the science of architectural acoustics.

SACD (*Super Audio CD*) Also known as *DSD* or *Direct Stream Digital*, joint trademark of Sony and Philips for their proposal for the next generation CD-standard. Sony and Philips have split from the DVD ranks to jointly propose their own solution comprised of a 1-bit, 64-times oversampled direct-stream digital SACD format. The original SACD proposal was for a hybrid disc comprising two layers: a high density (HD) DSD layer in the middle, and a standard density CD layer at the bottom. The two layers are read from the same side of the disc; the CD laser reads the bottom reflective layer through the semi-transmissive HD layer, while the middle layer is read by the HD laser delivering high-quality, multichannel sound without sacrificing backward compatibility. The HD layer has three tracks: the innermost is for two-channel stereo; the middle is a six-channel mix; and the outer is for such additional information as liner notes, still images and video clips. Maximum playing time is 74 minutes. This proposal turned out to be too expensive, so the SACD first release is a single-layer SACD-only disc.

SAE (*Society of Automotive Engineers*) The international trade organization comprised of 80,000 engineers, business executives, educators, and students representing 100 countries that functions as *the* resource for technical information and expertise used in designing, building, maintaining, and operating self-propelled vehicles for use on land or sea, in air or space.

sample rate conversion The process of converting one sample rate to another, e.g. 44.1 kHz to 48 kHz. Necessary for the communication and synchronization of dissimilar digital audio devices, e.g., digital tape machines to CD mastering machines.

sample-and-hold (S/H) A circuit that captures and holds an analog signal for a finite period. The input S/H proceeds the A/D converter, allowing time for conversion. The output S/H follows the D/A converter, smoothing glitches.

Sampling (Nyquist) Theorem A theorem stating that a band-limited continuous waveform may be represented by a series of discrete samples if the sampling frequency is at least twice the highest frequency contained in the waveform. See RaneNote: *Digital Dharma of Audio A/D Converters*.

sampling frequency or **sampling rate** The frequency or rate at which an analog signal is sampled or converted into digital data. Expressed in Hertz (cycles per second). For example, compact disc sampling rate is 44,100 samples per second or 44.1 kHz, however in pro audio other rates exist: common examples being 32 kHz, 48 kHz, and 50 kHz. [*Historical note re 44.1 kHz vs. 44.056 kHz: Since the first commercial digital audio recorders used a standard helical scan video recorder for storage, there had to be a fixed relationship between sampling frequency and horizontal video frequency, so these frequencies could be derived from the same master clock by frequency division. For the NTSC 525-line TV system, a sampling frequency of 44,055.94 Hz was selected, whereas for the PAL 625-line system, a frequency of 44,100 Hz was chosen. The 0.1% difference shows up as an imperceptible pitch shift.*] See RaneNote: *Digital Dharma of Audio A/D Converters*.

sampling The process of representing the amplitude of a signal at a particular point in time.

SAN (*storage area network*) A network connecting host computers to storage servers and systems. SAN technology allows high-speed connection of multiple workstations to a centralized hard-disk network (via fiber optics interconnection), allowing each workstation to access any drive from any location (e.g., control rooms in DAW recording studios).

SAR (*successive approximation register*) A type of analog-to-digital converter using a digital-to-analog converter to determine the output word successively, bit by bit.

sawtooth wave A periodic waveform characterized by a 50% duty cycle and a Fourier series consisting of both even- and odd-ordered, equal phase, sinusoidal harmonic components of its fundamental frequency. The amplitudes (coefficients multiplying the magnitude of the fundamental sine wave) of the odd-ordered harmonics are the same as a square wave, while the amplitudes (re the fundamental) for the even-ordered harmonics are $-1/n$, where n is the even harmonic number. Therefore the first few even harmonic multipliers are $-1/2$, $-1/4$, $-1/6$, ... etc., and the first few odd harmonic multipliers are $1/3$, $1/5$, $1/7$, ... etc.

Schottky, Walter (1886-1976) German physicist whose work in solid-state physics and electronics resulted in many inventions that bear his name (*Schottky effect, Schottky barrier, Schottky diode*). He also invented the tetrode and (with Erwin Gerlach) the ribbon microphone and ribbon tweeter.

SCMS (pronounced "scums") (*serial copy management system*) The copy protection scheme applied to consumer digital recording equipment — it does not apply to professional machines. This standard allows unlimited analog-to-digital copies, but only one digital-to-digital copy. This is done by two control bits (the *C* and *L* bits) contained within the digital audio data.

screeched The longest one-syllable word in the English language.

SCSI port (pronounced "scuzzy") (*small computer system interface*) A standard 8-bit parallel interface used to connect up to seven peripherals, such as connecting a CD-ROM player or document scanner to a microcomputer.

SD (*super density compact disc*) See: DVD.

SDDS (*Sony Dynamic Digital Sound*) Sony's competing format for the digital soundtrack system for motion picture playback. The signal is optically printed *outside* the sprocket holes, along both sides of the print. Sony recently developed a single camera system that records all three digital formats (Dolby Digital, DTS & SDDS) on a single inventory print, thus setting the stage for long term coexistence of all formats.

SDIF (*Sony digital interface format*) Sony's professional digital audio interface utilizing two BNC-type connectors, one for each audio channel, and a separate BNC-type connector for word synchronization, common to both channels. All interconnection is done using unbalanced 75 Ω coaxial cable of the exact same length (to preserve synchronization), and is not intended for long distances.

SDMI (*Secure Digital Music Initiative*) A multi-industry group defining a specification to protect digital music distribution.

self-noise *Microphones.* Residual noise, or the inherent noise level of a microphone when no signal is present. Microphone inherent self-noise is usually specified as the equivalent SPL level which would give the same output voltage, with typical values being 15-20 dB SPL.

SEMA (*Specialty Equipment Market Association*) An organization for the producers and marketers of specialty equipment products and services for the automotive aftermarket. Today's group grew out of the original SEMA started in 1963, known then as the "Speed Equipment Manufacturers Association" and includes aftermarket audio manufacturers.

semitone *Music.* An interval equal to a half tone in the standard diatonic scale. Also called half step, half tone. (AHD)

sensitivity 1. *Audio electromechanics.* The standard way to rate audio devices like microphones, headphones and loudspeakers. A standard input value is applied and the resultant output is measured and stated.

> **loudspeaker sensitivity**: the standard is to apply one watt and measure the sound pressure level (SPL) at a distance of one meter.

> **headphone sensitivity**: the standard is to apply one milliwatt and then measure the sound pressure level at the earpiece (using a dummy head with built-in microphones). See RaneNote: *Understanding Headphone Power Requirements.*

> **microphone sensitivity**: the standard is to apply a 1 kHz sound source equal to 94 dB SPL (one *pascal*) and then measure the output level and express it in mV/PA (millivolts per pascal). 2. *Audio electronics.* The minimum input signal required to produce a standard output level.

> **power amplifier sensitivity**: The input level required to produce one watt output into a specified load impedance, usually 4 or 8 Ω.

> **radio receiver sensitivity**: The input level required to produce a specified signal-to-noise ratio. Et cetera.

serial interface A connection which allows transmission of only one bit at a time. An example in the PC world is a RS-232 port, primarily used for modems and mice. A serial interface transmits each bit in a word in sequence over one communication link. See also: parallel interface.

serializer A parallel-to-serial data converter; used in buses and networks.

server A shared master computer on a local area network (LAN) used to store files and distribute them to clients upon demand.

servo-loop; servo-locked loop; servo-mechanism A self-regulating feedback system or mechanism. Typically a feedback system consisting of a sensing element, an amplifier, and a (servo)motor, used in the automatic control of a mechanical device (such as a loudspeaker). In audio, usually the name applies to a class of electronic control circuits comprised of an amplifier and a feedback path from the output signal that is compared with a reference signal. This topology creates an error signal that is the difference between the reference and the output signal. The error signal causes the output to do whatever is necessary to reduce the error to zero. A loudspeaker system with *motional feedback* is such a system. A sensor is attached to the speaker cone and provides a feedback signal that is compared against the driving signal to create more accurate control of the loudspeaker. Another example is Rane's *servo-locked limiter* which is an audio peak limiter circuit where the output is compared against a reference signal (the *threshold* setting) creating an error signal that reduces the gain of the circuit until the error is zero.

servo-locked limiter Rane Corporation trademark for their proprietary limiter circuit. See: servo-loop.

SFDR (*spurious free dynamic range*) A testing method used in quantifying high-speed data converters and high-frequency communication integrated circuits. It is the difference in dB between the desired output signal and any undesired harmonics found in the output spectrum. See: Intersil Application Note TB326 for measuring details.

Shannon, Claude E. (1916-2001) American mathematician and physicist who is credited as the father of information theory (For the mathematically advanced, see his famous paper, "A Mathematical Theory of Communication" published in 1948 in *The Bell*) . In his master's thesis Shannon showed how an algebra invented by the British mathematician, George Boole in the mid-1800s could represent the workings of switches and relays in electronic circuits. His paper has been called "possibly the most important master's thesis in the century." See RaneNote: *Digital Dharma of Audio A/D Converters.*

shaped triangular See: TPDF.

shelving response Term used to describe a flat (or shelf) endband shape when applied to program equalization. Also known as *bass* and *treble* tone control responses.

shielding, proper See Steve Macatee's *Considerations in Grounding and Shielding* and RaneNote: *Sound System Interconnection.*

show control See: MIDI show control.

SI (*International System of Units*) The International System of Units, universally abbreviated SI (from the French *Le Systme International d'Units*), is the modern metric system of measurement. SI is the dominant measurement system not only in science, but also in international commerce. See link for a downloadable copy of Barry N. Taylor's *Guide for the Use of the International System of Units (SI).* This free 86 page document is *the* definitive source of SI info.

sibilant *Linguistics. adj.* Of, characterized by, or producing a hissing sound like that of (s) or (sh): *the sibilant consonants; a sibilant bird call.* A sibilant speech sound, such as English (s), (sh), (z), or (zh). (AHD)

SID (*slew-induced distortion*) See: DIM/TIM.

side-chain In a signal processing circuit, such as one employing a VCA, a secondary signal path in parallel with the main signal path in which the condition or parameter of an audio signal that will cause a processor to begin working is sensed or detected. Typical applications use the side-chain information to control the gain of a VCA. The circuit may detect level or frequency or both. Devices utilizing side-chains for control generally fall into the classification of dynamic controllers.

sidetone *Telephony.* The feature of a telephone handset that allows you to hear yourself talk, acting as feedback that the phone is really working. Sidetones are actually short line echoes bled back into the earpiece. Too much sidetone sounds like an echo and too little sounds so quiet that people think the phone is broken. Sidetones are good for people but can cause acoustic feedback in teleconferencing systems if not treated properly.

sigma-delta See: delta-sigma modulation.

signal ground The common electrical reference point of a circuit, usually separate from the chassis ground but tied together at the power supply. See RaneNote: *Sound System Interconnection.*

signal levels Audio signal levels: see levels.

signal present indicator or **SIG PRES** An indicator found on pro audio signal processing units that lights once the input signal level exceeds a preset point. There is no standard specifying when a SIG PRES light should illuminate, although common practice makes it -20 dBu (77.5 mV), or the pro audio de facto standard line-level of +4 dBu (1.23 V).

signal-to-noise ratio See: S/N.

SIL (*speech interference level*) The numerical part of the RC noise rating.

Silicon Dust Nickname for microchips. Trademarked name first coined by National Semiconductor to describe the world's smallest op amp (*as of May 5, 1999*), the LMV921. Used in surface mount technology (SMT), they are about the size of a single letter on this page.

silver One of the English language words without a rhyme — others are "month," "orange" & "purple."

SIN (*signal induced noise*) Tongue-in-cheek term created by John K. Chester for cable shield induced noise found when the analog audio cable shield is grounded at one end only.

SINAD (pronounced "sin-add") or **S/N+D** (*signal-to-noise and distortion*) Acronym for the ratio: (signal + noise + distortion) / (noise + distortion). Or, as Metzler explains, it is the reciprocal of THD+N stated in decibels (dB). Originally developed for measuring FM receivers, it now also appears on A/D data sheets. Generally, the term "SINAD" is favored by the communication industry, while the audio industry uses "S/N+D," but they both mean the same thing. It is the preferred way to specify the dynamic range, or maximum S/N, since the noise and distortion products are measured in the presence of a signal. [*A signal is applied to the input, the output is passed through a notch filter to remove the signal and what remains is measured. Then the ratio of the rms value of the measured output signal to the rms value of everything else coming out (i.e., noise + distortion) is expressed in decibels.*] This gives a more accurate picture of real dynamic performance. Sometimes the measurement is stated for three reference levels of 0 dBFS, -20 dBFS, and -60 dBFS.

sine *Abbr.* **sin** *Mathematics.*1. The ordinate of the endpoint of an arc of a unit circle centered at the origin of a Cartesian coordinate system, the arc being of length *x* and measured counterclockwise from the point (1, 0) if *x* is positive or clockwise if *x* is negative. 2. In a right triangle, the ratio of the length of the side opposite an acute angle to the length of the hypotenuse. (AHD)

sine curve *Mathematics.* The graph of the equation $y = \sin x$. Also called sinusoid. (AHD)

sine wave *Physics.* A waveform with deviation that can be graphically expressed as the sine curve. (AHD)

sinusoid *Mathematics.* See: sine curve.

skin effect 1. *Electrical cable.* The tendency of high frequency (RF and higher) current to be concentrated at the surface of the conductor. 2. *Induction heating.* Tendency of an alternating current to concentrate in the areas of lowest impedance.

slapback See: slap echo below.

slap echo also called **slapback** 1. *Acoustics.* A single echo resulting from parallel non-absorbing (i.e., reflective) walls, characterized by lots of high frequency content. So-called because you can test for slap echo by sharply clapping your hands and listening for the characteristic sound of the echo in the mid-range. Slap echo smears a stereo sound field by destroying the critical phase relationships necessary to form an accurate sound stage. 2. *Recording.* Devices that simulate slap echo are popular in recording. One distinct repeat echo is added to an instrument sound resulting in a very live sound similar to what you would hear in an auditorium.

slew rate 1. The term used to define the maximum rate of change of an amplifier's output voltage with respect to its input voltage. In essence, *slew rate* is a measure of an amplifier's ability to follow its input signal. It is measured by applying a large amplitude *step function* (a signal starting at 0 V and "instantaneously" jumping to some large level [without overshoot or ringing], creating a step-like look on an oscilloscope) to the amplifier under test and measuring the slope of the output waveform. For a "perfect" step input (i.e., one with a rise time at least 100 times faster than the amplifier under test), the output will not be vertical; it will exhibit a pronounced slope. The slope is caused by the amplifier having a finite amount of current available to charge and discharge its internal compensation capacitor. 2. *Mathematics.* Slew rate is defined to be the maximum derivative of the output voltage with respect to time. That is, it is a measure of the worst case delta change of voltage over a delta change in time, or the rate-of-change of the voltage vs. time. For sinusoidal signals (*audio*), this equals 2 pi times the maximum frequency, times the maximum peak output voltage: SR = (2 pi) (Fmax) (Vpeak).

smoke From the *phlogiston* theory of electronics, it is smoke that makes ICs and transistors work. The proof of this is self-evident because every time you let the smoke out of an IC or transistor it stops working — elementary. This has been verified through exhaustive testing, particularly regarding power amplifier ICs and transistors. (Incidentally, wires carry smoke from one device to another.) [Origin unknown but classic.]

smoothing filter See: anti-imaging filter.

SMPTE (pronounced "simty") (*Society of Motion Picture and Television Engineers*) A professional engineering society that establishes standards, including a time code standard used for synchronization.

SMT (*surface mounting technology*) The science of attaching and interconnecting electronic devices, whose entire body projects in front of the mounting surface, as opposed to *through-hole devices* found on the earliest printed circuit boards. With surface mount technology all components sit on the surface of printed circuit boards and are soldered to conductive pads. With through-hole parts, component leads are placed through holes in the boards and then soldered from the back side. SMT is more cost-effective and allows far greater density of parts.

S/N or **SNR** (*signal-to-noise ratio*) An audio measurement of the residual noise of a unit, stated as the ratio of signal level (or power) to noise level (or power), normally expressed in decibels. The "signal" reference level must be stated. Typically this is either the expected nominal operating level, say, +4 dBu for professional audio, or the maximum output level, usually around +20 dBu. The noise is measured using a true rms type voltmeter over a *specified bandwidth*, and sometimes using weighting filters. All these thing must be stated for a S/N spec to have meaning. Simply saying a unit has a SNR of 90 dB means nothing, without giving the reference level, measurement bandwidth, and any weighting filers. A system's *maximum* S/N is called the dynamic range. See RaneNote: *Audio Specifications*.

S/N+D or **S/(N+D)** See: SINAD.

SNMP (*Simple Network Management Protocol*) The most common method by which network management applications can query a management agent using a supported MIB (Management Information Base). SNMP operates at the OSI Application layer. The IP (Internet Protocol)-based SNMP is the basis of most network management software, to the extent that today the phrase "managed device" implies SNMP compliance.

snollygoster Defined in 1895 as "a fellow who wants office, regardless of party, platform or principles and who ... gets there by the sheer force of monumental talknophical assumancy". [McQuain, *Never Enough Words*.]

Snow, William B. (~1900-~1979) American engineer best remembered for his foundation work for stereophonic reproduction in large rooms. See U.S. Patent 2,137,032 *Sound Reproducing System* (requires a free browser plug-in available from AlternaTIFF or InterneTIFF). His paper titled "Basic Principles of Stereophonic Sound, "*Stereophonic Techniques: An Anthology*, edited by John Eargle (Audio Engineering Society, ISBN 0-937803-08-1, NY, 1986, pp. 9-31) is considered the best introduction to this subject. Other papers of interest by Snow are collected in *Sound Reinforcement: An Anthology*, edited by David L. Klepper (Audio Engineering Society, NY, 1978).

soft clipping See: clipping.

solo A term used in recording and live-sound mixing to describe monitoring (via headphones) a single channel without affecting the main outputs (see: PFL) — same as *cueing*; however, it can also refer to certain console designs where it replaces the main mix with the soloed channel (called *destructive solo*).

sone A subjective unit of loudness, as perceived by a person with normal hearing, equal to the loudness of a pure tone having a frequency of 1,000 hertz at 40 decibels sound pressure level. (AHD)

sonorous 1. Having or producing sound. 2. Having or producing a full, deep, or rich sound. (AHD)

sound 1.a. Vibrations transmitted through an elastic material or a solid, liquid, or gas, with frequencies in the approximate range of 20 to 20,000 hertz, capable of being detected by human ears. Sound (in air) at a particular point is a rapid variation in the air pressure around a steady-state value (atmospheric pressure) — that is, sound is a *disturbance* in the surrounding medium. b. Transmitted vibrations of any frequency. c. The sensation stimulated in the ears by such vibrations in the air or other medium. d. Such sensations considered as a group. 2. Auditory material that is recorded, as for a movie. 3. Meaningless noise. 4. *Music.* A distinctive style, as of an orchestra or a singer. (AHD) See David Harrison's "Sound". See RaneNote: *Signal Processing Fundamentals*.

sound absorption See: absorption.

sound off To express one's views vigorously: *He was always sounding off about his boss.* (AHD)

sound pressure The value of the rapid variation in air pressure due to a sound wave, measured in pascals, microbars, or dynes — all used interchangeable, but *pascals* is now the preferred term. *Instantaneous* sound pressure is the peak value of the air pressure, often used in noise control measurements. *Effective* sound pressure is the rms value of the instantaneous sound pressure taken at a point over a period of time.

sound pressure level or **SPL** 1. The rms sound pressure expressed in dB re 20 microPa (the lowest threshold of hearing for 1 kHz). [As points of reference, *0 dB-SPL* equals the threshold of hearing, while *140 dB-SPL* equals irreparable hearing damage.] See: inverse square law 2. **Blue whales**, the largest living animals, also make the loudest sounds by any living source. Their low-frequency pulses have been measured at 188 dB-SPL and detected 530 miles away according to The Guinness Book of World Records.

Sound Recording History Fantastic site put together by David Morton.

SPARS (*Society of Professional Audio Recording Services*) Founded in 1979, a professional trade organization that unites the manufacturers of audio recording equipment and providers of services, with the users. Their goal is worldwide promotion of communication, education and service among all those who make and use recording equipment. Often confused with NARAS.

spatial Of, relating to, involving, or having the nature of space. (AHD)

Spatializer A single-ended spatial enhancement technique developed by Desper Products, Inc., a subsidiary of Spatializer Audio Labs, Inc. Widely licensed in both the consumer audio and multimedia computing markets, the Desper, or *Spatializer* process is normally used as a postprocessor. The *Spatializer* technology manipulates the original signal in a way that causes the listener to perceive a stereo image beyond the boundaries of the two loudspeakers. It claims to place sounds in front of the listener in an arc of 180 degrees, with excellent imaging and fidelity.

S/PDIF (*Sony/Philips digital interface format,* also seen w/o slash as SPDIF) A consumer version of the AES3 (old AES/EBU) digital audio interconnection standard based on coaxial cable and RCA connectors. See RaneNote: *Interfacing AES3 and S/PDIF.*

speech interference level (SIL) The numerical part of the RC noise rating.

Speakon® See: connectors.

spectra A plural of *spectrum.* In pro audio use, the distribution of frequency of a sound signal, especially: the distribution of sound energy, arranged in order of frequency wavelengths.

spectrum analyzer *Audio Test Equipment.* A type of electronic measurement device used to display the amplitude/frequency components of a continuous signal, as opposed to the amplitude/time domain oscilloscope. The formal IEEE definitions are "(1) An instrument generally used to display the power distribution of an incoming signal as a function of frequency. (2) An instrument that measures the power of a complex signal in many bands. The frequency bands can be either constant absolute bandwidth (e.g., FFT analyzer), or constant percentage bandwidth (e.g., RTA analyzer)."

spell checker A software program used by word processors to tell you that the following truism has no spelling errors: *"Dew knot trussed yore spell chequer two fined awl mistakes."*

SPICE (*simulation program with integrated circuit emphasis*) A computer circuit analysis program first developed and written by L. W. Nagel and D. O. Pederson of the EECS (Electrical Engineering and Computer Sciences) Department of UC Berkeley[1]. This was not the first simulation program by members of UC Berkeley's EECS Department. SPICE evolved from forerunners **BIAS**[2] and **CANCER**[3]. The SPICE program was used extensively for classroom instruction and graduate research. As such, each year it was refined and expanded by each new batch of graduate students (*yes, even I worked on SPICE, developing op amp models during by graduate years at UC Berkeley*) until it expanded beyond Berkeley's domain through licensing and the advent of mini and personal computers beginning in 1981. Indeed, **PSPICE (*Personal SPICE*)** developed in 1984 by Wolfram Blume (first doing business as *Blume Engineering,* then *MicroSim,* acquired by *OrCAD,* now owned by *Cadence*), the first version of SPICE for personal computers, is now the industry standard for circuit-simulation.

References
1. L.W. Nagel and D.O. Pederson, "Simulation Program with Integrated Circuit Emphasis (SPICE)," presented at the *16th Midwest Symposium on Circuit Theory,* Waterloo, Ontario, April 12, 1973.
2. W.J. McCalla and W.G. Howard, Jr., "BIAS-3 — A Program for the Nonlinear DC analysis of Bipolar Transistor Circuits," *IEEE J. Solid-State Circuits,* vol. SC-6, Feb. 1971, PP. 14-19.
3. L. Nagel and R. Rohrer, "Computer Analysis of Nonlinear Circuits, Excluding Radiation (CANCER)," *IEEE J. Solid-State Circuits,* vol. SC-6, Aug. 1971, pp. 166-182.

SPIF (*sales promotion incentive fund*) Same as no. 3 following.

spiff 1. To make attractive, stylish, or up-to-date: *spiffed up the old storefront.* 2. Attractiveness or charm in appearance, dress, or manners: *He may need more than spiff to get him through the bad patches ahead James Wolcott* [Possibly from dialectal *spiff* well-dressed] (AHD) 3. Giveaways (usually in the form of money) by manufacturers as added incentive ("make attractive") to personnel selling their goods. Compare with: swag.

spiral quad Same as *star quad*; see cables.

SPL controller See: leveler.

SPL See: sound pressure level.

splitter An audio device used to divide one input signal into two or more outputs. Typically this type of unit has one input with 6-16 (or more) outputs, each with a level control and often is unbalanced. See: distribution amplifier.

spooler Comes from the acronym SPOOL derived from *simultaneous peripheral operation on-line* (also *sequential peripheral operations on-line*). A program or piece of hardware that controls a buffer of data going to some output device, including a printer or a screen. Spooling temporarily stores programs or program outputs on magnetic tape, RAM or disks for output or processing. (Newton) ... *and you thought you were done learning for the day —- Ha!*

SQ Columbia's (CBS — *now Sony Music*) name for their quadraphonic sound system using a proprietary matrixing algorithm for encoding four-channel sound down to two-channels. See: Matrix Quad; Compare with: QS.

SQNR (*signal to quantization noise ratio* A measure of the quality of the quantization, or digital conversion of an analog signal. Defined as normalized signal power divided by normalized quantization noise power. The SQNR in dB is approximately equal to 6 times the number of bits of the ADC, for example, the maximum SQNR for 16 bits is approximately 96 dB.

square wave A periodic waveform characterized by a 50% duty cycle and a Fourier series consisting of odd-ordered, equal phase, sinusoidal harmonic components of its fundamental frequency with amplitudes (coefficients multiplying the magnitude of the fundamental sine wave) equal to $1/n$, where n equals the harmonic number. Therefore the first few harmonic amplitudes are $\frac{1}{3}$, $\frac{1}{5}$, $\frac{1}{7}$, $\frac{1}{9}$, etc. For a very cool pictorial, see Fourier Series: Square Wave Tool. And if you are missing the math, see Cuthbert Nyack's *Fourier Series of Square Wave.*

SRS® (*Sound Retrieval System*) A stereo image enhancement scheme invented by Arnold Klayman in the early '80s while working for Hughes Aircraft, and since 1993, marketed by SRS Labs, Inc. A standalone spatial enhancement scheme, SRS benefits from not requiring encoding of the signal, but thus prevents the audio producer from determining the location of individual sound effects. The results vary, being heavily dependent upon the original stereo mix. The goal is to extend the sound field well beyond the limitations of the loudspeakers, and make the overall sound seem more expansive. The elimination of the sweet spot is claimed.

state-variable filter An electronic filter based on state-variable techniques, first described by W. J. Kerwin, L. P. Huelsman, and R. W. Newcomb, "State variable synthesis for insensitive integrated circuit transfer functions," *IEEE J. Solid Circuits*, vol. SC-2, pp. 87-92, Sept. 1967. State-variable filters are also known as **KHN filters** in their honor. The concept of *state-variable* is one where a single variable defines one of the characteristics (or *states*) of a filter (e.g., the gain, or the center/corner frequency, or the Q). The state-variable approach yields independent adjustment of the transfer function pole and zero locations. [*The transfer function is a Laplace transform equation of the output divided by the input consisting of the ratio of two polynomials. Poles and zeros are the mathematical names for the solutions of the numerator polynomial —- called zeros because they cause the numerator to have zero value —- and denominator polynomial —- called poles because they cause the denominator to have zero value which makes the ratio infinity.*] This desirable independent adjustment feature allows the design of parametric EQs with independent adjustment of all three filter parameters, or constant-Q graphic EQs with amplitude-bandwidth independence (See RaneNote: *Constant-Q Graphic Equalizers*), or simultaneous low-pass and high-pass active crossovers (See RaneNote: *Linkwitz-Riley Crossovers*). The state-variable topologies also have lower component sensitivities that other designs, thus producing more production-friendly products. Most commonly seen with three op amps, they may be constructed using from one to four op amps.

standing wave See: room mode.

star quad mic cable See: cables.

Star-Spangled Banner The flag of the United States.

star topology 1. A set of three or more branches with one terminal of each connected at a common node. 2. A communications network based on a star pattern where all equipment is connected to a central location with a single path.

star-wired ring See: token ring.

steganography The science of communicating in a way that hides the existence of the actual communication. The practice of hiding information in a wider bandwidth carrier. This field covers the techniques used in digital watermarking schemes.

stereo or **stereophonic sound** 1. "The word *stereophonics* was derived by combining two Greek words: *stereo*, which means solid and implicates the three spatial dimensions (depth, breadth, and height), and *phonics*, which means the science of sound. Thus, stereophonics denotes the science of 3-dimensional sound" [Streicher Everest]. 2. Term applied to any system of recording (or transmission) using multiple microphones for capturing and multiple loudspeakers for reproduction the sound. *Stereo* as the term has become popularly used restricts the number of playback loudspeakers to two, but strictly speaking the term can apply to any number of loudspeakers. Although stereo was first demonstrated at the Paris Opera in 1881 (*really*) using carbon microphones and earphones, it would not become widespread until the work of Blumlein in the 1930s. Also see William B. Snow.

stereo 2-way or **stereo 3-way**, etc. See: active crossover.

stewardesses Longest English word typed using only the left hand.

stiction *Physics.* In positioning, the friction that prevents immediate motion when force is first applied to a body or surface at rest.

stopband The range of frequencies substantially attenuated by a filter as opposed to the range of frequencies unaffected by the filter. The opposite of passband.

STP (*shielded twisted-pair*) See: cables; also *Scientifically Treated Petroleum*, but that's another time and another story.

streaming media *Internet.* A process in which audio, video, and other multimedia is delivered just in time over the Internet or company intranet. Pioneered and named by Netscape, as a smarter way to deliver data, their browser immediately loaded text and then followed with graphics in real time as it arrived (*streamed in*), then Real Networks came along and applied this technology to audio and video.

structured audio See: MPEG-4.

subcode Non-audio digital data encoded on a CD that contains definable information such as track number, times, copy inhibit, copyright, etc.

subgroups See: groups.

submix See: groups.

subsonic Having a *speed* less than that of sound in a designated medium. (AHD) [Use infrasonic if referring to frequencies below human hearing range.]

subtend 1. *Mathematics.* To be opposite to and delimit: *The side of a triangle subtends the opposite angle.* 2. To underlie so as to enclose or surround: *flowers subtended by leafy bracts.* (AHD)

subwoofer A large woofer loudspeaker designed to reproduce audio's very bottom-end, i.e., approximately the last one or two octaves, from 20 Hz to 80-100 Hz. [*Actually misnamed since subsonic means slower than audio, while infrasonic means lower than audio, so it should be called an "infra-woofer."*]

successive approximation Early method of A/D conversion. For a detailed example see RaneNote: *Digital Dharma of Audio A/D Converters.*

supersonic Having, caused by, or relating to a *speed* greater than the speed of sound in a given medium, especially air. (AHD) [Use ultrasonic if referring to frequencies above human hearing range.]

suppression also **gain suppression** In teleconferencing the term used to describe the technique of instantaneous reduction of a sound system's overall gain to control acoustic feedback, and thus reduce echoes.

S-video Also called *Y/C video*, a two-channel video channel that transmits black and white, or luminance (Y), and color portions, or chrominance (C), separately using multiple wires. This avoids composite video encoding, such as NTSC, thus providing better picture quality. Found mostly on S-VHS and Hi8 products, and some Laserdisc and DVD players.

swag 1. *Slang* Stolen property; loot. [*According to Mercenary Audio: (pirate term) Stolen without a gun, but I can find no collaboration.*] 2. *Slang* Herbal tea in a plastic sandwich bag sold as marijuana to an unsuspecting customer. 3. *Australian* To travel about with a pack or *swag.* (AHD) 4. *Slang* Acronym for *scientific* (or *silly* or *sophisticated*)*wild ass guess.* 5. *Slang* Giveaways (usually in the form of merchandise "loot") by manufacturers as added incentive to personnel either selling or buying their goods. Compare with: spiff.

sweet spot Any location in a two-loudspeaker stereo playback system where the listener is positioned equidistant from each loudspeaker. The apex of all possible isosceles (two equal sides) triangles formed by the loudspeakers and the listener. In this sense, the sweet *spot* lies anywhere on the sweet *plane* extending forward from the midpoint between the speakers.

SWG (*standard wire gauge***)** British or Imperial standard. See: AWG.

symmetrical (reciprocal) response Term used to describe the comparative shapes of the boost/cut curves for variable equalizers. The cut curve exactly mirrors the boost curve.

synchronous A transmission process where the bit rate of the signal is fixed and synchronized to a master clock.

Syn-Aud-Con (*Synergetic Audio Concepts*) A private organization conducting audio seminars and workshops, sponsored by several pro audio companies.

T

3-dB down point See: passband.

3D sound A term used to describe a three-dimensional sound field. True 3D sound field positions sound anywhere in a semi-spherical shell surrounding the listener. Sound must come from anywhere directly behind to directly overhead to directly in front of the listener and all points left and right. It if does not, it is not 3D sound. The term is popularly misused by multimedia companies to describe systems, effects and techniques purported to create 3D sound from two sources and designed for two loudspeaker playback; however, the result is not 3D sound. It is enhanced two-dimensional sound. Strictly speaking, a broadening, widening, enhancing, or spreading of the left/right sound stage is not 3D. No two-loudspeaker system is capable of locating sounds directly to the rear of the listener; nevertheless, some of these systems truly impress. The best enhancement schemes come very close to recreating a quarter-spherical sound shell, extending to nearly 180 degrees left-to-right, approaching 90 degrees overhead, with greatly improved depth of field. For further information see the Ultimate Spatial Audio Index, and Links to the World of Spatial Sound.

10Base-T See: Ethernet.

21-gun salute Among the many "true origins," this is my favorite: A tribute for dignitaries created by Francis Hopkinson, a signer of the *Declaration of Independence*, and the designer of the first Stars and Stripes flag. As for the creation of the 21-gun salute, the story goes ...

Hopkinson was fond of doodling. As he sat in meetings during the momentous days as the Colonies debated the merits of independence from England, he wrote, over and over, the year:"1776." Idly adding up the numbers 1, 7, 7, and 6, the total, 21, intrigued him. Why not institute a 21-gun salute for dignitaries of the new republic? He submitted his idea to Congress, and it has been in use ever since. [Bartlett's Book of Anecdotes]

T-1 (*trunk level 1*) A digital transmission scheme utilizing two twisted-pair capable of handling a minimum of 24 voice channels. Used for connecting networks across remote distances. (Newton)

talent cueing See: IFB.

talkback 1. A recording console feature where a microphone mounted on the console allows the engineer to speak with the musicians during sessions — a very useful feature when the console is located in a soundproof control room, or out in the audience for sound reinforcement systems. 2. A proposed Rane product line aimed at the coffin market, since abandoned.

talk box A poor man's vocoder. Popularized by Peter Frampton and Joe Walsh in the '70s. See: Heil Talk Box for a demo of the original and most popular model.

talkover A term and function found on DJ mixers allowing the DJ to speak over the program material by triggering a ducker. Compare with: voiceover.

taper See: potentiometer.

tapir Any of several large, chiefly nocturnal, odd-toed ungulates (hoofed mammals) of the genus *Tapirus* of tropical America, the Malay Peninsula, and Sumatra, related to the horse and the rhinoceros, and having a heavy body, short legs, and a long, fleshy, flexible upper lip. (AHD) [*Don't confuse with "taper" above.*]

taste test or **tongue test** An actual voltage testing method recommended by Terrell Croft in his book *The American Electricians' Handbook*, published by McGraw-Hill in 1913. Here's the passage found on page 48:
> "The presence of low voltages can be determined by 'tasting.' The method is feasible only where the pressure is but a few volts and hence is used only in bell and signal work. Where the voltage is very low, the bared ends of the conductors constituting the two sides of the circuit are held a short distance apart on the tongue. If voltage is present a peculiar mildly burning sensation results which will never be forgotten after one has experienced it. The 'taste' is due to the electrolytic decomposition of the liquids on the tongue which produces a salt having a taste. With relatively high voltages, possible 4 or 5 V, due to as many cells of battery, it is best to first test for the presence of voltage by holding one of the bared conductors in the hand and touching the other to the tongue. Where a terminal of the battery is grounded, often a taste can be detected by standing on moist ground and touching a conductor from the other terminal to the tongue. Care should be exercised to prevent the two conductor ends from touching each other at the tongue, for if they do a spark can result that may burn."

And from the same book comes these words of wisdom for

testing for the presence of electricity by touching the two conductors:

"Electricians often test circuits for the presence of voltage by touching the conductors with the fingers. This method is safe where the voltage does not exceed 250 and is often very convenient for locating a blown-out fuse or for ascertaining whether or not a circuit is alive. Some men can endure the electric shock that results without discomfort whereas others cannot. Therefore, the method is not feasible in some cases."

[*I don't know how Mr. Croft died, but perhaps I could hazard a guess.* Thanks RH.]

Tchebysheff or **Tschebyscheff** See: Chebyshev.

tchotchke See: chachka.

TCP/IP (*transmission control protocol/internet protocol***)** A set of protocols developed by the Department of Defense in the '70s to link dissimilar computers across many kinds of networks and LANs. Popular with Ethernet users.

TDIF (*Teac digital interface format***)** Tascam's (Teac) 8-channel digital audio interface to their DA-88 digital multi-track recorder, using unbalanced signal transmission and a DB-25 type connector.

TDS (*time-delay spectrometry***)** A sound measurement theory and technique developed in 1967 by Richard C. Heyser at the Jet Propulsion Laboratories of the California Institute of Technology.

TEF (*time-energy-frequency***)** The term adopted to describe the entire spectrum of *TDS* measurements, including energy-time curves. Popularized by Richard Heyser through his participation in *Synergetic Audio Concepts* seminars. Made practical in 1979 by the Techron division of Crown International — Cal Tech's first TDS licensee, and introduced as the TEF System 10.

tele- Distance; distant: *telescope*. [Greek *tele-* meaning far off.] (AHD)

telecommunication Communicating over a distance by wire, fiber or wireless means.

teleconferencing An *audio* conference held by three or more persons over a distance. Normal usage refers to voice conferencing, also termed *audioconferencing* that includes all forms of audio. The term is sometimes extended to include video and document, or data, conferencing. Note that the term does not mean *telephone* conferencing, but rather *distance* conferencing, although telephone lines are often used. [*Thanks to RG at Q Factor for pointing out this important distinction.*] Contrast with: videoconferencing.

telemedicine A specialized form of videoconferencing optimized for medical uses. Also referred to as *medical conferencing*, it allows distance learning in medical education and delivers health care (including assisted medical operations) to patients and providers at a distance.

Telharmonium Invented and patented (US patent #580,035) by Thaddeus Cahill, in the 1890s, an amazing monstrosity weighing 7 tons that was the first device to successfully send music through a telephone connected to something similar to a gramophone cone that could be heard by an audience. Arguably the beginning of background music and synthesizers.

temperament *Music.* The building up of musical scales.

temporal Of, relating to, or limited by time. (AHD)

terminal strips See: connectors.

tetrode A type of vacuum tube having two grids, where one is used to reduce feedback related instabilities and oscillations.

thaumaturgy The working of miracles or magic feats, like designing and building a 24-bit audio converter that actually measures 144 dB dynamic range.

THD (*third-harmonic distortion***)** See: third-harmonic distortion.

THD (*total harmonic distortion***)** A measurement technique rarely used, but often confused with the THD+N technique described below. Many people mistakenly refer to a "THD" measurement when they really mean the "THD+N" technique. [*For completeness and the abnormally curious:* a true THD measurement consists of a computation from a series of individual harmonic amplitude measurements, rather than a single measurement. "THD" is the square root of the sum of the squares of the individual harmonic amplitudes. And the answer must specify the highest order harmonic included in the computations; for example, "THD through 8th harmonic." (from Metzler)] See RaneNote: *Audio Specifications.*

THD+N (*total harmonic distortion plus noise***)** The most common audio measurement. A single sine wave frequency of know harmonic purity is passed through the unit under test, and then patched back into the distortion measuring instrument. A measurement level is set; the instrument notches out the frequency used for the test, and passes the result through a set of band-limiting filters, adjusted for the bandwidth of interest (usually 20-20 kHz). What remains is noise (including any AC line [mains] *hum* or interference *buzzes*, etc.) and all harmonics generated by the unit. This composite signal is measured using a true rms detector voltmeter, and the results displayed. Often a resultant curve is created by stepping through each frequency from 20 Hz to 20 kHz, at some specified level (often +4 dBu), and bandwidth (usually 20 kHz; sometimes 80 kHz, which allows measurement of any 20 kHz early harmonics). [Note that the often-seen statement: "THD+N is x%," is meaningless. For a THD+N spec to be complete, it must state the *frequency, level,* and measurement *bandwidth*.] While THD+N is the most common audio test measurement, it is not the most useful indicator of a unit's performance. What it tells the user about *hum, noise and interference* is useful; however that information is better conveyed by the *signal-to-noise (S/N) ratio* specification. What it tells the user about harmonic distortion is not terribly relevant simply because it *is harmonically related to the fundamental,* thus the distortion products tend to get masked by the complex audio material. The various *intermodulation (IM) distortion* tests are better indicators of sonic purity. See RaneNote: *Audio Specifications.*

thermal noise See: Johnson noise.

theremin Considered the first electronic musical instrument, invented in 1919 by Russian born *Lev Sergeivitch Termen,* which he anglicized to *Leon Theremin.* The theremin is unique in that it is the only musical instrument played without being touched. Interestingly, when granted a US Patent in 1928, there were 32 prior patents referenced, going all the way back to Lee De Forest. A theremin works by causing two oscillators to "beat" together. The *beat frequency* equals the difference in frequency between the two signals. Beats are a physical phenomenon occurring in the air when sounds are mixed. A theremin uses one oscillator operating well above the upper limit of human hearing as a reference tone, and another oscillator whose frequency is varied by the proximity of a human hand, for instance, to a capacitive sensing element shaped like an antenna. A typical machine has two antennas and you play it by moving your hands nearer to and farther from the antennas. One antenna controls the volume of the sound, while the other controls the frequency, or pitch, of the sound. Used together you can creates sounds that can range from being very sci-fi-ish — a sort of quivering sound — as heard in early sci-fi movies like *The Day the Earth Stood Still,* to very complex jazz licks. The theremin even appears as Dr. Hannibal Lecter's favorite instrument in Thomas Harris' bestseller *Hannibal* (Delacorte, 1999).

It was the theremin that got Bob Moog (inventor of the *Moog Synthesizer* and considered the father of modern electronic music) interested in electronic music. His latest company Big Briar now makes some of the world's best theremins.

See the Theremin web ring for additional info; and to view the fascinating, bizarre, and stranger-than-fiction true-life story of Leon Theremin, check out the film (available on video), *Theremin: An Electronic Odyssey,* by Steven M. Martin (1994), including several performances by *Clara Rockmore,* perhaps the best theremin player ever.

thermionic valve See: vacuum tube and Fleming.

third-harmonic distortion The standard test used on analog magnetic tape recorders to determine the **maximum output level (MOL)**, which was defined to occur at the magnetization level at which a recorded 1 kHz sine wave reached "3 percent third-harmonic distortion." Of course, third-harmonic distortion is nothing more than a measurement of the amplitude of the third harmonic of the input frequency and is the most prominent distortion component in analog magnetic recording systems. The third-harmonic level was used as a convenient figure-of-merit because the 2nd harmonic is difficult to hear, since it tends to reinforce the pitch of the fundamental. The 3rd harmonic is easy to detect on pure tones (although less so on music), thus it makes a good benchmark for comparing sound "off tape" with the original. The distorted tone has an edge to it, containing a component one octave and a quint (interval of a fifth in music) above the fundamental. For this reason the third harmonic is also called a musical twelfth. Here's the interesting twist. This test was commonly abbreviated and listed on the specification sheet as "THD". Which, of course, was mistaken to mean "total harmonic distortion" instead of "third harmonic distortion." This led to it being mistakenly shortened to just "distortion," so you still find old analog tape date sheets, and many text books defining MOL as the point at which there exist "3% distortion," instead of the correct reference to "3% third-harmonic distortion" — quite different things.

third-octave Term referring to frequencies spaced every *three* octaves apart. For example, the third-octave above 1 kHz is 8 kHz. Commonly misused to mean one-third octave. While it can be argued that "third" can also mean one of three equal parts, and as such might be used to correctly describe one part of an octave split into three equal parts, it is potentially too confusing. The preferred term is one-third octave.

Thompson filters See: Bessel crossover.

THX Lucasfilm, Ltd. term meaning several things: 1) Their audio playback design and certification program for commercial cinema theaters; 2) Their audio playback specification for home cinema systems; 3) Approved audio/video playback equipment meeting their standards of quality and performance; and 4) DVDs, laserdiscs and VHS tapes mastered by them to meet their quality and performance standards. The term comes from two sources: George Lucas's first film *THX-1138* (student version; commercial version), and a somewhat tongue-in-cheek reference to *Tomlinson Holman's eXperiment,* after their original technical director, patentee and creative force behind all the above (who now runs TMH Corporation). See RaneNote: *Home Cinema Systems.*

THX Surround EX Surround-sound format that matrix-encodes a third surround channel into the existing left and right surround channels in a Dolby Digital signal. This channel drives a center rear loudspeaker. Compare with: DTS-ES.

TIA (*Telecommunications Industry Association*) Created in 1988 by a merger of the US Telecommunications Suppliers Association (USTSA) and the EIA's Information and Telecommunications Technologies Group (EIA/ITG). This organization works with the EIA in developing technical standards and collecting market data for the telecommunication industry.

Tice Clock An overt act of fraud perpetrated on the audio ignorant who suffer from acute aural hallucinations and beg to be separated from their money. See Bob Pease's wonderful "What's All This Hoax Stuff, Anyhow?"

tiger A great cat whose skin is striped, not just his fur.

TIM (*transient intermodulation distortion*) See: IM.

Timbre (pronounced "tambur") 1. The quality of a sound that distinguishes it from other sounds of the same pitch and volume. (AHD) 2. *Music.* The distinctive tone of an instrument or a singing voice.

time 1.a. A nonspatial continuum in which events occur in apparently irreversible succession from the past through the present to the future. b. An interval separating two points on this continuum. c. A number, as of years, days, or minutes, representing such an interval. d. A similar number representing a specific point on this continuum, reckoned in hours and minutes. 2. *Music.* a. The characteristic beat of musical rhythm: *three-quarter time.* b. The speed at which a piece of music is played; the tempo. (AHD) [Time is nothing more than a relationship between moving objects. Stop all movement and you stop time. An important concept in understanding just what *time* is, lies in understanding that *time is in the universe; the universe is not in time.* Which explains why it is not a valid question to ask, "How old is the universe?" The universe does not have an age; it is not in relationship with another moving object; it is not in time. *"Time is what keeps everything from happening all at once."* Unknown source.]

time delay No such thing; a misnomer. You cannot delay *time* (see above). Misused to mean *signal delay* or just *delay.*

tin-pan (*tinny piano*) From the cheap pianos associated with music publishers' offices that sounded like banging on tin pans. In the mid-1880s, gave birth to the name *Tin Pan Alley*, a district (*West 28th St. in Manhattan*) associated with musicians, composers, and publishers of popular music, or the publishers and composers of popular music considered as a group.

token ring A LAN baseband network access mechanism and topology in which a supervisory *"token"* (a continuously repeating frame [group of data bits] transmitted onto the network by the controlling computer; it polls for network transmissions) is passed from station to station in sequential order. Stations wishing to gain access to the network must wait for the token to arrive before transmitting data.

In a token ring topology, the next logical station receiving the token is also the nest physical station on the ring. This mechanism prevents collisions on this type of network. Normally connected as a *star-wired ring* where each station is wired back to a central point known as the *multistation access unit (MAU)*. The MAU forms a ring of the devices and performs the back-up function of restoring the ring should one of the devices crash or lose its cable connection.

tone 1. *Music.* a. A sound of distinct pitch, quality, and duration; a note. b. The interval of a major second in the diatonic scale; a whole step. c. A recitational melody in a Gregorian chant. 2.a. The quality or character of sound. b. The characteristic quality or timbre of a particular instrument or voice. (AHD)

tone controls The term most often referring to a two-band shelving equalizer offering amplitude control only over the highest (*treble*, from music, meaning the highest part, voice, instrument, or range) frequencies, and the lowest (*bass*, from music, meaning the lowest musical part) frequencies. Sometimes a third band is provided for boost/cut control of the midband frequencies. See also: Baxandall tone controls

tonic *Music.* Of or based on the keynote. (AHD)

topology *Electronics.* The interconnection pattern of nodes on a network. The logical and/or physical arrangement of stations on a network (e.g., *star topology*; *tree topology*; *ring topology*; *bus topology*, etc.). The geometric pattern or configuration of intelligent devices and how they are linked together for communications. (IEEE) *Mathematics.* "The branch of geometry concerned only with those basic properties of geometric figures that remain unchanged when the figures are twisted and distorted, stretched and shrunk, subjected to any 'schmooshing' at all as long as they're not ripped or torn. Size and shape are not topological properties since clay balls, dice, and oranges, for example, can be contracted, expanded or transformed into one another without ripping." (*Who's Counting?*, John Allen Paulos.)

toroid The name for any doughnut-shaped body. [*Mathematics*: a surface generated by a closed curve rotating about, but not intersecting or containing, an axis in its own plane. (AHD)] The shortened popular name for the doughnut-shaped (toroidal) transformers common to audio equipment; favored for their low hum fields.

TOSLINK(*Toshiba link*) A popular consumer equipment fiber optic interface based upon the S/PDIF protocol, using an implementation first developed by Toshiba.

total harmonic distortion See: THD and THD+N.

T-pad See: attenuator pad.

TPDF (*triangular probability density function*) Also called *triangular dither*. The most popular form of dither signal, described in detail in the landmark paper by Stanley Lipshitz, Robert Wannamaker, and John Vanderkooy, "Quantization and Dither: A Theoretical Survey," published in the *J. Audio Eng. Soc.*, Vol. 40, No. 5, 1992, pp. 355-375 *(issue available from the AES, but only recommended for the mathematically needy)*. As the name implies, TPDF describes a probability density function shaped like a triangle, instead of the more often seen bell-shaped curve. For dither use, the extremes represent the maximum possible quantization error of 1 LSB. Also very popular is a variant known as **shaped triangular** or **high-passed TPDF**, which is essentially high-pass filtered triangular dither that places most of the dither energy at higher frequencies making it less audible.

tracking power amplifiers A term used to describe audio power amplifier designs utilizing a variable power supply for the output, and a means of controlling the power supply based upon the input signal. This scheme improves efficiency. See: Class H Amplifiers and Compare with: rail-switchers.

trademarks See: USPTO.

transcendental number *Mathematics.* 1. Not capable of being determined by any combination of a finite number of equations with rational integral coefficients. 2. Not expressible as an integer or as the root or quotient of integers. Used of numbers, especially nonrepeating infinite decimals. (AHD)

transducer *Electrical.* A device, such as a microphone, or loudspeaker, that converts input energy of one form into output energy of another.

transform switch *Turntablist mixers.* This switch selects either *phono* or *line* as the channel source, but is commonly used for *transforming*, or quickly gating the source on and off.

transient response The reaction of an electronic circuit, or electromechanical device, or acoustic space to a non-repetitive stimulus such as a step or impulse response. It is the result to a sudden change in the input that is nonperiodic. For example, percussive instruments produce primarily transient sounds. The transient stimulus and resulting response are characterized by the amplitude and the rise time (and fall time if it is an impulse), overshoot, and settling time. The standard reference is to note the maximum amplitude and the time required to reach within 10% of the steady-state value. For a real world example of the comparative transient responses for a full-range and a 3-way loudspeaker system, see: Siegfried Linkwitz's: *Group delay and transient response*; also see: group delay.

transversal equalizer A multi-band variable equalizer using a tapped audio delay line as the frequency selective element, as opposed to bandpass filters built from inductors (real or synthetic) and capacitors. The term "transversal filter" does not mean "digital filter." It is the entire family of filter functions done by means of a tapped delay line. There exists a class of digital filters realized as transversal filters, using a shift register rather than an analog delay line, with the inputs being numbers rather than analog functions.

traveling wave Something vibrating creates a wave pattern that travels through a medium from one place to another.

tree topology A LAN topology that recognizes only one route between two nodes on the network. The map resembles a tree or the letter T.

triamp, triamplified, or triamplification Term used to refer to a 3-way active crossover where the audio signal is split into three paths, and using separate power amplifier channels for each driver.

triangle wave A periodic waveform characterized by a 50% duty cycle and a Fourier series consisting of odd-ordered, equal phase, sinusoidal harmonic components of its fundamental frequency with amplitudes (coefficients multiplying the magnitude of the fundamental sine wave) equal to $1/n^2$, where n equals the harmonic number. Therefore the first few harmonic amplitudes are 1/9, 1/25, 1/49, 1/81, etc. For a very cool pictorial, see Fourier Series: Triangle Wave Tool. And if you are missing the math, see: Cuthbert Nyack's *Fourier Series of Triangle Wave*.

triangular dither See: TPDF.

triple point of water A system is at the "triple point" when ice (solid), water (liquid), and vapor (gas) coexist in equilibrium. This point is the freezing point of water and is set by international agreement to equal 273.16 kelvin (0 degrees Celsius; 32 degrees Fahrenheit).

truncate To eliminate without round-off some low-order bits, often after performing an arithmetic computation.

Tschebyscheff See: Chebyshev.

TTL (*transistor transistor logic*) The workhorse digital logic integrated circuit family introduced as a standard product line in 1964.

TTM (*turntablist transcription methodology*) A system of music notation developed by John Carluccio in 1997, for turntablism (see below). His system uses a modified musical staff with the vertical axis representing the direction of rotation of the record and the horizontal axis representing time. A free descriptive pamphlet is available at Battle Sounds — look for: *Free Download: The Turntablist Transcription Methodology*.

turntablism A form of music founded by *turntablists* (see below), that is already mainstream enough that the Berklee College of Music publishing arm, Berklee Press has issued books and vinyl records for this music form. For further historical info see Miles White's "The Phonograph Turntable and Performance Practice in Hip Hop Music", and Christo Macais' "FAQ: Section 2: History of Turntablism".

turntablist A performing artist who uses two or more turntables as music sources from which he/she creates original results by quickly cutting and mixing the sounds of each, using specially designed performance mixers such as Rane's TTM 54i.

turntablist transcription methodology See: TTM.

tweeter High-frequency loudspeaker. See: crossover; also: ribbon tweeter.

twin-tone IMD See: IM.

TwinVQ (*transform-domain weighted interleave vector quantization*) Name of a music compression technology developed at the NTT Human Interface Laboratories in Japan. A transform coding method like MP3, AAC or AC-3.

twisted-pair Standard two-conductor copper cable, with insulation extruded over each conductor and twisted together. Usually operated as a balanced line connection. May be shielded or not. See: cables.

two-bit Costing or worth 25 cents: *a two-bit cigar.*

U

U Abbreviation for the "modular unit" on which rack panel heights are based. Per the EIA and ANSI standard *ANSI/EIA-310-D-1992 Cabinets, Racks, Panels, and Associated Equipment*, the modular unit is equal to 44.45 millimeters (1.75"). Panel heights are referred to as "*n*U" where *n* is equal to the number of modular units. Examples are 1U (1.75" high), 2U (3.5" high), 3U (5.25" high), etc. Popularly called *rack units* and often abbreviated "RU," which is technically incorrect but not misleading.

UART (*universal asynchronous receiver-transmitter*) The device that performs the bidirectional parallel-to-serial data conversions necessary for the serial transmission of data into and out of a computer.

UDP (*user datagram protocol*) A TCP/IP protocol describing how messages reach application programs within a destination computer. This protocol is normally bundled with IP-layer software. UDP is a transport layer, connectionless mode protocol, providing a (potentially unreliable, unsequenced, and/or duplicated) datagram mode of communication for delivery of packets to a remote or local user.

UDP/IP (*user datagram protocol/internet protocol*) See: UDP above.

UI (*user interface*) As compared with: GUI.

ULSI (*ultra-large-scale integration*) A logic device containing a million or more gates

ultrasonic Of or relating to acoustic frequencies above the range audible to the human ear, or above approximately 20,000 hertz. (AHD) Compare with: supersonic.

unbalanced line See: balanced line.

units of measurement See Rowlett's *How Many? A Dictionary of Units of Measurement* for a valuable list (with definitions) of the International System of Weights and Measures, the metric system, and all English customary units. Very highly recommended.

unity gain A gain setting of one, or a device having a gain of one, i.e., it does not amplify or attenuate the audio signal. The output equals the input. See RaneNote: *Unity Gain and Impedance Matching: Strange Bedfellows*.

unity power factor In an AC circuit, a power factor equal to one, which only occurs when the voltage and current are in phase, i.e., for a purely resistive circuit, or a reactive circuit at resonance.

unobtainium Reference to all those parts necessary to keep legacy audio devices running that you can never find — things like old ICs, connectors, etc. [*Origin unknown, but thanks to CD for passing it on.*]

UPS (*uninterruptible power supply*) A back-up power supply (commonly used with computers) that automatically continues to supply power when the main AC source fails.

upward expander See: expander.

URL (*uniform resource locator*) A Web address. A consistent method for specifying Internet resources in a way that all Web browsers understand. For example, "http://www.rane.com," is the URL for Rane's home page on the web. The "http" part tells the Web browser what protocol to use, and the remainder of the URL, "www.rane.com," is the Internet address.

USB (*universal serial bus*) A low-speed (12 Mbits/sec) serial bus that acts like a special purpose local area network. Originally proposed by a consortium of Compaq, Digital, IBM, Intel, Microsoft, NEC and Northern Telecom in March of 1995, it is now the standard PC serial connection. USB equipped machines typically have only three ports: USB, monitor, and Ethernet LAN . The USB port supports 63 devices, and eliminates the need for all specialized parallel, serial, graphics, modem, sound/game or mouse ports. USB is completely "plug and play," i.e., it detects and configures all devices automatically, and allows "hot swapping" of devices. See: IEEE-1394 for complementary high-speed system.

USPTO (*U.S. Patent Trademark Office*) Complete patent and trademark information is available free at this incredible website. To search, read and print any U.S. patent granted since 1790 (*really*) click here. [*To download exact full-page patent images, complete with diagrams, requires you have a TIFF plug-in. All Internet US patents are in TIFF image file format, using CCITT Group 4 compression, as mandated by international standards. This requires third-party software to view these images either directly or after conversion to another format, such as Adobe® PDF. A free, unlimited time TIFF plug-in offering full-size, unimpeded patent viewing and printing unimpeded by any advertising on Windows® x86 PCs is available from **AlternaTIFF**.*]

UTP (*unshielded twisted-pair*) See: cables.

UV (*ultraviolet*) Electromagnetic radiation at frequencies higher than visible light yet lower than those of x-rays. Commonly used to erase EPROMs and in wireless and fiber optic data transmission.

uxoriousness 1. Excessively submissive or devoted to one's wife. 2. "A perverted affection that has strayed to one's own wife." — Ambrose Bierce.

V

VA (*voltampere*) See: voltampere.

vaporware Refers to either hardware or software that exist only in the minds of the marketeers.

vacuum tube An electron tube where virtually all the air has been removed (creating a *vacuum*), thus permitting electrons to move freely, with low interaction with any remaining air molecules. (AHD) The first tube was a two-element diode, invented and patented by Ambrose Fleming in 1904, based on the Edison effect. Three years later, in 1907, Lee de Forest developed the first triode (known as the *Audion*) by adding a grid between the cathode (*emitter*) and the anode (*collector*), thus creating the first amplifier since a change of voltage at the grid produced a corresponding (but greater) change of voltage at the anode.

valance *Theater.* A part of the stage draperies, usually ornamental, which hangs in front of the main curtain.

valence *Chemistry.* The combining capacity of an atom or radical determined by the number of electrons that it will lose, add, or share when it reacts with other atoms. [AHD]

valve British term for vacuum tube, popularized because the first tube was known as the *Fleming valve* named for its inventor Ambrose Fleming.

VCA (*voltage-controlled amplifier*) An electronic circuit comprised of three terminals: input, output and control. The output voltage is a function of the input voltage and the control port. The gain of the stage is determined by the control signal, which is usually a DC voltage, but could be a current signal or even a digital code. Usually found as the main element in dynamic controllers, such as compressors, expanders, limiters, and gates. See: THAT Corporation's VCA History.

VDT (*video display terminal*) Computer monitor, or data terminal with a monitor.

variable-Q equalizer See: proportional-Q equalizer.

vector *Mathematics.* A quantity, such as velocity, completely specified by a magnitude and a direction.

vector diagram A drawing that shows the direction and magnitude of a quantity by a vector arrow. See RaneNote: *Linkwitz-Riley Crossovers up to 8th-Order: An Overview.*

vegetable diode See: LEVD.

velocity microphone See: ribbon microphone.

videoconferencing Video *and* audio communication held by two or more people over a distance using a codec at either end and linked by digital networks (T-1,ISDN, etc.). Contrast with: teleconferencing.

vinyl Common name for any phonograph record.

violet noise See: noise color.

virus A self-replicating program released into a computer system for mischievous reasons. Once triggered by some preprogrammed event (often time or date related), the results vary from humorous or annoying messages, to the destruction of data or whole operating systems. *Bad bad.*

VLSI (*very-large-scale integration*) Refers to the number of logic gates in an integrated circuit. By today's standards, a VLSI device could contain up to one million gates.

vocoder (*voice coder*) 1. Invented by Homer Dudley (no fooling) in 1936 at Bell Labs, and called a "phase vocoder." It was an electronic device for analyzing and synthesizing, or generating artificial speech. Homer Dudley was the first person to recognized that the basic information rate of speech is low and that if you broke it down into its basic components, these could be transmitted over a quite narrow bandwidth, and then reconstructed at the receiving end. Thus was born the speech synthesizer. The vocoder principal is based on determining the *formants*, or vowel sounds, of the speech signal, along with its fundamental frequency and any *noise* components such as *plosive* sounds (a speech sound produced by complete closure of the oral passage and subsequent release accompanied by a burst of air, as in the sound (p) in *pit*, or (d) in *dog*), hisses, or buzzes. Typically this is done by using two sets of filter banks — one for analysis and one for synthesis — and an "excitation analysis" block. The analysis filter bank is much like those used in real-time analyzers. The audio is presented to a bank of parallel connected bandpass filters, whose output levels are converted into DC voltage levels proportional to the signal passing through each bandpass filter. This captures the formant information. The excitation analysis block determines and codes the fundamental frequency and noise attributes. Reconstruction occurs by using the encoded DC levels, mixed with the excitation block output, to gate each output bandpass filter, which are then summed together to recreate a facsimile of the original speech signal. Early pictures and audio samples (*from* Prof. Edward A. Lee, UC Berkeley). 2. Once vocoder basics were established, they found new uses in electronic music applications. The MI (musical instrument) vocoder uses speech input to modulate another music instrument signal so that it "talks." Use of vocoders peaked in the '70s after being popularized by such notables as Wendy Carlos, Alan Parsons and Stevie Wonder. This vocoder version has two inputs, one for the vocal microphone and one for another instrument. Talking or singing into the microphone modulates or superimposes vocal characteristics onto the other instrument. Compare with: talk box.

voice *Music.* Musical sound produced by vibration of the human vocal cords and resonated within the throat and head cavities. [AHD]

voice coil See: loudspeaker.

voiceover 1. The voice of an unseen narrator, or of an on-screen character not seen speaking, in a movie or a television broadcast. 2. A film or videotape recording narrated by a voiceover. [AHD] Common examples of voiceovers include cartoon characters, documentary videos of all types, computer software tutorials, audio books, and automated telephone messages.

VoIP (*voice over Internet protocol*) The technology that allows you to transmit voice conversations (i.e., the ability to make telephone calls) and send faxes over a data network using the Internet Protocol. Think, *voice email.*

volatile Refers to a memory device that loses any data it contains when power is removed from the device. Examples would include static and dynamic RAMs.

volt *Abbr.* **E**, also **V**. The International System unit of electric potential and electromotive force, equal to the difference of electric potential between two points on a conducting wire carrying a constant current of one ampere when the power dissipated between the points is one watt. [After **Count Alessandro Volta**.] (AHD)

Volta, Count Alessandro (1745-1827) Italian physicist who invented the battery (1800). The volt is named in his honor. (AHD)

voltage follower See: buffer amplifier.

voltampere (*VA*) The product of rms voltage and rms current in an electronic circuit. It is the unit of apparent power in the International System of Units (SI).

VOM (*volt-ohm-milliammeter*) A portable test instrument for measuring voltage (volts), resistance (ohms) and current (amperes). Also see: VTVM.

vote "The instrument and symbol of a freeman's power to make a fool of himself and a wreck of his country."
— Ambrose Bierce.

VOX (*voice operated exchange*) Also called *voice operated relay*, originally a tape recorder feature where speech starts the recording process and silence stops it. However it is not restricted to tape recorders, for instance, cellular phones use VOX to save battery life, and teleconferencing systems use it to determine the number of active mics. See: NOM.

VRML(*virtual reality modeling language*) A developing standard for describing interactive 3D scenes delivered across the internet. In short, VRML adds 3D data to the Web. Heavily supported by Silicon Graphics (SGI) workstations, competing with Sun's Java loaded workstations.

VTVM (*vacuum tube voltmeter*) Antiquated term for a test instrument measuring voltage, resistance and current, constructed using vacuum tubes, which required plugging it into an AC voltage source, thus not portable. Characterized by having very high input impedance (compared to the standard VOM), that allowed more precise measurements. Replaced today by solid-state **DMM (digital multimeter)**.

vulcanized fiber See: fishpaper.

vulgar fractions Chiefly British term for common fractions, although sometimes used to mean improper fractions (those with a larger numerator than denominator). [Word History: Vulgar is an example of *pejoration*, the process by which a word develops negative meanings over time. The ancestor of vulgar, the Latin word *vulgris* (from *vulgus*, the common people), meant of or belonging to the common people, everyday, as well as belonging to or associated with the lower orders. Vulgris also meant ordinary, common (of vocabulary, for example), and shared by all.] (AHD)

VU meter (*volume unit*) The term *volume unit* was adopted to refer to a special meter whose response closely related to the perceived loudness of the audio signal. It is a voltmeter with standardized dB calibration for measuring audio signal levels, and with attack and overshoot (needle ballistics) optimized for broadcast and sound recording. Jointly developed by Bell Labs, CBS and NBC, and put into use in May, 1939, VU meter characteristics are defined by ANSI specification "Volume Measurements of Electrical Speech and Program waves, " C16.5-1942 (which is know incorporated into IEC 60268-17). 0 VU is defined to be a level of +4 dBu for an applied sine wave. The VU meter has relatively slow response. It is driven from a full-wave averaging circuit defined to reach 99% full-scale deflection in 300 ms and overshoot not less than 1% and not more than 1.5%. Since a VU meter is optimized for perceived loudness it is not a good indicator of peak performance. Contrast with: PPM.

VXCO (*voltage-controlled crystal oscillator* A crystal-based oscillator whose center frequency can be varied with an applied voltage.

W

W3 An abbreviation for World Wide Web.

walla The film industry term for background crowd noises in a movie.

Walla Walla A city in southeast Washington near the Oregon border south-southwest of Spokane. Founded in 1856 near the site of an army fort, it is a manufacturing center in an agricultural region famous for sweet yellow onions. In spite of its name, a quiet community.

WAN (*wide area network*) A computer and voice network bigger than a city or metropolitan area.

watermarking 1. *Paper* The act of adding a translucent design impressed on paper during manufacture and visible when the paper is held to the light. (AHD) 2. *Audio or video* Embedded data code within the digitized audio or video image that can be recovered but which will not affect the quality of the product. Various methods exist, but all consist of very short (2-5 microseconds long) pieces of code containing all the relevant data about the copyright owner and performance royalties. All make use of the science of steganography.

watt *Abbr.* **W** *Electricity* An International System unit of power equal to one joule per second. [After **James Watt**.] (AHD)

Watt, James (1736-1819) British engineer and inventor who made fundamental improvements in the steam engine, resulting in the modern, high-pressure steam engine (patented 1769). (AHD)

watts rms *No such thing.* See: apparent power and rms power.

.WAV File extension for a Wave file, the Microsoft format that is the de facto audio file format for PCs.

wavelength *Symbol* (Greek lower-case *lambda, ë*) The distance between one peak or crest of a sine wave and the next corresponding peak or crest. The *wavelength* of any frequency may be found by dividing the speed of sound by the frequency.

wavelet *Mathematics.* An algorithm used to efficiently compress and decompress the phase and frequency information contained in a transmitted signal.

Webcast The real time (continuous stream) delivery of audio and video from a server to a client. [*Think: broadcast.*]

Web ring A group of websites all sharing a common theme. For example, web rings exist for fans of certain bands, movies, TV shows, authors, racecar drivers, etc. Soon we will have a web ring for web rings.

weighting filters Special filters used in measuring loudness levels, and consequently carried over into audio noise measurements of equipment. The filter design "weights" or gives more attention to certain frequency bands than others. The goal is to obtain measurements that correlate well with the subjective perception of noise. [Technically termed *psophometric* (pronounced "so-fo-metric") filters, after the *psophometer*, a device used to measure noise in telephone circuits, broadcast, and other audio communication equipment. A psophometer was a voltmeter with a set of weighting filters.] Weighting filters are a special type of band-limiting filters designed to compliment the way we hear. Since the ear's loudness vs. frequency response is not flat, it is argued, we should not try to correlate flat frequency vs. loudness measurements with what we hear. Fair enough. Five weighting filter designs dominate (See: References: Metzler):

A-weighting The A-curve is a wide bandpass filter centered at 2.5 kHz, with ~20 dB attenuation at 100 Hz, and ~10 dB attenuation at 20 kHz, therefore it tends to heavily roll-off the low end, with a more modest effect on high frequencies. It is the inverse of the 30-phon (or 30 dB-SPL) equal-loudness curve of Fletcher-Munson. [*Editorial Note:* Low-cost audio equipment often list an A-weighted noise spec — not because it correlates well with our hearing — but because it helps "hide" nasty low-frequency hum components that make for bad noise specs. Sometimes A-weighting can "improve" a noise spec by 10 dB. Words to the wise: always wonder what a manufacturer is hiding when they use A-weighting.]

C-weighting The C-curve is "flat," but with limited bandwidth, with -3 dB corners of 31.5 Hz and 8 kHz, respectively.

ITU-R 468-weighting (*was CCIR, but since the CCIR became the ITU-R, the correct terminology today is ITU-R*) This filter was designed to maximize its response to the types of impulsive noise often coupled into audio cables as they pass through telephone switching facilities. Additionally it turned out to correlate particularly well with noise perception, since modern research has shown that frequencies between 1 kHz and 9 kHz are more "annoying" than indicated by A-weighting curve testing. The ITU-R 468-curve peaks at 6.3 kHz, where it has 12 dB of gain (relative to 1 kHz). From here, it gently rolls off low frequencies at a 6 dB/octave rate, but it quickly attenuates high frequencies at ~30 dB/octave (it is down -22.5 dB at 20 kHz, relative to +12 dB at 6.3 kHz).

ITU-R (CCIR) ARM-weighting or **ITU-R (CCIR) 2 kHz-weighting** This curves derives from the ITU-R 468-curve above. Dolby Laboratories proposed using an average-response meter with the ITU-R 468-curve instead of the costly true quasi-peak meters used by the Europeans in specifying their equipment. They further proposed shifting the 0-dB reference point from 1 kHz to 2 kHz (in essence, sliding the curve down 6 dB). This became known as the ITU-R ARM (*average response meter*), as well as the ITU-R 2 kHz-weighting curve. (See: R. Dolby, D. Robinson, and K. Gundry, "A Practical Noise Measurement Method," *J. Audio Eng. Soc.*, Vol. 27, No. 3, 1979) [*Before using these terms be aware that the ITU-R, even after 20 years, takes strong exception to having its name used by a private company to promote its own methodologies.*]

Z-weighting A new term defined in IEC 61672-1, the latest international standard for sound pressure level measurements. It stand for *zero*-weighting, or no weighting; i.e., a flat measurement with equal emphasis of all frequencies.

wet *Recording.* 1. The result of mixing the original recorded sound with the processed sound (reverb, chorusing, doubling, etc.). 2. Any sound with significant reverberation; not dead. Contrast with: dry.

wet circuit See below.

wet transformer *Telephony.* An analog audio transformer designed for both DC and AC operation. Derived from the term, *wet circuit*, referring to a circuit where voice signals are transmitted and also carries direct current. Contrast with: dry transformer.

WFAE (*World Forum for Acoustic Ecology*) "An interdisciplinary spectrum of individuals engaged in the study of the scientific, social, and cultural aspects of natural and human made sound environments."

Wheatstone bridge 1. An instrument used for measuring resistance. The circuit used is a 4-arm bridge, all arms of which are predominantly resistive. The bridge is a two-port network (i.e., it has two terminal pairs across opposite corners) capable of being operated in such a manner that when voltage is applied to one port, by suitable adjustment of the resistive elements in the network, zero output can be obtained at the signal output port (usually a meter). Under these circumstances the bridges is termed *balanced.*

[*Although the circuit used in a Wheatstone bridge was first described by **Samuel Hunter Christie** (1784-1865) — the son of James Christie, founder of the well-known auction house — in his paper "Experimental Determination of the Laws of Magneto-electric Induction" (1833), **Sir Charles Wheatstone** (1802-1875) received credit for its invention because of his adaptation of the circuit in 1843 for the measurement of resistance. Wheatstone also invented the concertina, the stereoscope and contributed significantly to the development of the telegraph.*]

white noise Analogous to white *light* containing equal amounts of all *visible* frequencies, white *noise* contains equal amounts of all *audible* frequencies (technically the bandwidth of noise is infinite, but for audio purposes it is limited to just the audio frequencies). From an *energy* standpoint white noise has constant power *per hertz* (also referred to as *unit bandwidth*), i.e., at every frequency there is the same amount of power (while pink noise, for instance, has constant power *per octave band* of frequency). A plot of white noise power vs. frequency is flat if the measuring device uses the same width filter for all measurements. This is known as a *fixed bandwidth* filter. For instance, a fixed bandwidth of 5 Hz is common, i.e., the test equipment measures the amplitude at each frequency using a filter that is 5 Hz wide. It is 5 Hz wide when measuring 50 Hz or 2 kHz or 9.4 kHz, etc. A plot of white noise power vs. frequency change is *not* flat if the measuring device uses a variable width filter. This is known as a *fixed percentage bandwidth* filter. A common example of which is ⅓-octave wide, which equals a bandwidth of 23%. This means that for every frequency measured the bandwidth of the measuring filter changes to 23% of that new center frequency. For example the measuring bandwidth at 100 Hz is 23 Hz wide, then changes to 230 Hz wide when measuring 1 kHz, and so on. Therefore the plot of noise power vs. frequency is not flat, but shows a 3 dB rise in amplitude per octave of frequency change. Due to this rising frequency characteristic, white noise sounds very bright and lacking in low frequencies. [Here's the technical details: noise *power* is actually its *power density spectrum* — a measure of how the noise power contributed by individual frequency components is distributed over the frequency spectrum. It should be measured in *watts/Hz*; however it isn't. The accepted practice in noise theory is to use *amplitude-squared* as the unit of power (purists justify this by assuming a 1 Ω resistor load). For electrical signals this gives units of *volts-squared/Hz*, or more commonly expressed as *volts/root-Hertz*. Note that the denominator gets bigger by the *square root of the increase in frequency*. Therefore, for an octave increase (doubling) of frequency, the denominator increases by the square root of two, which equals 1.414, or 3 dB. In order for the energy to remain constant (as it must if it is to remain white noise) there has to be an offsetting increase in amplitude (the numerator term) of 3 dB to exactly cancel the 3 dB increase in the denominator term. Thus the upward 3 dB/octave sloping characteristic of white noise amplitude when measured in constant percentage increments like ⅓-octave.] See: noise color.

wide-range curve Same as: X curve.

widget (perhaps alteration of *gadget*) 1. A small mechanical device or control; a gadget. 2. An unnamed or hypothetical manufactured article. (AHD) 3. As developed by *Guinness*, a small disk with a pinprick-size hole that fits inside their beer cans. As the beer is packaged, a small amount of stout is forced into the widget and held there under pressure. Once the pressure is released by opening the can, the beer is freed from the widget and a stream of bubbles flows upward. Now when the stout is poured, it looks like a pub-poured draught with the characteristic Guinness head (thick collar of foam), without the widget it looks like any other beer. It also reproduces the creamy texture and low carbonation of a draught pint. Now also used by *Murphy's* and *Beamish*.

Wintel A contraction of the words "Windows" and "Intel." Used to describe personal computers made from Intel microprocessors and running Microsoft Windows software. It is reported that this "Wintel standard" accounts for 80% of all PCs.

wire See: cables.

WOM (*write-only-memory*) Term coined by Signetics in 1972 for their 25000 Series 9046XN Random Access Write-Only-Memory integrated circuits. Based on SEX (Signetics EXtra secret) processes, these devices employ both enhancement and depletion mode P-Channel, N-Channel, and NEU-Channel MOS transistors (devices which simultaneously, randomly, or not at all, enhance or deplete regardless of gate polarity). The world's supply of WOMs was quickly consumed by newly designed airline baggage-handling equipment, where they are still used today to store the exact real-time location of each bag. WOM production was suddenly discontinued when it was discovered that the only copy of the mask code had been accidentally filed into a WOM location.

woofer Low-frequency loudspeaker. See: crossover.

word An ordered set of bits that is the normal unit in which information may be stored, transmitted, or operated upon within a given computer — commonly 16 or 32 bits.

word clock The synchronizing signal that indicates the sampling frequency or rate of sample words over a digital audio interface.

word length The number of bits in a word.

World Wide Web (*WWW* and/or *W3*) 1. A way to present resources and information over the Internet, or according to its inventor CERN , "The World Wide Web (W3) is the universe of network-accessible information, an embodiment of human knowledge." 2. Satirically called the *World Wide Wait.*

WOROM (*write-once read-only memory*) Systems in which data may be written once, but not erased and rewritten. Usually refers to CD-ROM technology that can be recorded once only.

wow A form of distortion due to very slow (~ 1 Hz) variations in rotational speed common to turntables and analog tape recorders. Heard as a slow variation in the pitch when played back. Compare with: flutter.

WPAN (*wireless personal-area network*) For instance, see Bluetooth and ZigBee.

write To record data on a medium.

WWW (*World Wide Web*) See: World Wide Web.

wye connector See: Y-connector.

WYSIWYG (pronounced "whizzy-wig") (*what you see is what you get*) Popular word processing term. Folklore says it was copied from a catchphrase from the old TV show *Rowan and Martin's Laugh-In* .

X

X The electronic symbol for reactance — the imaginary part of impedance.

X$_C$ The electronic symbol for capacitive reactance.

X$_L$ The electronic symbol for inductive reactance.

x-axis The horizontal axis of a two-dimensional Cartesian coordinate system, or one of three axes in a three-dimensional Cartesian coordinate system. (AHD)

X curve (*extended curve*) In the film sound industry an *X curve* is also known as the *wide-range curve* and conforms to ISO Bulletin 2969, which specifies for pink noise, at the listening position in a dubbing situation or two-thirds of the way back in a theater, to be flat to 2 kHz, rolling off 3 dB/oct after that. The *small-room X curve* is designed to be used in rooms with less than 150 cubic meters, or 5,300 cubic feet. This standard specifies flat response to 2 kHz, and then rolling off at a 1.5 dB/oct rate. Some people use a modified small-room curve, starting the roll-off at 4 kHz, with a 3-dB/oct rate. Compare with: Academy curve.

xerography The name created by the Haloid Company in 1946 (from the Greek *xeros* for dry and *graphein* for writing) for the process invented by Chester F. Carlson on October 22, 1938, which he named *electrophotography.* In 1960, Haloid-Xerox introduced the 914 copier, the first pushbutton, plain-paper, xerographic office machine. The company soon became known simply as **Xerox.**

X Generation See: Generation X.

Xilinx (pronounced *zi-links*; after *xi* the 14th letter of the Greek alphabet) Leading manufacturer of field-programmable logic devices.

XLR See: connectors.

XMF (*extensible music format*) A MIDI Manufacturers Association approved new standard that combines MIDI notes with DLS (downloadable sound) samples.

XOR Acronym for *exclusive OR*, a type of logic gate where a logic 1 output is based upon A or B inputs being present — but not both.

XT Official (FED-STD-1037C) abbreviation for crosstalk.

X-Y microphone technique A stereo recording technique where two cardioid microphones are placed facing each other, at an angle of 90 degrees, with the center of the source aimed at the center between them. Sometimes this technique is incorporated internally in a single microphone using two capsules. Also called the ***coincident-microphone technique*** Compare with: ORTF.

Y

Y 1. The electronic symbol for admittance — the inverse of impedance. 2. Abbreviation for luminance (black & white) video signal. 3. Chemical symbol for *yttrium* — my absolute favorite element, next to *ytterbium*.

Y2k (*year two thousand*)

YAG (*yttrium-aluminum-garnet*) A type of solid-state laser.

Yagi antenna Shortened form of *Yagi-Uda antenna*, a linear end-fire array consisting of a driven element, a reflector element, and one or more director elements — your basic TV antenna. [*Named after Hidetsugu Yagi (1886-1976), laboratory director of Shintaro Uda, professor at Tohoku University in Sendai, Japan.*]

yahoo A crude or brutish person; a boor. [*And you thought it was a search engine.*]

yapped *Book jargon.* Refers to the edge of the cover of a book bound in paper or other soft material. *Yapped edges* are not flush with the pages but extend beyond the edges of the book making them fragile.

y-axis The vertical axis of a two-dimensional Cartesian coordinate system, or one of three axes in a three-dimensional Cartesian coordinate system. (AHD)

YB (*yottabyte*) The number of bytes represented by 2 raised to the 80th power, i.e., 1,208,925,819,614,629,174,706,176 bytes.

Y/C video See: S-video.

Y-connector or **Y-cord** A three-wire circuit that is star connected. Also spelled *wye*-connector. It is okay to use a Y-connector to *split* an audio signal from an output to drive two inputs; it is not okay to use a Y-connector to try and *sum* or *mix* two signals together to drive one input. For details, see RaneNote: *Why Not Wye?*

Yellow Book Nickname for the Philips and Sony's ECMA-130 standard document that defines the format for CD-ROM (compact disc-read only memory) discs; available only to licensees. Compare with: Red Book and Green Book.

yield The number of devices that work as planned, specified as a percentage of the total number actually fabricated. Normally used to quantify a run of integrated circuits.

Y/N Software program "yes/no" response prompt. A "Y" or "N" keystroke is expected.

yottahertz One septillion (10^{24}) hertz. (AHD)

YRB (*Yellow Rat Bastard*) Website, magazine, clothes, music, newsletter, for the ultra hip, from NYC, of course. Contains adult content. Check it out — take the test.

YUV video The coding process used in CD-I in which the luminance signal (Y) is recorded at full bandwidth on each line and chroma values (U and V) are recorded at half bandwidth on alternate lines.

Z

Z The electronic symbol for impedance.

zaa zaa *Japanese.* An onomatopoetic word meaning hard rain, hail, the sound of a heavy downpour or rushing water.

zap To eradicate all or part of a program or database, sometimes by lightning, sometimes intentionally.

Zaphod Beeblebrox Douglas Adams' *Hitchhiker's Guide To The Galaxy*, President of the Universe character, famous for being able to scream a diminished fifth.

z-axis One of three axes in a three-dimensional Cartesian coordinate system. (AHD)

zeal "A certain nervous disorder afflicting the young and inexperienced." — Ambrose Bierce.

Zen The Sanskrit word for meditation.

zero Half of all the stored knowledge in computers. Compare with: one; See Kaplan's *The Nothing That Is* for its fascinating story.

zero crossing point *Electronics.* The point at which a signal waveform crosses from being positive to negative or vice versa. This is the instant the signal has zero value, which makes it the spot where you want to make changes with the least amount of zipper (or other) noise, e.g., change gain in VCAs, or activate switches, transfer data, etc.

zero lobing error *Electronic crossovers.* See: lobing error.

ZIF (*zero insertion force socket*) A standard IC-socket design requiring the user to move a lever to insert or remove the chip — as opposed to pressing and prying the chip manually — hence, *zero insertion force.* The lever actuator (hopefully) eliminates damaging the IC pins.

ZigBee (formerly known as **PURLnet**, **RF-Lite**, **Firefly**, and **HomeRF Lite**.) A low-cost, low-power, two-way, wireless communications standard between compliant devices anywhere in and around the home (*automation, toys, PC peripherals, etc.*), developed by Philips and others. Claiming lower cost, lower power consumption, higher density of nodes per network and simplicity of protocols, it is an alternative to Bluetooth.

Zippo® George G. Blaisdell invented the Zippo Windproof Lighter in 1932. The lighter was given its name as a derivation of the word "zipper" because the inventor liked the sound of the word, which had been patented in nearby Meadville, PA, in 1925 by B.F. Goodrich.

zipper noise Audible steps that occur when a parameter is being varied in a digital audio processor, analog VCA, digitally-controlled attenuator, etc.

Zobel network or **Zobel filter** [Also called *Boucherot cell* after Paul Boucherot who worked extensively with electrical networks and power.] 1. A filter designed according to image parameter techniques. 2. *Audio amplifiers.* Zobel networks are used in audio amplifiers to dampen out high frequency oscillations that might occur in the absence of loads at high frequencies. It is the commonly seen series resistor-capacitor combination located directly at the output of the driver stage, just before the output inductor. Typical values are 5-10 Ω in series with 0.1 microfarads. The network limits the rising impedance of a loudspeaker due to the speaker coil inductance. The output inductor found in most power amplifiers used to disconnect the load at high frequencies further aggravates this phenomenon. See Douglas Self's book for a good discussion of audio amplifier Zobel networks. 3. *Loudspeakers.* Some loudspeaker crossover designs include Zobel networks wired across the tweeter (high frequency) driver to compensate for the rise in impedance at high frequencies due to the inductance of the voice coil. The goal here is to try to keep the load seen by the crossover circuitry as resistive as possible. [After *Dr. Zobel of Bell Labs.*]

Zoetrope (pronounced ZOH-uh-trohp) A kind of mechanical cinema invented in 1834 by William George Horner. It was an early form of motion picture projector consisting of a drum containing a set of still images turned in a circular fashion to create the illusion of motion. Horner originally called it the *Daedatelum*, but Pierre Desvignes, a French inventor, renamed his version of it the Zoetrope (from Greek word root *zoo* for animal life and *trope* for "things that turn.") Like other motion simulation devices, the Zoetrope depends on the fact that the human retina retains an image for about 100 milliseconds so that if a new image appears in that time, the sequence was seem to be uninterrupted and continuous. It also depends on what is referred to as the *Phi phenomenon*, which observes that humans try to make sense out of any sequence of impressions, continuously relating them to each other.

z-transform A mathematical method used to relate coefficients of a digital filter to its frequency response, and to evaluate stability of the filter. It is equivalent to the Laplace transform of sampled data and is the building block of digital filters.

Z-weighting See: weighting filters.

zymurgist See: brewer.

zymurgy The scientific study of the process of fermentation in brewing and distilling.

Zyzyyzyski, Zyzeikkel The last name listed in the *1998 Snohomish County, Washington, U.S.A.* telephone directory — really (*but, alas, no more*).

zyzzyva (The last word in the English dictionary) Any of various tropical American weevils of the genus *Zyzzyva*, often destructive to plants. [New Latin *Zyzzyva* genus name probably from *Zyzza* former genus of leafhoppers.] (AHD)

RaneNotes — Technical Tutorials

Signal Processing Fundamentals

- **Sound**

- **Crossovers**

- **Equalizers**

- **Dynamic Controllers**

Dennis Bohn
Rane Corporation

RaneNote 134
© **1997 Rane Corporation**

SCREAMING TO BE HEARD

In space, no one can hear you scream — because there is no air or other medium for sound to travel. Sound needs a medium; an intervening substance through which it can travel from point to point; it must be carried on something. That *something* can be solid, liquid or gas. *They **can** hear you scream underwater* — briefly. Water is a medium. Air is a medium. Nightclub walls are a medium. Sound travels in air by rapidly changing the air pressure relative to its normal value (*atmospheric pressure*). Sound is a disturbance in the surrounding medium. A vibration that spreads out from the source, creating a series of expanding shells of high pressure and low pressure ... *high pressure ... low pressure ... high pressure ... low pressure*. Moving ever outward these cycles of alternating pressure zones travel until finally dissipating, or reflecting off surfaces (nightclub walls), or passing through boundaries, or getting absorbed — usually a combination of all three. Left unobstructed, sound travels outward, but not forever. The air (or other medium) robs some of the sound's power as it passes. *The price of passage: the medium absorbs its energy.* This power loss is experienced as a reduction in how *loud* it is (the term *loudness* is used to describe how loud it is from moment to moment) as the signal travels away from its source. *The loudness of the signal is reduced by one-fourth for each doubling of distance from the source.* This means that it is 6 dB less loud as you double your distance from it. [This is known as the *inverse square law* since the decrease is inversely proportional to the square of the distance traveled — for example, 2 times the distance equals a ¼ decrease in loudness, and so on.]

How do we *create* sound, and how do we *capture* sound? We do this using opposite sides of the same *electromagnetic* coin. Electricity and magnetism are kinfolk: If you pass a coil of wire through a magnetic field, electricity is generated within the coil. *Turn the coin over and flip it again:* If you pass electricity through a coil of wire, a magnetic field is generated. Move the magnet, get a voltage; apply a voltage, create a magnet — this is the essence of all *electromechanical* objects.

Microphones and loudspeakers are electromechanical objects. At their hearts there is a coil of wire (the *voice coil*) and a magnet (the *magnet*). Speaking causes sound vibrations to travel outward from your mouth. Speaking into a *moving-coil* (aka *dynamic*) microphone causes the voice coil to move within a magnetic field. This causes a voltage to be developed and a current to flow proportional to the sound — *sound has been captured*. At the other end of the chain, a voltage is applied to the loudspeaker voice coil causing a current to flow which produces a magnetic field that makes the cone move proportional to the audio signal applied — *sound has been created*. The microphone translates sound into an electrical signal, and the loudspeaker translates an electrical signal into sound. One capturing, the other creating. Everything in-between is just details. And in case you're wondering: yes; turned around, a microphone can be a loudspeaker (*that makes teeny tiny sounds*), and a loudspeaker can be a microphone (*if you SHOUT REALLY LOUD*).

SIMPLE DIVISION

Loudspeaker *crossovers* are a necessary evil. A different universe, a different set of physics and maybe we could have what we want: one loudspeaker that does it all. One speaker that reproduces all audio frequencies equally well, with no distortion, at loudness levels adequate for whatever venue we play. Well, we live here, and our system of physics does not allow such extravagance. The hard truth is, no one loudspeaker can do it all. We need at least two — more if we can afford them. *Woofers* and *tweeters*. A big woofer for the lows and a little tweeter for the highs. This is known as a *2-way system*. (Check the accompanying diagrams for the following discussions.) But with two speakers, the correct frequencies must be routed (or *crossed over*) to each loudspeaker.

Passive

At the simplest level a crossover is a *passive* network. A passive network is one not needing a power supply to operate — if it has a line cord, or runs off batteries, then it is not a passive circuit. The simplest passive crossover network consists of only two components: a *capacitor* connecting to the high frequency driver and an *inductor* (aka a *coil*) connecting to the low frequency driver. A *capacitor* is an electronic component that passes high frequencies (the *passband*) and blocks low frequencies (the *stopband*); an *inductor* does just the opposite: it passes low frequencies and blocks high frequencies. But as the frequency changes, neither component reacts suddenly. They do it gradually; they slowly start to pass (or stop passing) their respective frequencies. The *rate* at which this occurs is called the *crossover slope*. It is measured in *dB per octave*, or shortened to *dB/oct*. The slope increases or decreases so many dB/oct. At the simplest level, each component gives you a 6 dB/oct slope (a physical fact of our universe). Again, at the simplest level, adding more components increases the slope in 6 dB increments, creating slopes of 12 dB/oct, 18 dB/oct, 24 dB/oct, and so on. The number of components, or 6 dB slope increments, is called the *crossover order*. Therefore, a *4th-order* crossover has (at least) four components, and produces steep slopes of 24 dB/oct. The steeper the better for most drivers, since

speakers only perform well for a certain band of frequencies; beyond that they misbehave, sometimes badly. Steep slopes prevent these frequencies from getting to the driver.

You can combine capacitors and inductors to create a third path that eliminates the highest highs and the lowest lows, and forms a *mid-frequency* crossover section. This is naturally called a *3-way system*. (See diagram) The "mid" section forms a *bandpass* filter, since it only passes a specific frequency band. Note from the diagram that the high frequency passband and low frequency passband terms are often shortened to just *high-pass* and *low-pass*. A 3-way system allows optimizing each driver for a narrower band of frequencies, producing a better overall sound.

So why not just use passive boxes?

Problems

The single biggest problem is that one passive cabinet (or a pair) won't play loud enough and clean enough for large spaces. If the sound system is for your bedroom or garage, passive systems would work just fine — maybe even better. But it isn't. Once you try to fill a relatively large space with equally loud sound you start to understand the problems. And it doesn't take stadiums, just normal size clubs. It is really difficult to produce the required loudness with passive boxes. Life would be a lot easier if you could just jack everyone into their own headphone amp — like a bunch of HC 6 or HC 4 Headphone Amps scattered throughout the audience. Let *them* do the work; then everyone could hear equally well, and choose their own listening level. But life is hard, and headphone amps must be restricted to practice and recording.

Monitor speakers on the other hand most likely have passive crossovers. Again, it's a matter of distance and loudness. Monitors are usually close and not overly loud — too loud and they will feed back into your microphone or be heard along with the main mix — not good. Monitor speakers are similar to hi-fi speakers, where passive designs dominate — because of the relatively small listening areas. It is quite easy to fill small listening rooms with pristine sounds even at ear-splitting levels. But move those same speakers into your local club and they will sound thin, dull and lifeless. Not only will they not play loud enough, but they may *need* the sonic benefits of sound bouncing off close walls to reinforce and fill the direct sound. In large venues, these walls are way too far away to benefit anyone.

So why not use a *bunch* of passive boxes? You can, and some people do. However, for reasons to follow, it only works for a couple of cabinets. Even so, you won't be able to get the high loudness levels if the room is large. Passive systems can only be optimized so much.

Once you start needing multiple cabinets, active crossovers become necessary. To get good coverage of like frequencies, you want to stack like-drivers. This prevents using passive boxes since each one contains (at least) a high-frequency driver and a low-frequency driver. It's easiest to put together a sound system when each cabinet covers only one frequency range. For instance, for a nice sounding 3-way system, you would have low-frequency boxes (the big ones), then medium-sized mid-frequency boxes and finally the smaller high-frequency boxes. These would be stacked — or

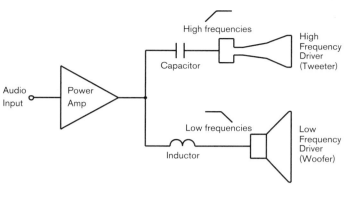

Passive 2-Way Crossover

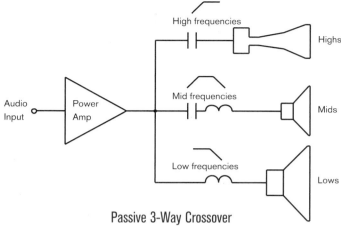

Passive 3-Way Crossover

hung, or both — in some sort of an *array*. A loudspeaker array is the optimum stacking shape for each set of cabinets to give the best combined coverage and overall sound. You've no doubt seen many different array shapes. There are tall towers, high walls, and all sorts of polyhedrons and arcs. The only efficient way to do this is with active crossovers.

Some smaller systems combine active and passive boxes. Even within a single cabinet it is common to find an active crossover used to separate the low- and mid-frequency drives, while a built-in passive network is used for the high-frequency driver. This is particularly common for super tweeters operating over the last audio octave. At the other end, an active crossover often is used to add a subwoofer to a passive 2-way system. All combinations are used, but each time a passive crossover shows up, it comes with problems.

One of these is power loss. Passive networks waste valuable power. The extra power needed to make the drivers louder, instead boils off the components and comes out of the box as heat — not sound. Therefore, passive units make you buy a bigger amp.

A couple of additional passive network problems has to do with their *impedance*. Impedance restricts power transfer; it's like resistance, only frequency sensitive. In order for the passive network to work exactly right, the *source impedance* (the amplifier's output plus the wiring impedance) must be as close to zero as possible and not frequency-dependent, and the *load impedance* (the loudspeaker's characteristics) must be fixed and not frequency-dependent (sorry — not in *this* universe; only on *Star Trek*). Since these things are not

possible, the passive network must be (at best), a simplified and compromised solution to a very complex problem. Consequently, the crossover's behavior changes with frequency — *not* something you want for a good sounding system.

One last thing to make matters worse. There is something called *back-emf* (back-*electromotive force*: literally, *back-voltage*) which further contributes to poor sounding speaker systems. This is the phenomena where, after the signal stops, the speaker cone continues moving, causing the voice coil to move through the magnetic field (now acting like a microphone), creating a *new* voltage that tries to drive the cable back to the amplifier's output! If the speaker is allowed to do this, the cone flops around like a dying fish. It does *not* sound good! The only way to stop back-emf is to make the loudspeaker "see" a dead short, i.e., zero ohms looking backward, or as close to it as possible — something that's *not gonna happen* with a passive network slung between it and the power amp.

All this, and not to mention that inductors saturate at high signal levels causing distortion — another reason you can't get enough loudness. Or the additional weight and bulk caused by the large inductors required for good low frequency response. Or that it is almost impossible to get high-quality steep slopes passively, so the response suffers. Or that inductors are way too good at picking up local radio, TV, emergency, and cellular broadcasts, and joyfully mixing them into your audio.

Such is life with passive speaker systems.

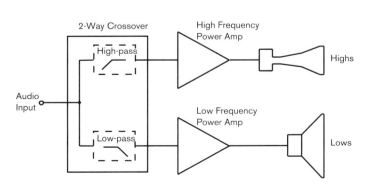

Active 2-Way Crossover

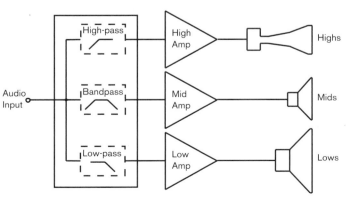

Active 3-Way Crossover

Active

Active crossover networks require a power supply to operate and usually come packaged in single-space, rack-mount units. (Although of late, *powered loudspeakers* with built-in active crossovers and power amplifiers are becoming increasingly popular.) Looking at the accompanying diagram shows how active crossovers differ from their passive cousins. For a 2-way system instead of one power amp, you now have two, but *they can be smaller for the same loudness level*. How *much* smaller depends on the *sensitivity* rating of the drivers (more on this later). Likewise a 3-way system requires three power amps. You also see and hear the terms *bi-amped*, and *tri-amped* applied to 2- and 3-way systems.

Active crossovers cure many ills of the passive systems. Since the crossover filters themselves are safely tucked away inside their own box, away from the driving and loading impedance problems plaguing passive units, they can be made to operate in an almost mathematically perfect manner. Extremely steep, smooth and well-behaved crossover slopes are easily achieved by active circuitry.

There are no amplifier power loss problems, since active circuits operate from their own low voltage power supplies. And with the inefficiencies of the passive network removed, the power amps more easily achieve the loudness levels required.

Loudspeaker jitters and tremors caused by inadequately damped back-emf all but disappear once the passive network is removed. What remains is the amplifier's inherent output impedance and that of the connecting wire. Here's where the term *damping factor* comes up. [Note that the word is damp-*ing*, not damp-*ning* as is so often heard; impress your friends.] Damping is a measure of a system's ability to control the motion of the loudspeaker cone after the signal disappears. No more dying fish.

Siegfried & Russ

Active crossovers go by many names. First, they are either 2-way or 3-way (or even 4-way and 5-way). Then there is the slope rate and order: 24 dB/octave (4th-order), or 18 dB/octave (3rd-order), and so on. And finally there is a name for the *kind* of design. The two most common being *Linkwitz-Riley* and *Butterworth*, named after Siegfried Linkwitz and Russ Riley who first proposed this application, and Stanley Butterworth who first described the response in 1930. Up until the mid '80s, the 3rd-order (18 dB/octave) Butterworth design dominated, but still had some problems. Since then, the development (pioneered by Rane and Sundholm) of the 4th-order (24 dB/octave) Linkwitz-Riley design solved these problems, and today is the norm.

What this adds up to is *active crossovers are the rule*. Luckily, the hardest thing about an active crossover is getting the money to buy one. After that, most of the work is already done for you. At the most basic level all you really need from an active crossover are two things: to let you set the correct crossover point, and to let you balance driver levels. That's all. The first is done by consulting the loudspeaker manufacturer's data sheet, and dialing it in on the front panel. (That's assuming a complete factory-made 2-way loudspeaker cabinent, for example. If the box is homemade, then both drivers must be carefully selected so they have the *same crossover frequency*, otherwise a severe response problem can result.) Balancing levels is necessary because high frequency drivers are more *efficient* than low frequency drivers. This means that if you put the same amount of power into each driver, one will sound louder than the other. The one that is the most efficient plays louder. Several methods to balance drivers are always outlined in any good owner's manual.

EQUALIZERS

You may have heard it said that equalizers are nothing more than glorified tone controls. That's pretty accurate and helps explain their usefulness and importance. Simply put, equalizers allow you to change the tonal balance of whatever you are controlling. You can increase (*boost*) or decrease (*cut*) on a band-by-band basis just the desired frequencies. Equalizers come in all different sizes and shapes, varying greatly in design and complexity. Select from a simple single-channel unit with 10 controls on 1-octave frequency spacing (a *mono 10-band octave equalizer*), all the way up to a full-featured, two-channel box with 31 controls on 1/3-octave frequency spacing (a *stereo 1/3-oct equalizer*). There are *graphic* models with slide controls (*sliders*) that roughly "graph" the equalizer's frequency response by the shape they form, and there are *parametric* models where you choose the frequency, amplitude, and bandwidth desired (the *filter parameters* — see diagram) for each band provided. Far and away, the simplest and most popular are the 1/3- and 2/3-octave graphics. They offer the best combination of control, complexity and cost.

In selecting graphic equalizers, the primary features to consider are the number of input/output channels, the number of boost/cut bands, the center-frequency spacing of each, and the *bandwidth behavior*. This last one may at first seem a bit odd, but it is perhaps the most important characteristic. Bandwidth behavior is either *constant-Q* or *variable-Q* (see diagrams). The *quality factor*, or *Q*, of a circuit relates to its bandwidth in an *inverse* manner. That is, narrow bandwidths result from high-Q circuits and wide bandwidths come from low-Q circuits. In the early '80s, Rane developed the first constant-Q designs to preserve the same shape (bandwidth) over the entire boost/cut range. In contrast, variable-Q designs have varying bandwidths (the shape changes) as a function of boost/cut amount. They start out very wide for small amplitude changes and become quite narrow for large changes. Rane's constant-Q design became the most popular, and changed the industry.

Using Equalizers

Equalizers can do wonders for a sound system. Let's start with loudspeaker performance. An unfortunate truth regarding budget loudspeakers is they don't sound very good. Usually this is due to an uneven frequency response, or more correctly a non-flat *power response*. An ideal cabinet has a flat power response. This means that if you pick, say, 1 kHz as a reference signal, use it to drive the speaker with exactly one watt, measure the loudness, and sweep the generator over the speaker's entire frequency range, *all frequencies will measure equally loud*. Sadly, with all but the most expensive speaker systems, they will not. Equalizers can help these frequency deficiencies. By adding a little here and taking away a little there, pretty soon you create an acceptable power response — and a whole lot better sounding system. It's surprising how just a little equalization can change a poor sounding system into something quite decent.

The best way to deal with budget speakers — although it costs more — is to commit *one* equalizer channel for *each* cabinet. This becomes a marriage. The equalizer is set, a security cover is bolted-on, and forever more they are inseparable. (Use additional equalizers to assist with the room problems.) And now for the hard part, but the most important part: If you do your measurements *outside* (no reflections off walls or ceiling) and *up in the air* (no reflections off the ground) you can get a very accurate picture of just the loudspeaker's response, free from room effects. This gives you the *room-independent* response. This is really important, because *no matter where this box is used, it has these problems*. Of course, you must make sure the cost of the budget speaker plus the equalizer adds up to substantially less than buying a really flat speaker system to begin with. Luckily (or should this be *sadly*) this is usually the case. Again, the truth is that *most* cabinets are not flat. It is only the very expensive loudspeakers that have world-class responses. (Hmmm ... maybe *that's* why they cost so much!)

The next thing you can do with equalizers is to improve the way each venue sounds. Every room sounds different — fact of life — fact of physics. Using exactly the same equipment, playing exactly the same music in exactly the same way, different rooms sound different — guaranteed. Each enclosed space treats your sound differently.

Reflected sound causes the problems. What the audience hears is made up of the *direct* sound (what comes straight out of the loudspeaker directly to the listener) and *reflected* sound (it bounces off *everything* before getting to the listener). And if the room is big enough, then *reverberation* comes into play, which is all the reflected sound that has traveled so far, and for such a (relatively) long time that it arrives and *re-arrives* at the listener delayed enough to sound like a second and third source, or even an *echo* if the room is *really* big.

It's basically a geometry problem. Each room differs in its dimensions; not only in its basic length-by-width size, but in its ceiling height, the distance from you and your equipment to the audience, what's hung (or not hung), on the walls, how many windows and doors there are, and where. Every detail about the space affects your sound. And regretfully, there is very little you can do about any of it. Most of the factors affecting your sound you cannot change. You certainly can't change the dimensions, or alter the window and door locations. But there are a few things you can do, and equalization is one of them. But before you equalize you want to optimize *how* and *where* you place your speakers. This is probably the number one item to attend to. Keep your loudspeakers out of corners whenever possible. Remove all restrictions between your speakers and your audience, including banners, stage equipment, and performers. What you want is for most of the sound your audience hears to come directly from the speakers. You want to minimize all reflected sound. If you have done a good job in selecting and equalizing your loudspeak-

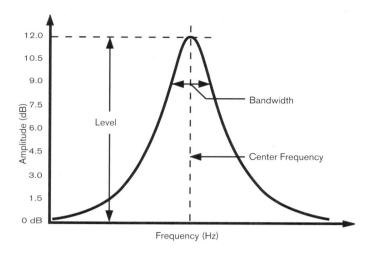

Bandpass Filter Parameters

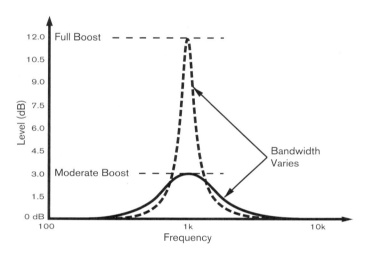

Variable-Q Graphic

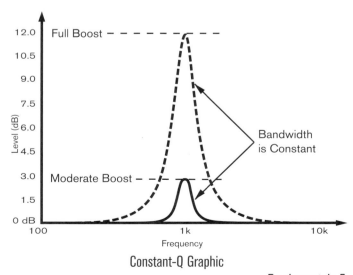

Constant-Q Graphic

ers, then you already know your direct sound is good. So what's left is to minimize the reflected sound.

Next use equalization to help with some of the room's more troublesome features. If the room is exceptionally bright you can beef up the low end to help offset it, or roll-off some of the highs. Or if the room tends to be boomy, you can tone-down the low end to reduce the resonance. Another way EQ is quite effective is in controlling troublesome *feedback* tones. Feedback is that terrible squeal or scream sound systems get when the audio from the loudspeaker gets picked-up by one of the stage microphones, re-amplified and pumped out the speaker, only to be picked-up again by the microphone, and re-amplified, and so on. Most often, this happens when the system is playing loud. Which makes sense, because for softer sounds, the signal either isn't big enough to make it to the microphone, or if it does, it is too small to build-up. The problem is one of an out-of-control, closed-loop, positive-feedback system building up until something breaks, or the audience leaves. Use your equalizer to cut those frequencies that want to howl; you not only stop the squeal, but you allow the system to play louder. The technical phrase for this is *maximizing system gain before feedback.*

It's important to understand at the beginning that you cannot *fix* room related sound problems with equalization, but you can *move* the trouble spots around. You can *rearrange* things sonically, which helps *tame* excesses. You win by making it sound better. Equalization helps.

Equalizers are useful in augmenting your instrument or voice. With practice you will learn to use your equalizer to enhance your sound for your best personal expression: deepen the lows, fill the middle, or exaggerate the highs — whatever you want. Just as an equalizer can improve the sound of a poor loudspeaker, it can improve the sound of a marginal microphone, or enhance any musical instrument. Equalizers give you that something extra, that *edge*. (We all know where "radio voices" *really* come from.)

Seeing Sound

To make loudspeaker and sound system measurements easy, you need a real-time analyzer (RTA). An RTA allows you to see the power response, not only for the loudspeaker, but even more importantly, for the whole system. Stand-alone RTAs use an LED or LCD matrix to display the response. A built-in *pink noise* generator (a special kind of shaped noise containing all audible frequencies, optimized for measuring sound systems) is used as the test signal. A measuring microphone is included for sampling the response. The display is arranged to show amplitude verses frequency. Depending upon cost, the number of frequency columns varies from 10 on 1-octave centers, up to 31 on 1/3-octave centers (agreeing with graphic equalizers). Amplitude range and precision varies with price. With the cost of laptop computers tumbling, the latest form of RTA involves an accessory box and software that works with your computer. These are particularly nice, and loaded with special memory, calculations and multipurpose functions like also being an elaborate SPL meter. Highly recommended if the budget allows. For a budget-effective alternative, see Rane's RA 27 for an easy to use, low-cost unit. Rane pioneered the simple

RTA with the RA 27's introduction in 1984. Not only was the RA 27 the first, but it remains the leader in affordable, easy-to-use, precise and reliable RTAs.

DYNAMIC CONTROLLERS

Dynamic controllers or *processors* represent a class of signal processing devices used to alter an audio signal based solely upon its *frequency content* and *amplitude level*, thus the term "dynamic" since the processing is completely program dependent. The two most common dynamic effects are *compressors* and *expanders*, with *limiters* and *noise gates* (or just "gates") being special cases of these.

The *dynamic range* of an audio passage is the ratio of the loudest (undistorted) signal to the quietest (just audible) signal, expressed in dB. Usually the maximum output signal is restricted by the size of the power supplies (you cannot swing more voltage than is available), while the minimum output signal is fixed by the noise floor (you cannot put out an audible signal less than the noise). Professional-grade analog signal processing equipment can output maximum levels of +26 dBu, with the best noise floors being down around -94 dBu. This gives a maximum *dynamic range* of 120 dB (equivalent to 20-bit digital audio) — pretty impressive number — but very difficult to work with. Thus were born dynamic processors.

Compressors

Compressors are signal processing units used to reduce (*compress*) the dynamic range of the signal passing through them. The modern use for compressors is to turn down just the loudest signals *dynamically*. For instance, an input dynamic range of 110 dB might pass through a compressor and exit with a new dynamic range of 70 dB. This clever bit of processing is normally done using a VCA (voltage controlled amplifier) whose gain is determined by a control voltage derived from the input signal. Therefore, whenever the input signal exceeds the threshold point, the control voltage becomes proportional to the signal's dynamic content. This lets the music peaks turn down the gain. Before compressors, a human did this at the mixing board and we called it *gain-riding*. This person literally turned down the gain anytime it got too loud for the system to handle.

You need to reduce the dynamic range because extreme ranges of dynamic material are very difficult for sound systems to handle. If you turn it up as loud as you want for the average signals, then along comes these huge musical peaks, which are vital to the *punch* and *drama* of the music, yet are way too large for the power amps and loudspeakers to handle. Either the power amps clip, or the loudspeakers *bottom out* (reach their travel limits), or both — and the system sounds *terrible*. Or going the other way, if you set the system gain to prevent these overload occurrences, then when things get nice and quiet, and the vocals drop real low, nobody can hear a thing. *It's always something.* So you buy a compressor.

Using it is quite simple: Set a *threshold* point, above which everything will be turned down a certain amount, and then select a *ratio* defining just how much a "certain amount" is. All audio below the threshold point is unaffected and all audio above this point is compressed by the ratio amount. The earlier example of reducing 110 dB to 70 dB requires a ratio setting of 1.6:1 (110/70 = 1.6). The key to understanding compressors is to always think in terms of *increasing level changes **in dB** above the threshold point*. A compressor makes these increases smaller. From our example, for every *1.6 dB increase* above the threshold point the output only *increases 1 dB*. In this regard *compressors make loud sounds quieter*. If the sound gets louder by 1.6 dB and the output only increases by 1 dB, then the loud sound has been made quieter.

Some compressors include *attack* and *release* controls. The *attack time* is the amount of time that passes between the moment the input signal exceeds the threshold and the moment that the gain is actually reduced. The *release time* is just the opposite — the amount of time that passes between the moment the input signal drops below the threshold and the moment that the gain is restored. These controls are very difficult to set, and yet once set, rarely need changing. Because of this difficulty, and the terrible sounding consequences of wrong settings, Rane correctly presets these controls to cover a wide variety of music and speech — one

less thing for you to worry about.

System overload is not the only place we find compressors. Another popular use is in the *making* of sound. For example when used in conjunction with microphones and musical instrument pick-ups, compressors help determine the final *timbre* (tone) by selectively compressing specific frequencies and waveforms. Common examples are "fattening" drum sounds, increasing guitar sustain, vocal "smoothing," and "bringing up" specific sounds out of the mix, etc. It is quite amazing what a little compression can do. Check your owner's manual for more tips.

Expanders

Expanders are signal processing units used to increase (*expand*) the dynamic range of the signal passing through it. However, modern expanders operate only *below the set threshold point*, that is, they operate only on low-level audio. Operating in this manner they make the *quiet parts quieter*. The term *downward expander* or *downward expansion* evolved to describe this type of application. The most common use is noise reduction. For example, say, an

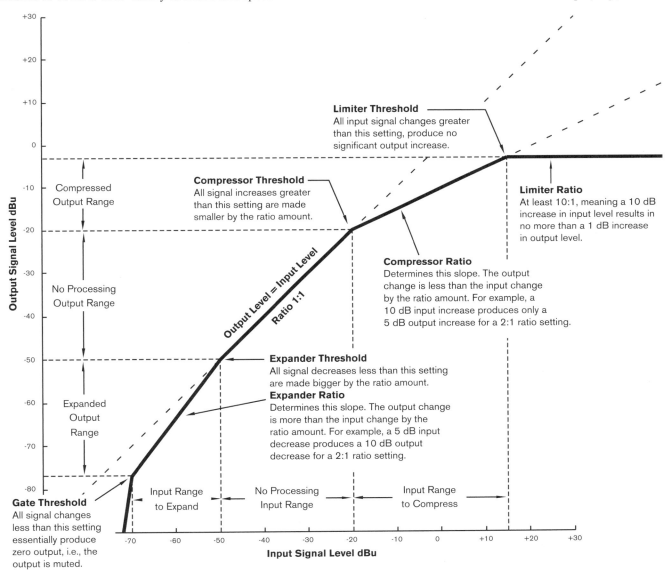

Gate/Expander/Compressor/Limiter Action

Fundamentals-7

expander's threshold level is set to be just below the quietest vocal level being recorded, and the ratio control is set for 2:1. What happens is this: when the vocals stop, the signal level drops below the set point down to the noise floor. There has been a step decrease from the smallest signal level down to the noise floor. If that step change is, say, -10 dB, then the expander's output attenuates 20 dB (i.e., due to the 2:1 ratio, a 10 dB decrease becomes a 20 dB decrease), thus resulting in a noise reduction improvement of 10 dB. It's now 10 dB quieter than it would have been without the expander.

Limiters

Limiters are compressors with fixed *ratios* of 10:1 or greater. Here, the dynamic action prevents the audio signal from becoming any bigger than the *threshold setting*. For example, say the threshold is set for +16 dBu and a musical peak suddenly comes along and causes the input to jump by 10 dB to +26 dB, the output will only increase by 1 dB to +17 dBu — basically remaining level. Limiters find use in preventing equipment and recording media overloads. A limiter is the extreme case of compression.

You will hear the term *pumping* used in conjunction with poorly designed or improperly set limiters. *Pumping* describes an audible problem caused by actually *hearing the gain change* — it makes a kind of "pumping" sound. This is particularly a problem with limiters that operate too abruptly. Rest assured that Rane limiters are designed not to have *any* audible side-effects.

Noise Gates

Noise gates (or *gates*) are expanders with fixed "infinite" downward expansion ratios. They are used extensively for controlling unwanted noise, such as preventing "open" microphones and "hot" instrument pick-ups from introducing extraneous sounds into your system. When the incoming audio signal drops below the *threshold* point, the gate prevents further output by reducing the gain to "zero." Typically, this means attenuating all signals by about 80 dB. Therefore once audio drops below the threshold, the output level basically becomes the residual noise of the gate. Common terminology refers to the gate "opening" and "closing." A gate is the extreme case of downward expansion.

Just as poorly designed limiters can cause pumping, poorly designed gates can cause *breathing*. The term *breathing* is used to describe an audible problem caused by being able to hear the noise floor of a product rise and lower, sounding a lot like the unit was "breathing." It takes careful design to get all the dynamic timing exactly right so breathing does not occur. Rane works very hard to make sure all of its dynamic processors have no audible funny business.

Another popular application for noise gates is to enhance musical instrument sounds, especially percussion instruments. Correctly setting a noise gate's *attack* (turn-on) and *release* (turn-off) adds "punch," or "tightens" the percussive sound, making it more pronounced — this is how Phil Collins gets his cool snare sound, for instance.

©Rane Corporation   10802 47th Ave. W.,   Mukilteo WA 98275-5098   TEL (425)355-6000   FAX (425)347-7757   WEB http://www.rane.com

Audio Specifications

- **Audio Distortion**
- **THD - Total Harmonic Distortion**
- **THD+N - Total Harmonic Distortion + Noise**
- **IMD – SMPTE - Intermodulation Distortion**
- **IMD – ITU-R (CCIF) - Intermodulation Distortion**
- **S/N or SNR - Signal-To-Noise Ratio**
- **EIN - Equivalent Input Noise**
- **BW - Bandwidth or Frequency Response**
- **CMR or CMRR - Common-Mode Rejection**
- **Dynamic Range**
- **Crosstalk or Channel Separation**
- **Input & Output Impedance**
- **Maximum Input Level**
- **Maximum Output Level**
- **Maximum Gain**
- **Caveat Emptor**

Dennis Bohn
Rane Corporation

RaneNote 145
© 2000 Rane Corporation

Objectively comparing pro audio signal processing products is often impossible. Missing on too many data sheets are the *conditions* used to obtain the published data. Audio specifications come with conditions. Tests are not performed in a vacuum with random parameters. They are conducted using rigorous procedures and the conditions must be stated along with the test results.

To understand the conditions, you must first understand the tests. This note introduces the classic audio tests used to characterize audio performance. It describes each test and the conditions necessary to conduct the test.

Apologies are made for the many abbreviations, terms and jargon necessary to tell the story. Please make liberal use of Rane's *Pro Audio Reference* (*www.rane.com/digi-dic.html*) to help decipher things. Also, note that when the term *impedance* is used, it is assumed a constant pure resistance, unless otherwise stated.

The accompanying table (back page) summarizes common audio specifications and their required conditions. Each test is described next in the order of appearance in the table.

Audio Distortion

By its name you know it is a measure of unwanted signals. *Distortion* is the name given to anything that alters a pure input signal in any way other than changing its magnitude. The most common forms of distortion are unwanted components or artifacts added to the original signal, including random and hum-related noise. A spectral analysis of the output shows these unwanted components. If a piece of gear is perfect the spectrum of the output shows only the original signal – nothing else – no added components, no added noise – nothing but the original signal. The following tests are designed to measure different forms of audio distortion.

THD. *Total Harmonic Distortion*

What is tested? A form of nonlinearity that causes unwanted signals to be added to the input signal that are *harmonically* related to it. The spectrum of the output shows added frequency components at 2x the original signal, 3x, 4x, 5x, and so on, but no components at, say, 2.6x the original, or any fractional multiplier, only whole number multipliers.

How is it measured? This technique excites the unit with a single high purity sine wave and then examines the output for evidence of any frequencies other than the one applied. Performing a spectral analysis on this signal (using a spectrum, or FFT analyzer) shows that in addition to the original input sine wave, there are components at harmonic intervals of the input frequency. Total harmonic distortion (THD) is then defined as the ratio of the rms voltage of the harmonics to that of the fundamental component. This is accomplished by using a spectrum analyzer to obtain the level of each harmonic and performing an rms summation. The level is then divided by the fundamental level, and cited as the total harmonic distortion (expressed in percent). Measuring individual harmonics with precision is difficult, tedious, and not commonly done; consequently, *THD+N* (see below) is the more common test. ***Caveat Emptor:*** *THD+N is always going to be a larger number than just plain THD. For this reason, unscrupulous (or clever, depending on your viewpoint) manufacturers choose to spec just THD, instead of the more meaningful and easily compared THD+N.*

Required Conditions. Since individual harmonic amplitudes are measured, the manufacturer must state the test signal *frequency*, its *level*, and the *gain* conditions set on the tested unit, as well as the *number of harmonics* measured. Hopefully, it's obvious to the reader that the THD of a 10 kHz signal at a +20 dBu level using maximum gain, is apt to differ from the THD of a 1 kHz signal at a -10 dBV level and unity gain. And more different yet, if one manufacturer measures two harmonics while another measures five.

Full disclosure specs will test harmonic distortion over the entire 20 Hz to 20 kHz audio range (this is done easily by sweeping and plotting the results), at the pro audio level of +4 dBu. For all signal processing equipment, *except mic preamps*, the preferred gain setting is unity. For mic pre amps, the standard practice is to use maximum gain. Too often THD is spec'd only at 1 kHz, or worst, with no mention of frequency at all, and nothing about level or gain settings, let alone harmonic count.

Correct: THD (5th-order) less than 0.01%, +4 dBu, 20–20 kHz, unity gain

Wrong: THD less than 0.01%

THD+N. *Total Harmonic Distortion + Noise*

What is tested? Similar to the THD test above, except instead of measuring individual harmonics this tests measures everything added to the input signal. This is a wonderful test since *everything* that comes out of the unit that isn't the pure test signal is measured and included – harmonics, hum, noise, RFI, buzz – everything.

How is it measured? THD+N is the rms summation of all signal components (excluding the fundamental) over some prescribed bandwidth. Distortion analyzers make this measurement by removing the fundamental (*using a deep and narrow notch filter*) and measuring what's left using a bandwidth filter (typically 22 kHz, 30 kHz or 80 kHz). The remainder contains harmonics as well as random noise and other artifacts.

Weighting filters are rarely used. When they are used, too often it is to hide pronounced AC mains hum artifacts. *An exception is the strong argument to use the ITU-R (CCIR) 468 curve because of its proven correlation to what is heard. However, since it adds 12 dB of gain in the critical midband (the whole point) it makes THD+N measurements bigger, so marketeers prevent its widespread use.*

[*Historical Note: Many old distortion analyzers labeled "THD" actually measured THD+N.*]

Required Conditions. Same as THD (*frequency, level & gain settings*), except instead of stating the number of harmonics measured, the residual noise bandwidth is spec'd, along with whatever weighting filter was used. The preferred value is a 20 kHz (or 22 kHz) measurement bandwidth, and "flat," i.e., no weighting filter.

Conflicting views exist regarding THD+N bandwidth measurements. One argument goes: it makes no sense to measure THD at 20 kHz if your measurement bandwidth doesn't include the harmonics. Valid point. And one supported by the IEC, which says that THD should not be tested any higher than 6 kHz, if measuring five harmonics using a 30 kHz bandwidth, or 10 kHz, if only measuring the first three harmonics. Another argument states that since most people can't even hear the fundamental at 20 kHz, let alone the second harmonic, there is no need to measure anything beyond 20 kHz. Fair enough. However, the case is made that using an 80 kHz bandwidth is crucial, not because of 20 kHz harmonics, but because it reveals other artifacts that can indicate high frequency problems. All true points, but competition being what it is, standardizing on publishing THD+N figures measured flat over 22 kHz seems justified, while still using an 80 kHz bandwidth during the design, development and manufacturing stages.

Correct: THD+N less than 0.01%, +4 dBu, 20–20 kHz, unity gain, 20 kHz BW

Wrong: THD less than 0.01%

IMD – SMPTE. *Intermodulation Distortion – SMPTE Method*

What is tested? A more meaningful test than THD, intermodulation distortion gives a measure of distortion products *not harmonically related* to the pure signal. This is important since these artifacts make music sound harsh and unpleasant.

Intermodulation distortion testing was first adopted in the U.S. as a practical procedure in the motion picture industry in 1939 by the Society of Motion Picture Engineers (SMPE – *no "T" [television] yet*) and made into a standard in 1941.

How is it measured? The test signal is a low frequency (60 Hz) and a *non-harmonically related* high frequency (7 kHz) tone, summed together in a 4:1 amplitude ratio. (*Other frequencies and amplitude ratios are used; for example, DIN*

favors 250 Hz & 8 kHz.) This signal is applied to the unit, and the output signal is examined for modulation of the upper frequency by the low frequency tone. As with harmonic distortion measurement, this is done with a spectrum analyzer or a dedicated intermodulation distortion analyzer. The modulation components of the upper signal appear as sidebands spaced at multiples of the lower frequency tone. The amplitudes of the sidebands are rms summed and expressed as a percentage of the upper frequency level.

[*Noise has little effect on SMPTE measurements because the test uses a low pass filter that sets the measurement bandwidth, thus restricting noise components; therefore there is no need for an "IM+N" test.*]

Required Conditions. SMPTE specifies this test use 60 Hz and 7 kHz combined in a 12 dB ratio (4:1) and that the peak value of the signal be stated along with the results. Strictly speaking, all that needs stating is "SMPTE IM" and the peak value used. However, measuring the peak value is difficult. Alternatively, a common method is to set the low frequency tone (60 Hz) for +4 dBu and then mixing the 7 kHz tone at a value of –8 dBu (12 dB less).

Correct: IMD (SMPTE) less than 0.01%, 60Hz/7kHz, 4:1, +4 dBu

Wrong: IMD less than 0.01%

IMD – ITU-R (CCIF). *Intermodulation Distortion – ITU-R Method*

What is tested? This tests for *non-harmonic* nonlinearities, using two equal amplitude, closely spaced, high frequency tones, and looking for beat frequencies between them. Use of beat frequencies for distortion detection dates back to work first documented in Germany in 1929, but was not considered a standard until 1937, when the CCIF (International Telephonic Consultative Committee) recommend the test. [*This test is often mistakenly referred to as the CCIR method (as opposed to the CCIF method). A mistake compounded by the many correct audio references to the CCIR 468 weighting filter.*] Ultimately, the CCIF became the radiocommunications sector (ITU-R) of the ITU (International Telecommunications Union), therefore the test is now known as the IMD (ITU-R).

How is it measured? The common test signal is a pair of equal amplitude tones spaced 1 kHz apart. Nonlinearity in the unit causes intermodulation products between the two signals. These are found by subtracting the two tones to find the first location at 1 kHz, then subtracting the second tone from twice the first tone, and then turning around and subtracting the first tone from twice the second, and so on. Usually only the first two or three components are measured, but for the oft-seen case of 19 kHz and 20 kHz, only the 1 kHz component is measured.

Required Conditions. Many variations exist for this test. Therefore, the manufacturer needs to clearly spell out the *two frequencies* used, and their *level*. The ratio is understood to be 1:1.

Correct: IMD (ITU-R) less than 0.01%, 19 kHz/20 kHz, 1:1, +4 dBu

Wrong: IMD less than 0.01%

S/N or SNR. *Signal-To-Noise Ratio*

What is tested? This specification indirectly tells you how noisy a unit is. S/N is calculated by measuring a unit's output noise, with no signal present, and all controls set to a prescribed manner. This figure is used to calculate a ratio between it and a fixed output reference signal, with the result expressed in dB.

How is it measured? No input signal is used, however the input is not left open, or unterminated. The usual practice is to leave the unit connected to the signal generator (with its low output impedance) set for zero volts. Alternatively, a resistor equal to the expected driving impedance is connected between the inputs. The magnitude of the output noise is measured using an rms-detecting voltmeter. Noise voltage is a function of bandwidth – wider the bandwidth, the greater the noise. This is an inescapable physical fact. Thus, a bandwidth is selected for the measuring voltmeter. If this is not done, the noise voltage measures extremely high, but does not correlate well with what is heard. The most common bandwidth seen is 22 kHz (*the extra 2 kHz allows the bandwidth-limiting filter to take affect without reducing the response at 20 kHz*). This is called a "flat" measurement, since all frequencies are measured equally.

Alternatively, noise filters, or weighting filters, are used when measuring noise. Most often seen is *A-weighting*, but a more accurate one is called the ITU-R (*old CCIR*) 468 filter. This filter is preferred because it shapes the measured noise in a way that relates well with what's heard.

Pro audio equipment often lists an A-weighted noise spec – not because it correlates well with our hearing – but because it can "hide" nasty hum components that make for bad noise specs. *Always wonder if a manufacturer is hiding something when you see A-weighting specs.* While noise filters are entirely appropriate and even desired when measuring other types of noise, it is an abuse to use them to disguise equipment hum problems. A-weighting rolls off the low-end, thus reducing the most annoying 2nd and 3rd line harmonics by about 20 dB and 12 dB respectively. Sometimes A-weighting can "improve" a noise spec by 10 dB.

The argument used to justify this is that the ear is not sensitive to low frequencies at low levels (´ la Fletcher-Munson equal loudness curves), but that argument is false. Fletcher-Munson curves document equal loudness of single tones. Their curve tells us nothing of the ear's astonishing ability to sync in and lock onto repetitive tones – like hum components – even when these tones lie beneath the noise floor. This is what A-weighting can hide. For this reason most manufacturers shy from using it; instead they spec S/N figures "flat" or use the ITU-R 468 curve (*which actually makes their numbers look worse, but correlate better with the real world*).

However, an exception has arisen: Digital products using A/D and D/A converters regularly spec S/N and dynamic range using A-weighting. This follows the semiconductor industry's practice of spec'ing delta-sigma data converters A-weighted. They do this because they use clever noise shaping tricks to create 24-bit converters with acceptable noise behavior. All these tricks squeeze the noise out of the audio bandwidth and push it up into the higher inaudible frequencies. The noise may be inaudible, but it is still measurable and can give misleading results unless limited. When used this way, the A-weighting filter rolls off the high frequency noise better than the flat 22 kHz filter and compares better with the listening experience. The fact that the low-end also rolls off is irrelevant in this application. (See RaneNote 137: *Digital Dharma of Audio A/D Converters*)

Required Conditions. In order for the published figure to have any meaning, it must include the *measurement bandwidth*, including any *weighting filters* and the *reference signal level*. Stating that a unit has a "S/N = 90 dB" is meaningless without knowing what the signal level is, and over what bandwidth the noise was measured. For example if one product references S/N to their maximum output level of, say, +20 dBu, and another product has the same stated 90 dB S/N, but their reference level is + 4 dBu, then the second product is, in fact, 16 dB quieter. Likewise, you cannot accurately compare numbers if one unit is measured over a BW of 80 kHz and another uses 20 kHz, or if one is measured flat and the other uses A-weighting. By far however, the most common problem is not stating *any* conditions.

Correct: S/N = 90 dB re +4 dBu, 22 kHz BW, unity gain
Wrong: S/N = 90 dB

EIN. *Equivalent Input Noise* or *Input Referred Noise*

What is tested? Equivalent input noise, or input referred noise, is how noise is spec'd on mixing consoles, standalone mic preamps and other signal processing units with mic inputs. The problem in measuring mixing consoles (and all mic preamps) is knowing ahead of time how much gain is going to be used. The mic stage itself is the dominant noise generator; therefore, the output noise is almost totally determined by the amount of gain: turn the gain up, and the output noise goes up accordingly. Thus, the EIN is the amount of noise *added* to the input signal. Both are then amplified to obtain the final output signal.

For example, say your mixer has an EIN of –130 dBu. This means the noise is 130 dB below a reference point of 0.775 volts (0 dBu). If your microphone puts out, say, -50 dBu under normal conditions, then the S/N at the input to the mic preamp is 80 dB (i.e., the added noise is 80 dB below the input signal). This is uniquely determined by the magnitude of the input signal and the EIN. From here on out, turning up the gain increases both the signal and the noise by the same amount.

How is it measured? With the gain set for maximum and the input terminated with the expected source impedance, the output noise is measured with an rms voltmeter fitted with a bandwidth or weighting filter.

Required Conditions. This is a spec where test conditions are critical. It is very easy to deceive without them. Since high-gain mic stages greatly amplify source noise, the *terminating input resistance* must be stated. Two equally quiet inputs will measure vastly different if not using the identical input impedance. The standard source impedance is 150 ohms. As unintuitive as it may be, *a plain resistor, hooked up to nothing, generates noise*, and the larger the resistor value the greater the noise. It is called *thermal noise* or *Johnson noise* (after its discoverer J. B. Johnson, in 1928)

and results from the motion of electron charge of the atoms making up the resistor. All that moving about is called thermal agitation (caused by heat – the hotter the resistor, the noisier).

The input terminating resistor defines the lower limit of noise performance. In use, *a mic stage cannot be quieter than the source.* A trick which unscrupulous manufacturers may use is to spec their mic stage with the input shorted – a big no-no, since it does not represent the real performance of the preamp.

The next biggie in spec'ing the EIN of mic stages is *bandwidth*. This same thermal noise limit of the input terminating resistance is a strong function of measurement bandwidth. For example, the noise voltage generated by the standard 150 ohm input resistor, measured over a bandwidth of 20 kHz (and room temperature) is –131 dBu, i.e., you cannot have an operating mic stage, with a 150 ohm source, quieter than –131 dBu. However, if you use only a 10 kHz bandwidth, then the noise drops to –134 dBu, a big 3 dB improvement. (*For those paying close attention: it is not 6 dB like you might expect since the bandwidth is half. It is a square root function, so it is reduced by the square root of one-half, or 0.707, which is 3 dB less*).

Since the measured output noise is such a strong function of bandwidth and gain, it is recommended to use no weighting filters. They only complicate comparison among manufacturers. Remember: if a manufacturer's reported EIN seems too good to be true, look for the details. They may not be lying, only using favorable conditions to deceive.

Correct: EIN = -130 dBu, 22 kHz BW, max gain, Rs = 150 ohms
Wrong: EIN = -130 dBu

BW. *Bandwidth* or *Frequency Response*

What is tested? The unit's bandwidth or the range of frequencies it passes. All frequencies above and below a unit's Frequency Response are attenuated – sometimes severely.

How is it measured? A 1 kHz tone of high purity and precise amplitude is applied to the unit and the output measured using a dB-calibrated rms voltmeter. This value is set as the 0 dB reference point. Next, the generator is swept upward in frequency (from the 1 kHz reference point) keeping the source amplitude precisely constant, until it is reduced in level by the amount specified. This point becomes the upper frequency limit. The test generator is then swept down in frequency from 1 kHz until the lower frequency limit is found by the same means.

Required Conditions. The reduction in output level is relative to 1 kHz; therefore, the 1 kHz level establishes the 0 dB point. What you need to know is how far down is the response where the manufacturer measured it. Is it 0.5 dB, 3 dB, or (*among loudspeaker manufacturers*) maybe even 10 dB?

Note that there is no discussion of an increase, that is, no mention of the amplitude *rising*. If a unit's frequency response rises at any point, especially the endpoints, it indicates a fundamental instability problem and you should run from the store. Properly designed solid-state audio equipment does not *ever* gain in amplitude when set for flat response (tubes or valve designs using output transformers are a different story and are not dealt with here). If you have ever wondered why manufacturers state a limit of "+0 dB", that is why. The preferred condition here is at least *20 Hz to 20 kHz* measured *+0/-0.5 dB*.

Correct: Frequency Response = 20–20 kHz, +0/-0.5 dB
Wrong: Frequency Response = 20-20 kHz

CMR *or* CMRR. *Common-Mode Rejection* or *Common-Mode Rejection Ratio*

What is tested? This gives a measure of a balanced input stage's ability to reject common-mode signals. *Common-mode* is the name given to signals applied simultaneously to both inputs. Normal *differential* signals arrive as a pair of equal voltages that are opposite in polarity: one applied to the positive input and the other to the negative input. A common-mode signal drives both inputs with the same polarity. It is the job of a well designed balanced input stage to amplify differential signals, while simultaneously rejecting common-mode signals. Most common-mode signals result from RFI (radio frequency interference) and EMI (electromagnetic interference, e.g., hum and buzz) signals inducing themselves into the connecting cable. Since most cables consist of a tightly twisted pair, the interfering signals are induced equally into each wire. The other big contributors to common-mode signals are power supply and ground related problems between the source and the balanced input stage.

How is it measured? Either the unit is adjusted for unity gain, or its gain is first determined and noted. Next, a generator is hooked up to drive both inputs simultaneously through two equal and carefully matched source resistors valued at one-half the expected source resistance, i.e., each input is driven from one-half the normal source impedance. The output of the balanced stage is measured using an rms voltmeter and noted. A ratio is calculated by dividing the generator input voltage by the measured output voltage. This ratio is then multiplied by the gain of the unit, and the answer expressed in dB.

Required Conditions. The results may be frequency-dependent, therefore, the manufacturer must state the *frequency tested* along with the CMR figure. Most manufacturers spec this at 1 kHz for comparison reasons. The results are assumed constant for all input levels, unless stated otherwise.

Correct: CMRR = 40 dB @ 1 kHz
Wrong: CMRR = 40 dB

Dynamic Range

What is tested? First, the maximum output voltage and then the output noise floor are measured and their ratio expressed in dB. Sounds simple and it is simple, but you still have to be careful when comparing units.

How is it measured? The maximum output voltage is measured as described below, and the output noise floor is measured using an rms voltmeter fitted with a bandwidth filter (with the input generator set for zero volts). A ratio is formed and the result expressed in dB.

Required Conditions. Since this is the ratio of the maximum output signal to the noise floor, then the manufac-

turer must state what *the maximum level* is, otherwise, you have no way to evaluate the significance of the number. If one company says their product has a dynamic range of 120 dB and another says theirs is 126 dB, before you jump to buy the bigger number, first ask, "Relative to what?" Second, ask, "Measured over what bandwidth, and were any weighting filters used?" You cannot know which is better without knowing the required conditions.

Again, beware of A-weighted specs. Use of A-weighting should only appear in dynamic range specs for digital products with data converters (*see discussion under S/N*). For instance, using it to spec dynamic range in an analog product may indicate the unit has hum components that might otherwise restrict the dynamic range.

Correct: Dynamic Range = 120 dB re +26 dBu, 22 kHz BW
Wrong: Dynamic Range = 120 dB

Crosstalk or *Channel Separation*

What is tested? Signals from one channel leaking into another channel. This happens between independent channels as well as between left and right stereo channels, or between all six channels of a 5.1 surround processor, for instance.

How is it measured? A generator drives one channel and this channel's output value is noted; meanwhile the other channel is set for zero volts (its generator is left hooked up, but turned to zero, or alternatively the input is terminated with the expect source impedance). Under no circumstances is the measured channel left open. Whatever signal is induced into the tested channel is measured at its output with an rms voltmeter and noted. A ratio is formed by dividing the unwanted signal by the above-noted output test value, and the answer expressed in dB. Since the ratio is always less than one (*crosstalk is always less than the original signal*) the expression results in *negative dB* ratings. For example, a crosstalk spec of –60 dB is interpreted to mean the unwanted signal is 60 dB below the test signal.

Required Conditions. Most crosstalk results from printed circuit board traces "talking" to each other. The mechanism is capacitive coupling between the closely spaced traces and layers. This makes it strongly frequency dependent, with a characteristic rise of 6 dB/octave, i.e., the crosstalk gets worst at a 6 dB/octave rate with increasing frequency. Therefore *knowing the frequency used for testing* is essential. And if it is only spec'd at 1 kHz (*very common*) then you can predict what it may be for higher frequencies. For instance, using the example from above of a –60 dB rating, say, at 1 kHz, then the crosstalk at 16 kHz probably degrades to –36 dB. But don't panic, the reason this usually isn't a problem is that the signal level at high frequencies is also reduced by about the same 6 dB/octave rate, so the overall S/N ratio isn't affected much.

Another important point is that crosstalk is assumed level independent unless otherwise noted. This is because the parasitic capacitors formed by the traces are uniquely determined by the layout geometry, not the strength of the signal.

Correct: Crosstalk = -60 dB, 20-20kHz, +4 dBu, channel-to-channel
Wrong: Crosstalk = -60 dB

Input & Output Impedance

What is tested? Input impedance measures the load that the unit represents to the driving source, while output impedance measures the source impedance that drives the next unit.

How is it measured? Rarely are these values actually measured. Usually they are determined by inspection and analysis of the final schematic and stated as a pure resistance in ohms. Input and output reactive elements are usually small enough to be ignored. (*Phono input stages and other inputs designed for specific load reactance are exceptions.*)

Required Conditions. The only required information is whether the stated impedance is balanced or unbalanced (*balanced impedances usually are exactly twice unbalanced ones*). For clarity when spec'ing balanced circuits, it is preferred to state whether the resistance is "floating" (*exists between the two lines*) or is ground referenced (*exists from each line to ground*).

The impedances are assumed constant for all frequencies within the unit's bandwidth and for all signal levels, unless stated otherwise. (*Note that while this is true for input impedances, most output impedances are, in fact, frequency-dependent – some heavily.*)

Correct: Input Impedance = 20 k ohms, balanced line-to-line

Wrong: Input Impedance = 20 k ohms

Maximum Input Level

What is tested? The input stage is measured *inside the unit* to establish the maximum signal level that causes clipping or a specified level of distortion.

How is it measured? This is not a field measurement. It is done during development by the design engineer using an adjustable 1 kHz input signal, an oscilloscope and a distortion analyzer.

Required Conditions. Whether the applied signal is balanced or unbalanced and the amount of distortion or clipping used to establish the maximum must be stated. The preferred value is balanced and 1% distortion, but often manufacturers use "visible clipping," which is as much as 10% distortion, and creates a false impression that the input stage can handle signals a few dB hotter than it really can. No one would accept 10% distortion at the measurement point, so to hide it, it is not stated at all – only the max value given without conditions. *Buyer beware.*

The results are assumed constant for all frequencies within the unit's bandwidth and for all levels of input, unless stated otherwise.

Correct: Maximum Input Level = +20 dBu, balanced, ≤1% THD

Wrong: Maximum Input Level = +20 dBu

Maximum Output Level

What is tested? The unit's output is measured to establish the maximum signal possible before visible clipping or a specified level of distortion.

How is it measured? The output is fixed with a standard load resistor and measured either balanced or unbalanced, using an oscilloscope and a distortion analyzer. A 1 kHz input signal is increased in amplitude until the output measures the specified amount of distortion, and that value is expressed in dBu. Next, the signal is swept through the entire audio range to check that this level does not change with frequency.

Required Conditions. Two important issues are present here: The first is the need to know whether a unit can swing enough unclipped volts for your application. The second is more difficult and potentially more serious, and that is the unit's ability to drive long lines without stability problems, or frequency loss.

The manufacturer must state whether the spec is for balanced or unbalanced use (*usually balanced operation results in 6 dB more swing*); what distortion was used for determination (*with the preferred value being 1% THD*); over what frequency range is this spec valid (*prefer 20 Hz – 20 kHz; watch out for just 1 kHz specs*); and what load impedance is guaranteed (*2k ohms or greater is preferred; 600 ohm operation is obsolete and no longer required except for specialized applications, with broadcast and telecommunications noted as two of them*).

This last item applies only to signal processing units designed as line drivers: These should specify a max cable length and the specs of the cable – by either specific brand & type, or give the max cable capacitance in pF/meter.

Correct: Max Output Level = +26 dBu balanced, 20-20 kHz, ≥2k ohms, ≤1% THD

Wrong: Max Output Level = +26 dBu

Maximum Gain

What is tested? The ratio of the largest possible output signal as compared to a fixed input signal, expressed in dB, is called the *Maximum Gain* of a unit.

How is it measured? With all level & gain controls set maximum, and for an input of 1 kHz at an average level that does not clip the output, the output of the unit is measured using an rms voltmeter. The output level is divided by the input level and the result expressed in dB.

Required Conditions. There is nothing controversial here, but confusion results if the test results do not clearly state whether the test was done using balanced or unbalanced outputs. Often a unit's gain differs 6 dB between balanced and unbalanced hook-up. *Note that it usually does not change the gain if the input is driven balanced or unbalanced, only the output connection is significant.*

The results are assumed constant for all frequencies within the unit's bandwidth and for all levels of input, unless stated otherwise.

Correct: Maximum Gain = +6 dB, balanced-in to balanced-out

Wrong: Maximum Gain = +6 dB

Caveat Emptor

Specifications Require Conditions Accurate audio measurements are difficult and expensive. To purchase the test equipment necessary to perform all the tests described here would cost you a minimum of $10,000. And that price is for computer-controlled analog test equipment, if you want the cool digital-based, dual domain stuff – double it. This is why virtually all purchasers of pro audio equipment must rely on the honesty and integrity of the manufacturers involved, and the accuracy and completeness of their data sheets and sales materials.

Tolerances or Limits Another caveat for the informed buyer is to always look for *tolerances* or *worst-case limits* associated with the specs. Limits are rare, but they are the gristle that gives specifications truth. When you see specs without limits, ask yourself, is this manufacturer NOT going to ship the product if it does not *exactly* meet the printed spec? Of course not. The product will ship, and probably by the hundreds. So what is the *real* limit? At what point will the product *not* ship? If it's off by 3 dB, or 5%, or 100 Hz – *what? When does the manufacturer say no?* The only way you can know is if they publish specification tolerances and limits.

Correct: S/N = 90 dB (± 2 dB), re +4 dBu, 22 kHz BW, unity gain

Wrong: S/N = 90 dB

Further Reading

1. Cabot, Richard C. "Fundamentals of Modern Audio Measurement," *J. Audio Eng. Soc.*, Vol. 47, No. 9, Sep., 1999, pp. 738-762 (Audio Engineering Society, NY, 1999).
2. Metzler, R.E. *Audio Measurement Handbook* (Audio Precision Inc., Beaverton, OR, 1993).
3. *Proc. AES 11th Int. Conf. on Audio Test & Measurement* (Audio Engineering Society, NY, 1992).
4. Skirrow, Peter, "Audio Measurements and Test Equipment," *Audio Engineer's Reference Book 2nd Ed,* Michael Talbot-Smith, Editor. (Focal Press, Oxford, 1999) pp. 3-94 to 3-109.
5. Terman, F. E. & J. M. Pettit, *Electronic Measurements 2nd Ed.* (McGraw-Hill, NY, 1952).
6. Whitaker, Jerry C. *Signal Measurement, Analysis, and Testing* (CRC Press, Boca Raton, FL, 2000)

Portions of this note appeared previously in the May/June & Sep/Oct 2000 issues of LIVESOUND! International magazine reproduced here with permission.

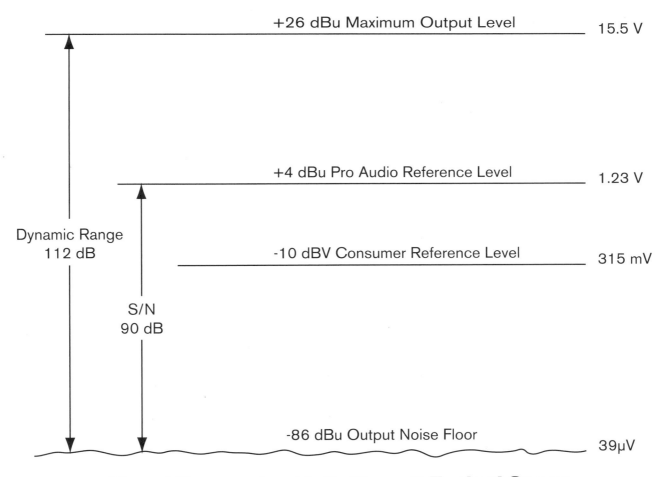

Signal Processing Definitions & Typical Specs

Common Signal Processing Specs With Required Conditions

Abbr	Name	Units	Required Conditions	Preferred Values*
THD	*Total Harmonic Distortion*	%	Frequency Level Gain Settings Harmonic Order Measured	20 Hz – 20 kHz +4 dBu Unity (Max for Mic Preamps) At least 5th-order (5 harmonics)
THD+N	*Total Harmonic Distortion plus Noise*	%	Frequency Level Gain Settings Noise Bandwidth *or* Weighting Filter	20 Hz – 20 kHz +4 dBu Unity (Max for Mic Preamps) 22 kHz BW (or ITU-R 468 Curve)
IM *or* IMD	*Intermodulation Distortion (SMPTE method)*	%	Type 2 Frequencies Ratio Level	SMPTE 60 Hz/7 kHz 4:1 +4 dBu (60 Hz)
IM *or* IMD	*Intermodulation Distortion (ITU-R method) (was CCIF, now changed to ITU-R)*	%	Type 2 Frequencies Ratio Level	ITU-R (or Difference-Tone) 13 kHz/14 kHz (or 19 kHz/20 kHz) 1:1 +4 dBu
S/N *or* SNR	*Signal-to-Noise Ratio*	dB	Reference Level Noise Bandwidth *or* Weighting Filter Gain Settings	re +4 dBu 22 kHz BW (or ITU-R 468 Curve) Unity (Max for Mic Preamps)
EIN	*Equivalent Input Noise* or *Input Referred Noise*	–dBu	Input Terminating Impedance Gain Noise Bandwidth or Weighting Filter	150 ohms Maximum 22 kHz BW (Flat – No Weighting)
BW	*Frequency Response*	Hz	Level Change re 1 kHz	+0/–0.5 dB (or +0/–3 dB)
CMR *or* CMRR	*Common Mode Rejection* or *Common Mode Rejection Ratio*	dB	Frequency *(Assumed independent of level, unless noted otherwise.)*	1 kHz
—	*Dynamic Range*	dB	Maximum Output Level Noise Bandwidth or Weighting Filter	+26 dBu 22 kHz BW (No Weighting Filter)
—	*Crosstalk (as –dB)* or *Channel Separation (as +dB)*	–dB or +dB	Frequency Level What-to-What	20 Hz – 20 kHz +4 dBu Chan.-to-Chan. & Left-to-Right
—	*Input & Output Impedance*	ohms	Balanced or Unbalanced Floating or Ground Referenced *(Assumed frequency-independent, with negligible reactance, unless specified.)*	Balanced No Preference
—	*Maximum Input Level*	dBu	Balanced or Unbalanced THD at Maximum Input Level	Balanced 1%
—	*Maximum Output Level*	dBu	Balanced or Unbalanced Minimum Load Impedance THD at Maximum Output Level Bandwidth Optional: Maximum cable length	Balanced 2k ohms 1% 20 Hz – 20 kHz Cable Length & Type (or pF/meter)
—	*Maximum Gain*	dB	Balanced or Unbalanced Output *(Assumed constant over full BW & at all levels, unless otherwise noted.)*	Balanced

* Based on the common practices of pro audio signal processing manufacturers.

©Rane Corporation 10802 47th Ave. W., Mukilteo WA 98275-5098 TEL (425)355-6000 FAX (425)347-7757 WEB http://www.rane.com

Selecting Mic Preamps

· **Mic Preamp Compatibility**

· **Mic Output Levels vs. Preamp Input Levels**

· **Mic Output Noise vs. Preamp Input Noise**

· **Conversion Tables for Mic Output Noise**

· **RMS Noise Summation for Mic & Preamp**

Dennis Bohn
Rane Corporation

RaneNote 148
© 2001 Rane Corporation

DIFFICULTIES

Selecting a power amplifier for a specific loudspeaker is easy; selecting a preamp for a specific microphone is not. Terminology is the problem. At one end we find power amplifier and loudspeaker manufacturers speaking the same language, or at least using the same vocabulary. Power amps are rated in watts and ohms, while loudspeakers are rated in ohms with a maximum power handling capability stated in watts.

Unfortunately, at the other end, microphone and preamp manufacturers do not speak the same language or use the same vocabulary. One is rated using sound pressure level (SPL) while the other rates itself in volts (dBu).

This note explains how to convert microphone specifications into preamp specifications, making selection and comparison easier. No math is involved since handy look-up tables do the math for you. Key terminology is explained and cross-referenced.

Acknowledgement. Acknowledgement usually comes at the end, however this technical note would not exist had it not been for an article authored by Tomlinson Holman, published in the September 2000 *Surround Sound Professional* magazine, titled "Capturing the Sound, Part 1: Dynamic Range." In that article Tom deftly demonstrated the difficulty in properly matching microphones and preamplifiers. His article motivated me to do this expanded and generalized note.

Worrisome Things

Buyer's guides for 2001 list microphones ranging in price from $50 to $8,000, and microphone preamplifiers from $150 to $4,500. Whether you spend $200 or $12,500 for one microphone and a preamp to go with it, it pays to make sure they are compatible. Luckily, knowing how to do this skillfully depends not on your budget – but rather on this free tech-note.

Selecting the right preamp for a given mic, or conversely selecting the right mic for a given preamp, involves two major things (and a bunch of minor ones):

· Input headroom – *Do you have enough?*
· Noise – *What will the preamp add to your mic?*

You need to determine whether the microphone under worst-case conditions is going to overload the preamp input stage and whether the preamp is going to materially degrade the noise performance of the microphone.

Actually, microphones have few specifications. Most are sold on sound, reputation and price. Specifications rarely enter into it. Even so, enough exist to make the right decision.

Other issues include the proper input impedance. Recently the trend is toward higher input impedances than classic designs, with many now rated 2 kilohms and higher. Since the connected impedance (i.e., mic plugged into the preamp) determines the noise performance, and the microphones are low impedance (150 - 200 ohms) then there is no noise penalty for providing higher input impedances.

Another thing to examine is phantom power. *Is it provided? Do you need it? Is it the correct voltage, and does it source enough current for your microphone?* This is an area where you need to make informed decisions. There is a huge myth circulating that microphones sound better running from 48 volts, as opposed to, say, 12 volts, or that you can increase the dynamic range of a microphone by using higher phantom power. *For the overwhelming majority of microphones both of these beliefs are false.* Most condenser microphones require phantom power in the range of 12-48 VDC, with many extending the range to 9-52 VDC, leaving only a very few that actually require just 48 VDC. The reason is that internally most designs use some form of current source to drive a low voltage zener (usually 5 volts; sometimes higher) which determines the polarization voltage and powers the electronics. The significance is that neither runs off the raw phantom power, they both are powered from a fixed and regulated low voltage source inside the mic. Increasing the phantom power voltage is never seen by the microphone element or electronics, it only increases the voltage across the current source. *But there are exceptions, so check the manufacturer, and don't make assumptions based on hearsay.*

Final selection details involve checking that the preamp's gain range is enough for your use, that there are overload indicators or metering to help in set up, that the plumbing is compatible with your wiring needs, and that the color doesn't clash with your tour jacket.

Preamp Input Overload

Determining input headroom compatibility requires knowing the microphone *sensitivity* rating and the *maximum SPL* allowed. The sensitivity rating is usually the easiest and least ambiguous number to find on the data sheet, rated at 1 kHz and expressed in millivolts per pascal (mV/Pa). One pascal is the amount of pressure resulting from a loudness level of 94 dB (written as 94 dB SPL). For example, a sensitivity rating of 20 mV/Pa tells you that when a sound equal to 94 dB SPL strikes the microphone element, it results in an output voltage of 20 millivolts.

The sensitivity rating gives you a voltage level at one reference point; now all you need is the mic's maximum SPL and you can calculate the maximum output voltage. Then you use this to compare against the maximum input voltage rating of the microphone preamp.

The maximum allowed sound pressure level is stated in several ways: *Maximum SPL* (often with a stated THD level), *Max Acoustic Input, Sound Pressure Level for X% THD*, all are variations for the same rating.

With these two specifications it is a simple matter to calculate the maximum output level in volts and convert that into the familiar *dBu* units found on microphone preamp data sheets. To make this even easier Table 1 is provided. To obtain the microphone maximum output level in dBu, find your microphone's sensitivity rating on the left side and then move right until you are directly below your microphone's maximum SPL rating. As an example, for a microphone with a sensitivity rating of 20 mV/Pa and a max SPL equal to 130 dB, Table 1 tells us that the maximum output voltage is +4 dBu. You now have what you need to compare preamps regarding maximum input level.

Another example using Table 1 is to block out all possibilities that could overload a specific preamp. For example, the shaded triangle area represents all those combinations that could overload Rane's handy-dandy MS 1b Mic Stage. The MS 1b's maximum input level is rated at +10 dBu, therefore all microphone sensitivity and max SPL combinations resulting in greater than +10 dBu are excluded from consideration. Used this way, any new microphones can be quickly checked for overload threat.

Caveats. Remember though, that this output level only occurs under the worst-case condition of sound pressure levels equaling the maximum allowed by the microphone. This means that if your application has sources that cannot achieve the maximum sound pressure levels, then you can relax your input overload requirement accordingly. For instance, if you know your source is never going to exceed, let's say, 110 dB SPL, and your microphone is rated for maximum levels of 130 dB, then you can take 20 dB off the levels shown in Table 1, and widen your preamp choices considerably.

Note also that input overloading is a strong function of the preamp's gain control setting. Most preamp manufacturers measure the maximum input level with the gain control set at minimum. This means there is a real danger that after carefully matching the output and input levels of a microphone and preamp, you find that the mic *still* overloads the preamp. This happens when the system needs the preamp gain turned

Table 1. Microphone Maximum Output Level (dBu)

Sensitivity		Maximum Sound Pressure Level (Max SPL) @ 1 kHz															
mV/Pa	dBu	120	122	124	126	128	130	132	134	136	138	140	142	144	146	148	150
2	-52	-26	-24	-22	-20	-18	-16	-14	-12	-10	-8	-6	-4	-2	0	2	4
4	-46	-20	-18	-16	-14	-12	-10	-8	-6	-4	-2	0	2	4	6	8	10
6	-42	-16	-14	-12	-10	-8	-6	-4	-2	0	2	4	6	8	10	12	14
8	-40	-14	-12	-10	-8	-6	-4	-2	0	2	4	6	8	10	12	14	16
10	-38	-12	-10	-8	-6	-4	-2	0	2	4	6	8	10	12	14	16	18
12	-36	-10	-8	-6	-4	-2	0	2	4	6	8	10	12	14	16	18	20
14	-35	-9	-7	-5	-3	-1	1	3	5	7	9	11	13	15	17	19	21
16	-34	-8	-6	-4	-2	0	2	4	6	8	10	12	14	16	18	20	22
18	-33	-7	-5	-3	-1	1	3	5	7	9	11	13	15	17	19	21	23
20	**-32**	-6	-4	-2	0	2	4	6	8	10	12	14	16	18	20	22	24
22	-31	-5	-3	-1	1	3	5	7	9	11	13	15	17	19	21	23	25
24	-30	-4	-2	0	2	4	6	8	10	12	14	16	18	20	22	24	26
26	-29	-3	-1	1	3	5	7	9	11	13	15	17	19	21	23	25	27
28	-29	-3	-1	1	3	5	7	9	11	13	15	17	19	21	23	25	27
30	-28	-2	0	2	4	6	8	10	12	14	16	18	20	22	24	26	28
32	-28	-2	0	2	4	6	8	10	12	14	16	18	20	22	24	26	28
34	-27	-1	1	3	5	7	9	11	13	15	17	19	21	23	25	27	29
36	-27	-1	1	3	5	7	9	11	13	15	17	19	21	23	25	27	29
38	-26	0	2	4	6	8	10	12	14	16	18	20	22	24	26	28	30
40	-26	0	2	4	6	8	10	12	14	16	18	20	22	24	26	28	30
42	-25	1	3	5	7	9	11	13	15	17	19	21	23	25	27	29	31
44	-25	1	3	5	7	9	11	13	15	17	19	21	23	25	27	29	31
46	-25	1	3	5	7	9	11	13	15	17	19	21	23	25	27	29	31
48	-24	2	4	6	8	10	12	14	16	18	20	22	24	26	28	30	32
50	-24	2	4	6	8	10	12	14	16	18	20	22	24	26	28	30	32

up (correspondingly reducing input headroom) and the microphone is used for a wide dynamic range source. Unless there is a person riding gain, or some provision for automatic input ranging, overload is STILL going to occur. This means that not only do you have to worry about matching your mic and preamp, but also about real-world sources and gain settings.

Noise

Microphones and preamps each have their own noise floors. When selecting a mic preamp you want to know to what degree the preamp's noise degrades the noise of your microphone. Different microphone technologies use different terminology to describe noise.

Dynamic Microphones. Dynamic microphone data sheets rarely list noise as a specification since there is no active circuitry to generate noise; there is only a magnet and a coil. This category of microphone is properly called electromagnetic or electrodynamic. The output noise is very low – so low they just don't list it. However, they do generate some noise and it is calculated by knowing the microphone's impedance.

Obtain the dynamic microphone impedance rating from the data sheet and use Table 2 to convert that into units of

Table 2. Output Noise for Dynamic Mics (20-20 kHz, 20°C/68°F)

Impedance Ohms	Noise dBu A-wtd
50	-141
100	-138
150	-136
200	-135
250	-134
300	-133
350	-132
400	-132
450	-131
500	-131
550	-130
600	-130

Selecting Mic Preamps-3

Table 3. Output Noise for Condenser Mics (dBu)

Sensitivity		Noise Floor (Equivalent Sound Pressure Level, dB-SPL, A-weighted)											
mV/Pa	dBu	6	8	10	12	14	16	18	20	22	24	26	28	30
2	-52	-140	-138	-136	-134	-132	-130	-128	-126	-124	-122	-120	-118	-116
4	-46	-134	-132	-130	-128	-126	-124	-122	-120	-118	-116	-114	-112	-110
6	-42	-130	-128	-126	-124	-122	-120	-118	-116	-114	-112	-110	-108	-106
8	-40	-128	-126	-124	-122	-120	-118	-116	-114	-112	-110	-108	-106	-104
10	-38	-126	-124	-122	-120	-118	-116	-114	-112	-110	-108	-106	-104	-102
12	-36	-124	-122	-120	-118	-116	-114	-112	-110	-108	-106	-104	-102	-100
14	-35	-123	-121	-119	-117	-115	-113	-111	-109	-107	-105	-103	-101	-99
16	-34	-122	-120	-118	-116	-114	-112	-110	-108	-106	-104	-102	-100	-98
18	-33	-121	-119	-117	-115	-113	-111	-109	-107	-105	-103	-101	-99	-97
20	-32	-120	-118	-116	-114	-112	-110	-108	-106	-104	-102	-100	-98	-96
22	-31	-119	-117	-115	-113	-111	-109	-107	-105	-103	-101	-99	-97	-95
24	-30	-118	-116	-114	-112	-110	-108	-106	-104	-102	-100	-98	-96	-94
26	-29	-117	-115	-113	-111	-109	-107	-105	-103	-101	-99	-97	-95	-93
28	-29	-117	-115	-113	-111	-109	-107	-105	-103	-101	-99	-97	-95	-93
30	-28	-116	-114	-112	-110	-108	-106	-104	-102	-100	-98	-96	-94	-92
32	-28	-116	-114	-112	-110	-108	-106	-104	-102	-100	-98	-96	-94	-92
34	-27	-115	-113	-111	-109	-107	-105	-103	-101	-99	-97	-95	-93	-91
36	-27	-115	-113	-111	-109	-107	-105	-103	-101	-99	-97	-95	-93	-91
38	-26	-114	-112	-110	-108	-106	-104	-102	-100	-98	-96	-94	-92	-90
40	-26	-114	-112	-110	-108	-106	-104	-102	-100	-98	-96	-94	-92	-90
42	-25	-113	-111	-109	-107	-105	-103	-101	-99	-97	-95	-93	-91	-89
44	-25	-113	-111	-109	-107	-105	-103	-101	-99	-97	-95	-93	-91	-89
46	-25	-113	-111	-109	-107	-105	-103	-101	-99	-97	-95	-93	-91	-89
48	-24	-112	-110	-108	-106	-104	-102	-100	-98	-96	-94	-92	-90	-88
50	-24	-112	-110	-108	-106	-104	-102	-100	-98	-96	-94	-92	-90	-88

dBu, A-weighted. This noise is the white noise generated by the resistance of the wire used to create the coil, plus a correction factor of 5 dB for A-weighting. (This is somewhat arbitrary, as true A-weighting may decrease the level anywhere from 3-6 dB depending upon the nature of the noise, but agrees with Holman's article and measured results).

The noise of the measuring standard 150 ohms (200 ohms for Europe) source resistor makes a good noise reference point. From Table 2, find that it equates to –136 dBu (A-weighted; –131 dBu when not). This means that you cannot have an operating mic stage, with a 150 ohm source, quieter than –136 dBu (A-weighted, 20°C/68°F, 20 kHz BW). Looking at Table 2 confirms that dynamic microphones, indeed, are quiet.

Use Table 4 to compare microphone output noise with preamplifier equivalent input noise (EIN). As an example, if your dynamic microphone's output noise equals –136 dBu and you are considering a preamplifier with a rated EIN of –136 dBu, then the difference between them is 0 dB and Table 4 lets you know that this preamp with this microphone will degrade the total noise by 3 dB. That is, the combination of mic and preamp adds 3 dB noise to the total. More on how this table works shortly.

Table 4. RMS Noise Summation for Connected Mic & Preamp

Preamp Noise vs. Mic Noise dB	Noise Added by Preamp dB
+6	7.0
+5	6.2
+4	5.5
+3	4.8
+2	4.1
+1	3.5
0	3.0
-1	2.5
-2	2.1
-3	1.8
-4	1.5
-5	1.2
-6	1.0
-7	0.8
-8	0.6
-9	0.5
-10	0.4
-11	0.3
-12	0.3
-13	0.2
-14	0.2
-15	0.1
-16	0.1
-17	0.1
-18	0.1
-19	0.1
-20	0.0

Condenser Microphones. Condenser, capacitor, or more properly, electrostatic microphone technology involves a polarizing voltage network and at least a buffer transistor built into the microphone housing, if not an entire preamp/biasing/transformer network – all of which contribute noise to the output. Electrostatic microphones are quite noisy compared to dynamic designs, but are very popular for other reasons.

Different manufacturers use different terminology on their electrostatic microphone specification sheets for noise: *Self-Noise*, *Equivalent Noise SPL*, *Equivalent Noise Level*, *Noise Floor*, and just plain *Noise* all describe the same specification. Microphone noise is referenced to the equivalent sound pressure level that would cause the same amount of output noise voltage and is normally A-weighted. This means the noise is given in units of dB SPL. A noise spec might read 14 dB SPL equivalent, A-weighted, or shortened to just 14 dB-A (*bad terminology, but common*). This is interpreted to mean that the inherent noise floor is equivalent to a sound source with a sound pressure level of 14 dB. Problems arise trying to compare the mic's noise rating of 14 dB SPL with a preamp's equivalent input noise (EIN) rating of, say, –128 dBu. *Talk about apples and oranges.*

Luckily (again) tables come to the rescue. Table 3 provides an easy look-up conversion between a microphone's output noise, expressed in equivalent dB-SPL, and its sensitivity rating, in mV/Pa, into output noise expressed in dBu, A-weighted. Using Table 3, a direct noise comparison between any microphone and any preamp is possible. The example shown by the half-toned column and row is for a microphone with a noise floor of 14 dB-SPL and a sensitivity rating of 20 mV/Pa, which translates into an output noise of –112 dBu, A-weighted.

Time to return to Table 4. Unfiltered electronic noise, whether from a resistor, a coil, an IC, or a transistor is white noise consisting of all audible frequencies occurring randomly. Due to this randomness you don't just add noise sources together, you must add them in an RMS (root mean square) fashion. Mathematically this means you must take the square root of the sum of the squares – which is why Table 4 is so handy – it does the RMS conversion for you.

Use Table 3 to convert your microphone's rated noise output into units of dBu. Find the difference in dB between your mic's output noise and the preamp's input noise. Find that difference in the left column of Table 4 and read what the preamp added noise will do to the microphone's noise in the right column. For example, if the mic's output noise translates into –120 dBu, and the preamp you are interested in has an EIN of –127 dBu, then the difference between the mic and the preamp is –7 dB, that is, the preamp is 7 dB quieter than the microphone. Table 4, at the row marked –7 dB, tells you that this preamp will degrade your microphone's noise by only 0.8 dB. Looking at Table 4 tells us that after about a 10 dB difference, the noise added by the preamp becomes insignificant.

Similar to Table 1, you can use Table 3 to map out a preamp's A-weighted noise to show the combinations that add insignificant noise. If you use a –10 dB difference figure as a guide, then the preamp's noise amounts to less than 0.4 dB increase. The shaded triangle area in Table 3 shows an example of this. The areas not shaded represent all possible combinations of microphone sensitivity and noise specifications that can be used with Rane's MS 1b Mic Stage, for instance, and add less than 0.4 dB of noise. If you allow 1 dB net added noise, then even more combinations are possible. (The shaded area is figured by taking the EIN of the MS 1b at –128 dBu, reducing it to –133 dBu with the 5 dB factor for A-weighting, and using the –10 dB difference found in Table 4 for 0.4 dB added noise, resulting in all combinations less than –123 dB being blocked out.)

DOING THE TWO-STEP

The following procedure summarizes this note for evaluating the compatibility of any microphone and any preamplifier:

Evaluating Input Overload Compatibility
1. Locate the microphone **Sensitivity** rating on the data sheet.
2. Find the **Maximum SPL** from the data sheet.
3. Using **Table 1**, find the microphone Sensitivity rating down the left side.
4. Find the Maximum SPL rating along the top of Table 1.
5. Move right along the Sensitivity rating row and move down the Max SPL rating column until they intersect and note the number – *this is the microphone's maximum output level expressed in dBu*.
6. From the microphone preamplifier's data sheet find the **Maximum Input Level** (in dBu).
7. Compare the mic's maximum output level obtained from Table 1 against the preamp's maximum input level obtained from its data sheet to determine compatibility.

Example Using Sample Data Sheets
1. Microphone's Sensitivity rating is 20 mV/Pa.
2. Microphone's Maximum SPL rating is 130 dB.
3. Table 1 shows the Sensitivity row marked 20 mV/Pa shaded.
4. Table 1 shows the Maximum SPL column for 130 dB shaded.
5. The intersecting point is at 4 dBu – *this is the maximum output level of the example microphone*.
6. The MS 1b Mic Stage data sheet lists the Maximum Input Level as +10 dBu.
7. Since this mic's max output level is +4 dBu and the preamp can handle +10 dBu, then this mic will not overload this preamp (when set for minimum gain).

Evaluating Noise Performance
Dynamic Mics
1. Find the impedance specification on the data sheet (use "actual" instead of "rated" if given the choice).
2. Use **Table 2** to find the **Output Noise** in dBu, A-weighted, by finding the closest impedance listed.
3. Find the EIN (equivalent input noise) in dBu rating on the preamplifier's data sheet.
4. Reduce the preamp's EIN by 5 dB to approximate A-weighting.
5. Calculate the difference between the microphone's output noise and the preamp's equivalent input noise (both expressed in dBu, A-weighted).
6. Use **Table 4** to determine how much total noise will be added by the proposed preamplifier.

Condenser Mics
1. Find the **Noise** rating on the microphone date sheet (this is stated as *Equivalent Noise Level*, *Self-Noise*, *Equivalent Noise SPL*, or *Noise Floor*), expressed in dB SPL, A-weighted.
2. Locate the microphone's **Sensitivity** rating on the data sheet.
3. Using **Table 3**, find the microphone Sensitivity rating down the left side.
4. Find the **Noise** rating in dB SPL, A-weighted along the top of Table 3.
5. Move along the Sensitivity rating row and move down the Noise column until they intersect and note the number – *this is the output noise converted to dBu, A-weighted*.
6. Find the **EIN** (equivalent input noise) in dBu rating on the preamplifier's data sheet.
7. Reduce the preamp's EIN by 5 dB to approximate A-weighting.
8. Calculate the difference between the microphone's output noise and the preamp's equivalent input noise (both expressed in dBu, A-weighted).
9. Use **Table 4** to determine how much total noise will be added by the proposed preamplifier.

Condenser Microphone Example Using Sample Data Sheets
1. Microphone's Equivalent Noise Level is 14 dB SPL, A-weighted.
2. Microphone's Sensitivity rating is 20 mV/Pa.
3. Table 3 shows the Sensitivity row marked 20 mV/Pa shaded.
4. Table 3 shows the Noise column for 14 dB SPL, A-weighted shaded.
5. The intersection point is at –112 dBu, A-weighted: *this is the output noise of the microphone*.
6. The MS 1b Mic Stage data sheet lists the Equivalent Input Noise as –128 dBu (no weighting).
7. Reducing this by 5 dB yields a preamp EIN of –133 dBu, A-weighted.
8. The difference between the microphone's output noise of –112 dBu, A-weighted and the preamp's EIN of –133 dBu, A-weighted is –11 dB.
9. Table 4 shows that the total noise added by the preamp is an insignificant 0.3 dB.

Mickey's Mics

Model MM-100
Super Heart-Shaped Gold Vapor Large Diaphragm
Condenser Microphone

"It's the best!" ... Anonymous, Mukilteo, WA

Unparalleled response with a pickup pattern following the locus of a fixed point on a circle that rolls on the circumference of another circle with the same radius.

SPECIFICATIONS

Transducer Principle	Condenser, or since 1950, Electrostatic
Pick-up Pattern	Super-Cardioid
Frequency Range	20 Hz – 20 kHz (±2 dB)
Sensitivity @ 1 kHz	20 mV/Pa
Impedance	150 ohms
Equivalent Noise Level	14 dB-SPL, A-weighted
Maximum SPL	130 dB (1 kHz, 0.5% THD)
Power Requirement	12-48 VDC Phantom Powering, 5 mA
Housing/Finish	Yttrium-Titanium/Glaring Fuchsia

MS 1b Microphone Stage

Features and Specifications

Parameter	Specification	Limit	Units	Conditions/Comments
Input Impedance	10k	1%	ohms	Balanced 5k + 5k
Gain Range	18 to 66	typ.	dB	
Phantom Power	+48	4%	volts	10 mA max.
Max. Input Level	+10/-32	min.	dBu	Gain 18/60, balanced output
Equivalent Input Noise	-128	typ.	dBu	20 kHz BW, Rs=150 ohms, Gain = 60 dB
S/N re 4 dB	96	typ.	dB	20 kHz BW, Rs=150 ohms, Gain = 18 dB
Dynamic Range	120/95	typ.	dB	Gain 18/66
CMRR	80	typ.	dB	Rs=150 ohms, 120 Hz, Gain = 60 dB
Frequency Response	30/45 to 200k	typ.	Hz	+0, -3dB, Gain 18/60 dB
THD+Noise	.007	typ.	%	+20 dBu, 55 Hz – 20 kHz, 22 kHz BW
Max. Output Level	+27/+22	min.	dBu	Balanced/Unbalanced, 2k ohm load
Output Impedance	50	1%	ohms	Each Leg

©Rane Corporation 10802 47th Ave. W., Mukilteo WA 98275-5098 TEL (425)355-6000 FAX (425)347-7757 WEB http://www.rane.com

12368 7-01   Selecting Mic Preamps-7

Home Cinema Systems

- **Dolby Pro-Logic & THX**

- **Home Theater Equalization**

- **THX 44 Equalizer**

- **THX 22 Equalizer**

- **SSE 35 Equalizer**

- **Interfacing Consumer & Pro Gear**

- **Troubleshooting & Alignment**

INTRODUCTION

A good home theater pulls you into the movie, letting you forget about flashing video light and amplified sound. A better playback system equals a better experience. Video quality at home can't match 35 mm projection, but the sound quality at home *can* surpass a commercial theater. Subjective opinion about audio reproduction is nothing new—we all know "experts" in the business who will tell you the "right" way to do it. There are several "right" ways of doing it, depending on your philosophy and taste. Realism, hearing through the directors ears, being blown away, and still having a system that sounds good when you play a CD is a multi-faceted goal. System component selection is important. Correct calibration is equally important. Rane equalizers are used in the finest recording studios in the world, including Lucasfilm's Skywalker Ranch. This is why Rane was originally approached to build the first equalizer for Home THX systems. This same technology is available for recreating the original studio mix in your living room.

Jeff Davies
Rane Corporation

RaneNote 132
© 1994-1999 Rane Corporation
Dolby is a trademark of Dolby Laboratories.
THX is a trademark of THX Ltd.
DTS is a trademark of Digital Theater Systems.
Radio Shack is a trademark of Tandy Corporation.

DOLBY PRO-LOGIC®

In a stereo system, the left and right speakers produce all the imaging, including center mono and ambient signals. In movies, the added center speaker is the *most* important channel in the system, while the surrounds produce the ambience. Dolby Pro-Logic derives four channels with full backward compatibility to stereo and mono, with minor compromises. Rather than re-explain how Dolby Pro-Logic works (*see References*), this note covers a few popular confusing topics.

Surround frequency response. The Dolby Pro-Logic surround output is mono. Decoder manufacturers may add their own stereo simulators to the mono surround output, delivering simulated left and right surround outputs. During Pro-Logic encoding, surround information gets a 100 Hz high pass filter and a 7 kHz low pass filter. Surround speakers only need to reproduce 100 Hz-8 kHz for Pro-Logic, but require full range for Dolby Digital and DTS systems (more on those later).

Center Channel Modes. *Normal* mode: Also called ***Small*** on some controllers. 20 Hz-20 kHz is delivered to the left and right outputs. 100 Hz-20 kHz is delivered to the center output. All material below 100 Hz is delivered to the left and right outputs. This is the mode preferred when using subwoofers (through a crossover, internal or external), and/or with a smaller center speaker that has less range than the left and right. ***Wide* mode:** Also called ***Large*** on some controllers. 20 Hz-20 kHz is delivered to left, center and right outputs. This mode is preferred when the left, center and right speakers are all full range and a subwoofer is either not used, or with a improves the "wrap-around" effect of the surround track.

***Surround Timbre Matching Equalization*:** An EQ correction curve matches front and surround response to our ears, to alleviate timbre shifts when sound pans from front to the rear.

***Crossover*:** A subwoofer output, crossed over at 80 Hz, derived from the LCR channels with a response of 20-80 Hz. All other channels reproduce 80 Hz-20 kHz. To be a Home THX System, other criteria in system response must be met.

Front THX speakers have wide horizontal dispersion and focused vertical dispersion. Within this listening window they must have a flat response and produce 105 dB without artifacts. Ceiling reflections can cause unpredictable imaging, acceptable for music but not for film reproduction. Living rooms are all shapes, sizes and textures, and controlling dispersion guarantees an accurate sound focus toward the screen. Smaller front speakers enable closer speaker placement and localization to the action. Subwoofer(s) take physical size away from the front speakers (more on that later).

Surround THX speakers are dipolar radiation in design, with opposite phase drivers aiming toward and away from the screen and the listener sitting in the "null" area, improving the diffuse effect, imitating a row of speakers as in a theater. Power must be flat to 102 dB without artifacts.

THX subwoofers produce an in-room response from 20-80 Hz at 105 dB without artifacts.

Power amplifiers must meet noise, phase, load and distortion specs, with power required to drive the speakers.

It is certainly alright to have a mixed system of THX and non-THX components. But to be a bona-fide *Home Ultra THX System*, it must include a THX approved controller, amps and speakers at a minimum and be aligned by a certified THX installer who has completed the course at Lucasfilm.

THX media. Lucasfilm's THX does *not* do any different encoding/decoding than Dolby Pro-Logic—they are the *same*. THX is just a *playback* system for material recorded in Dolby Pro-Logic. The THX Studio media program is designed to produce the highest visual and audio quality discs, but these do *not* require a THX system for playback. These discs look and sound fantastic on any Pro-Logic system, whether it is THX or not. The program came into existence because there was a lack of consistent quality control during the many steps of mastering. With a THX DVD, you can be assured you are getting the sharpest picture and best sound possible with the present state-of-the-art.

DOLBY DIGITAL®

Previously known as AC-3 on laserdiscs, Dolby Digital has been chosen as the standard for DVD and HDTV. Each channel delivers 20 Hz-20 kHz bandwidth to all five channels, along with a sixth "effects" channel used for additional subwoofer information. Crosstalk is much lower than Pro-Logic, providing a wide soundscape. Dolby Digital is not a replacement for THX, for some controllers add the benefits of timbre-matching and *dynamic* decorrelation to the surrounds. Even with discrete surround channels, dynamic decorrelation widens and prevents off-axis speaker localization of mono surround information.

DTS®

Digital Theater Systems' audio compression scheme applies to laserdisc and CD technology for home theater use. Though it has a smaller title library and controller support than Dolby Digital, it has a core of enthusiatic followers such as directors Steven Speilberg and James Cameron. It employs less compression than Dolby Digital, and proponents claim it has a much cleaner sound. A small but growing number of music CDs and DVDs are available in the DTS format.

EQUALIZATION

Equalizers somehow got a bad reputation in the hi-fi stereo world. Sure, there's the argument that the less electronics in the signal path, the fewer artifacts (noise, phase shifting, etc.). Check out the RaneNote, *Exposing Equalizer Mythology*. However, music recordings are rare that did not employ an equalizer at least once during production, and in the case of a movie soundtrack you can be assured there were several. Those bass and treble controls you've been using for years are crude broad-band equalizers. In a perfect listening environment, with flat speakers, you won't need an equalizer. The "flat" speaker has not been invented yet, and even if it existed the room would color it's sound. Speakers *sound* different in different rooms, for the room is an extention of the speaker enclosure. Most recording and film studios use equalizers to correct speaker and room response, even in carefully designed studios. Living rooms have even more random acoustics, and reproduction of the same audio as heard in a recording studio requires a similar equalizer.

A quality equalizer when used correctly, makes a system more accurate and transparent to its environment. Don't use an equalizer to solve a problem that can be solved with speaker placement—place the speakers, *then* EQ the room. Good speaker placement tips are usually found in the speaker's manual. An equalizer should be used minimally, with preferably no more than ±6 dB boost/cut. When setting the equalizer, try to use more cutting than boosting. Use a ⅓-octave spectrum analyzer, with multiple readings around the listening area for each channel, and averaged to set the EQ curves. Equalizers in a home theater fine-tune the room, and help timbre-match non-matching speakers. A lot of sounds pan between the LCR channels, so the same speaker model should be used whenever possible. Employing equalization is even *more* important when adding a different model center channel speaker to a stereo pair.

To decide whether or not an equalizer is really necessary, try running a ⅓-octave spectrum analyzer in the room to see the differences between channels. If all channels average flat within ±3 dB, you're just plain lucky.

Left, Center, and Right.
Most room equalization curves have one thing in common.

Higher frequencies require less EQ, while the room affects frequencies below 1 kHz and gets worse as they get lower. Looking at a ⅓-octave analyzer with good speakers, the lower octaves will have greater dips and peaks, while the upper octaves may have few if any adjustments. The Rane **THX 44** equalizer was specified by Lucasfilm with this in mind. Rather than use ⅓-octave sliders across the spectrum, the LCR channels get the ⅓-octave treatment from 80 to 800 Hz.

Each channel has two tunable parametric bands that smooth the higher frequencies more accurately with fewer controls and circuitry. Two tunable parametric bands are also provided for the subwoofer. Since the THX 44 is intended as a *system-flattening* EQ, it is intended to be set *once* in the final stages of system alignment. A security cover is provided to prevent temptation to play with all those little sliders. Though THX 44 meets the Lucasfilm standards, it is an ideal system equalizer for all Pro-Logic and 5.1 digital systems. And speaking of 5.1, add a **THX 22** to the surround channels for the same equalization control all around the room.

For systems that need equalization but budget or space considerations rule out the THX 44, the **SSE 35** is a single rack space three channel graphic equalizer intended for home theater. ⅔-octave sections are provided for the LCR channels above 160 Hz, and ⅓-octave sections are provided for Left and Right (or subwoofer channels) below 100 Hz. Crossovers provide mono or stereo subwoofer outputs if desired, adding a crossover to controllers or subwoofers without one (*see Subwoofers below*). The SSE 35 is a sweetener for systems that allow connections between the processor and power amplifiers, and a must-have when a different model center channel speaker is used. The SSE 35 was designed for Dolby Pro-Logic systems, but in Dolby Digital systems use the SSE 35 without the subwoofer crossover. Additionally, the SSE 35 works well in systems that are primarily used for stereo music listening with occasional home theater use—see the Subwoofer section for more on this subject.

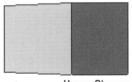

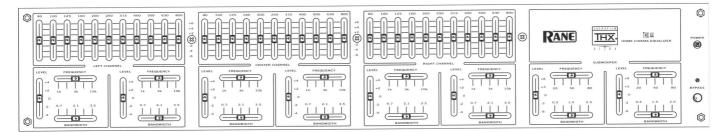

Rane THX 44 Home Cinema Equalizer

SURROUNDS

Equalizing the surround speakers has less of an impact than equalizing the front channels in Dolby Pro-Logic systems, but more important for 5.1 digital systems. Proper surround placement should have the effect of enveloping the listener in a subtle, non-localized sound. Depending on the room, interior decorator, and speaker design intentions, surround speakers may be mounted on the side walls, back walls, aiming down, up, or any way to *maximize* room reflections to give a multiple speaker effect. This is the *opposite* goal of the front speakers that must keep attention toward the screen. A matter of preference exists for some 5.1 digital users that like a point/source surround, but this is less like an actual movie theater and may not translate with how the director intended the surround sound field. Any localized sound to the back or side that makes you want to look over your shoulder is not good, until they come up with 360° screens. Surrounds "fit" in the system better when they have the same relative timbre to the front speakers. In-wall surrounds benefit from equalization when chosen for their appearance over sound. Even though Dolby Pro-Logic surround information rolls off below 100 Hz and above 7 kHz, there will still be some signal present outside of this range. This is unintended "leakage" from the Dolby Pro-Logic decoder, and doesn't need to be boosted by the equalizer—leave it flat outside of this range; the front speakers will reproduce it. Even with 5.1 digital systems, equalizing the surrounds is not as important as equalizing the front channels, but the purist will use the same ⅓-octave equalization as the front channels.

The best choice for surrounds is the Rane **THX 22** Stereo Equalizer. It has the same 1/3-octave graphic/parametric combo and look as the THX 44, in a single rack height chassis. It may also be used in any stereo application, such as auxiliary speakers in a home where the main system serves another room or rooms for music. For those who would rather not deal with a parametric, use the Rane ME 60. It is the easiest equalizer to use with a 1/3-octave realtime analyzer.

SUBWOOFER

Fact: low frequencies require a larger speaker enclosure to provide the larger wavelengths. Since a small center channel speaker needs to be placed close to the screen, and speakers and drivers need to be matched for left, center and right, large full range enclosures are impractical for the front channels—hence the need for subwoofers. Two subwoofers provide greater room coverage, though one can be sufficient if placed correctly. A second subwoofer will activate different room nodes and provide more even coverage throughout the room, but if incorrectly placed can cause more problems by cancelling frequencies at the listening position. Frequencies below 100 Hz are hard to localize, and movie soundtracks are mixed with this in mind. *Tip: to place a subwoofer, put it in the primary listening chair, and turn on the pink noise. Crawl around places in the room where the subwoofer might go, reading your SPL meter (try corners). The place that gives you the loudest reading is the best place to put the subwoofer.*

The reasons for using stereo left/right subwoofers can use the same points. Two subs can smooth out different resonances from different parts of the room. Music CDs often carry stereo information in the sub range, especially in some classical recordings. Turning off the main speakers and just listening to stereo subs proves the point. Symphonic and pipe organ works reveal a wealth of out-of-phase sub information that is not directly localizable, but perceivably stereo. If a stereo recording has out-of-phase sub material, it may be cancelled out in a summed mono system.

So—if the system is primarily a home theater, mono sub(s) can suffice; if watching movies is secondary to playing music, stereo subwoofers or large full range speakers are called for. Movie soundtracks sound just as good with stereo subwoofers, and music sounds even better. The **SSE 35** is one of the few components available that delivers stereo subwoofer outputs.

Equalizing a subwoofer is admittedly not an easy task. Using pink noise and a spectrum analyzer is tricky, several readings must be taken and averaged, and a ⅓-octave analyzer won't tell you the narrow problem frequencies that get even

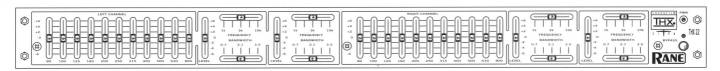

Rane THX 22 Stereo Equalizer

THX 44 or THX 22 GRAPHIC EQUALIZATION CHART

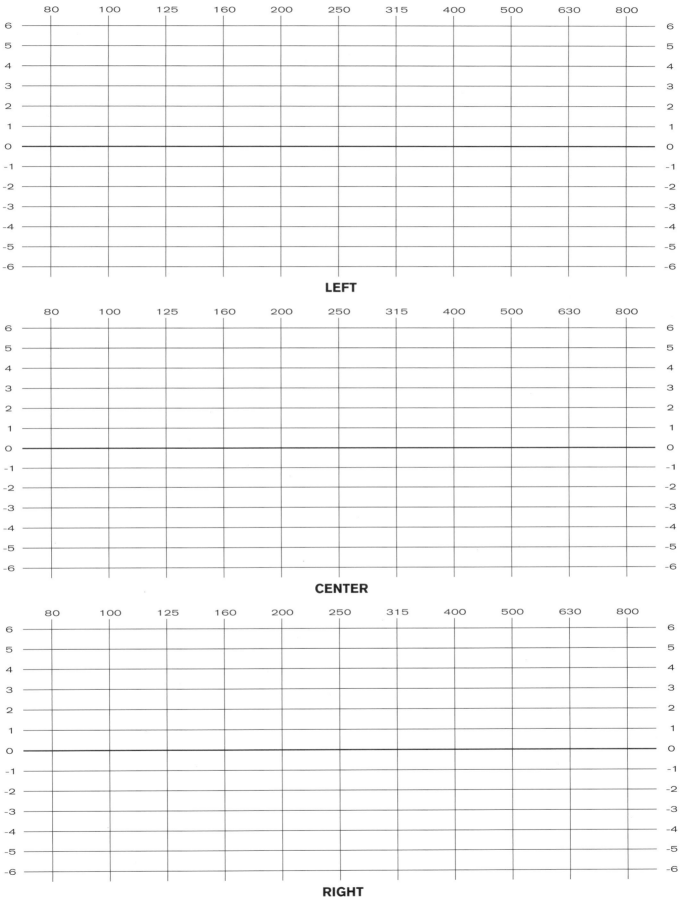

LEFT

CENTER

RIGHT

Home Cinema-5

more specific in the sub range. A frequency generator and an SPL meter might show general problems, but use your ears as the final judge. Just run some pink noise through the subwoofer, and listen for an even, low roar without any coloration. You might find a strong resonance at one particular frequency. Be sure you're not hearing rattles coming from the environment, these need to be dealt with mechanically.

A parametric equalizer is called for once the best subwoofer position is found and rattles have been dealt with. The **THX 44** has a two band version, which should be enough if you are using a THX approved subwoofer. For more bands, see the Rane PE 17 in the professional products division.

Setting a parametric by ear is a bit of an art—someone with good tuning ears can use the following method: Begin with all LEVEL controls set at "0". One band at a time, turn up the Boost control about 6 dB. The BANDWIDTH should be pretty tight, about a tenth of an octave. Sweep the FREQUENCY control slowly until you hear an obvious volume increase at a certain frequency (you can use an SPL meter or your ears). There's your problem point, so sweep a little and listen to how wide of a "bump" it is, and adjust the BANDWIDTH control to fit the bump. Now pull the BOOST control down to a negative setting where things sound smooth. Repeat this process for the other bands as necessary.

SUBWOOFER CROSSOVER

A crossover takes the audio spectrum and divides it, so that frequencies below the crossover point are sent to the sub, and frequencies above are sent to the main speakers. This lets the whole system have a wider dynamic range with less distortion. Bass requires a lot of power to reproduce correctly, and the subwoofer needs it's own amplifier. A crossover circuit for the subwoofer is found in all THX controllers, frequency set at 80 Hz. Dolby Pro-Logic components may have a sub output added, but it is just a summed mono signal with maybe a low pass filter that removes nothing from the LCR channels. Some powered subwoofers also may claim to have a crossover, but in reality it's just a 6 or 12 dB per octave low pass filter that does nothing to reduce the drain and increase the headroom of the main speakers. In all Dolby Pro-Logic center modes (except Wide or Large), a bass-splitting circuit only sends information over 100 Hz to the center and surround outputs and keeps the bass in the left and right channels. Sure, some low frequency material exists at the center and surround outputs, but is leakage, rolled off, hard to localize, and nothing that isn't already in the left and right channels, so don't fret about trying to reproduce it in the surrounds. All are good arguments to the benefits of a 5.1 digital system, which has the dedicated subwoofer channel with no crossover required. However, some smart controllers will include a subwoofer crossover anyway to route bass information from non-5.1 sources to the subwoofer — check your manual.

INTERFACING CONSUMER AND PRO GEAR

The THX 44, THX 22, ME 60 and SSE 35 all sport RCA connectors to make connection easy, following the consumer audio standard. Questions arise with non-RCA balanced equipment, such as a Rane RPE 228d Programmable Equalizer or PE 17 Parametric Equalizer. Here's a can of worms that books are written about, but here are a few basics, starting with definitions and ending with a cure.

Balanced: One audio signal on three wires: positive (+) signal, negative (–) return signal, and a shield ground. The audio signal voltage is on the (+) and (–) wires, and the shield protects the two from outside interference as well as providing a ground reference. Use balanced connections in professional installations where cable lengths exceed 10 feet (3 meters). Balanced is also sometimes referred as +4 dBu because of it's high typical signal. Connectors can be XLR (Cannon or 3-pin), screw terminal, or ¼" TRS (tip-ring-sleeve) phone plugs.

Unbalanced: One audio signal on two wires: positive (+) signal, and a grounded shield. Since the shield also contains the (–) signal, it is more susceptible to outside interference. This is usually not a problem with short cable runs (under 10 feet or 3 meters). Unbalanced is sometimes referred as –10 dBV because of its lower typical signal. Connectors are usually RCA or ¼" TS (tip-sleeve) phone plugs.

Connecting these two systems cause level mismatches, ground loops and hums, and headaches for anyone attempting to get the two to talk to each other. For more in-depth information on grounding solutions and custom cables, refer to the RaneNote, *Sound System Interconnection*.

Rule #1. Any signal that is running on an unbalanced (2-conductor) cable longer than 10 feet (3 meters) is likely to hum. The longer the cable, the worse the hum. Balanced equipment, isolation transformers or interface boxes can help, but any line over 10 feet must use *two conductors with shield*.

In consumer (unbalanced) systems:
1. Locate the equipment as close as possible to each other.
2. Keep cables as short as possible, using good quality shielded cables.
3. Keep AC cables away from signal cables. Never run them parallel to each other.

Rule #2. Audio equipment designers don't read the same textbooks regarding signals and grounding schemes. Some will have great ideas that are compatible with their own equipment, but not with the rest of the world. The worst offenders are grounding rules. Some ground their chassis—others don't. Some connect sleeve to chassis ground—others to signal ground. Some have grounding AC line cords—some don't. Some include RF suppression, some don't. Rack mounting sometimes solves ground problems, other times causes ground problems. Even though the *Audio Engineering Society* has decreed that pin 2 is 'hot' on balanced XLR connectors, some still use pin 3 out of habit. Often the answer lies in trial and error, one unit at a time along the signal chain, from the amp back to the source. When you get to a piece that does appear to cause hum, it may be just in the interconnection — you'll get a "no problem found" reply on the bill if you send it in for repair. Good sources to help avoid this, along with *Sound System Interconnection*, are in the references. Troubleshoot along the signal chain from the speaker

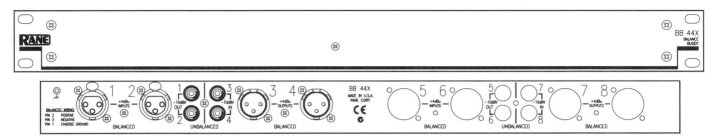

Rane BB 44X Balance Buddy, Front and Rear Panels

back to the audio source, one component, one wire at a time, following rules and checking grounds. There are unfortunately no easy steps to follow, just several items to try.

1. Before changing any grounds, turn off the system or at least turn down the volume to prevent pops or nasty surprises.
2. Try a different or better quality signal cable. Different cable companies use different shielding practices.
3. Try connecting a heavy guage wire from one chassis to another, possibly by a rear panel screw and a star washer.
4. Try reversing the polarity on non-polarized AC plugs.
5. For RF suppression, ferrite beads or ferrite cable clamps can be installed at the input connector.

Rane makes a couple of solutions to get out of all this, the Rane **BB 44X** and the **BB 22**. The BB 44X is a 19" W x 1.75 " H box with no controls, only XLR and RCA connectors. There is no power supply or active electronics to introduce any noise into the system. It uses high grade transformers to isolate, balance or unbalance, and level match between +4 dBu and -10 dBV signals (depending on how you connect it). There are two female and two male XLR connectors, each going through a transformer to an RCA connector, equating to stereo in and stereo out of a balanced device. The **OPTION 88** accessory expands the 4 channels into 8 within the same enclosure, providing 4-in and 4-out. The BB 44X solves all grounding problems when used with properly wired cables. The BB 22 is half of a BB 44x, simply converting two unbalanced RCA inputs to two balanced XLR outputs in a small 5" box. No more overloaded inputs. No more ground loop. No more hum.

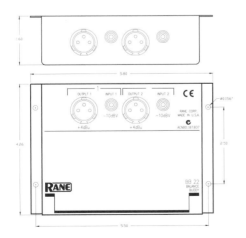

Rane BB 22 Balance Buddy, Top and Rear Panels

(jacks are only on the rear).

ALIGNING A HOME CINEMA

Once everything is hooked up correctly, situated, rattle and hum removed, the tuning stage can finally begin. Basic tools required are a ⅓-octave realtime analyzer and a hand held SPL meter.

Most installers use a Radio Shack SPL meter—it works, it's inexpensive, and easy to find. Set it to *C Weighting, Slow*. It's primary job is balancing loudness of all channels during the Dolby test signal found on all decoders. Place the meter at arms length in the central listening position. Seated ear height is the best, but do try keeping it away from reflective surfaces or seat cushions. Setting the meter to read 75 dB on all channels during the Dolby test sequence check with the preamp volume at "0" will bring the system to Dolby Reference Level. In other words, the living room is calibrated to the same volume of a Dolby Stereo movie theater, and is the "proper" level to watch a movie. If your preamp does not have a 0 dB indicator of this level tied to the volume control, you could mark or create one, say at "noon" or "2 o'clock" and set channel levels at the power amps.

Choose an analyzer that is ⅓-octave, with a flat response mic and a pink noise source, and preferably with a memory averaging function. Setting EQ correctly requires mic readings from different listening area locations and then averaging them. Goldline and Audio Control are good analyzer manufacturers. Minimize any background noises like ventilation systems, traffic, or wild animals because these may throw off analyzer readings. It is not necessary to endure pink noise at high volume. 75 dB is recommended, but can 65 work as well. Ear plugs are allowed.

If the amplifiers have level controls, turn them all down. Connect the pink noise output of the analyzer directly to each input channel of the equalizer. With the equalizer set flat (all sliders at 0), turn up the amplifier level so the SPL meter reads 75 dB. Beginning with the center channel, analyze, average, and flatten each channel one at a time per the analyzer instructions. Getting the pink noise to be read flat on the analyzer within ±3 dB is the goal.

Don't be picky with irregularities above 1 kHz. The purpose is to correct the power response in the room, not redesign the speaker. The lower the frequency, the more the room affects it.

If the amplfiers don't have front volume controls, connect the pink noise with an RCA "wye" cable to a left and right aux input. With Dolby Pro-Logic on, the center channel produces the noise. Start with center and then do left, then right. Disconnecting the right channel moves the noise to the left, and vice versa. This method only works for the front channels.

If you need to equalize your surrounds and the power amplifier doesn't have level controls, run the pink noise into the left input on your processor temporarily, set the mode to Stereo or Bypass (so that no processing will occur) and take the left preamp output to each surround equalizer channel in turn, thereby using the volume control on your processor.

If you are aligning a THX or 5.1 digital system or are using an R-2 Analyzer, refer to the Home THX Audio System Room Equalization Manual available from Lucasfilm or the Rane website. The equalizer is not set any differently for a THX system, it's just a more comprehensive manual.

ANALYZING WITH NO ANALYZER

Sometimes an analyzer just isn't available without great expense or wait, but with a less than $60 investment, equalizers can be aligned and systems greatly improved. Tools: the Radio Shack SPL meter, and an audio test CD. This method doesn't average readings throughout the room, but works great for creating the "sweet spot" for one listener in the center of the room.

There are several audio test CDs available at better record and hi-fi stores, but look for one with $\frac{1}{3}$-octave test signals on individual tracks. This method can be useful before installing an equalizer to see how flat the system is. Get a pencil and plot the band readings with the supplied chart to see the response of the room before equalization.

Start by aligning the system to Dolby level as described above. Adjust the output from all the speakers in the system to 75 dB, with the subwoofer disconnected or its amplifier off.

Begin with the processor in Dolby Pro Logic Mode. The test signals appear primarily in the center channel. Switch your processor to Center Only mode if available—if not, disconnect the other speakers or channels or turn their amplifiers off. Select the CD track that corresponds to the first slider on the EQ. On the THX 44 or THX 22 it would be 80 Hz. On the SSE 35 it would be 160 Hz. Slide the filter on the EQ until the SPL reading hovers around 75 dB.

Advance the CD track to adjust the next slider and adjust the equalizer. In most rooms you will find more variance in the 80 to 800 Hz range. To double check your adjustments, go back to the track you started with and advance tracks, watching the meter for any bands that deviate.

In Dolby Pro-Logic, mono signals go to the center. The 1/3-octave frequencies on the test disc are mono, and go to the center when left and right are connected. To get signal to the left channel, disconnect the CD player's right output. Reverse this to get right channel signal. After reconnecting left and right amplifiers and speakers, analyze and equalize each in turn.

Do the sub channel last. Reconnect the subs, and connect both CD channels, with center in OFF mode or disconnected. You will find an usually large amount of level variations from 40 through 100 Hz. These variations change in different locations in the room. Look at the meter reading range as the needle is waving, and use the center of that range to go by. Just try to correct major peaks and valleys, and trust your ears for an uncolored sound.

Make sure you re-test all channel levels with the Dolby TEST signal and the SPL meter to 75 dB when you are done with the equalization process.

LISTEN

You may now trust your ears to adjust the subwoofer. If there are differences between the front channels, use the center channel as a reference and get the left and right to sound similar. This is where higher frequency controls above 1 kHz are better adjusted by ear than trusting the meter or analyzer. Most people find that a completely flat equalizer setting can sound overly bright. Not equalizing much above 1 kHz helps, and allowing a natural rolloff of high frequencies in the front channels, but not much more than -3 dB at 16 kHz.

The above approach is a shortcut to doing the room with an averaging analyzer, but it allows demonstrable results. Just listen with the equalizer *in* the system, and *bypassed*. Use the enclosed security cover to guard your valuable settings, and keep a record with the supplied equalization charts.

REFERENCES

1. J. Sehring, "The Advantages of Stereo Subwoofers", *Audio*, February 1994.
2. D. Bohn, "Exposing Equalizer Mythology", *Rane Note,* 1986
3. T. Holman "New Factors in Sound for Cinema and Television", presented at the 89th Convention of the Audio Engineering Society, Los Angeles, CA, 1990 September 21-25.
4. Lucasfilm LTD, "Home THX System Room Equalization Manual", 1993
5. D. Bohn, "Sound System Interconnection", *Rane Note*, 1985
6. G. Davis and R. Jones, "Sound Reinforcement Handbook", Yamaha Corporation, Hal Leonard Publishing.
7. P. Giddings, "Audio System Design and Installation", Howard Sams Books #22672
8. R. Dressler, "Dolby Pro Logic Surround Decoder Principles of Operation", Dolby Laboratories 1988, 1993
10. H. Ott, "Noise Reduction Techniques in Electronic Systems", Wiley Interscience

©Rane Corporation   10802 47th Ave. W.,   Mukilteo WA 98275-5098   TEL (425)355-6000   FAX (425)347-7757   WEB http://www.rane.com

Digital Dharma of Audio A/D Converters

- **Data Conversion**

- **Binary Numbers**

- **The Story of Harry & Claude**

- **Quantization**

- **Successive-Approximation**

- **PCM & PWM**

- **Delta-Sigma Modulation & Noise Shaping**

- **Dither**

- **Life After 16 – A Little Bit Sweeter**

Dennis Bohn
Rane Corporation

RaneNote 137
© 1997 Rane Corporation

INTRODUCTION

Among the many definitions for the wonderful word "dharma" is the essential function or nature of a thing. That is what this note is about: the essential function or nature of audio analog-to-digital (A/D) converters. Like everything else in the world, the audio industry has been radically and irrevocability changed by the digital revolution. No one has been spared. Arguments will ensue forever about whether the true nature of the real world is analog or digital; whether the fundamental essence, or *dharma,* of life is continuous (analog) or exists in tiny little chunks (digital). Seek not that answer here. Here we shall but resolve to understand the dharma of audio A/D converters.

Data Conversion

It is important at the onset of exploring digital audio to understand that once a waveform has been converted into digital format, *nothing can occur to change its sonic properties*. While it remains in the digital domain, it is only a series of digital words, representing numbers. Aside from the gross example of having the digital processing actually fail and cause a word to be lost or corrupted into none use, nothing can change the sound of the word. It is just a bunch of "ones" and "zeroes." There are no "one-halves" or "three-quarters". The point being that *sonically*, it begins and ends with the conversion process. Nothing is more important to digital audio than data conversion. Everything in-between is just arithmetic and waiting.

That's why there is such a big to-do with data conversion. It really is that important. Everything else quite literally is just details. We could go so far as to say that data conversion is the art of digital audio while everything else is the science, in that it is data conversion that ultimately determines whether or not the original sound is preserved (and this comment certainly does not negate the enormous and exacting science involved in truly excellent data conversion.)

Since analog signals continuously vary between an infinite number of states and computers can only handle two, the signals must be converted into *binary digital words* before the computer can work. Each digital word represents the value of the signal at one precise point in time. Today's common word length is 16-bits or 32-bits. Once converted into digital words, the information may be stored, transmitted, or operated upon within the computer.

In order to properly explore the critical interface between the analog and digital worlds, it is necessary to review a few fundamentals and a little history.

Binary Numbers

Whenever we speak of "digital," by inference, we speak of computers (throughout this paper the term "computer" is used to represent any digital-based piece of audio equipment). And computers in their heart of hearts are really quite simple. They only can understand the most basic form of communication or information: yes/no, on/off, open/closed, here/gone – all of which can be symbolically represented by two things – any two things. Two letters, two numbers, two colors, two tones, two temperatures, two charges – it doesn't matter. Unless *you* have to build something that will recognize these two states – now it matters. So, to keep it simple we choose two numbers: one and zero ... a "1" and a "0." Officially this is known as binary representation, from Latin *bini* two by two. In mathematics this is a base-2 number system, as opposed to our decimal (from Latin *decima* a tenth part or tithe) number system, which is called base-10 because we use the ten numbers 0-9.

In binary we use only the numbers 0 and 1. "0" is a good symbol for no, off, closed, gone, etc., and "1" is easy to understand as meaning yes, on, open, here, etc. In electronics it is easy to determine whether a circuit is open or closed, conducting or not conducting, has voltage or doesn't have voltage. Thus the binary number system found use in the very first computer, and nothing has changed today. Computers

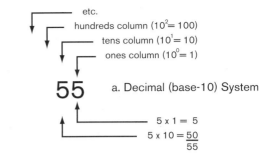

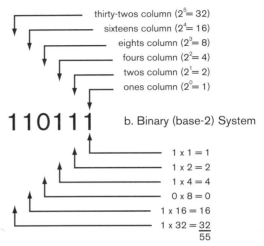

Figure 1. Number Representation Systems

just got faster and smaller and cheaper, with memory size becoming incomprehensibly large in an incomprehensibly small space.

One problem with using binary numbers is they become big and unwieldy in a hurry. For instance, it takes six digits to express my age in binary, but only two in decimal. But, in binary, we better not call them "digits" since "digits" implies a human finger or toe, of which there are ten, so confusion reigns. To get around that problem John Tukey of Bell Laboratories dubbed the basic unit of information (as defined by Shannon – more on him later) a *binary unit*, or "binary digit" which became abbreviated to "bit." A bit is the simplest possible message representing one of two states.

So, I'm 6-bits old! Well, not quite. But it takes 6-bits to express my age as 110111. Let's see how that works. I'm fifty-five years old. So in base-10 symbols that is "55," which stands for 5-1s plus 5-10s. You may not have ever thought about it, but each digit in our everyday numbers represents an additional power of 10 beginning with 0. That is, the first digit represents the number of 1s (10^0), the second digit represents the number of 10s (10^1), the third digit represents the number of 100s (10^2), and so on. We can represent any size number by using this shorthand notation.

Binary number representation is just the same except substituting the powers of 2 for the powers of 10 [any base number system is represented in this manner]. Therefore (moving from right to left) each succeeding bit represents $2^0 = 1$, $2^1 = 2$, $2^2 = 4$, $2^3 = 8$, $2^4 = 16$, $2^5 = 32$, etc. Thus, my age breaks down as 1-1, 1-2, 1-4, 0-8, 1-16, and 1-32, represented as "110111," which is 32+16+0+4+2+1 = 55 ...or *double-nickel* to you cool cats. Figure 1 shows the two examples.

Now let's take a brief look at how all this came about.

The Story of Harry & Claude

The French mathematician Fourier unknowingly laid the groundwork for A/D conversion in the late 18th century. All data conversion techniques rely on looking at, or *sampling*, the input signal at regular intervals and creating a digital word that represents the value of the analog signal at that precise moment. The fact that we know this works lies with Nyquist.

Harry Nyquist discovered while working at Bell Laboratories in the late '20s and wrote a landmark paper[1] describing the criteria for what we know today as sampled data systems. Nyquist taught us that for periodic functions, if you sampled at a rate that was at least twice as fast as the signal of interest, *then no information (data) would be lost upon reconstruction.* And since Fourier had already shown that all alternating signals are made up of nothing more than a sum of harmonically related sine and cosine waves, then audio signals are *periodic functions* and can be sampled without lost of information following Nyquist's instructions. This became known as the *Nyquist frequency*, which is the highest frequency that may be accurately sampled, and is one-half of the *sampling frequency*. For example, the theoretical Nyquist frequency for the audio CD (compact disc) system is 22.05 kHz, equaling one-half of the standardized sampling frequency of 44.1 kHz.

As powerful as Nyquist's discoveries were, they were not without their dark side: the biggest being *aliasing* frequencies. Following the Nyquist criteria (as it is now called) guarantees that no information will be lost; it does not, however, guarantee that no information *will be gained.* Although by no means obvious, the act of sampling an analog signal at precise time intervals is an act of *multiplying* the input signal by the sampling pulses. This introduces the possibility of generating "false" signals indistinguishable from the original. In other words, given a set of sampled values, we cannot relate them specifically to one unique signal. As Figure 2 shows, the same set of samples *could* have resulted from any of the three waveforms shown … and from all possible sum and difference frequencies between the sampling frequency and the one being sampled. All such false waveforms that fit the sample data are called "aliases." In audio, these frequencies show up mostly as intermodulation distortion products, and they come from the random-like white noise, or any sort of ultrasonic signal present in every electronic system. Solving the problem of aliasing frequencies is what improved audio conversion systems to today's level of sophistication. And it was Claude Shannon who pointed the way.

Shannon is recognized as the father of information theory: while a young engineer at Bell Laboratories in 1948, he defined an entirely new field of science. Even before then his genius shined through for, while still a 22-year-old student at MIT he showed in his master's thesis how the algebra invented by the British mathematician George Boole in the mid-1800s, could be applied to electronic circuits. Since that time, *Boolean algebra* has been the rock of digital logic and computer design.[2]

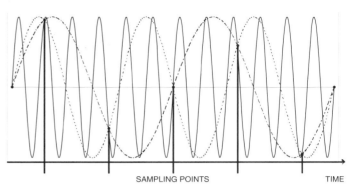

Figure 2. Aliasing Frequencies

SAMPLING POINTS — TIME

Shannon studied Nyquist's work closely and came up with a deceptively simple addition. He observed (and proved) that if you restrict the input signal's bandwidth to less than one-half the sampling frequency *then no errors due to aliasing are possible.* So bandlimiting your input to no more than one-half the sampling frequency *guarantees no aliasing.* Cool – only it's not possible.

In order to satisfy the Shannon limit (as it is called – Harry gets a "criteria" and Claude gets a "limit") you must have the proverbial brick-wall, i.e., infinite-slope filter. Well, this isn't going to happen, not in this universe. You cannot guarantee that there is absolutely no signal (or noise) greater than the Nyquist frequency. Fortunately there is a way around this problem. In fact, you go all the way around the problem and look at it from another direction.

If you cannot restrict the input bandwidth so aliasing does not occur, then solve the problem another way: Increase the sampling frequency until the aliasing products that do occur, do so at ultrasonic frequencies, and are effectively dealt with by a simple single-pole filter. This is where the term "oversampling" comes in. For full spectrum audio the minimum sampling frequency must be 40 kHz, giving you a useable theoretical bandwidth of 20 kHz – the limit of normal human hearing. Sampling at anything significantly higher than 40 kHz is termed *oversampling*. In just a few years time, we have seen the audio industry go from the CD system standard of 44.1 kHz, and the pro audio quasi-standard of 48 kHz, to 8-times and 16-times oversampling frequencies of around 350 kHz and 700 kHz respectively. With sampling frequencies this high, aliasing is no longer an issue.

Okay. So audio signals can be changed into digital words (*digitized*) without loss of information, and with no aliasing effects, as long as the sampling frequency is high enough. How is this done?

[1] Nyquist, Harry, "*Certain topics in Telegraph Transmission Theory*," published in 1928.
[2] See Clive Maxfield's book *Bebop to the Boolean Boogie* (HighText ISBN 1-878707-22-1, Solana Beach, CA, 1995) for the best treatment around.

A/D Converters-3

# Bits	# Divisions	Resolution/Div	Max % Error	Max PPM Error
8	$2^7 = 128$	39 mV	0.78	7812.00
16	$2^{15} = 32,768$	153 µV	0.003	30.50
20	$2^{19} = 524,288$	9.5 µV	0.00019	1.90
24	$2^{23} = 8,388,608$	0.6 µV	0.000012	0.12

Table 1. Quantization Steps For ±5 Volts Reference

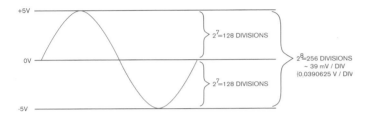

Figure 3. 8-Bit Resolution

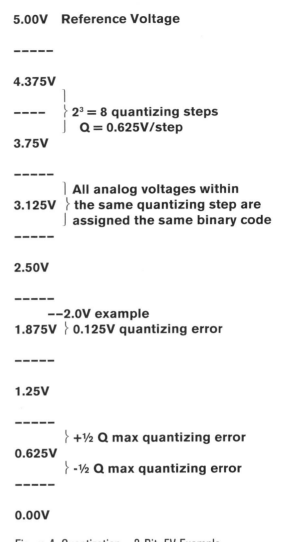

Figure 4. Quantization – 3-Bit, 5V Example

Quantization

Quantizing is the process of determining which of the possible values (determined by the number of bits or voltage reference parts) is the closest value to the current sample – i.e., you are assigning a *quantity* to that sample. Quantizing, by definition then, involves deciding between two values and thus always introduces error. How big the error, or how accurate the answer, depends on the number of bits. The more bits, the better the answer. The converter has a reference voltage which is divided up into 2^n parts, where n is the number of bits. Each part represents the same value. Since you cannot resolve anything smaller than this value, there is error. *There is always error in the conversion process.* This is the *accuracy* issue.

The number of bits determines the converter accuracy. For 8-bits, there are $2^8 = 256$ possible levels as shown in Figure 3. Since the signal swings positive *and* negative there are 128 levels for each direction. Assuming a ±5 V reference[3], this makes each division, or bit, equal to 39 mV (5/128 = .039). Hence, an 8-bit system cannot resolve any change smaller than 39 mV. This means a worst case accuracy error of 0.78%. Table 1 compares the accuracy improvement gained by 16-bit, 20-bit and 24-bit systems along with the reduction in error. (Note: this is not the only way to use the reference voltage. Many schemes exist for coding, but this one nicely illustrates the principles involved.) Each step size (resulting from dividing the reference into the number of equal parts dictated by the number of bits) is equal and is called a *quantizing step* (also called *quantizing interval* – see Figure 4). Originally this step was termed the *LSB* (least significant bit) since it equals the value of the smallest coded bit, however it is an illogical choice for mathematical treatments and has since be replaced by the more accurate term quantizing step.

The error due to the quantizing process is called *quantizing error* (no definitional stretch here). As shown earlier, each time a sample is taken there is error. Here's the not obvious part: *the quantizing error can be thought of as an unwanted signal which the quantizing process adds to the perfect original.* An example best illustrates this principle. Let the sampled input value be some arbitrarily chosen value, say, 2 volts. And let this be a 3-bit system with a 5 volt reference. The 3-bits divides the reference into 8 equal parts ($2^3 = 8$) of 0.625 V each, as shown in Figure 4. For the 2 volt input example, the converter must choose between either 1.875 volts or 2.50 volts, and since 2 volts is closer to 1.875 than 2.5, then it is the best fit. This results in a quantizing error of - 0.125 volts, i.e., the quantized answer is too small by 0.125 volts. If the input signal had been, say, 2.2 volts, then the quantized answer would have been 2.5 volts and the quantizing error would have been +0.3 volts, i.e., too big by 0.3 volts.

---

[3] A single +5 V supply is probably more common today, but this illustrates the point.

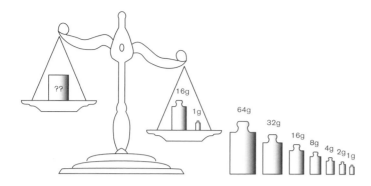

Figure 5A. Successive Approximation Example

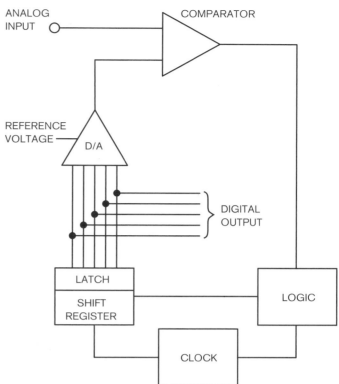

Figure 5B. Successive Approximation A/D Converter

These alternating unwanted signals added by quantizing form a quantized error waveform, that is a kind of additive broadband noise that is generally uncorrelated with the signal and is called *quantizing noise*. Since the quantizing error is essentially random (i.e. uncorrelated with the input) it can be thought of like *white noise* (noise with equal amounts of all frequencies). This is not quite the same thing as thermal noise, but it is similar. *The energy of this added noise is equally spread over the band from dc to one-half the sampling rate.* This is a most important point and will be returned to when we discuss delta-sigma converters and their use of extreme oversampling.

Successive Approximation

Successive approximation is one of the earliest and most successful analog-to-digital conversion techniques. Therefore, it is no surprise it became the initial A/D workhorse of the digital audio revolution. Successive approximation paved the way for the delta-sigma techniques to follow.

The heart of any A/D circuit is a comparator. A comparator is an electronic block whose output is determined by comparing the values of its two inputs. If the positive input is larger than the negative input then the output swings positive, and if the negative input exceeds the positive input, the output swings negative. Therefore if a reference voltage is connected to one input and an unknown input signal is applied to the other input, you now have a device that can *compare* and tell you which is larger. Thus a comparator gives you a "high output" (which could be defined to be a "1") when the input signal exceeds the reference, or a "low output" (which could be defined to be a "0") when it does not. A comparator is the key ingredient in the successive approximation technique as shown in Figures 5A & 5B.

The name *successive approximation* nicely sums up how the data conversion is done. The circuit evaluates each sample and creates a digital word representing the closest binary value. The process takes the same number of steps as bits available, i.e., a 16-bit system requires 16 steps for *each sample*. The analog sample is successively compared to determine the digital code, beginning with the determination of the biggest (most significant) bit of the code.

The description given in Daniel Sheingold's *Analog-Digital Conversion Handbook* (see References) offers the best analogy as to how successive approximation works. The process is exactly analogous to a gold miner's assay scale, or a chemical balance as seen in Figure 5A. This type of scale comes with a set of graduated weights, each one half the value of the preceding one, such as 1 gram, ½ gram, ¼ gram, $\frac{1}{8}$ gram, etc. You compare the unknown sample against these known values by first placing the heaviest weight on the scale. If it tips the scale you remove it; if it does not you leave it and go to the next smaller value. If that value tips the scale you remove it, if it does not you leave it and go to the next lower value, and so on until you reach the smallest weight that tips the scale. (When you get to the last weight, if it does not tip the scale, then you put the next highest weight back on, and that is your best answer.) The sum of all the weights on the scale represents the closest value you can resolve.

In digital terms, we can analyze this example by saying that a "0" was assigned to each weight removed, and a "1" to each weight remaining – in essence creating a digital word equivalent to the unknown sample, with the number of bits equaling the number of weights. And the quantizing error will be no more than ½ the smallest weight (or ½ *quantizing step*).

As stated earlier the successive approximation technique must repeat this cycle for each sample. Even with today's technology, this is a very time consuming process and is still limited to relatively slow sampling rates, but it did get us into the 16-bit, 44.1 kHz digital audio world.

A/D Converters-5

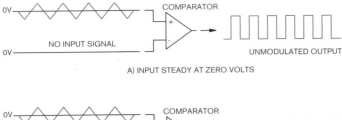

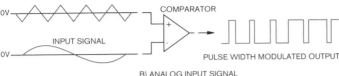

Figure 6. Pulse Width Modulation (PWM)

PCM (Pulse Code Modulation) and PWM (Pulse Width Modulation)

The successive approximation method of data conversion is an example of pulse *code* modulation, or PCM. Three elements are required: sampling, quantizing, and encoding into a fixed length digital word. The reverse process reconstructs the analog signal from the PCM code. The output of a PCM system is a series of digital words, where the word-size is determined by the available bits. For example the output is a series of 8-bit words, or 16-bit words, or 20-bit words, etc., with each word representing the value of one sample.

Pulse *width* modulation, or PWM is quite simple and quite different from PCM. Look at Figure 6. In a typical PWM system, the analog input signal is applied to a comparator whose reference voltage is a triangle-shaped waveform whose repetition rate is the sampling frequency. This simple block forms what is called an *analog modulator*.

A simple way to understand the "modulation" process is to view the output with the input held steady at zero volts. The output forms a 50% duty cycle (50% high, 50% low) square wave. As long as there is no input, the output is a steady square wave. As soon as the input is non-zero, the output becomes a pulse-width *modulated* waveform. That is, when the non-zero input is compared against the triangular reference voltage, it varies the length of time the output is either high or low.

For example, say there was a steady DC value applied to the input. For all samples when the value of the triangle is less than the input value, the output stays low, and for all samples when it is greater than the input value, it changes state and remains high. Therefore, if the triangle starts higher than the input value, the output goes high; at the next sample period the triangle has increased in value but is still more than the input, so the output remains high; this continues until the triangle reaches its apex and starts down again; eventually the triangle voltage drops below the input value and the output drops low and stays there until the reference exceeds the input

again. *The resulting pulse-width modulated output, when averaged over time, gives the exact input voltage.* For example if the output spends exactly 50% of the time with an output of 5 volts, and 50% of the time at 0 volts, then the *average* output would be exactly 2.5 volts.

This is also an FM, or frequency-modulated system – the varying pulse-width translates into a varying frequency. And it is the core principle of most Class-D switching power amplifiers. The analog input is converted into a variable pulse-width stream used to turn-on the output switching transistors. The analog output voltage is simply the average of the on-times of the positive and negative outputs. Pretty amazing stuff from a simple comparator with a triangle waveform reference.

Another way to look at this, is that this simple device actually *codes a single bit of information*, i.e., a comparator is a *1-bit A/D converter*. PWM is an example of a 1-bit A/D encoding system. And a 1-bit A/D encoder forms the heart of delta-sigma modulation.

Delta-Sigma Modulation & Noise Shaping

After nearly thirty years, delta-sigma modulation (also sigma-delta[4]) has only recently emerged as the most successful audio A/D converter technology. It waited patiently for the semiconductor industry to develop the technologies necessary to integrate analog and digital circuitry on the same chip. Today's very high-speed "mixed-signal" IC processing allows the total integration of all the circuit elements necessary to create delta-sigma data converters of awesome magnitude[5].

How the name came about is interesting. Another way to look at the action of the comparator is that the 1-bit information tells the output voltage which direction to go based upon what the input signal is doing. It looks at the input and compares it against its last look (sample) to see if this new sample is bigger or smaller than the last one – that is the information transfer: bigger or smaller, increasing or decreasing. If it is bigger than it tells the output to keep increasing, and if it is smaller it tells the output to stop increasing and start decreasing. It merely reacts to the *change*. Mathematicians use the Greek letter "delta" (symbol Δ) to stand for deviation or small incremental change, which is how this process came to be known as "delta modulation." The "sigma" part came about by the significant improvements made from summing or integrating the signal with the digital output before performing the delta modulation. Here again, mathematicians use the Greek letter "sigma" (symbol Σ) to stand for summing, so "delta-sigma" became the natural name.

Essentially a delta-sigma converter digitizes the audio signal with a very low resolution (1-bit) A/D converter at a very high sampling rate. It is the oversampling rate and subsequent digital processing that separates this from plain delta modulation (no sigma).

---

[4] The name *delta-sigma modulation* was coined by Inose and Yasuda at the University of Tokyo in 1962, but due to a translation misunderstanding, words were interchanged and taken to be *sigma-delta*. Both names are still used, but only *delta-sigma* is actually correct.

[5] Leung, K., et al., "A 120 dB dynamic Range, 96 kHz, Stereo 24-bit Analog-to-Digital Converter," presented at the 102nd Convention of the Audio Engineering Society, Munich, March 22-25, 1997.

Referring back to the earlier discussion of quantizing noise it is possible to calculate the theoretical sine wave signal-to-noise (S/N) ratio (actually the signal-to-*error* ratio, but for our purposes it's close enough to combine) of an A/D converter system knowing only *n*, the number of bits. Doing a bit (sorry) of math shows that the value of the added quantizing noise relative to a maximum (full-scale) input equals $6.02n + 1.76$ dB for a sine wave. For example, a perfect 16-bit system will have a S/N ratio of 98.1 dB, while a 1-bit delta-modulator A/D converter, on the other hand, will have only 7.78 dB!

To get something of a intuitive feel for this, consider that since there is only 1-bit, the amount of quantization error possible is as much as ½-bit. That is, since the converter must choose between the only two possibilities of maximum or minimum values, then the error can be as much as half of that. And since this quantization error shows up as added noise, then this reduces the S/N to something on the order of around 2:1 or 6 dB.

One attribute shines true above all others for delta-sigma converters and makes them a superior audio converter: simplicity. The simplicity of 1-bit technology makes the conversion process very fast, and very fast conversions allows use of extreme oversampling. And extreme oversampling pushing the quantizing noise and aliasing artifacts way out to megawiggle-land, where it is easily dealt with by digital filters (typically 64-times oversampling is used, resulting in a sampling frequency on the order of 3 MHz).

To get a better understanding of how oversampling reduces audible quantization noise, we need to think in terms of noise power. From physics you may remember that power is conserved – i.e., you can *change* it, but you cannot create or destroy it; well, quantization noise power is similar. With oversampling the quantization noise power is spread over a band that is as many times larger as is the rate of oversampling. For example, for 64-times oversampling, the noise power is spread over a band that is 64 times larger, reducing its power density in the audio band by 1/64th. See Figures 7A-E for example.

Noise shaping helps reduce in-band noise even more. Oversampling pushes out the noise, but it does so uniformly, that is, the spectrum is still flat. Noise shaping changes that. Using very clever complex algorithms and circuit tricks, noise shaping contours the noise so that it is reduced in the audible regions and increased in the inaudible regions. Conservation still holds, the total noise is the same, but the amount of noise present in the audio band is decreased while simultaneously increasing the noise out-of-band – then the digital filter eliminates it. Very slick.

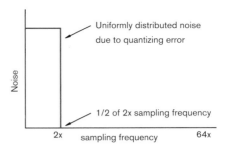

A. Original Noise Power Distribution

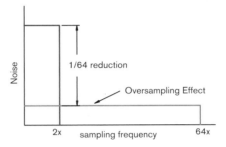

B. Reduction & Redistribution due to Oversampling

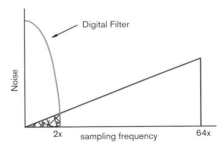

C. Noise Shaping "Tilts" Distribution

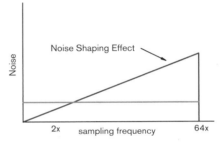

D. Digital Filter Eliminates Out-of-Band Noise

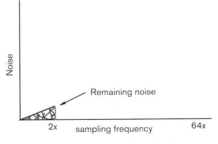

E. Remaining Noise Distribution.

Figure 7A-E. Noise Power Redistribution & Reduction due to Oversampling, Noise Shaping and Digital Filtering.

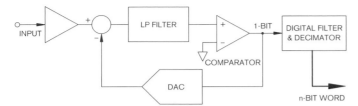

Figure 8. Delta-Sigma A/D Converter

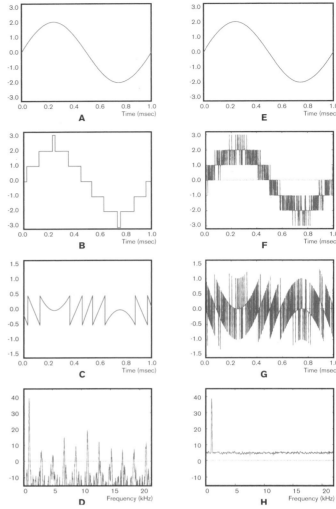

Figure 9. A. Input Signal. B. Output Signal [no dither]. C. Total Error Signal [no dither]. D. Power Spectrum of Output Signal [no dither]. E. Input Signal. F. Output Signal [with dither]. G. Total Error Signal [with dither]. H. Power Spectrum of Output Signal [with dither].[8]

As shown in Figure 8, a delta-sigma modulator consists of three parts: an analog modulator, a digital filter and a decimation circuit. The analog modulator is the 1-bit converter discussed previously with the change of integrating the analog signal before performing the delta modulation. (The integral of the analog signal is encoded rather than the change in the analog signal, as is the case for traditional delta modulation.) Oversampling and noise shaping pushes and contours all the bad stuff (aliasing, quantizing noise, etc.) so the digital filter suppresses it. The decimation circuit, or *decimator*, is the digital circuitry that generates the correct output word length of 16-, 20-, or 24-bits, and restores the desired output sample frequency. It is a digital sample rate reduction filter and is sometimes termed *downsampling* (as opposed to oversampling) since it is here that the sample rate is returned from its 64-times rate to the normal CD rate of 44.1 kHz, or perhaps to 48 kHz, or even 96 kHz, for pro audio applications. The net result is much greater resolution and dynamic range, with increased S/N and far less distortion compared to successive approximation techniques – all at lower costs.

Dither – Not All Noise Is Bad[6]

Now that oversampling helped get rid of the bad noise, let's add some *good noise – dither* noise.

Just what is *dither*? Aside from being a funny sounding word, it is a wonderfully accurate choice for what is being done. The word "dither" comes from a 12th century English term meaning "to tremble." Today it means to be in a state of indecisive agitation, or to be nervously undecided in acting or doing. Which, if you think about it, is not a bad description of noise.

Dither is one of life's many trade-offs. Here the trade-off is between noise and resolution. Believe it or not, we can introduce dither (a form of noise) and increase our ability to resolve very small values. Values, in fact, smaller than our smallest bit — now that's a good trick. Perhaps you can begin to grasp the concept by making an analogy between dither and anti-lock brakes.[7] Get it?

No? Okay, here's how this analogy works: With regular brakes, if you just stomp on them, you probably create an unsafe skid situation for the car — not a good idea. Instead, if you rapidly tap the brakes, you control the stopping without skidding. We shall call this "dithering the brakes." What you have done is introduce "noise" (tapping) to an otherwise rigidly binary (*on* or *off*) function.

So by "tapping" on our analog signal, we can improve our ability to resolve it. By introducing noise, the converter rapidly switches between two quantization levels, rather than picking one or the other, when neither is really correct. Sonically, this comes out as noise, rather than a discrete level with error. Subjectively, what would have been perceived as distortion is now heard as noise.

---

[6] This section is included because of the confusing surrounding the term. However, it is noted that with the truly astonishing advances made in A/D converter resolution technology of the past two years, the need for dither in A/D converters has essentially disappeared, making this section more of historical interest. Dither is still necessary for word-length reduction in other digital processing.

[7] Thanks to Bob Moses, PAVO, for this great analogy.

[8] From Pohlmann, *Principles of Digital Audio, 3rd ed.*, p.44.

Lets look at this is more detail. The problem dither helps to solve is that of quantization error caused by the data converter being forced to choose one of two exact levels for each bit it resolves. It cannot choose *between* levels, it must pick one or the other. With 16-bit systems, the digitized waveform for *high frequency, low signal levels* looks very much like a steep staircase with few steps. An examination of the spectral analysis of this waveform reveals lots of nasty sounding distortion products. We can improve this result either by adding more bits, or by adding dither. Prior to 1997, adding more bits for better resolution was straightforward, but expensive, thereby making dither an inexpensive compromise; today, however, there is less need.

The dither noise is added to the low-level signal before conversion. The mixed noise causes the small signal to jump around, which causes the converter to switch rapidly *between* levels rather than being forced to choose between two fixed values. Now the digitized waveform still looks like a steep staircase, but each step, instead of being smooth, is comprised of many narrow strips, like vertical Venetian blinds. The spectral analysis of this waveform shows almost no distortion products at all, albeit with an increase in the noise content. The dither has caused the distortion products to be pushed out beyond audibility, and replaced with an increase in wideband noise. Figure 9 diagrams this process.

Life After 16 – A Little Bit Sweeter

Current digital recording standards allow for only 16-bits, yet it is safe to say that for all practical purposes 16-bit technology is history[9]. Everyone who can afford the up-grade is using 20- and 24-bit data converters and (temporarily, until DVD-Audio becomes common) *dithering* (vs. truncating) down to 16-bits.

Here is what is gained by using 20-bits:
* 24 dB more dynamic range
* *24 dB less residual noise*
* 16:1 reduction in quantization error
* Improved jitter (timing stability) performance

And if it is 24-bits, add **another 24 dB** *to each of the above and make it a* **256:1** *reduction in quantizing error, with essentially zero jitter!*

As stated in the beginning of this note, with today's technology, analog-to-digital-to-analog conversion is *the* element defining the sound of a piece of equipment, and if it's not done perfectly then everything that follows is compromised.

With 20-bit high-resolution conversion, low signal-level detail is preserved. The improvement in fine detail shows up most noticeably by reducing the quantization errors of low-level signals. Under certain conditions, these course data

steps can create audio passband harmonics not related to the input signal. Audibility of this quantizing noise is much higher than in normal analog distortion, and is also known as *granulation noise*. 20-bits virtually eliminates granulation noise. Commonly heard examples are musical fades, like reverb tails and cymbal decay. With only 16-bits to work with, they don't so much fade, as collapse in noisy chunks.

Where it really matters most is in measuring very small things. It doesn't make much difference when measuring big things. If your ruler measures in whole inch increments and you are measuring something 10 feet long, the most you can be off is ½ inch. Not a big deal. However, if what you're measuring is less than an inch, and your error can be as much as ½ inch, well, now you've got an accuracy problem. This is exactly the problem in digitizing small audio signals. Graduating our audio digital ruler finer and finer means we can accurately resolve smaller and smaller signal levels, allowing us to capture the *musical details*. Getting the exact right answer *does* result in better reproduction of music.

A/D Converter Measuring Bandwidth Note

Due to the oversampling and noise shaping characteristics of delta-sigma A/D converters, certain measurements must use the appropriate bandwidth or inaccurate answers result. Specifications such as signal-to-noise, dynamic range, and distortion are subject to misleading results if the wrong bandwidth is used. Since noise shaping purposely reduces audible noise by shifting the noise to inaudible higher frequencies, taking measurements over a bandwidth wider than 20 kHz results in answers that do not correlate with the listening experience. Therefore, it is important to set the correct measurement bandwidth to obtain meaningful data.

---

[9] Historical Footnote: The reason the British divided up the pound into 16 ounces is not as arbitrary as some might suspect, but, rather, was done with great calculation and foresightedness. At the time, you see, technology had advanced to where 4-bit systems were really quite the thing. And, of course, 4-bits allows you to divide things up into 16 different values (since $2^4 = 16$). So one pound was divided up into 16 equal parts called "ounces," for reasons to be explained at another time. Similarly, the roots of a common American money term come from a simple 3-bit system. A 3-bit system allows eight values (since $2^3 = 8$), so if you divide up a dollar into eight parts, each part is, of course, 12.5 cents. Therefore you would call two parts (or *two-bits*, as we Americans say) a "quarter" — obvious.

References

1. Candy, James C. and Gabor c. Temes, eds. *Oversampling Delta-Sigma Data Converters: Theory, Design, and Simulation* (IEEE Press ISBN 0-87942-285-8, NY, 1992).
2. "Delta Sigma A/D Conversion Technique Overview," *Application Note AN 10* (Crystal Semiconductor Corporation, TX, 1989).
3. Pohlmann, Ken C. *Advanced Digital Audio* (Sams ISBN 0-672-22768-1, IN, 1991).
4. Pohlmann, Ken C. *Principles of Digital Audio, 3rd ed.* (McGraw Hill ISBN 0-07-050469-5, NY, 1995).
5. Sheingold, Daniel H., ed. *Analog-Digital Conversion Handbook, 3rd ed.* (Prentice-Hall ISBN 0-13-032848-0, NJ, 1986).
6. "Sigma-Delta ADCs and DACs," *1993 Applications Reference Manual* (Analog Devices, MA, 1993).
7. *The American Heritage Dictionary of the English Language, 3rd ed.* (Houghton Miffin ISBN 0-395-44895-6, Boston, 1992).
8. Watkinson, John. *The Art of Digital Audio, 2nd ed.* (Focal Press, ISBN 0-240-51320-7, Oxford, England, 1994).

©Rane Corporation   10802 47th Ave. W.,   Mukilteo WA 98275-5098   TEL (425)355-6000   FAX (425)347-7757   WEB http://www.rane.com

Unity Gain & Impedance Matching: Strange Bedfellows

- **Unity Gain and Balancing**

- **Impedance Matching**

- **Cross-Coupled Output Stages**

INTRODUCTION

This paper discusses the pitfalls (often subtle) of our industry's failure to define and standardize what "unity gain" means, and the conditions necessary to measure it. It further discusses how people improperly use one piece of misinformation (impedance matching) to correct for this lack of standardization. All done, without knowing discrepancies exist between different pieces of equipment, and without knowing impedance matching is unnecessary, signal degrading, and wasteful.

For me, it began with a phone call. The caller said he wanted to know our output impedance so he could add the proper load impedance.

"Why would you want to do such a thing?" I asked.

"Because I want to maintain unity gain through each piece of signal processing gear," he replied.

That gave me pause. Then I laughed and realized what he was doing right, and what he was doing wrong.

The problem stems from another case of our industry working without proper guidelines and standards. This one involves the conditions used to establish unity gain. Lately, the popular trend of including unity gain detent points and reference marks only aggravates things.

This Note identifies and explains the problem. Once understood, the solution becomes easy – and it doesn't involve impedance matching.

Dennis Bohn
Rane Corporation

RaneNote 124
© **1991 Rane Corporation**

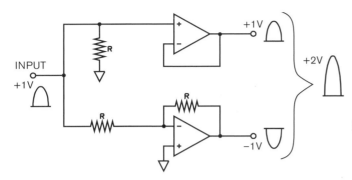

Figure 1. Differential line driving circuit.

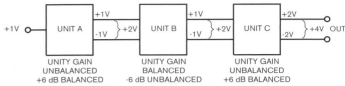

Figure 2. Example of signal increase due to different unity gain definitions.

UNITY DOES NOT ALWAYS EQUAL ONE

It begins with an understanding of unity gain. Simple enough. Ask anyone and they will tell you unity gain means that if I put, say, 1 V in, I get 1 V out, i.e., a gain of one, or unity. Nothing could be easier. That is until that same someone asks the question,

"Is that unity gain balanced, or unbalanced?"

Herein lies the problem. Today we find that many (most?) pro audio signal processors have a gain difference of 6 dB between unbalanced and balanced out (exceptions to this are units with output transformers, or cross-coupled output stages – see Appendix). This x2 difference results from differentially driving the line. Figure 1 shows how an input signal drives one side of the line positively and the other side negatively (each line driving amplifier has a gain of one, but together they yield a gain a two). For example, a +1 V peak AC input signal drives one side to +1 V while simultaneously driving the other side to -1 V. This gives a balanced output level of +2 V peak (the *difference* between +1 V and -1 V). Alternatively, that same input signal drives an unbalanced line to +1 V peak. Thus, there is a 6 dB disparity between an unbalanced and a balanced output — a gain difference factor of two.

Here, unity equals two.

NO STANDARDS

This brings us to the part about no standards. Without a standard defining the specified conditions for unity gain, manufacturers make their own decision as to what "unity gain" means. For one, it means 1 V in gives 1 V out unbalanced, and 2 V out balanced. For another, it means 1 V in gives 1 V out balanced, and ½ V out unbalanced. For yet others, it means 1 V in gives 1 V out (using transformers), or 2 V out (using cross-coupled stages), either balanced *or* unbalanced. Very confusing.

Figure 2 shows how this creates problems. Here different definitions result in a gain of 12 dB, *with all controls seemingly set for unity*.

IMPEDANCE MATCHING

Impedance matching went out with vacuum tubes, Edsels and beehive hairdos. Modern transistor and op-amp stages do not require impedance matching. If done, *impedance matching degrades audio performance*.

Modern solid-state devices transfer *voltage* between products, not *power*. Optimum power transfer requires impedance matching. Optimum voltage transfer does not. Today's products have high input impedances and low output impedances. These are compatible with each other. Low impedance output stages drive high impedance input stages. This way, there is no loading, or signal loss, between stages. No longer concerned about the transfer of power, today's low output/high input impedances allow the almost lossless transfer of signal voltages.

What then, does impedance matching have to do with unity gain? Well, it shouldn't have anything to do with it. But because of different manufacturer's definitions, it is one way (brute force) of correcting gain discrepancies between products. *Impedance matching introduces a 6 dB pad between units*. Let's see how this works.

Look at Figure 3. Here we see a real world interface between two units. The positive and negative outputs of the driving unit have an output impedance labeled R_{OUT}. Each input has an impedance labeled R_{IN}. Typically these are around 100 Ω for R_{OUT} and 20k Ω for R_{IN}. Georg Ohm taught us that 100 Ω driving 20k Ω (looking only at one side for simplicity) creates a voltage divider, but a very small one (-0.04 dB). This illustrates the above point about achieving almost perfect voltage transfer, *if impedance matching is not done*.

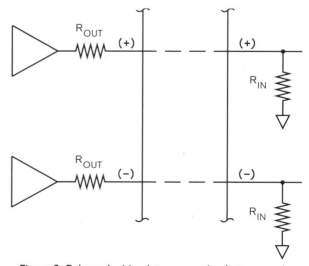

Figure 3. Balanced wiring interconnection between units.

If it is done, you lose half your signal. Here's how: impedance matching these units involves adding 100 Ω resistors (equal to R_{OUT}) to each input (paralleling R_{IN}). The new input impedance now becomes essentially the same as the output impedance (100 Ω in parallel with 20 kΩ equals 99.5 Ω), therefore matching. Applying Ohm's law to this new circuit tells us that 100 Ω driving 100 Ω creates a voltage divider of ½. That is, ½ of our signal drops across R_{OUT} and ½ drops across R_{IN}, for a voltage loss of 6 dB. We lose half our signal in heat across R_{OUT}. Not a terribly desirable thing to do; yet, it does fix our unity gain problem.

Back to Figure 2. By selectively impedance matching only between Units A and B, we introduce a 6 dB pad. This cancels the 6 dB gain resulting from using balanced outputs with this unit. This changes the output of Unit A to ±½ V, or +1 V balanced. Since Unit B already is unity gain balanced, then we do *not* impedance match, and its output is also ±½ V. We do impedance match Unit C's output and now Unit C passes this +1 V signal to its output as ±½ V, and finally we get a true unity gain result from all three boxes. One volt in, produces one volt out — balanced.

PREFERRED ALTERNATIVE TO IMPEDANCE MATCHING

The preferred alternative to impedance matching is ridiculously easy — turn the level control down 6 dB. Of course this means the unity gain mark, or detent position, loses its meaning, but this is far better than losing half your signal.

Many users do not view this issue as a problem. There are so many other variables that require turning level controls up or down that this just becomes part of the overall system gain setting. Most units have sufficient headroom to allow for an unexpected 6 dB of gain without hurting anything.

Besides, the unity gain mark/detent is only a reference point. The whole reason manufacturers give you level controls, is to allow setting the gain you need for your system. If it were important for them to remain at unity, they would not be there. They are yours. You paid for them. Use them.

SUMMARY

Unity gain and impedance matching: a strange dichotomy. One solves the other, but badly.

Impedance matching is not necessary and creates many ills. It reduces signal levels and dynamic range by 6 dB (and possibly signal-to-noise by the same amount). The large currents necessary to drive the low matching-impedance usually degrades total harmonic distortion. And the extra current means excess heat and strain on the power supply, creating a potentially unreliable system.

Simply turning the level control down (or up, as the situation dictates), is the best solution for unity gain disparities.

Rane's Standard:
"Unity Gain" is defined as 'balanced in' to 'balanced out'. For unbalanced units, "unity gain" is modified to mean 'balanced or unbalanced in' to 'unbalanced out'.

APPENDIX: UNDERSTANDING CROSS-COUPLED OUTPUT STAGES

Cross-coupled output stages have been around for a long time[1]. So has their marketing rhetoric. Some of the many grand claims are even true. Understanding cross-coupled output stages begins with the following: *The only purpose of cross-coupling techniques is to mimic an output transformer under unbalanced conditions. They offer no advantages over conventional designs when used balanced.* Understanding cross-coupled *circuitry* begins with an understanding of output transformers (Figure 4). Here we see a typical configuration. The output amplifier drives the primary winding of the transformer (with one side grounded), and the secondary winding floats (no ground reference) to produce the positive and negative output legs of the signal. An output transformer with a turns ratio of 1:2 (normal), produces a 2 V output signal for a 1 V input signal, i.e., there exists a difference of potential between the two output leads of 2 V. The diagram shows how a 1 V peak input signal produces ±1 V peak output signals (relative to ground), or a differential floating output of 2 V peak. (Alternatively, two op-amps could differentially drive the primary; and use a turns ratio of 1:1 to produce the same results.)

So, 1 V in, produces 2 V out – a gain of 6 dB. Simple. Note that because the output signal develops across the secondary winding, it does not matter whether one side is grounded or not. Grounding one side gives the same 2 V output. Only this time it references to ground instead of floating. *There is no gain change between balanced and unbalanced operation of output transformers.*

Contrast this with the active output stage of Figure 1. Here, grounding one side reduces the output from 2 V to 1 V. Though this is a one time gain reduction (correctable by increasing the level 6 dB), it bothers some. Mark off points.

Of more concern is the 6 dB lost of headroom. A desirable aspect of differentially driving interconnecting lines is the ability to get 6 dB more output level from the same power supply rails. Most audio products use op-amps running from ±15 V rails. A single op-amp drives an unbalanced line to around ±11 V peak (+20 dBu). Using two op-amps to drive the line differentially doubles this to ±22 V peak (one goes positive, while the other goes negative), a value equal to +26 dBu. Mark off more points for loss of headroom.

Mark off even more points for potential distortion (depends on op-amps, and exact configuration), oscillation,

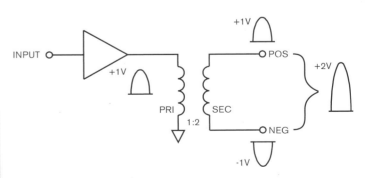

Figure 4. Balancing output transformer

and failure, resulting from asking one side to drive a short (the result of grounding one side for unbalanced operation).

These three things: 6 dB loss of gain, 6 dB loss of headroom, and the questionable practice of allowing an op-amp to drive a short, sparked creation of the cross-coupled output stage. It solves two out of three.

Cross-coupled output stages do two things active differential output stages do not. They maintain the same gain either balanced or unbalanced. And they protect themselves from having to drive a short. But *they still have 6 dB loss of headroom*.

A point not understood by many users. They believe that cross-coupled output stages behave exactly like transformers. Not true. They have the same headroom limitation as all op-amp designs operating from ±15 V power supplies. (Some equipment uses ±18 V, but this only results in a 2 dB difference for unbalanced.)

MCI's original design[1] appears in Figure 5. MCI used two op-amps, wired such that the opposite output subtracted from twice the input signal (not particularly obvious, but true). That way, each side's gain looks like a gain of one for balanced operation, i.e., 1 V in, gives ±1 V out. Yet shorting one side (running unbalanced) gives a gain of two (nothing to subtract).

Since cross-coupled and normal differential output stages use essentially the same parts (and therefore cost the same), a fair question is why don't you see more of the former? The answer lies in the perils of positive feedback.

Inherent to the operation of cross-coupled output stages is positive feedback. The subtraction process created by cross-coupling opposite outputs, has an undesirable side effect of being positive feedback. Because of this, op-amp matching, resistor ratio matching and temperature compensation becomes critical. If not done properly, cross-coupled stages drift and eventually latch-up to the supply rails. (This is why you see so many variations of Figure 5, with all sorts of excess baggage glued on. Things like capacitive-coupled AC feedback, fixed loading resistors, high-frequency gain roll off capacitors, offset trims, etc.) The difficulty in controlling these parameters in high volume production, leads most manufacturers to abandon its use.

Recently, Analog Devices helped solve these problems by putting all the elements into one integrated circuit[2]. Their monolithic IC version (which Rane uses in select products) operates on the same principles as MCI's, although Analog Devices uses three op-amps to drive the input differentially. Here precise control and laser trimming guarantees stable performance, and opens up a new chapter in cross-coupled output stage use.

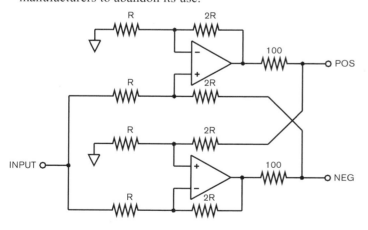

Figure 5. MCI cross-coupled output circuit[1].

REFERENCES

1. T. Hay, "Differential Technology in Recording Consoles and the Impact of Transformerless Circuitry on Grounding Technique," presented at the 67th Convention of the Audio Engineering Society, *J. Audio Eng. Soc. (Abstracts)*, vol. 28, p. 924 (Dec. 1980).
2. "SSM-2142 Balanced Line Driver," *Audio/Video Reference Manual*, pp. 7-139 (Analog Devices, Norwood, MA, 1992).

Reproduced with permission from *S&VC*, vol. 8, no. 9, Sept. 20, 1990, pp. 10-20.

Setting Sound System Level Controls

- **Decibel: Audio Workhorse**

- **Dynamic Range: What's Enough?**

- **Headroom: Maximizing**

- **Console/Mic Preamp Gain Settings**

- **Outboard Gear I/O Level Controls**

- **Power Amplifier Sensitivity Controls**

- **Active Crossover Output Attenuators**

- **Using the RaneGain™ Test Set**

Dennis Bohn
Rane Corporation

RaneNote 135
© **1997 Rane Corporation**

IMPORTANCE

Correctly setting a sound system's gain structure is one of the most important contributors to creating an excellent *sounding* system. Conversely, an improperly set gain structure is one of the leading contributors to *bad* sounding systems. The cost of the system is secondary to proper setup. The most expensive system set wrong never performs up to the level of a correctly set inexpensive system. Setting all the various level controls is not difficult; however, it remains a very misunderstood topic.

The key to setting level controls lies in the simple understanding of *what* you are trying to do. A few minutes spent in mastering this concept makes most set-ups intuitive. A little common sense goes a long way in gain setting.

A dozen possible procedures exist for correctly setting the gain structure of any system. What follows is but one of these, and is meant to demonstrate the *principles* involved. Once you master the fundamental principles, you will know what to do when confronted with different system configurations.

DECIBELS, DYNAMIC RANGE & MAXIMIZING HEADROOM

Audio-speak is full of jargon, but none so pervasive as the *decibel.* Those unfamiliar or rusty with decibel notation, and its many reference levels, are directed to the sidebar offered as review or introduction. Mastering gain, or level control settings also requires an understanding of *dynamic range* and *headroom.*

Dynamic range is the ratio of the loudest (undistorted) signal to that of the quietest (discernible) signal in a piece of equipment or a complete system, expressed in decibels (dB*).* For signal processing equipment, the maximum output signal is ultimately restricted by the size of the power supplies, i.e., it cannot swing more voltage than is available. While the minimum output signal is determined by the noise floor of the unit, i.e., it cannot put out a discernible signal smaller than the noise (generally speaking). Professional-grade analog signal processing equipment can output maximum levels of +26 dBu, with the best noise floors being down around -94 dBu. This gives a maximum *unit dynamic range* of 120 dB — a pretty impressive number coinciding nicely with the 120 dB dynamic range of normal human hearing (from just audible to painfully loud).

For sound systems, the maximum loudness level is what is achievable before *acoustic feedback*, or system squeal begins. While the minimum level is determined by the overall background noise. It is significant that the audio equipment noise is usually swamped by the HVAC (heating, ventilating & air conditioning) plus audience noise. Typical minimum noise levels are 35-45 dB SPL (sound pressure level), with typical loudest sounds being in the 100-105 dB SPL area. (Sounds louder than this start being very uncomfortable, causing audience complaints.) This yields a typical useable *system dynamic range* on the order of only 55-70 dB — quite different than unit dynamic ranges.

Note that the dynamic range of the system is largely out of your hands. The lower limit is set by the HVAC and audience noise, while the upper end is determined by the comfort level of the audience. As seen above, this useable dynamic range only averages about 65 dB. Anything more doesn't hurt, but it doesn't help either.

Headroom is the ratio of the *largest* undistorted signal possible through a unit or system, to that of the *average* signal level. For example, if the average level is +4 dBu and the largest level is +26 dBu, then there is *22 dB of headroom*.

Since you can't do anything about the system dynamic range, your job actually becomes easier. All you need worry about is *maximizing unit headroom*. But how much is enough?

An examination of all audio signals reveals music as being the most dynamic (*big surprise*) with a *crest factor* of 4-10.

Crest factor is the term used to represent the ratio of the peak (crest) value to the *rms (root mean square — think average)* value of a waveform. For example, a sine wave has a crest factor of 1.4 (or 3 dB), since the peak value equals 1.414 times the rms value.

Music's wide crest factor of 4-10 translates into 12-20 dB. This means that musical peaks occur 12-20 dB higher than the "average" value. This is why headroom is so important. *You need 12-20 dB of headroom in each unit to avoid clipping.*

PRESET ALL LEVEL CONTROLS IN THE SYSTEM

After all equipment is hooked-up, verify system operation by sending an audio signal through it. *Do this first before trying to set any gain/level controls.* This is to make sure all wiring has been done correctly, that there are no bad cables, and that there is no audible hum or buzz being picked up by improperly grounded interconnections (See the *Sound System Interconnections* RaneNote).

Once you are sure the system is operating quietly and correctly, then you are ready to proceed.

Turn down all power amplifier level/sensitivity controls.

Turn *off* all power amplifiers. (This allows you to set the maximum signal level through the system without making yourself and others stark raving mad.)

Set all gain/level controls to their *off* or *minimum* settings.

Defeat all dynamic controllers such as compressors/limiters, gate/expanders, and enhancers by setting the Ratio controls to 1:1, and/or turning the Threshold controls way up (or down for gate/expanders).

Use no *equalization* until after correctly setting the gain.

CONSOLE/MIC PREAMP GAIN SETTINGS

A detailed discussion of how to run a mixing console lies outside the range of this Note, but a few observations are relevant. *Think about the typical mixer signal path.* At its most basic, each input channel consists of a mic stage, some EQ, routing assign switches and level controls, along with a channel master fader. All of these input channels are then mixed together to form various outputs, each with its own level control or fader. To set the proper mixer gain structure, you want to maximize the overall S/N (signal-to-noise) ratio. *Now think about that a little:* because of the physics behind analog electronics, each stage contributes noise as the signal travels through it. (Digital is a bit different and is left to another Note and another day.) Therefore each stage works to *degrade* the overall signal-to-noise ratio. Here's the important part: *The amount of noise contributed by each stage is* (relatively) independent of the signal level passing through it. So, the bigger the input signal, the better the output S/N ratio (in general).

The rule here is to take as much gain as necessary to bring the signal up to the desired average level, say, +4 dBu, *as soon as possible.* If you need 60 dB of gain to bring up a mic input, you don't want to do it with 20 dB here, and 20 dB there, and 20 dB some other place. You want to do it all at once at the input mic stage. For most applications, *the entire system S/N (more or less) gets fixed at the mic stage.* Therefore set it for as much gain as possible without excessive clipping. Note the wording *excessive* clipping. A little clipping is not audible in the overall scheme of things. Test the source for its expected *maximum input level*. This means, one at a time, having the singers sing, and the players play, as loud as they expect to sing/play during the performance. Or, if the source is recorded, or off-the-air, turn it up as loud as ever expected. Set the input mic gain trim so the mic OL (overload) light just occasionally flickers. *This is as much gain as can be taken with this stage.* Any more and it will clip all the time; any less and you are hurting your best possible S/N.

(Note that a simple single mic preamp is set up in the same manner as a whole mixing console.)

OUTBOARD GEAR I/O LEVEL CONTROLS

All outboard unit level controls (except active crossovers — see below) exist primarily for two reasons:
- They provide the flexibility to operate with all signal sizes. If the input signal is too small, a gain control brings it up to the desired average level, and if the signal is too large, an attenuator reduces it back to the desired average.
- Level controls for equalizers: the need to provide make-up gain in the case where significant cutting of the signal makes it too small, or the opposite case, where a lot of boosting makes the overall signal too large, requiring attenuation.

Many outboard units operate at "unity gain," and do not have *any* level controls — what comes in (magnitude-wise) is what comes out. For a perfect system, *all* outboard gear would operate in a unity gain fashion. *It is the main console's (or preamp's) job to add whatever gain is required to all input signals.* After that, all outboard compressors, limiters, equalizers, enhancers, effects, or what-have-you need not provide gain beyond that required to offset the amplification or attenuation the box provides.

With that said, you can now move ahead with setting whatever level controls *do* exist in the system.

Whether the system contains one piece of outboard gear, or a dozen, gains are all set the same way. Again, the rule is to maximize the S/N through each piece of equipment, thereby maximizing the S/N of the whole system. And that means setting things such that your *maximum system signal* goes straight through every box without clipping.

RaneGain Test Set

The RaneGain (RG) test set is a handy tool kit based on techniques first developed by Pat Brown of *Syn-Aud-Con* for use in quickly setting sound system gain controls. It consists of two pieces: a self-contained, phantom-powered 400 Hz generator and a separate audio Transducer housed in an XLR connector. The RG Generator plugs into any mic input on a mixing console (or separate mic preamp) having phantom power in the range of 12-48 VDC, providing a convenient sound source. The RG Transducer plugs into the output of each unit and sounds a warning whenever the output level is clipped. See the RaneGain data sheet (*www.rane.com/ranegain.html*) for additional details.

SETTING SIGNAL PROCESSING LEVEL CONTROLS

First, a sound source is connected to the mixing console (or separate mic preamp) to provide the *maximum system signal* output, then this signal is used to set the outboard units.

The most convenient sound source is one built into the mixer or preamp. If a built-in generator is available, use that; if not, use an external oscillator, such as the RaneGain generator or other test equipment. Connect the generator to an unused channel in the mixing console or to the input of the mic preamp. Carefully set the generator level and the channel input fader so the mic stage does not overload. Next, adjust the master output fader (or preamp output level control) for the largest level possible without clipping the output stage. Determine this maximum level using any of the four methods: *RaneGain Test Set, OL Light, Oscilloscope,* or *AC Voltmeter* described below.

- **RaneGain Test Set** Plug the RG Transducer into the console's (or preamp's) master balanced output XLR jack. Turn up the master output fader (or preamp output level control) until the Transducer first sounds; reduce the level until the Transducer stops. This is now the *maximum system signal* output.

- **OL Light** Adjust the sound source until the master output overload (OL) indicator just begins to light (or the output meter indicates an OL condition). This is now the *maximum system signal* output, although it is a conservative maximum since most OL indicators come on several dB before actual clipping.

- **Oscilloscope** Using the RG Transducer or OL light are fast and convenient ways to set levels. However, a better alternative is to use an oscilloscope and actually *measure* the output to see where excessive clipping really begins. This method gets around the many different ways that OL points are detected and displayed by manufacturers. *There is no standard for OL detection.* If you want the absolute largest signal possible before real clipping, you must use either the RG Transducer or an oscilloscope.

- **AC Voltmeter** If the RG Transducer or an oscilloscope is out of the question, another alternative is to use an AC voltmeter (preferably with a "dB" scale). Here, instead of relying on the OL indicator, you choose a very large output level, say, +20 dBu (7.75 Vrms) and *define that as your maximum level.* Now set everything to not clip at this level. This is a reasonable and accurate way to do it, but is it an appropriate maximum? Well, you already know (from the above discussion) that you need 12- 20 dB of headroom above your average signal. It is normal pro audio practice to set your average level at +4 dBu (which, incidentally, registers as "0 dB" on a true VU meter). And since all high quality pro audio equipment can handle +20 dBu in and out, then this value becomes a safe maximum level for setting gains, giving you 16 dB of headroom — plenty for most systems.

Outboard gear gain/level controls fall into three categories:
- No controls
- One control, either Input or Output
- Both Input & Output Controls

Obviously, the first category is not a problem!

If there is only one level control, regardless of its location, set it to give the maximum output level either by observing the OL light, or the RG Transducer, or the oscilloscope, or by setting an output level of +20 dBu on your AC voltmeter.

With two controls it is very important to set the *Input control* first. Do this by turning up the Output control just enough to observe the signal. Set the Input control to barely light the OL indicator, then back it down a hair, or set it just below clipping using your oscilloscope, or until the RG Transducer buzzes. Now set the Output control also to just light the OL indicator, or just at clipping using the scope, or just buzzing. (Note: there is no good way to optimally set an input control on a unit with two level controls, using only an AC voltmeter.)

For Rane digital audio products, like the Rane RPM series of Multiprocessors, where input A/D (analog-to-digital) metering is provided with software, setting the input level gain is particularly easy and *extremely important*: Using the maximum system signal as the input, open up the Input Trim box and simply slide the control until the 0 dBFS indicator begins lighting. This indicates the onset of "digital clipping," and is definitely something you want to avoid, so this is the maximum gain point.

SETTING POWER AMPLIFIERS

If your system uses active crossovers, for the moment, set all the crossover output level controls to maximum.

Much confusion surrounds power amplifier controls.

First, let's establish that power amplifier "level/volume/gain" controls are *input sensitivity* controls. (no matter *how* they are calibrated.) They are not *power* controls. They have absolutely *nothing to do with output power.* They are sensitivity controls, i.e., these controls determine exactly what input level will cause the amplifier to produce full power. Or, if you prefer, they determine just how *sensitive* the amplifier is. For example, they might be set such that an input level of +4 dBu causes full power, or such that an input level of +20 dBu causes full power, or whatever-input-level-your-system-may-require, causes full power.

They do not *change* the available output power. They only change the required input level to produce full output power.

Clearly understanding the above, makes setting these controls elementary. You want the *maximum system signal* to cause full power; therefore set the amplifier controls to give full power with your maximum input signal using the following procedure:

1. Turn the sensitivity controls all the way down (least sensitive; fully CCW; off).
2. Make sure the device driving the amp is delivering max (unclipped) signal.
3. Warn everyone you are about to make a LOT of noise!
4. Cover your ears and turn on the first power amplifier.
5. Slowly rotate the control until clipping just begins. Stop! This is the maximum possible power output using the maximum system input signal. In general, if there is never a bigger input signal, this setting guarantees the amplifier cannot clip. (Note: if this much power causes the loud-speaker to "bottom out," or distort in any manner, then you have a mismatch between your amp and speaker. *Matching speakers and amps is another subject beyond this note.*)
6. Repeat the above process for each power amplifier.
7. Turn the test signal off.

ACTIVE CROSSOVER OUTPUT LEVEL CONTROLS

Setting the output attenuators on active crossovers differs from other outboard gear in that they serve a different purpose. These attenuators allow setting different output levels to each driver to correct for efficiency differences. This means that the same voltage applied to different drivers results in different loudness levels. This is the loudspeaker *sensitivity* specification, usually stated as so many dB SPL at a distance of one meter, when driven with one watt. Ergo, you want to set these controls for equal maximum loudness in each driver section. Try this approach:

1. Turn down all the crossover outputs *except for the lowest frequency band*, typically labeled "Low-Out." (Set one channel at a time for stereo systems.)
2. If available, use pink noise as a source for these settings; otherwise use a frequency tone that falls mid-band for each section. Turn up the source until you verify the console is putting out the maximum system signal level (somewhere around the console clipping point.) Using an SPL meter (*Important: turn off all weighting filters; the SPL meter must have a flat response mode*) turn down this one output level control until the maximum desired loudness level is reached, typically around 100-105 dB SPL. Very loud, but not harmful. (1-2 hours is the Permissible Noise Exposure allowed by the U.S. Dept. of Labor Noise Regulations for 100-105 dB SPL, A-weighted levels.)

Okay. You have established that with this maximum system signal this driver will not exceed your desired maximum loudness level (at the location picked for measurement). Now, do the same for the other output sections as follows:

1. *Mute* this output section — *do not turn down the level control; you just set it!* If a Mute button is not provided on the crossover, disconnect the cable to the power amp.
2. Turn up the next output section: either "High-Out" for 2-way systems, or "Mid-Out" for 3-way systems, until the *same maximum loudness level* is reached. Stop and mute this output.
3. Continue this procedure until all output level controls are set.
4. Un-mute all sections, and turn off the test source.

Congratulations! You have finished correctly setting the gain structure for your system. Now you are ready to adjust EQ and set all dynamic controllers. Remember, after EQ-ing to *always reset the EQ level controls for unity gain*. Use the Bypass (or Engage) pushbuttons to "A/B" between equalized and un-equalized sound, adjusting the overall level controls as required for equal loudness in both positions.

SUMMARY

Optimum performance requires correctly setting the gain structure of sound systems. It makes the difference between excellent sounding systems and mediocre ones. The proper method begins by taking all necessary gain in the console, or preamp. All outboard units operate with unity gain, and are set to pass the *maximum system signal* without clipping. The power amplifier sensitivity controls are set for a level appropriate to pass the maximum system signal without excessive clipping. Lastly, active crossover output controls are set to correct for loudspeaker efficiency differences.

REFERENCES

1. Murray, John & Pat Brown, "A Gain Structure Guide," *LIVE SOUND! International*, pp. 18-24, Mar/Apr 1997. Thanks to John and Pat for inspiration and some content for this RaneNote.
2. *The Syn-Aud-Con Newsletter.* Various issues; you need them all — subscribe: 1-800-796-2831.

©Rane Corporation   10802 47th Ave. W.,   Mukilteo WA 98275-5098   TEL (425)355-6000   FAX (425)347-7757   WEB http://www.rane.com

Practical Line-Driving Current Requirements

- **Line Driving Requirements**

- **Bandwidth vs. Impedance Table**

- **Spectral Distribution of Audio**

- **Line Driving Current**

- **IC Current Rating Table**

Dennis Bohn
Rane Corporation

RaneNote 126
© 1991 Rane Corporation

INTRODUCTION

Successfully driving audio lines requires good line drivers. A fact no one argues. What constitutes a good line driver, however, encourages great debate. This note examines the technical problems involved in driving audio lines, and sets down useful guidelines for successful line drivers.

Of particular concern is identifying realistic requirements. Separating relevance from truth, in line drivers. That is, while it may be *true* that one line driver's performance exceeds another; is this extra capacity *relevant* to the real world problems of driving audio lines with real audio signals? Or are you paying extra for capabilities you do not need, and cannot use?

Examining the important electrical parameters of audio lines defines the minimum specifications for line drivers. Once understood, these parameters form the basis for evaluation of different output stages.

WHAT'S NEEDED?

Well, first you need all the obvious things: Stable into reactive loads. Swing at least ±11 volts peak (+20 dBu). Be reliable. Run cool. Achieve the cost objectives. All these things are taken simply for granted. This is just good common sense design.

This leaves two additional, very important criteria:
- Low Output Impedance
- High Output Current

The problem comes about in quantifying these characteristics: Just how low an output impedance? And how much current? The remainder of this note sheds light on these questions.

SIMPLIFYING A COMPLEX PROBLEM

Let's dispel a myth right away: Practically speaking, electrical engineering transmission line theory does *not* apply to real world audio lines [1]. In spite of all the hysterical audiophile hi-fi (and lately pro audio) press to the contrary. This pseudo-science babble is nothing more than a (quite successful) disinformation campaign designed to separate a largely uninformed, and therefore, largely gullible consumer base from its discretionary income. (I've become convinced there is absolutely *nothing* audiophiles will not believe.) Madison Avenue at its worst. All under the guise of "informed experts". The only thing these people are informed experts on, is how to take your money.

Here's what they're not telling you: *transmission line effects are a function of the wavelength of the signals being transmitted.* The wavelength of audio signals is directly proportional to the speed of propagation through the medium being discussed. As an example, consider the wavelength of a 20 kHz signal. In air, with a standardized (0°C, 0% RH) velocity of 1087 ft/sec, it is *.65 inches* (1087/20 kHz). Very short.

In wire, with a standardized velocity of about 0.7 (very conservative estimate) times the speed of light, i.e., 186,000 miles/sec x .7 = 130,200 miles/sec, it is *6.5 MILES*. Very long. And for all lower frequencies, it is even longer.

Electrically, a long line is defined as one in which the length equals, or exceeds, the shortest wavelength of the transmitted signal. For 20 kHz audio signals, 6.5 miles is a long line; for 1 kHz tones, 130 miles is a long line. From a transmission line viewpoint, telephone engineers deal with long lines; sound contractors do not. Don't let the wire mountebanks (look it up) tell you different.

Okay, enough tutorial and editorial, back to the note.

So, transmission theory is out. This paves the way for simple R-C modeling of our audio line. Figure 1 shows an R-C circuit that models the practical audio lines encountered everyday by sound contractors. The output impedance (overwhelmingly resistive) of each leg of the output line drivers appear labeled R_{OUT}. The distributed balanced cable capacitance is lumped into one equivalent loading capacitor labeled C_{WIRE}. And the balanced input impedance (again, largely resistive) is labeled R_{LOAD}. The actual wire resistance is small enough to ignore (R_{LOAD} swamps all its effects). Similarly, for runs of 200' or more, the cable capacitance (normally 10-100 times greater) dominates all unit input RFI filtering capacitance.

From here, it is a small step to the equivalent half-circuit show in Figure 2. This is a conceptually easier, yet technically accurate model, analogous to examining an unbalanced line. R_o is the total balanced output resistance (twice R_{OUT}, typically 100-600 ohms). C_W is the total balanced cable capacitance (34 pF/ft for Belden 8451; other cable is as good as 20 pF/ft, or as bad as 60 pF/ft). R_L is the total balanced input resistance (typically 20k-100k ohms).

CABLE AS A LOW-PASS FILTER

Some intuition and a little circuit knowledge helps predict the frequency response of Figure 2 (see Figure 3). At low frequencies, the impedance of the capacitor is high enough it is essentially out of the circuit. This leaves a resistive voltage divider made up of R_o and R_L. In modern designs, the output resistance is so small compared to the input resistance that

this results in a neglible loss, e.g., 0.1 dB for R_o=100 ohms and R_L=10k ohms. First-order approximations treat this as 0 dB. (This example points out why you do not want to match output and input resistances. If done, you create a voltage divider of 1/2, since R_o=R_L. A permanent loss of 6 dB of signal—not a good idea.)

At high frequencies, the impedance of the capacitor is low enough it essentially shorts all signal to ground. This accounts for the shape shown in Figure 3—a low-pass filter. The term, f_c, designates the corner frequency. This is defined as the frequency where the impedance of the capacitor equals the source resistance. This results in a loss of 3 dB, relative to the passband, hence, the -3 dB point. (It's not 6 dB like resistors, due to the phase angle created by the capacitor. This is phasor arithmetic.)

The exact corner frequency is given by the equivalent parallel resistance of R_o and R_L. Since R_o is much smaller than R_L, their parallel resistance essentially equals R_o. For example, the parallel result of R_o=100 ohms and R_L=10k ohms is 99 ohms. First-order approximations treat this as R_o.

The point of all this is that *the output resistance of the line driver and the cable capacitance are critical factors in determining the bandwidth of the connected system.* Combinations of high output resistance and large cable capacitance seriously shortchange expected wide bandwidth systems. Table 1 gives the -3 dB frequency bandwidth as a function of output resistance and cable length. As can be seen, large output resistances and long cable runs do not produce wide bandwidth systems. For example, a unit with 200 ohms output resistance drives 1000 feet of Belden 8451 cable with excellent bandwidth. Yet, the same unit, changed to 600 ohms output resistance, restricts line driving to less than 500 feet for the same bandwidth. Since this is true, why do some manufacturers use larger output resistors than others? For stability reasons. Cable capacitance creates excess phase shift in the feedback networks of line drivers. Discrete output resistors buffer this capacitance and minimizes excess phase shift. This results in more stable operation. Different manufacturer's output stage designs require different output resistors. Therefore, strictly from a designer's stability standpoint, the bigger, the better, in output resistors.

Your application dictates what you need, sometimes job by job. Knowing your cable lengths, the required frequency response (70.7 volt systems, paging and AM/FM background sources, for example, cannot use 20 kHz bandwidth) and using Table 1 as a guideline, allows evaluation of the suitability of any specific output resistance for your application. In general, balanced output impedances of 200 ohms, or less, work fine for most installations.

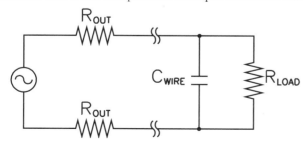

Figure 1. Simple R-C model for balanced line.

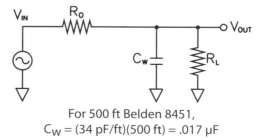

For 500 ft Belden 8451,
C_W = (34 pF/ft)(500 ft) = .017 μF

Figure 2. Equivalent half-circuit for Figure 1.

CHARGING AND DISCHARGING CABLE CAPACITANCE 20,000 TIMES A SECOND

Charging and discharging cable capacitance 20,000 times a second takes a lot of current. Luckily, it's not necessary to do this to large levels. If so, hardly any line drivers would qualify.

Many articles discuss the current requirements needed to drive 600 ohm lines, which is not terribly relevant, since they are rarer than a flat loudspeaker. However, what they do not discuss and what does exist, are the current requirements necessary to drive cable capacitance. The line capacitance must be charged and discharged at a rate equal to the maximum slew rate of the system. For audio this is usually a value based upon 20 kHz. Slew rate is the maximum rate of change of voltage with respect to time. That is, you must swing so many volts in so many seconds. Analysis goes like this:

current required: $I = C\, dv/dt$

where dv/dt is maximum slew rate of system

slew rate: $dv/dt = 2\,\pi f\, V_{peak}$

for f = 20kHz: $dv/dt = (1.25 \times 10^5)(V_{peak})$

If C is expressed in microfarads, the required current can be simplified to:

$I = C\, V_{peak}/8$

This is for 20 kHz signals *only*, with C given in μF.

For example, suppose you want to drive a 1000' of Belden 8451 to +26 dBu levels (22 volts peak) with 20 kHz. How much current must the line driver deliver? Table 1 tells us that the capacitance is .034 μF, therefore:

$I = (.034)(22/8) = 93.5\text{mA}$

This is a *lot* of current. Very few line drivers have this capacity. If you like wasting your client's money, then insist on line drivers (for this application) that put out 100 mA.

RELEVANCE TO THE RESCUE

Luckily, reality tempers this problem to something manageable. While it is true you need 93.5 mA to satisfy the above example, it is also true that the example is contrived and not even close to being real. You simple do not *ever* have 20 kHz signals at +26 dBu levels. If you did, you would smoke every high-frequency driver in the house.

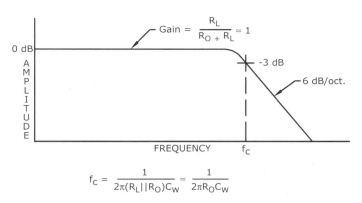

$$f_C = \frac{1}{2\pi(R_L\|R_O)C_W} \approx \frac{1}{2\pi R_O C_W}$$

Figure 3. Frequency response of equivalent half-circuit.

By examining the worst case spectral distribution of audio signals, we can predict the maximum required line driver current. This amount of current guarantees no slew limiting when driving the specified cable.

What 20 kHz levels are real? This is harder to answer than first imagined. The one thing all researchers agree on is that high frequencies are much smaller than low frequencies. Just *how much* smaller is harder to put a handle on. For music, IBM's Voss [2] claims discovery of a 1/f relationship between frequencies and level, i.e., inversely proportional—double the frequency, halve the amplitude. This says that music contains high frequencies with a natural roll-off rate of 6 dB/octave. An earlier Cabot, et al., study [3] generally supports this.

If music naturally rolls off at a 6 dB/octave rate, where does it peak? Referring again to Cabot's study, which includes review of much previous work, all data seems to peak generally in the octave around 250 Hz. If we apply the 1/f rule to these figures, then the expected response around 20 kHz would be about 38 dB less than those around 250 Hz! This seems quite extreme, but is substantiated by other studies (and agrees with IEC/DIN noise spectrum standards). Yet, other studies show that the type of music plays an important role in determining the exact peaking and rolloff rate. For example, high frequencies found within popular music tends toward larger magnitudes than classical orchestral music.

If this applies to music, does it apply to speech? Well, sort of. Like music, speech high frequency magnitudes are

Table 1. Bandwidth as a function of output resistance and cable length.

CABLE LENGTH BELDEN 8451 (34 pF/ft)

Balanced Out Ohms	500' (.017μF)	1000' (.034μF)	1500' (.051μF)	2000' (.068μF)
50	187.0 kHz	93.6 kHz	62.4 kHz	46.8 kHz
100	93.6 kHz	46.8 kHz	31.2 kHz	23.4 kHz
150	62.4 kHz	31.2 kHz	20.8 kHz	15.6 kHz
200	46.8 kHz	23.4 kHz	15.6 kHz	11.7 kHz
300	31.2 kHz	15.6 kHz	10.4 kHz	7.8 kHz
400	23.4 kHz	11.7 kHz	7.8 kHz	5.8 kHz
600	15.6 kHz	7.8 kHz	5.2 kHz	3.9 kHz

Line Driving-3

significantly lower than those of low frequencies. Beranek's data [4] shows the typical male speech power spectrum peaking at around 500 Hz, and dropping off at a 8 dB/octave rate above 1 kHz. This is close to music's 1/f fall, but a little steeper and peaking about an octave later. Female speech tends to peak another octave higher, with a similar rolloff rate.

Some generalities are possible. What's needed is an ultra-conservative this-will-never-get-you-into-trouble guideline. Here is mine: *To calculate current (only), I figure real audio signals (speech or music) stay flat out to 5 kHz and then rolloff at a 6 dB/octave rate.*

Understand this takes the worst case studies, and then builds in at least another two-to-one safety margin. Very conservative, but it correctly models the shape of real music and speech signals. And it is not nearly as conservative as assuming a flat 20 kHz spectra. That is totally unfounded. Remember *this is only for current calculations*. Line driver *voltage* response must remain absolutely flat to 20 kHz.

Calculating maximum current availability based on the above premise guarantees no slew limiting when driving cable. If this *ever* gets you into trouble, do two things:
• Replace all your fried high-frequency drivers.
• Call me, and I'll bring the beer and we'll discuss which is more audible, slew limiting or blown drivers!

CALCULATING MAXIMUM CURRENT DEMANDS

My rule of "flat to 5 kHz with a 6 dB/octave rolloff thereafter" makes for simple current calculations. Since 20 kHz is two octaves away, the amplitude will be 12 dB less, which is a factor of four. And 20 kHz is four times 5 kHz. So they cancel. That is, the frequency is four times greater, but the amplitude is four times less, so they cancel. This means we can calculate our current requirements using:
• A frequency of 5 kHz.
• The expected maximum signal level.
• The total cable capacitance.

Let's go back to our original example. Now we use 5 kHz instead of 20 kHz. Since slew rate is directly proportional to frequency, and current is directly proportional to slew rate, our new formula is simply ¼ of our old one:

I = C V$_{peak}$/32

Since we are being conservative, we can fill-in a worst case value of +26 dBu for V$_{peak}$. This yields a simplified formula for *peak* current as follows:

I = 0.7 C (where C is in µF)

So, for our example with .034 µF (1000' of Belden 8451), we need:

I = (0.7)(.034) = 23.8 mA peak (16.8 mA rms)

Or, approximately ¼ what we previously calculated. Moral of the story: *Don't pay for what you don't need.*

If the load impedance is less than about 10k ohms, you must include extra current for driving the resistance. So if the load impedance really is 600 ohms (for mystical, strange and unknown reasons), add the following for +26 dBu levels:

22 V $_{peak}$/600 = 36.7 mA peak (25.9 mA rms)

But we cannot simple add them (life is never simple, you know that). Due to the phase relationship between resistors and capacitors, currents through them do not add like normal numbers. Instead they add by taking the square root of the sum of the squares (phasor arithmetic), i.e.,

(25.9 mA² + 16.8 mA²)$^{1/2}$ = 30.9 mA rms

Therefore, our example of driving 1000' of cable, terminated in 600 ohms, to +26 dBu levels, requires approximately 31 mA from the output devices.

Okay, but how do you tell whether any particular device has that much current? Check the data sheet, ask the manufacturer, or consult the schematic and see if the output ICs show up in Table 2. In general, Rane products use 5534s and SSM2142s as output line drivers. Check the individual schematics, or contact the factory, for the exact devices used in any specific product.

Table 2. Current ratings of popular ICs used as output line drivers.

(Vs=±15 VDC; TA=25°C; all data typical instantaneous values)

IC	RMS CURRENT	PEAK CURRENT	MANUFACTURER
AD845	35 mA	50 mA	Analog Devices
HA4741	11 mA	15 mA	Harris
HA5221	40 mA	56 mA	Harris
LM627	24 mA	33 mA	National Semiconductor
LM6321*	212 mA	300 mA	National Semiconductor
LT1028	28 mA	40 mA	Linear Technology
LT1115	28 mA	40 mA	Linear Technology
NE5532	27 mA	38 mA	Philips / Signetics
NE5534	27 mA	38 mA	Philips / Signetics
SSM2134	42 mA	60 mA	Analog Devices/PMI
SSM2142	42 mA	60 mA	Analog Devices/PMI
TL074	12 mA	17 mA	Texas Instruments
TLE2027	25 mA	35 mA	Texas Instruments

*High speed buffer; requires op amp.

REFERENCES

1. Jim Brown, "The Effects of Cable on Signal Quality," *Sound & Video Contractor*, Vol. 8, No. 9, Sep. 20, 1990, pp. 22-33.
2. (Richard F. Voss,) "IBM Researcher Discovers 1/f Distribution In Music," *Electronic Engineering Times*, p.11, Monday, February 19, 1979.
3. Richard C. Cabot, C. Roy Genter II and Thomas Locke, "Sound Levels and Spectra of Rock Music," presented at the 60th Convention of the Audio Engineering Society, *J. Audio Eng. Soc. (Abstracts)*, vol. 26, p. 586 (Jul/Aug 1978), preprint 1358.
4. Leo Beranek, *Acoustics* (Amer. Inst. of Physics, New York, 1986) p. 407.

©Rane Corporation   10802 47th Ave. W.,   Mukilteo WA 98275-5098   TEL (425)355-6000   FAX (425)347-7757   WEB http://www.rane.com

Constant-Voltage Audio Distribution Systems: 25, 70.7 & 100 Volts

- **Background – Wellspring**

- **U.S. Standards – Who Says?**

- **Basics – Just What *is* "Constant" Anyway?**

- **Voltage Variations – Make Up Your Mind**

- **Calculating Losses – Chasing Your Tail**

- **Wire Size – How Big is Big Enough?**

- **Rane Constant-Voltage Transformers**

Dennis Bohn
Rane Corporation

RaneNote 136
© **1997 Rane Corporation**

Background – Wellspring

Constant-voltage is the common name given to a general practice begun in the late 1920s and early 1930s (becoming a U.S. standard in 1949) governing the interface between power amplifiers and loudspeakers used in *distributed sound systems*. Installations employing ceiling-mounted loudspeakers, such as offices, restaurants and schools are examples of distributed sound systems. Other examples include installations requiring long cable runs, such as stadiums, factories and convention centers. The need to do it differently than you would in your living room arose the first time someone needed to route audio to several places over long distances. It became an economic and physical necessity. Copper was too expensive and large cable too cumbersome to do things the home hi-fi way.

Stemming from this need to minimize cost, maximize efficiency, and simplify the design of complex audio systems, thus was born constant-voltage. The key to the solution came from understanding the electric company cross-country power distribution practices. They elegantly solved the same distribution problems by understanding that what they were distributing was *power*, not voltage. Further they knew that power was voltage times current, and that power was conserved. This meant that you could change the *mix* of voltage and current so long as you maintained the same *ratio*: 100 watts was 100 watts – whether you received it by having 10 volts and 10 amps, or 100 volts and 1 amp. The idea bulb was lit. By stepping-up the voltage, you stepped-down the current, and vice-versa. Therefore to distribute 1 megawatt of power from the generator to the user, the power company steps the voltage up to 200,000 volts, runs just 5 amps through relatively small wire, and then steps it back down again at, say, 1000 different customer sites, giving each 1 kilowatt. In this manner large gauge cable is only necessary for the short direct run to each house. Very clever.

Applied to audio, this means using a transformer to step-up the power amplifier's output voltage (gaining the corresponding decrease in output current), use this higher voltage to drive the (now smaller gauge wire due to smaller current) long lines to the loudspeakers, and then using another transformer to step-down the voltage at each loudspeaker. Nothing to it.

U.S. Standards– Who Says?

This scheme became known as the *constant-voltage distribution method*. Early mention is found in *Radio Engineering, 3rd Ed.* (McGraw-Hill, 1947), and it was standardized by the American Radio Manufacturer's Association as SE-101-A & SE-106, issued in July 1949[1]. Later it was adopted as a standard by the EIA (Electronic Industries Association), and today is covered also by the *National Electric Code (NEC)*[2].

Basics – Just What *is* "Constant" Anyway?

The term "constant-voltage" is quite misleading and causes much confusion until understood. In electronics, two terms exist to describe two very different power sources: "constant-current" and "constant-voltage." Constant-current is a power source that supplies a fixed amount of current regardless of the load; so the output voltage varies, but the current remains constant. Constant-voltage is just the opposite: the voltage stays constant regardless of the load; so the output current varies but not the voltage. Applied to distributed sound systems, the term is used to describe the action of the system *at full power only*. This is the key point in understanding. *At full power the voltage on the system is constant and does not vary as a function of the number of loudspeakers driven*, that is, you may add or remove (subject to the maximum power limits) any number of loudspeakers and the voltage will remain the same, i.e., constant.

The other thing that is "constant" is the amplifier's output voltage at rated power – and *it is the same voltage for all power ratings*. Several voltages are used, but the most common in the U.S. is 70.7 volts rms. The standard specifies that all power amplifiers put out 70.7 volts at their rated power. So, whether it is a 100 watt, or 500 watt or 10 watt power amplifier, the maximum output voltage of each must be the same (constant) value of 70.7 volts.

Figure 1 diagrams the alternative series-parallel method, where, for example, nine loudspeakers are wired such that the net impedance seen by the amplifier is 8 ohms. The wiring must be selected sufficiently large to drive this low-impedance value. Applying constant-voltage principles results in Figure 2. Here is seen an output transformer connected to the power amplifier which steps-up the full-power output voltage to a value of 70.7 volts (or 100 volts for Europe), then each loudspeaker has integrally mounted step-down transformers,

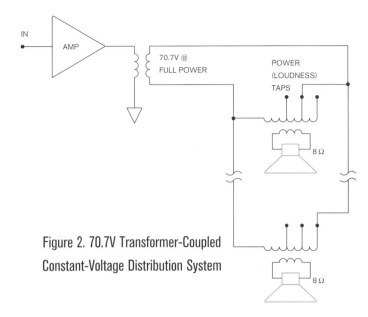

Figure 2. 70.7V Transformer-Coupled Constant-Voltage Distribution System

converting the 70.7 volts to the correct low-voltage (high current) level required by the actual 8 ohm speaker coil. It is common, although not universal, to find power (think loudness) taps at each speaker driver. These are used to allow different loudness levels in different coverage zones. With this scheme, the wire size is reduced considerably from that required in Figure 1 for the 70.7 volt connections.

Becoming more popular are various *direct-drive* 70.7 volt options as depicted in Figure 3. The output transformer shown in Figure 2 is either mounted directly onto (or inside of) the power amplifier, or it is mounted externally. In either case, its necessity adds cost, weight and bulk to the installation. An alternative is the direct-drive approach, where the power amplifier is designed from the get-go (I always wanted to use that phrase, and I sincerely apologize to all non-American readers from having done so) to put out 70.7 volts

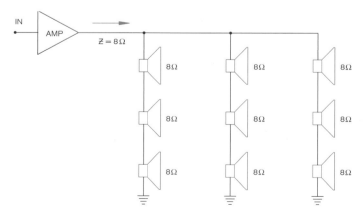

Figure 1. Low-Inpedance Series-Parallel 8 ohm Direct Drive Constant-Voltage-2

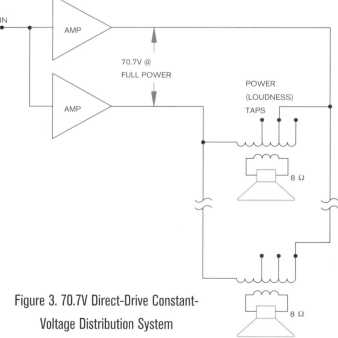

Figure 3. 70.7V Direct-Drive Constant-Voltage Distribution System

at full power. An amplifier designed in this manner does not have the current capacity to drive 8 ohm low-impedance loads; instead it has the high voltage output necessary for constant-voltage use — same power; different priorities. Quite often direct-drive designs use bridge techniques which is why two amplifier sections are shown, although single-ended designs exist. The obvious advantage of direct-drive is that the cost, weight and bulk of the output transformer are gone. The one disadvantage is that also gone is the isolation offered by a real transformer. Some installations require this isolation.

Voltage Variations – Make Up Your Mind

The particular number of *70.7* volts originally came about from the second way that constant-voltage distribution reduced costs: Back in the late '40s, UL safety code specified that all voltages above 100 volts peak ("max open-circuit value") created a "shock hazard," and subsequently *must be placed in conduit* – expensive – bad. Therefore working backward from a maximum of 100 volts peak (conduit not required), you get a maximum rms value of 70.7 volts (Vrms = 0.707 Vpeak). [It is common to see/hear/read "70.7 volts" shortened to just "70 volts" – it's sloppy; it's wrong; but it's common – accept it.] In Europe, and now in the U.S., 100 volts rms is popular. This allows use of even smaller wire. Some large U.S. installations have used as high as 210 volts rms, with wire runs of over one mile! Remember: the higher the voltage, the lower the current, the smaller the cable, the longer the line. [For the very astute reader: The wire-gauge benefits of a reduction in current exceeds the power loss increases due to the higher impedance caused by the smaller wire, due to the current-squared nature of power.] In some parts of the U.S., safety regulations regarding conduit use became stricter, forcing distributed systems to adopt a 25 volt rms standard. This saves conduit, but adds considerable copper cost (lower voltage = higher current = bigger wire), so its use is restricted to small installations.

Calculating Losses – Chasing Your Tail

As previously stated, modern constant-voltage amplifiers either integrate the step-up transformer into the same chassis, or employ a high voltage design to direct-drive the line. Similarly, constant-voltage loudspeakers have the step-down transformers built-in as diagrammed in Figures 2 and 3. The constant-voltage concept specifies that amplifiers and loudspeakers need only be rated in watts. For example, an amplifier is rated for so many watts output at 70.7 volts, and a loudspeaker is rated for so many watts input (producing a certain SPL). Designing a system becomes a relatively simple matter of selecting speakers that will achieve the target SPL (quieter zones use lower wattage speakers, or ones with taps, etc.), and then adding up the total to obtain the required amplifier power.

For example, say you need (10) 25 watt, (5) 50 watt and (15) 10 watt loudspeakers to create the coverage and loudness required. Adding this up says you need 650 watts of amplifier power – simple enough – but alas, life in audioland is never easy. Because of real-world losses, you will need about 1000 watts!

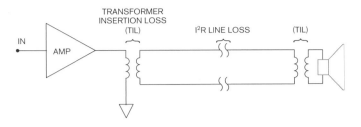

Figure 4. Transformer & Line Insertion Losses

Figure 4 shows the losses associated with each transformer in the system (another vote for direct-drive), plus the very real problem of line-losses. *Insertion loss* is the term used to describe the power dissipated or lost due to heat and voltage-drops across the internal transformer wiring. This lost power often is referred to as I^2R losses, since power (in watts) is current-squared (abbreviated I^2) times the wire resistance, R. This same mechanism describes line-losses, since long lines add substantial total resistance and can be a significant source of power loss due to I^2R effects. These losses occur physically as heat along the length of the wire.

You can go to a lot of trouble to calculate and/or measure each of these losses to determine exactly how much power is required[3], however there is a Catch-22 involved: Direct calculation turns out to be extremely difficult and unreliable due to the lack of published insertion loss information, thus measurement is the only truly reliable source of data. The Catch-22 is that in order to measure it, you must wait until you have built it, but in order to build it, you must have your amplifiers, which you cannot order until you measure it, after you have built it!

The alternative is to apply a very seasoned rule of thumb: *Use 1.5 times the value found by summing all of the loudspeaker powers.* Thus for our example, 1.5 times 650 watts tells us we need 975 watts.

Wire Size – How Big Is Big Enough?

Since the whole point of using constant-voltage distribution techniques is to optimize installation costs, proper wire sizing becomes a major factor. Due to wire resistance (usually expressed as ohms per foot, or meter) there can be a great deal of engineering involved to calculate the correct wire size. The major factors considered are the maximum current flowing through the wire, the distance covered by the wire, and the resistance of the wire. The type of wire also must be selected. Generally, constant-voltage wiring consists of a twisted pair of solid or stranded conductors with or without a jacket.

For those who like to keep it simple, the job is relatively easy. For example, say the installation requires delivering 1000 watts to 100 loudspeakers. Calculating that 1000 watts at 70.7 volts is 14.14 amps, you then select a wire gauge that will carry 14.14 amps (plus some headroom for I^2R wire losses) and wire up all 100 loudspeakers. This works, but it may be unnecessarily expensive and wasteful.

Really meticulous calculators make the job of selecting wire size a lot more interesting. For the above example, looked at another way, the task is not to deliver 1000 watts to

100 loudspeakers, but rather to distribute 10 watts each to 100 loudspeakers. These are different things. Wire size now becomes a function of the geometry involved. For example, if all 100 loudspeakers are connected up daisy-chain fashion in a continuous line, then 14.14 amps flows to the first speaker where only 0.1414 amps are used to create the necessary 10 watts; from here 14.00 amps flows on to the next speaker where another 0.1414 amps are used; then 13.86 amps continues on to the next loudspeaker, and so on, until the final 0.1414 amps is delivered to the last speaker. Well, obviously the wire size necessary to connect the last speaker doesn't need to be rated for 14.14 amps! For this example, the fanatical installer would use a different wire size for each speaker, narrowing the gauge as he went. And the problem gets ever more complicated if the speakers are arranged in an array of, say, 10 x 10, for instance.

Luckily tables exist to make our lives easier. Some of the most useful appear in Giddings[3] as Tables 14-1 and Table 14-2 on pp. 332-333. These provide cable lengths and gauges for 0.5 dB and 1.5 dB power loss, along with power, ohms, and current info. Great book. Table 1 below reproduces much of Gidding's Table 14-2[4].

Rane Constant Voltage Transformers

Rane offers several models of constant-voltage transformers. The design of each is a true transformer with separate primary and secondary windings—not a single-winding autotransformer as is sometimes encountered. The MA 6S transformers are sold individually, and are designed to mount on a separate 3U rack space mounting panel sold separately. For the U.S. market, a tapped secondary is provided offering a choice of 70.7 V or 25 V output voltages. The model **TF 170** is rated 100 watts, while the model **TF 370** is rated for 300 watts. For the European market a 100 watt, 100 V secondary is available as model **TF 110**. The mounting kit for all these models is ordered as a **KTM 6** and mounts (6) 100 W or (3) 300 W or any combination thereof. See the KTM 6 data sheet for more information.

The MA 3 transformers are also sold individually and mount directly inside the unit. The choices are **TF 407** rated 40 W, 70.7 V and **TF 410** rated 40 W, 100 V.

Table 1: 70.7V Loudspeaker Cable Lengths and Gauges for 1.5 dB Power Loss

Wire Gauge >		22	20	18	16	14	12	10	8
Max Current (A) >		5	7.5	10	13	15	20	30	45
Max Power (W) >		350	530	700	920	1060	1400	2100	3100
Load Power	**Load Ohms**				**Maximum Distance in Feet**				
1000	5	0	0	0	0	185	295	471	725
500	10	0	93	147	236	370	589	943	1450
400	12.5	0	116	184	295	462	736	1178	1813
250	20	117	186	295	471	739	1178	1885	2900
200	25	146	232	368	589	924	1473	2356	3625
150	33.3	194	309	490	785	1231	1962	3139	4829
100	50	292	464	736	1178	1848	2945	4713	7250
75	66.6	389	618	981	1569	2462	3923	6277	9657
60	83.3	486	774	1227	1963	3079	4907	7851	12079
50	100	584	929	1473	2356	3696	5891	9425	14500
40	125	729	1161	1841	2945	4620	7363	11781	18125
25	200	1167	1857	2945	4713	7392	11781	18850	29000

References

[1] Langford-Smith, F., Ed. *Radiotron Designer's Handbook, 4th Ed.* (RCA, 1953), p. 21.2.

[2] Earley, Sheehan & Caloggero, Eds. *National Electrical Code Handbook*, 5th Ed. (NFPA, 1999).

[3] See: Giddings, Phillip *Audio System Design and Installation* (Sams, 1990) for an excellent treatment of constant-voltage system designs criteria; also Davis, D. & C. *Sound System Engineering, 2nd Ed.* (Sams, 1987) provides a through treatment of the potential interface problems.

[4] Reproduced by permission of the author and Howard W. Sams & Co.

©Rane Corporation   10802 47th Ave. W.,   Mukilteo WA 98275-5098   TEL (425)355-6000   FAX (425)347-7757   WEB http://www.rane.com

Evolution of the DJ Mixer Crossfader

- **History**

- **Curves**

- **Pots - VCAs - Magnetics**

- **Performance**

Rick Jeffs
Rane Corporation

RaneNote 146
© **1989 Rane Corporation**

ORIGINATION

The DJ mixer crossfader was originally developed as a control for implementing smooth fades from one program source to another, but where did the idea come from? Fading between two independent sources was first accomplished by DJs using *two rotary knobs*. They would maintain constant acoustic energy (equal loudness) in the room while carefully fading from one program source to another. Some expertise was required to accomplish this effect accurately and consistently. It became obvious that if a way could be found to fade from one source to another with a single control, the task would be much easier and repeatable for the less experienced.

Panning circuits were already used in recording studios to move a single source from *left-to-right* while maintaining constant acoustic energy. While the requirements for a single source panning circuit were well defined, those for maintaining constant acoustic energy while fading from *one source to another* were *not*.

The exact origin of the first use of a crossfader in the DJ world has proven difficult to track down. It seems certain to have come out of the broadcast industry, where the term "fader" has been in use since at least the '50s (mentioned throughout the *Radiotron Designer's Handbook*, 4th ed., 1952) and the term "cross-fading" shows up in the *Tremaine's Audio Cyclopedia* in 1973. The earliest example documented so far was designed by Richard Wadman, one of the founders of the British company Citronic. It was called the model SMP101, made about 1977, and had a crossfader that doubled as a L/R balance control or a crossfade between two inputs.

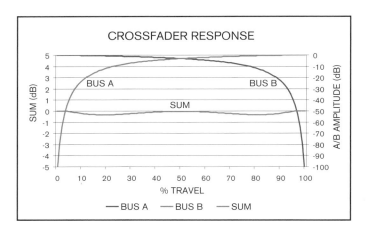

Figure 1: Constant-Power Response

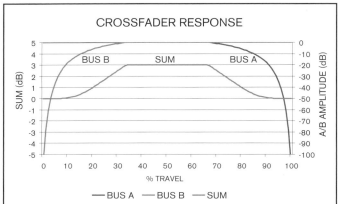

Figure 3: Medium Taper for Cut In and Pump-It-Up

1st Generation Curve Shape

Knowledgeable engineers noted that if two source signals of equal RMS amplitude were statistically random and incoherent, a slight modification to the standard panning circuit would allow constant energy fading between sources. The new control was called a *crossfader* and has achieved wide use and acceptance. Figure 1 shows the classic constant-power response.

The curve shown in Figure 1 only yields constant-power fading when *the original source signal assumptions are true.*

Limitations: It wasn't long before the basic crossfader topology showed some limitations. Disco dance music with a dominant beat challenged the original assumption of *random*. As beat matching source signals gained popularity, the assumption of *incoherence* became invalid. Those who had mastered the skill of two-knob-fading scoffed at the idea of a crossfader control, and were now saying "we told you so." It was apparent the traditional crossfader lacked flexibility.

In addition to the fundamental, smooth crossfade response shown in Figure 1, DJs wanted to perform more complex mixing functions. They wanted to *add* one dance song to another without losing energy in *either* until fully mixed. They wanted to *cut* in a beat and then *pump it up*. They wanted to *cut* one program in and out without affecting the other. Figures 2-4 show some of the tapers required for various effects.

2nd Generation Curve Slope

It was soon clear that one crossfader response curve was not suitable for all applications. No matter how skilled the DJ, it was not possible to achieve all of the desired effects. At first, the applications were distinct enough that manufacturers could design special mixers by selecting one of the tapers shown in Figures 1-4 for specific applications. However, as DJ performances became more sophisticated and competitive, a fixed taper became inadequate. DJs wanted to mix it up. By now they were familiar with the results possible with the various tapers and wanted them all. For performing DJs, the days of the application specific crossfader were over.

3rd Generation Curve Slope

The solution was to provide a second control that would allow the DJ to change the taper of the crossfader.

Limitations: At this point, most designers had lost track of the original constant-power crossfader taper. Implementations had become careless and undefined. Defined standards did not exist for the tapers shown in Figures 2-4. When crossfader taper control was added, it was not surprising that the range and shape of tapers was haphazard. Each implementation performed differently, causing confusion among performers.

The best passive controls could not meet the increasing demands on performance and usage. Passive controls are rated for a maximum number of operations, while maintain-

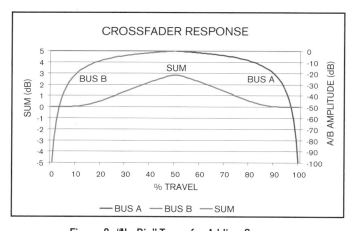

Figure 2: "No Dip" Taper for Adding Sources

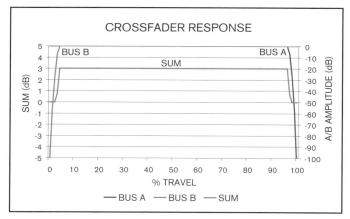

Figure 4: Sharp Taper for Cut and Scratch

ing given travel noise and force specifications. As the number of operations increases, travel noise goes up and travel force changes. Even high-quality controls with cycle life ratings as high as 100,000 to 300,000 require frequent service or replacement.

4th Generation Curve Slope

The high maintenance requirements of passive crossfader controls resulted in unacceptable service costs and down time. It was bothersome to disassemble a mixer just to clean and lubricate the controls. Replacement required costly factory service and could leave a DJ without income for weeks. The solution was to design mixers with field serviceable crossfaders. While doing nothing to resolve the reliability problems, the *removable crossfader* did help reduce service costs and down time.

5th Generation Curve Slope

To improve performance and extend service life, audio was removed from the crossfader control and processed in a voltage-controlled amplifier (VCA) or some other voltage/current controlled element. The crossfader control was only used to develop a DC control signal. However, this implementation was found only on expensive mixers. This practice greatly reduced travel noise and extended service life, but the performance of affordable VCAs was limited. In addition, crossfader tapers were still poorly defined as were the controls used to alter the tapers. Implementations were complex and consistency was poor.

Rane developed an *Active Crossfader*™ design, featuring high quality VCAs, low cost, and simplicity. The classic response of the design is shown in Figure 1. In addition to providing an accurate constant-power response, the circuit produced the optimum integration time for removing travel noise without noticeably affecting the reaction time of the control. The *Active Crossfader* topology created an excellent foundation for more sophisticated designs.

MUSICAL INSTRUMENT CONNECTION

A new art form emerged from hip-hop. Turntablist (scratch DJs) take small bits and pieces of music from different locations on vinyl records and create new compositions. A mixer and a couple of turntables become their instrument. This emerging art form again put demands on crossfaders that current state-of-the-art designs could not meet.

The following is a list of the new requirements:
• Music instrument quality and performance.
• Accuracy, reliability and repeatability for all functions.
• More than a 10-times increase in crossfader usage over previous applications.
• Crossfader with a taper range adjustable from constant-power to less than a .1 inch (2.5mm) pitch between full off and maximum level.
• Mechanically durable crossfader control with a knob that provided a fine music instrument feel.
• Crossfader taper control with smooth and predictable settings.
• Reverse operation of the crossfader.

In addition to the new crossfader demands, *all of the same demands were now placed on the input (or program) faders.*

None of the existing designs met all of the new demands. In addition, many manufacturers were timid about providing *any* product for fear of service liability problems. Available products were either very expensive with limited performance and feature-sets, or cheap throw-away toys with virtually no warranty.

Rane accepted the challenge and designed a performance mixer meeting all of the new demands, with music instrument quality and reliability. Because the combination of features was complex, and performance requirements very high, it was apparent that the new design would need new technology.

The challenge was to find an active or VCA topology that would provide the required performance without excessive cost or complexity. A single, low-cost, high performance, quad gain core that provided crossfader *and* input fader gain control for a stereo, two bus system was one answer. The actual audio signal path is very simple, yet the topology allows complex control.

This patent pending design isolates all audio from the control elements, greatly extending the life and performance of the controls.

The taper of the crossfader is adjustable from the gentle, constant-power curve shown in Figure 1, to the steep taper shown in Figure 4. Careful control of attack and decay rates yields low noise and smooth performance. In addition to predictable taper control, the design provides crossfader reversal.

Because the input faders use the same VCA design as the crossfader, these controls also have excellent control isolation, performance and reliability. As with the crossfader, implementation of accurate taper control (shown in Figure 5) and reversal functions, is possible without affecting audio quality.

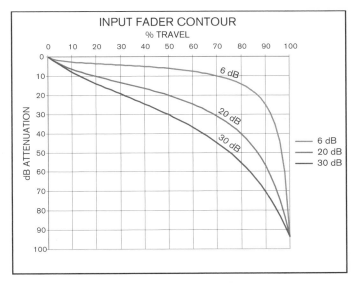

Figure 5 Input Fader Taper Control.

MAGNETICS

The new Rane magnetic fader (*patent pending*) is the fastest, most accurate, and longest lasting on the planet. The design uses non-contact technology previously reserved for the most demanding aerospace and industrial applications. *No travel noise - no bleed – ever.*

Unlike *optical* non-contact faders, Rane's *magnetic* fader is impervious to smoke, moisture, temperature, ambient light and aging. (*You know, only the stuff you run into at every club.*) The electrical performance of the new fader is – *literally* – unaffected by use. The mechanical life exceeds *10 million* operations.

Rane's magnetic fader accurately translates hand motion into precise audio level control. This system provides more flexible curve selection and fader assignment options than ever before. And they are the first to offer true morphing between curves.

It is common for a crossfader to undergo millions of operations over the life of a mixer. High-quality potentiometers used with VCAs yield 100,000 to 500,000 operations. More exotic, doped-plastic-element potentiometers yield 2 million operations. *In all cases, contact-based controls generate travel noise and exhibit electrical performance decline with use.* Non-contact fader technology is the only way to fully address the needs of the professional performance DJ.

Non-contact controls sense position without the use of electrical contacts. This eliminates both travel noise and electrical performance decline as parts wear. Possible methods include optical (*light and a shutter*), sonic (*sound and a receiver*), inductive (*coupling between coils of wire*), capacitive (*coupling between conductive plates*) and magnetic (*sensing the strength of a magnetic field*). Each of these methods varies in complexity, accuracy and immunity to environmental changes.

Rane favors magnetic position sensing due to its unique combination of *simplicity, accuracy* and *environmental immunity*. How does it work? It's as simple as 1-2-3:

1) Finite Element Analysis (FEA) is used to map the flux density field of a small, rare-earth magnet. [*FEA is a computer-based modeling technique.*]

2) A stationary Hall effect sensor is used to measure the flux density of the moving magnet. [*Hall effect, named after its discoverer E.H. Hall, describes a voltage that is generated by the effect of an external magnetic field acting perpendicularly to the direction of the current.*]

3) The location of the magnet (*your hand*) is determined by comparing the measured flux density value to a stored master flux density map.

[*For more details on Hall effect sensors, Lorentz forces and other exciting things see the Pro Audio Reference. Meanwhile, if you can't wait, Rick Jeffs explains: "When a perpendicular magnetic field is present, a Lorentz force is exerted on the current flowing in a thin sheet of semiconductor material (Hall element). This force disturbs the current distribution, resulting in a potential difference (voltage) across the output. The stronger the magnetic field, the greater the voltage difference."*]

Rane uses only the finest materials: nickel-plated neodymium-iron-boron magnets, space age plastic with embedded Teflon®, surface-passivated and polished stainless steel bearing rods and stainless steel handle. The result is a control offering unprecedented feel, control and years of accurate, carefree operation.

The new Rane magnetic fader is the fastest, most accurate, and longest lasting on the planet. See it on the TTM 56.

SUMMARY

In the end, the crossfader has provided functionality far beyond what was originally envisioned. Advanced topologies allow mixing styles not possible with two knobs (can you imagine scratching on a UREI; however, we must concede that some traditional mixing tasks are best accomplished with the two knob method.)

While disco dance, hip-hop and scratch are well established genre, new mixing styles are evolving at a rapid pace: Trance - progressive trance - techno - deep tech - electro - jungle - breaks - funk/breaks - hip hop - scratch - house grooves - hard house - deep house - funky house - disco house - drum 'n' bass - acid - live music.

What's next? As mixing styles continue to evolve, so will the performance mixer. There may soon be as many styles of performance mixers as there are guitars. The invention of non-contact fader controls has answered the need for reliable controls. The use of microprocessor based methods of translating hand motion into virtually any desired response answers the need for versatility. One thing is for sure; the evolution isn't over! Performers continue to demand new levels of performance and reliability, and designers continue to respond.

A condensed version ran in *DJ Times*, June 1999

Superior Audio Requires Fixed-Point DSPs

- **Dynamic Range**

- **Proper Gain Setting**

- **Right Tool for the Right Job**

Greg Duckett
Terry Pennington
Rane Corporation

RaneNote 153
© 2002 Rane Corporation

Introduction

The mountebanks are at it again, hawking their goods by telling tall tales. This new tale states that for pro audio applications floating-point DSPs are better than fixed-point DSPs – not quite so, as you will learn. Read on to see why you may be paying too much and receiving too little when it comes to buying DSP signal processors.

A lot of confusion has been stirred up recently in the audio industry over the issue of DSP internals. This particular deception goes like this: "Our box uses 32-bit floating point DSP chips, while their box uses only 24-bit fixed-point DSP chips. Obviously 32 is better than 24." Obviously – if you don't know the facts. What they fail to point out is the "rest of the story," which is that the 24-bit fixed-point DSP box can operate in "double-precision" mode, making it a 48-bit box. And in this case, 48 really is better than 32, only it has little to do with size. Given today's choices, fixed-point is superior to floating-point for audio. It may not forever be the case, but for today it is.

Here is the executive summary of why fixed-point DSPs make for superior audio:

1. Less dynamic range (yes, in DSPs used for audio, this can be a feature).
2. Double-precision capable 48-bit processing.
3. Programming flexibility that can guarantee proper behavior under the adverse conditions presented by audio signals — truly one of nature's oddest phenomena.
4. Lower-power consumption (floating point hardware is more complicated than fixed point; more transistors require more watts).

With that said, let's back up and review a few things.

A truly objective comparison of DSP architectures is not easy; in fact, it may not be possible. In the end, it is the application and the skill of the software programmer implementing the application that determines superior audio performance. But people don't want to hear that. They want the easy answer. Everyone is looking for the secret word, the single number that defines the difference and makes the duck drop down and deliver a $100 bill (*apologies made to all readers who have not seen the original* You Bet Your Life, *NBC 1950-1961, TV shows hosted by Groucho Marx*). Yet the truth is that there is no single number that quantifies the differences. Not the number of bits, the MIPS or FLOPS rate, the clock rate, the architecture, or any one thing.

Two distinct types of DSP implementations dominate pro audio applications: one utilizes *fixed-point* processing while the other features a *floating-point* solution. Both produce the same results under most conditions; however, it is the word "most" that creates the difference.

Looking under the hood of an IEEE 32-bit floating-point processor and a 24-bit fixed-point processor reveals that each DSP design offers the same 24-bit processing precision — *precision* is not the issue. The defining difference is that the fixed-point implementation offers double precision, while the floating-point device features increased dynamic range. In floating-point processors scaling the data increases dynamic range, but scaling does not improve precision, and in fact degrades performance for audio applications (more on this later). And it turns out that the strength of the fixed-point approach is the weakness of the floating-point, giving fixed-point a double advantage.

The benefit is most obvious in low frequency audio processing. This is important since most of the energy in audio lies in the low-frequency bands (*music and speech have an approximate 1/f spectrum characteristic, i.e., each doubling of frequency results in a halving of amplitude*). The simple truth is that the floating-point technique struggles with large amplitude, low-frequency computations. In fact, building a high-Q, low frequency digital filter is difficult no matter what method you use, but all things considered fixed-point double-precision is superior to floating-point single-precision.

To thoroughly explain, in a scientific engineering manner, the advantages and disadvantages of the two techniques as they relate to broadband audio applications is a vastly complex subject and lies beyond the scope of this article. An objective direct comparison involves a steep slippery slope of complexities, qualifications and definitions, all necessary in order to avoid apples to oranges error. A task as daunting as this has already been done by Dr. Andy Moorer[1] (cofounder of the Stanford University Center for Computer Research in Music and Acoustics, then CTO at the Lucasfilm Droid Works, then cofounder of Sonic Solutions, and now Senior Computer Scientist at Adobe Systems) and is recommended for the detail-curious and mathematically courageous. The goal here is to draw a simplified illustration of the audio challenges faced by each DSP solution. (See the *Let's Be Precise About This...* section for a more in-depth mathematically oriented example — sorry, but mathematics is all we are dealing with here.)

Dynamic Range

Higher dynamic range is better, yes? Just as lower distortion is better and lower noise is better. We're reminded of a sales guide published by a hi-fi manufacturer in the mid-seventies: This guide had a "lower is better" and "higher is better" approach to equipment specifications. The author of that promotional material would be shocked to hear an audio manufacturer claim that higher dynamic range can be a problem. Nonetheless, it is a fact when examined in relationship to the ultra-high dynamic range capabilities of the 32-bit floating-point processors found in some of the current DSP audio signal processors.

As mentioned earlier, both DSP designs have a 24-bit processor for the mainstream functions. The fixed-point technique adds double precision giving it 48-bit processing power, while the floating-point design adds an 8-bit exponent. The 8-bit exponent gives the floating-point architecture an astonishing dynamic range spec of 1500 dB (8-bits = 256, and 2^{256} equals approximately 1500 dB) which is used to manipulate an operating window, within which its 24-bit brain operates. Floating-point processors automatically scale the data to keep it within optimum range. This is where the trouble lies and this is why fixed-point is better than floating-point for audio. It is not that the dynamic range is the problem so much as the automatic scaling over a 1500 dB range that is the problem. Fixed-point, with its 48-bits, gives you 288 dB of dynamic range – enough for superior audio – but the programmer has to scale the data carefully. Floating-point programmers leave it up to the chip, but, unless they are careful, that creates serious errors and noise artifacts. All the jumping about done by the continuous signal boosting and attenuating can produce annoying noise pumping.

The new mythmakers flaunt their DSP dynamic range as a plus, but it only shows their weakness. *The dynamic range specification of a DSP chip has little to do with the overall dynamic range of the finished product.* The dynamic range of the "box" is bounded by the A/D converter on its input, to some extent on the processing in the center of the device, of which the DSP chip is a part, and on the D/A converter on the output (*even without converters the output of both DSP types is a 24-bit fixed-point word*). The dynamic range of a DSP chip is the ratio between the largest and smallest numbers it can handle. If a DSP device sporting an advertised dynamic range of 1500 dB resides between the input converters and the output converters its contribution to the overall dynamic range of the product is limited to the dynamic range of the converters. Is this a bad thing? No, not in itself.

What's bad about a floating-point processor with a dynamic range of 1500 dB is that it scales its processing range based on the amplitude of the signal its dealing with, but when dealing with signals of differing amplitudes (i.e., real audio), the scaling may not be optimized for the mixed result. When dealing with audio signals the installer cannot simply ignore the subtleties of system setup because they have a floating-point processor in their box.

Consider the typical audio mixer scenario: At any given moment a mixer can have multiple levels present at its many input ports. Input-1 might have a high-level sample to deal with while Input-2 has a very low level, Input-3 somewhere in the middle of its upper and lower limits and so on. A 32-bit floating-point DSP chip makes a determination about the appropriate window within which to work on a sample-by-sample basis but finally represents its calculations in the same 24-bit manner as its fixed-point counterpart. Even in a simple two-channel stereo processor signal levels between channels, while similar in average level, can be vastly different instantaneously due to phase differences.

Nothing is gained by using a floating-point device in an audio application but much may be lost. It does not have the 48-bit double precision capability of a fixed-point solution, and noisy artifacts may be added.

Importance of Proper Gain Setting

The reality here is that so long as we have finite precision/ dynamic range in the converters and DSPs, the installer plays the final and most important role in maintaining the proper processing window alignment for a given installation. Improperly set gain structure can overload fixed-point processors. While floating-point DSPs give the flexibility to misadjust the system (too much internal gain) without noticeable internal clipping, they still suffer the unintended consequences of the misalignment (say, in trying to mix two channels of very different audio levels) that floating-point processors cannot fix. They merely mask the problem from the installer's view. Or, worse, produce audible and annoying rise in quantization noise when filters are used below 100 Hz. In this sense the fixed-point processors force the installer to maintain the 144 dB processing window by avoiding internal clipping through proper gain structure/setup and so make maintaining overall quality easier than floating-proper processor based boxes.

Double Precision

The double precision 48-bit processing is used when long time constants are required. This occurs when low frequency filters are on the job and when compressors, expanders and limiters are used with their relatively slow attack and release times. If 24 bits are all that are available when more precision is required, the results are a problem. The function misbehaves and the least damaging result is poor sound quality. The worst result is amplifier or loudspeaker damage due to a misbehaving DSP crossover, making double precision a must-have for superior audio.

Examples and Counterexamples

Floating-point evangelists like to use an example where the processor is set up for 60 dB attenuation on the input and 60 dB make-up gain on the output. Leaving aside the absurdity of this fabricated example, let's use it to make our fixed-point-is-better point: add a second input to this example, with the gain set for unity, a 0 dBu signal coming in, and configure the processor to sum both these channels into the output and listen to the results — you will not like what you hear.

Another revealing example is how you never hear floating-point advocates talk about low-frequency/high-Q filter behavior. The next time you get the opportunity, set up a floating-point box parametric filter for use as a notch filter with a center frequency of 50 Hz and a Q of 20. First listen to the increase in output noise. Now run an input sweep from 20 Hz to 100 Hz and listen to all the unappetizing sounds that result. Audio filters below about 100 Hz require simultaneous processing of large numbers and small numbers — something fixed-point DSPs do much better than their floating-point cousins.

Free the Developers

The real determinant of quality in audio DSP is the skill of the programmers. They must devise accurate and efficient algorithms; the better their understanding of the (sometimes-arcane) math, the better the algorithm; the better the algorithm, the better the results. Fixed-point processing delivers a load of responsibility to the hands of the developer. It also delivers an equal amount of flexibility. A talented engineer with a good grasp of exactly what is required of a DSP product can fashion every detail of a given function down to the last bit. This is not so with floating-point designs. They offer an ease of programming that is seductive, making them popular when engineering talent is limited, but not the best choice. On one hand it is easier to program but on the other hand it is less controlled as to the final results — and, as we all know, that is what is important.

The Right Tool for the Right Job

If fixed-point DSP devices are so good, then why do floating-point DSPs exist? Fair enough question. They exist because DSP applications differ widely. Some of the more popular floating-point applications are found in physics, chemistry, meteorology, fluid dynamics, image recognition, earthquake modeling, number theory, crash simulation, weather modeling, and 3-D graphics. If you are designing an image processor, a radar processor, anything to do with astronomy, or a mathematics matrix inverter, the choice is clearly a floating-point solution. As always, the application dictates the solution.

This is not to say that floating-point DSPs will never have their day in achieving superior audio — it's just not today. What will it take? Here are some pretty nasty "ifs" necessary for floating-point to overtake fixed-point: *if* it is a 56-bit floating-point processor (i.e., 48-bit mantissa plus 8-bit exponent) or 32-bit with double-precision (requiring a large accumulator), *if* the parts run at the same speed as the equivalent fixed-point part, *if* they use the same power, and *if* they cost the same, then the choice is made.

Another possibility is if the floating point DSPs evolve to offer significantly more processing power for the same price (enough to overcome the low-frequency, high-Q issues in firmware) and offer a compatible peripheral chip set, then this could tip the scales even if they still offer only a 32-bit fixed numerical format.

Further Study

Digital audio is a vast and complex subject with many subtleties when it comes to superior signal processing. An article this short touches only some of the important issues. Selecting just one book from all the possibilities for recommendation for further study is easier than it may seem. That book is John Watkinson's *The Art of Digital Audio, 3rd ed.* (Focal Press ISBN 0-240-51587-0, Oxford, England, 2001). The title says it all. One of the best digital audio references you can own.

References

1. Moorer, James A. (www.jamminpower.com) "48-Bit Integer Processing Beats 32-Bit Floating Point For Professional Audio Applications," presented at the 107th Convention of the Audio Engineering Society, New York, September 24-27, 1999, preprint no. 5038.

Fixed vs. Floating DSPs-3

The Big and the Small

Over and over in audio DSP processing you run into the same simple arithmetic repeated over and over: multiply one number by another number and add the result to a third number. Often the result of this multiply-and-add is the starting point for the next calculation, so it forms a running total, or an accumulation, of all the results over time. Naturally enough, adding the next sample to the previous result is called an "accumulate" and it follows that a multiply followed by an accumulate is called a MAC. MAC's are the most common of all operations performed in audio DSP, and DSP processors typically have special hardware that performs a MAC very, very quickly.

As results accumulate, errors also accumulate. As well, the total can get large compared to the next sample. To show this in action return to the mythical 3-digit processors. Say we have the series of numbers shown in the row labeled "Samples" in Table 1; a strange looking set of numbers, perhaps, but it represents the first part of a simple sine wave. Multiply the first number by a small constant (say, 0.9) and add the result to the second number: 0*0.9 + 799= 799. Multiply this result by 0.9 and add it to the third number: 799*0.9 + 1589= 2308. And again: 2308*0.9 + 2364= 4441. Continue this pattern and it forms a simple digital filter. The results using double precision fixed-point are shown in the row labeled "Fixed-Point Results" in Table 1.

What about the floating-point processor? Start with exponent = 0. The results are: 0, 799, … the next number is too big, so increase the exponent to 1 … 2290, 4420, etc. Notice that the floating-point values are smaller than they should be because the limited precision forces the last one or two digits to be 0. It's easy to see that each result has an error, and the errors are carried forward and accumulate in the results. Algorithms with long time constants, such as low frequency filters, are especially prone to these errors.

You'll also notice that the accumulated values are getting larger than the input samples. The long time constant in low frequency filters means that the accumulation happens over a longer time and the accumulated value stays large for a longer time. Whenever the input signal is near zero (at least once every cycle in a typical audio signal) the samples can be small enough that they are lost; because the accumulated value is large, the samples fall entirely outside the precision range of the floating point processor and are interpreted as zero. The double precision available in the fixed point processor helps the programmer to avoid these problems.

Sample #	Samples	Fixed-Point Results	Floating-Point Results
1	0	0	0
2	799	799	799
3	1589	2308	2290
4	2364	4441	4420
5	3115	7112	7080
6	3835	10236	10200
7	4517	13729	13600
8	5154	17510	17300
9	5739	21498	21200

Table 1: Results Between Floating- and Fixed-Point Accumulation

Let's Be Precise About This …

An example is the best way to explain how you lose precision when floating-point processors scale data. Assume you have two mythical 3-digit radix-10 (i.e., decimal) processors. One is "fixed-point", and one is "floating-point." For simplicity, this example uses only positive whole numbers. (On real fixed- or floating-point processors, the numbers are usually scaled to be between 0 and 1.)

The largest number represented in single precision on the fixed-point processor is 999. Calculations that produce numbers larger than 999 require double precision. This allows numbers up to 999999.

Let the floating-point processor use 2 digits for the exponent, making it a 5-digit processor. This means it has a dynamic range of 0 to 999×10^{99} = HUGE number. To see how this sometimes is a problem, begin with the exponent = 0. This allows the floating-point processor only to represent numbers up to 999 – same as the fixed-point single-precision design. Calculations that produce numbers larger than 999 require increasing the exponent from 0 to 1. This allows numbers up to 9990. *However*, notice that the smallest number (greater than zero) that can be represented is $1 \times 10^1 = 10$, *meaning numbers between 1-9 cannot be represented (nor 11-19, 21-29, 31-39, etc.).* Increasing the exponent to 3 only makes matters worst, but you can cover (almost) the same range as the fixed point processor (up to 999000); however the smallest number now represented is $1 \times 10^3 = 1000$, *meaning numbers between 1 and 999 cannot be represented.* And the next increment is $2 \times 10^3 = 2000$, meaning the represented number jumps from 1000 to 2000. So that now numbers between 1001 to 1999 cannot be represented. With exponent = 3, each increment in the mantissa of 1 results in an increase in the number of 1000, and another 999 values that cannot be represented.

Is this as big a problem as it first appears – well, yes and no. At first it looks like the floating-point processor has lost the ability to represent small numbers for the entire calculation's time, but the scaling happens on a *per-sample* basis. The loss of precision only occurs for the individual samples with magnitude greater than 999. Now you might think that everything is fine, because the number is big and it does not need the values around zero. But a few wrinkles cause trouble. When calculations involve large and small numbers *at the same time*, the loss of precision affects the small number and the result. This is especially important in low-frequency filters or other calculations with long time constants. Another wrinkle is that this happens automatically and beyond the control of the programmer. If the programmer does not employ the right amount of foresight, it could happen at a bad time with audible results.

In the fixed-point case, the programmer must explicitly change to double precision – there is nothing automatic about it. The programmer changes to double precision at the start of the program section requiring it and stays there till the work is done.

©Rane Corporation 10802 47th Ave. W., Mukilteo WA 98275-5098 USA

TEL (425)355-6000 FAX (425)347-7757 WEB http://www.rane.com

13209 7-02

Grounding and Shielding Audio Devices

- **Pin 1 Problem**

- **Balanced vs. Unbalanced**

- **Shield Grounding**

- **Connectors**

Stephen Macatee
Rane Corporation

RaneNote 151
© 1995, revised 2002 Rane Corporation

INTRODUCTION

Now that the Audio Engineering Society has adopted the "pin 2 is hot" standard, the question of what to do with pin 1 is being addressed. A recommended practices document is being created covering interconnection of professional audio equipment. How and where to connect pin 1 is too complex to be issued as a standard; thus only a recommended practice is being developed. The recommended practices may affect manufacturers who choose to follow them.

Many shield-wiring practices exist in the audio industry today. The majority of available literature on the subject prescribes clear solutions to any wiring problem, yet problems are rampant due to inconsistent variations on the well-documented ideal. Two clear groups have developed on either side of a hard-to-straddle fence — the balanced world and the unbalanced world.

Over the years, the declining cost of professional audio equipment has facilitated its use in more and more home studio environments. As home studios incorporate professional, balanced equipment into their systems, the unbalanced and balanced worlds collide. Home studios adding balanced equipment to their traditionally unbalanced gear also add connectivity problems. Professional users never consider unbalanced gear, yet still have connectivity problems.

The performance of any interconnection system is dependent on input/output (I/O) circuit topologies (specific balanced or unbalanced schemes), printed circuit board layout, cables and connector-wiring practices. Only wiring practices, both in the cable and in the box, are covered here. The I/O circuit topologies are assumed ideal for this discussion to focus on other interconnection issues.

The Audio Engineering Society recommendation will address a simple issue, the absurdity that one can not buy several pieces of pro audio equipment from different manufacturers, buy off-the-shelf cables, hook it all up, and have it work hum and buzz-free. Almost never is this the case. Transformer isolation and other interface solutions are the best solutions for balanced/unbalanced interconnections, though they are too costly for many systems. Even fully balanced systems can require isolation transformers to achieve acceptable performance. Some consider isolation transformers the *only* solution. These superior solutions are not covered here.

Another common solution to hum and buzz problems involves disconnecting one end of the shield, even though one can not buy off-the-shelf cables with the shield disconnected at one end. The best end to disconnect is unimportant in this discussion. A one-end-only shield connection increases the possibility of radio frequency (RF) interference since the shield may act as an antenna. The fact that many modern day installers still follow the one-end-only rule with consistent success indicates that acceptable solutions to RF issues exist, though the increasing use of digital technology increases the possibility of future RF problems. Many successfully and consistently reduce RF interference by providing an RF path through a small capacitor connected from the lifted end of the shield to the chassis.

The details of noise-free interconnections and proper grounding and shielding are well covered in other literature. They are not revisited here. Readers are encouraged to review the References listed for further information. Most of these materials have been applicable in the audio industry for well over 60 years, though they have not been implemented or embraced by many.

Balanced vs. Unbalanced Shields

For the ensuing discussion, the term shield is qualified with the description balanced or unbalanced. An unbalanced return conductor physically resembles a shield and provides shielding for electric fields, but magnetic fields are not shielded. Though this is also true for balanced shields, the twisted-pair construction of balanced cables provides much greater immunity to magnetic field interference. Unbalanced cable shields also carry signal in the form of return current, further alienating unbalanced shields from "true" shields. Shield is defined by Ott [1] as "... a metallic partition placed between two regions of space. It is used to control the propagation of electric and magnetic fields from one place to another." Balanced interconnection provides the superior interface of the two.

The "Pin 1" Problem

Many audio manufacturers, consciously or unconsciously, connect balanced shields to audio signal ground; pin 1 for 3-pin (XLR-type) connectors, the sleeve on ¼" (6.35mm) jacks. Any currents induced into the shield modulate the ground where the shield is terminated. This also modulates the signal referenced to that ground. Normally great pains are taken by circuit designers to ensure "clean and quiet" audio signal grounds. It is surprising that the practice of draining noisy shield currents to audio signal ground is so widespread. Amazingly enough, acceptable performance in some systems is achievable, further providing confidence for the manufacturer to continue this improper practice — unfortunately for the unwitting user. The hum and buzz problems inherent in balanced systems with signal-grounded shields has given balanced equipment a bad reputation. This has created great confusion and apprehension among users, system designers as well as equipment designers.

Similar to the "pin 2 is hot" issue, manufacturers have created the need for users to solve this design inconsistency. Until manufacturers provide a proper form of interconnection uniformity, users will have to continue their struggle for hum-free systems, incorporating previously unthinkable practices.

The Absolute, Best Right Way to Do It

Clearly, the available literature prescribes balanced interconnection as the absolute best way to interconnect audio equipment. The use of *entirely* balanced interconnection with *both* ends of the shield connected to *chassis ground* at the point of entry provides the best available performance.

The reasons for this are clear and have been well-documented for over 60 years. Using this scheme, with high-quality I/O stages, *guarantees* hum-free results. This scheme differs from current practices in that most manufacturers connect balanced shields to signal ground, and most users alter their system wiring so only one end of the shield is connected. Due to these varied manufacturer and user design structures, an all-encompassing recommendation with proper coverage of both balanced and unbalanced interconnection is essential.

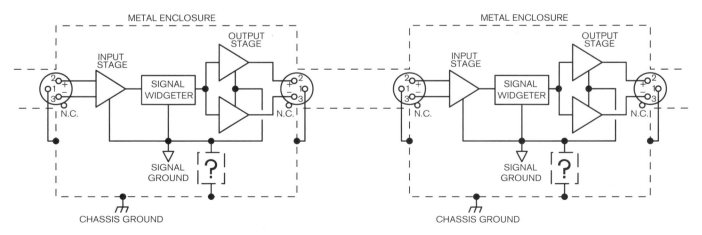

Figure 1. Balanced cable shields should function as an extention of the enclosure.

Conceptually, it is easiest to think of shields as an extension of the interconnected units' boxes (see Figure 1). Usually, metallic boxes are used to surround audio electronics. This metal "shell" functions as a shield, keeping electromagnetic fields *in* and *out* of the enclosure. For safety reasons, the enclosures in professional installations are required by law to connect to the system's *earth* ground (which in many systems is not the planet Earth — an airplane is a good example).

A SPECULATIVE EVOLUTION OF BALANCED AND UNBALANCED SYSTEMS

One may ask, if the balanced solution is best, why isn't all equipment designed this way? Well, reality takes hold; unbalanced happens.

Back in the early days of telephone and AC power distribution a specific class of engineers evolved. They learned that telephone and AC power lines, due to their inherently long runs, must be balanced to achieve acceptable performance. (To this day, many telephone systems are still balanced and unshielded.) In the 1950s, hi-fi engineers developed systems that did not necessitate long runs, and used unbalanced interconnection. The less expensive nature of unbalanced interconnection also contributed to its use in hi-fi. These two classes of engineers evolved with different mind-sets, one exclusively balanced, the other exclusively unbalanced. The differing design experience of these engineers helped form the familiar balanced and unbalanced audio worlds of today.

Now add spice to the pot with the continued price decrease and praise devoted to balanced, "professional" audio interconnections with the desire for better audio performance at home, and one sees the current trend of merging balanced and unbalanced systems arise. Home studio owners, previously on the unbalanced side of the fence, dream to jump but unfortunately straddle the fence, getting snagged on the fence's ground barbs when connecting their new balanced equipment (Figure 2).

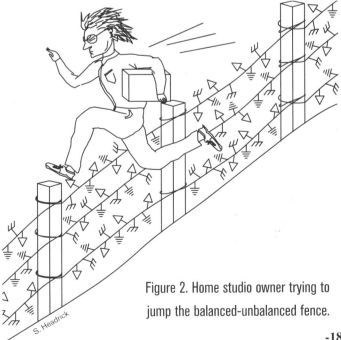

Figure 2. Home studio owner trying to jump the balanced-unbalanced fence.

S. Headrick

How Could This Happen?

To fulfill their users' desires to "go" balanced, hi-fi designers started upgrading equipment to balanced. From an unbalanced designer's mind-set, connecting the new balanced circuit's shield to ground is almost subconscious. The issue of which ground connects to the shield is alien or unknown. The old unbalanced "shield" (really the return signal conductor, not a true shield) is already "grounded." Without appropriate balanced interconnection research, this hi-fi mind-set may not think to *add* a chassis-grounded shield around the existing 2-conductor cable. This redefines the "old" return conductor as a "new" negative signal carrier, not as a shield. It was perhaps the convenience of the situation and this mind-set that started improper signal grounding of balanced shields in the first place. Little treatment of this subject is given in educational institutions, and many systems happen to work satisfactorily even with improperly grounded shields.

Other designers, upgrading to balanced interconnections, may have realized that by connecting the shield to signal ground, interfacing to unbalanced equipment is made simpler since signal ground (needed for unbalanced interconnection) will be available on the cable. (This unfortunately allows easy use of ¼" mono connectors.) This still creates the same problem, signal-grounded balanced shields. Signal-grounded shields on balanced equipment create ground loops in the audio path and modulate the audio signal ground, wreaking havoc with most systems. This practice penalizes those who want to realize the superior performance of balanced interconnections and has given balancing a bad reputation.

A third possible reason for signal-grounded balanced shields arises if designers change phantom powered microphone inputs to balanced line-level inputs, and do not use caution. The phantom power return currents travel through the shield, requiring shield connection to the signal ground. When changing this topology to line-level balanced inputs, the designer may not think to change the shield connection to chassis ground. This issue is further complicated by manufacturers who incorporate ground-lift switches in their products. These switches disconnect chassis and signal ground. Thus care should be taken to ensure that phantom power return currents always have a return path to their power supply, regardless of the ground-lift switch position.

Manufacturers who started in balanced fields, such as the telephone and broadcast industries, used chassis-grounded shields when maximum protection from electromagnetic interference (EMI, including RF) was necessary. Perhaps users from these balanced fields assumed that all balanced equipment had chassis-grounded shields. When improperly-wired manufacturer's equipment was installed, they discovered hum and buzz problems. They solved them with isolation transformers, by disconnecting one end of the shield, or by simply not using that manufacturer's equipment. The feedback to inform manufacturers of their improper shielding practices never developed. Manufacturers may have suggested isolation transformers or cable rewiring solutions instead of addressing the cause of the problem: signal-grounded balanced shields. Again, some systems with signal-grounded shields work acceptably, causing further and future bewilderment.

The History Lesson

The lesson to be learned from this account involves keeping in mind these audio interconnection issues when specifying, designing, or upgrading other connectivity systems such as AES3 (formerly AES/EBU), SPDIF, and other electrical interfaces. Balanced and unbalanced systems are not designed to interface together directly. As the audio industry embraces more digital products, interconnection systems must be clearly designed and specified for use within the limits of their electrical interfaces. Multiple conductor connectors, carrying either digital or analog signals, present even more challenges. The distance between units is an important issue. Keeping interconnects balanced and chassis-ground-shielded provides the best possible immunity from electromagnetic interference, regardless of cable lengths. Unbalanced interconnection may be less expensive to manufacture and sell, but is perhaps more expensive to install — hum and buzz-free.

The Audio Engineering Society is to be applauded for assembling and disseminating this information to those who may be unfamiliar with it. Manufacturers and, more importantly, users will eventually be rewarded.

CHASSIS GROUND vs. SIGNAL GROUND

Let us examine the distinction between chassis and signal ground in audio devices. Chassis ground is generally considered any conductor which is connected to a unit's metal box or chassis. The term *chassis ground* may have come about since units with 3-conductor line cords connect the chassis to earth ground when plugged in to a properly wired AC outlet. In units with a 2-conductor line cord (consumer equipment), the chassis does not connect to earth ground, though the chassis is normally connected to the *signal ground* in the box in both unbalanced/consumer and in balanced/pro equipment.

Signal ground is the internal conductor used as the 0 V reference potential for the internal electronics and is sometimes further split into digital and analog ground sections. Further signal ground splits are also possible, though it is important to remember that all "divisions" of signal ground connect together in one place. This is usually called a *star* grounding scheme.

It is easy to confuse chassis ground and signal ground since they are usually connected together — either directly or through one of several passive schemes. Some of these schemes are shown in Figure 3. The key to keeping an audio device immune from external noise sources is knowing *where*

and *how* to connect signal ground to the chassis.

First let's examine *why* they must be tied together. We'll cover *where* and *how* in a moment. There are at least two reasons why one should connect signal ground and chassis ground together in a unit.

One reason is to decrease the effects of coupling electrostatic charge on the chassis and the internal circuitry. External noise sources can induce noise currents and electrostatic charge on a unit's chassis. Noise currents induced into the cable shields also flow through the chassis — since the shields terminate (or should terminate) on the chassis. Since there is also coupling between the chassis and the internal circuitry, noise on the chassis can couple into the internal audio. This noise coupling can be minimized by connecting the signal ground to the chassis. This allows the entire grounding system to fluctuate with the noise, surprisingly providing a quiet system. Further coupling reduction is gained when the chassis is solidly bonded to a good earth ground — either through the line cord, through the rack rails or with an independent technical or protective ground conductor. This provides a *non-audio* return path for any externally induced noise.

The second reason to connect signal ground to chassis is the necessity to keep the signal grounds of two interconnected units at very nearly the same voltage potential. Doing so prevents the loss of system dynamic range where the incoming peak voltage levels exceed the power supply rails of the receiving unit.

Unbalanced units connect successive signal grounds together directly through each interconnecting cable — the sleeve of each RCA cable. This, and the fact that the chassis is generally used as a signal ground conductor, keeps the signal ground impedance of unbalanced systems very low. Many may agree that unbalanced systems are helped by the fact that the chassis are normally *not* earth grounded. This allows an entire unbalanced system to float with respect to earth ground. This eliminates the potential for multiple return paths for the audio grounding system, since there is not a second path (ground loop) through the earth ground conductor. Low signal ground impedance between units is essential for acceptable operation of all non-transformer-isolated systems, balanced and unbalanced.

The design of balanced interconnection does not connect signal grounds directly together. The negative conductor provides the required signal return current. To avoid loss of dynamic range, balanced systems use a different method of keeping signal ground potentials small.

Since the cable shield already connects the two chassis together, simply connecting signal ground to the chassis in each box keeps the signal ground potentials between units small. The key is how to connect them. Since the cables between units also provide the shortest (and therefore the lowest impedance) path between two units, using the cable shield to minimize the signal ground potentials between units is quite effective.

Now that we know why one must connect signal ground to chassis, let's discuss *how* to connect them. The schemes in Figure 3 appear straight forward enough, but what is not shown is precisely where and how the conductors connect together.

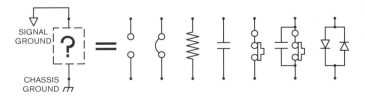

Figure 3. Some passive schemes for connecting signal ground to chassis.

It all comes down to paying close attention to where currents flow. As discussed above, the shield noise currents flow through the chassis and shunt to earth ground on units with 3-conductor line cords. The key issue is that these noise currents do not flow through a path shared by any audio currents. It seems so simple, and is — especially to draw (see Figure 3 again). The hard part is implementing the proper layout scheme.

Connecting signal ground to the chassis in each unit can only be done in *one* place in each unit. If done twice, one leaves the possibility open that the noise currents will flow through a path shared by audio.

There are two schools of thought on where to connect the signal ground to the chassis. They are both versions of the star ground scheme mentioned above. The first connects a trace (or wire) directly from the audio power supply ground terminal and connects to the chassis ground point (see Figure 4). It is important, in both "schools", that no other signal currents be allowed to flow through this trace. Do not allow this trace to share any other return currents from other signal-grounded circuit points, such as the input or output circuit's ground. This keeps chassis noise currents from flowing through the same trace which is a return path for an audio signal. Also keep in mind that this trace may contain noise currents and should be kept away from noise sensitive circuitry. This is a star grounding scheme which uses a point originating at the output of the power supply as the center of the star. There are two common locations in the power supply for the star's center: the output terminal of the power supply and the point between the AC filter capacitors.

Another school of thought on where to connect signal ground to the chassis simply moves the center of the star ground to the input jack's ground. This scheme makes the most sense for unbalanced units and balanced units equipped with ¼" connectors where use of mono plugs is possible.

MANUFACTURER ISSUES TO ADDRESS

Implementing their users' desires to "upgrade" to balanced, traditionally unbalanced manufacturers are faced with an important issue: How do you solve the balanced/unbalanced incompatibility problem? If you sell your product to a mixed balanced/unbalanced market, a suggested method of interconnection must be available. Isolation transformers and active interface boxes are the best solution and should be offered as the best interconnection alternative. However, persuading unbalanced customers to buy an expensive interface solution is much harder than the lower performance option of rewiring their cables. (The "add-on" transformer solution is analogous to a software company releasing a new software revision which renders your existing files incompatible unless an additional file conversion program is purchased.)

Through careful rewiring of the cables, acceptable interconnection solutions are achievable in some systems. (One of Rane's most popular RaneNotes, *Sound System Interconnection*, is one example of the "custom" wiring needed in some systems.) This same cable re-wiring solution holds whether the equipment is wired with signal ground or with chassis ground on the balanced circuit's shields.

SOLUTIONS FOR MIXED BALANCED AND UNBALANCED SYSTEMS

It is obvious from the vast quantity of literature that for fully balanced operation, the shield should connect to chassis ground at the point of entry. This is also true for unbalanced operation when a third shield conductor is available; connect the shield to chassis ground at the point of entry. However, this is only valid when 2-conductor shielded cable is used.

Shielded 2-Conductor Connectivity

Figure 5 shows recommended wiring for all combinations of balanced and unbalanced I/O interconnections when 2-conductor shielded cable is used. Figure 5 also includes the two most common manufacturer shield-grounding schemes; signal-grounding the shield and chassis-grounding the shield. Identifying these schemes for every unit in a system is essential to debug system hum and buzz. This is no simple task since chassis and signal grounds are connected together. The goal is to find out if the manufacturer connected them together is such a way that shield currents do not affect the audio signal. The dashed lines in Figure 5 represents the units' chassis boundary. Connections between dashed lines are functions of the cable. Connections outside these lines are the manufacturer's choosing, whether conscious or unconscious.

Figure 5 is arranged such that the top and left most figure (5a) is the theoretical "best" way to connect equipment with optimal results. The "best" way being, everything completely balanced with all shields (pin 1s) connected to chassis ground at the point of entry. As one moves down or to the right, degradation in performance is expected. Whether a system operates acceptably or obeys these theoretical predictions is too system-specific to predict accurately. However, one must start somewhere.

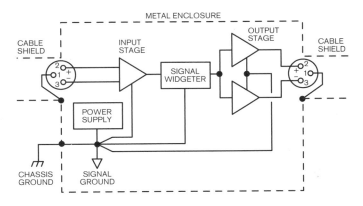

Figure 4. Star ground scheme for connecting signal ground to chassis. Star center may be connected at power supply, or at input ground.

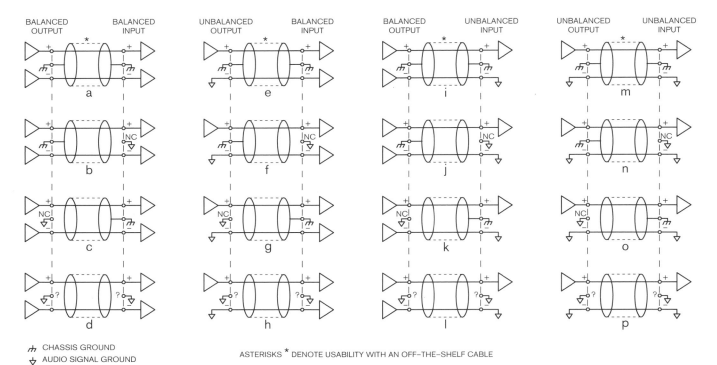

Figure 5. Interconnectivity using shielded 2-conductor cable only. Asterisks denote usability with off-the-shelf cable.

The quality and configuration of the input and output circuits are omitted from Figure 5 and the ensuing discussion, to focus on cable wiring and the internal wiring of the units. The I/O circuitry is assumed ideal.

Fully Balanced

Fully balanced systems (left column in Figure 5) provide the best performance when both ends of the shield connect to units with chassis-grounded shields (Figure 5a). When units with signal-grounded shields are encountered, disconnect the shield at the signal-grounded end (Figures 5b & 5c). This keeps the induced shield currents out of the audio signal ground. If both units involved have signal-grounded shields, you have entered the twilight zone (Figure 5d). This is perhaps the most common scheme. Most disconnect one end of the shield, specifically which end is disconnected creates strong political debates and is left for the individual user to decide [6]. Never disconnect both ends of a shield.

Unbalanced Output Driving Balanced Input

The second column in Figure 5 shows unbalanced outputs driving balanced inputs. Again, only shielded 2-conductor cable is used. The best case here has both ends of the shield connected to units whose shield is chassis-grounded (Figure 5e). Some may argue that the induced noise on the signal conductors may be injected into the "sending" unit through the unbalanced output stage. This is a function of the system and output circuit, and is quite likely. Disconnecting the shield at the unbalanced output might reduce this problem.

When units with signal-grounded shields are encountered, disconnect the shield at the signal-grounded end (Figures 5f & 5g). This keeps the noisy shield currents out of the audio signal ground. If both units involved have signal-grounded shields, you've entered the twilight zone again (Figure 5h). Support your one-end-only political party (Figure 5l).

Balanced Output Driving Unbalanced Input

The third column in Figure 5 is the most troublesome, balanced outputs driving unbalanced inputs. Since the input stage is not balanced, induced noise on the signal conductors is not rejected. If you must use an unbalanced input, use as short an input cable as possible. This reduces the induced noise. There's a reason it's hard to find and buy unbalanced RCA cables longer than 12 feet. Figure 5i shows both ends of the cable shield connected to units with chassis-grounded shields. If the units are far apart, the chance of the shield currents inducing noise on the signal conductors is greater. Keeping this cable very short reduces the shield current and therefore reduces the noise that is *not* rejected by the unbalanced input stage. Most systems may require disconnecting one end of the shield for the Figure 5i case. Even a small current in the shield may prove too much for an unbalanced input stage. Again, support your favorite one-end-only political position.

Disconnect the shield at units with signal-grounded shields (Figures 5j & 5k). If both ends have signal-grounded shields, run for your favorite one-end-only political party. (Figure 5l).

This scheme connects the balanced output's negative output to signal ground, rather than a high impedance input. Many balanced output circuits will attempt to drive this signal ground, causing great distortion and potentially damaging the output stage. Other balanced output stages are termed "floating" balanced. (Analog Devices SSM-2142 Balanced Line Driver chip is one example.) Also called a cross-coupled output, these circuits mimic the performance of fully balanced transformer solutions and are designed so the negative output can short to signal ground. If you find or use this scheme, be sure that the balanced output stage can properly handle signal ground on its negative output.

Full Unbalanced

Fully unbalanced systems do not provide a 3-conductor connector to enable proper use of a shield. In the unlikely event you run across one, use the wiring in the fourth column (Figure 5m-p). Again keeping cable lengths short will reduce noise problems, with or without a shield.

Most home audio systems are fully unbalanced. Millions of these systems work virtually hum and buzz-free every day, due to their small nature, short cable runs and 2-conductor AC line cords. The headaches begin when one tries to add a balanced unit to such a system. In unbalanced home audio products neither of the line cord's conductors connects to the chassis, since plugging older, non-polarized AC plugs into an improperly wired outlet would place the "hot" wire on the unit's chassis. Lack of the third pin on the line cord prevents ground loops in home systems since a second path to ground, or between units, is unavailable. Professional audio equipment generally comes equipped with a 3-wire line cord. The third wire (green wire) is required to connect to the chassis. This provides the second ground path (loop) from one unit to the next.

Connector Choice

Connector type was purposely left out of Figure 5 and the above discussion since connector choice adds another layer of complexity to interconnection systems. The most troublesome culprit is the ¼" connector. Mono ¼" connectors are used on most musical instruments and in phone systems. Stereo ¼" connectors are used for headphones, balanced interconnection, effect and insert send/return loops, relay switch closure points, and an extravagant collection of other miscellaneous connections. Murphy's Law tells us, if you provide such a diverse selection of ¼" interconnection options, they will be hooked up improperly. The audio industry's problem is that many of these options are completely incompatible. A properly wired mono ¼" connector has signal ground on the sleeve, a properly wired balanced ¼" connector has chassis ground on the sleeve. Interconnecting this combination should not be achievable — much like trying to connect 120 VAC to an RCA jack (see Figure 6). The ¼" connectors low cost, high availability, and small size all contribute to its widespread and varied use. Undoubtedly the numerous interconnection uses of such a popular connector arose for these reasons.

Sadly, the possibility of including connector type in a recommended practices document is slim. The duplicate connectors on many audio components contributes to higher costs and wastes millions of dollars worth of connectors that are never used. Some manufacturers are attempting to

eliminate the ¼" connector to avoid the confusion and problems when ¼" jacks are used. This is a step in the right direction, though the high density allowed by these connectors requires less valuable rear-panel real estate. Most marketing departments prefer thirty connectors per inch, making the currently available 3-pin (XLR) alternative markedly unpopular. What is needed is a 3-pin connector solution that requires less space than the traditional XLR connector. A locking, stackable 3-pin mini-DIN comes to mind.

Terminal block and Euroblock connector types are used when separate cable-end connectors are unnecessary or impractical. These connection solutions provide the user with the most wiring options when both signal and chassis ground terminals are available. This allows the *user* to decide which wiring practice to incorporate. This is the most desirable solution, though most studio equipment does not call for these connector types.

"Hidden" Balanced I/O Solution

An interesting solution for mono interconnection incorporates unshielded balanced stages, much like most telephone systems. Figure 7 shows this configuration. This allows off-the-shelf mono cables to be used to connect unbalanced or unshielded-balanced I/Os to a system. Though not as ideal as a shielded balanced interconnection, systems with mono connectors, like home theatre systems, benefit from this configuration. Keeping cable lengths short is essential and not difficult in a home environment.

One advantage of such a system, besides making it impossible, on fully balanced systems, to get signal ground on an external cable, is that it provides an easy upgrade path to balanced signal connections. The manufacturer need only change the connector to a 3-pin version. Also crucial for this solution is the need to have either cross-coupled output stages or an output that does not mind a grounded negative output, since the negative output may connect to signal ground.

A slight disadvantage lies with the common use of non-twisted pair cables in off-the-shelf mono cables. Using twisted cable with this unshielded balanced scheme greatly improves the achievable performance.

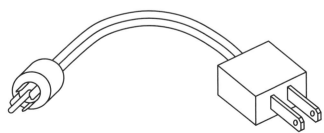

Figure 6. Difficult-to-find connector type.

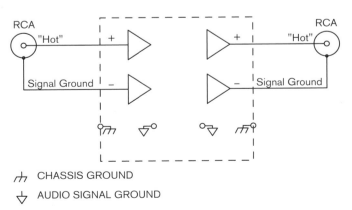

$\perp\!\!\!\perp$ CHASSIS GROUND

$\triangledown$ AUDIO SIGNAL GROUND

Figure 7. "Hidden" Balanced Interconnection.

The Muncy Solution

Neil Muncy is an electroacoustic consultant and veteran of years of successful system design. His long standing solution to these issues provides real-world proof of the guaranteed performance achievable with fully balanced systems wired per the Audio Engineering Society recommendation. Mr. Muncy implements what I call the Muncy solution and alters every piece of gear so it has balanced inputs and outputs with both ends of the shield connected to chassis ground at the point of entry. Decades of this practice, and the early research and discipline to understand the basic physics required to implement it properly, have given Mr. Muncy the drive to tirelessly tour the country dispersing his findings. Mr. Muncy's seminars educate those who are ignorant of the "right" way to wire balanced equipment, and show the advantages gained when every piece of gear in the system is wired accordingly.

CURRENT MANUFACTURER SOLUTIONS

Let's examine manufacturer's choices regarding signal-grounding or chassis-grounding balanced cable shields. The problems of signal-grounding balanced shields have already been covered. Users choose to live with hum & buzz, alter off-the-shelf cables by disconnecting one end of the shield or, even in fully balanced systems, use isolation transformers. All are senseless alternatives for inconsistent manufacturing methods. Their advantages and disadvantages are outlined in Tables 1 and 2.

Table 1. Signal-Grounded Balanced Shields

Advantages	Disadvantages
Permits mono ¼" cable use if proper I/O stage is present.	Hum and Buzz are present. Must alter cables to interface with many components. Use of isolation transformers and/or interface boxes needed in some systems. Most manufacturers do it this way.

Table 2. Chassis-Grounded Balanced Shields

Advantages (with ideal I/O circuitry)	Disadvantages
Use of off-the-shelf cable is permitted. No hum and buzz occurs. No isolation transformers or add-on solutions are needed.	Mono ¼" cables cannot be used. Few manufacturers do it this way.

For the manufacturer, several shield connectivity choices are available.

1. Keep or change shield connections to *chassis ground*.
Manufacturers who chassis-grounded balanced shields originally must still recommend isolation transformers, cable altering and the technical support that go with these hum and buzz solutions. This is unfortunately necessary, since not all balanced equipment has chassis-grounded shields. Ideally, if *all* balanced equipment were suddenly and miraculously chassis grounded on both ends at the point of entry, off-the-shelf cables could be used in every system, leaving only the I/O circuitry to dictate system performance.

2. Change shield connections to *signal ground*.
Though this would be a step backward, it is still a choice. Most equipment is connected this way and most users have found their own costly "add-on" interconnection solutions.

3. Offer the shield connection choice to the user.
Provide both options. Two independent screw terminals (one signal, one chassis), a switch or a jumper option permit the user to wire as they please. More on this later.

MANUFACTURER SOLUTIONS FOR EFFICIENTLY AND EFFECTIVELY CONNECTING BALANCED SHIELDS TO CHASSIS

Printed Circuit Board Mounted Jacks

The printed circuit mounted jack provides manufacturers with the most cost-effective solution for transferring cable signals to a printed circuit board. On the board, most manu-facturers connect the balanced shield conductor (to signal ground) with a board trace. For optimum balanced perfor-mance connect the shield to chassis ground at the *point of entry*. This means that the shield conductor, to avoid spraying any induced RF energy into the box, never passes the chassis' outer plane. This is not a simple task. Currently no printed circuit mounted 3-conductor connectors provide this optimum solution.

Terminal Strips

When both signal and chassis ground terminals are provided on terminal block or Euroblock connector types, the user decides which wiring practice to incorporate. This is a desirable solution, though a lot of equipment does not call for these connector types. Providing a Pem nut, screw and toothed washer near the cable terminals, instead of an additional chassis-grounded screw terminal, prevents the shield conductor from entering the enclosure — supplying the ultimate interconnection solution. (This is why Rane terminal strips and Euroblock inputs and outputs have a PEM nut, screw and tooth washer above the shield connection.) Users select their preferred wiring practice, and the shield can not spray RF into the enclosure. Maintaining the shield around the signal conductors all the way to the I/O terminals is important. Keeping the Pem screw near the terminals is therefore essential.

Panel Mount Jacks with Wires

Panel mount jacks require the manufacturer to connect a wire from a terminal pin to the printed circuit board or chassis. This is a good solution for chassis-grounding a shield, though this allows the shield to enter the enclosure. Keep the wire short, the gauge large, and the path to chassis away from sensitive circuits. "Wire" is a four letter word to many manufacturers, and some consider them too costly due to their labor intensive nature. Achieving consistent results with hand-wired connections is difficult, making the PC mounted jack solution more desirable.

L-Bracket or Standoff Solution

A circuit board trace run to a nearby chassis-grounded point is another option. Use of an L-bracket, standoff or similar mechanical connection to the chassis provides mechanical stability, but also consumes valuable rear panel and/or PC board real estate at the same time. Important here is avoiding long traces and keeping the trace away from sensitive areas since it acts as a noise source when shield currents are large or noisy.

Jumper Options

Not as "friendly" as the screw terminal solution, an internal jumper option provides user configuration of internal shield connection points. This allows the use of XLR or ¼" connectors yet still gives the user control of shield wiring practices. Providing a separate, external switch for this function is not cost effective. Two issues arise with this solution. The first is that there is no external visual indication showing shield connection point. The second issue to address is which position to ship the jumpers in.

The first problem is nothing new. Most manufacturers do not specify where their shields are connected. The unit's manual or schematic, if available, may indicate what ground connects to the shield. The schematic symbols used for grounds are not standardized, though there is an Audio Engineering Society standards group addressing drafting symbols to solve the dangling triangle mystery. Proper schematics indicate which symbols represent signal and chassis grounds. The second issue's answer is clear — chassis-grounding the balanced shield is the "best" default option, though offering the choice supplies an elegant solution for parties on both sides of the fence. For fully balanced systems, defaulting the shield jumper to chassis provides the best solution, but only when all interconnected units have chassis-grounded shields. Other units with signal-grounded shields short-circuit the shield currents to signal ground when connected, causing potentially nasty modulation of the signal ground. This makes the other guy appear the culprit, but does nothing to solve the problem. Clearly users must be able to determine manufacturer shield wiring practices. Additionally, to support both "one-end-only" shield connection parties, separate input and output jumpers must be provided (see Figure 8).

Neutrik Solution

Neutrik AG, Liechtenstein, offers snap-in, printed circuit mount jacks with metal brackets which pierce the inside of the chassis when external mounting screws are installed. This chassis-pierced bracket also has a separate pin available through the printed circuit board. The sharp piercing tab provides the electrical connection between the chassis housing and printed circuit board. This solves the problems of the labor intensive wire and the need to connect to a chassis point, providing the best solution for manufacturers *and* users. [Neutrik's popular "combo" receptacles — combined female XLR & female ¼" connectors — provide this piercing tab feature.] Unfortunately, depending on the available height in a given unit, these jacks have trouble fitting in a single rack space unit due to their slightly larger height. Hopefully other jacks with this built-in feature will become available, providing manufacturers with a cost effective solution to this grounding problem.

OTHER SUGGESTIONS

Many years ago RCA developed their own guidelines for rear panel I/O practices. Some manufacturers and users practice their own methods of left to right interconnection customs. AC and speaker level I/O on one side, microphone and lower level signals on the other side. This permits easier rack wiring and decreases crosstalk between cable runs in the rack and along cable paths. While the recommended practices document may not dictate product design at such a basic level, this type of thinking benefits everyone. With multi-manufacturer standardized network-controlled products popping up everywhere, now is the time to address these basic features. Users with "standardized" interconnection systems, designed with the user in mind by informed engineers, will spend less time debugging and installing systems. This allows more installations per day, generates better, quieter systems and provides more business with smiling users *and* manufacturers.

FIBER IS THE FUTURE

Digital fiber optic interconnection solves all the above problems of electrical interconnection systems, though one must face a new set of problems. However, when one adds up the debugging costs of eliminating hum from electrical systems, fiber may not seem as expensive.

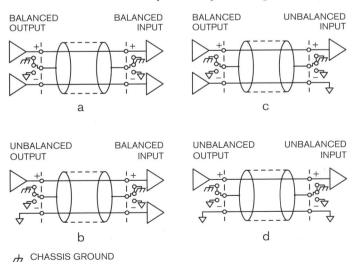

CHASSIS GROUND

AUDIO SIGNAL GROUND

Figure 8. User-Selectable Shield Connections.

CONCLUSION

Balanced and unbalanced interconnection are two very different beings. The incompatibility between these two configurations, whether using analog or digital signals, must be considered when designing, specifying, installing or upgrading equipment and systems. Literature on the subject of grounding and shielding audio devices dictates chassis-grounding balanced shields. Most manufacturers, however, signal ground their balanced shields. Speculation about how and why this practice materialized was explored. The Audio Enginnering Society is developing a recommended practices document which also condones chassis-grounding balanced shields, among other things. It was shown that the manufacturer choice of signal-grounding or chassis-grounding balanced shields does not affect the cable re-wiring and other technical support solutions normally recommended when interconnection of balanced and unbalanced equipment is needed. Therefore manufacturers need not hesitate in addressing their "pin 1 problems," and should provide users with the *real* benefits of balanced interconnection by providing chassis ground on balanced shields. Efficient and effective ways of doing this were also discussed.

Also covered was the importance of reducing signal ground voltages between interconnected units by carefully and properly connecting chassis ground to signal ground, in one place, in each unit. Vitally important is the manner in which one connects these two grounds together. The same care must be taken when connecting I/O cable shields to the chassis ground. One must avoid common impedance coupling in the shield-to-chassis trace to ensure optimum performance from balanced interconnection.

The goal of the Audio Engineering Society in recommending these balanced interconnection solutions is to reduce or eliminate the need for interconnection work-arounds through education and information sharing. This is the mission statement of the Audio Engineering Society in the first place. Systems installed with chassis-grounded balanced shields on all units, with well-twisted interconnection cables operate hum and buzz-free, leaving only the input and output circuit topology specifications to dictate system performance.

The Audio Engineering Society recommendation's purpose is not to create another "pin 2 is hot" war. In reality, users and installers have found acceptable solutions for "the pin 1 problem" of signal-grounded balanced shields and are unlikely, nor will they be able, to suddenly change over to not using alternatives. Manufacturers specify I/O connector type on data sheets, similarly, we should specify shield connection practices in equipment specifications, on the chassis, or at least in the manual, thus providing users with required information for proper system configuration.

REFERENCES

1. Ott, Henry W., *Noise Reduction Techniques in Electronic Systems* (John Wiley and Sons, Inc., NY, 1976).
2. Morrison, Ralph, *Grounding and Shielding Techniques in Instrumentation* (John Wiley and Sons, Inc., NY, 1967).
3. Morrison, Ralph, *Noise and Other Interfering Signals* (John Wiley and Sons, Inc., NY, 1992).
4. Giddings, Philip, *Audio System Design and Installation* (Howard W. Sams, 1990).
5. Jung, Walt and Garcia, Adolfo, *Op Amps in Line-Driver and Receiver Circuits, Part 2*, (Analog Dialogue Vol. 27, No. 1, 1993).
6. Whitlock, Bill, "System Problems and Equipment Manufacturers" (*Systems Contractor News,* September 1997).
7. Perkins, Cal, *Measurement Techniques for Debugging Electronic Systems and Their Interconnection*, (Proceedings of the 11th International AES Conference, Portland, OR, May, 1992).
8. *Sound System Interconnection*, (Rane Corporation, Mukilteo, WA, 1985).
9. Metzler, Bob, *Audio Measurement Handbook*, (Audio Precision, Portland, OR, 1993).

A version of this RaneNote was published in the Journal of the Audio Engineering Society, Vol. 43, No. 6, June, 1995.

Sound System Interconnection

- Cause and prevention of ground loops

- Interfacing balanced and unbalanced

- Proper pin connections and wiring

- Chassis ground vs. signal ground

- Ground lift switches

Rane Technical Staff

RaneNote 110
© 1985, 1995 Rane Corporation

INTRODUCTION

This note, originally written in 1985, continues to be one of our most useful references. It's popularity stems from the continual and perpetual difficulty of hooking up audio equipment without suffering through all sorts of bizarre noises, hums, buzzes, whistles, etc.— not to mention the extreme financial, physical and psychological price. As technology progresses it is inevitable that electronic equipment and its wiring should be subject to constant improvement. Many things *have* improved in the audio industry since 1985, but unfortunately wiring isn't one of them. However, finally the Audio Engineering Society (AES) is trying to do something about it, by working on a recommended practice document for interconnection of pro audio equipment.

Rane's policy is to accommodate rather than dictate. However, this document contains suggestions for external wiring changes that should ideally only be implemented by trained technical personnel. Safety regulations require that all original grounding means provided from the factory be left intact for safe operation. No guarantee of responsibility for incidental or consequential damages can be provided. *(In other words, don't modify cables, or try your own version of grounding unless you really understand exactly what type of output and input you have to connect.)*

GROUND LOOPS

Almost all cases of noise can be traced directly to ground loops, grounding or lack thereof. It is important to understand the mechanism that causes grounding noise in order to effectively eliminate it. Each component of a sound system produces its own ground internally. This ground is usually called the audio *signal* ground. Connecting devices together with the interconnecting cables can tie the signal grounds of the two units together in one place through the conductors in the cable. Ground loops occur when the grounds of the two units are also tied together in another place: via the third wire in the line cord, by tying the metal chassis together through the rack rails, etc. These situations create a circuit through which current may flow in a closed "loop" from one unit's ground out to a second unit and back to the first. It is not simply the presence of this current that creates the hum—it is when this current flows through a unit's audio signal ground that creates the hum. In fact, even without a ground loop, a little noise current always flows through every interconnecting cable (i.e., it is impossible to eliminate these currents entirely). The mere presence of this ground loop current is no cause for alarm if your system uses properly implemented and *completely* balanced interconnects, which are excellent at rejecting ground loop and other noise currents. Balanced interconnect was developed to be immune to these noise currents, which can never be entirely eliminated. What makes a ground loop current annoying is when the audio signal is affected. Unfortunately, many manufacturers of balanced audio equipment design the internal grounding system improperly, thus creating balanced equipment that is not immune to the cabling's noise currents. This is one reason for the bad reputation sometimes given to balanced interconnect.

A second reason for balanced interconnect's bad reputation comes from those who think connecting unbalanced equipment into "superior" balanced equipment should improve things. Sorry. Balanced interconnect is not compatible with unbalanced. The small physical nature and short cable runs of completely unbalanced systems (home audio) also contain these ground loop noise currents. However, the currents in unbalanced systems never get large enough to affect the audio to the point where it is a nuisance. Mixing balanced and unbalanced equipment, however, is an entirely different story, since balanced and unbalanced interconnect are truly *not compatible*. The rest of this note shows several recommended implementations for all of these interconnection schemes.

The potential or voltage which pushes these noise currents through the circuit is developed between the independent grounds of the two or more units in the system. The impedance of this circuit is low, and even though the voltage is low, the current is high, thanks to Mr. Ohm, without whose help we wouldn't have these problems. It would take a very high resolution ohm meter to measure the impedance of the steel chassis or the rack rails. We're talking thousandths of an ohm. So trying to measure this stuff won't necessarily help you. We just thought we'd warn you.

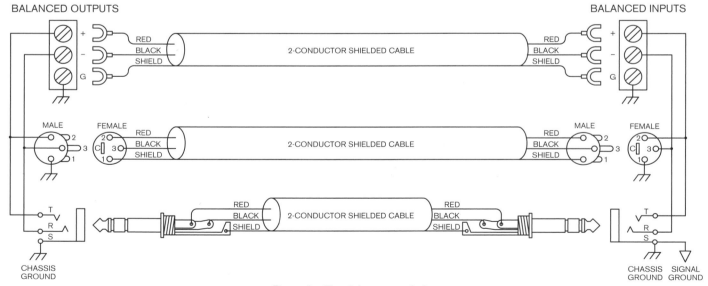

Figure 1a. The right way to do it.

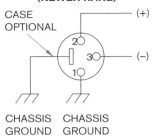

| COMMON (WRONG) PRACTICE | RECOMMENDED PRACTICE (NEWER RANE) |

Figure 1b. Recommmended practice.

THE ABSOLUTE BEST RIGHT WAY TO DO IT

Use balanced lines and *tie the cable shield to the metal chassis (right where it enters the chassis) at both ends of the cable.*

A balanced line requires three separate conductors, two of which are signal (+ and −) and one shield (see Figure 1a). The shield serves to guard the sensitive audio lines from interference. Only by using balanced line interconnects can you *guarantee* (yes, *guarantee*) hum-free results. Always use twisted pair cable. Chassis tying the shield at each end also *guarantees* the best possible protection from RFI [radio frequency interference] and other noises [neon signs, lighting dimmers].

Neil Muncy[1], an electroacoustic consultant and seasoned veteran of years of successful system design, chairs the AES Standards Committee (SC-05-05) working on this subject. He tirelessly tours the world giving seminars and dispensing information on how to successfully hook-up pro audio equipment[2]. He makes the simple point that it is absurd that you cannot go out and buy pro audio equipment from several different manufacturers, buy standard off-the-shelf cable assemblies, come home, hook it all up and have it work hum and noise free. *Plug and play.* Sadly, almost never is this the case, despite the science and rules of noise-free interconnect known and documented for over *60 years* (see References for complete information).

It all boils down to using balanced lines, only balanced lines, and nothing but balanced lines. This is why they were developed. Further, that you *tie the shield to the chassis, at the point it enters the chassis, and at both ends of the cable* (more on 'both ends' later).

Since standard XLR cables come with their shields tied to pin 1 at each end (the shells are not tied, nor need be), this means equipment using 3-pin, XLR-type connectors *must tie pin 1 to the chassis* (usually called chassis ground) — not the audio signal ground as is most common.

Not using *signal ground* is the most radical departure from common pro-audio practice. Not that there is any argument about its validity. There isn't. **This is the right way to do it**. So why doesn't audio equipment come wired this way? Well, some does, and since 1993, more of it does.

That's when Rane started manufacturing some of its products with balanced inputs and outputs tying pin 1 to chassis. So why doesn't everyone do it this way? Because life is messy, some things are hard to change, and there will always be equipment in use that was made before proper grounding practices were in effect.

Unbalanced equipment is another problem: it is everwhere, easily available and inexpensive. All those RCA and ¼" TS connectors found on consumer equipment; effect-loops and insert-points on consoles; signal processing boxes; semi-pro digital and analog tape recorders; computer cards; mixing consoles; et cetera.

The next several pages give tips on how to successfully address hooking up unbalanced equipment. Unbalanced equipment when "blindly" connected with fully balanced units starts a pattern of hum and undesirable operation, requiring extra measures to correct the situation.

THE NEXT BEST RIGHT WAY TO DO IT

The quickest, quietest and most foolproof method to connect balanced and unbalanced is to **transformer isolate all unbalanced connections**. See Figure 2.

Many manufacturers provide several tools for this task, including Rane. Consult your audio dealer to explore the options available.

The goal of these adaptors is to allow the use of *standard cables*. With these transformer isolation boxes, modification of cable assemblies is unnecessary. Virtually any two pieces of audio equipment can be successfully interfaced without risk of unwanted hum and noise.

Another way to create the necessary isolation is to use a *direct box.* Originally named for its use to convert the high impedance, high level output of an electric guitar to the low impedance, low level input of a recording console, it allowed the player to plug "directly" into the console. Now this term is commonly used to describe any box used to convert unbalanced lines to balanced lines.

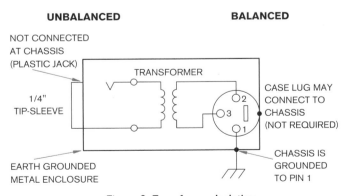

Figure 2. Transformer Isolation

THE LAST BEST RIGHT WAY TO DO IT

If transformer isolation is not an option, special cable assemblies are a last resort. The key here is to prevent the shield currents from flowing into a unit whose grounding scheme creates ground loops (hum) in the audio path (i.e., most audio equipment).

It is true that connecting both ends of the shield is theoretically the best way to interconnect equipment –though this assumes the interconnected equipment is internally grounded properly. Since most equipment is *not* internally grounded properly, connecting both ends of the shield is not often practiced, since doing so usually creates noisy interconnections.

A common solution to these noisy hum and buzz problems involves disconnecting one end of the shield, even though one can not buy off-the-shelf cables with the shield disconnected at one end. The best end to disconnect is a matter of personal preference and should be religiously obeyed; choose inputs or outputs and always lift the side you choose (our drawings happen to disconnect the input end of the cable—the output of the driving unit). If one end of the shield is disconnected, the noisy hum current stops flowing and away goes the hum — but only at low frequencies. A one-end-only shield connection increases the possibility of high frequency (radio) interference since the shield may act as an antenna. Many reduce this potential RF interference by providing an RF path through a small capacitor (0.1 or 0.01 microfarad ceramic disc) connected from the lifted end of the shield to the chassis. The fact that many modern day installers still follow this one-end-only rule with consistent success indicates this and other acceptable solutions to RF issues exist, though the increasing use of digital and wireless technology greatly increases the possibility of future RF problems.

If you've truly isolated your hum problem to a specific unit, chances are, even though the documentation indicates proper chassis grounded shields, the suspect unit is not internally grounded properly. Here is where special test cable assemblies, shown in Figure 3, really come in handy. These assemblies allow you to connect the shield to chassis ground *at the point of entry*, or to pin 1, or to lift one end of the shield. The task becomes more difficult when the unit you've isolated has multiple inputs and outputs. On a suspect unit with multiple cables, try various configurations on each connection to find out if special cable assemblies are needed at more than one point.

See Figure 4 for suggested cable assemblies for your particular interconnection needs. Find the appropriate output configuration (down the left side) and then match this with the correct input configuration (across the top of the page.) Then refer to the following pages for a recommended wiring diagram.

GROUND LIFTS

Many units come equipped with ground lift switches. In only a few cases can it be shown that a ground lift switch improves ground related noise. (Has a ground lift switch ever *really* worked for you?) In reality, the presence of a ground lift switch greatly reduces a unit's ability to be "properly" grounded and therefore immune to ground loop hums and buzzes. Ground lifts are simply another Band-Aid® to try in case of grounding problems. It is, however, true that an entire system of properly grounded equipment, without ground lift switches, is guaranteed (yes guaranteed) to be hum free. The problem is most equipment is *not* (both internally and externally, AC system wise) grounded properly.

Most units with ground lifts are shipped so the unit is "grounded" — meaning the chassis is connected to audio signal ground. (This should be the best and is the "safest" position for a ground lift switch.) If after hooking up your system it exhibits excessive hum or buzzing, there is an incompatibility somewhere in the system's grounding

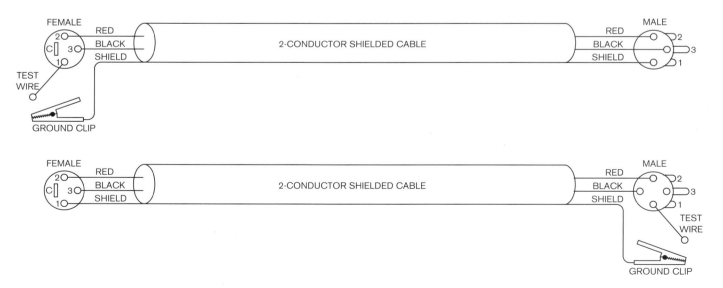

Figure 3. Test cables

configuration. In addition to these special cable assemblies that may help, here are some more things to try:

1. Try combinations of lifting grounds on units supplied with lift switches (or links). It is wise to do this with the power off!

2. If you have an entirely balanced system, verify all chassis are tied to a good earth ground, for safety's sake and hum protection. Completely unbalanced systems never earth ground anything (except cable TV, often a ground loop source). If you have a mixed balanced and unbalanced system, do yourself a favor and use isolation transformers or, if you're cheap, try the special cable assemblies described here and expect it to take many hours to get things quiet. May the Force be with you.

3. Balanced units with outboard power supplies (wall warts or "bumps" in the line cord) do *not* ground the chassis through the line cord. Make sure such units are solidly grounded by tying the chassis to an earth ground using a star washer for a reliable contact. (Rane always provides this chassis point as an external screw with a toothed washer.) Any device with a 3-prong AC plug, such as an amplifier, may serve as an earth ground point. Rack rails may or may not serve this purpose depending on screw locations and paint jobs.

FLOATING, PSEUDO, AND QUASI-BALANCING

During inspection, you may run across a ¼" output called floating unbalanced, sometimes also called psuedo-balanced or quasi-balanced. In this configuration, the sleeve of the output stage is not connected inside the unit and the ring is connected (usually through a small resistor) to the audio signal ground. This allows the tip and ring to "appear" as an equal impedance, not-quite balanced output stage, even though the output circuitry is unbalanced.

Floating unbalanced often works to drive either a balanced or unbalanced input, depending if a TS or TRS standard cable is plugged into it. When it hums, a special cable is required. See drawings #11 and #12, and do not make the cross-coupled modification of tying the ring and sleeve together.

SUMMARY

If you are unable to do things correctly (i.e. use fully balanced wiring with shields tied to the *chassis* at the point of entry, or transformer isolate all unbalanced signals from balanced signals) then there is no guarantee that a hum free interconnect can be achieved, nor is there a definite scheme that will assure noise free operation in all configurations.

WINNING THE WIRING WARS

- Use balanced connections whenever possible.
- Transformer isolate all unbalanced connections from balanced connections.
- Use special cable assemblies when unbalanced lines cannot be transformer isolated.
- Any unbalanced cable must be kept under 10 feet (3 m) in length. Lengths longer than this will amplify all the nasty side effects of unbalanced circuitry's ground loops.
- When all else fails, digitize everything with fiber optics and enter a whole new realm of problems.

REFERENCES

1. Neil A. Muncy, "Noise Susceptibility in Analog and Digital Signal Processing Systems," presented at the 97th AES Convention of Audio Engineering Society in San Francisco, CA, Nov. 1994.

2. *Grounding, Shielding, and Interconnections in Analog & Digital Signal Processing Systems: Understanding the Basics*; Workshops designed and presented by Neil Muncy and Cal Perkins, at the 97th AES Convention of Audio Engineering Society in San Francisco, CA, Nov. 1994.

3. The entire June 1995 AES Journal, Vol. 43, No. 6, available $6 members, $11 nonmembers from the Audio Engineering Society, 60 E. 42nd St., New York, NY, 10165-2520.

4. Phillip Giddings, *Audio System Design and Installation* (SAMS, Indiana, 1990).

5. Ralph Morrison, *Noise and Other Interfering Signals* (Wiley, New York, 1992).

6. Henry W. Ott, *Noise Reduction Techniques in Electronic Systems*, 2nd Edition (Wiley, New York, 1988).

7. Cal Perkins, "Measurement Techniques for Debugging Electronic Systems and Their Instrumentation," *The Proceedings of the 11th International AES Conference: Audio Test & Measurement,* Portland, OR, May 1992, pp. 82-92 (Audio Engineering Society, New York, 1992).

8. Macatee, *RaneNote*: "Grounding and Shielding Audio Devices," Rane Corporation, 1994.

9. Philip Giddings, "Grounding and Shielding for Sound and Video," *S&VC*, Sept. 20th, 1995.

Band-Aid is a registered trademark of Johnson & Johnson

CABLE CONNECTORS	MALE BALANCED XLR	¼" BALANCED TRS (TIP-RING-SLEEVE)	¼" UNBALANCED TS (TIP-SLEEVE)	UNBALANCED RCA
FEMALE BALANCED XLR (NOT A TRANSFORMER, NOR A CROSS-COUPLED OUTPUT STAGE)	1	2	3 B	4 B
FEMALE BALANCED XLR (EITHER A TRANSFORMER OR A CROSS-COUPLED OUTPUT STAGE)	1	2	5	6
¼" BALANCED TRS (NOT A TRANSFORMER, NOR A CROSS-COUPLED OUTPUT STAGE)	7	8	9 B	10 B
¼" BALANCED TRS (EITHER A TRANSFORMER OR A CROSS-COUPLED OUTPUT STAGE)	7	8	11	12
¼" FLOATING UNBALANCED TRS (TIP-RING-SLEEVE) (SLEEVE IN UNIT = NC)	21 A	22 A	11	12
¼" UNBALANCED TS (TIP-SLEEVE)	13	14	15 A	16 A
UNBALANCED RCA	17	18	19 A	20 A

Figure 4. Interconnect chart for locating correct cable assemblies on the following pages.
Note: (A) This configuration uses an "off-the-shelf" cable.
Note: (B) This configuration causes a 6 dB signal loss. Compensate by "turning the system up" 6 dB.

FROM OUTPUT

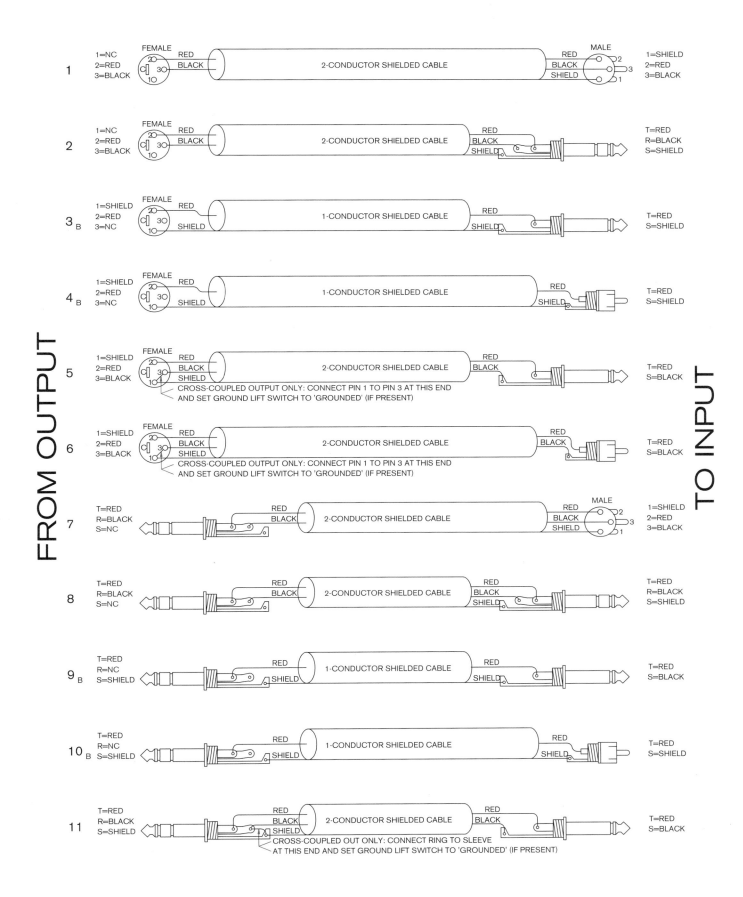

FROM OUTPUT

TO INPUT

1
1=NC
2=RED
3=BLACK
FEMALE
RED
BLACK
2-CONDUCTOR SHIELDED CABLE
RED
BLACK
SHIELD
MALE
1=SHIELD
2=RED
3=BLACK

2
1=NC
2=RED
3=BLACK
FEMALE
RED
BLACK
2-CONDUCTOR SHIELDED CABLE
RED
BLACK
SHIELD
T=RED
R=BLACK
S=SHIELD

3 B
1=SHIELD
2=RED
3=NC
FEMALE
RED
SHIELD
1-CONDUCTOR SHIELDED CABLE
RED
SHIELD
T=RED
S=SHIELD

4 B
1=SHIELD
2=RED
3=NC
FEMALE
RED
SHIELD
1-CONDUCTOR SHIELDED CABLE
RED
SHIELD
T=RED
S=SHIELD

5
1=SHIELD
2=RED
3=BLACK
FEMALE
RED
BLACK
SHIELD
2-CONDUCTOR SHIELDED CABLE
RED
BLACK
T=RED
S=BLACK
CROSS-COUPLED OUTPUT ONLY: CONNECT PIN 1 TO PIN 3 AT THIS END
AND SET GROUND LIFT SWITCH TO 'GROUNDED' (IF PRESENT)

6
1=SHIELD
2=RED
3=BLACK
FEMALE
RED
BLACK
SHIELD
2-CONDUCTOR SHIELDED CABLE
RED
BLACK
T=RED
S=BLACK
CROSS-COUPLED OUTPUT ONLY: CONNECT PIN 1 TO PIN 3 AT THIS END
AND SET GROUND LIFT SWITCH TO 'GROUNDED' (IF PRESENT)

7
T=RED
R=BLACK
S=NC
RED
BLACK
2-CONDUCTOR SHIELDED CABLE
RED
BLACK
SHIELD
MALE
1=SHIELD
2=RED
3=BLACK

8
T=RED
R=BLACK
S=NC
RED
BLACK
2-CONDUCTOR SHIELDED CABLE
RED
BLACK
SHIELD
T=RED
R=BLACK
S=SHIELD

9 B
T=RED
R=NC
S=SHIELD
RED
SHIELD
1-CONDUCTOR SHIELDED CABLE
RED
SHIELD
T=RED
S=BLACK

10 B
T=RED
R=NC
S=SHIELD
RED
SHIELD
1-CONDUCTOR SHIELDED CABLE
RED
SHIELD
T=RED
S=SHIELD

11
T=RED
R=BLACK
S=SHIELD
RED
BLACK
SHIELD
2-CONDUCTOR SHIELDED CABLE
RED
BLACK
T=RED
S=BLACK
CROSS-COUPLED OUT ONLY: CONNECT RING TO SLEEVE
AT THIS END AND SET GROUND LIFT SWITCH TO 'GROUNDED' (IF PRESENT)

Interconnection-7

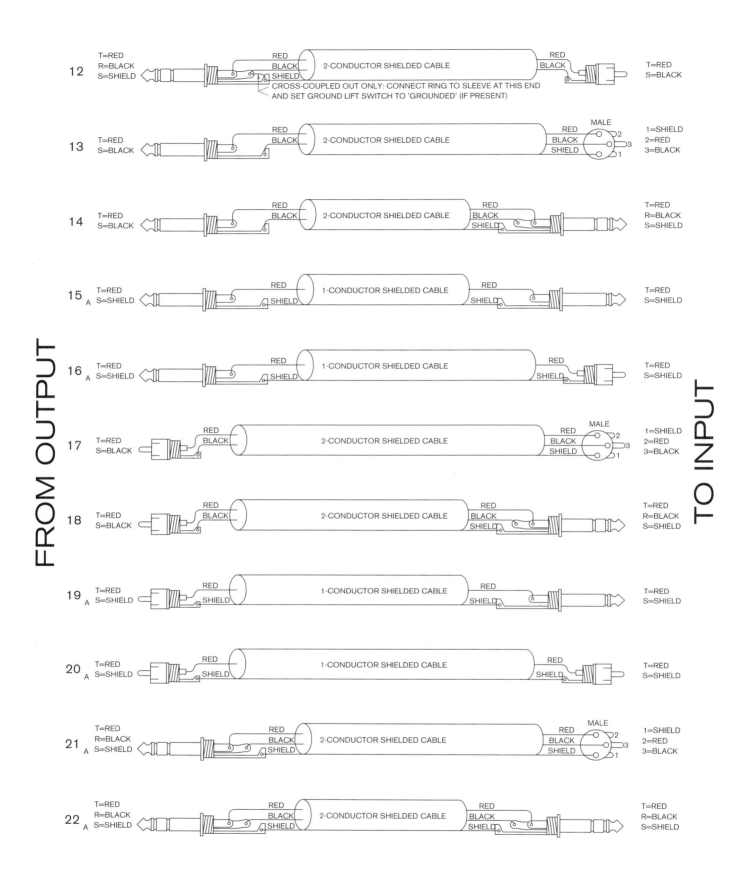

FROM OUTPUT

TO INPUT

12 T=RED R=BLACK S=SHIELD   RED BLACK SHIELD   2-CONDUCTOR SHIELDED CABLE   RED BLACK   T=RED S=BLACK
CROSS-COUPLED OUT ONLY: CONNECT RING TO SLEEVE AT THIS END
AND SET GROUND LIFT SWITCH TO 'GROUNDED' (IF PRESENT)

13 T=RED S=BLACK   RED BLACK   2-CONDUCTOR SHIELDED CABLE   RED BLACK SHIELD   MALE 2 3 1   1=SHIELD 2=RED 3=BLACK

14 T=RED S=BLACK   RED BLACK   2-CONDUCTOR SHIELDED CABLE   RED BLACK SHIELD   T=RED R=BLACK S=SHIELD

15 A T=RED S=SHIELD   RED SHIELD   1-CONDUCTOR SHIELDED CABLE   RED SHIELD   T=RED S=SHIELD

16 A T=RED S=SHIELD   RED SHIELD   1-CONDUCTOR SHIELDED CABLE   RED SHIELD   T=RED S=SHIELD

17 T=RED S=BLACK   RED BLACK   2-CONDUCTOR SHIELDED CABLE   RED BLACK SHIELD   MALE 2 3 1   1=SHIELD 2=RED 3=BLACK

18 T=RED S=BLACK   RED BLACK   2-CONDUCTOR SHIELDED CABLE   RED BLACK SHIELD   T=RED R=BLACK S=SHIELD

19 A T=RED S=SHIELD   RED SHIELD   1-CONDUCTOR SHIELDED CABLE   RED SHIELD   T=RED S=SHIELD

20 A T=RED S=SHIELD   RED SHIELD   1-CONDUCTOR SHIELDED CABLE   RED SHIELD   T=RED S=SHIELD

21 A T=RED R=BLACK S=SHIELD   RED BLACK SHIELD   2-CONDUCTOR SHIELDED CABLE   RED BLACK SHIELD   MALE 2 3 1   1=SHIELD 2=RED 3=BLACK

22 A T=RED R=BLACK S=SHIELD   RED BLACK SHIELD   2-CONDUCTOR SHIELDED CABLE   RED BLACK SHIELD   T=RED R=BLACK S=SHIELD

©Rane Corporation   10802 47th Ave. W.,   Mukilteo WA 98275-5098   TEL (425)355-6000   FAX (425)347-7757   WEB http://www.rane.com

Why Not Wye?

(or, "Successful Monoing Of Your Low End")

- **Splitting Signals**
- **Subwoofing in Mono**
- **Unbalanced Summing**
- **Balanced Summing**
- **Output Impedances**

Dennis Bohn
Rane Corporation

RaneNote 109
© **1991 Rane Corporation**

INTRODUCTION

Wye-connectors (or "Y"-connectors, if you prefer) should never have been created.

Anything that can be hooked-up wrong, will be. You-know-who said that, and she was right. A wye-connector used to *split* a signal into two lines is being used properly; a wye-connector used to *mix* two signals into one is being abused and may even damage the equipment involved.

Here is the rule: Outputs are low impedance and must *only* be connected to high impedance *inputs*—never, never tie two outputs directly together—never. If you do, then each output tries to drive the very low impedance of the other, forcing both outputs into current-limit and possible damage. As a minimum, severe signal loss results.

MONOING YOUR LOW END

One of the most common examples of tying two outputs together is in "monoing" the low end of multiway active crossover systems. This combined signal is then used to drive a sub-woofer system.

Since low frequencies below about 100 Hz have such long wavelengths (several feet), it is very difficult to tell where they are coming from (like some of your friends). They are just there—everywhere. Due to this phenomenon, a single sub-woofer system is a popular cost-effective way to add low frequency energy to small systems.

So the question arises as how best to do the monoing, or summing, of the two signals? It is done very easily by tying the two low frequency outputs of your crossovers together using the resistive networks described below. You do *not* do it with a wye-cord.

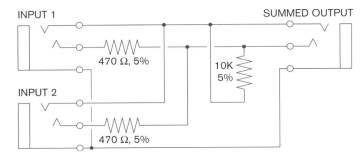

Figure 1. Unbalanced Summing Box

SUMMING BOXES

Unbalanced Summing Box

Figure 1 shows the required network for sources with unbalanced outputs. Two resistors tie each input together to the junction of a third resistor, which connects to signal common. This is routed to the single output jack. The resistor values can vary about those shown over a wide range and not change things much. As designed, the input impedance is about 1k ohms and the line driving output impedance is around 250 Ω. The output impedance is small enough that long lines may still be driven, even though this is a passive box. The input impedance is really quite low and requires 600 Ω line-driving capability from the crossover, but this should not create problems for modern active crossover units.

The rings are tied to each other, as are the sleeves; however, the rings and sleeves are not tied together. Floating the output in this manner makes the box compatible with either balanced or unbalanced systems. It also makes the box ambidextrous: It is now compatible with either unbalanced (mono, 1-wire) or balanced (stereo, 2-wire) ¼" cables. Using mono cables shorts the ring to the sleeve and the box acts as a normal unbalanced system; while using stereo cables takes full advantage of the floating benefits.

Balanced Summing Boxes

Figures 2 and 3 show wiring and parts for creating a balanced summing box. The design is a natural extension of that appearing in Figure 1. Here both the tip (pin 2, positive) and the ring (pin 3, negative) tie together through the resistive

networks shown. Use at least 1% matched resistors. Any mismatch between like-valued resistors degrades the common-mode rejection capability of the system.

TERMITES IN THE WOODPILE

Life is wonderful and then you stub your toe. The corner of the dresser lurking in the night of this Note has to do with applications where you want to sum two outputs together *and* you want to continue to use each of these outputs separately. If all you want to do is sum two outputs together and use *only* the summed results (the usual application), skip this section.

The problem arising from using all three outputs (the two original and the new summed output) is one of channel separation, or crosstalk. If the driving unit truly has zero output impedance, than channel separation is not degraded by using this summing box. However, when dealing with real-world units you deal with finite output impedances (ranging from a low of 47 Ω to a high of 600 Ω). Even a low output impedance of 47 Ω produces a startling channel separation spec of only 27 dB, i.e., the unwanted channel is only 27 dB below the desired signal. (Technical details: the unwanted channel, driving through the summing network, looks like 1011.3 Ω driving the 47 Ω output impedance of the desired channel, producing 27 dB of crosstalk.)

Now 27 dB isn't as bad as first imagined. To put this into perspective, remember that even the best phono cartridges have channel separation specs of about this same magnitude. So, stereo separation is maintained at about the same level as a home system.

For professional systems this may not be enough. If a trade-off is acceptable, things can be improved. If you scale all the resistors up by a factor of 10, then channel separation improves from 27 dB to 46 dB. As always though, this improvement is not free. The price is paid in reduced line driving capability. The box now has high output impedance, which prevents driving long lines. Driving a maximum of 3000 pF capacitance is the realistic limit. This amounts to only 60 feet of 50 pF/foot cable, a reasonable figure. So, if your system can stand a limitation of driving less than 60 feet, scaling the resistors is an option for increased channel separation.

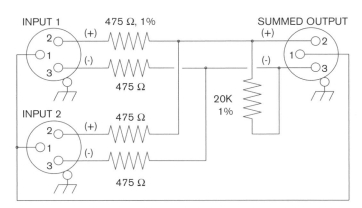

Figure 2. Balanced summing box using XLR connectors

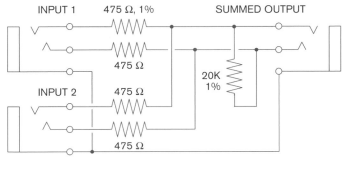

Figure 3. Balanced summing box using ¼" TRS connectors

©Rane Corporation   10802 47th Ave. W.,   Mukilteo WA 98275-5098 USA   TEL (425)355-6000   FAX (425)347-7757   WEB http://www.rane.com

Constant-Q
Graphic Equalizers

- **Filter Fundamentals**
- **LRC & Gyrator Equalizers**
- **Parametric Equalizers**
- **Constant-Q Equalizers**
- **Interpolating Constant-Q Equalizers**

Constant-Q Graphic Equalizers

- **Filter Fundamentals**
- **LRC & Gyrator Equalizers**
- **Parametric Equalizers**
- **Constant-Q Equalizers**
- **Interpolating Constant-Q Equalizers**

INTRODUCTION

Few would argue the necessity of equalizers for quality sound reinforcement systems. They are an essential tool that every sound person keeps in their bag of tricks for establishing high quality sound. Without equalizers the system is left without nearly enough knobs to turn to try and correct for room difficulties, speaker anomalies, and individual performer preferences.

In 1982, Rane Corporation pioneered a new type of graphic equalizer called a Constant-Q Graphic Equalizer to solve one of the most annoying problems that plagued all previous 1/3-octave designs. Namely, that the bandwidth of the filters was a function of the slider position; only at the extreme boost/cut positions were the filter bandwidths truly 1/3-octave wide. At all modest boost/cut positions the filter bandwidths exceeded one octave. For true "graphic" operation, and real control of a system's frequency response, this was an unacceptable design.

The new Constant-Q graphic equalizer circuit topology allows true 1/3-octave bandwidth control at all slider positions. Finally, equalizers are available that are accurately "graphic" in the picture formed by their slider positions. Gone is the misleading picture formed by conventional designs: if a single slider is boosted 3 dB then only that 1/3-octave frequency band is being affected, unlike other equalizers where the real picture is over one octave wide.

The advantages of the Constant-Q design go far beyond yielding a more accurate picture; they provide a degree of adjustment never before possible. Crucial subtle refinements of frequency response are for the first time possible, allowing for an unequaled clarity of sound reproduction.

Dennis Bohn
Terry Pennington
Rane Corporation

RaneNote 101
© 1982 & 1987 Rane Corporation

This latest version combines *Note 101: Constant-Q Graphic Equalizers* and *Note 117: The Rane GE 30 Interpolating Constant-Q Equalizer* into one comprehensive technical document covering all aspects of constant-Q equalizer design. Although some material is dated, the basic information is still a valuable introduction to what is now a standard, and what was then (in 1982) a radical new approach to equalizer design.

GRAPHICS AND PARAMETRICS

Equalizers fall into two very large categories: graphics and parametrics. Graphic equalizers further divide into two groups dominated respectively by 15 band 2/3 octave equalizers and 30 band 1/3-octave equalizers. Functionally, parametrics fall between 15 band and 30 band equalizers. The 15 band graphic equalizers offer great economy but very little flexibility or control. Parametrics give great control flexibility at an increased cost, but are limited to only being able to correct four, five or at most eight frequency spots per equalizer. The 30 band equalizer is the preferred choice by sound professionals at a cost equal to, or slightly higher than parametrics, but with the ease and convenience of being able to apply correction to 30 places.

Graphic equalizers get their name from the fact that the relative positions of the 15 or 30 sliders supposedly form a "graphic" picture of the frequency response correction being applied (that they do not, is why Rane developed Constant-Q equalizers.) Parametrics get their name from the fact that all three "parameters" of the filters are fully adjustable, i.e., center frequency, amplitude and bandwidth. In graphic equalizers, the center frequencies are fixed at standard ISO (International Standards Organization) locations; likewise, the bandwidths are normally set at either one, 2/3 octave, or 1/3-octave widths.

To understand the inherent problems with conventional equalizers and to follow the evolution of Rane's unique Constant-Q approach requires a brief review of equalizer filter fundamentals.

FILTER FUNDAMENTALS

As a review and to establish clear definitions of terminology, Figure 1 shows the frequency response of a typical equalizer filter.

Equalizer correction is accomplished by band-pass filters, each designed to function over a different range of frequencies. A filter is just like a sieve; it passes some things and blocks others. In this case it passes certain frequencies and blocks all others. A filter may be designed to pass just a single frequency, or it may pass all frequencies above or below a certain one, or it may pass only a specific band of frequencies. The latter is termed a *bandpass filter*.

Bandpass filters are characterized by three parameters as shown in Figure 1. *Amplitude* refers to the maximum gain through the filter and occurs at a specific *center frequency*, f_0. The filter is said to have a certain *bandwidth*, defined as the span of frequencies between the points where the amplitude has decreased 3 dB with respect to that of the center frequency. The interpretation of Figure 1 proceeds as follows: The filter has a *passband* between frequencies f_1 and f_2 and an upper and lower *stopband* outside these frequencies. It has a gain of 12 dB (a gain of 4) at f_0: so frequencies around f_0 are made larger by a factor of about 4 while those frequencies significantly outside the f_1-f_2 window are not amplified at all. *Bandwidth* is usually expressed in *octaves*. One octave is a doubling of frequency; therefore a bandpass filter with passband boundary frequencies f_1 and f_2 of, say, 100 Hz and 200 Hz respectively, is said to be one octave wide. One-third

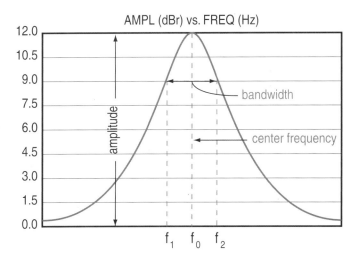

Figure 1. Bandpass Filter Parameters

octave is a 26% increase in frequency ($2^{1/3} = 1.26$); therefore, boundary frequencies of 100 Hz and 126 Hz respectively would be 1/3-octave wide.

The *Quality Factor*, or "Q", of a filter is a close relative to bandwidth. *It is defined to be the center frequency divided by the bandwidth in Hertz*. For example, a filter centered at 1000 Hz that is 1/3-octave wide has -3dB frequencies located at 891 Hz and 1123 Hz respectively, yielding a bandwidth of 232 Hz. Q, therefore, is 1000 Hz divided by 232 Hz, or 4.31.

With suitable circuitry wrapped around it, a band-pass filter may be designed to give an adjustable amplitude characteristic that can be either boosted or cut. The frequency response of such a circuit appears as Figure 2 and forms the heart of any equalizer.

If variable controls are put onto each of the three parameters described in Figure 1, a *parametric* equalizer is realized. The user now has individual control of *where* the center frequency is located, the *width* over which the filter will act, and *amount* of boost or cut.

CONVENTIONAL EQUALIZERS– DESIGN & PROBLEMS

The conventional variable-Q equalizer suffers from a great deal of filter overlap at low corrective settings (which gives it its "combining" characteristics) and a severe degradation of its bandwidth at high settings, making its performance very unpredictable.

Conventional graphics are overwhelmingly of one basic design, namely, LRC equalizers (Gyrators are LRC designs painted a different color—more on this later). An LRC design gets its name from the need for an inductor (electronic abbreviation: "L"), a resistor (R) and a capacitor (C) for each filter section.

The problems inherent in any LRC design arise when the bandwidth determining factors are examined. As mentioned earlier, bandwidth and Q are intimately related. High Q's mean narrow bandwidths and vice versa. At the slider end points the Q of the filter is very high but at all intermediate slider positions it degrades. There is a different value of Q for

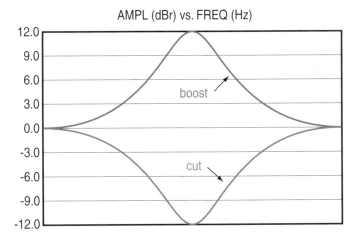

AMPL (dBr) vs. FREQ (Hz)

Figure 2. Typical Equalizer Response

every possible slider position. What this means is that the bandwidth of the filter is different for each slider position, being the narrowest at the extreme slider positions and becoming wider and wider as the slider is moved toward center. This is why a single slider on a conventional one-third octave equalizer affects over three times the bandwidth expected when boosting or cutting modest amounts.

Gyrators are solid-state equivalents to inductors and solve all of the really nasty problems inherent with real-world inductors. Inductors are big, bulky, heavy and expensive. They make marvelous antennas for hum pick-up and must be shielded and positioned very carefully if they are not to turn a wonderful design into a system full of hummingbirds. All of which adds more cost.

Gyrators are used therefore to replace the inductors in LRC designs. They allow for very cost-effective, easily designed equalizers. The only drawback is that they do not in any way alter the bandwidth versus slider position problem. Q is adversely affected by the slider position in exactly the same manner.

So called, "combining" filters are really a misnomer, since they are yet another manifestation of LRC equalizers. The name comes about in the manner that the individual LRC filter sections are summed together to obtain the final output.

Most commonly, the LRC network is duplicated 15 or more times, with all slider pots in parallel and tied to one master op amp. This indeed does work, although the intersection caused by all these parallel networks makes things a little squirrelly and must be compensated for by tweaking each section. A far better solution is to add one or more summing op amps and break up the chain into several series-parallel networks, or "combining" circuits, as they have become known. The end result is a much more predictable design, that gives a smoother resultant curve.

All of this is fine, it just has nothing to do with the bandwidth versus slider position problem. What is needed is a completely different approach—one not based on LRC equalizer topology at all. A new design.

PARAMETRIC EQUALIZERS

It should be obvious by now, that parametric equalizers must be based upon totally different topology than are graphic equalizers, since all three parameters are *independently* adjustable.

Well, some are and some are not.

Some parametrics (I will be kind and not name them) offer adjustment of amplitude, center frequency and bandwidth that are not independent. But since you can adjust each, they get away with it. Those parametrics that offer truly independent adjustment (and there are many) are indeed based on different topology. The heart of these designs is a bandpass section called a *state-variable filter*. A state-variable filter is one where all three parameters are *separately* adjustable. Notice the word is "separately", not "independently". Most state-variable designs allow center frequency to be independently adjusted, but require bandwidth and gain to be adjusted *in a certain order*. One of the ways around this dilemma is to do the amplitude function separate from the filter, thus allowing each filter section to have its gain fixed. Then, by clever selection of component values, *both* center frequency and bandwidth become independent from each other.

Parametrics offer such flexibility with such complexity that they can be their own worst enemy. Their complexity causes two serious drawbacks: cost and limited bands. With three control knobs per band, very few bands are possible per instrument—typically, only four or five. Their flexibility can also be a mixed blessing: they are very difficult to use because you cannot, at a glance, tell where you are with regards to frequency position, degree of boost/cut, or bandwidth. Translating from 1/3-octave realtime analyzer readings to a parametric requires some intuitive concentration.

For all these reasons, 1/3-octave equalizers, with their graphical picture of boost/cut, fixed center frequencies, and narrow bandwidths offer the ultimate in control for quality sound systems.

If only someone would fix that damn bandwidth versus slider position problem...

CONSTANT-Q GRAPHIC EQUALIZERS

The development of the Constant-Q graphic equalizer is the logical next step after reviewing and clearly understanding designs and problems of LRC equalizers and parametrics. It's the result of applying the very best parametric equalizers topology to graphic equalizers.

The filter sections are now totally isolated from the effects of the amplitude slide pots with respect to center frequency and bandwidth; allowing each filter to be designed for the precise center frequency and narrow bandwidth required. The result is unequaled freedom between bandwidth and slider position. A freedom to make subtle adjustments a reality without resorting to racks of parametrics or being forced to 1/6-octave graphic overkill.

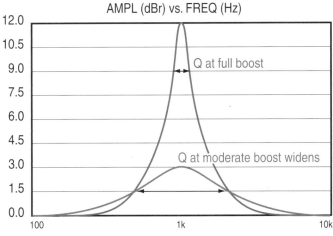

AMPL (dBr) vs. FREQ (Hz)

Figure 3. Conventional Graphic

Figure 4. Constant-Q Graphic

But, does it work? Confucius say, "One picture…

Figures 3, 4 and 5 nearly speak for themselves. In Figure 3, the results from a highly regarded, expensive, California-designed, graphic equalizer are shown. Note that the 1/3-octave wide bandwidth at the 12 dB boost position degrades drastically when only boosted 3 dB, while in Figure 4 the constant-Q graphic equalizer design holds its narrow band-width almost perfectly. For a really telling picture, look at Figure 5, where a very expensive import 1/3-octave graphic is shown with alternate sliders of 800 and 1.25 kHz boosted 12 dB (the 1 kHz slider is centered); compare the results to the constant-Q design under identical conditions. Which one is really a "graphic" equalizer?

Ah, but how well do they combine? Quite nicely, actually. Compare Rane's constant-Q equalizer and conventional designs—at maximum boost with both units rated for +12 dB, the conventional unit's combined output yields around +18 dB gain with about 4 dB of ripple, while the constant-Q unit produces only +15 dB of gain, with less than 3 dB of ripple.

INTERPOLATING CONSTANT-Q

The term "interpolating" equalizer is not used solely to confuse the uninitiated. It is so called because its design allows one to reach any frequency on or between ISO prescribed center frequencies. To *interpolate* is to come to a realization somewhere between two numbers or entities, and this is exactly what interpolating constant-Q equalizers do.

Realtime analyzers were designed to work with equalizers, or was it the other way around? In any event, there are now more ways to analyze a room than just with the realtime approach. If you are only concerned with the indications of a realtime analyzer, then it is not important to be able to dial in correction *between* the centers of the filters. However, if you can view anomalies in between, it should then be possible to adjust for these indications with the processing instrumentation. In light of this it is incumbent on the manufacturers of equalization products to allow this. Rane has done just that by designing *interpolating* constant-Q equalizers.

Such things as dual channel fourier analysis, MLSSA, and the TEF analyzer have changed the way audio professionals adjust a sound system. These new test devices make it possible for the sound system operator to view and correct deficiencies in the sound spectrum that are as narrow as a few cycles. This sort of critical evaluation is not possible with a realtime analyzer and should, therefore, change the way equalizer designers view their task.

The constant-Q equalizer bandwidth does not change with amplitude. Its fixed 1/3-octave bandwidth will, however, *allow small ripples to develop between two adjacent bands*, as seen in Figure 6. This ripple may fall at a frequency requiring adjustment as indicated by the sophisticated test equipment now being used. This occurrence may limit its usefulness in this application.

You see a very small dip between the peaks at the center frequencies. This is the "ripple" that the interpolating equalizer avoids.

The interpolating equalizers from Rane are really another category of equalizer. This advancement in equalization provides the best of all of the three previously mentioned categories. Its filter bandwidths will not vary as its controls are adjusted. Its "filter combining" characteristics will not degrade when large amounts of correction are required, and its filters will interact predictably when two adjacent filters are used to reach a frequency between the ISO frequency centers.

In providing this flexibility, the actual bandwidths have been adjusted only slightly wider than that required by a conventional realtime. This assures the best possible convergence of two filters while maintaining a fixed, predictable bandwidth that is narrow enough to satisfy the needs of those using 1/3-octave realtime analyzers. Should one attempt to use two filters to adjust a node between center frequencies, the interpolating constant-Q equalizer will allow this without the ripple associated with normal constant-Q designs.

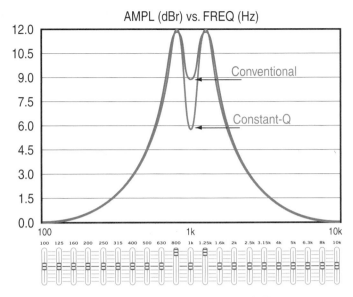

Figure 5. Alternate Sliders Boosted 6 dB

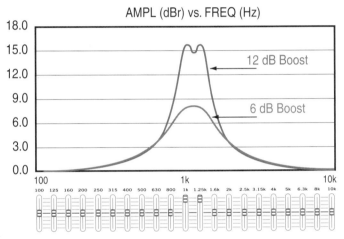

Figure 6. Constant-Q EQ with Two Adjacent Sliders Boosted
6 dB and 12 dB

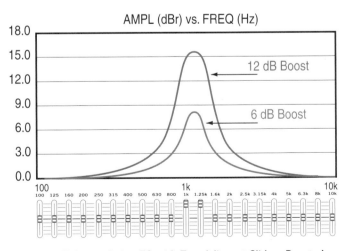

Figure 7. Interpolating EQ with Two Adjacent Sliders Boosted
6 dB and 12 dB

INTERPOLATING VS. COMBINING

The term "combining" has been bandied about in the audio world for almost as long as there have been equalizers. The term is a bit of a misnomer in that the filters themselves do not combine. The resultant curve produced by an equalizer is a combination of the individual filter magnitudes which are set by the controls on the equalizer. The curve at the output will be such a combination, regardless of the design philosophy of the equalizer. The lack of combining attributed to the constant-Q devices as they have been known is purely a function of the bandwidth of their filters. The bandwidth of a constant-Q equalizer is fixed and the bandwidth of a conventional equalizer is not. Configuring a constant-Q equalizer for optimum filter combining will be the ideal. This provides optimum performance on and in between the ISO center frequencies.

Since these effects are a direct result of the filter bandwidth, any equalizer exhibiting variable bandwidth cannot be relied upon to perform predictably over its control range. Only an interpolating equalizer will deliver the necessary results at all times at all settings. There will be no degradation of bandwidth and no changes in adjacent filter summation—just reliable performance.

Comparing Figures 6 and 7 tells the story. Figure 7 was generated through an interpolating GE 30. Notice that the combined peak of the 800 Hz and 1 kHz filters are the same, level not withstanding. This is the kind of performance required under the scrutiny of today's test equipment and the ever more critical ears of modern humanity. The center frequency can be fine tuned, as in a parametric, by raising or lowering an adjacent band. The result will always be a smooth response.

SUMMARY

Rane introduced constant-Q equalizers in the mid-eighties. Now, most equalizer manufacturers produce constant-Q models. When using a 1/3-octave analyzer, a constant-Q equalizer gives the best, most accurate results, and truly delivers "graphic" representation of the equalization curve with the front panel sliders. Actual use of an equalizer rarely (and shouldn't) require full boost or cut in any band, and the more realistic ±3 to ±6 dB corrections on a conventional equalizer requires over-compensating adjacent bands to arrive at the correct curve. What you see is what you get with a constant-Q.

The interpolated peak exhibited by Figure 7 satisfies the requirements of today's sophisticated measurement equipment. Simultaneous adjustment of any two adjacent sliders allows precise control of the response peak at frequencies between ISO standard points. By adjusting each slider up or down relative to each other, the peak may be moved to the right or left to give continuous coverage of all frequencies between the ISO boundaries. Control like a parametric, with the convenience of a graphic, without the trade-offs of a conventional equalizer. Only from Rane.

Constant-Q-5

ADDITIONAL READING

RaneNote: Exposing Equalizer Mythology, (Rane Corporation, 1986).
RaneNote: Operator Adjustable Equalizers: An Overview, (Rane Corporation,1990).
"Constant-Q Graphic Equalizers," *J. Audio Eng. Soc.*, vol. 34, pp. 611-626 (Sept., 1986).

Operator Adjustable Equalizers: An Overview

- Equalizer History
- Industry Choices
- Terminology & Definitions
- Active & Passive
- Graphics & Parametrics
- Constant-Q & Proportional-Q
- Interpolating & Combining
- Phase Shift Examples
- References

Dennis Bohn
Rane Corporation

RaneNote 122
© 1990 Rane Corporation
Reprinted with permission from the Audio Engineering Society from The Proceedings of the AES 6th International Conference: Sound Reinforcement, 1988 May 5-8, Nashville.

INTRODUCTION

This paper presents an overview of operator adjustable equalizers in the professional audio industry. The term "operator adjustable equalizers" is no doubt a bit vague and cumbersome. For this, the author apologizes. Needed was a term to differentiate between fixed equalizers and variable equalizers.

Fixed equalizers, such as pre-emphasis and de-emphasis circuits, phono RIAA and tape NAB circuits, and others, are subject matter unto themselves, but not the concern of this survey. Variable equalizers, however, such as graphics and parametrics are very much the subject of this paper, hence the term, "operator adjustable equalizers." That is what they are—equalizers adjustable by operators—as opposed to built-in, non-adjustable, fixed circuits.

Without belaboring the point too much, it is important in the beginning to clarify and use precise terminology. Much confusion surrounds users of variable equalizers due to poorly understood terminology.

What types of variable equalizers exist? Why so many? Which one is best? What type of circuits prevail? What kind of filters? Who makes what? Hopefully, the answers lie within these pages, but first, a little history.

A LITTLE HISTORY

No really big histories exist regarding variable equalizer use. Good short histories appear in [1]-[3]. An expanded short history follows.

Hurrah for Hollywood. Mother Nature and Hollywood spawned the first use of variable equalizers for sound improvement. Motion pictures with sound brought audio playback systems into theaters for the first time. Soon, some people's attention focused on just how bad these reproduction systems sounded. John Volkman was one of these people. It was the '30s and Volkman worked for RCA. Credit John with being the first person to use a variable equalizer to improve reproduced sound. He applied this new tool to equalize a motion picture theater playback system.

While Bell Labs used fixed equalizers earlier than this for correcting audio transmission losses [4], Volkman represents one of the first uses of an external variable equalizer as an added component to an installed system. Telephone applications involved integrating equalization as part of the receiving electronics, as opposed to thinking of the equalizer as a separate entity.

During the same period Volkman experimented with equalizers for reproduced sound, Hollywood found uses for them in producing sound. Langevin, Cinema Engineering, and others [4], created outboard operator adjustable equalizers for post-production sound effects and speech enhancement. Langevin Model EQ-251A represents very early use of slide controls. While not a graphic equalizer in today's sense, it was the forerunner. The EQ-251A featured two slide controls, each with switched frequency points. One slider controlled a bass shelving network with two corner frequency choices, while the other provided peaking boost/cut with four switchable center frequencies. This passive unit looked and performed equal to anything manufactured today.

Art Davis's company, Cinema Engineering, developed the first recognizable graphic equalizer [4]. Known as the type 7080 Graphic Equalizer, it featured 6 bands with boost/cut range of 8 dB, adjustable in 1 dB steps. (After Art Davis moved to Altec, he designed a 7 band successor to the 7080 known as the Model 9062A. A hugely successful graphic equalizer selling into the '70s.) Being an active design, the 7080 allowed signal boosting without loss—a nice feature. (With passive units, boosting of signals requires an initial broad band signal loss and then reducing the loss on a band-by-band basis. For example, flat might represent 16 dB loss while a 6 dB boost represented only 10 dB loss. It was all a matter of reference point.)

Another innovative feature of the 7080 was the first use of staggered mixing amps to aid in smooth combining of the equalized audio signal. Cinema Engineering designed 3 mixing amplifiers for 6 bands. Using this approach, no amplifier mixed adjacent bands. The center frequencies were 80Hz, 200Hz, 500Hz, 1.25kHz (labeled 1.3kHz), 3.2kHz (labeled 3kHz), and 8kHz. The amplifiers mixed 80Hz + 1250Hz, 200Hz + 3200Hz, and 500Hz + 8kHz respectively. Using separate amplifiers to mix signals spaced 4 octaves apart, resulted in seamless recombination at the output. (Later Art Davis would use a similar technique in the design of the first Altec-Lansing active graphic equalizers.)

Not much happened during the '40s and early '50s due to World War II and its aftermath. Most applications of variable equalizers involved post-production work. No serious success at room equalization is known. Then in 1958, Wayne Rudmose (a professor at Southern Methodist University, Dallas, Texas) successfully applied new theories about acoustic equalization to the Dallas Love Field Airport. Dr. Rudmose published his monumental work [5] and sound system equalization was born.

In 1962, Texas made another major contribution to variable equalizer history. This time it was the University of Texas (Austin) and a physics professor named C.P. Boner. Dr.s Boner and Rudmose were contemporaries and friends, having co-authored a paper 23 years earlier [6] . Boner, acknowledged by many, as the father of acoustical equalization, built organs as a hobby. From his organ/room tuning experiences and acoustical physics knowledge grew a profoundly simple theory. Boner reasoned that when feedback occurs, it did so at one precise frequency, and to stop it all you had to do was install a very narrow notch filter at that frequency. He went to one of his former students whose company made precision filters for instrumentation and asked him to design a narrow band audio filter. Gifford White agreed, and launched White Instruments into the new field of acoustic equalization.

Armed with White equalizers, Boner established the foundation theory for acoustic feedback, room-ring modes, and room-sound system equalizing techniques [7]-[10]. Expanding Boner's work was a student of Wayne Rudmose named William Conner. In 1967, Conner published a concise paper [11] still considered among the best to describe the theory and methodology of sound system equalization.

Also in 1967, Art Davis, along with Jim Noble and Don Davis (not related) developed the industry's first 1/3-octave variable notch filter set (passive) for Altec-Lansing. Don Davis presented the paper to the Audio Engineering Society in October, 1967 [12]. Dubbed the "Acousta-Voice" system, it ushered in the modern age of sound system equalization and represented the ultimate in speed and convenience. The Acousta-Voice system proved another path existed for the control of room-ring modes. As an alternative to Boner's narrow-band notching technique, 1/3-octave "broad-band" filters produced the same results.

The rest, as they say, is history. A 20 year history that witnessed an explosion of variable equalizer developments. Among the most noteworthy being the 1/3-octave graphic equalizer, the parametric equalizer, use of integrated circuits, development of the gyrator (synthetic inductor), active LC and RC designs, development of constant-Q (bandwidth) graphic equalizers, and the application of microprocessors for control and memory. All of these developments, in this author's opinion, fall into the category of improvements—albeit, very important improvements—rather than qualifying as new concepts applied to variable equalizers. Recently, however, two categorically new concepts appeared.

The first is transversal equalizers: In 1984, Industrial Research Products introduced the first variable equalizer based on analog transversal filter technology [13] (more on transversal filters later).

The second is digital equalizers: In 1987, Yamaha introduced the DEQ7 Digital Equalizer, the first stand-alone variable equalizer based on digital signal processor (DSP) technology [14]. A combination "graphic" (bad terminology since there is no graphical representation of settings) and parametric, the DEQ7 featured 30 different built-in configurations. Also in 1987, Roland previewed a digital parametric equalizer [15], the first variable equalizer to include the new digital audio transmission standard developed by the Audio Engineering Society [16].

CHOICES, CHOICES, CHOICES

Figure 1 shows the breadth of operator adjustable equalizers. And this covers only the manually adjustable analog units—microprocessor-controlled and full-digital designs are omitted. Such are your choices as a user.

Estimates suggest only 25% of the equalizers sold find their way into serious permanent sound systems. Uses for the remaining 75%, split between program enhancement and sound reinforcement.

Program enhancement primarily appears in live performance, recording studio, broadcast, and post-production marketplaces. Within these markets equalizers do everything from simple band limiting to complex sound manipulation.

Sound reinforcement uses equalizers everywhere from small lounge acts to large touring companies. Most applications are for compensating ragged loudspeaker power responses rather than attempting any sort of serious room equalization. This is true for monitor loudspeaker systems as well as mains. Yet, the equalizer is the crucial link in vastly improving the system's sound.

With such diverse applications it is not surprising to find so many choices. To understand the choices, however, is first to understand the terminology.

TERMINOLOGY

Equalizer terminology deserves better positioning than the back of the book. So instead of a complete glossary at the end, an abbreviated glossary appears now. To confuse and make sure you are paying attention, this will not be in alphabetical order. Hopefully, appearing in order of importance for understanding equalizers.

Passive Equalizer. A variable equalizer requiring no power to operate. Consisting only of passive components (inductors, capacitors and resistors) passive equalizers have no AC line cord. Favored for their low noise performance (no active components to generate noise), high dynamic range (no active power supplies to limit voltage swing), extremely good reliability (passive components rarely break), and lack of RFI interference (no semiconductors to detect radio frequencies).

Disliked for their cost (inductors are expensive), size (and bulky), weight (and heavy), hum susceptibility (and need careful shielding), and signal loss characteristic (passive equalizers always reduce the signal). Also inductors saturate easily with large low frequency signals, causing distortion. Used primarily for notching in permanent sound systems.

Active Equalizer. A variable equalizer requiring power to operate. Available in many different configurations and designs. Favored for low cost, small size, light weight,

loading indifference, good isolation (high input and low output impedances), gain availability (signal boosting possible), and line-driving ability.

Disliked for increased noise performance, limited dynamic range, reduced reliability, and RFI susceptibility. Used everywhere.

Graphic Equalizer. A multi-band variable equalizer using slide controls as the amplitude adjustable elements. Named for the positions of the sliders "graphing" the resulting frequency response of the equalizer. Only found on active designs. Both center frequency and bandwidth are fixed for each band.

Rotary Equalizer. A multi-band variable equalizer using rotary controls as the amplitude adjustable elements. Both active and passive designs exist with rotary controls. Center frequency and bandwidth are fixed for each band.

Parametric Equalizer. A multi-band variable equalizer offering control of all the "parameters" of the internal bandpass filter sections. These parameters being amplitude, center frequency and bandwidth. This allows the user to not only control the amplitude of each band, but also to shift the center frequency and widen or narrow the affected area. Available with rotary and slide controls.

Sub-categories of parametric equalizers exist for units allowing control of center frequency but not bandwidth. For rotary control units the most used term is quasi-parametric. For units with slide controls the popular term is para-graphic. The frequency control may be continuously variable or switch selectable in steps.

Cut-only parametric equalizers (with adjustable bandwidth or not) are called notch equalizers, or band-reject equalizers.

Transversal Equalizer. A multi-band variable equalizer using a tapped time delay line as the frequency selective element, as opposed to bandpass filters built from inductors (real or synthetic) and capacitors. The term "transversal filter" does not mean "digital filter." It is the entire family of filter functions done by means of a tapped delay line. There exists a class of digital filters realized as transversal filters, using a shift register rather than an analog delay line, the inputs being numbers rather than analog functions. To date, however, due to expensive hardware, digital transversal filter realization of variable equalizers remains in the laboratory. The only available transversal equalizers today are from Industrial Research Products [13], employing all-pass analog filters for the tapped delay line.

Cut-Only Equalizer. Term used to describe graphic equalizers designed only for attenuation. (Also referred to as notch equalizers, or band-reject equalizers). Usually applied to active designs. The flat (0 dB) position locates all sliders at the top of the front panel. Comprised only of notch filters (normally spaced at 1/3-octave intervals), all controls start at 0 dB and reduce the signal on a band-by-band basis. Used only in permanent sound systems. Proponents of cut-only philosophy argue that boosting runs the risk of reducing system headroom.

Boost/Cut Equalizer. The most common graphic equalizer. Available with 10 to 31 bands on octave to 1/3-octave spacing. The flat (0 dB) position locates all sliders at the center of the front panel. Comprised of bandpass filters, all

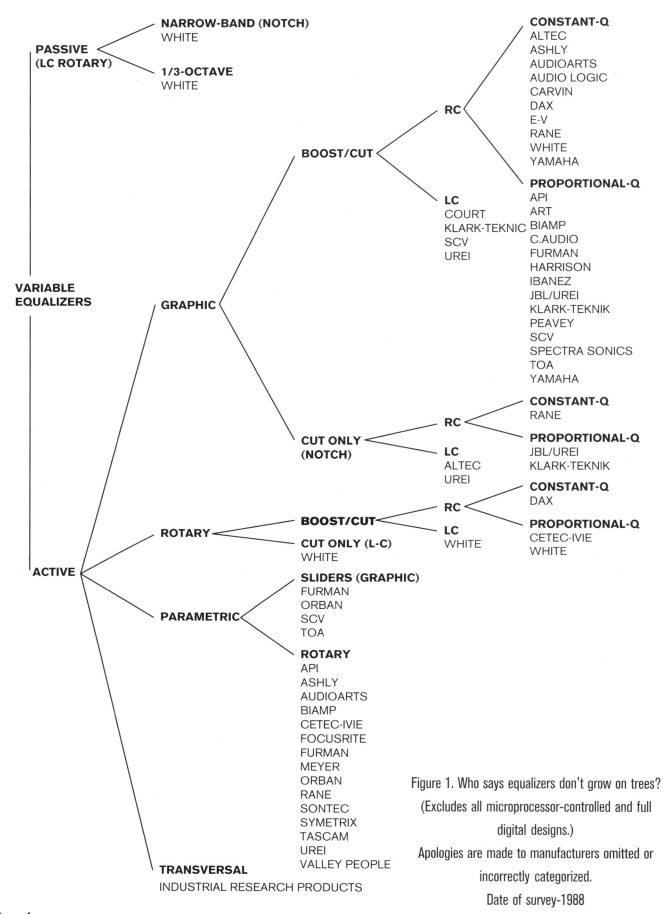

Figure 1. Who says equalizers don't grow on trees?
(Excludes all microprocessor-controlled and full
digital designs.)
Apologies are made to manufacturers omitted or
incorrectly categorized.
Date of survey-1988

controls start at their center 0 dB position and boost (amplify or make larger) signals by raising the sliders, or cut (attenuate or make smaller) the signal by lowering the sliders on a band-by-band basis. Commonly provide a center-detent feature identifying the 0 dB position. Used by all branches of the professional audio industry. Boost capability necessary for all forms of program equalization. Proponents of boosting in permanent sound systems argue that cut-only use requires make-up gain which runs the same risk of reducing system headroom.

Narrow-Band Filter. Term popularized by C.P. Boner to describe his patented (tapped toroidal Inductor) passive notch filters. Boner's filters were very high Q (around 200) and extremely narrow (5 Hz at the -3 dB points). Boner used large numbers (around 100-150) of these sections in series to reduce feedback modes [9].

Today's usage extends this terminology to include all filters narrower than 1/3-octave. This includes parametrics, notch filter sets, and certain cut-only variable equalizer designs.

1/3-Octave. Term used to describe variable equalizers with the bands located on standard ISO (International Organization for Standardization) recommended 1/3-octave center spacing.

Generally for boost/cut equalizers, not only are the filters located on 1/3-octave spacing but they are also 1/3-octave wide, measured at the -3 dB points referenced from the maximum boost or cut point (symmetrical boost/cut responses assumed). Fig. 2 diagrams this reference point.

Cut-only (notch or band-reject) equalizers unfortunately offer no such standardization on bandwidth measurement points. If referenced as being 1/3-octave wide, you will find two schools of thought as illustrated by Fig. 3. One manufacturer may use the same definition as given above for boost/cut

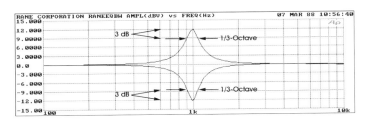

Figure 2. Symmetrical boost/cut response showing   1/3-octave bandwidth.

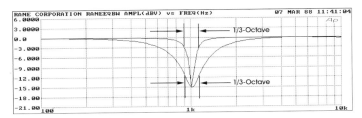

Figure 3. Cut-only (notch or band-reject) response showing different 1/3-octave measurement points.

designs while another uses a new definition. The new definition measures the -3 dB points from the 0 dB reference line. Applications exist for both approaches. Some permanent sound system installations require the narrower design while other applications need the wider response. The narrower response is more selective, but less efficient. There are also many variations between these two extremes.

LC Filter (Also LCR, LRC, etc.). Passive filter comprised of capacitors (C), resistors (R), and inductors (electronic symbol "L"; why "L?" Well, you see they couldn't use "I" because that was being used for current). Note that both active and passive equalizers use LC filters. In active units, the actual filter element is passive; the active elements act as buffers, mixers and gain blocks.

RC Filter. Active filter made from resistors (R), capacitors (C) and an amplifier (either tubes, transistors, or integrated circuits).

Two main categories exist. The first uses active RC networks to synthesize inductors (gyrators) and then create bandpass or band-reject filters based on original LC designs. The second uses active RC networks s directly to create bandpass or band-reject filters.

Q (Bandwidth). The quality factor, or "Q," of a filter is an inverse measure of the bandwidth. To calculate Q, divide the center frequency by the bandwidth measured at the -3 dB (half-power) points. For example, a filter centered at 1 kHz that is 1/3-octave wide has -3 dB frequencies located at 891 Hz and 1123 Hz respectively, yielding a bandwidth of 232 Hz (1123-891). The quality factor, Q, is therefore 1 kHz divided by 232 Hz, or 4.31.

Going the other way is a bit sticky. If Q is known and the bandwidth (expressed in octaves) is desired, direct calculation is not obvious—nor easy. Development of a direct expression appears in [17], along with a hand-held calculator program to make this easier.

Proportional-Q Equalizer (also Variable-Q). Term applied to graphic and rotary equalizers describing bandwidth behavior as a function of boost/cut levels. Paul Wolff of API recommends the term "proportional-Q" as being more accurate and less ambiguous than "variable-Q." If nothing else, "variable-Q" suggests the unit allows the user to vary (set) the Q, when no such controls exist.

Fig. 4 shows proportional-Q response for 4 different boost settings. The bandwidth varies inversely proportional to boost (or cut) amounts, being very wide for small boost/cut levels and becoming very narrow for large boost/cut levels. The skirts, however, remain constant for all boost/cut levels. Compare with Fig. 5.

Constant-Q Equalizer (also Constant-Bandwidth). Term applied to graphic and rotary equalizers describing bandwidth behavior as a function of boost/cut levels. Since Q and bandwidth are inverse sides of the same coin, the terms are fully interchange-able.

Fig. 5 shows constant-Q response for 4 different boost settings. The bandwidth remains constant for all boost/cut levels. For constant-Q designs, the skirts vary directly proportional to boost/cut amounts. Small boost/cut levels produce narrow skirts and large boost/cut levels produce wide skirts.

Equalizers-5

Equalize/Attenuate. Original terms used by Art Davis to signify direction of equalization. Equalize meant to make bigger and attenuate meant, of course, to make smaller. Replaced today by boost/cut terminology.

Lift/Dip. Popular European term meaning boost/cut.

Peaking Response. Term used to describe a bandpass shape when applied to program equalization. Fig. 2 shows a peaking response.

Shelving Response. Term used to describe a flat (or shelf) end-band shape when applied to program equalization. Fig. 6 shows shelving responses. Also known as bass and treble tone control response. Ambiguities exist when describing shelving equalization controls regarding corner frequencies. Fig. 6 shows the two conflicting definition points. Comer frequency 1 represents the normal engineering definition of the ±3 dB point. Corner frequency 2, however, represents a definition point more relevant to the user. Normally a user wants to know the available boost/cut amount at the top or bottom of the shelving response.

Symmetrical (Reciprocal) Response. Term used to describe the comparative shapes of the boost/cut curves for variable equalizers. Fig. 2 shows symmetrical or reciprocal responses.

Asymmetrical (Non-reciprocal) Response. Term used to describe the comparative shapes of the boost/cut curves for variable equalizers. Fig. 7 shows asymmetrical or non-reciprocal responses.

Gyrator Filters. Term used to describe a class of active filters using gyrator networks. Gyrator is the name given for RC networks that mimic inductors. A gyrator is a form of artificial inductor where an RC filter synthesizes inductive characteristics. Used to replace real inductors in filter design.

Discrete Equalizer. A variable equalizer comprised solely of separate (discrete) transistors, as opposed to designs using integrated circuits. Currently, it is believed only API makes discrete equalizers.

Combining (Interpolating) Equalizer. Term used to describe the summing response of adjacent bands of variable equalizers. If two adjacent bands, when summed together, produce a smooth response without a dip in the center, they are said to combine well.

Good combining or interpolating characteristics come from designs that buffer adjacent bands before summing, i.e., they use multiple summing circuits. If only one summing circuit exists for all bands, then the combined output exhibits ripple between center frequencies.

Altec-Lansing first described Art Davis's buffered designs as combining, and the terminology became commonplace. Describing how well adjacent bands combine is good terminology. However, some variations of this term confuse people. The phrase "combining filter" is a misnomer, since what is meant is not a filter at all, but rather whether adjacent bands are buffered before summing. The other side of this misnomered coin finds the phrase "non-combining filter." Again, no filter is involved in what is meant. Dropping the word "filter" helps, but not enough. Referring to an equalizer as "non-combining" is imprecise. All equalizers combine their filter outputs. The issue is how much ripple results.

For these reasons, Rane [18] suggested the term "interpolating" as an alternative. Interpolating means to insert between two points, which is what buffering adjacent bands accomplishes. By separating adjacent bands when summing, the midpoints fill in smoothly without ripple.

Fig. 8 plots the summed response of adjacent filters showing good combining or interpolation between bands for an interpolating constant-Q equalizer. Fig. 9 plots similar results for a proportional-Q equalizer. Fig. 10 plots the summed response of adjacent filters showing combined response with ripple for either constant-Q or proportional-Q designs not buffering adjacent filters. Demonstrated here is the lack of interpolation between centers.

Minimum-Phase Filters (or Minimum Phase Shift Filters). A much confused term, having little meaning for today's variable equalizers. There seem to be two issues intertwined here. The first concerns minimum-phase filters and the implication that some equalizers do not use mini-

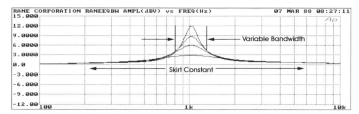

Figure 4. Proportional-Q (Variable-Q) equalizer performance.

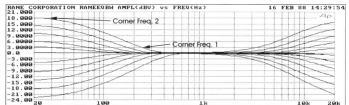

Figure 6. Equalization curves showing shelving response.

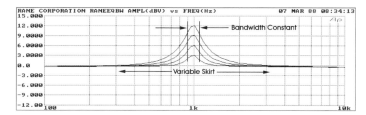

Figure 5. Constant-Q (bandwidth) equalizer performance.

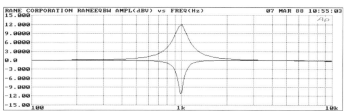

Figure 7. Asymmetrical (non-reciprocal) boost/cut curves.

mum-phase filters. From a strict electrical engineering viewpoint [19], [20], the precise definition of a minimum-phase function is a detailed mathematical concept involving positive real transfer functions, i.e., transfer functions with all zeros restricted to the left half s-plane. References [21] & [22] demonstrate that all equalizer designs based on 2nd-order bandpass or band-reject networks have minimum-phase characteristics. This says, in essence, all variable equalizers on the market today use minimum-phase filters.

The second issue involves minimum phase shift filters. There is an implication that some equalizers produce less phase shift than others. Again, this does not seem to be the case. All 2nd-order bandpass or band-reject filters (active or passive) shift phase the same amount. (The bandwidth of this phase shift differs for various 2nd-order responses, but the phase shift is the same.). And when used to create boost/cut responses, do so with the same phase shift. Different phase responses do exist, but they are a function of boost/cut levels and individual filter bandwidths. That is, there will be less phase shift for 3 dB of boost/cut than 12 dB; and a 1-octave filter set will have a wider phase response than a 1/3-octave unit (but the number of degrees of phase shift will be the same). Figs.11 and 12 demonstrate this. In Fig. 11, the phase responses for different levels of boost appear (cut responses are identical but mirror image). This verifies Pennington's [23] rule-of-thumb regarding 10 degrees of phase shift per 3 dB of amplitude change. Fig. 12 shows the bandwidth variation for this phase shift for wider and narrower bandpass responses.

This completes the most common variable equalizer terms. Other terms exist—lots—but this is the foundation for understanding the remaining variations and alternatives.

FILTER TYPES

Passive. Audio use of fixed passive equalizers dates back 50 years to Hollywood's early experiments with program sweetening. Harry Kimball published the definitive design book of the times [24].

Even before Rudmose and Boner, Frank Bies of Bell Labs described passive attenuation equalizer use for correcting overall gain-frequency characteristics [25]. These two papers represent early guidelines for fixed passive equalizer designs. The most successful topology was the bridged-T section. When applying variable techniques to bridged-T sections, however, the nuisance characteristic of changing loss appeared. That is, as you varied the amplitude you also varied the net loss through the filter section. Soloman and Broneer [26] did the pioneering work for designing constant-loss variable passive equalizers (constant-loss in the sense that varying the attenuation did not change the net loss).

They showed that redrawing a Wheatstone bridge creates a bridged-T equalizer (Fig. 13). In Fig. 13 the boxes labeled Z1 and Z2 consist of variously configured reactive (inductors & capacitors) elements. Named constant-S (S is the symbol for insertion loss) equalizers, Soloman and Broneers work paved the way for commercial passive variable equalizers employing constant-K (impedances independent of frequency) designs. Fig.14a shows a band-reject constant-S variable equalizer, while Fig. 14b shows the simpler commer-

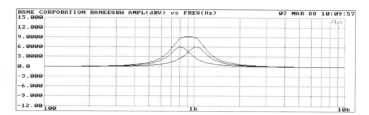

Figure 8. Summed response of adjacent filters showing good combining or interpolation between bands of interpolating constant-Q equalizer.

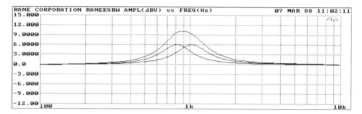

Figure 9. Summed response of adjacent filters showing combining or interpolation between bands for proportional-Q equalizer.

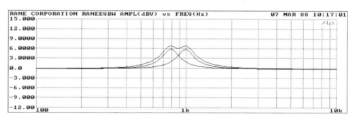

Figure 10. Summed response of adjacent filters showing combined response with ripple, for constant-Q or proportional-Q designs, not buffering adjacent filters.

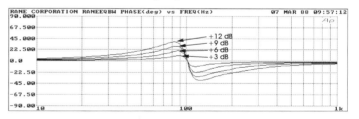

Figure 11. Phase response of 2nd-order bandpass filter used to produce four boost levels for 1/3 octave equalizer.

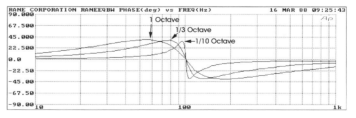

Figure 12. Phase responses for 2nd-order bandpass filter used to produce + 12dB boost levels for three bandwidths.

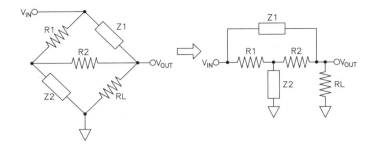

Figure 13. Wheatstone bridge to bridged-T equalizer re-drawing.

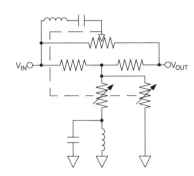

Figure 14a. Constant-S variable band-reject filter.

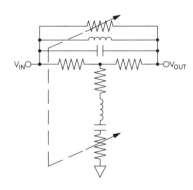

Figure 14b. Altec-Lansing Acousta-Voice band-reject filter section.

Figure 15. Series resonant network.

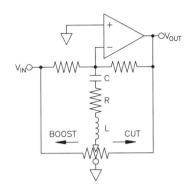

Figure 16. Active LC equalizer based on Baxandall negative feedback tone control circuit [27].

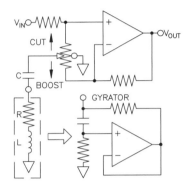

Figure 17. Active LC circuit showing gyrator substitution for inductor.

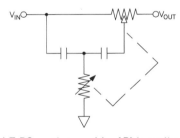

Figure 18. Bridged-T RC section used by API in active proportional-Q equalizer.

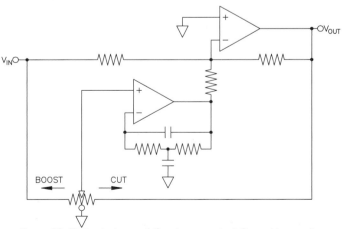

Figure 19. First private-use 1/3-octave constant-Q graphic equalizer circuit developed by Thurmond [30].

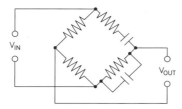

Figure 20a. Passive Wien-bridge.

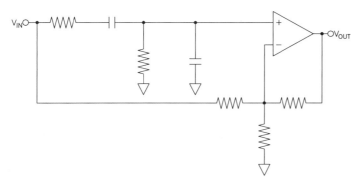

Figure 20b. Active Wien-bridge band-reject filter.

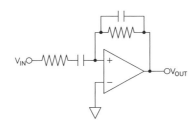

Figure 20c. Active Wien-bridge bandpass filter.

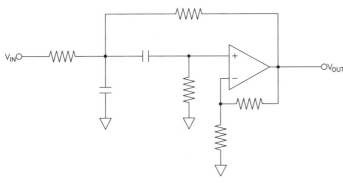

Figure 21. Voltage-controlled voltage source (VCVS) bandpass filter section.

cial network as first used by Altec-Lansing in their Acousta-Voice system.

Active LC. Active LC designs commonly use the simpler series resonant network (Fig. 15) over the more complex bridged-T configuration. A popular topology, based on Peter Baxandall's famous negative feedback tone control circuit [27] appears as Fig. 16. The LCR series resonant circuit creates a bandpass filter function. The slider routes the bandpass filter either to the input for boosting or to the output for cutting. This design is indicative of approaches used by White [21] and others.

Another often used design appears as Fig.17. Here the series resonant circuit is routed between the amplifier's inputs. When connected to the positive input, it acts as a frequency selective attenuator; and when connected to the negative input, it acts as a frequency selective gain booster. Altec [2], UREI and others favor this design.

Active RC Proportional-Q. Active RC filter techniques provide the means for creating very cost-effective designs. The most popular approach makes use of gyrators [28], [29]. This synthetic inductor replaces the series resonant circuit as shown in Fig.17. This is the most common proportional-Q design and perhaps a dozen different manufacturers use it. This is the simplest gyrator form; many others exist.

API, Audio Products, Inc. developed a unique proportional-Q approach that uses the bridged-T RC filter section shown in Fig. 18 as the variable building block. Many such buffered sections string together in series. Although drawn as single elements in Fig. 18, the capacitors are really a bank of capacitors selected by the frequency control.

Active RC Constant-Q. Credit goes to Bob Thurmond for development of the first private-use constant-Q, 1/3-octave graphic equalizer in 1973 [30]. (Commercially available constant-Q graphic equalizer designs did not become available until 1981 [31]). Thurmond used the Baxandall derived design shown in Fig. 16 and replaced the series resonant circuit with an active RC filter using a bridged-T feedback circuit. Fig. 19 shows a simplified diagram for this design. Today, Altec [2], Carvin, Dax and others use this basic topology, differing only in the type of bandpass filter used.

Active RC bandpass filters based on various non-gyrator topologies, appear in all constant-Q equalizer designs. Some use Wien-bridge based active filters as shown in Fig.20, but most use Huelsman's [32] designs derived from the monumental work of Sallen and Key in 1955 [33]. These appear as Figs.s 21 and 22.

Another commonly used technique relays on a circuit developed by many, but patented by Ken Gundry of Dolby Laboratories [34]. No mention appears in the patent regarding constant-Q performance advantages or parametric equalizer use, yet these are the most often seen variations. Fig. 23 shows this circuit. Comparing Figs.s 19 and 23 reveals their similarity. The main difference being Fig. 23 separates the boost/cut functions using two amplifiers. Rane, White and others use variations of Fig. 23 in their constant-Q graphic products.

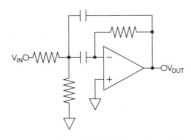

Figure 22. Multiple feedback (MFB) bandpass filter section.

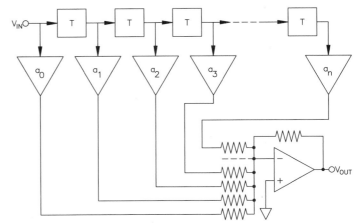

Figure 25. Transversal filter graphic equalizer.

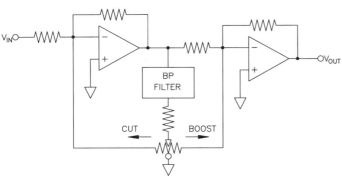

Figure 23. First commercially available 1 /3-octave constant-Q
graphic equalizer circuit [31].

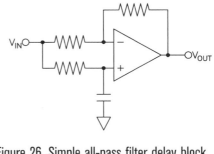

Figure 26. Simple all-pass filter delay block.

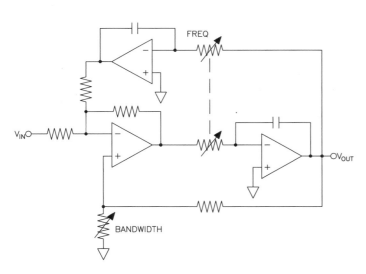

Figure 24. State-variable non-inverting bandpass filter section.

Parametric Equalizers. Parametric equalizer designs use many of the same circuits as constant-Q graphic equalizers (historically, the parametrics were first). By adding independently variable frequency and bandwidth controls, you create a parametric equalizer. A popular way to do this is to use a state-variable active filter as shown in Fig. 24. Carefully designed state-variable topology allows completely independent control over frequency and bandwidth without changing the amplitude. Relegating the amplitude control function outside of the state-variable filter then completes a true parametric equalizer. Any of Fig.s 17,19, or 23 work as parametrics with the bandpass function being replaced with the state-variable design of Fig. 24.

Transversal Equalizers. Transversal filter equalizers are constant-Q designs based on a tapped delay line as shown in Fig.25. Each tap roughly represents an area of the frequency response affected. Scaling each of these outputs by a "tap weight" (constants $a1$, $a2$, etc.) and summing the results, produces any desired frequency response. Active filters can be designed either in the frequency or time domain with the same results. Frequency and time are inexorably linked by physics. Transversal filters take advantage of this knowledge by modifying the frequency response using time delay (also the foundation for all digital filters).

Analog transversal filter designs require using either analog delay lines (bucket-brigade devices) or all-pass active filters. The simplest all-pass filter appears in Fig. 26. It produces a flat amplitude response with changing phase shift. (Interchanging the positions of the non-inverting input resistor/capacitor network produces either phase-lead or phase-lag characteristics). This circuit starts with zero degrees at DC, yields 90 degrees at the design frequency, and ends up with 180 degrees at high frequencies. Since time is nothing more than phase shift divided by frequency, you can use a string of phase shifters to create time delay (although it is frequency-dependent time delay; frequency independent time delay requires bucket-brigade devices or digital techniques). An all-pass filter approach produced the first transversal equalizer by IRP [13] in 1984.

CONCLUSION

So, there you have it—15 categories to choose from. To sum up, as the great London auctioneer Mr. Christie said, in 1770, "The whole of which is truly neat."

This many categories exist primarily due to simple historical evolution. As technology evolved, so did equalizer design. A natural course of events. Transistor and integrated circuit developments led to active designs. Invention of gyrators created a new category. Proliferation of modern active RC filter designs created new ways of doing old tricks, and old ways to do new tricks. And, today, digital technology propels us into a whole new generation of equalizers.

My personal favorite is the parametric. It allows you to go anywhere and do anything. Yet, there are those who claim the best parametric will not sound as good as old passive bridged-T designs. Perhaps, but that cannot be objectively proven. Tightly controlled A-B testing demonstrates that all equalizers designs, creating the same exact frequency curve (important—it must be identical) are indistinguishable. It does not matter whether they are passive or active, proportional-Q or constant-Q, LC or RC, fixed band or parametric, or operate in the frequency or time domain. With apologies to Gertrude Stein, a transfer function is a transfer function is a transfer function.

Differences do exist, but they are in areas other than those described above. Secondary considerations such as noise performance, dynamic range, and transient stability all enter into explaining perceived sonic attributes.

Many designs are decades old, while others are but a few years. The latest is not necessarily the best, although, we like to think so. Each new development is embraced as the ultimate—for a while. Then, we tend to migrate back to proven ways that are comfortable and known, if for no other reason. This, too, is not always best. Ours is a human industry, with human quirks.

The decision as to which is best is a personal one. Many subjective things enter into the selection process. There are those who swear by one design over another and will never be convinced otherwise. Nothing can be done about this, nor should we try. Objectively, much could be written regarding the performance virtues of each design. Nevertheless, suffice it to say, applications exists for all these designs. Eventually, the market determines lasting favorites. For now, *vive la difference*.

REFERENCES

1. T. Uzzle, "Boost vs. Cut," Altec-Lansing Corp., Application Note AN-6 (1981).
2. G. Ballou, Ed., *Handbook for Sound Engineers: The New Audio Cyclopedia* (H.W. Sams, Indianapolis, 1987).
3. D. Davis and C. Davis, *Sound System Engineering*, 2nd. Ed., (H.W. Sams, Indianapolis, 1987).
4. H. Tremaine, *Audio Cyclopedia,* 2nd. Ed., (H.W. Sams, Indianapolis, 1973).
5. W. Rudmose, "Equalization of Sound Systems," *Noise Control*, vol. 24 (Jul. 1958).
6. C.P. Boner, H. Wayne [Rudmose] Jones and W.J. Cunningham, "Indoor and Outdoor Response of an Exponential Horn," *J. Acoust. Soc. Am.*, vol. 10, p. 180 (1939).
7. C.P. Boner, "Sound Reinforcement Systems in Reverberant Churches," presented at the 67th Meeting of the Acoustical Society of America, New York, May 8, 1964.
8. C.P. Boner and C.R. Boner, "Minimizing Feedback in Sound Systems and Room-Ring Modes With Passive Networks," *J. Acoust. Soc. Am.*, vol. 37, p. 131 (Jan. 1965).
9. ---- ----, "A Procedure for Controlling Room-Ring Modes and Feedback Modes in Sound Systems with Narrow-Band Filters," *J. Audio Eng. Soc.*, vol. 13, pp. 297-299 (Oct. 1965).
10. ---- ----, "Behavior of Sound System Response Immediately Below Feedback," *J. Audio Eng. Soc.*, vol. 14, pp. 200-203 (Jul. 1966).
11. W. Conner, "Theoretical and Practical Considerations in the Equalization of Sound Systems," *J. Audio Eng. Soc.*, vol. 15, pp. 194-198 (Apr. 1967).
12. D. Davis, "A 1/3-Octave Band Variable Notch Filter Set for Providing Broadband Equalization of Sound Systems," presented at the 33rd Convention of the Audio Engineering Society, *J. Audio Eng. Soc. (Abstracts)*, vol. 16, p. 84 (Jan. 1968).
13. "Transversal Equalizer DG-4017," Industrial Research Products, Inc., data sheet (1984).
14. "Digital Equalizer DEQ7," Yamaha, data sheet (1987).
15. T. Thomas, "Digital Processing for the Digital Age," *Roland Users Group*, vol. 6, pp.60-62 (Jan. 1988).
16. "AES Recommended Practice for Digital Audio Engineering—Serial Transmission Format for Linearly Represented Digital Audio Data (AES3-1985 & ANSI S4.40-1985)," *J. Audio Eng. Soc.*, vol. 33, pp. 975-984 (Dec. 1985).
17. D. Bohn, "Bandpass Filter Design," *Studio Sound,* vol. 25, pp. 36-37 (Jan. 1983).
18. T. Pennington, "The Rane GE 30 Interpolating Constant-Q Equalizer," *Rane Note 117* (now available as "Constant-Q Graphic Equalizers," *Rane Note 101*), Rane Corp., 1987
19. *IEEE Standard Dictionary of Electrical and Electronics Terms (ANSI/IEEEStd100-1984)*, 3rd ed., p.548 (IEEE, New York, 1984).
20. H. Blinchikoff and A. Zverev, *Filtering in the Time and Frequency Domains*, pp. 89-91 (Wiley, New York, 1976).
21. C. Van Ryswyk, "Filters for Equalization: Active or Passive?" presented at the 55th Convention of the Audio Engineering Society, *J. Audio Eng. Soc. (Abstracts)*, vol. 24, p. 851 (Dec. 1976), preprint 1177.
22. R.A. Greiner and M. Schoessow, "Design Aspects of Graphic Equalizers," presented at the 69th Convention of the Audio Engineering Society, *J. Audio Eng. Soc. (Abstracts)*, vol. 29, p. 556 (July/Aug. 1981), preprint 1767.
23. T. Pennington, "Constant-Q," *Studio Sound*, vol. 27, pp. 82-85 (Oct. 1985).
24. H.R. Kimball, *Motion Picture Sound Engineering* (Van Nostrand, New York, 1938).
25. F. Bies, "Attenuation Equalizers," *J. Audio Eng. Soc.*, vol. 1, pp. 125-136 (Jan. 1953).
26. B. Soloman and C. Broneer, "Constant-S Equalizers," *J. Audio Eng. Soc.*, vol.6, pp. 210-215 (Oct. 1958).
27. P. Baxandall, "Negative Feedback Tone Control—Independent Variation of Bass and Treble Without Switches," *Wireless World,* vol. 58, p. 402 (Oct. 1952).
28. R. Riordan, "Simulated Inductors Using Differential Amplifiers," *Electron. Lett.*, vol. 3, pp. 50-51 (Feb. 1967).
29. T.H. Ishimoto, "Applications of Gyrators in Graphic Equalizers," presented at the 63rd Convention of the Audio Engineering Society, *J. Audio Eng. Soc. (Abstracts)*, vol. 27, p. 598 (July/Aug. 1979) preprint
30. G.R. Thurmond, "New Devices for Equalization," presented at the 52nd Convention of the Audio Engineering Society, *J. Audio Eng. Soc. (Abstracts)*, vol. 23, p. 827 (Dec. 1975) preprint 1076.
31. D. Bohn, "Constant-Q Graphic Equalizers," *J. Audio Eng. Soc.*, vol. 34, pp. 611-626 (Sep. 1986).
32. W. Kerwin and L. Huelsman, "The Design of High Performance Active RC Bandpass Filters," *IEEE Int. Conv. Rec.*, vol. 14, pt. 10, pp. 74-80 (1960).
33. R. Sallen and E. Key, "A Practical Method of Designing RC Active Filters," *IRE Trans. Circuit Theory*, vol. CT-2, pp. 74-85 (Mar. 1955).
34. K. Gundry, "Adjustable Equalizers Useable in Audio Spectrum," U.S. Patent 3,921,104 (Nov. 1975).

©Rane Corporation   10802 47th Ave. W.,   Mukilteo WA 98275-5098   TEL (425)355-6000   FAX (425)347-7757   WEB http://www.rane.com

Exposing Equalizer Mythology

- **Combining Filters**

- **Phase Behavior**

- **Marketing Buzzwords**

- **Constant-Q**

- **Passive and Active Equalizers**

Introduction

John Roberts is one of my heroes. John wrote a regular column for the now defunct magazine *Recording Engineer/ Producer* entitled "Exposing Audio Mythology". "Laying to Rest… or at least exposing the false premises upon which they are based… some of the Pro-Audio Industry's more obvious 'Old Wives Tales' "— such was the opening for John's first column. Great stuff, you could almost hear the theme music and see the masked rider off in the distance.

He originally intended to do a few columns on the most flagrant abuses, that was in early 1983. He continued until mid-1986. Every issue, without fail, he waged war on the myth-sayers. John is resting now. Myth exposing is too much for one person. I'm arrogant enough, and angry enough, to help out. So I thought I would expose some of the most popular myths regarding equalizers.

Dennis Bohn
Rane Corporation

RaneNote 115
© **1986 Rane Corporation**

MYTH #1: There exists such a thing as a combining filter.

Many contractors are very confused over just what a combining filter is. So am I. Filter designers have many names for different types of filters: Butterworth, Chebyshev, Bessel, etc., but combining isn't one of them. The problem here is with the use of the word filter. We must distinguish between what is being thought and what is being said. Within the context of using this phrase lies the real intent, i.e., how much ripple exists in the output.

The outputs of filter banks combine (or actually, re-combine) to form a resultant curve characterized by an overall shape and a ripple content with associated phase shift. How this combining takes place and the bandwidth of the individual filters dictates the amount of ripple. The type of filter used has nothing to do with it. Combining is done by electronically summing together all of the filter outputs. It is not a filter at all: it is a means of summing individual filter's outputs. All equalizers combine their filter outputs. It is wrong to say an equalizer is non-combining. The only examples of non-combining filters are real time analyzers and crossovers. An example of the misuse of this term concerns comparison between constant-Q and conventional graphic equalizers. (Conventional, as used here, refers to any graphic equalizer that is not constant-Q.) The popular, albeit false, belief is that conventional equalizers use combining filters, while constant-Q designs use non-combining filters. Both designs sum their outputs together. The difference lies in the smoothness of the combined curves. The fallacy lies in taking the answer out of context.

Setting a conventional equalizer to have the same bandwidth as a constant-Q design produces a combined result exactly the same if the number of summers is the same. However, the only condition where this occurs is either full boost or full cut. Most users do not understand this is the only position where the affected bandwidth is one-third octave wide (for one-third designs). At all other boost/cut settings the bandwidth degrades to over one octave wide. There is no doubt that if two adjacent filters located one-third octave apart degrade to where each is one octave wide, then the summed result will be very smooth. There is also no doubt that this is no longer a one-third octave equalizer. It now acts as an octave equalizer. If that is what is required, then a conventional equalizer is the correct choice; however, if one-third octave control is required, then only a constant-Q design will do.

MYTH #2: Minimum Phase behavior is an important criteria when buying an equalizer.

Minimum phase is one of the few things you *don't* have to worry about when buying an equalizer. It's not that it isn't important, it is. It's just that no known examples of commercial equalizers that are *not* minimum phase even exist. None. Forget all the marketing hype to the contrary.

A precise definition of minimum phase is a detailed mathematical concept involving positive real transfer functions, i.e., transfer functions with all zeros restricted to the left half s-plane. If the last sentence produced a zero in the middle of your brain, don't worry. All you need to know is minimum phase behavior is not a problem in any equalizer you may consider purchasing.

Here again is an example of sloppy rhetoric. A failure to communicate clearly what is being thought. Somewhere years ago some marketing type needed a term, a buzz word if you will, for distinguishing his company's equalizer from everybody else's. Some engineer dropped the term minimum phase and the marketing guy went nuts. That's it, thought he; never mind that it doesn't fit what is trying to be said, it sounds good. Nice and high-tech, so he used it to try to build a smoke screen between comparable products.

What they wanted to say was their product could create boost/cut curves with less phase shift than their competitors, and that this was a good thing. Problem was, here comes the engineer again to say this simply wasn't true. Any two equalizers producing the same curve do so with *exactly* the same phase shift. Same universe, same physics, same results—much to marketing's chagrin. So they compromised on claiming their product had MINIMUM PHASE characteristics. Never mind that all the competition also had minimum phase behavior. The customer wouldn't know that. The promotion implied that the other products didn't. Let the buying public figure out otherwise.

Okay, now you know otherwise. Don't be hoodwinked by this buzz word.

MYTH #3: Only one brand of equalizer exhibits complementary phase performance.

Speaking of buzz words, here's a beaut: *complementary phase shift*. Somebody worked overtime on this campaign. I guess what gets me so angry about this issue is the arrogance of the manufacturer. The underlying premise is that the pro audio public is so gullible they will believe anything, if presented profoundly. Well, they are wrong. All of you are a whole lot smarter than they give you credit for. Street smarts go a long way in solving problems.

Complementary phase shift means nothing more than the equalizer displays symmetrical boost/cut curves (and is minimum phase). The boost curves are mirror images of the cut curves. That means the phase shift of the boost is also a mirror image of the cut. If two things are mirror images of each other, they are complementary. Nothing too profound.

Now, it is not true all equalizers exhibit symmetrical boost/ cut curves. Therefore, not all equalizers have complementary phase shift. At least two of the more popular brands do not. So, if you perceive this to be an important parameter when buying an equalizer, you are correct in asking whether the unit has symmetrical boost/cut curves. I can give you a list of a dozen manufacturers whose equalizers do. In truth, every example of graphic equalizer I'm familiar with has symmetrical boost/cut curves, as well as most of the parametrics on the market. In fact, you have to look long and hard to find examples of equalizers that are *not* complementary phase performers. As I said, I know of two, there may be more.

The correct question at this point is why do you care if the equalizer has complementary phase shift? Damned, if I know. I can tell you why they say it is important, and I can tell you why they are misleading you.

The popular demonstration involves setting up one channel with an arbitrary curve and then adjusting the other channel for the opposite response. Passing a signal through both channels in series produces a flat frequency response. No phase shift. No time delay. Now this result seems to have overwhelmed them. They describe the results as bizarre, remarkable and baffling. I can find no one else that is the least bit surprised. This is one of the few places where your intuition is correct.

If you take two equalizers set for complementary curves and put them in series you get a response of *unity*. You do not get an all-pass response, as they claim. There is no amplitude variation, no phase shift, and no time delay. Basic sophomore electrical engineering tells us why. Something called a transfer function represents each channel. This mathematical equation completely describes the amplitude, phase and time response of a signal passing through that channel. The complementary channel's transfer function is the reciprocal of the first. Putting them in series causes the two transfer functions to multiply. Anything times the reciprocal of itself produces the answer of unity, i.e., $(1/X)(X)=1$. Nothing too difficult here. *One* is not the transfer function of an all-pass filter. *One* is the transfer function of a piece of wire.

So what does all this have to do with what kind of equalizer you may want to buy? Not much, really. The implication is that you must have a complementary phase equalizer to correct for a room's frequency anomalies — not true. Any equalizer that produces the opposite room response works — and works just as well.

MYTH #4: Constant-Q means non-symmetrical boost/cut curves.

Until 1986, I wouldn't have considered this an official myth. At that time, F. Alton Everest published a book, entitled Successful Sound System Operation (TAB Books No. 2606). It is a well done introduction to the business of sound reinforcement, and I recommend it to anyone just starting out. His treatment of constant-Q equalizers (p. 252), however, needs some revising.

Mr. Everest states erroneously and unequivocally that constant-Q equalizers characterized themselves by having asymmetrical boost/cut curves. (This occurred from a misreading of a popular parametric equalizer's data sheet; something easy to do.) This myth involves a mixing of two separate issues.

Reciprocity of boost/cut curves and constant-Q have nothing to do with each other. You can find *constant-Q* symmetrical and non-symmetrical equalizers and you can find *non-constant-Q* symmetrical and non-symmetrical equalizers. The terms characterize two different aspects of an equalizer. Constant-Q refers to the bandwidth behavior for different amounts of boost or cut. If the bandwidth stays constant as a function of boost/cut amounts, then it is constant-Q. If it does not, then it is not a constant-Q design.

If the cut curves are mirror images of the boost curves, then the equalizer has symmetrical (or *reciprocal*) response. If the curves are not mirror images of each other, then the equalizer is of the non-symmetrical school.

Two separate issues, both available in any combination from several manufacturers. Your choice.

MYTH #5: Given identical equalizers, one passive and one active, the passive unit will sound different.

The key to whether this is a myth involves the crucial word, identical. If two equalizers do not produce the *exact* transfer function, then they will definitely sound different. That is not the issue here. At issue, is whether there exists some sound quality attributable to active or passive circuits per se. There does not.

A transfer function exists characterizing every equalizer's output behavior to a given input change. Any two equalizers with the sum transfer function, when operating within the constraints necessary to behave according to that function, will give the same results no matter what physical form makes up the equalizer. In general, any equalizer response can be implemented by many different types of circuits, both active and passive. The perceived differences between equalizers designed for the same response function must be explained by factors other than whether the equalizer is active or passive. Some characteristics that can contribute to the misbehavior of the circuit are nonlinearities that occur because the components are being used improperly or stressed beyond their linear operating region. Sometimes the perceived differences are nothing more than one circuit is quieter than another.

Any two equalizers with the same frequency domain transfer function will behave the same in the time domain. The transfer function determines responses such as overshoot, ringing, and phase shift regardless of implementation.

Nothing mysterious exists within the realm of active and passive equalizers. Simple electronic theory explains all differences between these two, if differences exist. If not, they will perform and sound the same to the objective observer. Never assume that because an equalizer is active or passive it is automatically better or worse for your application. Study your needs and consult with knowledgeable people to make the correct equalizer selection.

MYTH #6: An ideal equalizer would add no phase shift when boosting or cutting.

Phase shift is not a bad word. It is the glue at the heart of what we do, holding everything together. That it has become a maligned term is most unfortunate. This belief stands in the way of people really understanding the requirements for room equalization.

The frequency response of most performing rooms looks like a heart attack victim's EKG results. Associated with each change in amplitude is a corresponding change in phase response. Describing them as unbelievably jagged is being conservative. Every time the amplitude changes so does the phase shift. In fact, it can be argued that phase shift is the stuff that causes amplitude changes. Amplitude, phase and time are all inextricably mixed by the physics of sound. One does not exist without the others.

An equalizer is a tool. A tool that allows you to correct for a room's anomalies. It must be capable of reproducing the exact opposite response of the one being connected. This requires precise correction at many neighboring points with the associated phase shift to correct for the room's opposing phase shift. *It takes phase shift to fix phase shift*. Simple as that.

One way people get into trouble when equalizing rooms is using the wrong type of equalizer. If an equalizer is not capable of adding the correct amount of phase shift, it will make equalizing much more difficult than it has to be. The popularity of the many constant-Q designs has come about because of this phenomenon. Equalizers that produce broad smooth curves for modest amounts of boost/cut make poor room equalizers, and good tone modifiers. They lack the ability to make amplitude and phase corrections close together. Lacking the ability to make many independent corrections with minimal interference to neighboring bands restricts their usage primarily to giving a shape to an overall response rather than correcting it. Serious correcting requires sharp constant-Q performance, among many other things.

Only by adding many precise, narrow phase shift and amplitude corrections do you truly start equalizing a system's blurred phase response. You do not do it with gentle smooth curves that lack the muscle to tame the peakedness of most rooms. Broad smooth curves do not allow you to correct for the existing phase shift. Its just that simple, you must pre-shape the signal in both amplitude and phase. And that requires narrow filters that preserve their bandwidths at all filter positions.

©Rane Corporation   10802 47th Ave. W.,   Mukilteo WA 98275-5098   TEL (425)355-6000   FAX (425)347-7757   WEB http://www.rane.com

Linkwitz-Riley Crossovers

- **ZERO LOBING ERROR**

- **24 dB/OCTAVE SLOPES**

- **STATE VARIABLE SOLUTION**

- **TIME CORRECTION**

The assumption is made that the reader is familiar with active crossovers and how they are used in professional sound systems. For those who are not and want to review the basics, one of the best references will be found in an article entitled. "Crossover Basics". by Richard Chinn, in the September 1986 issue of STEREO REVIEW.

Dennis Bohn
Rane Corporation

RaneNote 107
© **1983 Rane Corporation**

INTRODUCTION

What's a Linkwitz-Riley, and why do I care? First off, its not "what's", but "who": Siegfried Linkwitz and Russ Riley are two Hewlett-Packard R&D engineers who wrote a paper[1] in 1976 describing a better mousetrap in crossover design. Largely ignored (or unread) for the past several years, it is now receiving the attention it deserved in 1976. Typical of most truly useful technical papers, it is very straight-forward and unassuming. A product of careful analytical attention to details, with a wonderfully simple solution.

The, "why do I care?", part is easily answered by stating that a Linkwitz-Riley crossover will give you a clearer and more accurate sound system. Period. It will automatically clean up the messiness that mars most systems at their crucial crossover points. (It is at the crossover points that most systems lose it.)

It is seldom whether to cross over, but rather, how to cross over. Active crossovers have proliferated over the past few years at a rate equal to the proverbial lucky charm. The potential crossover buyer must choose from among a dozen different manufacturers and designs. Some are adequate; some are even good; but none seem to offer just the right mix of features, technology and cost. Until now.

An attempt will be made within this Note to present the essence of a Linkwitz-Riley design, and to introduce Rane's answer to a truly affordable crossover that features the very best technology, with exactly the right features.

A 4th-order state variable active filter[2] has been developed by Rane Corporation to implement the Linkwitz-Riley alignment for crossover coefficients. In addition to the active crossover, the unit features a variable time delay circuit so the user may effectively "move" the drivers into front-to-back alignment. With both these tools, the professional sound person now has the means to smooth out and perfect the crucial crossover region, resulting in a sound system that exhibits unsurpassed clarity and accuracy.

A PERFECT CROSSOVER

Mother nature gets the blame. Another universe, another system of physics, and the quest for a perfect crossover might not be so difficult. But we exist here and must make the best of what we have. And what we have is the physics of sound, and of electromagnetic transformation systems that obey these physics.

A perfect crossover, in essence, is no crossover at all. It would be one driver that could reproduce all frequencies equally well. Since we cannot have that, then second best would be multiple speakers, along the same axis, with sound being emitted from the same point, i.e., a coaxial speaker that has no time shift between drivers. This gets closer to being possible, but still is elusive. Third best, and this is where we really begin, is multiple drivers mounted one above the other with no time shift, i.e., non-coincident drivers adjusted front-to-rear to compensate for their different points of sound propagation. Each driver would be fed only the frequencies it is capable of reproducing. The frequency dividing network would be, in reality, a frequency gate. It would have no phase shift or time delay. It's amplitude response would be absolutely flat and its roll-off characteristics would be the proverbial brick wall. (Brings a tear to your eye, doesn't it?)

Using digital technology, such a crossover is possible, but not at a price that is acceptable to most working musicians. What is possible at an affordable price is a very good compromise known as the Linkwitz-Riley crossover.

LINKWITZ-RILEY CROSSOVER

What distinguishes the Linkwitz-Riley crossover design from others is its perfect combined radiation pattern of the two drivers at the crossover point. Stanley P. Lipshitz[3] has coined the term "lobing error" to describe this crossover characteristic. It's a good term and should spread through the industry as the standard. It derives from the examination of the acoustic output plots (at crossover) of the combined radiation pattern of the two drivers (see Figures 1 & 2). If it is not perfect. the pattern forms a lobe that exhibits an off-axis frequency dependent tilt with severe amplitude peaking.

Interpretation of Figure 1 is not particularly obvious. Let's back up a minute and add some more details. For simplicity, only a two way system is being modeled. The two drivers are mounted along the vertical center of the enclosure (there is no side-to-side displacement, i.e., one driver is mounted on top of the other.) Any front-to-back time delay between drivers has been corrected. The figure shown is a polar plot of the side-view, i.e., the angles are vertical angles.

It is only the vertical displacement sound field that is at issue here. All of the popular crossover types (constant voltage[4], Butterworth all-pass[5], etc.) are well behaved along the horizontal on-axis plane. To illustrate the geometry involved here, imagine attaching a string to the speaker at the mid-point between the drivers. Position the speaker such that the mid-point is exactly at ear level. Now pull the string taut and hold it up to your nose (go on, no one's looking). The string should be parallel to the floor. Holding the string tight, move to the left and right. This is the horizontal on-axis plane. Along this listening plane, all of the classic crossover designs exhibit no problems. It is when you lower or raise your head below or above this plane that the problems arise. This is the crux of Siegfried Linkwitz's contribution to crossover design. After all these years and as hard as it is to believe, he was the first person to publish an analysis of what happens off-axis with non-coincident drivers (not-coaxial). (Others may have done it before, but it was never made public record.)

Figure 1A represents a side view of the combined acoustic radiation pattern of the two drivers emitting the same single frequency. That is, a plot of what is going on at the single crossover frequency all along the vertical plane. The pattern shown is for the popular 18 dB/octave Butterworth all-pass design with a crossover frequency of 1700 Hz and drivers mounted 7 inches apart[1].

What is seen is a series of peaking and cancellation nodes. Back to the string. Holding it taut again and parallel to the floor puts you on-axis. Figure 1A tells us that the magnitude of the emitted 1700 Hz tone will be 0 dB (a nominal reference point). As you lower your head, the tone will increase in loudness until a 3 dB peak is reached at 15 degrees below parallel. Raising your head above the on-axis line will cause a reduction in magnitude until 15 degrees is reached where there will be a complete cancellation of the tone. There is another cancellation axis located 49 degrees below the on-axis. Figure 1B depicts the frequency response of the three axes for reference.

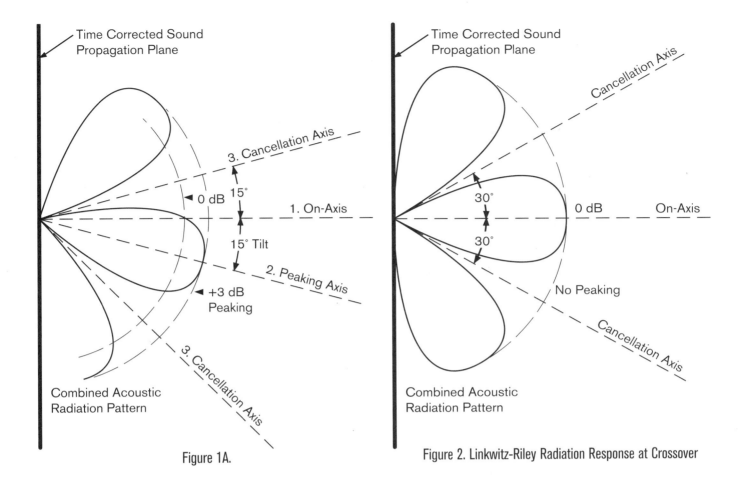

Figure 1A.

Figure 2. Linkwitz-Riley Radiation Response at Crossover

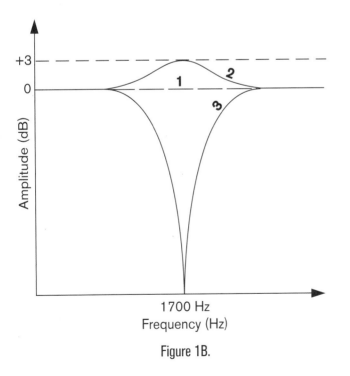

Figure 1B.

Figure 1. Butterworth All-Pass Design Radiation Pattern at Crossover.

For a constant voltage design, the response looks worse, having a 6 dB peaking axis located at -20 degrees and the cancellation axes at +10 and -56 degrees, respectively. The peaking axis tilts toward the lagging driver in both cases, due to phase shift between the two crossover outputs.

The cancellation nodes are not due to the crossover design, they are due to the vertically displaced drivers. (The crossover design controls *where* cancellation nodes occur, not *that* they occur.) The fact that the drivers are not coaxial means that any vertical deviation from the on-axis line will result in a slight, but very significant differences in path lengths to the listener. This difference in distance traveled is effectively a phase shift between drivers. And this causes cancellation nodes — the greater the distance between drivers, the more nodes.

In distinct contrast to these examples is Figure 2, where the combined response of a Linkwitz-Riley crossover design is shown. There is no tilt and no peaking. Just a perfect response whose only limitation is the dispersion characteristics of the drivers used. The main contributor to this ideal response is the in-phase relationship between the crossover outputs.

Two of the cancellation nodes are still present but are well defined and always symmetrical about the on-axis plane. Their location changes with crossover frequency and driver mounting geometry (distance between drivers). With the other designs, the peaking and cancellation axes change with frequency and driver spacing.

Let's drop the string and move out into the audience to see how these cancellation and peaking nodes affect things. Figure 3 shows a terribly simplified, but not too inaccurate stage-audience relationship with the characteristics of Figure 1 added.

The band is cooking and then comes to a musical break. All eyes are on the flautist, who immediately goes into her world-famous 1700 Hz solo. So what happens? The people in the middle hear it sweet, while those up front are blown out of their seats, and those in the back are wondering what the hell's all the fuss!

Figure 4 shows the identical situation but with the Linkwitz-Riley characteristics of Figure 2 added. Now the people in the middle still hear everything sweet, but those up front are not blown away, and those in the back understand the fuss!

I think you get the point.

Now let's get real. I mean really real. The system isn't two way, it's four way. There isn't one enclosure, there are sixteen. No way are the drivers 7 inches apart — try 27. And time corrected? Forget it.

Can you even begin to imagine what the vertical off-axis response will look like with classic crossover designs? The further apart the drivers are, the greater the number of peaks and cancellations, resulting in a multi-lobe radiation pattern. Each crossover frequency will have its own set of patterns, complicated by each enclosure contributing even more patterns. And so on.

(For large driver spacing the Linkwitz-Riley design will have as many lobes as other designs, except that the peaks are always 0 dB, and the main lobe is always on-axis.)

Note that all this is dealing with the direct sound field, no multiple secondary arrivals or room interference or reverberation times are being considered. Is it any wonder that when you move your realtime analyzer microphone 3 feet you get a totally different response?

Now let me state clearly that using a Linkwitz-Riley crossover will not solve all these problems. But it will go a long, long way toward that goal.

The other outstanding characteristic of the Linkwitz-Riley alignment is the rolloff rate of 24 dB/octave (Figure 5). With such a sharp drop-off, drivers can be operated closer to their theoretical crossover points without the induced distortion normally caused by frequencies lying outside their capabilities. Frequencies just one octave away from the crossover point are already attenuated by 24 dB (a factor or about 1/16). The importance of sharp cutoff rate and in-phase frequency response of the crossover circuitry cannot be over-stressed in contributing to smooth overall system response.

A summary of the characteristics of a Linkwitz-Riley crossover reads:

1. Absolutely flat amplitude response through out the pass-band with a steep 24 dB/octave rolloff rate after the crossover point.
2. The acoustic sum of the two driver responses is unity at crossover. (Amplitude response of each is -6 dB at crossover, i.e., there is no peaking in the summed acoustic output)
3. Zero phase difference between drivers at crossover. (Lobing error equals zero, i.e., no tilt to the polar radiation pattern.) In addition, the phase difference of zero degrees through crossover places the lobe of the summed acoustic output on axis at all frequencies.
4. The low pass and high pass outputs are everywhere in phase. (This guarantees symmetry of the polar response about the crossover point)
5. All drivers are always wired the same (in phase).

A casual reading of the above list may suggest that this is, indeed, the perfect crossover. But such is not so. The wrinkle involves what is known as "linear phase". A Linkwitz-Riley crossover alignment is not linear phase: meaning that the amount of phase shift is a function of frequency. Or, put into time domain terms, the amount of time delay through the filter is not constant for all frequencies. Which means that some frequencies are delayed more than others. (In technical terms, the network has a frequency-dependent group delay. but with a very gradually changing characteristic.)

Is this a problem? Specifically, is this an audible "problem"? In a word, no.

Much research has been done on this question[6-9], with approximately the same conclusions: given a slowly changing non-linear phase system, the audible results are so minimal as to be non-existent; especially in the face of all of the other system non-linearities. And with real-world music sources (remember music?), it is not audible at all.

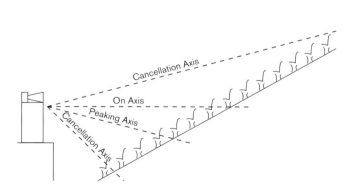

Figure 3. Butterworth All-Pass Crossover Stage-Audience Relationship

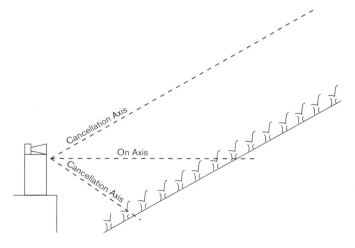

Figure 4. Linkwitz-Riley Crossover Stage Audience Relationship

STATE VARIABLE SOLUTION

One of the many attractions of the Linkwitz-Riley design is its utter simplicity, requiring only two standard 2nd-order Butterworth filters in series. The complexities occur when adjustable crossover frequencies are required.

After examining and rejecting all of the standard approaches to accomplish this task, Rane developed a 4th-order state-variable filter specifically for implementing the Linkwitz-Riley crossover. The state-variable topology was chosen over other designs mainly for the following reasons:

1. It provides simultaneous high-pass and low-pass outputs that are always at exactly the same frequency.
2. Changing frequencies can be done simultaneously on the high-pass and low-pass outputs without any changes in amplitude or Q (quality factor).
3. The sensitivities of the filter are very low. (Sensitivity is a measure of the effects of non-ideal components on an otherwise, ideal response.)
4. It offers the most cost-effective way to implement two 4th-order responses with continuously variable crossover frequencies.

TIME OR PHASE CORRECTION

Implicit in the development of the theory of a Linkwitz-Riley crossover design is the key assumption that the sound from each driver radiates from the some exact vertical plane, i.e., that the drivers have no time delay with respect to each other. The crossover then prohibits any lobing errors as the sound advances forward simultaneously from the two drivers. Figure 6 illustrates such a front-to-back displacement, which causes the lobing error shown in Figure 7a.

A Linkwitz-Riley crossover applied to drivers that are not time-corrected loses most of its magic. The lobing error is no longer zero; it exhibits a frequency dependent tilt with magnitude errors as shown in Figure 7b.

This being the case, Rane incorporates either adjustable time delay or phase shift circuits into its Linkwitz-Riley crossovers.

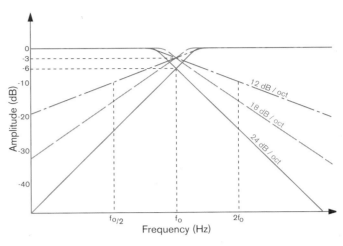

Figure 5. Frequency Response of 4th-order Linkwitz-Riley Active Crossover

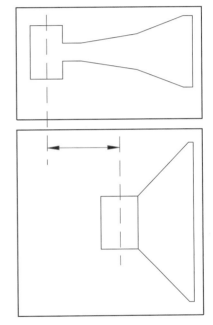

Figure 6. Driver Displacement

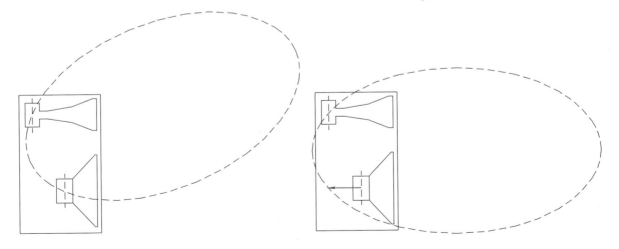

Figure 7. Adding Delay to the Forward Driver Time-Aligns the Phase of Both Drivers, Reducing Lobing Error.

Figure 7a Without Time Alignment.

Figure 7b. With Time Alignment.

REFERENCES

1. S. H. Linkwitz "Active Crossover Networks for Non-coincident Drivers," *J. Audio Eng. Soc.*, vol. 24, pp. 2-8 (Jan/Feb 1976).

2. D. Bohn. "A Fourth Order State Variable Filter for Linkwitz-Riley Active Crossover Designs," presented at the 74th Convention of the Audio Engineering Society, New York, Oct. 9-12,1983, preprint no. 2011.

3. S. P. Lipshitz and J. Vanderkooy, "A Family of Linear-Phase Crossover Networks of High Slope Derived by Time Delay," *J. Audio Eng. Soc.*, vol. 31, pp. 2-20 (Jan/Feb 1983).

4. R. H. Small, "Constant-Voltage Crossover Network Design," *J. Audio Eng. Soc.*, vol. 19, pp. 12-19 (Jan 1971).

5. J.R. Ashley and A. L. Kaminsky. "Active and Passive Filters as Loudspeaker Crossover Networks," *J. Audio Eng. Soc.*. vol. 19. pp. 494-502 (June 1971).

6. B. B. Bauer, "Audibility of Phase Shift," *Wireless World*, (Apr. 1974).

7. S. P. Lipshitz, M. Pocock, and J. Vanderkooy. "On the Audibility of Midrange Phase Distortion in Audio Systems," *J. Audio Eng. Soc.*, vol. 30, pp. 580-595 (Sep 1982).

8. R. Lee. "Is Linear Phase Worthwhile," presented at the 68th Convention of the Audio Engineering Society, Hamburg, Mar 17-20, 1981, preprint no. 1732.

9. H. Suzuke. S. Morita. and T. Shindo. "On the Perception of Phase Distortion," *J. Audio Eng. Soc.*, vol. 28, no. 9, pp. 570-574 (Sep 1980).

10. RaneNote, "Linkwitz-Riley Crossovers Up to 8th-Order," 1989.

©Rane Corporation   10802 47th Ave. W.,   Mukilteo WA 98275-5098   TEL (425)355-6000   FAX (425)347-7757   WEB http://www.rane.com

Linkwitz-Riley Active Crossovers up to 8th-Order: An Overview

- Linkwitz-Riley Alignment
- Butterworth Alignment
- 1st to 8th Order Filters
- Vector Diagrams
- Transient Response
- Phase Response

Dennis Bohn
Rane Corporation

RaneNote 119
© 1989 Rane Corporation (rev. 12/01)

INTRODUCTION

In 1976, Siegfried Linkwitz published his famous paper [1] on active crossovers for non-coincident drivers. In it, he credited Russ Riley (a co-worker and friend) with contributing the idea that cascaded Butterworth filters met all Linkwitz's crossover requirements. Their efforts became known as the Linkwitz-Riley crossover alignment. In 1983, the first commercially available Linkwitz-Riley active crossovers appeared from Sundholm and Rane [2].

Today, the de facto standard for professional audio active crossovers is the 4th-order Linkwitz-Riley (LR-4) design. Offering in-phase outputs and steep 24 dB/octave slopes, the LR-4 alignment gave users the tool necessary to scale the next step toward the elusive goal of perfect sound.

Now a new tool is available: the 8th-order Linkwitz-Riley (LR-8) active crossover [3]. With incredibly steep slopes of 48 dB/octave, the LR-8 stands at the door waiting for its turn at further sound improvements. Using a LR-8 cuts the already narrow LR-4 crossover region in half. Just one octave away from the crossover frequency the response is down 48 dB. The LR-8 represents a major step closer to the proverbial brick wall, with its straight line crossover region.

Before exploring the advantages of LR-8 designs, it is instructional to review just what Linkwitz-Riley alignments are, and how they differ from traditional Butterworth designs of old.

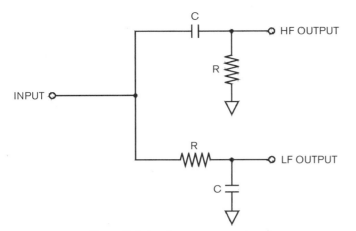

Figure 1. 1st order crossover network

1st-Order Network

It begins with a resistor and a capacitor. It never gets more complicated than that—just resistors and capacitors: lots and lots of resistors and capacitors. Resistors are the great emancipators of electronics; they are free of frequency dependence. They dissipate energy without frequency prejudice. All frequencies treated equally. Capacitors, on the other hand, selectively absorb energy; they store it, to be released at a later time. While resistors react instantly to any voltage changes within a circuit, capacitors take time to charge and discharge.

Capacitors are so frequency dependent, they **only** pass signals with frequency associated with them. Direct-current (what we call zero frequency) will not pass at all; while, at the other end of the spectrum, very high frequencies will not absorb. Capacitors act like a piece of wire to high frequencies; hardly there at all.

We use these facts to create a crossover network. Figure 1 shows such a circuit. By interchanging the positions of the resistor and capacitor, low-pass (low frequencies = LF) and high-pass (high frequencies = HF) filters result. For the low-pass case (LF), the capacitor ignores low frequencies and shunts all high frequencies to ground. For the high-pass case (HF), the opposite occurs. All low frequencies are blocked and only high frequencies are passed.

1st-Order Amplitude Response

Using 1kHz as an example and plotting the amplitude versus frequency response (Figure 2) reveals the expected low-pass and high-pass shapes. Figure 2 shows that the 1st-order circuit exhibits 6 dB/octave slopes. Also, that 6 dB/octave equals 20 dB/decade. Both ways of expressing steepness are useful and should be memorized. The rule is: **each order, or degree, of a filter increases the slopes by 6 dB/octave or 20 dB/decade**. So, for example, a 4th-order (or 4th-degree—interchangeable terms) circuit has 24 dB/octave (4x6 dB/octave) or 80 dB/decade (4x20 dB/decade) slopes.

Using equal valued resistors and capacitors in each of the circuits causes the amplitude responses to 'cross over' at one particular frequency where their respective -3 dB points intersect. This point represents the attenuation effect resulting when the impedance of the capacitor equals the resistance of the resistor.

The equivalent multiplying factor for -3 dB is .707, i.e., a signal attenuated by 3 dB will be .707 times the original in level. Ohms law tells us that if the voltage is multiplied by .707, then the current will also be multiplied by .707. Power is calculated by multiplying voltage times current. Therefore, a voltage multiplied by .707, and a current multiplied by .707, equals 0.5 power. So the -3 dB points represent the one-half power point—a useful reference.

Lastly, Figure 2 shows the flat amplitude response resulting from summing the LF and HF outputs together. This is called **constant voltage**, since the result of adding the two output voltages together equals a constant. The 1st-order case is ideal in that **constant power** also results. Constant-power refers to the summed power response for each loudspeaker driver operating at the crossover frequency. This, too, results in a constant. Since each driver operates at ½ power at the crossover frequency, their sum equals one—or unity, a constant.

1st-Order Phase Response

Much is learned by examining the phase shift behavior (Figure 3) of the 1st-order circuit. The upper curve is the HF output and the lower curve is the LF output. The HF curve starts at +90° phase shift at DC, reduces to +45° at the crossover frequency and then levels out at 0° for high fre-

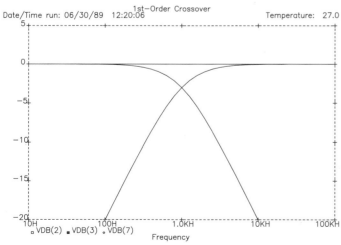

Figure 2. 1st-order amplitude response

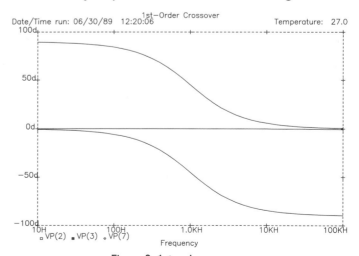

Figure 3. 1st-order response

quencies. The LF curve starts with 0° phase shift at DC, has -45° at the crossover frequency and levels out at -90° for high frequencies.

Because of its reactive (energy storing) nature each capacitor in a circuit contributes 90° of phase shift, either positive or negative depending upon its application. Since the HF section places the capacitor directly in the signal path, this circuit starts out with +90° phase shift. This is called **phase lead**. The LF section, which starts out with 0° and eventually becomes -90° is called **phase lag**.

Examination of Figure 3 allows us to formulate a new rule: **each order, or degree, of a crossover network contributes ±45° of phase shift at the crossover frequency** (positive for the HF output and negative for the LF output).

Once again, Figure 3 shows the idealized nature of the 1st-order case. Here the result of summing the outputs together produces 0° phase shift. Which is to say that the summed amplitude and phase shift of a 1st-order crossover equals that of a piece of wire.

1st-Order Group Delay Response

We shall return to our rules shortly, but first the concept of **group delay** needs to be introduced. Group delay is the term given to the ratio of an incremental change in phase shift divided by the associated incremental change in frequency (from calculus, this is the first-derivative). The units for group delay are seconds. If the phase shift is **linear**, i.e., a constant rate of change per frequency step, then the incremental ratio (first-derivative) will be constant. We therefore refer to a circuit with linear phase shift as having **constant group delay**.

Group delay is a useful figure of merit for identifying linear phase circuits. Figure 4 shows the group delay response for the Figure 1 1st-order crossover circuit. Constant group delay extends out to the crossover region where it gradually rolls off (both outputs are identical). The summed response is, again, that of a piece of wire.

The importance of constant group delay is its ability to predict the behavior of the LF output **step response**. A circuit with constant group delay (linear phase shift) shows no overshoot or associated damping time to a sudden change (step) in input level (Figure 5). The circuit reacts smoothly to

the sudden change by rising steadily to meet the new level. It does not go beyond the new level and require time to settle back. We also refer to the step response as the **transient** response of the circuit. The transient response of the summed outputs is perfect since their sum is perfectly equal to one.

For clarity purposes normally only the step response of the LF network is shown. Nothing is learned by examining the step response of the HF network. A step response represents a transition from one DC level to another DC level, in this case, from -1 volt to +1 volt. A HF network, by definition, does not pass DC (neither does a loudspeaker), so nothing particularly relevant is learned by examining its step response. To illustrate this, Figure 5 shows the HF step response. It begins and ends with zero output since it cannot pass DC. The sharp edge of the input step, however, contains much high frequency material, which the HF network passes. So, it begins at zero, passes the high frequencies as a pulse, and returns to zero.

The HF and LF outputs are the exact complement of each other. Their sum equals the input step exactly as seen in Figure 5. Still, we learn everything we need to know by examining only the LF step response; looking for overshoot and ringing. From now on, just the LF output will be shown.

Vector Diagrams

A vector is a graphical thing (now we're getting technical) with magnitude and direction. We can use vectors to produce diagrams representing the instantaneous phase shift and amplitude behavior of electrical circuits. In essence, we freeze the circuit for a moment of time to examine complex relationships.

We shall now apply our two rules to produce a vector diagram showing the relative phase shift and amplitude performance for the 1st-order crossover network at the single crossover frequency (Figure 6a). By convention, 0° points right, +90° points up, -90° points down, and ±180° points left. From Figures 2 & 3 we know the HF output amplitude is -3 dB with +45° of phase shift at 1 kHz, and the LF output is -3 dB with -45° phase shift. Figure 6a represents the vectors as being .707 long (relative to a normalized unity vector) and rotated up and down 45°. This shows us the relative phase difference between the two outputs equals 90°.

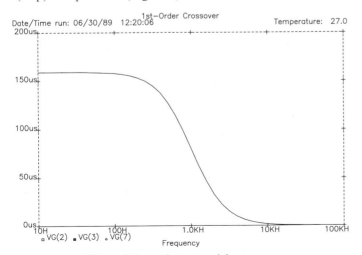

Figure 4. 1st-order group delay response

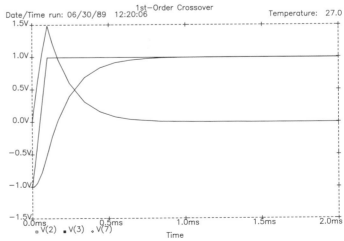

Figure 5. 1st-order transient response

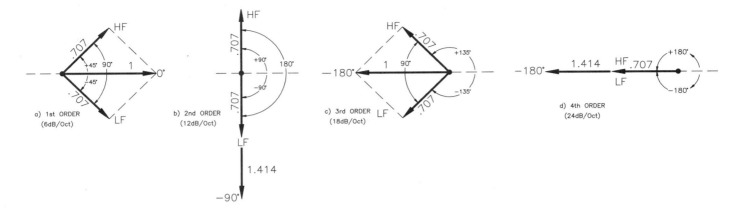

Figure 6. 1st through 4th-order butterworth vector diagrams

Next we do vector addition to show the summed results. Vector addition involves nothing more complex than mentally moving one of the vectors to the end of the other and connecting the center to this new end point (it is like constructing a parallelogram). Doing this, results in a new vector with a length equal to 1 and an angle of 0°. This tells us the recombined outputs of the HF and LF networks produce constant voltage (i.e., a vector equal to 1), and is in phase with the original input of the circuit (i.e., a vector with 0° phase rotation).

The 1st-order case is ideal when summed. It yields a piece of wire. Since the responses are the exact mirror images of each other, they cancel when summed, thus behaving as if neither was there in the first place. Unfortunately, all optimized higher order versions yield flat voltage/power response, group delay or phase shift, **but not all at once**. Hence, the existence of different alignments and resultant compromises.

2nd, 3rd & 4th-Order Butterworth Filters

There are many types of filters (most named after mathematicians). Each displays a unique amplitude characteristic throughout the passband. Of these, only **Butterworth** filters have an absolutely flat amplitude response. For this reason, Butterworth filters are the most popular for crossover use. Butterworth filters obey our two rules, so we can diagram them for the 2nd, 3rd and 4th-order cases (Figures 6b-6d). The 2nd-order case has ±90° phase shift as shown. This results in the outputs being 180° out of phase. Vector addition for this case produces a zero length vector, or complete cancellation. The popular way around this is to reverse the wiring on one of the drivers (or, if available, electronically inverting the phase at the crossover). This produces a resultant vector 90° out of phase with the input and 3 dB (1.414 equals +3 dB) longer. This means there will be a 3 dB amplitude bump at the crossover region for the combined signals.

The 3rd-order Butterworth case (Figure 6c) mimics the 1st-order case at the crossover frequency, except rotated 180°. Hence, we see the HF vector rotated up 135° (3x45°) and the LF vector rotated down the same amount. The phase shift between outputs is still 90°. The resultant is constant voltage (unity) but 180° out-of-phase with the input.

The 4th-order Butterworth diagram (Figure 6d) shows the HF vector rotated up 180° and the LF vector rotated down the same amount. The phase difference between outputs is now zero, but the resultant is +3 dB and 180° out-of-phase with the input. So, the 4th-order and the inverted phase 2nd-order produce 3 dB bumps at the crossover frequency.

Linkwitz-Riley Alignment

Two things characterize a Linkwitz-Riley alignment: 1) In-phase outputs (0° between outputs) at *all* frequencies (not just at the crossover frequency as popularly believed by some) and 2) Constant voltage (the outputs sum to unity at all frequencies).

Linkwitz-Riley in-phase outputs solve one troublesome aspect of crossover design. The acoustic lobe resulting from both loudspeakers reproducing the same frequency (the crossover frequency) is always on-axis (not tilted up or down) and has no peaking. This is called zero lobing error. In order for this to be true, however, both drivers must be in correct time alignment, i.e., their acoustic centers must lie in the same plane (or electrically put into equivalent alignment by adding time delay to one loudspeaker). Failure to time align the loudspeakers defeats this zero lobing error aspect. (The lobe tilts toward the lagging loudspeaker.)

Examination of Figure 6 shows that the 2nd-order (inverted) and 4th-order Butterworth examples satisfy condition 1), but fail condition 2) since they exhibit a 3 dB peak. So, if a way can be found to make the amplitudes at the crossover point -6 dB instead of -3 dB, then the vector lengths would equal 0.5 (-6 dB) instead of .707 (-3 dB) and sum to unity— and we would have a Linkwitz-Riley crossover.

Russ Riley suggested cascading (putting in series) two Butterworth filters to create the desired -6 dB crossover points (since each contributes -3 dB). Voila! Linkwitz-Riley alignments were born.

Taken to its most general extremes, cascading any order Butterworth filter produces 2x that order Linkwitz-Riley. Hence, cascading (2) 1st-order circuits produces a 2nd-order Linkwitz-Riley (LR-2); cascading (2) 2nd-order Butterworth filters creates a LR-4 design; cascading (2) 3rd-order Butterworth filters gives a LR-6, and so on. (Starting with LR-2, every other solution requires inverting one output. That is, LR-2 and LR-6 need inverting, while LR-4 and LR-8 don't.)

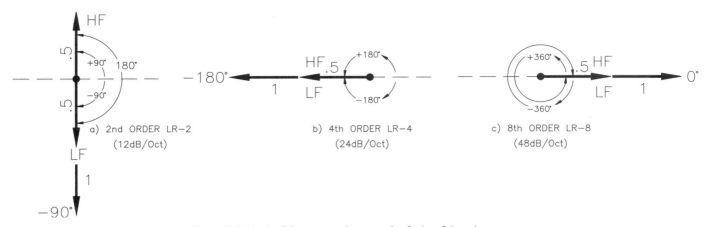

Figure 7. Linkwitz-Riley vector diagrams for 2nd to 8th-order cases.

LR-2, A Transient Perfect 2nd-Order Crossover

As an example of this process, let's examine a LR-2 design. Referring to Figure 1, all that is required is to add a buffer amplifier (to avoid interaction between cascaded filter components) to each of these two outputs and then add another resistor/capacitor network identical to the first. We now have a 2nd-order Linkwitz-Riley crossover.

The new vector diagram looks like Figure 7a. Each vector is .5 long (from the fact that each 1st-order reduces by 0.707, and .707 x .707 = .5) with phase angles of $\pm 90°$. Since the phase difference equals 180°, we invert one before adding and wind up with a unity vector 90° out of phase with the original.

Figure 8 shows the amplitude response. The crossover point is located at -6 dB and the slopes are 12 dB/octave (40 dB/decade). The summed response is perfectly flat. Figure 9 shows the phase response. At the crossover frequency we see the HF output (upper trace) has +90° phase shift, while the LF output (lower trace) has -90° phase shift, for a total phase difference of 180°. So, we invert one before summing and the result is identical to the LF output.

These results differ from the 1st-order case in that the summed results do not yield unity (a piece of wire), but instead create an all-pass network. (An all-pass network is characterized by having a flat amplitude response combined with a smoothly changing phase response.) This illustrates

Garde's [4] famous work.

Cascading two linear phase circuits results in linear phase, as shown by the constant group delay plots (all three identical) of Figure 10. And constant group delay gives the transient perfect LF step response shown in Figure 11.

LR-4 and LR-8 Alignments

Looking back to Figure 7b., we see the vector diagrams for 4th and 8th-order Linkwitz-Riley designs. The LR-4 design shows the resultant vector is unity but 180° out of phase with the input at the crossover frequency.

Cascading (2) 4th-order Butterworth filters results in an 8th-order Linkwitz-Riley design. Figure 7c. shows the vector diagram for the LR-8 case. Here, we see the phase shift for each output undergoes 360° rotation returning to where it began. The resultant vector is back in.phase with the original input signal. So, not only, are the outputs in phase with each other (for all frequencies), they are also in phase with the input (at the crossover frequency).

8th-Order Comparison

A LR-8 design exhibits slopes of 48 dB/octave, or 160 dB/decade. Figure 12 shows this performance characteristic compared with the LR-4, 4th-order case for reference. As expected, the LR-4 is 80 dB down one decade away from the

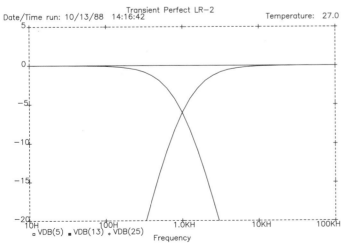

Figure 8. LR-2 amplitude response

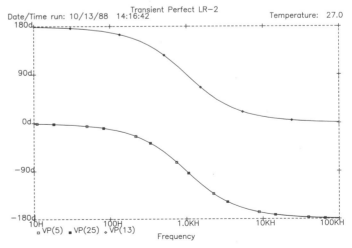

Figure 9. LR-2 phase response

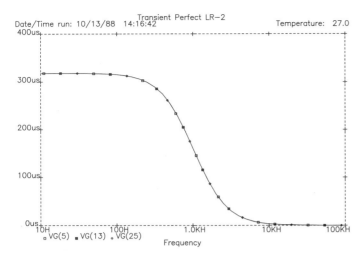

Figure 10. LR-2 group delay

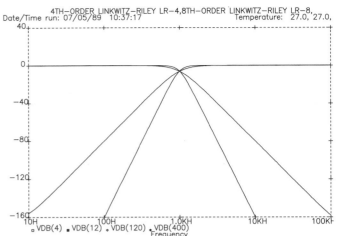

Figure 12. LR-4 and LR-8 slopes

corner frequency, while the LR-8 is twice that, or 160 dB down. Of interest here, are the potential benefits of narrowing the crossover region by using a LR-8 alignment.

Figure 13 magnifies the responses shown in Figure 12 to reveal a clearer picture of the narrower crossover region, as well as showing the flat summed responses. (The slight difference in summed amplitudes at the crossover frequency is due to a slight gain difference between the two circuits.) The critical crossover region for the LR-8 case is one-half of what it is for the LR-4 case. The exact definition of where the crossover region begins and ends is ambiguous, but, by whatever definition, the region has been halved.

As an example of this, a very conservative definition might be where the responses are 1 dB down from their respective passbands. We would then refer to the crossover region as extending from the -1 dB point on the low-pass response to the -1 dB point on the high-pass response. For LR-8, these points are 769 Hz and 1301 Hz respectively, yielding a crossover region only ¾-octave wide. As a comparative reference, the LR-4 case yields -1 dB points at 591 Hz and 1691 Hz, for a 1.5-octave wide region.

For the LR-8 case, it is interesting to note that the -1 dB point on the low-pass curve corresponds almost exactly to the

-20 dB point on the high-pass curve (the exact points occur at 760 Hz and 1316 Hz). So if you want to define the region as where the response is down 20 dB, you get the same answer. The entire region for the LR-8 case is ¾-octave wide, or it is one-half this number for each driver. That is, the loudspeaker driver (referred to as 'driver' from now on) has to be well behaved for only about 0.4 octave beyond the crossover point. This compares with the 4th-order case where the same driver must behave for 0.8 octave.

The above is quite conservative. If other reference points are used, say, the -3 dB points (895 Hz & 1117 Hz), then the LR-8 crossover region is just 1/3-octave wide, and drivers only have to stay linear for 1/6-octave. (1/6-octave away from the crossover frequency the drive signal is attenuated by 12 dB, so the output driver is operating at about 1/16 power.)

The extremely steep slopes offer greater driver protection and linear operation. Beyond the driver's linear limits all frequencies attenuate so quickly that most nonlinearities and interaction ceases being significant. Because of this, the driver need not be as well behaved outside the crossover frequency. It is not required to reproduce frequencies it was not designed for. For similar reasons, power handling capability can be improved for HF drivers as well. And this

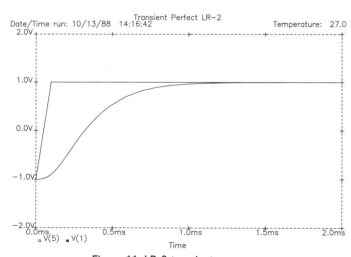

Figure 11. LR-2 transient response

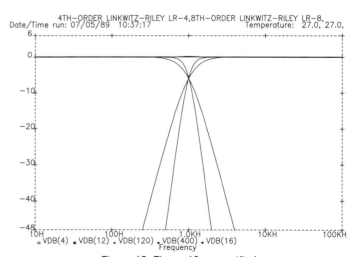

Figure 13. Figure 12 mangnified

narrower crossover region lessens the need for precise driver time alignment since the affected spectrum is so small.

The caveat, though, is an increased difficulty in designing good systems with sharp slopes. The loudspeakers involved have differing transient responses, polar patterns and power responses. This means the system designer must know the driver characteristics thoroughly. Ironically, sometimes loudspeaker overlap helps the system blend better even when on-axis amplitude response is flat.

LR-8 Phase Response

Figure 14 shows the respective phase response for LR-4 (upper trace) and LR-8 (lower trace) designs. As predicted by the vector diagram in Figure 7b, the LR-4 case has 180° (4x45°) of phase shift at the crossover frequency. Thus, the output signal is out-of-phase with the input signal at the crossover frequency for the LR-4 case. Both outputs are in-phase with each other, but out-of-phase with the input.

The LR-8 design eliminates this out-of-phase condition by bringing the outputs back in sync with the input signal at the crossover frequency. The lower trace shows the 360° phase shift for the LR-8 alignment.

LR-8 Transient Response

Butterworth functions do not have linear phase shift and consequently do not exhibit constant group delay. (First-order networks are not classified as Butterworth.) Since Linkwitz-Riley designs (higher than LR-2) are cascaded Butterworth, they also do not have constant group delay.

Group delay is just a measure of the non-linearity of phase shift. A direct function of non-linear phase behavior is overshoot and damping time for a step response. The transient behavior of all Linkwitz-Riley designs (greater than 2nd-order) is classic Butterworth in nature. That is, the filters exhibit slight overshoot when responding to a step response, and take time to damp down.

Figure 15 compares LR-8 and LR-4 designs and shows the greater overshoot and damping time for the 8th-order case. The overshoot is 15% for the LR-4 case and twice that, or about 30%, for the LR-8 case. As expected, the LR-8 design takes about twice as long to damp down. The initial rise-time differences are due to the group delay value differences.

Is It Audible?

The conservative answer says it is not audible to the overwhelming majority of audio professionals. Under laboratory conditions, some people hear a difference on non-musical tones (clicks and square waves).

The practical answer says it is not audible to anyone for real sound systems reproducing real audio signals.

Linkwitz-Riley Power Response

Linkwitz-Riley alignments produce constant voltage response (voltage vectors sum to unity) at the crossover frequency, but they may produce constant power. At the crossover frequency, each voltage output is ½ of normal. This produces ½ the normal current into the loudspeakers. Since power is the product of voltage times current, the power is ¼ of normal. Considering a simple two-way system, the combined total power at the crossover frequency will be ½ of normal (¼ from each driver), producing a dip of 3 dB at the crossover frequency in the overall power response, *provided there is no additional phase shift contributed by the drivers themselves — such is never the case.*

The power response of loudspeakers with noncoincident drivers is a complex problem. See the Vanderkooy and Lipshitz[5] study for complete details.

These responses are just for the electronic filters. For real world results including driver response, see Siegfried Linkwitz's website at www.linkwitzlab.com/frontiers.htm#F.

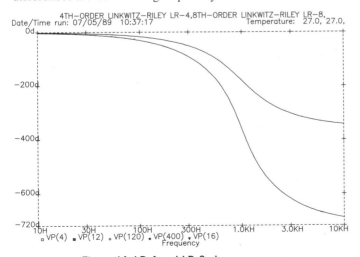

Figure 14. LR-4 and LR-8 phase response

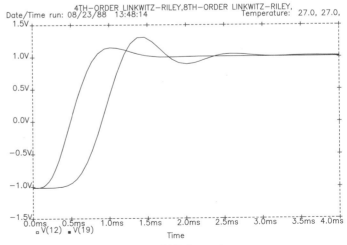

Figure 15. LR-4 and LR-8 transient response

References

1. S. Linkwitz, 'Active Crossover Networks for Non-Coincident Drivers,' *J. Audio Eng. Soc.,* vol. 24, pp. 2-8 (Jan./Feb. 1976).

2. D. Bohn, 'A Fourth-Order State-Variable Filter for Linkwitz-Riley Active Crossover Designs,' presented at the 74th Convention of the Audio Engineering Society, *J. Audio Eng. Soc.* (Abstracts), vol. 31, p. 960 (Dec. 1983), preprint 2011.

3. D. Bohn, 'An 8th-Order State-Variable Filter for Linkwitz-Riley Active Crossover Designs,' presented at the 85th Convention of the Audio Engineering Society, *J. Audio Eng. Soc.* (Abstracts), vol. 36, p. 1024 (Dec. 1988), preprint 2697.

4. P. Garde, 'All-Pass Crossover Systems,' *J. Audio Eng. Soc.,* vol. 28, pp. 575-584 (Sep. 1980).

5. J. Vanderkooy & S.P. Lipshitz, "Power Response of Loudspeakers with Noncoincident Drivers — The Influence of Crossover Design," *J. Audio Eng. Soc.*, Vol. 34, No. 4, pp. 236-244 (Apr. 1986).

A Bessel Filter Crossover, and Its Relation to Others

- **Crossovers**

- **Bessel Functions**

- **Phase Shift**

- **Group Delay**

Ray Miller
Rane Corporation

RaneNote 147
© 1998, 2002 Rane Corporation

INTRODUCTION

One of the ways that a crossover may be constructed from a Bessel low-pass filter employs the standard low-pass to high-pass transformation. Various frequency normalizations can be chosen for best magnitude and polar response, although the linear phase approximation in the passband of the low-pass is not maintained at higher frequencies. The resulting crossover is compared to the Butterworth and Linkwitz-Riley types in terms of the magnitude, phase, and time domain responses.

A BRIEF REVIEW OF CROSSOVERS

There are many choices for crossovers today, due especially to the flexibility of digital signal processing. We now have added incentive to examine unconventional crossover types. Each type has its own tradeoffs between constraints of flatness, cutoff slope, polar response, and phase response. See [1] and [2] for more complete coverage of crossover constraints and types. Much of the content of this paper is closely related to previous work by Lipshitz and Vanderkooy in [3].

Our sensitivity to frequency response flatness makes this one of the highest priorities. It is often used as a starting point when choosing a crossover type.

Cutoff slopes of at least 12 dB per octave are usually chosen because of limitations in the frequency range that drivers can faithfully reproduce. Even this is less than optimal for most drivers.

Polar response is the combined magnitude versus listening angle from noncoincident drivers [4]. The ideal case is a large lobe in the polar response directly in front of the drivers, and happens when low-pass and high-pass outputs are in-phase.

The phase response of a crossover is one of its most subtle aspects, and so is often ignored. A purely linear phase shift, which is equivalent to a time delay, is otherwise inaudible, as is a small non-linear phase shift. Still, there is evidence that phase coloration is audible in certain circumstances [5], and certainly some people are more sensitive to it than others.

A first-order crossover is unique, in that it sums with a flat magnitude response and zero resultant phase shift, although the low-pass and high-pass outputs are in phase quadrature (90 degrees), and the drivers must perform over a huge frequency range. The phase quadrature that is characteristic of odd-order crossovers results in a moderate shift in the polar response lobe.

In spite of this, third-order Butterworth has been popular for its flat sound pressure *and* power responses, and 18 dB per octave cutoff slope.

Second-order crossovers have historically been chosen for their simplicity, and a usable 12 dB per octave cutoff.

Fourth-order Linkwitz-Riley presents an attractive option, with flat summed response, 24 dB per octave cutoff, and outputs which are always in phase with each other, producing optimal polar response.

Steeper cutoff slopes are known to require higher orders with greater phase shift, which for the linear phase case is equivalent to more time delay.

A number of other novel and useful designs exist which should be considered when choosing a crossover. Generating the high-pass output by subtracting the low-pass output from an appropriately time-delayed version of the input results in a linear phase crossover, with tradeoffs in cutoff slope, polar response, and flatness [1]. Overlapping the design frequencies and equalizing the response can result in a linear phase crossover [3], with a tradeoff in polar response. A crossover with perfect polar response can be designed with a compromise in phase response or cutoff slope [6].

WHAT IS A BESSEL CROSSOVER?

The Bessel filter was not originally designed for use in a crossover, and requires minor modification to make it work properly. The purpose of the Bessel filter is to achieve approximately linear phase, linear phase being equivalent to a time delay. This is the best phase response from an audible standpoint, assuming you don't want to correct an existing phase shift.

Bessels are historically low-pass or all-pass. A crossover however requires a separate high-pass, and this needs to be derived from the low-pass. There are different ways to derive a high-pass from a low-pass, but here we discuss a natural and traditional one that maximizes the cutoff slope in the high-pass. Deriving this high-pass Bessel, we find that it no longer has linear phase. Other derivations of the high-pass can improve the combined phase response, but with tradeoffs.

Two other issues that are closely related to each other are the attenuation at the design frequency, and the summed response. The traditional Bessel design is not ideal here. We can easily change this by shifting the low or high-pass up or down in frequency. This way, we can adjust the low-pass vs. high-pass response overlap, and at the same time achieve a phase difference between the low-pass and high-pass that is nearly constant over all frequencies. In the fourth order case this is 360 degrees, or essentially in-phase. In fact, the second and fourth order cases are comparable to a Linkwitz-Riley with slightly more rounded cutoff!

BESSEL LOW-PASS AND HIGH-PASS FILTERS

The focus of this paper is on crossovers derived using traditional methods, which begin with an all-pole lowpass filter with transfer function (Laplace Transform) of the form $1/p(s)$, where $p(s)$ is a polynomial whose roots are the poles.

The Bessel filter uses a $p(s)$ which is a Bessel polynomial, but the filter is more properly called a Thomson filter, after one of its developers [7]. Still less known is the fact that it was actually reported several years earlier by Kiyasu [8].

Bessel low-pass filters have maximally flat group delay about 0 Hz [9], so the phase response is approximately linear in the passband, while at higher frequencies the linearity degrades, and the group delay drops to zero (see Fig. 1 and 2). This nonlinearity has minimal impact because it occurs primarily when the output level is low. In fact, the phase response is so close to a time delay that Bessel low-pass and all-pass filters may be used solely to produce a time delay, as described in [10].

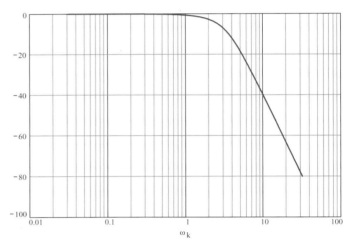

Fig. 1 Fourth-Order Bessel Magnitude

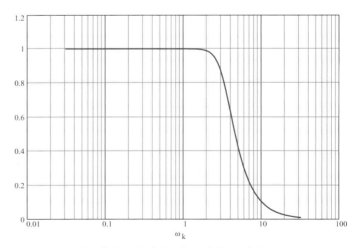

Fig. 2 Fourth-Order Bessel Group Delay

The high-pass output transfer function may be generated in different ways, one of which is to replace every instance of s in the low-pass with $1/s$. This "flips" the magnitude response about the design frequency to yield the high-pass. Characteristics of the low-pass with respect to 0 Hz are, in the high-pass, with respect to infinite frequency instead. A number of other high-pass derivations are possible, but they result in compromised cutoff slope or polar response (see [1]). These are beyond the scope of this paper.

This popular method results in the general transfer function (1); (2) is a fourth-order Bessel example.

$$\frac{1}{c_0 + c_1 \cdot \left(\frac{1}{s}\right) + c_2 \cdot \left(\frac{1}{s}\right)^2 + \ldots + c_n \cdot \left(\frac{1}{s}\right)^n} = \frac{s^n}{c_n + c_{n-1} \cdot s + c_{n-2} \cdot s^2 + \ldots + c_0 \cdot s^n} \quad (1)$$

$$\frac{1}{1 + \left(\frac{1}{s}\right) + \frac{9}{21} \cdot \left(\frac{1}{s}\right)^2 + \frac{2}{21} \cdot \left(\frac{1}{s}\right)^3 + \frac{1}{105} \cdot \left(\frac{1}{s}\right)^4} = \frac{s^4}{\frac{1}{105} + \frac{2}{21} \cdot s + \frac{9}{21} \cdot s^2 + s^3 + s^4} \quad (2)$$

Note the reversed coefficient order of the high-pass as compared to the low-pass, once it's converted to a polynomial in s, and an added n^{th}-order zero at the origin. This zero has a counterpart in the low-pass, an implicit n^{th}-order zero at infinity! The nature of the response of the high-pass follows from equation (3) below, where s is evaluated on the imaginary axis to yield the frequency response.

$$s = j\omega, \quad p\left(\frac{1}{j\omega}\right) = p(-j\omega_h), \quad \omega_h = \frac{1}{\omega} \quad (3)$$

The magnitude responses of the low-pass and the high-pass are mirror images of each other on a log-frequency scale; the negative sign has no effect on this. The phase of the low-pass typically *drops* near the cutoff frequency from an asymptote of zero as the frequency is *increased*, and asymptotically approaches a negative value. However, in addition to being mirror images on a log-frequency scale, the phase of the high-pass is the negative of the low-pass, which follows from the negative sign in (3). So the phase *rises* from zero at high frequency, and approaches a positive value asymtotically as the frequency is *decreased*. This results in offset curves with similar shape. Any asymmetry of the s-shaped phase curve is mirrored between the low-pass and high-pass. See Figure 5 for a second-order example, where the phase curve also has inherent symmetry.

One special case is where the denominator polynomial p(s) has symmetric coefficients, where the nth coefficient is equal to the constant term; the $(n-1)^{st}$ coefficient is equal to the linear term, etc. This is the case for Butterworth and therefore the Linkwitz-Riley types [3]. A fourth-order Linkwitz-Riley is given as an example in equation (4).

$$\frac{1}{1 + 2 \cdot \sqrt{2} \cdot s + 4 \cdot s^2 + 2 \cdot \sqrt{2} \cdot s^3 + s^4} \quad (4)$$

When this is the case, coefficient reversal has no effect on p(s), and the high-pass differs from the low-pass only in the numerator term s^n. This numerator can easily be shown to produce a constant phase shift of 90, 180, 270, or 360 degrees (360 is in-phase in the frequency domain), with respect to the low-pass, when frequency response is evaluated on the

imaginary axis. For the second-order case $s^2 = (j\omega)^2 = -\omega^2$ and the minus sign indicates a polarity reversal (or 180-degree phase shift at all frequencies).

NORMALIZATIONS

Filter transfer functions are normalized by convention for

$$\omega_0 = 1, \left(f = \frac{1}{2 \cdot \pi} \text{ Hz}\right)$$

and are then designed for a particular frequency by replacing every instance of s in the transfer function by

$$\frac{s}{\omega_0}, \quad \omega_0 = 2 \cdot \pi \cdot f_0$$

This has the effect of shifting the magnitude and phase responses right or left when viewed on a log-frequency scale. Of course, it doesn't affect the shapes of these response curves, since when the transfer functions are evaluated:

$$f\left(\frac{s}{\omega_0}\right) = f\left(\frac{j\omega}{\omega_0}\right) = f(jy), \quad y = \frac{\omega}{\omega_0} \quad (5)$$

where y is a constant multiple of the variable frequency. The group delay, being the negative derivative of the phase with respect to angular frequency, is also scaled up or down.

This process can also be used to adjust the overlap between the low-pass and high-pass filters, so as to modify the summed response. After this is done, the filters are still normalized as before, and may be designed for a particular frequency. Adjusting the overlap will be done here with a normalization constant u, which will be applied equally but oppositely to both the low-pass and high-pass. In the low-pass, s is replaced by (s/u), and in the high-pass, s is replaced by (su). The low-pass response is shifted right (u > 1) or left (u < 1) when viewed on a log frequency scale, and the high-pass response is shifted in the opposite direction.

These overlap normalizations may be based on the magnitude response of either output at the design frequency, chosen for the flattest summed response, for a particular phase shift, or any other criterion.

Normalization influences the symmetry of p(s), but perfect symmetry is not achievable in general. This means that it will not always be possible to make the low-pass and high-pass phase response differ *exactly* by a constant multiple of 90 degrees for some normalization. The situation can be clarified by normalization for $c_n = 1$, as done by Lipshitz and Vanderkooy in [1] and [5], where $c_0 = 1$ for unity gain at 0 Hz. This form reveals any inherent asymmetry. Equation (6) shows the general low-pass, while (7) is the fourth-order Bessel denominator. Note that it becomes *nearly* symmetric, and relatively similar to the Linkwitz-Riley in (4).

$$c_0 = 1$$

$$s \longrightarrow \frac{s}{\sqrt[n]{c_n}}$$

$$\frac{1}{c_0 + c_1 \cdot s + c_2 \cdot s^2 + \ldots + c_n \cdot s^n} \longrightarrow \frac{1}{1 + k_1 \cdot s + k_2 \cdot s^2 + \ldots + k_n \cdot s^n} \quad (6)$$

$$1 + s + \frac{9}{21} \cdot s^2 + \frac{2}{21} \cdot s^3 + \frac{1}{105} \cdot s^4 \longrightarrow 1 + 3.2011 \cdot s + 4.3916 \cdot s^2 + 3.1239 \cdot s^3 + s^4 \quad (7)$$

PHASE-MATCHED BESSELS

The textbook low-pass Bessel is often designed for an approximate time delay of

$$t_o = \frac{1}{\omega_o}$$

rather than for the common -3 dB or -6 dB level at the design frequency used for crossovers. This design will be used as a reference, to which other normalizations are compared. The low-pass and high-pass have quite a lot of overlap, with very little attenuation at the design frequency, as shown in Figure 3, for a second-order Bessel with one output inverted.

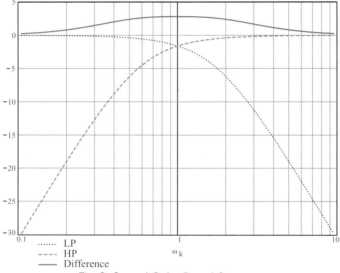

Fig. 3 Second-Order Bessel Crossover

Bessel polynomials of degree three or higher are not inherently symmetric, but may be normalized to be nearly symmetric by requiring a phase shift at the design frequency of 45 degrees per order, negative for the low-pass, positive for the high-pass. This results in a fairly constant relative phase between the low-pass and high-pass at all other frequencies. Equation (8) shows an equation for deriving the normalization constant of the fourth-order Bessel, where the imaginary part of the denominator (7) is set to zero for 180-degree phase shift at the design frequency.

$$s = j\omega_p, \quad \omega_p - \frac{2}{21}\cdot\omega_p^3 = 0, \quad u = \frac{1}{\omega_p} = \frac{1}{\sqrt{10.5}} \quad (8)$$

This normalization is not new, but was presented in a slightly different context in [5], with a normalization constant of 0.9759, which is the square of the ratio of the phase-match u in equation (8) to the u implied by equations (6) and (7), the fourth root of $\frac{1}{105}$.

Since the phase nonlinearity of the high-pass is now in the passband, the crossover resulting from the sum of the two approaches phase linearity only at lower frequencies. This doesn't preclude it from being a useful crossover.

The summed magnitude response of the Bessel normalized by the 45-degree criterion is fairly flat, within 2 dB for the second-order and fourth-order. We may adjust the overlap slightly for flattest magnitude response instead, at the expense of the polar response. Figures 4-6 show the results of four

normalizations for the second-order filter. The -3 dB and phase-match normalizations are illustrated in Figures 5 and 6. Note that for the second-order phase-match design, low-pass and high-pass group delays are exactly the same.

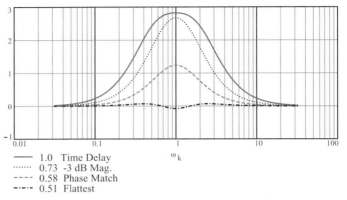

— 1.0 Time Delay
⋯⋯ 0.73 -3 dB Mag.
--- 0.58 Phase Match
-⋅-⋅- 0.51 Flattest

Fig. 4 Comparison of Second-Order Bessel Sums

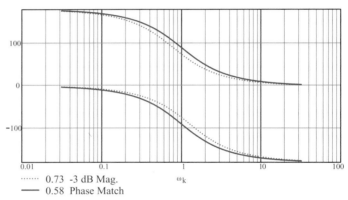

⋯⋯ 0.73 -3 dB Mag.
— 0.58 Phase Match

Fig. 5 Comparison of Second-Order Phase

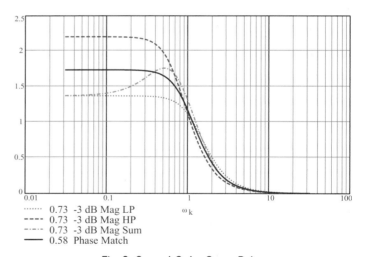

⋯⋯ 0.73 -3 dB Mag LP
--- 0.73 -3 dB Mag HP
-⋅-⋅- 0.73 -3 dB Mag Sum
— 0.58 Phase Match

Fig. 6 Second-Order Group Delay

The fourth-order is illustrated in Figures 7-9, Figure 7 being a 3-D plot of frequency response versus normalization. Figure 8 shows four cases, which are cross-sections of Figure 7. The phase-match case has good flatness as well as the best polar response. The fourth-order Linkwitz-Riley is very similar to the Bessel normalized by 0.31. The third-order Bessel magnitude has comparable behavior.

In a real application, phase shifts and amplitude variations in the drivers will require some adjustment of the overlap for best performance. The sensitivity of the crossover response to normalization should be considered [2].

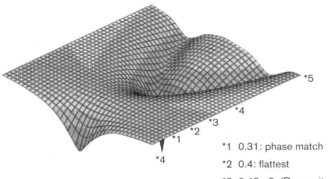

*1 0.31: phase match

*2 0.4: flattest

*3 0.48: -3 dB magnitude

*4 0.64: cancellation

*5 1.0: time delay design

Fig. 7 Summed Fourth-Order Bessel Frequency Response vs. Normalization. Normalization values are relative to time delay design.

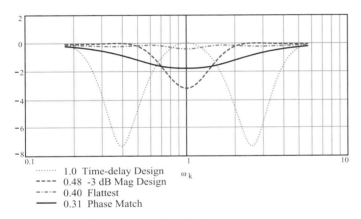

.... 1.0 Time-delay Design
- - - - 0.48 -3 dB Mag Design
- · - · 0.40 Flattest
——— 0.31 Phase Match

Fig. 8 Summed Fourth-Order Responses

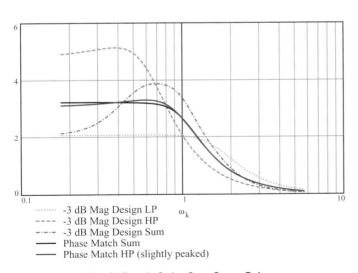

.... -3 dB Mag Design LP
- - - - -3 dB Mag Design HP
- · - · -3 dB Mag Design Sum
——— Phase Match Sum
——— Phase Match HP (slightly peaked)

Fig. 9 Fourth-Order Sum Group Delays

COMPARISON OF TYPES

Butterworth, Linkwitz-Riley, and Bessel crossovers may be thought of as very separate types, while in fact they are all particular cases in a continuous space of possible crossovers. The separate and summed magnitude responses are distinct but comparable, as can be seen by graphing them together (Figure 10). The Bessel and Linkwitz-Riley are the most similar. The Butterworth has the sharpest initial cutoff, and a +3dB sum at crossover. The Linkwitz-Riley has moderate rolloff and a flat sum. The Bessel has the widest, most gradual crossover region, and a gentle dip in the summed response. All responses converge at frequencies far from the design frequency.

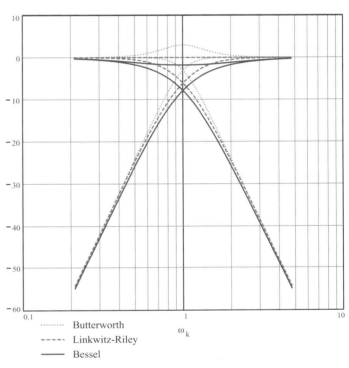

.... Butterworth
- - - - Linkwitz-Riley
——— Bessel

Fig. 10 Fourth-Order Magnitudes

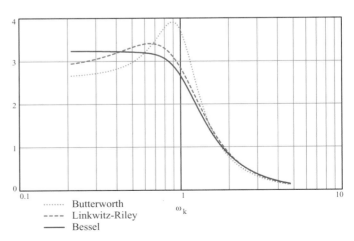

.... Butterworth
- - - - Linkwitz-Riley
——— Bessel

Fig. 11 Fourth-Order Group Delays

Bessel-5

Normalization with respect to time delay design	Low-pass Denominator Polynomial	High-pass Denominator Polynomial
1	$1+s+\frac{1}{3}\cdot s^2$	$\frac{1}{3}+s+s^2$
1	$1+s+\frac{2}{5}\cdot s^2+\frac{1}{15}\cdot s^3$	$\frac{1}{15}+\frac{2}{5}\cdot s+s^2+s^3$
1	$1+s+\frac{9}{21}\cdot s^2+\frac{2}{21}\cdot s^3+\frac{1}{105}\cdot s^4$	$\frac{1}{105}+\frac{2}{21}\cdot s+\frac{9}{21}\cdot s^2+s^3+s^4$
$\frac{1}{\sqrt{3}}=0.5774$	$1+\sqrt{3}\cdot s+s^2$	$1+\sqrt{3}\cdot s+s^2$
0.4030	$1+2.481\cdot s+2.463\cdot s^2+1.018\cdot s^3$	$1.018+2.463\cdot s+2.481\cdot s^2+s^3$
$\frac{1}{\sqrt{10.5}}=0.3086$	$1+3.240\cdot s+4.5\cdot s^2+3.240\cdot s^3+1.050\cdot s^4$	$1.050+3.240\cdot s+4.5\cdot s^2+3.240\cdot s^3+s^4$

Table 1 - Bessel Crossovers of Second, Third, and Fourth-Order, Normalized First for Time Delay Design, then for Phase Match at Crossover

The phase responses also look similar, but the amount of peaking in the group delay curve varies somewhat, as shown in Figure 11. There is no peaking in the Bessel low-pass, while there is a little in the high-pass for orders > 2. The summed response has only a little peaking. The group delay curve is directly related to the behaviour in the time domain, as discussed in [11]. The most overshoot and ringing is exhibited by the Butterworth design, and the least by the Bessel.

Often when discussing crossovers, the low-pass step response is considered by itself, while the high-pass and summed step response is usually far from ideal, except in the case of the linear phase crossover; this has been known for some time [12], but step-response graphs of higher-order crossovers are generally avoided out of good taste!

Table 1 gives Bessel crossover denominators normalized for time delay and phase match. Note the near-perfect symmetry for the (last three) phase-match cases.

SUMMARY

It is seen that a Bessel crossover designed as described above is not radically different from other common types, particularly compared to the Linkwitz-Riley. It does not maintain linear phase response at higher frequencies, but has the most linear phase of the three discussed, along with fairly good magnitude flatness and minimal lobing for the even orders. It is one good choice when the drivers used have a wide enough range to support the wider crossover region, and when good transient behaviour is desired.

A version of this RaneNote was presented at the 105th Convention of the Audio Engineering Society, San Francisco, CA, 1998

REFERENCES

[1] S.P. Lipshitz and J. Vanderkooy, "A Family of Linear-Phase Crossover Networks of High Slope Derived by Time Delay", *J. Aud. Eng. Soc*, vol 31, pp2-20 (1983 Jan/Feb.).

[2] Robert M. Bullock,III, "Loudspeaker-Crossover Systems: An Optimal Choice," *J. Audio Eng. Soc*, vol. 30, p486 (1982 July/ Aug.)

[3] S.P. Lipshitz and J. Vanderkooy, "Use of Frequency Overlap and Equalization to Produce High-Slope Linear-Phase Loud-speaker Crossover Networks," *J. Audio Eng. Soc*, vol. 33, pp114-126 (1985 March)

[4] S.H. Linkwitz, "Active Crossover Networks For Non-Coincident Drivers, " *J. Audio Eng Soc*, vol. 24, pp 2-8 (1976 Jan/Feb.).

[5] S.P. Lipshitz, M Pocock and J. Vanderkooy "On the Audibility of Midrange Phase Distortion in Audio Systems," *J. Audio Eng. Soc*, vol 30, pp 580-595 (1982 Sept.)

[6] S.P. Lipshitz and J. Vanderkooy, "In Phase Crossover Network Design," *J. Audio Eng. Soc*, vol 34, p889 (1986 Nov.)

[7] W.E. Thomson, "Delay Networks Having Maximally Flat Frequency Characteristics," *Proc IEEE*, part 3, vol. 96, Nov. 1949, pp. 487-490.

[8] Z. Kiyasu, "On A Design Method of Delay Networks," *J. Inst. Electr. Commun. Eng.*, Japan, vol. 26, pp. 598-610, August, 1943.

[9] L. P. Huelsman and P. E. Allen, *Introduction to the Theory and Design of Active Filters*," McGraw-Hill, New York, 1980, p. 89.

[10] Dennis G. Fink, "Time Offset and Crossover Design," *J. Audio Eng Soc*, vol. 28:9, pp601-611 (1980 Sept)

[11] Wieslaw R. Woszczyk, "Bessel Filters as Loudspeaker Crossovers," Audio Eng. Soc. Preprint 1949 (1982 Oct.)

[12] J.R. Ashley, "On the Transient Response of Ideal Crossover Networks," *J. Audio Eng. Soc*, vol 10, pp241-244 (1962 July)

©Rane Corporation   10802 47th Ave. W., Mukilteo WA 98275-5098 USA   TEL (425)355-6000   FAX (425)347-7757   WEB http://www.rane.com

Squeeze Me, Stretch Me: The DC 24 Users Guide

- **DYNAMICS 101**

- **THRESHOLD & RATIO CONTROLS**

- **COMPRESSORS & LIMITERS**

- **GATES & EXPANDERS**

- **SPLIT BAND PROCESSING**

- **GUITAR, BASS & RECORDING**

INTRODUCTION

Compressors, expanders, and their cohorts – limiters and gates, are all in the business of automatically controlling the volume, or dynamics of sound. Lumped together they can be called dynamic controllers, which would also have to include your hand on the fader and the fat man dancing in front of the midrange cabinet.

Used wisely, often in conjunction with each other or with equalization or filtering, dynamic controllers can improve the intelligibility of voice and the subjective effect of music. But in the wrong hands they can sound terrible, and compressors are the worst offenders.

Our goal is to de-mystify dynamic controllers as best we can within the limitations of printed media. By understanding a given tool's strengths and weaknesses, you can put it to it's best use.

Roger Nichols - "I have used the DC 24 on every album project I have done since I've had it". He has had a DC 24 since 1988. Projects include mixdown on Riki Lee Jones *Flying Cowboys*, recording and mixdown on Donald Fagens *Kamakiriad*, and numerous others.

Walter Becker - "The DC 24 is great for bass and guitar. I suggest you check it out". Walter is a member of the popular group, *Steely Dan*.

Jeff Davies
Dennis Bohn
Rane Corporation

RaneNote 130
© 1993 Rane Corporation

DYNAMICS 101: A PRIMER

Let's start with what a dynamic controller actually does. No matter how you cut it, these are electronic volume controls. It is a hand on a control, turning the volume down and turning it up again. The hand is really quick and really accurate, but it's just turning a volume control.

SIGNAL CHAIN

Conceptually, dynamic controllers have two internal paths, the signal and the side chains. The signal chain is the path the main signal takes through the unit: through the input circuits, the gain control device and then through the output circuits. The signal chain goes through the "volume control" in the "hand on a control" analogy.

SIDE CHAIN

The side chain is the hand which turns the control. Side chain circuitry examines the input signal and issues a control voltage to adjust the amplification of the signal. There are a number of parameters governing side chain activity, but the four most commonly discussed are threshold, ratio (or slope), attack time and release time. Some dynamic controllers offer adjustment of each of these parameters, while others have one or more preset at an optimum setting for the application.

THRESHOLD

The threshold, like crossing through a doorway, is the point at which gain adjustment begins. When the input signal is below the threshold, a dynamic controller should be like a straight wire. Above, the side chain asserts itself and turns the volume down.

RATIO

Once the threshold is exceeded, just how far the volume goes down depends on the ratio (or slope) setting. An ordinary preamp or a straight wire has a ratio of 1:1, that is, the output level tracks the input level perfectly. A 2dB change at the input produces a 2dB change at the output. A severe ratio is perhaps 8:1 or 10:1. For a 10:1 ratio, a 10 dB blast at the input would rise only 1 dB at the output – *heavy* compression. Kinder, gentler ratios are in the 2:1 to 3:1 range.

ATTACK TIME

Attack time is the time which passes between the moment the input signal exceeds the threshold and the moment that the gain is actually reduced. Attack times generally range between 1ms and 30ms.

RELEASE TIME

Release time is the time which passes between the moment the input signal drops below the threshold and the moment that the gain is restored. Typical release times are between .1 seconds and 4 seconds.

Some of the oldest compressors were called levelers, which are becoming popular again. They had very slow attack times and very long release times to provide volume adjustment of overall program level for broadcast. If you shouted repeatedly, the level would slowly fall off for about 30 seconds, then it would take another minute or so to recover.

COMPRESSORS

A compressor, when the input signal reaches the level set by the Threshold control, begins turning down the signal by an amount set by the Ratio control. Most modern compressors make the loud signals quieter, but do not make the quiet parts louder. (However, by keeping the loud signals under control, you can turn up the output level which will make the quiet parts louder along with the rest of the signal.) Some compressor designs actually do raise quiet signals below the threshold. These designs might be called "upward expanders".

LIMITERS

A limiter is a special form of compressor set up especially to reduce peaks for overload protection. In other words, it is a compressor with a maximum ratio. A compressor is usually set up to change the dynamics for purposes of aesthetics, intelligibility, or recording or broadcast limitations. Once the threshold of a limiter is reached, no more signal is allowed through. A limiter has a relatively high threshold, very fast attack and release times and a very high ratio, approaching infinity:1.

EXPANDERS

An expander is a compressor running in reverse. *Above* the threshold, a compressor reduces the gain; *below* the threshold an expander reduces the gain. A compressor keeps the loud parts from getting too loud, an expander makes the quiet parts quieter.

GATES

A gate is an expander with the ratio turned up. With the proper settings (low threshold and a high ratio), a gate can be applied to remove noise between louder sounds, and is often called a noise gate for the way it can lock out background noise.

GATE / EXPANDERS

A low ratio acts as an expander that turns quieter signals down, while a high ratio acts as a gate that shuts signals off.

SIDE CHAIN EXTRA #1: SEND/RETURN

The gain control voltage is derived from the side chain audio. If you were to put a signal with treble boost into the side chain audio, it would not effect the treble in the main signal path, but it would cause the high frequencies to cross the threshold sooner or more often. Large peaks of treble could be set to cause heavy compression with virtually no compression at other times. What we've just designed here is the basic de-esser, a circuit to remove excess sibilance. With a bass boost you can make a de-thumper and with a midrange boost a de-nasaler. Most compressors have a send and return available in a side chain loop to patch in an equalizer for these purposes.

SIDE CHAIN EXTRA #2: SLAVE

Many compressors and expanders make the side chain control voltage available to connect to a neighboring unit, or to tie internal channels together. This is called slaving or linking the compressors, and it causes the units to compress simultaneously when only one has an input over the threshold. This feature is normally used to preserve stable stereo imaging, or to preserve spectral balance when the compressors are used in the high and low frequency ranges of a mono signal.

THIS IS ALL VERY INTERESTING. SO WHAT'S THE PROBLEM?

The problem is that heavy compression (low threshold and a high ratio), almost always has nasty side effects. In the first place, the timbre of the sound itself changes; it becomes "hard" and "closed" and not nearly as sweet and open as the sounds you envisioned when you got into this business. Second, attack times optimized for pleasant compression will not track initial transients quickly enough, and many instruments audibly suffer. Third, heavy compression will usually be accompanied by "breathing," i.e., the background noise rises way out of proportion to the foreground sound as the compressor releases. Bottom line: it just doesn't sound good. Take anybody's compressor, run just about any sound through it, compress it severely and run the results on Family Feud: survey says, 89% of the audience won't like it.

SO WHAT'S THE SOLUTION?

Many designs have appeared throughout the years to produce gentle, smooth, natural-sounding compression. They include tubes, FETs, VCAs, soft-knee compressors, electro-optical attenuators, and self-adjusting attack and release times. Today, some digital workstations compress without snipping transients, by looking ahead into the digital future. Is that cheating or what? So what has Rane done to make its compressors sound so great?

An independent panel of judges has studied Rane's compressor designs and unanimously decided there has been no cheating. Rane has combined a number of perfectly even handed, meat-and-potatoes ideas to make its compressors so capable and transparent that we just *seem* like we're not being fair.

IDEA NUMBER ONE

Use self-adjusting attack and release times. The compressor and expander sections in the DC 24 change attack and release times automatically to suit the program material by using dedicated RMS-sensing ICs in the side chain. If the input is predominantly low-frequency, the times are made more gradual and slowed. If a quick transient comes flashing down the wires, the times are tightened to deal with it. Our experience has shown that attack and release controls, when present, are confusing and easy to misalign.

IDEA NUMBER TWO

Combine an expander/gate function with the compressor. The expander/gate, the compressor (and the limiter: see Idea Number Three) in the DC 24 can be used independently, but a big reason they are together is to share the work of clean compression. An expanded or gated source of sound exhibits less "breathing" when compressed. Instead of looking for another patch cord when you realize you need a bit of gating, you just turn a control.

IDEA NUMBER THREE

Combine a peak limiter function with the compressor. Tracking with this idea of burden-sharing, Rane has put a peak limiter in the same path as the expander and the compressor in the DC 24. With a limiter right there, you won't be asking the compressor to clamp the wild excursions. The limiter, with auto-attack, auto-release and adjustable threshold optimized, will play level police while the compressor persuades more gently.

Rane designed a patented servo-locked limiting circuit, which places the limiter within a servo loop and effectively stops peaks from exceeding the threshold. The attack time varies with the source material, but is never allowed to produce diode-like hard clipping.

REALLY GREAT IDEA NUMBER FOUR, WHICH DESERVES ITS OWN SECTION

Here's the special twist in the DC 24: the two sections, fabulous as they are, can also be assigned to *different frequency ranges* of the same channel of sound. This is not a new idea, but it's a great idea. In the past, the difficulty has been that split-band compression has required a lot of equipment: at least two compressors and a set of bandpass filters per channel, or a very expensive difficult-to-set large unit. What the DC 24 offers is not just innovative engineering but a lot of powerful, interactive functions crammed into one rack space.

SPLIT-BAND DYNAMIC PROCESSING

We haven't talked much about split-band processing, but it's one of the easiest ways to compress transparently. Broadcast stations have used split-band compression for years, often dividing the spectrum into four or five bands. When it's done right, the radio station sounds great: loud, present, with no squashing or pumping at all.

The great Dolby noise reduction systems, from Dolby A all the way through B, C, S and SR, all use some variation on compression, expansion and band-splitting. Dolby's goal has always been maintenance of the purity of sound, with no artifacts of the processing. It works.

Split-band compression works well for several reasons: You can optimize each set of dynamic processors (the compressor, expander and limiter) to a particular range of audio. That is, the ratio and threshold controls can be suited to each part of the spectrum.

You can decide to process different ranges of an instrument differently. You could use no compression at all on the low end of a bass, with heavy compression on the top end to put the string slaps in balance with the bottom. Or you could tighten the boomy bottom up with compression but leave the top less controlled for that open feeling.

Any massive anomaly like a low frequency breath noise for example, only triggers gain reduction within its range, leaving the desired vocal unaltered. And the decidedly unmusical phenomenon of a popped 'P' sucking the overall level back 10 dB is a thing of the past.

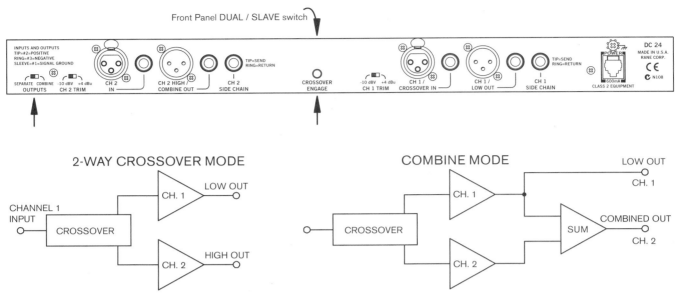

2-WAY CROSSOVER MODE

COMBINE MODE

Figure 1. Results of the Separate / Combine and Dual switches in Crossover Mode.

VISUALIZING ALL THIS

Figure 1 shows a couple of different configurations, depending on the positions of the Crossover / Dual / Combine switches that truly make the DC 24 a multi-function unit. It can be a two way crossover, with independent processing on the low and high outputs. The outputs can be summed with the Separate/Combine switch, and the Crossover can be switched in (see rear panel above), so that processing the low and highs separately can take place in a mono or send/return application. Even though the outputs are summed at Channel 2's output, Channel 1 is still outputting the lows which might be valuable to a bass player running a full range along with a bass bin (see Figure 1).

Figure 2 shows how the gate/expander, compressor, and limiter all can work together on the same program material in a single channel. The vertical axis is the output level, and the horizontal axis is the input level. When all Ratios are set at 1:1, the input and output of the circuit are the same as illustrated by the straight diagonal line running at 45° across the graph. Each of the Threshold controls acts like a "hinge point", activating gain reduction only when the input signal reaches the level set by this control. The Ratio controls how much of an "angle" the hinge will bend, or more realistically how much gain reduction will occur once the threshold is reached. Graphically, the ratio can swing this hinge from 45° (no processing) to almost 90° (full ratio). It is also possible, by adjusting the Thresholds, to have each of these circuits overlap and interact

with each other to develop a dynamic curve. The solid black line shows the curve produced when the controls are set as shown.

In this example, the gate/expander circuit works on the quiet parts, and the compressor and limiter work on the louder parts. The gate/expander can range from just turning down the quiet parts a little to a lot. The compressor and limiter are a lot more flexible when used separately at different thresholds, even though they have the same job of keeping the loud stuff under control. Got it?

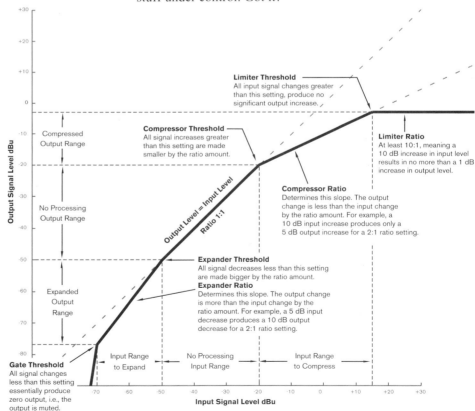

Figure 2. Compressor / Limiter / Gate Input to Output Graph

DC 24 APPLICATIONS

STARTING OUT

Sometimes it's neccessary to start from scratch. The panel above shows where the controls should be for *no* processing. Then you can adjust each section one at a time.

TWO CHANNEL COMPRESSOR/LIMITER

In this case, the audio path on channel 1 is completely separate from channel 2, allowing you to use it as a stereo unit or for doing two completely different processes to two completely different signals. For stereo use, the front panel has a "Dual/Slave" mode switch that allows you to slave channel 2 to channel 1. This assures that both signals are affected identically. In this application, the crossover is disengaged (this button is located in the middle of the rear panel.) The "Separate/Combine" switch on the rear panel should be in the "Separate" mode. Set the rear panel "-10/+4" switches accordingly, depending on whether you are running your system at -10 dBV or +4 dBu levels.

CROSSOVER WITH BUILT-IN LIMITING

Let's say that you want to run a bi-amped system and process the low end a little differently than the high end. This is a handy way of saving your woofers from over-excursion. In this application the crossover is engaged and set at the recommended crossover point for your speakers, let's just say 1.2k for the sake of example. In this instance the Separate/Combine switch on the far left of the rear panel is set on Separate. Your input would connect to the Channel 1 input jack. This gives you a separate output on Channel 1 (signals below 1.2k, the "lows") and everything from 1.2k and above on Channel 2 (the "highs"). This setup allows you to better contain the low end without unnecessarily limiting the high end. A crossover *and* a processor all in one rack space!

GUITAR

John Albani (Canadian Musician Magazine)- "By now, I'm sure that you have heard that a low stage volume is essential to your sound man getting a better house mix. Well, here are a few suggestions on how to achieve a lower volume without sounding like you're playing out of a transistor radio.

"Marshalls and other 4 x 12 cabinets give a great 'chunky' sound, but it is also accompanied by an annoying 'woofing' on the lower end. This stereo compressor has the unique feature of becoming a two-way crossover with independent low end and high end compressors. With this I was able to achieve what was previously only possible with the dynamics section of the SSL console that was used for my guitar sounds on the Lee Aaron "Bodyrock" album. Take the preamp output

of the loop into the DC 24 Channel 1 Input. The Channel 2 Output should return to the main amp input of the effects loop or the power amp (via your effects). Set the switches to Dual / Crossover / Combine. Now you can set a crossover point on the front panel (try around 400 Hz) and compress the bottom end at a 10:1 ratio. While chugging on a chord where you notice a lot of woofing, set the gain reduction with the Threshold control to read 6 dB. When you hit an open chord, there should be no gain reduction. If there is, back off on the Threshold, not on the Ratio. Now compress the top end between a 1.5:1 to 2:1 ratio, with 3 dB gain reduction when an open chord is hit, to give your sound a lot more attack. Also, no matter where you play on the neck, the bottom end of the sound will be even, without woofing, giving your overall tone punch and clarity.

"Warning: Do not over compress the top end or the pick attack will be slurred. If you want to hear more attack, turn up the top end Level of the DC 24 after setting the above-mentioned compression for the top end.

"Right now you are 99% on your way to retaining your sound or bettering it, without blasting everyone to Palookaville, or deafening your sound man.

"On stage you must work within the tonal range of your instrument. I hear guitarists with huge sounds that are great until the bass player fires up. He can't hear because the bottom from the 4 x 12s is blurring out his bottom end. So you end up in a volume war, which puts you out of the front mix. Try this: Once you have the sound you like, back off on the bottom Level control of the DC 24. Your bass player is already operating in that tonal range and you won't miss the sub lows when he's playing with you anyway."

BASS

Now for you bass guitar players out there...How many times have you been yanked out of the mix by your soundman because you're overdriving the system? You'd love to be able to keep the high-end attack without booming on the low end. Well, try this. Set the switches to Crossover *in*, Separate/Combine to Combine, and Dual Mode on the front panel. Now, plug into Channel 1 from your preamp output, and come out of Channel 2 into your amp. What you have done is split your mono signal, with a crossover point, then you've run it through separate processors and combined the signal back together on the Output of Channel 2.

Where does the unit go in the signal chain? Well, that depends on how you want it to function. If it's a comp/limiter for the input signal, it would go after the bass (if the bass has a line-level output) and before the preamp. If it's to function as a limiter to protect the speakers in the bass rig, it would go after the preamp and before the power amp. Another method

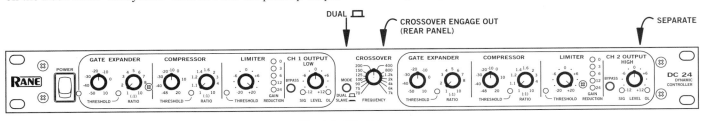

"Straight Wire" Setup

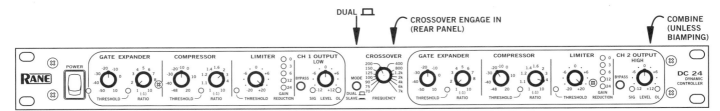

Bass Guitar Setup

is to insert the unit in the effect loop of the preamp. This allows the bass signal to be affected by the pre-amp first, then the comp/limiter, and then sent to the power amp. This can be desirable with tube pre-amps.

This unit can also be used for biamp rigs. For this, it is placed in the signal chain after the preamp and before the power amps. The output from the preamp is the signal that is processed and split at the selected crossover point. For biamp purposes, the Combine/Separate switch should be in the Separate position. Channel 1 processes the lows and channel 2 processes the highs. The low and high outputs are independent and correspond to Channels 1 and 2.

The DC 24 has two great advantages over other compressors–the crossover and the dual channels. It gives you complete control of the signal and processing of it. This is something that wasn't available before in a single unit. One stereo or two mono comp/limiters and one crossover would be required to do what the DC 24 does in a single rack space. This unit solves many compressor blues. For more attack, you can turn up the Level on the top end. Notice that when you stop playing, that amp buzz and hiss goes away. Nice, huh?

Dave Freeman (Bassics Magazine)- "I tested this unit in the combine mode with the crossover set at 200 Hz. I used my 4 string Music Man bass, famous for its ear splitting high end, as test in different channel settings. I set Channel 1 (low end) for mild compression at 2:1 with the Threshold at -10 dB. I set Channel 2 (high end) for heavy compression at 6:1, and the Threshold at -20 dB. I turned the volume and the treble controls on the bass on full, and slapped and popped like a madman. So what happened? Well, the high end was compressed down to the low end level. The sound was balanced and didn't have a compressed tone. I could slap away 'til my fingers went numb without having the comp/limiter clamp down on the entire signal. Impressive results!

"I then tested the unit with my 5 string Ken Smith bass. I set the lows for mild compression at 2:1 at -20 dB Threshold. I set the high end for the same compression but with the Threshold at -10 dB. I wanted just a bit on the bottom for the low B string and less processing on the highs. I slapped and popped on all the strings including the low B. The result was slight processing on the lows which tightened the bottom, but didn't make it *sound* controlled or processed. The highs had subtle compression that sounded natural, unlike others that 'breathe' when compressing."

RECORDING

Use it on bass guitar, piano, drums, vocals–anywhere you've used a compressor/limiter before. The DC 24 gives you more control and a less tortured sound. In fact, split-band processing works so well that a DC 24 sounds good compressing an entire mix (two required for stereo in split-band mode).

Of special interest are instruments which have large level differences in their different tonal ranges. String pops on a bass are one, but flute is another. The higher tones require more breath and are much louder than the lower. Another good application would be a drum mix or submix. A split-band compressor does a better job of smoothing the performance out.

Roger Nichols (Engineer)- He uses the DC 24 primarily on bass and guitar. He sets the Crossover at 100 Hz, the Gates and Compressors to 1:1, and engages the Combine and Dual Mode switches. This gives him separate Limiters to control the high and low peaks separately on a mono signal.

Brent Hurtig (EQ Magazine)- "In the studio, the crossover has some different applications. With Combine selected and the Crossover engaged, a signal entering Channel 1 is split into two bands. These two bands again may receive separate processing. What's different here, though, is that the two bands' signals are merged at the Channel 2 Output. This little exercise allows you to apply different amounts of compression and limiting to the low and high ends of a piano. Or let's say the saxophonist sounds great, but every time she hits the high C she pins the meters: Just the high end of the sax could be limited. Very clever.

"You also can use the Separate mode in the studio. With this setting, the crossover acts like a low pass filter to signals in Channel 1, and like a high pass filter to signals in Channel 2. We found some great sounding guitar, vocal, and keyboard tones using the DC 24 in this equalizer-like manner."

Digital Recording: Use it to compress an extremely wide dynamic range into a signal that won't go into digital overload, i.e. clipping. The limiter is the primary circuit here to keep things under control, but a little compression with its threshold set just under the limiter threshold setting will help keep the limiting even more subtle. Also, the gate can be set just above the noise floor with a low threshold and high ratio to remove mixer or tape hiss between cuts. To control a stereo mix, set the switches to Normal / Separate / Slave.

©Rane Corporation   10802 47th Ave. W.,   Mukilteo WA 98275-5098   TEL (425)355-6000   FAX (425)347-7757   WEB http://www.rane.com

Good Dynamics Processing

- **A COMPRESSOR**
    - **Threshold**
    - **Ratio**
    - **Attack time**
    - **Release time**
    - **Gain control**
    - **Hold time**
    - **Compression caused distortion**
    - **Signal measurement**
    - **What to look for when buying**

- **A LIMITER**

- **A DOWNWARD EXPANDER**
    - **What to look for in an expander**

- **A GATE**

- **HOW TO "KICK THE TIRES" OF A GATE**

Ray Bennett
Rane Corporation

RaneNote 141
© **1998 Rane Corporation**

A COMPRESSOR

Producing a good, effective compressor is not a trivial task. It has to "rein in" excessive program dynamics without being unduly intrusive. It does this by reducing the gain in the audio path when the signal level exceeds a pre-determined threshold. Four important parameters need to be controlled. Refer to Figure 1 for the following definitions.

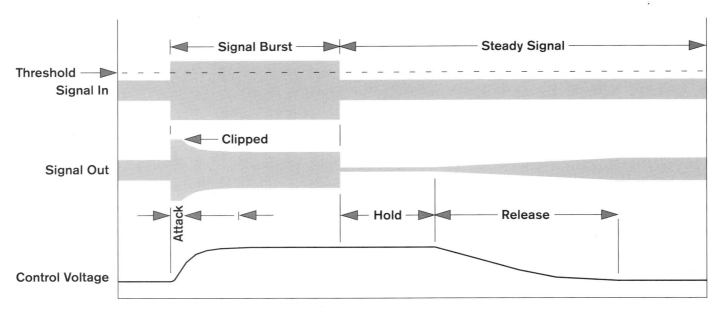

Figure 1. Short Segment of Signal Dynamics

Note that the signal increase is too fast to keep under control with the illustrated attack time. In this case, either the attack time must be decreased, or the high frequency content must be limited. Although not totally obvious, limiting the high frequency content also limits the rate-of-change of the signal level—that is, the sound can only get louder at some maximum rate.

Threshold

The signal level above which the compressor reduces system gain. This parameter is almost always adjustable. Note that a threshold that exceeds the system clip level is essentially a bypass function. A workable range for this control is –40 dBu to +20 dBu. Notice that if the threshold is set to a low level of –40 dBu, the compressor begins to look very much like a Leveler or Automatic Gain Control (AGC).

Ratio

A measure of how much the gain will be reduced under given conditions. A ratio of 2:1 means that once the signal level exceeds the threshold, the output signal level is allowed to increase by only 1 dB for every 2 dB of input increase. The desired setting during use should be the minimum that will provide the required overload protection. Normal ratio for a compressor ranges from 1.5:1 to 10:1. This parameter is almost always adjustable. Note that a ratio of 1:1 is analogous to a functional bypass.

Attack time

How long the compressor takes to control the signal after the actual overload occurs. In a good compressor with adjustable attack time, expect a range of adjustment from 500 microseconds (us) to 100 milliseconds (ms). Some manufacturers specify this time from the beginning of overload to some arbitrary gain reduction – perhaps –3 dB. Others specify it from the start of overload to the time the gain stops changing. Perhaps the most meaningful is to specify from start of overload to when the system gain is within, say, 3 dB of the final control point for 10 dB of gain reduction. Unfortunately, in the war of specsmanship, this measurement suffers by

comparison. In a system where this parameter is adjustable, ridiculously short times are often spec'd just to look good. Some manufacturers state the attack time as from onset of a very large, very fast overload to the *beginning* of gain control. This is an artificially short time since it really doesn't reflect how long it takes to get the overload under control. The important consideration is "how long does it take to control an overload?" Equally important as speed, is the *shaping* of the attack function. If badly done, even a slow attack will sound abrupt and "clicky." Unfortunately, the buyer is not usually informed as to this critical part of the design. This is where a reviewer's article could pay off, as well as a carefully done listening test by the potential buyer. If during testing, the compressor sounds intrusive when the attack is reduced below 1 ms, try a different compressor.

Release time

How long the compressor takes to relinquish control once the overload passes. Same problems of specification as the attack time, but of less consequence. Normal adjustment range is from 100 ms to 3 sec or more. A short release time of 100 to 500 ms is a good starting range for spoken voice, while the longer times are better for instrumental music. This time inversely affects the distortion added by the compression process, as will be shown. Release time is usually adjustable. Here again, the buyer is at the mercy of the designer. Much has been done with release circuitry over the years to produce good compressors. Terms like "program dependant" and "dynamics dependant" abound. Some have genuine meaning, while some are hype to get the buyer's attention. Bottom line? How does it sound when compressing?

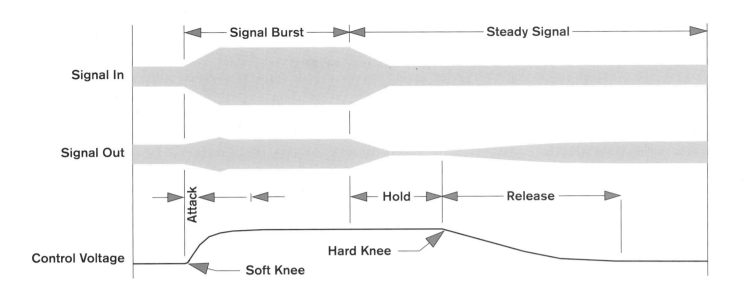

Figure 2. Signal Dynamics with Limited Frequency Response

In this example, note that the signal attack time is slow enough to be kept under control. The hold time, if adjustable, could have been shorter.

Gain control

This is sometimes called "make up gain." It is used to adjust the output level to the desired optimum. This control usually has a range of plus and minus 15 to 20 dB. A center detent at 0 dB of gain is often provided. Beware of too much control, as it makes it difficult to adjust to the desired value. Some feel that ±10 dB is plenty. The author believes ±15 dB is a good range. If the user is employing lots of compression, then more gain range might be appropriate. However, if subtlety is the buyer's style, 10 dB may be better.

In addition, the following terms may be encountered:

Hold time

How long the compressor takes to *begin* the release process once the overload passes. Not normally spec'd in a compressor, but a valid parameter nonetheless.

If provided, the hold time allows the operator to maintain the important "tail" of cymbals, triangles, etc., without distorting the dynamics. In most compressors, this is accomplished by making the release time quite long. A hold function allows the operator to more accurately tailor the compressor function to the dynamics of the program material. If the adjustment is provided, it should be from 50 ms to 1 sec or more. Adjusting the hold time entails using the minimum setting that preserves the program dynamics. Speech would require minimum hold, while solo instruments such as vibraphone would probably sound better with a hold time of 1-2 seconds.

Compression caused distortion

This is largely ignored but is very significant. In one U.S. made compressor, which is generally considered to be quite good, operating with 10 dB of compression, minimum release time, ratio of 10:1, at a frequency of around 100 Hz, the distortion exceeds 5% THD (Total Harmonic Distortion)! This is not at all abnormal. As the release time is increased, this distortion decreases but never goes away completely. There is a technique that will eliminate it completely, but that is the subject of another paper. Incidentally, the author believes this distortion often causes the operator to adjust the release time longer than should be used. The assumption is that the sound improved because of the longer release time, but perhaps it actually sounded better because of the reduced distortion (to a point). The condition that saves the day is that this distortion is relatively difficult to hear, since it tends to be masked by the program dynamics that brought it about in the first place. The same effect masks occasional clipping. For example the cannons in the *1812 Overture* are almost totally clipped but still manage to sound reasonably good. Try treating a vocal that way and the singer will probably be unrecognizable.

The source of this compressor caused distortion is ripple remaining superimposed on the control voltage presented to the voltage-controlled amplifier (VCA). Because the rectification and log conversion is full-wave, the ripple is at twice the signal frequency. The release time acts as a single pole low-pass filter, which reduces this ripple at the rate of 6 dB per octave. That is, as the signal frequency goes up, so does the ripple frequency. As the ripple frequency increases one octave, it is reduced in amplitude by 6 dB (by one half) by the action of the release filter. Since the release filter is set to around 0.5 seconds or more, its implied "rolloff frequency" (-3 dB point) is 0.32 Hz or less. (The formula is freq = 1/(2*pi*TC) where TC is the time constant – 0.5 sec in this example.) One would think that 0.32 Hz is so far below any signal of interest that there just can't be any ripple remaining. If the VCA didn't deal with it the way it does, that supposition would be true; however, the VCA functions by multiplying the control voltage times the signal voltage. This means that the ripple (at twice the signal frequency) multiplied times the input signal causes even-ordered harmonics. Often the designer has worked hard in the design process to eliminate the generation of these harmonics elsewhere in the audio path, only to generate them in the VCA.

Signal measurement

Much has been written concerning the proper rectification/log conversion process used to measure the incoming signal level. Some advocate peak logging, while others say that RMS log conversion is the only way to go. It must be kept in mind that, by definition, RMS log conversion requires averaging over several cycles of the signal. At most frequencies this makes the attack time unacceptably long. Often a compromise is used where the averaging time for the log conversion process is essentially a peak function at low frequencies and RMS at high signal frequencies. In- between it's anyone's guess. This sounds sloppy, but in practice, it works quite well. Ultimately, the release time filter converts the peak log to an averaged peak log. Since the logging process reduces the apparent extremes in the signal dynamics, this averaging is a reasonably good first-order approximation. One way to improve the ripple removal is to use a two-pole release filter. This two-pole approach reduces the ripple twice as fast – 12 dB per octave at the cost of more circuitry. Another advantage to using two-pole filtering (both attack and release) is the shaping of the transitions (the "knees") tends to be much smoother and less abrupt. The attack and release can be adjusted to be faster while still allowing the compression process to sound good. Unfortunately, unless the manufacturer "brags" about the method used, there really isn't any easy way to tell how the circuitry was designed. The bottom line remains the same – How does it sound? Keep in mind, how it sounds is the *only thing that will remain in your recording.* All the fancy lights, expensive extruded front panel, stainless steel cabinet, etc won't be in the credits.

What to look for when buying a compressor

A compressor is enough of an investment that, like a new car, it should be "test driven.". Look at the front panel. The function of each knob and switch should be clear and understandable. If the salesman has trouble explaining it so that the function makes sense, consider another brand or another salesman. Turn the knobs, feel the "action." It should be smooth, not "gritty." While this may seem silly for some, it is a good indication of how much effort the builder puts into buying quality parts. Listen to it carefully with program material similar to what will be used in the buyer's situation. Adjust for minimum attack, maximum ratio, mid-range release (perhaps 0.5 sec). Adjust the threshold until the gain reduction meter shows 10 dB or so of gain reduction with no

clipping during the loud music. No gain reduction meter or clip indicator? This is a good time to look at another brand. There should be at least a threshold light to help set the control levels. Once the unit is set up, listen very carefully to the transition from quiet material to the loud transients, such as drumbeats. There should be nothing added by the compressor except decreased dynamic range. If it sounds worse when compressing, look elsewhere. Understand that the rather extreme compression that was just set up will sound somewhat "squashed", but it shouldn't sound "clicky" or "nasty." The click sound usually comes from the attack not being shaped properly, while the nasty, distorted sound is simply the result of a poor compressor. This is the area that the buyer should try to get the best possible performance for the money being spent. Once this part is satisfied, the buyer can look for attractive graphics, lots of lights and extra functions. Be careful about paying extra for a function that isn't needed. Although, one extra function that is almost imperative is a limiter with separate controls. Often, a downward expander is also included. Depending on the intended use, this may be worthwhile.

A LIMITER

What makes a good limiter? One that is used infrequently but effectively. As will be shown, an effective limiter has constraints that preclude it sounding good. That may seem like a contradiction, but it really isn't. That's not to say that there aren't good limiters – there certainly are. There just aren't *good* limiters that make good *compressors*.

A Rane DC 24 is an example of a good feature set. It has two channels of compression, limiting, and downward expansion.

If we make it a condition that the limiter cannot pass any signal that exceeds some threshold, then we automatically impose certain restrictions as follows:

To prevent transient overload, it must have an attack time faster than the fastest rise time expected. See Figures 1 & 2. The fastest rise time may be defined as one divided by the highest system frequency. This frequency is estimated as four times the –3 dB rolloff of the system for a single processing device. "Four times" is an arbitrary and conservative constraint. It assumes that the highest frequency will be 12 dB lower in amplitude than the program material due to the 6 dB per octave rolloff attributable to the high frequency limitation. The 6 dB figure is correct only if the system rolloff is defined by a single filter. If several devices are in sequence in the audio path and they have similar rolloffs, the maximum frequency can be downgraded to two times the rolloff of the system. For the sake of discussion, let's assume there are two devices in the path and they each rolloff around 50 kHz at 6 dB per octave each. We estimate the highest frequency of interest at 100 kHz. Therefore, the attack time required is 1/100 kHz, or 10 us. An attack time this short represents a possible, but challenging goal.

A more common approach is to allow very short transients to pass through and be clipped by the system. Generally speaking this isn't too objectionable. In fact, it probably sounds better than allowing the attack time to be as fast as 10 us, for reasons to be explained. A common compromise seems to be 100 us to 1ms for the attack time. Slower than 1 ms and the clipped peaks become wide enough to be quite audible. To avoid second-order effects, the fast attack transfer function must have "gentle transitions" known commonly as "soft knees." All this means is that as the change is made from no limiting to full limiting, the transition be performed smoothly rather than abruptly. If this isn't done, the engaging of the limiter introduces an audible click. This artifact is one of the main reasons operators "dial in" a relatively slow attack time in limiters with this parameter adjustable. *The operator finds the occasional clipping preferable to the click.* Consequently, if the click can be minimized, a faster attack time can be used. As the attack time becomes faster, this click becomes more difficult to avoid. Discussion abounds on the ideal shaping for this transfer function. Most common is an RC (exponential) charge with some diode action to "soften" the start of the limiting.

The limiter must have enough control ratio to guarantee the signal can't clip once it has begun to decrease system gain. Normally, the ratio of a limiter ranges from around 20:1 to "infinity." With an infinite ratio, once the input signal exceeds the limiter's threshold, the output is not allowed to increase at all. A 20:1 limiter is easily attainable in a "feedforward limiter" while a "feedback limiter" is required for an infinite ratio. A *feedforward* limiter is one, which measures the input level, then calculates the gain applied by other functions to obtain the assumed output level. It sounds complicated, but it isn't that bad. A *feedback* limiter simply measures the output level then generates whatever control voltage is necessary to prevent that level from exceeding the threshold. Why use one over the other? In a system where other dynamic gain control is used, such as a compressor, there is already a voltage available that indicates the level in dB of the input signal. In a feedback limiter, the rectification and logging (if any) must be added at the output. Also, all limiters add distortion to the audio. Some of the reasons have already been discussed. Another source of distortion is the ripple remaining on the control voltage. This ripple is inversely proportional to the release time and the signal frequency. If a half-wave rectifier is used (common if applied at the output), the ripple is at the signal frequency and double the amplitude compared to that left by full-wave rectification. With full-wave rectification, the ripple is twice the signal frequency. Also, if the rectified voltage is converted to a log function, it leaves less ripple than a simple, rectified voltage. This ripple causes distortion in the VCA as it did in the compressor, only worse. A serious problem with the feedback limiter is that the distortion caused by the limiter is already present in the signal being measured. In other words, the limiter reprocesses the distortion along with the signal and adds increasingly complex distortion. Fortunately, this "second-pass" distortion is much reduced in level. The ripple voltage may be minimized by use of a multiple-order release filter. However, as the order of the filter increases, it becomes more difficult to obtain reasonably short attack times. A second-order filter is a workable compromise. All this means is that the first release filter is followed by a second nearly identical filter. This reduces the ripple by 6 dB (by one half) at a given signal frequency compared to the standard first-

order release filter at the expense of additional circuitry. Nearly all limiters use a single-order filter for this function.

Another parameter is the release time. If too short, the action of the limiter sounds choppy; if too long, the limiter "breaths". That is, after the offending overload, the limiter holds the system gain down too long. As the gain is brought back to normal, the increase in level is audible – not very pleasant. Also, as mentioned above, as the release time is shortened, the distortion increases. For a limiter operating with a release time of perhaps 500 ms, at 500 Hz this distortion easily exceeds several percent THD. It is quite audible. This may be improved by using a second-order release filter as mentioned, but ultimately the best fix is to use the limiter as little as possible.

A serious limiter *must* use full-wave rectification to measure the signal level. Let's assume in a half-wave system that the positive peaks are measured. It is entirely possible to have a major overload on the negative half of the signal only. In such a case, the overload wouldn't be detected and there wouldn't be any limiting. Full wave rectification adds so little to the cost that the choice is trivial. Unfortunately, the buyer has no easy means to determine the method used. If the ratio is mentioned and it's greater than about 20:1, it is *probably* a feedback limiter. A feedback limiter "tacked on" to another function (usually a compressor) is *not likely* to sound good if used heavily.

Normally the limiter is part of some other function, such as a compressor, as in the Rane DC 24. A limiter by itself is difficult to evaluate. It should be listened to with a compressor ahead of the limiter in the sound processing. With the compressor set up and functioning normally, have the clip light come on *occasionally*. Adjust the threshold of the limiter to just light on the loudest music peaks, and then only briefly. The clip light *should not come on except very rarely*. The limiter should be considered "disaster prevention." With it operating as described, its action should be quite unobtrusive. If it can be heard working, it probably is either not set up properly or is a bad limiter. It is the author's opinion that there are a lot more bad limiters than good ones. Fortunately, if used carefully, even a bad one won't be a total disaster. However, it *must be fast enough* to avoid clipping on all but the most difficult program material. If it can't do this properly, it's no better than a really bad compressor.

A DOWNWARD EXPANDER

The function of a good downward expander is to increase the *apparent* dynamic range of the system by decreasing the gain during the relatively quiet times thereby moving the apparent noise floor downward. It does this by comparing the signal level to a threshold. When the signal level drops below this threshold, the expander decreases the system gain by some ratio. This ratio is the same as defined in the compressor, only opposite in sense. The difference between this ratio and that of the compressor is that the gain of the expander decreases when the input signal is *below* the threshold. Expanders usually operate with a rather gentle ratio – perhaps 1.5:1 to 2.5:1. Occasionally higher ratios are used, but the audio tends to take on an odd breathing sound as the background noise comes and goes due to the expander's action.

To be effective, the dynamics of the expander must have moderately fast attack and fairly slow release times. The attack is the time spent restoring the system gain to normal when the signal level increases. Times of 0.5 ms to 1.5ms work well. The release is the time spent reducing system gain when the signal decreases. For the release, a time of 0.5 sec to 1.5 sec is common. The waveform of the control voltage must avoid sudden changes. Transitions must happen smoothly with a decidedly "soft knee." This is especially important with the downward expander since the audio will be, by definition, rather quiet at the threshold. Without audio dynamics to mask the gain adjustment, it must be done smoothly and gently or the action adds objectionable artifacts to the sound. To recap, the five determinates of the dynamics of a good downward expander are:

Threshold. The signal level below which the expander begins to reduce the system gain. This parameter is almost always adjustable and typically ranges from –50dBu to 0 dBu.

Ratio. The rate at which the gain reduces expressed as a ratio of output level change to input level change, such as 2:1. The normal range of adjustment is 1:1 (bypass) to 5:1 or so.

Release Time. The time it takes the expander to reduce system gain after the signal has dropped below the threshold level. If this parameter is adjustable, it is set to fit the dynamics of the particular audio source. Speech typically requires a fairly short release time while music sounds better with a longer release time. Adjustment range should be from 100 ms to 3 sec or more.

Attack Time. The time it takes the expander to restore the system gain after the signal level rises above threshold. A variety of methods exist to define this time, but it seems to be less of a problem than with a Gate, Limiter, or Compressor. The most descriptive is to declare the time it takes the expander to increase the gain to within some percentage of the final level after the signal is suddenly restored. This time may depend on how much the input level exceeds the threshold. Attack time is usually fixed. If it is adjustable, it should range from 0.5 ms to 10 ms. If it is fixed, an attack time from 1 to 5 ms would be appropriate.

Depth of gain reduction. This refers to the limit of the gain reduction caused by the expander. As a practical matter, it's usually limited to perhaps 60 dB of gain reduction. Sometimes the amount of gain reduction is adjustable to keep the system from sounding "dead." If the depth is fairly modest, this becomes a "ducking" function. If the system gain is decreased to a very low level, the constraints placed on the control dynamics are relaxed. For example, if the system is not passing audio due to heavy downward expansion, the transition at the beginning of the attack time is not so critical. However, the apparent attack time appears longer because of the time it takes the control to transit through the relatively inaudible region.

What to look for in an expander

Normally an expander is packaged as part of some other processing function, such as a compressor or a gate. A good listening test for an expander is to set the threshold *higher* than the threshold of the companion compressor. This would *not* be a normal setting, but the overall control function

should still be smooth and without "odd anomalies." All this means is that it shouldn't "go wacky" even though the controls are set in a non-standard way. When operating by itself, it should be possible to set the controls so that the expander doesn't breath excessively nor sound choppy. An expander is particularly effective with spoken material. Subtle control should normally be the goal – avoid extremes. If the ratio is fixed, make sure it is gentle, perhaps 1.5:1 or so. Make sure there is a way to defeat the expander if the program material doesn't require it – a real bypass function is better than a very low threshold. If a mic is available for the listening test, set the threshold to substantially decrease the gain with no input to the mic. While listening with earphones, say something like "putt, putt, putt" into the mic. Make sure the expander "comes alive" quickly enough to include all of the "p" sound. If the release is adjustable, it should be possible to set it such that the gain decrease after the input ends is not overly noticeable, yet the softer "t" sound isn't chopped off. If used properly, the expander should do a good job of cleaning up a sound track during the quiet times without making it sound like the background noise is "doing pushups."

A GATE

An excellent gate is a very challenging balance of constraints. A gate is a device used to pass or not pass audio, based on the signal level. Refer to Figure 3. If the level exceeds an established threshold, the audio is passed (the gate is "open"). If the level is below the threshold, the audio is blocked (the gate is "closed"). It's never "partially open" except during transitional times. A deceptively simple definition. The easy approach is to use the equivalent of a simple switch – either on or off. Indeed, some are done that way. Unfortunately, they sound terrible.

By definition, sound is present when the switch is "thrown." The rapid change in level causes a serious "click" to be added to the audio. This happens both when the gate is opened and when closed. Various tricks are added to avoid these artifacts and that is where the design challenge happens. One method, which has some acceptance is to only open or close the gate when the actual signal waveform crosses zero volts (remember, it's alternating voltage). If the VCA is a reasonably good one, no output signal is produced at that instant. The problem is that most waveforms resulting from a percussion instrument have a very large initial transition followed by smaller "tremors." By the time the threshold is exceeded and the next zero crossing happens, the main event is over. The loud drum "rim shot" is reduced to a dull thud, for example.

Another approach is to use a downward expander with a very high ratio and a very fast attack. The problem with this method is that almost no downward expander is capable of the dramatic attack times required. The attack time is defined as the time required for the gate to open, or pass signal, after the signal level exceeds the established threshold. To be effective, this time must be less than 100 us. One gate measured, advertises 5 us, although in actual tests it didn't do anything before 100 us, and it took an additional 50 us to actually control the signal! Another gate has been measured at 20 us

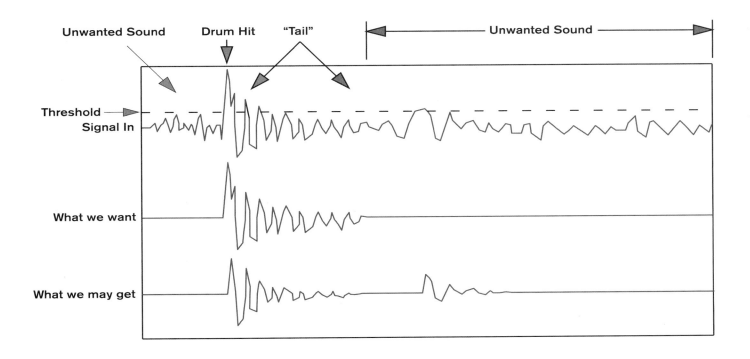

Figure 3. Typical Gate Dynamics

In this example, what we want isn't going to sound like what we may get! First, part of the drum hit is lost. Second, the end of the tail is attenuated too soon. Third, unwanted sound is picked up. In a really good gate, the drum will sound exactly the same as the original, only the unwanted sound will be gone. Incidentally, part of the solution to this problem may be to reposition the microphone to remove some of the unwanted sound. No gate can perform magic, though with the right settings it can seem like it.

(start of +20 dBu burst of 20 kHz to *beginning* change of control voltage). In addition, this gate uses an analog delay to "hold back" the audio path to give the gate time to open. It appears to open before the increase in signal level happens. These are rather expensive but effective tricks just to make a "switch" sound good.

The following parameters are required in a superior gate:

Threshold. The signal level above which the gate opens to pass audio. The operator almost always adjusts this parameter. A normal control range is from −50 dBu to +20 dBu. A threshold setting *below* the noise floor becomes a bypass –gate always open.

Attack Time. The time from when the signal exceeds the threshold to when the gate opens. Unfortunately, it is often defined as when the gate just begins to open in order to "improve the spec's." This is probably the first specification a prospective buyer should look at when evaluating a gate. When an attack time of less than 100 us is specified, be suspicious of how it was measured. This parameter is sometimes adjustable, often by a 2-position switch (fast and faster). If adjusted by potentiometer, it needs to be set fast enough to include all of the percussive rise time of the audio. If it won't open that fast, go buy a better gate. The attack time should be adjustable, or fixed, to 500 us or *less*. A reasonable maximum is 1.5 ms.

Release Time. The time from when the signal drops below the threshold to when the gate closes. This parameter is usually adjustable. It is set to include the "tail" of the sound before the switch completely closes. For a kick drum, this time is fairly short, while for a triangle it may be as long as 4 seconds. The range of adjustment should be from 100 ms to 4 sec or more.

The following parameters are optional:

Hold Time. Companion to the release control. The time from when the signal drops below the threshold to when the gate just *begins* to close. If present, this parameter is normally adjustable by the operator and ranges from 10 ms to 4 seconds. This parameter is used to preserve the dynamics of the "tail" of a sound, such as a cymbal or bell. If used thoughtfully with the release time the over all quality of the transition is much improved.

Depth of Cut. The amount of gain reduction when the gate is "switched off." Since a VCA is usually used for the actual gain control element, a total switch function is not practical. Also, in some situations, total gain reduction is not wanted. If total silence isn't necessary while the gate is closed, the attack time is improved by limiting the gain reduction. Therefore, this parameter is sometimes adjustable. It should range from 90 dB reduction to 0 dB (effective bypass). A depth of 60 dB to 40 dB would be typical.

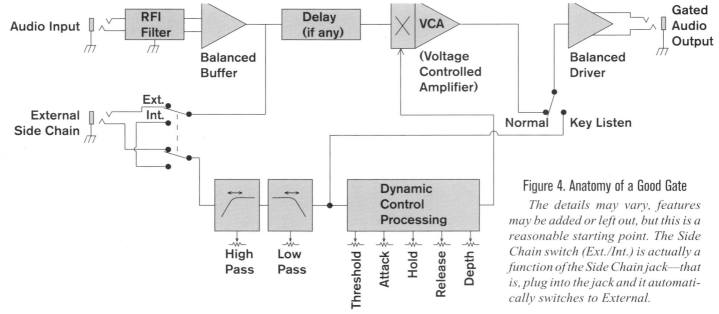

Figure 4. Anatomy of a Good Gate

The details may vary, features may be added or left out, but this is a reasonable starting point. The Side Chain switch (Ext./Int.) is actually a function of the Side Chain jack—that is, plug into the jack and it automatically switches to External.

High-Pass and Low-Pass Filters. These are applied in the control signal path (referred to as the "side chain") **not** the actual audio signal path. Usually there is a switch called a "key listen switch" that allows listening to the control signal to judge the affect of the filtration. Often there is a back panel jack called the "side chain jack" that allows this control signal path to be interrupted and modified externally then returned to control the gating. Any delay in this signal path degrades the attack time of the gate, so filters should be used sparingly since **all** filters introduce delay (we'll save the semantics of "lead" and "lag" for another discussion).

An analog delay in the audio path. If used, it is essential that the curve of the delay-versus-frequency be smooth and free of sudden changes. Ideally, it would seem that a constant delay would be best, however, a delay that varies **smoothly** with frequency works well. In any case, its function is to delay the audio path slightly to give the gate time to react before too much of the signal transition has occurred. This delay should range from 10 us to 100 us or more. If it is too long it will cause other problems. This delay is difficult to evaluate in testing. The only practical approach is to measure phase shift at a rather low frequency. Incidentally, this delay thoroughly "trashes" a square wave, or any other complex wave when viewed on an oscilloscope, due to phase dispersal. Fortunately, the signal sounds unchanged, but it certainly doesn't look unchanged.

Notice that there is no reference to "ratio." For those who insist on thinking in terms of a downward expander, the ratio of a gate is infinite. That is, above the threshold it's on and below the threshold it's off. Nothing in between other than transitional shaping.

Note that, because of the very fast attack time required, shaping of the attack function is very important. This alone will make or ruin an otherwise good gate. The real secret is a very fast turn on done carefully and smoothly – not a trivial task. Most, but not all, gates that are fast enough to be effective have a serious "click" at the turn on-transition.

HOW TO "KICK THE TIRES" OF A GATE

The best way is to play a drum track recording which has picked up low levels of some other instrument. The drum should be a snappy snare, preferably with lots of "rim shots." The sound to look for is a sharp percussive attack with some trailing sound. With the audio signal passing through the gate, adjust the threshold to trigger on the drum but not quite trigger on the background sound. Set the attack time for the minimum. There should be no "click" added even at minimum attack time. Listen very carefully to the drum sound while enabling and disabling the gate action. The sound of the drum *should not change* while the background sound between drum hits should be gone. Adjust the release and hold controls for the best result. This is the essential purpose of a gate. If it can't do it well, find a gate that will. Take heart – good gates do exist.

In summation, let it be said – buyer, be careful. Don't expect top performance if you're shopping for the lowest price. By the same token, a high price doesn't ensure the best sound. If you don't need "gimmicks", don't be talked into them. The beautifully done, extruded front panel may look really sharp, but it doesn't make a recording sound one bit better. If the cabinetry is tinny and cheap looking, the circuit design *may* also be minimal and of poor quality, but this isn't necessarily true. Review articles are a good starting point, but be careful of the reviewer's personal prejudices – they may not coincide with those of the buyer. Listen to the opinions of colleagues, again with a view to personal prejudice. When all is said and done – listen to the equipment. Make the test as representative of the buyer's actual situation as possible. Listen carefully, be critical. If something sounded funny, don't necessarily believe the salesman's claim that there's "something wrong with the recording." If necessary, the buyer should provide a recording for the listening. Make sure the equipment can be returned if it doesn't work out. After all, the ultimate test is how the potential hit recording sounds. Will it go platinum or just be another "not bad" recording?

Limiters Unlimited

- **Auto-Slave**

- **Protecting Loudspeakers**

- **Protecting Systems**

- **Signal Overload Protection**

- **Limiting Volume**

INTRODUCTION

Limiters are in the protection business, limiting audio systems to safe levels. These limits protect loudspeakers, protect the audio signal from clipping, protect the neighbors, and protect ears.

A limiter continuously monitors the audio signal, looking for levels exceeding its adjustable threshold. A limiter normally operates at unity gain and has no effect on the signal. If excessive levels are detected, the Voltage Controlled Attenuator (VCA) automatically reduces the gain. If the level never exceeds the threshold, the signal remains unaffected.

Monty Ross
Rane Corporation

RaneNote 127
© 1991 Rane Corporation

AUTO-SLAVE, EXTENDING YOUR LIMITS

In the applications and examples that follow, you will read about multi-channel limiters with *auto-s/ave*. Auto-slaving provides the ability to tie together the circuitry that controls the VCA's of two or more limiters. Each limiter channel maintains its independent threshold adjustment. The amount of gain reduction is shared with all slaved channels when any one has exceeded its threshold. Figure 1 shows a simplified block diagram of a quad limiter with this feature.

PROTECTING LOUDSPEAKERS WITH LIMITERS

Loudspeakers manufacturers provide recommended power ratings for their drivers. These ratings are not absolute, and should be used only as a guide. Sound contractors' diverse experiences using loudspeakers sometimes lead them to formulate their own power ratings. Limiters allow for real world applications. With a limiter you can customize your speaker protection scheme for maximum reliability.

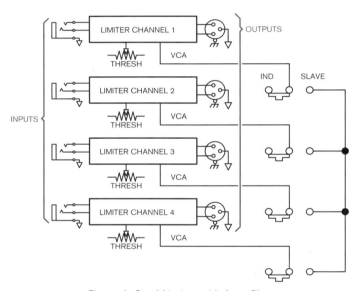

Figure 1. Quad Limiter with Auto-Slave

It is important to note that midrange and tweeter (high-frequency) drivers cannot handle as much power as woofers (low-frequency drivers). Therefore it is especially important that tweeters and midranges are protected by different limiter thresholds than the woofer.

Multi-amped systems often use limiters for speaker protection. Limiters are typically placed at the input of each power amplifier for each driver. In Figure 2 we show a tri-amped system protected by a limiter. Set each limiter's threshold to match the power handling of each driver. Whenever the high, mid or low limiters reach their set limit threshold, all three bands limit by the same amount. This is due to the three slaved channels in the limiter, assuring the system's spectral balance stays constant. (If only one band limited and the other two increased in volume, the result would be an abrupt change in the tonal balance of the system.) This clever trick provides the least audible and most effective form of multi-amped system power limiting.

TAKING YOUR SYSTEM TO THE LIMIT

A properly designed system has the ability to operate as loudly as needed for the application. When limiters are introduced into a system their thresholds are set to protect the systems' components.

Sometimes limiting occurs before a satisfactory volume level is reached. For example, a touring band could perform in a venue that is much bigger than its equipment can handle. Higher power speakers or more powerful amplifiers may be called for. This permits higher limit levels to be set, thus allowing a louder system.

ALL SYSTEMS UNDER CONTROL

Signal overload problems may occur when cascading multiple audio signal processors. Take for example a parametric equalizer with a single band boosted by 10 dB to flatten a room. If a loud note in this same frequency range is present, the overload light on the equalizer illuminates. By then it is too late, the signal is clipped. Additionally, overloading could be overlooked if the overload indicators are

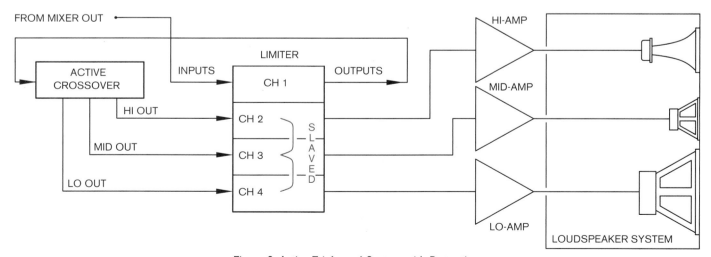

Figure 2. Active Tri-Amped System with Protection

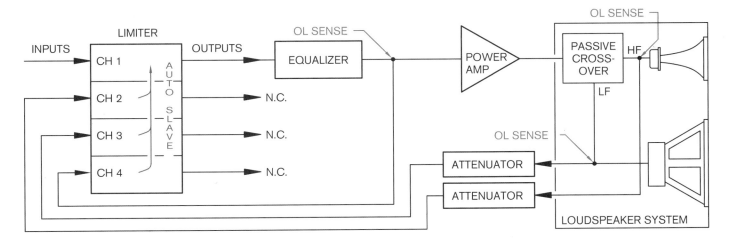

Figure 3. Signal Overload Protection

obscured by security covers or a closed rack. This problem is corrected by adding a 4-channel limiter with all four channels slaved together as shown in Figure 3. The first channel is the primary input limiter and up to 3 points are simultaneously monitored by the limiter's other 3 channels. The *threat* of overload automatically activates the limiter rather than lighting an LED, thus preventing overload altogether. Simply add a wye connector in the audio path anywhere you need protection and connect it to one of the 3 other inputs. When any single processor nears an unwanted level, the first channel limits the gain at the input of the whole system, preventing overload.

REIGN OVER YOUR VOLUME

A benefit of limiters is their automatic gain control ability. No one needs to be present to watch and change the levels of a system once you properly set the thresholds. A limiter prevents the need to gain ride a system. In this sense, the limiter acts as a compressor. Increase the volume so that the quiet parts are loud enough to be heard and the limiter automatically prevents the loud passages from clipping the amplifiers or overpowering the speakers.

Professional audio systems are often operated by untrained people. Take a music/paging system in a restaurant for instance. The owner of a restaurant wants specific levels of music in certain dining rooms so his customers or neighboring businesses will not be annoyed. Placing a limiter in the audio chain will prevent everyday users from turning the volume up too loud. The limiter's circuit tends the shop.

Another application involves hearing. We sometimes take our hearing for granted. Hearing is non-linear and constantly changing. When the sounds our ears pick up get loud (sensitivity to loudness varies with different people), some automatic systems come into play. Some of these changes are aural (involuntary muscular responses in the ear) and some are neural (the way the brain responds to impulses from the ear). The mechanism between the ear and brain begins to shut down in an attempt to protect itself. This action manifests itself by dulling your hearing senses. The natural response to this is to boost the volume or EQ controls to compensate for the perceived drop in level. Extended exposure to high sound levels can result in permanent hearing damage. Limiters help control these levels. When using a limiter for this purpose we recommend security covers to make the settings tamper proof.

SUMMARY

Put limiters in the signal path—anywhere there is a place where signals can't be monitored by someone or where there might be too much signal. At the output of the signal source, at the input of an equalizer, at the input of a mixer, at the input of a power amplifier or at the input to an active crossover. You can be very creative with limiters to achieve your particular goal. Especially if your limiter has an auto-slave option..

REFERENCES

1. M. Ross, "An Investigation into How Amplifier Clipping is Said to Burn-Out Loudspeakers, and How Limiters Can Save Them," presented at the 89th Convention of the Audio Engineering Society, *J. Audio Eng. Soc. (Abstracts)*, vol. 38, p.870 (Nov 1990), Preprint 2956.

©Rane Corporation   10802 47th Ave. W.,   Mukilteo WA 98275-5098   TEL (425)355-6000   FAX (425)347-7757   WEB http://www.rane.com

03182 8-97   Limiters-3

Power Amplifier Clipping and its Effects on Loudspeaker Reliability

- **Harmonic Theory**

- **Power Ratings**

- **Blown Tweeters**

- **Clipping and its Indicators**

- **Limiter Protection**

Monty Ross
Rane Corporation

RaneNote 128
© 1991 Rane Corporation

INTRODUCTION

Power amplifier clipping is quite common. This note examines the clipping phenomenon which *allegedly* damages loudspeakers. We suggest that this form of distortion is not the cause. Rather, we show that amplitude compression of the audio spectrum is the culprit. Rane limiters provide a solution to amplitude compression, thus preventing loudspeaker failure.

WHY DO LOUDSPEAKERS NEED PROTECTING?

All loudspeaker drivers have power handling limits. Once exceeded, damage occurs. There are several ways a loudspeaker suffers *power* damage. A couple of these warrant explanation.

The first is over-excursion of the diaphragm. The diaphragm of a loudspeaker is the radiating surface that moves in response to an electrical signal. This surface may be conical, domed or flat in shape, and it creates sound by physically pushing and pulling the air in the room. The laws of physics say that in order to play louder or to reproduce lower frequencies, the diaphragm must move further toward its mechanical limits. If it is asked to move still farther, it experiences over-excursion. This most often occurs in woofers but can affect midranges or tweeters if low frequencies are not limited. If the loudspeaker cannot handle over-excursion, mechanical destruction of the driver is likely the result.

Another enemy of loudspeakers is heat, generated by power losses in the voice coils. No device is 100% efficient. For loudspeakers, 1 watt of input power does not produce 1 watt of acoustic energy. In fact most loudspeakers are typically well under 10% efficient [1] [3]. These losses convert to heat that builds up in the voice coils, causing mechanical deformation, like melting of the voice coil former. It causes weakening of the structure by charring the voice coil former, which later shakes apart. The heat causes the glues to bubble up, fill the air gap and glue the voice coil solidly in the gap. Often the voice coil wire melts like a fuse link, resulting in an open driver. Obviously we wish to prevent this.

Music power-handling capability for multi-way loudspeakers always presents a problem to the loudspeaker user and designer. Users who must replace blown tweeters often feel they didn't do anything wrong, because their amplifier only put out 50 watts and their speaker had a 200 watt rating.

Yet, the tweeter blew up. This recurring problem motivated engineers to find out why this happens. Many opinions developed. Some of these have been scientifically verified—others remain theory.

CONFLICTING "FACTS"

Studies show the typical spectral energy for different types of music have high frequency energy considerably lower in level than low frequency energy [2]. This knowledge has further complicated the studies of how tweeters get destroyed. It seems that woofers should blow rather than tweeters if the high frequencies are lower in amplitude.

Loudspeaker manufacturers use this knowledge about the energy distribution of music when they design their products. This knowledge allows them to make better sounding tweeters because they can use lighter moving structures. Smaller wire in the voice coils can be used because there is significantly less power in the high frequency ranges. Since smaller wire is lighter, it takes less energy to move. For a speaker system rated to handle a given number of watts, the tweeter by itself can probably handle less than one-tenth that amount.

From all this came a theory that spread quickly through the industry. Since there is more musical energy at low frequencies than high frequencies, there is not enough high frequency power to blow out tweeters. Therefore, high frequencies loud enough to burn out tweeters must come from somewhere else. Where do they come from?

Well, it was reasoned, if there is enough low frequency energy to clip the amplifier, then it perhaps would produce enough high frequency distortion products (as a result of clipping) to blow up the tweeter.

This theory convinced many in the early 70's and slowly evolved into "fact". While doing research into the reliability

Table 1. Harmonic Amplitudes of a 100 Hz Square Wave, 0dB = 100 Watts (Instantaneous Power)

Harmonic	Amplitude	in dB	Watts	Frequency
1	1	0	100	100 Hz
2	0	-∞	0	200 Hz
3	1/3	-9.54	11.12	300 Hz
4	0	-∞	0	400 Hz
5	1/5	-13.98	4	500 Hz
6	0	-∞	0	600 Hz
7	1/7	-16.9	2.04	700 Hz
8	0	-∞	0	800 Hz
9	1/9	-19.1	1.23	900 Hz
10	0	-∞	0	1 kHz
11	1/11	-20.8	0.83	1.1 kHz
12	0	-∞	0	1.2 kHz
13	1/13	-22.3	0.589	1.3 kHz
⋮	⋮	⋮	⋮	⋮

and protection of power amplifiers, I had to study how the typical consumer used amplifiers and speakers. I found that clipping is a common occurrence and is not as audible as most people think. I also found that the operation of many clipping indicators is very slow and does not always show actual clipping. (Many manufacturers slow them down, using their own rule of thumb for how much clipping can occur until it lights the indicator.)

Newer and better sounding amplifiers, including amplifiers with soft clipping circuits, still blew tweeters. But amplifiers with higher power were having fewer incidences of blown tweeters. This appeared to reinforce the theory that clipping caused tweeter blowouts. One thing was clear, when clipping occurred, tweeters blew.

If you're getting the idea I don't believe in the clipping/ harmonic theory, you're right. So let's investigate the phenomena further.

WHEN SINE WAVES CLIP

When sine waves clip severely they resemble square waves in shape, introducing massive distortion. In the extreme case, a perfect square wave has the highest level of harmonic components (See Fig. 1). A less clipped sine wave has components at the same frequencies but at lower levels.

Let's look at the square wave example shown in Table 1 (at left). Fourier analysis shows the harmonic structure.

As you can see, the total amount of instanaeous power left to make it through an ideal 1kHz crossover (and on to the tweeter) is less than two watts (0.83 + 0.589 = 1.419W). Hardly a problem. And remember, this simulates severe overdrive of a 100 watt amplifier with a sine wave to make an ideal square wave. Driving it harder will not increase the harmonics.

This analysis shows if a small tweeter that only handles 5 or 10 watts is used in a 100 watt speaker system it would not blow out, even under square wave conditions. Yet it does.

It takes a lot more than this to cause major failure. So what's happening?

Compression is what's happening [3].

Today's newer higher quality amplifiers have greater dynamic range and sound better when clipped with musical transients than older amplifier designs. So it is more likely for a user to overdrive and clip newer amplifiers on low frequency dynamic peaks because of lower audible distortion. This results in compression of the dynamics of the music. The high frequencies get louder but the low frequencies can't. This may be heard as an increase in brightness of the sound. Some may simply interpret it as louder with no change in tonal balance.

For example, in a 100 watt amplifier, as you turn up the level, the low frequency components will limit (clip) at 100 watts. Meanwhile the high frequency components continue to increase until they (the high frequencies) approach the 100 watt clipping point.

The graphs in Figures 2, 3 & 4 are scaled in volts. With an 8 ohm load the 100 watt level corresponds to 40 volts peak. Below clipping, the low frequencies reach 100 watts (40 volts peak) but the high frequencies are only 5 or 10 watts (9 to 13 volts peak).

Let's assume a musical signal with low and high frequency components driving a 100 watt (8 ohms) amplifier. We use a low level/high frequency sinewave mixed with a high level/low frequency sinewave burst. (See Fig.2). The high frequencies reproduced by the tweeter are at least 10dB lower in level than the low frequencies. Now as we turn up the amplifier to clip the signal (3dB overdrive—See Fig.3). Notice that only the low frequency burst portion of the waveform clips but the high frequency portion increases in level. The clipping, of course, produces harmonics but not nearly as much as the square waves discussed earlier. The amplitude of the high frequencies went up by 3dB in relation to the low frequency fundamental. (3dB compression).

If you overdrive the amplifier by 10dB, the high frequency amplitude goes up by 10dB. This goes on dB for dB as you turn up the volume, until the high frequency reaches the 100 watt level. Meanwhile the peak level of the low frequency portion can not increase above 100 watts (See Fig. 4). This now represents nearly 100% compression (no difference between HF amplitude and LF amplitude).

Now it is easy to see how the high frequency portion exceeds the 5 or 10 watts tweeter rating. Sure, clipping is producing extra harmonics but *they never approach the levels of the amplified high frequency source signals.*

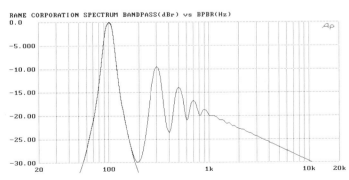

Figure 1. Harmonic Comnponents of a 100 Hz Squarewave vs. a 100 Hz Sinewave.

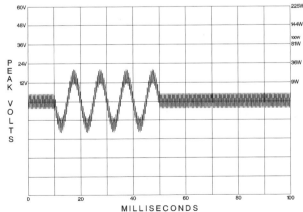

Figure 2. Low Level, High Frequency Sinewave Mixed with a High Level, Low Frequency Sinewave Burst.

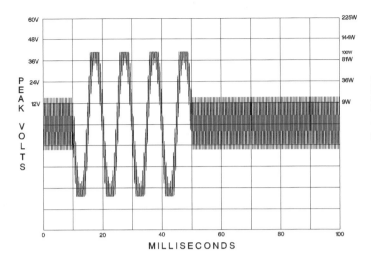

Figure 3. 100 W Amp with 3 dB Overdrive

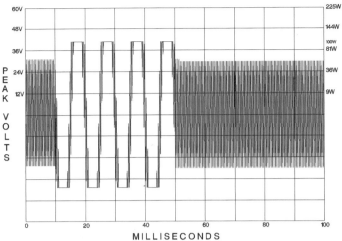

Figure 4. 100 W Amp with 10 dB Overdrive

It may be argued that the signal's distortion would be intolerable. Don't fool yourself. It really surprises people how much clipping they tolerate before they cannot listen anymore. Just disconnect the clipping indicator on a power amplifier and see how loud someone drives it. Watch the amplifier output with an oscilloscope. There will be a surprising level of clipping. 10 dB clipped off the top of low frequency transients is not an uncommon occurrence when the purpose is to impress your neighbors.

WHAT CAN WE DO ABOUT IT?

If we can prevent an amplifier from clipping, we could better utilize our loudspeakers. Limiters play an important role in preventing clipping and the resulting amplitude compression. The Rane MA 6S power amplifier, DC 24 dynamic controller, CP 64 and CP 52 commercial processors, VP 12 voice processor, and the RPM 26 multifunction processor are all products that limit. These limiters prevent the compression mentioned earlier because when *any frequency reaches threshold all frequencies are turned down by the same amount.*

The MA 6S six channel power amplifier is specifically designed not to clip by the use of its internal voltage controlled attenuators on each channel.

The DC 24 limiters have user adjustable threshold controls. This allows you to customize your total system for maximum reliability with no compromise on sound quality.

The FVL 22 has an Auto-Slave feature which allows you to slave the two channels together. When using the Auto-Slave mode for bi-amping, or stereo program, the spectral balance is preserved and amplitude compression is eliminated.

REFERENCES

[1] K. Blair Benson, *Audio Engineering Handbook,* (McGraw-Hill, New York, 1988)

[2] R. A. Greiner and Jeff Eggars, "The Spectral Amplitude Distribution of Selected Compact Discs," *Journal of the Audio Engineering Society,* vol. 37, pp.346-275 (April, 1989)

[3] Carlo Zuccatti, "Thermal Parameters and Power Ratings of Loudspeakers" *Journal of the Audio Engineering Society,* vol. 38, pp.34-39 (Jan-Feb, 1990)

Understanding Headphone Power Requirements

- **Headphone Sensitivity**

- **Listing of Headphones**

- **HC 6 Power vs. Loudness**

- **HC 4 / MH 4 Power vs. Loudness**

- **Table of Common Sound Pressure Levels**

Dennis Bohn

Rane Corporation

RaneNote 100
© **1983 Rane Corporation**

INTRODUCTION

Much confusion abounds regarding headphone power requirements. This Rane Note is intended to disperse some of the mist surrounding headphone specifications and hopefully give you a clearer understanding of how much power is really needed for your application.

HEADPHONE SENSITIVITY

Headphone manufacturers specify a "sensitivity" rating for their products that is very similar to loudspeaker sensitivity ratings. For loudspeakers, the standard is to apply 1 watt and then measure the sound pressure level (SPL) at a distance of 1 meter. For headphones, the standard is to apply 1 milliwatt (1 mW = 1/1000 of a watt) and then measure the sound pressure level at the earpiece (using a dummy head with built-in microphones). Sensitivity is then stated as the number of dB of actual sound level (SPL) produced by the headphones with 1 mW of input; headphone specifications commonly refer to this by the misleading term "dB/mW." What they really mean is dB SPL for 1 mW input.

Think about these sensitivity definitions a moment: headphone sensitivity is rated using 1/1000 of a watt; loudspeaker sensitivity is rated using 1 watt. So a quick rule-of-thumb is that you are going to need about 1/1000 as much power to drive your headphones as to drive your loudspeakers since both of their sensitivity ratings are similar (around 90-110 dB SPL). For example, if your hi-fi amp is rated at 65 watts, then you would need only 65 mW to drive comparable headphones. (Actually you need less than 65 mW since most people don't listen to their loudspeakers at 1 meter.) And this is exactly what you find in hi-fi receivers—their headphone jacks typically provide only 10-20 mW of output power.

Take another moment and think about all those portable tape players. They sound great, and loud. Why, you can even hear them ten feet away as the teenage skateboarder that ran over your foot escapes.

Power output? About 12 mW.

THE LIST

As an aid in finding out how much power is available from either the HC 6 or HC 4 Headphone Consoles, we have compiled a listing of popular headphones. Included is a column giving the maximum SPL obtainable using the HC 6 or HC 4 and any particular headphone—ultimately, it all gets down to actual SPL. The power rating really doesn't matter at all—either it's loud enough or it isn't (of course it has to be clean power, not clipped and distorted). The SPL numbers shown are for maximum *continuous* SPL; for momentary peak SPL add 3 dB.

Note that the maximum achievable SPL varies widely for different models and manufacturers, ranging from a low of 107 dB to a harmful 146 dB! The table also shows there is very little relationship between headphone impedance and sensitivity, and that power output *alone* means nothing, since in one case 80 mW produces a maximum SPL of 107 dB, yet in another case the same 80 mW yields an SPL of 124 dB!

Sensitivity (dB) is the measured sound pressure level with 1 mW of power. The **Max Power (mW)** columns are typical continuous average (rms) power, 20 Hz-20 kHz, with THD less than 0.1%.

If headphones are not yet owned, or replacements are desired, use this listing as a guide for selecting headphones with sufficient sensitivity for the maximum desired SPL. *Note: headphones with an impedance of less than 32 ohms are not recommended for use with the HC 6 or the HC 4.*

Manufacturer	Model	Impedance (ohms)	Sensitivity (dB)	HC 4 Max Power (mW)	HC 4 Max SPL (dB)	HC 6 Max Power (mW)	HC 6 Max SPL (dB)
AKG	K141M	600	98	89	117	80	117
	K240M, K240DF	600	88	89	107	80	107
	K270S	75	92	239	115	380	118
	K301	100	94	225	118	285	119
	K401, K501	120	94	220	117	290	119
Audio-Technica	ATH-COM1, ATH-COM2, ATH-908	40	90	220	113	440	116
	ATH-910	40	92	220	115	440	118
	ATH-P5	40	100	220	123	440	126
	ATH-M40	60	100	238	123	400	126
	ATH-D40	66	102	235	126	295	127
	ATH-M2X, ATH-M3X	45	100	230	123	435	126
Beyerdynamic	DT150	250	97	160	119	175	119
	DT211, DT311	40	98	220	121	440	124
	DT250	80	98	240	121	360	123
	DT411	250	102	160	124	175	124
	DT 531	250	95	160	116	175	116
	DT431, DT331	40	86	220	109	440	112
	DT770PRO, DT990PRO	600	96	89	115	80	115
	DT801, DT811, DT511	250	94	160	116	175	116
	DT901, DT911	250	98	160	120	175	120
Fostex	T-5	44	96	225	119	435	122
	T-7	70	98	240	121	385	124
	T-20	50	96	233	120	425	122
	T-40	50	98	233	122	425	124
Grado	SR 325	40	96	220	119	440	122
Hosa	HDS-701	40	91	220	114	440	117
Koss	A/250, A/200, A/130, TD/80	60	98	238	123	320	125
	R/200	60	84	238	108	400	110
	R/100, R/45	60	85	238	109	400	111
	R/90, HD/2, SB/15	60	100	238	123	400	126
	R/80, R/35S, R/20, Porta Pros	60	101	238	124	400	127
	R/70B, R/55B, SB/50, SB/35	60	101	238	124	400	127
	R/40	60	90	238	114	400	116
	R/30S	60	106	238	130	400	132
	R/10	60	103	238	127	400	129
	TD/75	60	95	238	119	400	121
	TD/65	90	101	235	124	340	126
	TD/61	38	93	212	116	440	119
MB Quart	QP 805	300	98	145	120	80	117
Sennheiser	HD 400, 433, 435, 470	32	94	200	117	450	121
	HD25	70	120	240	144	380	146
	HD445	52	97	235	121	390	123
	HD25SP	85	100	235	123	350	125
	HD265, 525, 535, 545, 565	150	94	207	117	190	117
	HD455, 475	60	94	238	118	400	120
	HD465	100	94	225	118	285	119
	HD 570	120	95	220	110	290	120
	HD580, 600	300	97	145	118	80	116
Sony	MDR-V100MK2	32	98	200	121	450	125
	MDR-85	40	102	220	125	440	128
	MDR-V600, MDR-D77	45	106	230	129	435	132
	MDR-CD10	32	96	200	119	450	123
	MDR-CD550, CD750	45	100	230	123	435	126
	MDR-CD6	45	110	230	133	435	136
	MDR-CD850, CD950	32	102	200	125	450	129
	MDR-CD1000, CD3000	32	104	200	127	450	131
	MDR-D33, MDR-D55, MDR-7504	45	104	230	127	435	130
	MDR-7506	63	106	240	129	400	132
	MDR-7502	45	102	230	125	435	128
Stanton	ST PRO, DJ PRO 1000	32	100	200	123	450	127
Telex	PH-6	600	105	89	124	80	124
Yamaha	RH5MA	32	98	200	121	450	125
	RH1	32	90	200	113	450	116
	RH2	32	95	200	118	450	122
	RH3	60	95	238	119	400	121
	RH10M	40	102	220	125	440	128
	RH40M	32	103	200	126	450	130

Sound Pressure Level Equivalents

SPL-dB	Common Example	SPL-dB	Common Example
140	Irreparable damage	60	Normal conversation
130	Jet aircraft taking off	50	Elevator music
120	Threshold of pain / Thunder	40	Normal home background (kids asleep)
110	Threshold of discomfort	30	Studio background
100	Dirt bike / Riveter	20	Rustling of leaves / Quiet whisper
90	Start of unsafe levels	10	Butterfly swoop
80	Average factory	0	Threshold of hearing
70	Kids at play		

Permissible Noise Exposures

Extracted from the U.S. Department of Labor Noise Regulations

Duration Per Day, Hour	Sound Level (dB), A-Weighting
8	90
6	92
4	95
3	97
2	100
1½	102
1	105
½	110
¼ or less	115

©Rane Corporation   10802 47th Ave. W.,   Mukilteo WA 98275-5098   TEL (425)355-6000   FAX (425)347-7757   WEB http://www.rane.com

Cost-Effective Noise Masking Systems

- **RA 30 Pink Noise**

- **Zones and Speaker Arrays**

INTRODUCTION

As the popularity of noise masking systems grows, so too does the cost of the equipment to implement it. However, like other sound system needs, Rane products can contribute a great deal to the cost-effectiveness of noise masking systems without sacrificing reliability or operational requirements.

Properly designed noise masking systems are an art form unto themselves. Their requirements far exceed what can be accomplished in this short space. The purpose of this note is to introduce noise masking designers to Rane products useful in their craft.

Terry Pennington
Roy Gill
Dennis Bohn
Rane Corporation

RaneNote 116
© 1987 Rane Corporation

REALTIME ANALYZERS

Rane's RA 30 Realtime Analyzer is ideally suited for generating the pink noise signal required to ideally mask ambient noise and conversation in open-plan office environments. Any Rane equalizer may be used to contour the pink noise output. The analyzer is used to set the one-third octave equalizer for the smoothest sounding noise within the environment.

NOISE SOURCE

Most noise masking authorities think the best pink noise sources are generated by pseudo-random digital techniques. The generator in the RA 30 is just such a device. Figure 1 shows a plot of the pink noise output produced by the Rane noise generator. As you can see, it is extremely flat with respect to "log" frequency. This is ideally what is desired as the basis of any masking system. The digital circuitry employed by Rane's design generates an output which is in reality white noise. This signal, modified by a pink noise curve, appears at the pink noise output jack of the units. The output is activated by the front panel pink noise switch.

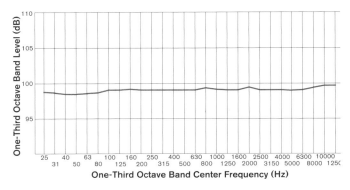

Figure 1. RA 30 Pink Noise Frequency Response

BASIC SYSTEM

Figure 2 illustrates the internal functional blocks of a typical noise masking generator. All of these blocks are duplicated in the Rane RA 30 when connected to a graphic equalizer. Connecting the system requires only patching the pink noise output of the RA 30 to the equalizer input, then connect the distribution and amplification electronics to the output of the equalizer. The downstream electronics may be in the form of a Rane SM 26B to provide the necessary splits and level controls for individual zones, followed by a Rane MA 6S power amplifier. The output of the amplifier may then be fed directly to low impedance loudspeakers or to a constant voltage transformer system such as the Rane KTM 6 Multichannel Transformer kit. In any event, the result is an extremely cost effective noise masking system with a minimum of components. Figure 3 depicts such a system.

MULTIPLE ARRAY NOISE MASKING

Simple noise masking systems use one equalized noise generator, distributing the shaped noise throughout the ceiling array. While cost effective, these simple systems too often are, themselves, a distraction. When this happens, the system gets switched off and the customer feels noise masking doesn't work and they wasted their money.

The evolution of successful noise masking produced the following guidelines (from "Acoustics of Open Plan Rooms," by Rollins Brook and "Sound System Design," by Chris Foreman in Glen Ballou, Ed., *Handbook For Sound Engineers* [Howard W. Sams & Co, Indianapolis, 1987]) for creating unnoticeable, yet very effective systems:
- Use three carefully equalized noise sources
- Interlace noise sources driving speaker arrays
- Disperse noise evenly in all areas (±2 dB)
- Use adequate amplification to avoid clipping
- Use separate EQ for the paging source
- Do not attenuate noise during paging

These guidelines result in a fairly complex and expensive system. Luckily, Rane products can help reduce both.

The most random signal results from the use of exactly three noise sources (more do not add more). This way, no two adjacent speakers emit the same sound. Each neighbor produces a randomly different sound. Experience has shown this approach creates the least distracting and most effective masking.

A non-irritating and successful noise source mimics the shape and range of normal speech. This means a maximum frequency range of about 200 Hz to 5 kHz, with an overall rolloff of 5-6 dB/octave beginning at 200 Hz and extending to around 5 kHz. With perfect speakers and no room interference, this can be done with a single capacitor. With actual speakers and normal rooms, this takes a one-third octave equalizer. Such is the cost of living in the real world.

An RA 30 may be used for each zone providing redundancy of pink noise generation. The ME 30B equalizer locations are arbitrary. Placing them between the Mixer and the MA 6S works just as well. Other Rane equalizers may be substituted of course, depending on space, 1/3 or 2/3-octave resolution or U.L. requirements (see Figure 4).

The SRM 66 Matrix Mixer is ideal for this application. Assign the mic to all outputs while routing the noise generators as shown. You even have a couple extra inputs left for music sources.

An MA 6S/KTM 6 combination drives the ceiling array. The MA 6S can alternatively handle three channels for noise masking, with the other three for background music in other offices, or simply bridged for three 300 watt zones.

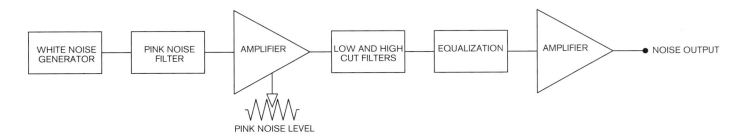

Figure 2. Typical Noise Masking Generator

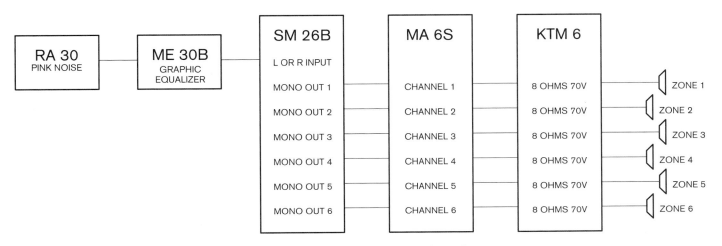

Figure 3. Basic Noise Masking System Example

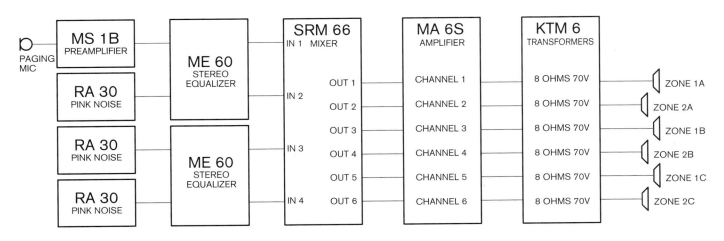

Figure 4. Multiple Array Noise Masking System Example

Noise Masking-3

The outputs drive the loudspeakers in an interlaced array as shown by Figure 5. No two adjacent speakers receive the same source. This is not the wiring nightmare it first appears. Notice that the speakers still wire daisychained, just diagonal instead of straight.

The noise must be as uniform as possible throughout the office environment. This demands lots of speakers. The most successful systems extend the noise signal into ancillary areas (storage rooms, copying/FAX centers, closets, etc.) adding even more speakers.

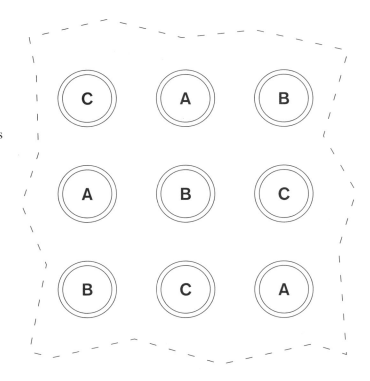

Figure 5. Noise Masking Ceiling Array

REFERENCE

"Acoustics of Open Plan Rooms," by Rollins Brook and "Sound System Design", by Chris Foreman in Glen Ballou, Ed., *Handbook For Sound Engineers,* Howard W. Sams & Co, Indianapolis, 1987.

©Rane Corporation   10802 47th Ave. W.,   Mukilteo WA 98275-5098   TEL (425)355-6000   FAX (425)347-7757   WEB http://www.rane.com

Mix-Minus Speech Reinforcement with Conferencing

- **Controlling Acoustic Levels**

- **Speech Reinforcement Zones**

- **Using Delays to Enhance the Sound System**

- **ECS with Zones –**

  - **Two Zone Mix-Minus using the Aux Out of the ECM 82e**

  - **Six Zone Mix-Minus using the Post-Gate Outputs of the ECM 82e**

- **Applying NAG in the Real World**

- **Noise Masking**

- **Feedback Eliminator**

Mike Slattery
Rane Corporation

RaneNote 140
© **1997 Rane Corporation**

INTRODUCTION

Large conference rooms require speech reinforcement so people at all locations can adequately hear each other. To perform speech reinforcement without acoustic feedback is difficult, add Conferencing and it becomes complex. This RaneNote gives insight into acoustic proprieties of speech reinforcement and applications using Rane Conferencing products.

Controlling Acoustic Levels

The following operations neglect any effect of room echo or room acoustics.

Terms used for calculating properties:

D0 - Distance from talker to the farthest listener.
D1 - Distance from the source mic to the nearest loudspeaker.
D2 - Distance from the listener to the nearest loudspeaker.
Dn - Distance from the talker to the nearest listener.
Ds - Distance from the talker to the microphone.
NOM - Number of Open Mics

When audio travels from a source, its *Sound Pressure Level* (SPL) attenuates by half for every doubling of the distance. The formula for calculating the SPL attenuation is known as the inverse square law and is stated as:

Without speech reinforcement.
Inverse Square Law:
SPL Attenuation = **Dn** SPL – 20Log(**D0/Dn**)

When applying sound reinforcement to a large conference room, first you need to know the room's *Potential Acoustic Gain* (PAG). This allows you to determine the maximum amount of sound reinforced, in decibels, achievable before feedback occurs.

The PAG formula:
PAG = 20Log((**D0 * D1**)/(**Ds * D2**))

If **NOM** is greater than 1 then:
PAG = 20Log((**D0 * D1**)/(**D2 * Ds**)) – 10Log**NOM**

When using PAG to setup system gain, it is customary to add 6 dB of *Feedback Stability Margin* (FSM). Systems that operate at 6 dB below their PAG are usually free of feedback problems.

PAG = 20Log((**D0 * D1**)/(**D2 * Ds**)) – 10Log**NOM** - 6 dB

How much sound reinforcement is needed to achieve an average SPL at a distant listener's position relative to the non-reinforced SPL at a near listener's position?

This *Needed Acoustical Gain* or NAG is the gain in decibels required by sound reinforcement to achieve an equivalent acoustic level at the farthest listener equal to what the nearest listener would hear without sound reinforcement.

The NAG formula:
NAG = 20Log(**D0/Dn**)

NAG must be less than or equal to PAG to avoid feedback.

Example:
    D0 - 20 feet
    D1 - 10 feet
    D2 - 6 feet
    Dn - 4 feet
    Ds - 2 feet

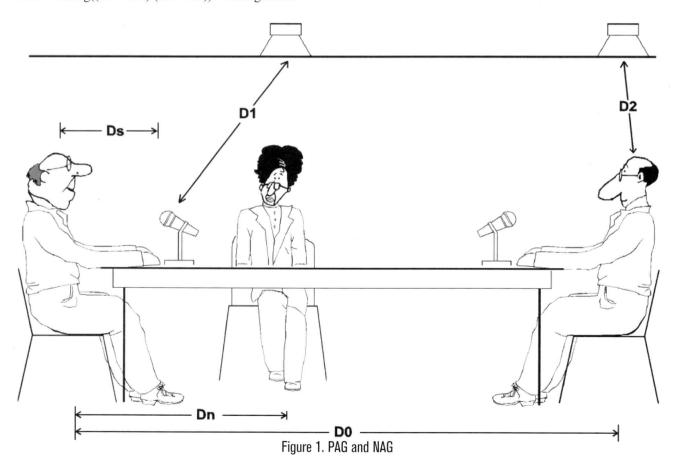

Figure 1. PAG and NAG

Calculating PAG and NAG

Loudspeakers are placed throughout the conference room. The closest loudspeaker to the talker is placed 10 feet from the talker's microphone. The closest loudspeaker to the farthest listener is placed 6 feet from the listener.

1. How much acoustic gain can the sound system supply without causing feedback if only 1 microphone is on? (PAG)
2. How much acoustic gain is required for the farthest listener to hear at an equivalent level to the nearest listener? (NAG)
3. Can the farthest listener receive enough gain without feedback?

1. Using the PAG formula:
$$\textbf{PAG} = 20Log((\textbf{D0} * \textbf{D1})/(\textbf{D2} * \textbf{Ds})) - 10Log\textbf{NOM} - 6 \text{ dB}$$

$$PAG = 20Log((20*10)/(6*2) - 6 \text{ dB}$$
$$PAG = 18 \text{ dB (to nearest whole dB)}$$

2. Using the NAG formula:
$$\textbf{NAG} = 20Log(\textbf{D0/Dn})$$

$$NAG = 20Log(20/4)$$
$$NAG = 14 \text{ dB}$$

3. Since PAG is the maximum calculated level that is obtainable without feedback and it is 4 dB greater than the calculated NAG level, the sound system should operate without feedback.

Speech Reinforcement Zones

To perform speech reinforcement in a large conference room or auditorium, it is best to use automatic microphone mixers and divide the room into zones. The zones are made up of both microphone and loudspeaker groups. A microphone group is a mix of the post-gate outputs from the individual microphones within a zone. Each loudspeaker group has it own amplifier to allow selective audio sources to be played within a zone. Grouping microphones within a zone allows a microphone group to be played at selected loudspeaker groups. Zoning allows microphones within a zone to be played on loudspeakers of other zones while disabling them from being played within their own zone. This is typically called a *mix-minus* zone system.

Some system designers use relays to disable a loudspeaker group when a microphone within its zone gates-on. *Do not use this type of design with acoustic echo cancellers.* Changes in the acoustic properties of a room, caused by switching loudspeakers, will cause the echo canceller to loose its adaptation and return echo.

The simplest example of using zones for speech reinforcement uses only two zones, with each zone having one microphone and one ceiling loudspeaker. A microphone and ceiling loudspeaker are placed at each end of a conference table. Zone 1 contains the left microphone and ceiling loudspeaker and Zone 2 contains the right microphone and ceiling loudspeaker. To perform speech reinforcement, Zone 1's microphone's audio signal is feed only to Zone 2's ceiling loudspeaker and Zone 2's microphone's audio signal is feed only to Zone 1's ceiling loudspeaker.

Using Delays to Enhance the Sound System

Sound travels through 70° F air at about 1.13 feet per millisecond. In a large conference room using speech reinforcement, this delay causes the listener to perceive the direction of the talker from the ceiling loudspeakers and not directly from the talker. This delay-related phenomena is one aspect of the *Haas Effect* or *precedence effect*.

The Haas Effect is described as:

When two loudspeakers are referenced with the same signal, the sound image direction is centered between the two loudspeakers. As one of the loudspeakers is delayed up to 10 milliseconds, the sound image direction is shifted towards the non-delayed loudspeaker. For the sound image to be restored to the center position, the delayed loudspeaker level must be increased by 10 dB. Increasing the level of the delayed loudspeaker also adds to the loudspeakers SPL. If the delay is between 10 to 30 milliseconds, the delayed loudspeaker contributes a sense of liveliness but not direction. Increasing the delay by 50 milliseconds or more causes the listener to become aware of the delayed loudspeaker.

By utilizing the Haas Effect in a speech reinforcement system, the sound image direction is maintained from the talker and not the loudspeakers. This is achieved by using delays in the sound system to align each microphone group to its reinforcement zone. To determine the amount of delay required between each microphone group and its loudspeaker groups, measure the distance from the center talker of one microphone group to each center listener of the zones that the

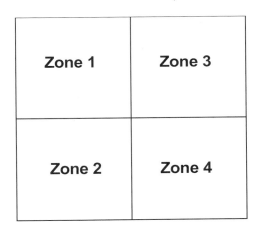

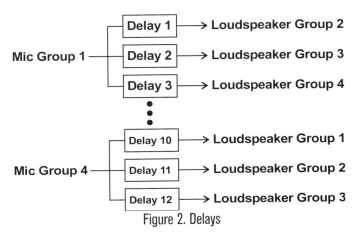

Figure 2. Delays

talkers microphone is reinforced. Add to the measurement the distance from the listener to his closest loudspeaker. Using the measured distance for each zone, calculate the delay and add 10 milliseconds (See above formula). Apply the calculated delay time to each zone for the microphone group. *The number of delays required to perform this task is staggering for a large number of zones.* For example, a system with four zones may require three delays per zone (a delay for each microphone group within a zone) for a total of twelve delays!

Another method for aligning a microphone group to a zone is to use programmable delays for each zone and speech detection for each microphone group. For this to work, the programmable delay must have fast recallable memories without producing audio artifacts during delay changes. Each delay must have a memory setting stored for each microphone group. When speech is detected within a microphone group, all delays must recall their setting for that group. This type of system is achievable with ECS and the RPM 26v by using the contact closure outputs on the ECM 82e mixer and programmable delays available in the RPM 26v.

ECS with Zones

ECS provides three methods for creating microphone groups within a zone. In choosing the type of method, first determine the number of microphones within a zone to create the microphone group. If a microphone group can be placed on one ECM 82e, then the Mix or Aux output of an ECM 82e can be used to create the microphone group. If a single microphone group cannot be produced from one ECM 82e mixer, then the Post-Gate Output of an ECM 82e must be used with a separate matrix mixer to create the microphone group. Using the Mix output of the ECM 82e provides for a Mixer Gate feature, which improves system stability. *Unfortunately, if an echo canceller is placed in the ECM 82e then the Mix out has about a 40 millisecond delay.* Therefore, when using an acoustical echo canceller with distances between zones of less than 40 feet, it is not wise to use the Mix out. The **Aux Output** is processed before the echo canceller and only requires the internal Aux Output switch be placed in Post-Gate mode (factory default).

Two Zone Mix-Minus Using the ECM82e's Aux Out

Figure 3 illustrates how two ECM 82eAs and an ECB 62e can perform a simple two zone mix-minus system using the Aux out of the ECM 82eA and two ports on the ECB 62e to create the zones. This is performed by assigning Mixer 1's Aux output to Zone 2's loudspeakers and Mixer 2's Aux Output to Zone 1's loudspeakers. To play the Program audio (audio from the VCR and Hybrid) at the two zones the audio matrix must include these two inputs. Connecting Port 1's output to Port 6's input allows for the Program Audio level to be changed without changing the speech reinforcement level.

Feedback Warning: Connecting an output port to another input port may result in feedback if the matrix routing is not set properly. (See Fig. 4)

The RPM 26v performs audio processing of the speech reinforcement system. Some of the audio processing features include bandwidth reduction, equalization, delay compensation and compression. DSP program 9 is chosen for its large number of parametric filters. Although this program is normally used as a two-way crossover, its crossovers can be bypassed using the advanced mode by a right mouse click. Placing the RPM 26v between the Aux outputs of the ECM 82eAs and the ECB 62e allows for audio processing of the speech reinforcement material without affecting the program material. (See Fig. 5)

To create zones:
1. Make a map of the microphone and loudspeaker placements: (See Fig. 3)
2. Divide the table into the number of required zones, or that you are able to work with.
3. Determine which microphones go with each ECM 82eA mixer to create a microphone group.
4. Assign the loudspeakers to a zone.
5. Setup the matrix routing for the ECB 62e. (See Fig. 4)

Figure 4. RaneWare ECS Port Screen

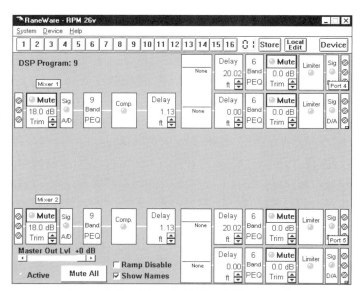

Figure 5. RaneWare RPM 26v DSP Program 9

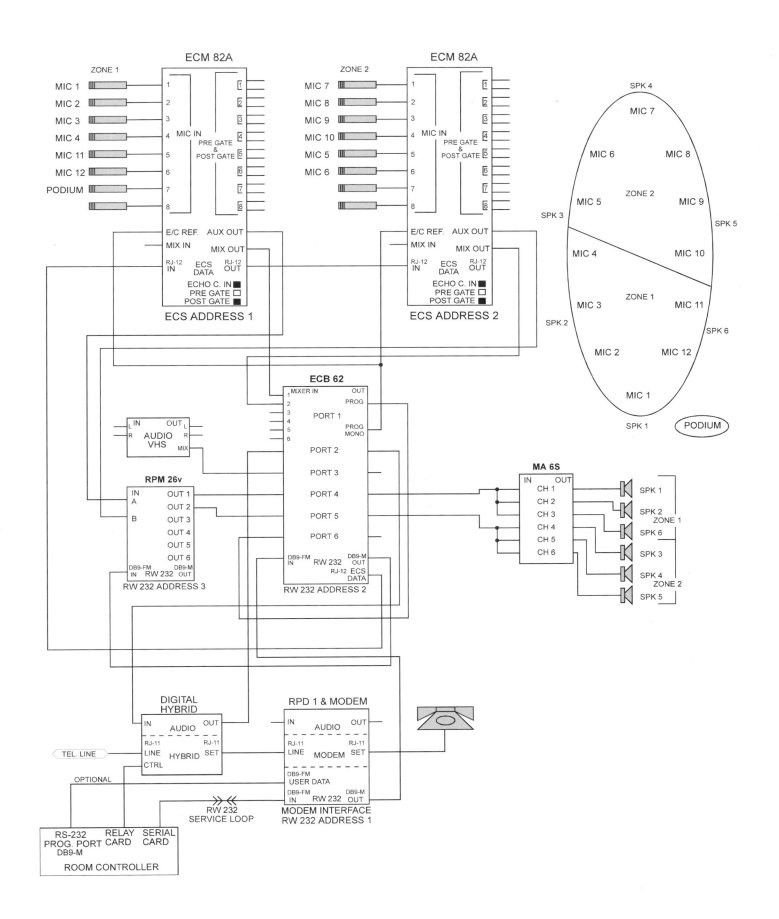

Figure 3. 2-Zone Mix-Minus

Six Zone Mix-Minus Using ECM 82's Post-Gate Outputs

Figure 6 illustrates how the Post-Gate outputs of the ECM 82e are used for speech reinforcement. This system has superior program and speech reinforcement audio performance above the method using the Aux output of the ECM 82eA. This improved performance is achieved by using a separate program loudspeaker and a matrix mixer. Separating the program from the speech reinforcement audio allows for audio processing to be performed on the speech reinforcement audio without affecting the program audio.

In this application delays were not required, thereby eliminating the need for microphone grouping. This allows for Post-Gate outputs to be fed directly to a 16 x 8 audio matrix mixer. This mixer is then used to create the speech reinforcement zones using the matrix routing. *Since microphone grouping is not used in this example, performing the Haas Effect with delays is not practical.* Without individual microphone groups the audio received at a zone contains a mix of all of the microphones fed to the loudspeakers for that zone. This will cause problems if delays are used.

Using a matrix mixer in conjunction with the Post-Gate outputs of the ECM 82eA reduces the number of microphones in a zone and increases PAG by allowing a greater distance between microphones and loudspeakers. This method also allows for individual NAG level adjustments for each microphone within a Zone.

Since there are six zones, three RPM 26v's are used to perform audio processing for the speech reinforcement system. Some of the audio processing features include bandwidth reduction, equalization and compression. DSP program 9 is chosen for its large number of parametric filters. Although this program is normally used as a two-way crossover, its crossovers can be bypassed using the advanced mode with a right mouse click.

To create zones:
1. Make a map of the microphone and loudspeaker placements: (See Fig. 6)
2. Divide the table into the number of required zones, or that you are able to work with.
3. Determine which microphones go with each ECM 82eA mixer to create a microphone group.
4. Assign the loudspeakers to a zone.
5. Setup the matrix routing. (See Fig. 7)
6. Setup the NAG level for each input of the Matrix Mixer.

Zone	Speaker	Mic/Input	Input Route
1	1	5, 6, 7, 8, 9, 10, Prog	12, 13, 8, 9, 10, 11, 14
2	2	7, 8, 9, 10, Prog	8, 9, 10, 11, 14
3	3	Pod, 1, 11, 12, Prog	7, 1, 5, 6, 14
4	4	Pod, 1, 2, 3, 4, 11, 12, Prog	7, 1, 2, 3, 4, 5, 6, 14
5	5	Pod, 1, 2, 3, 4, Prog	7, 1, 2, 3, 4, 14
6	6	5, 6, 7, Prog	12, 13, 8, 14

Figure 7. Matrix Routing Chart

Pod = Podium

Prog = Program

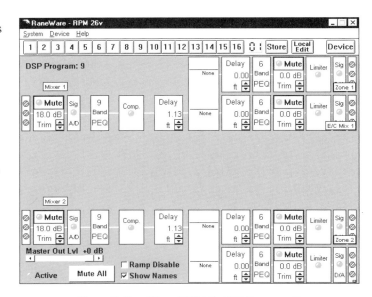

Figure 8. RaneWare RPM 26v DSP Program 9

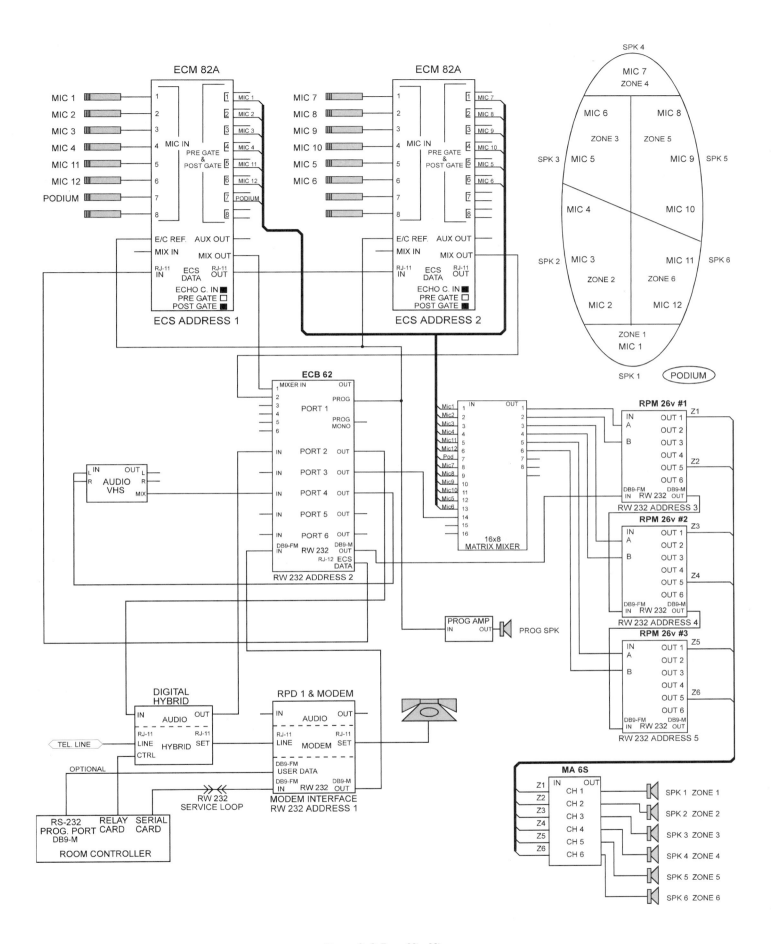

Figure 6. 6-Zone Mix-Minus

Applying NAG in the Real World

Using the system of Figure 6, the following procedure describes a method to apply NAG. Since room acoustics is a major contributor of the level settings for PAG and NAG, you might find it easier to set the NAG levels of a microphone to a loudspeaker zones by using a sound level meter and a portable pink noise source with loudspeaker. The following is a step-by-step procedure that first determines a system level set at the power amp using the microphone and loudspeaker that are farthest from each other (**Zr**). This will be the maximum level required by the speech reinforcement system. After determining the system level, the other routing levels for this microphone to a zone (**Zt**) can be set by using a sound level meter or a version of NAG called *Route Attenuation Level* (RAL).

In this system the Podium is 30 feet from the chair at Zone 4 and the microphones are 4 feet apart.

Zr - Distance from noise source to Zone reference.
Zt - Distance from noise source to test zone.

The RAL formula:
$$RAL = 20Log(Zt/Zr)$$

Do not adjust microphone gains at the ECM 82As to set NAG levels.

1. Setup the input levels and equalization for the RPM 26v's.
2. Setup the system level at the MA 6S amp by starting with the microphone that is farthest from a loudspeaker. In this example, the Podium Mic is the farthest from Zone 4's loudspeakers.
   a. Disable all Mics. *Tip: If you use one of the canned ECS files, Memory 16 can be used to enable and disable Mics.*
   b. Enable the Podium Mic and apply 80 dB SPL of pink noise source to it. *Tip: If you use one of the canned ECS files, Memory 16 can be used to set this level.*
   c. Place a sound level meter pointing towards the loudspeaker at the listening position for the person at Mic 7.
   d. Set the route level for the Podium Mic to Zone 4 (matrix mixer input 7 to output 4) to 0 dB.
   e. Set the system level by adjusting Zone 4's loudspeaker level at channel 4 of the MA 6S Amp so that 71 dB SPL is received at this position. Set all other MA 6S input levels to the same.

3. Using this Mic, setup the NAG for its next closest zone.
   a. Place a sound level meter pointing towards the loudspeaker at the listening position for the person in the center of this zone.
   b. Set the route attenuation level for this Mic to the Zone under test using its calculated value or use a sound level meter.
   Calculating RAL for the Podium Mic to Zone 3:
   Zr = 32 feet
   Zt = 22 feet
   RAL = 20Log(22/32)
   RAL = 3 dB
4. Repeat step 3 for all remaining zones that this Mic is reinforced in. Use the Routing Chart of Fig. 7.
5. Apply the noise source on the next test Mic.
   a. At the farthest zone, place a sound level meter pointing towards the loudspeaker at the listening position for the person in the center of this zone.
   b. Set the route level for this Mic for a 71 dB SPL.
   c. Go to step 3.
6. Repeat step 5 for all remaining Mics.

Noise Masking

Providing a method for noise masking allows individuals to talk "off-record" without being easily heard by others in the room. This method is commonly used in courtroom applications. Since noise masking may need to be selected in different areas, use a matrix mixer to select the masked zones. The noise source on the ECB 62e is program-selectable for this function.

Feedback Eliminator

Installing feedback eliminators at each loudspeaker group can help maintain system stability by reducing feedback. The typical feedback eliminator performs this function using high-Q adaptable notch filters. When using feedback eliminators with echo cancellers, bypass the far-end audio around the feedback eliminator. If the feedback eliminator cannot be bypassed, connect the output of the feedback eliminator to the echo canceller's reference on the ECM 82.

Reference

Glen M. Ballou, *Handbook for Sound Engineers Second Edition* (SAMS, 1991)

©Rane Corporation   10802 47th Ave. W.,   Mukilteo WA 98275-5098   TEL (425)355-6000   FAX (425)347-7757   WEB http://www.rane.com

09515 2-00

Controlling Audio Systems with ActiveX

- **ActiveX**

- **Network Hardware**

- **CobraNet**

- **Ethernet**

Stephen Macatee
Devin Cook
Rane Corporation

RaneNote 152
© **1999 Rane Corporation**

INTRODUCTION

Control of audio systems and transport of audio over computer networks are newsworthy topics in the professional audio industry. Several schemes are available today. Using ActiveX is not new to the audio industry, but controlling CobraNet devices with ActiveX is. The secondary problem of incorporating real world relays, switches, indicators and existing non-networked, serially-controlled audio and interface products needs addressing to transition into our future. Also, the ability to link on-screen controls to such relays, switches, indicators and equipment must be supported.

To implement such control over Ethernet networks, Microsoft ActiveX controls have been employed as a control implementation. A brief primer on ActiveX as well as ActiveX advantages and disadvantages are discussed. With years of work on the old topic of true cross-manufacturer interoperability still not generating the critical mass it once was, a view toward these topics is also revisited. This paper attempts to show that the nirvana of true manufacturer interoperability — regardless of protocol — is achievable over networks without the need for manufacturers to agree — except on Microsoft ActiveX.

BACKGROUND

Much has been written on the varying needs, implementations, benefits and pitfalls of system control. The Audio Engineering Society (AES) has held conferences and paper sessions on computer-controlled audio systems[1]. With the seemingly constant drop in price and availability of computers, it is easy to anticipate further and even ubiquitous incorporation of computers as the control platform of choice for professional audio systems. Thousands of systems already incorporate personal computers, Macintosh and other computers.

The natural evolution of audio and control over standard Ethernet computer networks already taking place furthers the need to enable disparate computer-controllable devices to share both a common user interface and the transport mechanism over Ethernet. Peak Audio's CobraNet technology offers one such solution which uses Ethernet for transport and SNMP (Single Network Management Protocol) for control. Others to watch for increased applicability in the pro audio world include the currently consumer and professional audio-deployed IEEE 1394 (FireWire) and USB. ATM and other technologies from the computer industry will continue to infiltrate the conservative pro audio world.

The complexity of audio systems continues to grow, driven by users' requirements and expectations and the constant march of technology. The need for untrained users to easily control such complex systems is perhaps the hardest thing to provide when equipment from multiple manufacturers is incorporated into a single system.

Control interfaces began with device front panel controls and evolved through the following: wired and wireless remotes, MIDI, RS-232, RS-422, RS-485, DMX512, etc. The list continues through Ethernet and many other proprietary and non-proprietary schemes. Yet, with all these control and several transport schemes to choose from, it is still difficult to control disparate products from a common user interface and have the results work cohesively.

The dream of a common hardware and software approach permitting cross-manufacturer interoperability has lost a lot of steam since the Lone Wolf days of the pro audio industry. Much is learned from examining where we've been; where we're going; how we got here; why we were going there in the first place and what mistakes were made along the way.

The Lone Wolf dream of linking all manufacturers' products together with a common user interface and transport mechanism created great excitement and anticipation. The idea was simple, but the implementation proved too difficult. The Lone Wolf dream failed due to sale of the technology before it worked well enough for the scaleable needs of the industry, as well as the sudden licensing of too many manufacturers before the resources to support them were in place. One thing is certain, Lone Wolf and SC-10 succeeded by providing the audio industry with a vision and the facility for cooperation toward that vision. It is now taking the technology of the computer industry to get us there though.

The need for a common communications and transport protocol applicable across disparate components from many manufacturers was achieved by the computer industry many years ago. It is often discussed that many standards come about through the necessity of one or more entities in an industry having the initiative to solve the problem at hand. Then others recognize its significance and jump on the bandwagon thus creating the momentum for a future standard, and/or competitive alternate solutions are developed. As is happening in many industries, adopting techniques and technology from the long-standing and significantly larger computer industry with its enticing economies of scale and other advantages seems a worthwhile venture. This is where the ActiveX rubber meets the road.

ACTIVEX BACKGROUND

Microsoft ActiveX controls are of concern to the pro audio community. This technology allows designers of computer-controlled sound systems to create common front-end software control panels that operate different manufacturers' units, without having to know anything about their internal code or protocols. This is powerful. If manufacturers incorporate ActiveX controls, systems designers will not be limited to products offered by a single, platform-specific manufacturer.

Each ActiveX control is made up of Properties and Events. ActiveX control Properties are values associated with the control which include things such as level settings, mute condition and meter readings. ActiveX control Events tell the computer something has happened, such as a switch closure, button press or clip detection. ActiveX allows the manufacturer to create an object (a piece of software code) which fully describes a device, while hiding the implementation details such as protocol from the programmer. By hiding the communication details, there is no need for manufacturers to agree on protocol. This lack of a protocol standard means that cooperation between manufacturers is not required. It allows each manufacturer to choose the best protocol for their devices.

For example, no longer would you need to know that the 17th byte of a 32-byte status message meant that the unit's second output channel was muted. With an ActiveX control, you might simply refer to the device's output 2 mute status as "Device1.Out2Mute."

WHAT IS ACTIVEX ANYWAY?

ActiveX is a Microsoft-developed software technology released in 1996. ActiveX, formerly called OLE (Object Linking and Embedding), is based on the Component Object Model (COM), but provides substantially different services to developers. An ActiveX control is a unit of executable code, such as an .exe file, that follows the ActiveX specification for providing software objects. This technology allows programmers to assemble reusable software controls into applications and services. However, software development using ActiveX technology should not be confused with Object-Oriented Programming (OOP). OOP is concerned with creating objects, while ActiveX is concerned with making objects work together. Simply stated, ActiveX is a technology that lets a program – the ActiveX control – interact with other programs over a network, regardless of the language in which they were written. ActiveX controls can do similar things as Java, but they are quite different. Java is a programming language, while ActiveX controls can be written in any language (e.g., Visual Basic, C, C++, even Java). Also, ActiveX runs in a variety of applications, while Java and Javascript usually run only in Web browsers. ActiveX controls can be used in web pages and within visual programming languages such as Borland's Delphi, Sybase's PowerBuilder, Microsoft's Visual Basic and even in tools such as Adobe's GoLive and National Instrument's LabVIEW.

For pro audio applications, objects are the sliders, buttons, indicators and other graphical screen entities. The objects have properties: slider position, slider range, on or off for buttons and indicators. Once the screen objects are chosen and placed, ActiveX controls can link the objects' properties to other ActiveX controls such as the device parameters inside an audio device. For example, linking a slider to the ActiveX control for a device's level control. Then, moving the level control graphic slider varies the audio level and vice-versa.

Here's an example: A computer is used to control an audio system over an Ethernet network and something on the computer's screen controls some function of the system. The idea is to place controls on the computer screen and link them, using ActiveX, to a parameter in the system. What's important is that only the controls required by the computer's end-user need be displayed. Additionally, more detailed interfaces including hidden or password-protected web pages can then be created to provide any level of system parameter access desirable — from complete system control, to a lone system power button, or anything in-between. No longer are systems limited to the number of security levels provided by a vendor's software, nor are you limited to controlling a single system parameter per screen control. For example, you can link multiple ActiveX controls to a single screen object, thus adjusting EQ level simultaneously with master level control and limiter threshold. You can also program actions when certain events occur, such as triggering audio playback or turning a system off at a certain time or adjusting delay time as the temperature changes.

You can control different parameters inside the same device from different computers on the network as well as control the same parameter from multiple computers. This is one of the major advantages of networks – multiple control locations automatically update when changes are made by any control location.

However, ActiveX controls are not limited to just Ethernet implementations. You can create RS-232 or MIDI capable ActiveX controls. For audio networking purposes, Ethernet-enabled ActiveX controls are discussed here. It is wise as a development architecture to separate the communications code from the other software development pieces to allow portability of ActiveX controls onto other transport mechanisms.

One of many popular software packages used to create user interface web pages for computer-controlled systems is Microsoft's FrontPage. Web pages may or may not be accessible over the Internet. Using FrontPage or any of the many ActiveX-ready software packages, ActiveX provides, literally, an infinite number of programming possibilities.

The procedure for using ActiveX with FrontPage is simple: insert a manufacturer-supplied ActiveX control in your web page. Set the control's Properties – such as the IP address and name for the manufacturer's device. As needed, insert a button (or scroll bar, check box…) and set its Properties like the button's name, value and control range. Use Microsoft's Script Wizard that is included with FrontPage to link the button's Events to the device's internal ActiveX parameter(s) or link other Events and Actions as needed for your application.

NETWORKING RELAYS, SWITCHES AND INDICATORS

Many systems must incorporate relays, switches and luminous indicators for control, event or status indication. The Rane Via 10 Ethernet Bridge ships with ActiveX controls which allow its logic port states to be linked to a web page ActiveX control . The device's logic ports are capable of driving relays or LEDs, or reading switches, relays or any zero to 5 volt source. Thus, on-screen objects can be linked with these real world hardware tools to incorporate their use in networked systems. Applications for the zero to five volt input port include switches, but temperature or humidity sensors, potentiometers or any variable 5 volt source are suitable. Since this is a networked system, multiple locations can control and monitor the logic ports, and the on-screen status always remains linked to the hardware tools – change either and their states always correspond. This product is one way of implementing relays, et cetera into network controlled systems.

CONTROLLING EXISTING EQUIPMENT

Using existing RS-232-based and other serially-controlled equipment on a network is a likely requirement as the audio industry transitions into the network world. It may be some time before Ethernet control jacks are found on a wide variety pro audio equipment. Until then, carrying RS-232 data over an Ethernet network can be achieved in several ways. Several vendors sell inexpensive RS-232-to-Ethernet adapters. The previously mentioned Rane product simultaneously supports both the logic ports and the proprietary RW 232 protocol of Rane products. Also, many CobraNet devices offer asynchronous transport of RS-232 data. You are still faced with RS-232's one-to-one Master-Slave issues with these devices. Some CobraNet devices now incorporate memories that are recallable from contact closures. These memory closures can also be transported over the network allowing a single switch to recall memories in multiple, similarly-equipped CobraNet devices.

Logic ports on existing devices can drive or be driven from relays that are monitored by the network. Or, combining existing ports with those on the previously mentioned Rane device's logic ports, one can easily incorporate non-networked products into networks. Applications for these input and output logic ports include memory changes and/or system monitoring.

ActiveX-3

ACTIVEX EXPERIENCES

ActiveX control of system parameters provides several advantages:

World Unity

ActiveX unifies divergent protocols from multiple manufacturers without the need for cooperation. ActiveX can significantly widen product choices for system designers and end-users, providing economies of scale, cost, availability, flexibility and serviceability.

Manufacturers need only develop ActiveX implementations for parameters requiring network control. Though, easier said than done, it's a small price given the advantages and direction of the pro audio industry. For some applications and products, ActiveX may eliminate the need for a manufacturer to implement a customized software user interface for a product or products.

Customization and Unlimited Security Levels

ActiveX permits easy customization of user interfaces and access levels, thereby avoiding constraints to the security levels offered by individual products or manufacturers. Complete interface customization, specific for the system end-user or the installer can easily be incorporated. The use of full color graphics with photos of the system controls or its components can be placed and scaled on a computer screen. The common password-protected web pages and firewalls of the computer world offer the security necessary for any system.

Third Party Software Support & Availability

ActiveX is supported by many software vendors who offer third-party education and support avenues. Sources of information abound for those who want to dive into this technology. Development of ActiveX controls is possible using any of the previously mentioned tools. With a variety of ActiveX capable packages available, needs from the simple to the advanced are satisfied.

Microsoft's Visual C++ includes a library called Active Template Library (ATL) which is designed to allow programmers to avoid the inefficiencies of other less efficient approaches to ActiveX. While ATL does allow development of ActiveX files that can be more size and time efficient, the drawback to this approach is the added difficulty in debugging the code.

Same Business Model as AMX & Crestron

ActiveX offers the same business model to the audio industry as room controller software providers. Many sound contractors either have in-house programmers for such software development or this service is contracted out. Additionally, these same sound contractors may already have a web master on staff that is capable of ActiveX implementations for sound system control.

Those who have followed the trends in room controller technology already recognize the industry's acceptance of Ethernet and IP-based implementations. Thus, it is a simple step for room control developers to support ActiveX controls. Plus, their development tools are already web-publishing based, so current room control developers should have a small learning curve in the ActiveX world.

Therefore, for network systems with one or more PCs as the main controller, instead of assigning AMX or Crestron programmers the system control programming tasks, you find a web site provider who can implement the system control front-ends.

The success or failure of this new relationship remains the same: the system's control implementation relies on the system designer's ability to communicate the needs to the software provider. This is no different than the current room controller business model.

Non-proprietary and Ubiquitous

ActiveX controls are widespread and non-proprietary. Web page creators have been utilizing ActiveX controls for years, thus providing a large and knowledgeable group of ActiveX-familiar providers. ActiveX also provides the ability for these providers to create their own customized ActiveX controls. The color, apparent texture, size, shape, shading, look and feel of each control can be created completely from scratch and designed to match any on-screen décor imaginable.

Fits well into existing PCs

ActiveX is easily incorporated into existing PCs running Windows and Internet Explorer avoiding the need to create a new technology, protocol or hardware-based solution.

Multiple, Simultaneous Control Locations

While not an ActiveX advantage, the combination of network technologies and protocols permits incorporation of multiple simultaneous control locations. This was a previously difficult task in the control industry because serial streams such as RS-232 and RS-485 are unable to share multiple masters. With web-based architectures like ActiveX, controls on multiple web pages offer simultaneous control of the same system parameter(s) from many locations. For the CobraNet ActiveX controls implemented, Simple Network Management Protocol (SNMP) was used to provide the control capabilities found in computer network management, control and diagnostics tools such as Hewlett-Packard's OpenView. The case where changes made from a device's front panel are reflected in multiple network control screens is also satisfied. This is one of the major advantages of networks – multiple control locations can automatically be updated when changes are made by any control location.

Another advantage to network technology is its inherent redundancy ability. With careful network design, both the control and audio transport paths offer automatic fault redundancy.

ActiveX controls also have limitations.

Signal Indication

Perhaps the most important need within controlled systems is the need for accurate and trustworthy on-screen signal indicators. ActiveX control signal indicators have yet to be implemented within a CobraNet system.

Timing

ActiveX has timing limitations, particularly as the number of controls on a single web page are increased. As controls are added to a page, more RAM is used and the multiplexed processing time allotted for each control is diminished thus creating practical timing limits. The response times are not easily measured or calculated. Timing is a function of the computer's speed, the network's speed which can be constantly changing, the ActiveX control's size and code efficiencies and – in the case of CobraNet-based systems – how often the CobraNet interface and the CobraNet device itself scans for network and/or hardware changes. In the CobraNet case, the ActiveX control data is being transported over SNMP.

While it is impractical to suggest precise delay times for system changes, a unicast CobraNet system with 120 ActiveX controls on a single page, utilizing four, 24-port managed switches, with 64 audio channels and two simultaneously running web pages appeared to have a response time around one second. This is not heart warming, but the intent is to communicate performance levels to allow applicability decisions.

Time-critical applications such as show control and synchronized events may not be deterministic enough for ActiveX.

Uncommon and New to the Audio Industry

Few pro audio manufacturers offer ActiveX implementations of their software-controlled parameters which creates a Herculean obstacle for significant implementations across multiple manufacturers' products. Also, there is no current support for ActiveX in Netscape or the Macintosh world.

There are certainly other ways to implement cross-manufacturer control. For CobraNet-based systems, CobraCAD software from Peak Audio offers significant advantages through its use of SNMP – particularly as the CobraCAD package matures and the use of SNMP for control may offer fewer obstacles as the future unfolds. No other currently available tools seem to offer the advantages of ActiveX for the pro audio industry.

CONCLUSION

ActiveX provides a viable solution to the problem of user interface across disparate equipment in computer-controlled systems – particularly CobraNet and other Ethernet-based systems. While no solution – including ActiveX – can solve all problems, ActiveX appears to be a viable one at this juncture for the above issues.

REFERENCES

1. Proceedings of the AES 13th International Conference on Computer-Controlled Sound Systems (Audio Engineering Society, NY, 1994).

2. Tanenbaum, Andrew S. *"Computer Networks"* 3rd edition (Prentice Hall, ISBN 0-13-349945-6, New Jersey, 1996).

3. Perkins, David & Evan McGinnis, *"Understanding SNMP MIBs"* (Prentice Hall, ISBN 0-13-437708-7, Upper Saddle River, 1997).

4. Bates, Jonathan, *"Creating Lightweight Components with ATL"* (Sams, ISBN 0-672-31535-1, Indianapolis, 1999).

5. Cook, Devin, *"Emerging Standards for Networked Audio System Control,"* RaneNote 144, 1998.

Interfacing AES3 & S/PDIF

- **Initials, Acronyms & Standards**

- **AES3 (AES/EBU) & S/PDIF Differences**

- **AES-3id Variation**

- **Conversion Cautions**

- **Converting AES3, AES-3id & S/PDIF**

OVERVIEW

Mainstream digital audio dates from the introduction of the compact disc in the early '80s, making it about twenty years old. Today two serial interfaces coexist: **AES3** (aka **AES/EBU**) for professional use and **S/PDIF** for consumer products. Simple low-cost passive conversion between them is possible – even easy – but it is also filled with cautions. The old rule that direct connection between AES/EBU and S/PDIF equipment is bad practice is relaxed today with new receiver chips tolerant to either interface. With that said, let's explore this tangled nest.

Dennis Bohn
Rane Corporation

RaneNote 149
© 2001 Rane Corporation

INITIALS, ACRONYMS & STANDARDS

The professional digital audio interface known as AES/EBU is initialism for *Audio Engineering Society/European Broadcasting Union*, the two organizations that created the first two-channel digital audio serial interface standard in 1985. Issued as AES3-1985, it was subsequently revised & reissued, with the latest version (as of 2001) being ***AES3-1992 (r1997) AES Recommended Practice for Digital Audio Engineering – Serial transmission format for two-channel linearly represented digital audio data.*** It was also made an American National Standard, issued as **ANSI S4.40-1992**, and an international standard, issued as **IEC 60958-4**. The importance is that *all* of these documents cover the same serial interface, which is now correctly called the **AES3** interface, instead of AES/EBU, and will be used for the rest of this RaneNote.

In the consumer universe we find the acronym **S/PDIF** (also seen without the slash as **SPDIF**) created from *Sony/Philips digital interface format*. This was also made an international standard and issued as **IEC 60958-3** (same number, different dash as the professional version), and it conforms with the EIAJ (*Electronic Industry Association Japan*) standard **CP-1201** (renumbered **CP-340**).

AES-3id-1995 AES information document for digital audio engineering – Transmission of AES3 formatted data by unbalanced coaxial cable is the same format as AES3 but instead of 110-ohm balanced line, it is a 75-ohm unbalanced line using BNC connectors and carried over the same coaxial interface as consumer S/PDIF. AES3id (*the hyphen is dropped for simplicity*) is a special AES3 subset for broadcast applications and long distance runs. (*For long distance high-frequency transmission, unbalanced coax is superior to balanced lines due to the high capacitance of shielded twisted-pair cable.*) Conversion between AES3 and AES3id is very similar to S/PDIF.

[**Note** AES3 is a professional (only) audio standard and S/PDIF is a consumer (only) audio standard, while IEC 60958 and EIAJ CO-1201 cover both consumer and professional definitions.]

[**Caution** *Do not confuse S/PDIF with* **SDIF** *(no P); they are very different. SDIF, developed and used exclusively by Sony on early professional machines, is mono and not self-clocking, consequently requiring three cables for interconnection: two for the stereo channels and one for the synchronization clock.*]

DIFFERENCES BETWEEN AES3 AND S/PDIF

The following table summarizes the differences in the electrical characteristics of AES3 and S/PDIF interfaces:

	AES3[1]	AES3id[2]	S/PDIF[3]
Interface	Balanced	Unbal	Unbal
Connector	XLR-3	BNC	RCA
Impedance	110 Ω	75 Ω	75 Ω
Output Level	2-7 V_{p-p}	1.0 V_{p-p}	0.5 V_{p-p}
Max Output	7 V_{p-p}	1.2 V_{p-p}	0.6 V_{p-p}
Max Current	64 mA	1.6 mA	8 mA
Min Input[5]	0.2 V	0.32 V	0.2 V
Cable	STP[4]	Coax	Coax
Max Distance	100 m	1000 m	10 m

Table 1 indicates a large difference between the minimum output level and the minimum input level (2 V vs. 0.2 V for AES3 for instance). The difference is accounted for by two factors: 1) Half the signal is loss due to the impedance matching required for high-speed transmission lines (*output impedance equals input impedance creating a 6 dB pad*); and 2) Signal loss driving long cables.

CONVERSION CAUTION

You can convert one electrical interface to another with just a few parts, but the protocol used in AES3 and S/PDIF is not exactly the same and that can cause problems. The basic data formats are identical, but there is a bit in the channel status frame that tells which is which, and assigns certain bits different meanings.

This sets the stage for incompatibilities. Many older units are sticklers about what's what in each bit, and even though a given signal faithfully complies with the standard, some equipment will still reject it. Fortunately, many units are flexible and tolerant so simple resistor or transformer converters work. But be warned that a converter that works fine with one unit is no guarantee that it will work fine with all units.

Remember that even though the *audio data* is the same between AES3 and S/PDIF, they have different *subcode* formats. AES3 converted to 75-ohm coax is *not* S/PDIF, and S/PDIF converted to XLR balanced is *not* AES3. Nor is AES3id 75-ohm BNC the same as 75-ohm RCA S/PDIF – it may work, but it is not the same. They are still in their native format; just the transmission medium has changed. Going from S/PDIF to AES3 has a higher degree of success than the other way around. AES3 signals often are not recognized as valid by S/PDIF inputs. Whether they will work in your application depends on the equipment chosen.

Therefore the following passive circuits convert only the signal level and impedance, and not other protocol details (e.g., sample rate, consumer/professional status, nor correct any block errors in the data stream).

Examining the table reveals the difference in levels as the most troubling. The minor impedance mismatch is easily taken care of, but the levels and drive currents are another matter entirely for a passive converter. (*If you add power supplies to the converter then it becomes straightforward, but that is the subject of another Note and another day.*)

---

[1]AES3-1992 (r1997); [2]AES-3id-1995; [3]IEC 60958-3; [4]Shielded twisted-pair; [5] V_{min} for eye pattern T_{min} of 50% of T_{nom} (*eye pattern* is a measurement method for determining transmission quality.)

AES3 to AES3id or S/PDIF

IF (*BIG if*) you know that either the transmitter or the receiver is transformer coupled and the interconnect distance is short then a simple resistor divider will match the impedances and change the level as shown in Fig. 1. This is the AES3id recommended network for creating a 12-dB pad (4:1 voltage divider) and converting the AES3 110 ohm balanced output impedance into 75 ohms for driving the AES3id input. Therefore an average output level of 4 volts will be reduced to 1 volt. Since this exceeds the max allowed for S/PDIF, use the values shown in parenthesis to create an 18-dB pad (8:1 voltage divider) producing 0.5 volt output for the same 4 volts input. (*Other average AES3 output voltages require different resistors – consult AES3id for value graph*).

Transformers make the best passive impedance matchers, plus provide the benefits of ground isolation, high-frequency rejection, DC blocking and short-circuit protection. Impedance matching is easily handled by selection of the appropriate turns ratio (1.21:1 for 110-ohm to 75-ohm – *it's the square of the turns ratio for impedance*) and careful attention to winding details allow wideband high-frequency transformers (you need ~12.5 MHz). The best and safest converter includes the transformer.

If you are not sure about the transformer isolation of the equipment interfacing, use a store-bought impedance matching transformer that comes complete with connectors and a separate resistor voltage divider network as shown in Fig. 2. This T-network is a 75-ohm:75-ohm bi-directional attenuator. The attenuation is a little less than that of Fig. 1 for the same (*assumed*) 4-volt AES3 input because the transformer reduces the voltage level by a factor of 1.21:1 (down to 3.3 volts) as well as matching the impedances.

Sources:
Store-Bought: *Neutrik* NADITBNC series (www.neutrikusa.com/products/accessories/aes-ebu.html)
Or *C4 Audio Systems* SA XM BF series (www.proaudio.uk.com/dip/c4home.htm)

Alternatively, build the impedance matching transformer into the resistor network, as shown in Fig. 3.

Sources:
DIY (do-it-yourself): *Scientific Conversion* SC961-04 (SMT) or SC976-012 (thru-hole) (http://www.scientificconversion.com/Scproduc.html)
Or *Schott* P/N 22523 (thru-hole) (www.schottcorp.com/products/search.asp)

AES3id or S/PDIF to AES3

This conversion only requires impedance matching since the levels are smaller than AES3, but compatible. No satisfactory resistor-only network exists to convert between AES3id or S/PDIF and AES3 even though one appears in the AES3id document. While the network given matches the impedance, it does so with an attenuation of the input signal, running the risk of making it too small for the AES3 receiver, and it does not create the balanced 110-ohm lines that an AES3 receiver needs. Therefore it is recommended to use a transformer for this conversion as shown in Fig. 4. Note that this adapter is identical to that shown in Fig. 3, only driven backwards. Using the store-bought converter with a male-to-female adapter allows it to be fully bi-directional – or build your own using the recommended transformers. *BUT DO NOT FORGET that the levels coming out of an AES3 transmitter are too large for the typical AES3id or S/PDIF input so you must add the attenuator. Going the other way you do not need the attenuator since all AES3 receivers can handle the smallest in-spec AES3id or S/PDIF output signal as long as a minimum of 200 mV arrives.*

AES3id to S/PDIF & Vice-versa

Since both formats use 75-ohm coaxial cable, connecting an *AES3id output* to an *S/PDIF input* is simple. All that is needed is to provide compatible hardware hook-up and a 6-dB pad (2:1 attenuator). As long as connecting distances are short, the simple T-network shown in Fig. 5 does the job.

S/PDIF outputs may be connected directly to *AES3id inputs* – no adapter is required (but don't forget the formatting caveats mentioned above).

NOTE that even though the network is symmetrical and functions normally in either direction, it is to be used only to interface between an *AES3id output* and an *S/PDIF input*. If this adapter is used the other way around, to connect an S/PDIF output to an AES3id input, the attenuation may make the S/PDIF signal too small for the AES3id receiver to acquire.

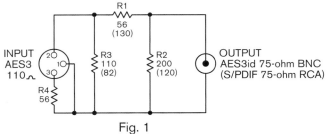

Fig. 1

AES3 to AES3id & S/PDIF Converter
Resistor Impedance Matching Voltage Divider
110Ω to 75Ω; 4:1 (12 dB) PAD
AES3 4V out = AES3id 1V in
(or 8:1 [18 dB] PAD; AES3 4Vout = S/PDIF 0.5V in)

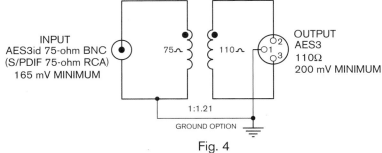

Fig. 4

AES3id or S/PDIF to AES3 Converter

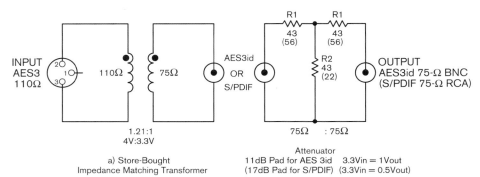

a) Store-Bought
Impedance Matching Transformer

Attenuator
11dB Pad for AES 3id   3.3Vin = 1Vout
(17dB Pad for S/PDIF)   (3.3Vin = 0.5Vout)

Fig. 2

AES3 to AES3id & S/PDIF Converter
using separate transformer and voltage dividing network.

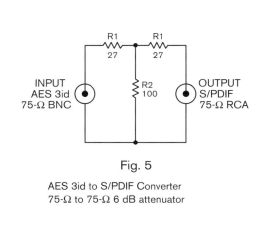

Fig. 5

AES 3id to S/PDIF Converter
75-Ω to 75-Ω 6 dB attenuator

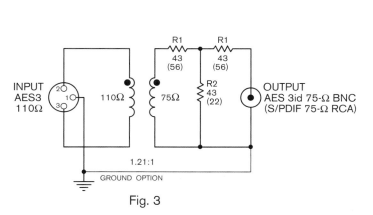

Fig. 3

AES3 to AES 3id & S/PDIF Converter
Transformer Impedance Matching & Resistor Voltage Divider
110Ω to 75Ω; 4:1 (12 dB) PAD
AES3 4Vout = AES3id 1V in
(AES3 4Vout = S/PDIF 0.5Vin)

©Rane Corporation   10802 47th Ave. W.,   Mukilteo WA 98275-5098   TEL (425)355-6000   FAX (425)347-7757   WEB http://www.rane.com

Interfacing Audio and POTS

(Plain Old Telephone Service)

- **Analog Telephone Overview**

- **Characteristics**

- **Simple Interface**

INTRODUCTION

In the USA, in spite of all the hoopla about digital-this, digital-that and fiber-optic-whatever, the truth is that many small commercial paging and music-on-hold applications still involve interfacing with the plain old telephone service, or "POTS". (*By contrast, if you work in the EU business place, then you will rarely run into POTS, since it has almost all been converted to ISDN.*) Meanwhile, back in the USA: if you are lucky, the telephone system you get to work with will provide a line-level auxiliary analog audio feed, but if not, then this Note's for you.

Dennis Bohn
Rane Corporation

RaneNote 150
© 2002 Rane Corporation

ANALOG TELEPHONE OVERVIEW

An analog telephone line, at its simplest, is nothing more than a 600 Ω balanced line. One pair of wires carries duplex[1] audio and 48 VDC for telephone operation. The 48 VDC is current limited by series resistors (one in each leg), therefore phones "on-hook" (no current drawn) typically measure 48 VDC, while phones "off-hook" (current drawn) typically measure 6 - 8 VDC.

Basically all phones work the same, yet many different systems coexist throughout the word. Major differences are found in wiring practices and connectors, line impedances, and loop currents, signaling tones and safety regulations. International harmonization is slowly changing this. The system described here is typical for the United States.

Long distance lines separate transmit and receive audio paths and use 4-wire cable (two pairs). Converting 2-wire local wiring to 4-wire long distance wiring requires a hybrid[2] and is not the subject of this note.

(Teleconferencing applications require complex digital hybrids containing acoustic echo cancelling technology. See *RaneNote: Mix-Minus Speech Reinforcement with Conferencing [ECS]* for details.)

What is of concern here is how to add or remove audio from a normal telephone circuit without interfering with the operation of, or being harmed by, the telephone lines.

A *phone patch*, or *phone tap*, is necessary to interface line-level analog audio to and from POTS. The phone patch allows connecting standard audio equipment to a phone line, while isolating the audio equipment from ring tone and line voltage. It operates in parallel with the telephone, with a circuit design that disturbs normal operation very little due to its high impedance input (*if the hold resistor is not needed*)

POTS Characteristics (TYPICAL)

Bandwidth	300 - 3.3 kHz (3 kHz BW)
Signal-to-noise	45 dB
Average Level	-9 dBm† (275 mV)
Impedance	600 Ω
Connector	RJ-11
Cable	2-Wire (twisted pair)
DC Voltage	48 V[3] (±6 V typ)
Polarity	Positive (*tip*, or *red* wire) tied to earth ground[4]; so it measures −48 VDC (relative to *ring* or *green* wire)
DC Current	20-26 mA (typ)
DC Resistance	200-300 Ω (typ)
AC Ring Volts & Freq.	90 Vrms, 20 Hz (2 secs on, 4 secs off)

† 0 dBm = 1 mW (0.775V) into 600 Ω

SIMPLE POTS INTERFACE WITH CAUTIONS

A single transformer and capacitor creates a POTS interface in a pinch; however adding a few more components greatly improves the performance. The transformer provides the necessary isolation, while the capacitor blocks the DC voltage from the transformer.

The diagram shows an enhanced version discussed next:

The MOV (metal-oxide varistor), or any similar transient voltage suppressor, is required due to the extreme lightning-induced voltage spikes that can travel on telephone lines (*thousands of volts*). It needs a maximum operating voltage of at least 250 Vrms. This seems extreme for a 48 VDC powered line, but the telephone company tests their lines by adding as much as another 200 V, so you must guard against the worst case.

It is not necessary to add a matching capacitor to the other leg of the transformer primary (to preserve the line balance) as will be seen shortly. Use a non-polar type since the polarity of the DC voltage cannot be guaranteed and oftentimes reverses with different operating modes. The value is not critical and depends on the reflected impedance seen by the series capacitor. Normal usage for this type of phone patch is either to drive a high impedance (≥10 kΩ) input of a recorder or an amplifier, or, if used in the opposite direction (i.e., to add audio to the phone line), driven from a low impedance (≤300 Ω) output. The voltage rating must be high enough to withstand the usual DC voltage (and variations) plus the AC ring voltage; a value of 250 Vrms is recommended. Since a 1µF/250V non-polar capacitor can be quite large (and expensive), consider paralleling two or more small non-polar caps (e.g., two 0.47µf/250V, or three 0.33µF/250V rated, etc.).

The resistor, R1, is necessary if the circuit must hold the line, i.e., look-like a phone off-hook. It must be selected to draw enough DC current to drop about 6 V. A big problem comes in predicting this value. The DC source is typically 48 V, but can vary anywhere from 42-54 V, and sometimes *much* more (24-60 V).

Resistor R2 is a good idea to make the line driving impedance higher when using the patch to *add audio* (*total equals R2 + line driver output impedance*).

Luckily when designing a phone patch you do not have to worry much about what the telephone line looks like when the phone is on-hook. This is good because while described as a 600 Ω balanced line, the on-hook line (*the off-hook line is quite different, and will be discussed next*) never measures 600 Ω, nor is it very well balanced. Variations from 500-2500 Ω are reported for the ungrounded side of the line, simultaneous with the grounded side measuring 0-700 Ω – hardly a balanced line. Plus the DC resistance of the telephone cabling

---

[1] Duplex means two-way; full duplex is redundant, but, alas, has been misused so long that it is here to stay; half duplex means one-way and is correct usage.

[2] The name comes from the original use of a *hybrid coil* (special transformer) in the telephone whose function was to keep the send and receive signals separated.

[3] 48 VDC was selected because it qualifies as safe low voltage (<50

VDC) in most countries and is easily created from four car batteries wired in series.

[4] The positive terminal is earth grounded to minimize electrochemical reactions on wet telephone wiring. When the wires are at negative potential compared to the ground the metal ions flow from ground to the wire instead of the reverse situation where the metal from the wire migrates causing corrosion.

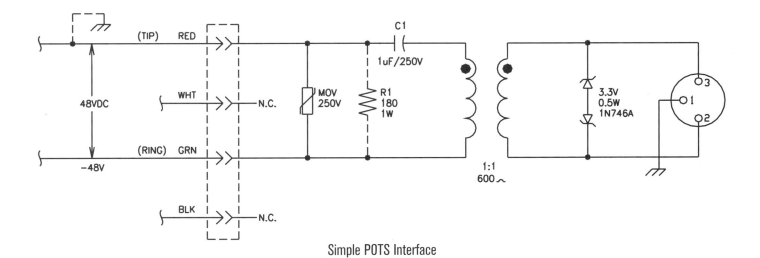

Simple POTS Interface

is not trivial, easily amounting to as much as 1500 Ω for locations a few miles from the central office (26 AWG is common, measuring 440 Ω/mile).

Once the phone is answered, the system goes into off-hook mode and sends out the dial tone. Now the line is predictable with the balanced output impedance measuring about 400 Ω (±25%), split evenly between the two lines, with the voltage ranging from 42 V to as high as 80 V. Still not well balanced, but a lot closer than the on-hook values.

The back-to-back zener diodes in the secondary clamp any high voltage (including any ring voltage that may appear) that gets through the transformer and protects the downstream equipment. Their value is pretty arbitrary and is determined by what the interfaced unit can withstand. The 1N746s limit the output to 4 V peak-to-peak, or 1.4 Vrms. Likewise the power rating need not be excessive; ½-watt is enough.

Circuit Summary
1. Provide isolation (transformer).
2. Block DC voltage (series capacitor).
3. If required, provide DC path to hold the line (parallel resistor).
4. Provide primary protection (parallel MOV)
5. Provide secondary protection (zener diodes).
6. Protect against too low secondary impedance (series resistor)

DIY (do-it-yourself) Transformer Sources

Telephony has been around for so long that most electronic supply stores carry interfacing transformers (600 Ω to 600 Ω, analog audio transformer with telephone grade frequency response and distortion performance). They come in two types: "wet" and "dry," referring to whether they are designed to pass direct current (DC) – *wet* transformers withstand DC currents without saturating, *dry* transformers do

not. For the diagram shown you want a dry transformer, which is smaller and less expensive than wet ones. Most modern telephone circuits use dry transformers.

Three shown, but typical of many:
Bourns Cat. # LM-LP 1001 (thru-hole):
www.bourns.com/pdf/LMNP.pdf
Or SM-LP-5001 (SMT):
www.bourns.com/pdf/SMLP5001.pdf
Radio Shack Cat. # 273-1374 (wire leads):
www.radioshack.com
Tamura Cat. # MET-46 (thru-hole):
z17.zland.com/ps/tamura/customer.nsf
Other good sources include **Prem Magnetics**
www.premmag.com)
and **Midcom**
www.midcom-inc.com/products/analog).

Store-Bought Phone Patch Sources

The following are simple telephone interfaces. They are not *hybrids*. They are used simply to put audio on or take audio off POTS. They are *not for teleconferencing* and will not work due to their lack of acoustic echo cancelling technology. These are for non-conference applications only.

The models differ greatly in features and price, so do your homework before spending momma's hard-earned money.
Comrex Telephone Coupler TCB-2
www.comrex.com/couplers.htm
Excalibur HC-1 Handi-Coupler
www.bradleybroadcast.com/2001/telephone.htm
JPS Communications RTU-200
www.jps.com/products/prodinfo/rtu200.html
PSC Phone Tap
www.professionalsound.com/catalog/ph-tap.html
Radio Shack
www.radioshack.com

Pro Audio Company Names: Mysterious Initials — What They Mean

ACE *Audio Composite Engineering.* Now in a strategic alliance with QSC.

ACO Pacific from *ACOoustics.*

AEI Music *Audio Environments Inc.* Now merged with DMX Music.

AKG Acoustics *Akustische u. Kino-Gerte* (Acoustic and Cinematography Equipment)

AKM *Asahi Kasei Microsystems Co., Ltd.*

ALESIS A loose acronym for *Algorithmic Electronic Systems* adjusted to make spelling and pronunciation easier. One of two companies born from the ashes of MXR (Alesis is now owned by Numark).

ALLISON Research After the name of Paul C. Buff's first wife. See: PAL STUDIOS.

ALTEC LANSING *All Technical Products* plus *Lansing* from partner *James B(ullough) Lansing,* who left in 1946 to form a new company: JBL.

AMPEG *Amplified Peg* In 1946, Everett Hull, an accomplished pianist and bass player, organized a partnership with Stanley Michaels under the name "Michaels-Hull Electronic Labs." Their mission was to produce a new microphone pickup that Hull designed. The pickup was fitted on the end of an upright bass and was dubbed the Amplified Peg or "Ampeg" for short.

AMEK According to founder Graham Langley, there is no particular significance to the name.

AMPEX After the initials of founder *Alexander M. Poniatoff* plus *EXcellence.*

AMS Neve *Advanced Music Systems,* now merged with *Neve,* after Rupert Neve, father of modern audio console technology.

AMX Modified initials for the company's original name: *Advanced Microcomputer Systems,* but due to conflicts with the other "AMS" (above), they made it "AMX" — changed to Panja in 1999, then back to AMX in 2001.

APHEX *Aural Perception Heterodyne Exciter*

API *Automated Processes, Inc.* also *Audio Products, Inc.* "Automated Processes" was chosen out of frustration to avoid the repeated name rejection by NY State when incorporating, according to Lou Lindauer, founder (all 26 of the names originally picked were rejected). When Paul Wolff bought the company in 1985, he could not continue to use the original name for legal reasons, so he came up with "API Audio Products." When he sold the company to the ATI Group in 1999, they incorporated under the original "Automated Processes" name. Got it?

APT *Audio Processing Technology*

ART *Applied Research & Technology*; one of two companies born from the ashes of MXR (ART is now owned by Yorkville).

ARX *Audio Research X*; evolved from *Audio Research & Technology* after its initials became confused with those of *Applied Research & Technology,* so they replaced "& Technology" with "X" and registered it worldwide.

ASHLY Audio After *Larry Ashley,* one of the five founders of the original sound company (which evolved into manufacturing). They chose his name for the alphabetical advantage, then modified it by dropping the "e" to prevent conflict with another company; in addition, it added a little intrigue.

ASPI Digital *Atlanta Signal Processors, Inc.,* now owned by and renamed Polycom.

ASTATIC Meaning *a-static,* that is, *without static,* from their original line of radio microphones.

ATI *Audio Technologies, Incorporated.* Founded in 1979 by principals Samuel B. Wenzel and Edward M. Mullin.

ATI *Audio Toys, Incorporated.* Founded in 1988 as *Audio Teknology, Inc.,* the company later renamed itself to prevent confusion with the above ATI.

B&O *Bang & Olufsen* After founders *Peter Boas Bang* and *Svend Andreas Grn Olufsen* who started this famous Danish company in 1925.

B&W Loudspeakers *Bowers & Wilkins*

BASF *Badische Aniline Soda Ash Fabrik* Famous brand name, whose slogan was "The First Name In Magnetic

Media," now owned by EMTEC, who retired the BASF brand name in 2002.

BBE Sound *Barcus Berry Electronics* after founders Les Barcus & John Berry, inventors of the first piezo crystal transducer for a musical instrument. Today Barcus-Berry exists as a separate company from BBE Sound.

BELLARI After David DiFrancisco's uncle, Albert Bellari, who immigrated from Italy in the early 1900s; a division of Rolls.

BGW Systems *Brian Gary Wachner*, founder.

BOSE After Amar Bose, PhD professor at MIT, who founded the company in 1964.

BOZAK After founder *Rudy Bozak*, who is credited with designing and manufacturing the first DJ mixer, the Bozak CMA 10-2DL that UREI copied after Bozak stopped production and issued as the famous UREI Model 1620, and much later (after UREI stopped production) Rane redesigned, modernized and sells as the Rane Model 2016.

BSS Audio *Brooke Siren Systems* after founders Chas Brooke and Stan Gould.

CAD Professional Microphones *Conneaut Audio Devices* from Conneaut, OH, their location.

CALREC *Calder Recordings*; shortened from Calder Valley Sound Recording Group

CEDAR Audio *Computer Enhanced Digital Audio Restoration*

CERWIN-VEGA Originally named Vega Associates by founder Gene Czerwinski, who upon incorporation in 1973 added a shortened anglicized version of his last name as a prefix.

CITRONIC Manufacturing began in founder Richard Wadman's garage in the English town called Bromham. Being in a small village, Wadman's house existed on a plot of land that did not have a street name. The house was built on "Site 2" on a designated plot of building land. It became known therefore only as *Site 2* which, through usage, came to be called "cittoe". Eventually the address became Cittoe, with no number. When Wadman registered the company he combined his house name and a shorten form of "electronic" to form Citronic.

CTI Audio *Conneaut Technologies* from Conneaut, OH, their location.

CTS Chicago Telephone Supply after the location and original product line when founded in 1896.

DAR *Digital Audio Research*

dbx *David Blackmer's eXpander*, founder, who went on to found Earthworks.

DDA *Dearden Davies Associates*, after founders Gareth Davies and David Dearden, whose new company is Audient

DIGIGRAM *Digital Gramophone* per Neil Glassman, president of this French company.

DMX Music *Digital Music Express* Now merged with AEI Music.

DOD *David O. DiFrancesco*, founder, whose new company is Rolls.

DTS *Digital Theater Systems*

DUKANE *Dupage* and *Kane* counties in St. Charles, IL, the county boundaries where they are located; originally named *Operadio* when they first manufactured battery-operated radios.

EAW *Eastern Acoustic Works* Now owned by Mackie.

EMTEC *European Multimedia Technologies* Owner of the (now retired) BASF brand name.

E-MU Systems *Electronic Music Systems*

ENSONIQ Name created by founder Bob Yannes from the made-up *ensonic* replacing the "c" with "q" because Compaq was getting lots of publicity with its start-up company in 1983.

E-V *Electro-Voice* Founder Al Kahn (with Lou Borroughs) built a PA system for Notre Dame football coach Knute Rockne to use when he was in his coaching tower. Rockne called it his "electric voice." Mr. Kahn reworked it to "Electro-Voice" and changed the original name of his company from Radio Engineers to Electro-Voice. [*Thanks to Keith Clark, Install Editor at ProSoundWeb for the info and the confirming research. Also See: Kahn, Al 1953 — a history of the company*]

EVENTIDE The original company name was Eventide Clockworks, chosen by founder Richard Factor because "eventide" means "evening" and he started out by making digital clocks for DJs after hours. For the whole wonderful story see *Who/What/Where is "Eventide Clockworks"?* Today, in addition to his role running Eventide, he is busy helping to privatize SETI (search for extraterrestrial intelligence), serving as the SETI League's first president.

FOCUSRITE An off-the-shelf *shell company name* (a pre-registered U.K. legal entity) used initially to quickly establish a company, normally changed after startup, however Rupert Neve liked it, because it proved memorable and many people find it analogous to accurate listening.

FOSTEX Believed a combination of *Foster* (parent company) plus *EXcellence*.

FSR "Just stands for FSR," states Phyllis Gillick, Inside Sales.

GHS Strings *Gould, Holcomb* and Solko the initials of the original founders that started the company in 1964.

GLYPH Named after a symbolic figure that is usually engraved or incised. Since "glyphs" contain recorded history and in many cases stories or multimedia, it is a natural name choice for Glyph Technologies storage connotations. The logo is Hunab Ku, the Mayan god representing the milky way (Mayan astronomers developed the 365-day calendar based on the stars movement). Hunab Ku was the "maker of movement and measure."

GT Electronics *Groove Tubes* Founded by Aspen Pittman.

HHB Communications *Half-Human Band*: name of their rock group in the '70s.

IED *Innovative Electronic Designs*

ICEpower *Intelligent, Compact and Efficient* A division of B&O dedicated to digital audio power conversion technologies and products.

IRP Professional Sound Products *Industrial Research Products*

ISP Technologies *Intelligent Signal Processing* New company formed by James Waller who founded Rocktron in the early '80s and sold it to GHS Strings in 2000.

JBL *James Bullough Lansing*; after selling his interests in Altec Lansing, he used his full name for his new company, which soon became known by their famous initials.

JVC *Japan Victor Company*

KEF *Kent Engineering & Foundry*, by founder Raymond Cooke in Kent, U.K.

KRK Systems *Keith R. Klawitter*, founder.

LAB.GRUPPEN *"Lab Association"* is an accurate translation of the original Swedish name selected in 1979 by electronic engineer founders Kenneth Andersson and Dan Bavholm. The use of the dot was a stylish element selected to make their name stand apart from a field dominated by hyphens and spaces — little did they know what awaited them with the dot-com revolution of the '90s. The choice of the word "LAB" stemmed from the love of the Disney character Gyro Gearloose, the great engineer inventor created by Carl Barks, and the many cartoon signs marked "LAB" hung up to help Gyro find his way to the laboratory.

MACKIE After *Greg Mackie* who previously founded TAPCO and Audio Control.

MAMA *Musical Archives, Musical Archives* Founded in 1989 by Gene Czerwinski (Cerwin-Vega founder) to preserve the music of culturally significant artists (by not requiring them to be commercially successful), whose CDs consistently are Grammy nominees, with at least one Grammy winner.

MBHO *Mikrofonbau Haun Obrigheim* Translates roughly into "Handmade microphones by Herbert Haun, founder, in Obrigheim, Germany. Maker of legendary microphones since 1962, marketed variously as Peerless MT and MT Quart. For their first three decades, MBHO capsules and complete microphones were sold to other manufacturers; now they are sold direct through normal distribution channels. One favorite large diaphragm condenser model (MBHN 608 CL) is known as "the lollypop," while another popular pressure zone design (MBNM 630 C-N-PZ) is known as "the frog."

MIPRO *Microphone Professionals*

MOTU *Mark of the Unicorn*

MUZAK *Music + Kodak*

MXR *"Mixer"* Defunct company started by Keith Barr (Alesis), Terry Sherwood (ART) and Michael Liacona (Whirlwind) that spawned ART & ALESIS. Today the new owner Jim Dunlop has resurrected the name and products.

NEUTRIK Shortened form of Neuelektrik ("new electrical") to distinguish this company from a previous one.

NHT *Now Hear This*

NVISION *n* for any number, *Vision* for visual resolution; put them together *n+Vision* and you get any number of scan lines at any data rate, which is HDTV, their business.

NXT *New Transducers Ltd.*

OTARI The name of a small village where the founder Mr. M. Hosoda was born. The name Otari is actually derived from a Chinese word "o" meaning little and "tari" meaning valley, together meaning little valley, hence the little valley called Otari where Mr. Hosoda was born.

PAL Studios Not an acronym or initial, but simply the name "pal" meaning friend or buddy. The name of inventor, engineer, composer, arranger and multi-instrumentalist, Paul C. Buff's original recording studio in Cucamonga, CA where he recorded Frank Zappa (*and taught him recording technology*), as well as creating the original sound of west coast surf music (*recording, for example, The Surfaris "Wipe Out" in 1962*). The name was taken from his mother and stepfather's recording label named PAL. (*Paul's day-job* was at General Dynamics, which Frank Zappa nicknamed *"The Bomb Factory."*) His next company was named Allison Research after his first wife. In 1980 he merged Allison Research with Bob Todrank's Valley Audio and formed Valley People. The name derived from the 225-acre art/music colony he and Bob developed in the '70s. Paul's latest company is White Lightning in Nashville.

PANJA In 1999, the new name for AMX, purportedly (not confirmed) derived from a Swahili word loosely meaning "machete" used to describe their products that allow "cutting the ties" between the Internet and the PC. Changed back to AMX in 2001.

PAS *Professional Audio Systems*

PEAVEY After founder Hartley Peavey, a 1965 Mississippi State business graduate.

PEZ Derived from *pfefferminz*, the German word for peppermint. [*This one is here to see if you are paying attention.*]

PMC *Professional Monitor Company*

PRG *Production Resource Group*

QSC Audio Products *Quilter Sound Company* after founder *Patrick Quilter.*

RADAR *random access digital audio recorder* The world's first 24-track hard disk digital audio recorder, originally developed by Creation Technologies, and distributed by Otari. Today, the team that created RADAR bought that division from Creation and formed iZ Technology headed by the original founder, Barry Henderson.

RANE An *anagram* made from the four letters common to the founder's first and last names.

RCF *Radio Cine Forniture*, Italian company owned by Mackie.

ROLLS Founder David DiFrancesco states, "Just a name we pulled out of the blue; it is short and "rolls" off the tongue."

RPG Diffusor Systems *Reflection-Phase Grating* Note the "o" rather than an "e" in *Diffusor* — it is the European spelling favored by Manfred Schroeder.

SADiE *Studio Audio Disk Editor*, but it is also *Studio Audio Distribution in Europe* for their German subsidiary, SADiE GmbH, and *Studio Audio Digital Equipment* for their American subsidiary, SADiE Inc., America, and for that nice human touch, it is the name of founder Joe Bull's grandmother. Interestingly, the small "i" was added in the beginning to clearly differentiate the company from the singer "Sade."

SAMSON Technologies *Sam's sons*; founders are the sons Jerry and Paul of Sam Ash (Sam Ash Music).

SEK'D *Studio fr Elektronische Klangerzeugund der Universitt Dresden* (Studio for electronic Klangerzeugund of the University of Dresden)

SESCOM *Scientific Electronic Systems Company*

SHURE After founder Sydney N. Shure in 1925. Originally named Shure Radio Company, located in Chicago, it was renamed Shure Brothers after his brother, Samuel J. joined the company. Even though Samuel left the company in the '30s, the name was not changed until 1999, when it became Shure Incorporated.

SONY Latin *sonus* (sound) plus English slang nickname *Sunny* (young, bright & cute), drop an "n" and *voilà*. In 1946, the company was founded by Akio Morita and Masaru Ibuka, and named *Tokyo Telecommunications Engineering Corp.* As the company grew and aimed at world markets, Morita changed the name in 1958, claiming that "Sony" was pronounceable in any language and easily remembered.

SPL *Signal Perfection, Ltd.*

SPL *Sound Performance Lab*

SRS Labs *Sound Retrieval System*

SSL *Solid State Logic*

SSM *Solid State Micro Technology for Music*; originally *Solid State Music Technology*, which changed when ownership changed; subsequently bought out by PMI, who was then acquired by Analog Devices, the current owner.

SWR *Steve W. Rabe*, founder.

TAD Pioneer *Technical Audio Devices*

TAPCO *Technical Audio Products Company*, Greg Mackie's first audio company, acquired by Electro-Voice, now EVI Audio, who retired the TAPCO brand name, and was subsequently bought by Telex.

TASCAM *TEAC Audio Systems Corporation America*; In the late 1960's TEAC formed a special R&D group named *TASC (TEAC Audio Systems Corp.)* for the purpose of researching ways to apply TEAC's recording technology for musicians and recording studios. TASCAM was established in 1971 for the purpose of distributing TASC products in the U.S. and conducting additional market research.

TC ELECTRONIC Only the founder, Kim Rishøj, knows for sure, but it is believed by well-placed sources to be an anagram for *"eccentric lot."*

TEAC *Tokyo Electro Acoustic Company*; originally founded as *Tokyo Television Acoustic Company* in August 1953, but later changed "Television" to "Electro" and then just TEAC.

THAT *Travaline, Hebert and Tyler*, or *Tyler, Hebert and Travaline,* founders — take your pick. There is no T-name order priority all previously worked at **dbx.**

TL Audio *Tony Larking*, founder.

TOA Electronics Exact origin lost, however it is believed to derive from the two Japanese sounds closest to the original kanji characters representing the company. These were "to", possibly shortened from "toyo" meaning the East or the Orient (eastern Asia), or "toi" meaning "far," combined with possibly another contraction of "ajia" meaning Asia, or "wa" shortened form of "wafu" meaning Japanese, together they mean *"Far East,"* or *"Eastern Asia."* Today, to emphasis the worldwide nature of the company, the name is spelled out *T-O-A*, not pronounced.

TOLECO Systems *The Oliver Electric Company* after the founder's cat. Today the cat's dead and the company's defunct.

TRACE ELLIOT No Mr. Trace; no Mr. Elliot; only a late night in a British pub, *The Victoria*, in 1979, where Fred Friedlein proclaimed he wanted a serious, professional sounding, double-barreled name (like Klark-Teknik, Mesa/Boogie, or Seymour Duncan). He selected "trace" since it referred to a sine wave and a wave was featured on Fred's other company's logo, the *Soundwave* music shop in Romford Essex, East London. Wanting the second name to sound very classy and British he accepted "Elliot" suggested by Andy Perry, their Australian technical designer. The company was sold to Kaman in 1992; bought back by management in 1997; and then sold again in 1998 to Gibson, the current owner.

UREI *United Recording Electronics Industries*

VAC *Valve Amplification Company*

XTA The letters do not stand for anything per John Austin, founder.

VALLEY PEOPLE See: PAL Studios.

ZSYS *z-systems* from *z-domain* or z-transform, the mathematical space used in designing DSP algorithms — their primary product — and coincidentally, works well with the founder's name: Glenn Zelniker.

Annotated List of Pro Audio Reference Books

Alexander, Robert, *The Inventor of Stereo, The Life and Works of Alan Dower Blumlein* (Focal Press ISBN 0-240-51577-3 Oxford, England, 1999). [*At last, a magnificent biography of a man finally restored to his rightful place in history.*]

American Heritage Dictionary of the English Language, 4th ed. (Houghton Mifflin ISBN 0-395-82517-2 , Boston, 2000). [*If you only own one dictionary, make it this one.*]

Ballou, Glen, ed., *Handbook For Sound Engineers, Third Edition* (Focal Press ISBN 0-240-80454-6, Boston, 2002). [*Very uneven reference, but contains good information. The book is divided into chapters written by twenty-seven authors, resulting in great differences in treatment, tone and thoroughness of subject matter. Some sections are excellent and useful to a sound engineer; some are not. A fully-searchable and hyperlinked CD-ROM would have helped.*]

Barber, David W., *Better Than It Sounds* (Sound And Vision ISBN 0-920151-22-1, Toronto, 1998). [*Humorous musical quotations.*]

Bartlett's Book of Anecdotes (Little, Brown Co. ISBN 0-316-08267-8, New York, 2000). [*Fun stuff; I don't know how many are true, but fun anyway.*]

Beckmann, Petr, *A History of Pi* (The Golem Press ISBN 0-911762-18-3, Boulder, CO, 1977). [*If the origin of key mathematical symbols interests you, then you'll love this.*]

Benson, K. Blair, ed., *Audio Engineering Handbook* (McGraw-Hill, New York, 1988). [*This is a great compilation of articles written by some of the best in the business. Too bad it is out of print. A lot of the material is done at an advanced level and quite difficult, but valuable. Contains the best article I've found on audio standards, written by Daniel Queen, retired AES Standards Manager.*]

Beranek, Leo L., *Acoustics* (McGraw-Hill, New York, 1954; Reissued 1986 by Acoustical Society of America ISBN 0-88318-494-X). [*The classic text. Long out-of-print, but now available. Difficult, but definitive.*]

———, *Music, Acoustics & Architecture* (Wiley , New York, 1962). [*Another gem from Dr. Beranek — this time in non-technical language — the essential meaning of acoustics to the performance and appreciation of music.*]

———, *Noise Reduction* (McGraw-Hill, New York, 1960). [*Written in 1960, for a special MIT summer program, this book went on to become the foundation for modern noise control.*]

Bierce, Ambrose, *The Devil's Dictionary* (Oxford University Press, ISBN 0-195-12627-0, Oxford, 1998). [*Originally published in the late 1890s by "The Wickedest Man in San Francisco" — this is better than therapy.*]

Blauert, Jens, *Spatial Hearing; The Psychophysics of Human Sound Localization; Revised Edition* (MIT Press ISBN 0-262-02413-6 Cambridge, MA, 1997). [*Everything known about human sound localization, between two covers.*]

Blesser, Barry, "An Interdisciplinary Synthesis of Reverberation Viewpoints," *J. Audio Eng. Soc.,* vol. 49, pp. 867-903 (2001 October 2001). [*This is the best overview available describing the enormous complexity of reverberation, showing how various disciplines contribute to our understanding.*]

Bohn, Dennis A., "Operator Adjustable Equalizers: An Overview," *The Proceeding of the AES 6th International Conference: Sound Reinforcement* (Audio Engineering Society ISBN 0-937803-13-8, New York, 1989). [*Hey, you have to promote yourself at least once — that's the rule.*]

Croft, Terrell, *The American Electrician's Handbook, 2nd ed.* (McGraw-Hill, New York, 1921). [*A gem of a book: leather bound, all edges gilt, wonderful!*]

Davis, Don & Carolyn Davis, *Sound System Engineering, 2nd ed.* (Sams ISBN 0-672-21857-7, Indianapolis, 1987). [*The textbook written by the husband and wife team that founded Synergetic Audio Concepts (Syn-Aud-Con), and pioneered sound system seminars.*]

Davis, Gary & Ralph Jones, *Yamaha Sound Reinforcement, 2nd ed.* (Hal Leonard ISBN 0-88188-900-8, Milwaukee, 1989). [*It's hard to find affordable, useful and accurate pro audio references— this is all three. The best $/page/ information-content value around.*]

Deketh, J., *Fundamentals of Radio-Valve Technique* (Philips Technical Library reprinted by Audio Amateur Press ISBN 1-882580-23-0 Peterborough, NH, 1999). [*First published in English in 1949, this handy book has been newly reprinted by Audio Amateur Press (available from Old Colony). This is one of the classic tube texts, and deserves a place on your shelf if you have any vacuum tube, or valve, interest at all.*]

Feucht, Dennis L., *Handbook of Analog Circuit Design* (Academic Press ISBN 0-12-254240-1, San Diego, 1990). [*A rare find: a textbook that is truly useful and practical. Which isn't surprising once you know he was a real world Tektronix engineer. Particularly good at giving insight into circuits. His book is also available in CD-ROM format; see his website.*]

Frederiksen, Thomas M., *Intuitive Analog Electronics* (McGraw-Hill ISBN 0-07-021962-1, New York, 1989). [*Only a very few technical writers have the real gift — Bob Pease, John Watkinson, Jim Williams, and more recently, Clive Maxfield, all come to mind, but before any of them, came Tom Frederiksen; Tom has true gift. I was most fortunate to have learned directly from Tom, as were a couple of the other aforementioned. It simply cannot be written or said clearer or more interestingly than the way Tom does it. (FYI: He has a whole "Intuitive" series — five titles that I know of. Find them, search them out, you won't be disappointed.)*]

Giddings, Philip, *Audio System Design and Installation* (Howard W. Sams ISBN 0-672-22672-3, Indianapolis, 1990). [*Don't let the title fool you, this is* the *book on interconnection wiring, grounding, shielding and AC power.*]

Hale, Constance, *Sin and Syntax: How to Craft Wickedly Effective Prose* (Broadway Books ISBN 0-7679-0308-0, New York, 1999). [*By the author of* Wired Style *and a former editor of* Wired *magazine, a must-have guide that goes way beyond the "rules" of modern language and good writing.*]

Helmholtz, Hermann, *On The Sensations of Tone* (Dover ISBN 0-486-60753-4, New York, 1980). [*One of the world's greatest scientific classics — a genuine treasure. Written in 1885, and still considered one of the best sources for physiological acoustics.*]

Holman, Tomlinson, *Sound For Film And Television* (Focal Press ISBN 0-240-80291-8 Boston 1997) [*From the man who invented and developed Lucasfilm's THX program, and now a professor at the University of Southern California School of Cinema-Television.*]

Howare, David M. & James Angus, *Acoustics And Psychoacoustics* (Focal Press ISBN 0-240-51428-9 Oxford, England 1998) [*A beautiful blend of acoustics and psychoacoustics from musical and scientific perspectives. Minimal math.*]

IEEE 100: The Authoritative Dictionary of IEEE Standards Terms, 7th ed. (IEEE ISBN 0-7381-2601-2, New York, 2000). [*The definitive answers for electrical & electronic terminology disputes.*]

Kaplan, Robert, *The Nothing That Is: A Natural History of Zero* (Oxford University Press ISBN 0-19-512842-7 New York, 2000). [*If the origin of key mathematical symbols interests you, then you'll love this.*]

Kordyban, Tony, *Hot Air Rises and Heat Sinks: Everything You Know About Cooling Electronics Is Wrong* (ASME Press ISBN 0791800741, 1998). [*A collection of myths, mistakes, and "lessons learned" from practicing engineers involved in the field of electronic equipment cooling. In between headaches, Tony Kordyban joyfully explains why everything you know about cooling electronics is wrong. A MUST-HAVE book for anyone involved in cooling electronics.*]

Krauss, Herbert L., Charles W. Bostian & Frederick H. Raab, *Solid State Radio Engineering* (John Wiley & Sons ISBN 0-471-03018-X, New York, 1980). [*Written in 1980, and still the acknowledged leader, this is one of the best books ever penned about classic analog radio. With the advent of digital radio, there will never be another text of this caliber on this topic.*]

Lampen, Stephen H., *Wire, Cable & Fiber Optics for Video & Audio Engineers, 3rd ed.* (McGraw-Hill ISBN 0-07-038134-8, New York, 1998) [*Trust me, you need this book — there is none better on this subject.*]

Langford-Smith, Fritz., *Radiotron Designer's Handbook, 4th ed.* (Originally published by the Wireless Press for Amalgamated Wireless Valve Company Pty. Ltd., Sydney, Australia in 1934; revised three times to produce the 4th (and final) edition in 1952; reproduced and distribute by RCA Electronic Components, Harrison, NJ for the last time in May, 1968; resurrected and reissued as a 1,000 page paperback by Newnes (Butterworth-Heinemann) ISBN 0-7506-3635-1, Oxford, England, 1997) [*Along with Tremaine's book below, this is another of the ancient-audio sacred texts. This tome is a comprehensive reference covering basic audio principles and the practical design of all types of classic radio receivers, audio amplifiers and record-producing equipment up to the invention of the transistor. This is the book you consult to learn how they did compressors in the very old days, for instance.*]

Maor, Eli, *e: The Story of a Number* (Princeton University Press ISBN 0-691-03390-0, Princeton, NJ, 1994). [*If the origin of key mathematical symbols interests you, then you'll love this.*]

Maxfield, Clive, *Bebop to the Boolean Boogie* (HighText Publications ISBN 1-878707-22-1, Solana Beach, CA, 1995). [*Try it; you'll love it.*]

McQuain, Jeffrey, *Never Enough Words* (Random House ISBN 0-679-45804-2 New York, 1999). [*Wonderful source for Americanisms. Where else are you going to find out that "teetotaciously exflunctified" means "totally worn out." Sports figures are accused of "talking trash," well, this is what is called "talking tall."*]

Metzler, Bob., *Audio Measurement Handbook* (Audio Precision, Beaverton, OR, 1993; FAX (503) 641-8906). [*Just how do you measure transient intermodulation distortion, anyway? Bob explains.*]

Moore, Brian C., *An Introduction to the Psychology of Hearing, 4th ed.* (Academic Press ISBN 0-12-505627-3, San Diego, CA 1997). [*Uncommonly clear explanations of the most complex hearing issues, from the leading researcher in the field.*]

Morton, David, *Off The Record: The Technology and Culture of Sound Recording in America* (Rutgers University Press ISBN 0-8135-2747-3, New Brunswick, NJ 2000). [*Great history full of surprises especially regarding dictation and answering machines. Be sure and check out his Dead Recording Media website.*]

Moses, Bob, "Asynchronous Serial Communications," *The Proceedings of the AES 13th International Conference: Computer-Controlled Sound Systems* (Audio Engineering Society ISBN 0-937803-25-1, New York, 1994). [*A great primer on all things asynchronous, from the originator of Rane's website.*]

Nahin, Paul J., *An Imaginary Tale: The Story of [the square root of minus one]* (Princeton University Press ISBN 0-691-02795-1, Princeton, NJ, 1998). [*If the origin of key mathematical symbols interests you, then you'll love this.*]

Newton, Harry, *Newton's Telecom Dictionary, 17th ed.*(CMP Books ISBN 1-57820-069-5, New York, 2001). [*Telecommunication's magnum opus — there is nothing else like it.*]

Olson, Harry F., *Acoustical Engineering* (Van Nostrand, New York 1957; reissued 1991 by Professional Audio Journals, Inc., Philadelphia, PA Available from Old Colony). [*Along with Beranek's* Acoustics *above, these two form the definitive bookends for all later acoustics books.*]

———, *Musical Engineering* (McGraw Hill, New York 1952) [*An audio master presents the first unified engineering treatment of all the elements that enter into the production and reproduction of music.*]

Pease, Robert A., *Troubleshooting Analog Circuits* (Butterworth Heinemann ISBN 0-7506-9184-0, Boston, 1991). [*Bob Pease is legendary among analog circuit designers, and his monthly column, "What's All This … Stuff, Anyhow?" in Electronic Design magazine is one of the most read and loved columns of all time. No better book on analog troubleshooting than this. "In all my years of designing/building/fixing audio gear, whenever something goes wrong, the right answer is always in this book (virtually no math, either)," writes Bill Coe, Sluggo Audio.*]

Pickles, James O., *An Introduction to the Physiology of Hearing, 2nd ed.* (Academic Press ISBN 0-12-554754-4, San Diego, CA 1988). [*An excellent complement to Moore's book above on the* psychology, *this covers the* physiology *of hearing.*]

Pohlmann, Ken, ed., *Advanced Digital Audio* (Sams ISBN 0-672-22768-1, Carmel, IN, 1991). [*Difficult subjects clearly explained by this acclaimed professor of music engineering at the University of Miami — an accurate, authoritative digital audio resource.*]

Read, Oliver, *The Recording and Reproduction of Sound* (Sams, Indianapolis, 1949; 2nd ed. 1952). [*Another of the almost mythical early texts on audio. Illustrated with fantastic photographs. Long out-of-print but available through used book services and stores.*]

Roederer, Juan G., *The Physics and Psychophysics of Music, 3rd ed.* (Springer-Verlag ISBN 0-387-94366-8, New York, 1995). [*Originally written in 1970 and now in its third edition, this is one of the first, and my all-time favorite book on psychoacoustics, or the "music of science," as professor Roederer prefers.*]

Rumsey, Francis and John Watkinson, *The Digital Interface Handbook, 2nd edition* (Focal Press ISBN 0-240-51396-7, Oxford, England, 1995). [*Finally, a valuable reference on this complex topic.*]

Self, Douglas, *Audio Power Amplifier Design Handbook, 2nd edition* (Newnes ISBN 0-7506-4527-X, Oxford, England, 2000). [*For all the books written on audio, there are surprisingly few on power amplifiers. Of the few seen, I prefer this one. Written by a real-world, experienced, working, multi-degreed (Cambridge & Sussex) engineer, it is rational, reliable, accurate and truly useful. Highly recommended. Recommended even higher is his website that is just chock-full of wonderful stuff.*]

Slone, G. Randy, *High-Power Audio Amplifier Construction Manual* (McGraw-Hill ISBN 0-07-134119-6, New York, 1999). [*A very valuable do-it-yourself book; highly recommended.*]

Streicher, Ron and F. Alton Everest, *The New Stereo Soundbook, 2nd ed.* (Audio Engineering Associates ISBN 0-9665162-0-6, Pasadena, CA, 1998). [*The best book so far on mic-ing and recording stereophonic sound.*]

Talbot-Smith, Michael, *Audio Engineer's Reference Book, 2nd ed.* (Focal Press ISBN 0-240-51528-5, Oxford, England, 1999). [*Perhaps this book is best taken literally, i.e., if you already are an audio engineer then this your reference book. However, if you are not an audio engineer, then I think this should not be your only reference book. It covers a lot of ground, from the math and physics of audio, all the way through digital audio transmission and standards. Too much, I think, for any one volume. The info is there, but it is quite sparse and difficult in places. This book takes work, but has value.*]

Transnational College of LEX, *Who Is Fourier? A Mathematical Adventure* (Language Research Foundation ISBN 0-9643504-0-8, Belmont, MA, Third Printing 1998). [*A very different book, deceptively simple in style — almost comic book-like — but, I believe the best book on Fourier ever. Buy it; give it a chance — don't be put off by the style. I bet you learn something and tell all your friends to get a copy. It's that good.*]

Tremaine, Howard M., *Audio Cyclopedia, 2nd ed.* (Howard W. Sams ISBN 0-672-20675-7, Indianapolis, 1973). [*One of the ancient-audio wonders. Although terribly outdated, and long out-of-print, this is still the best all-around pro audio reference for the fundamentals. And, if you dig, you can still find copies in used bookstores.*]

Watkinson, John, *The Art of Digital Audio, 3rd ed.* (Focal Press ISBN 0-240-51587-0, Oxford, England, 2001). [*The title says it all. One of the best digital audio references you can own.*]

———, *The Art of Sound Reproduction* (Focal Press ISBN 0-240-51512-9, Oxford, England, 1998). [*Don't even ask; if John wrote, you need it. Outstanding overview of the entire audio field — all the theoretical background necessary to understand sound reproduction.*]

———, *Compression in Video & Audio* (Focal Press ISBN 0-240-51394-0, Oxford, England, 1995). [*Want to know all about MUSICAM, Dolby AC, JPEG and MPEG? This is your book.*]

———, *An Introduction to Digital Audio* (Focal Press ISBN 0-240-51378-9, Oxford, England, 1995). [*Less rigorous than the one below, but no less valuable. An excellent first book on digital audio.*]

Weis, Elisabeth and John Belton, *Film Sound: Theory And Practice* (Columbia University Press ISBN 0-231-05637-0, New York, 1985). [*More historical and theoretical than Holman's book above, thus a nice complement.*]

Welch, Walter L. and Leah Brodbeck Stenzel Burt, *From Tinfoil to Stereo* (University Press of Florida ISBN 0-8130-1317-8, Gainesville, FL, 1994). [*The most comprehensive history of the phonograph and sound recording, starting with its inception in 1877 to the time of the Great Crash in 1929. Considered the fundamental reference book of sound recording history.*]

Whitaker, Jerry C., *Signal Measurement, Analysis, and Testing* (CRC Press ISBN 0-8493-0048-7, Boca Raton, LA, 2000). [*Finally a good textbook on these topics. From theory to practical, great book.*]

White, Glenn D., *The Audio Dictionary, 2nd ed.,* (University of Washington Press ISBN 0-295-97088-X, Seattle, 1991). [*None better. You need this book.*]

———, *The Audio Dictionary, 2nd ed., CD-ROM Version* (University of Washington Press ISBN 0-295-97540-7, Seattle, 1998). [*Very useful CD-ROM version of the above, complete with color graphics and sound. There is also a combo book and CD-ROM version ISBN 0-295-97541-5.*]

Williams, Jim, *Analog Circuit Design.* (Butterworth Heinemann ISBN 0-7506-9166-2, Boston, 1991). [*A must-have for anyone interested in analog circuit design by one of the analog gurus of all time.*]

Williams, Tim, *EMC for Product Designers, 3rd Ed.* (Newnes ISBN 0-7506-4930-5, Oxford, England, 2001). [*The best practical book dealing with achieving EMC immunity and emissions for CE marking. Also check out his new book below.*]

Williams, Tim and Keith Armstrong, *EMC for Systems and Installations* (Newnes ISBN 0-7506-4167-3, Oxford, England, 2000). [*The best practical book dealing with achieving EMC immunity and emissions for CE marking. Also check out his first book above.*]

Woram, John M., *Sound Recording Handbook* (Howard W. Sams ISBN 0-672-22583-2, Indianapolis, 1989). [*Among the dozens of recording books this one stands tall, from another of the audio-teaching masters.*]

Acquiring New Books

Amazon.Com *www.amazon.com*

Barnes & Noble *www.barnesandnoble.com*

Internet Bookshop (London) and Amazon.co.uk: *Often the best prices on British books are from British sources, although it is hard to find discounted new technical books anywhere.* *www.bookshop.co.uk, www.amazon.co.uk*

CMP Books (formerly Telecom Books): *There is no better source for all things telecom.* *www.cmpbooks.com*

Music Books Plus: *Good selection of mainstream audio books.* *www.musicbooksplus.com*

Old Colony Sound Lab: *Excellent for most audio books & especially books on loudspeakers and tubes (valves).* *www.audioxpress.com*

Opamp Technical Books: *Another great source for audio books.* *opampbooks.com*

ProSoundWeb Bookstore *A new source for books on pro audio, live sound and recording. Nice job of presenting and describing each book. The books are actually bought through Amazon.com but ProSoundWeb gets a small commission that helps keep their very useful website afloat, so help them out the next time you need a book.* *www.prosoundweb.com*

Acquiring Out-of-Print Books

Some of the books listed are out-of-print and unavailable through normal book sources, however they are among the most useful. Try to locate them through your local used bookstores — absolutely worth the trouble.

In addition try any/all of the following used and rare book search sites:

Advanced Book Exchange *www.abebooks.com*
Alibris *www.alibris.com*
Bookfinder *www.bookfinder.com*
Powell's *www.powells.com*

Also now Amazon.com automatically searches their used book suppliers when you search for new books, and there is a Barnes & Noble Out of Print, Used & Rare Book search page.

Notes

Notes

Notes

Notes

Notes

Useful Rules and Abbreviations when using the International System of Units (SI) and Other Terminology

- The goal is to make quantity values as independent from language as possible.

- Numbers combined with units are *never* spelled out. They are always written as Arabic numbers not words. And units are always abbreviated, *never* spelled out. Examples:

  5 V *not*: five V

  40 W *not*: 40 watts

  the current was 12 A *not*: the current was 12 amps

  not: the current was twelve amperes.

- Unit names when written out are *never* capitalized. Example:

  watts *not*: Watts

  amperes *not*: Amperes

  volts *not*: Volts

- Unit symbols or abbreviations are *always* capitalized when derived from a person's name. Examples:

  ampere is A, farad is F, *but* second is s and meter is m

  But, as always, there is an exception:

  liter is L (to avoid confusion between lowercase l and the number 1)

- For clarity, state the units for each number. Example:

  20 Hz – 20 kHz *not*: 20–20kHz

  10 MHz to 100 MHz *not*: 10 to 100 MHz

- Always space the symbol from the number. Examples:

  35 mA *not*: 35mA

  25 °C *not*: 25°C

  11 kΩ *not*: 11k Ω

  4 kHz *not*: 4k Hz

- Unit symbols are never pluralized. Examples:

  80 W *not*: 80 Ws

  15 cm long *not*: 15 cms long

Useful Information

International System of Units (SI) Names & Symbols and Other Terminology Common to Pro Audio

Name	Symbol	Name	Symbol
ampere	A	micrometer	μm
bit or bits	spell out	microsecond	μs
bytes	spell out	milliampere	mA
decibel	dB	millihenry	mH
degree (angle)	°	millimeter	mm
farad	F	millivolt	mV
gauss	Gs	minute (time)	min
gram	g	minute (angle)	'
henry	H	nanosecond	ns
hertz	Hz	oersted	Oe
hour	h	ohm	Ω
inch	in	pascal	Pa
joule	J	picofarad	pF
kelvin	K	second (time)	s
kilohertz	kHz	second (angle)	"
kilohm	$k\Omega$	siemens	S
liter	L	tesla	T
megahertz	MHz	volt	V
meter	m	watt	W
microfarad	μF	weber	Wb

SI Prefixes for Decimal Numbers

Factor	Name	Symbol	Factor	Name	Symbol
10^{24}	yotta	Y	10^{-1}	deci	d
10^{21}	zetta	Z	10^{-2}	centi	c
10^{18}	exa	E	10^{-3}	milli	m
10^{15}	peta	P	10^{-6}	micro	μ
10^{12}	tera	T	10^{-9}	nano	n
10^{9}	giga	G	10^{-12}	pico	p
10^{6}	mega	M	10^{-15}	femto	f
10^{3}	kilo	k	10^{-18}	atto	a
10^{2}	hecto	h	10^{-21}	zepto	z
10^{1}	deka	da	10^{-24}	yocto	y

SI Prefixes for Binary Numbers

Factor	Name	Symbol	Origin	Derivation
2^{10}	kibi	Ki	kilobinary: $(2^{10})^1$	kilo: $(10^3)^1$
2^{20}	mebi	Mi	megabinary: $(2^{10})^2$	mega: $(10^3)^2$
2^{30}	gibi	Gi	gigabinary: $(2^{10})^3$	giga: $(10^3)^3$
2^{40}	tebi	Ti	terabinary: $(2^{10})^4$	tera: $(10^3)^4$
2^{50}	pebi	Pi	petabinary: $(2^{10})^5$	peta: $(10^3)^5$
2^{60}	exbi	Ei	exabinary: $(2^{10})^6$	exa: $(10^3)^6$